INTERNATIONAL CONSTRUCTION LAW

The construction industry routinely operates across international borders, which means that construction professionals need to have a good understanding of how legislation in different jurisdictions might affect their work. This book is an in-depth analysis of international construction law from all the major jurisdictions of the world, alongside their relevant contract law principles, helping the reader to prepare for the complexity of an international construction project.

The book begins by introducing the major families of law, before looking at individual jurisdictions. Each chapter is written by an experienced legal professional operating in that region and covers subjects such as: taking over, defects liabilities, warranties, design issues, termination, bonds and guarantees, limitation of liability, and more. The systems included are:

- German civil system (Germanic code);
- French civil system (Napoleonic code);
- English common law system;
- GCC countries civil law system (with emphasis on UAE, Qatar, Saudi Arabia, and Egypt);
- Nordic legal system;
- Chinese civil system.

Finally, the book will discuss the national standard construction contracts used in the differing legal systems and the widely used FIDIC contracts.

The combination of truly international coverage with the practical insight of experienced practitioners means that this book will be invaluable to any professional involved in the construction industry including lawyers, project managers, contractors, and investors as well as academics in the field.

Dr. Wolfgang Breyer is founder and managing partner of Breyer Rechtsanwälte, a boutique law firm practicing exclusively in the field of construction and architectural law. In addition, Dr. Breyer is the founder and chairman of the International Construction Law Association (ICLA), a member of the International Academy of Construction Lawyers (IACL), founder of the International Construction Practice and Law MBE program at the University of Stuttgart, and a founding member of the Leading Construction Lawyers International Alliance (LCL).

CONSTRUCTION PRACTICE SERIES

Series editors: Philip Britton and Phillip Capper

Construction Contract Variations
Michael Sergeant and Max Wieliczko
Holman Fenwick Willan LLP

Delay and Disruption in Construction Contracts
Fifth Edition
Andrew Burr

The Law of Construction Disputes
Second Edition
Cyril Chern

Construction Insurance and UK Construction Contracts
Third Edition
Roger ter Haar QC, Marshall Levine and Anna Laney

Construction Law
Second Edition
Julian Bailey

International Contractual and Statutory Adjudication
Andrew Burr

Remedies in Construction Law
Second Edition
Roger ter Haar QC

Professional Negligence in Construction
Second Edition
Ben Patten and Hugh Saunders

Litigation in the Technology and Construction Court
Adam Constable QC, Lucy Garrett QC and Calum Lamont

Chern on Dispute Boards
Practice and Procedure
Fourth Edition
Cyril Chern

The Law of Construction Disputes
Third Edition
Cyril Chern

Construction Arbitration and Alternative Dispute Resolution
Theory and Practice Around the World
Edited by Renato Nazzini

Adjudication in Construction Law
Second Edition
Darryl Royce

International Construction Law
An Overview
Edited by Wolfgang Breyer

For more information about this series, please visit:
www.routledge.com/Construction-Practice-Series/book-series/CPS

INTERNATIONAL CONSTRUCTION LAW

AN OVERVIEW

EDITED BY WOLFGANG BREYER

informa law
from Routledge

First published 2024
by Informa Law from Routledge
4 Park Square, Milton Park, Abingdon, Oxon OX14 4RN

and by Informa Law from Routledge
605 Third Avenue, New York, NY 10158

Informa Law from Routledge is an imprint of the Taylor & Francis Group, an informa business

British Library Cataloguing-in-Publication Data
A catalogue record for this book is available from the British Library

Library of Congress Cataloging-in-Publication Data
Names: Breyer, Wolfgang, editor.
Title: International construction law : an overview / edited by Wolfgang Breyer.
Description: Abingdon, Oxon [UK] ; New York, NY : Routledge, 2023. |
Series: Construction practice series | Includes bibliographical references and index. |
Identifiers: LCCN 2023026003 (print) | LCCN 2023026004 (ebook) | ISBN 9781138945470 (hardback) | ISBN 9781032586427 (paperback) | ISBN 9781315671376 (ebook)
Subjects: LCSH: Building laws. | Construction industry—Law and legislation.
Classification: LCC K3538 .I5811 2023 (print) | LCC K3538 (ebook) | DDC 343.07/869—dc23/eng/20230531
LC record available at https://lccn.loc.gov/2023026003
LC ebook record available at https://lccn.loc.gov/2023026004

ISBN: 978-1-138-94547-0 (hbk)
ISBN: 978-1-032-58642-7 (pbk)
ISBN: 978-1-315-67137-6 (ebk)

DOI: 10.4324/9781315671376

Typeset in Times New Roman
by Deanta Global Publishing Services, Chennai, India

CONTENTS

TABLE OF CASES

Sapphire International Petroleum Ltd. v The National Iranian Oil Company (1964) 13 ICLQ 1011, 1012 7
Saxa, Inc. v DFD Architecture, Inc., 312 S. W. 3d 224 (Tex. App. 2010) 610
Sayers v International Drilling Co NV [1971] 1 WLR 1176 (CA) (Sayers case) 10
Schneider Electric Buildings Critical Systems, Inc. v Western Surety Co., 149 A. 3d 778 (Md. App. 2016) 607
Scottish Power UK Plc v BP Exploration Operating Co Ltd & Ors [2016] 2 EWCA Civ 1043, 1 November 2016 83
Scrivener v Pask (1865-66) L.R. 1 C.P. 715 68
Selectmove Ltd, Re [1995] 2 All E.R. 531 67
Semco Salvage & Marine Pty Ltd v Lancer Navigation [1997] UKHL 2 60
Sennett v Tape Estate [1986] SJ No. 223, 45 Sask R 314 (QB) 15
Sexton v Horton (1926) 38 C.L.R. 240 56
Sharn Importing Ltd. v Babchuk [1971] BCJ No. 477, 21 DLR (3d) 349 (SC) 10
Sidhu v British Airways Plc [1997] 1 All E.R. 193 54
Sigurdson v Farrow, [1981] AJ No. 996, 121 DLR (3d) 183 (QB) 15
Sika Contracts Ltd v BL Gill and Closeglen Properties Ltd (1978) 9 B.L.R. 11 68
Sir Lindsay Parkinson v Commissioners of His Majesty's Works [1950] 1 All ER 208 115
Skanska Construction (Regions) Ltd v Anglo Amsterdam Corp Ltd [2002] 84 Con. L.R. 100 109
Skeate v Beale (1840) 11 Ad & E 983 74
Sloan & Co. v Liberty Mut. Ins. Co., 653 F.3d 175, 180 (3d Cir. 2011) 354
Slutsky-Peltz Plumbing & Heating Co., Inc. v Vincennes Community School Corporation, 556 N.E. 2d 344 (Ind. App. 1990) 602, 603, 610
Soleimany v Soleimany [1999] QB 785 (CA) 8
Solle v Butcher [1950] 1 K.B. 671 73
Southern Foundries (1926) Ltd v Shirlaw [1940] A.C. 701 70
Southway Group Ltd v Wolff (1991) 57 B.L.R. 33 77
Spice Girls Ltd v Aprilia World Service BV [2002] EWCA Civ 15 72
Spring Ltd v London Borough of Camden [2012] BLR 83 125
Spurrier v La Cloche [1902] AC 446 (PC) 9
SSE Generation Ltd v Hochtief Solutions AG and anor [2016] ScotCS CSOH 177 111
State ex rel. Johnson Controls, Inc. v Tucker, LLC, 729 S. E. 2d 808 (W. Va. 2012) 601
State Government Insurance Commission v Trigwell [1979] HCA 40; (1979) 142 CLR 617 56
Sterling v Taylor, 40 Cal. 4th 757, 55 Cal. Rptr. 3d 116, 152 P.3d 420 (2007) 368
Stevenson, Jacques & Co v McLean (1880) 5 QBD 346 64
Stevenson v Watson (1879) 4 CPD 148 99
Stilk v Myrick (1809) 2 Camp. 317 67
St John Shipbuilding & Dry Dock Co. v Kingsland Marine Corp [1981] FCJ No. 603, 126 DLR (3d) 322 (CA) 4, 17
St John Shipping Corp v Joseph Rank Ltd [1957] 1 Q.B. 267 74
Stocznia Gdanska SA v Latvian Shipping Co (Repudiation) [2002] EWCA Civ 889 ....80, 82
Stormont Main Working Men's Club v J Roscoe Milne Partnership (1988) 13 ConLR 187 98
St. Paul Mercury Ins. Co. v Capitol Sprinkler Inspection, Inc., 573 F. Supp. 2d 152, 172 (D.D.C. 2008) 359
Sunlite International Inc v Trans-Canada Resources Ltd., [1978] AJ No. 798, [1978] 5 WWR 345 (TD) 14
Superior Energy Services LLC v Cabinda Gulf Oil Company, Ltd., 2013 WL 6406324 (N. D. Cal., 6 December 2013) 606
Sutcliffe v Thackrah [1974] AC 727 60
Tate v Latham [1897] 1 QB 502 110
Taylor v Allon [1965] 1 All E.R. 557 64
Temloc Ltd v Errill Properties Ltd 39 BLR 30 (1 January 1988) 84
Thod Investment Ltd. (cob Jeff Parry Promotions) v André-Philippe Gagnon Inc [2005] AJ No. 1105, 2005 ABQB 601, 385 AR 199 (Master) 9
Thomas Bates & Son Ltd v Wyndham's (Lingerie) Ltd [1981] 1 W.L.R. 505 73

TABLE OF LEGISLATION

EDITOR BIOGRAPHY

Wolfgang Breyer
Dr. Wolfgang Breyer is founder and managing partner of Breyer Rechtsanwälte, a boutique law firm practicing exclusively in the field of construction and architectural law. In addition, Dr. Breyer is the founder and chairman of the International Construction Law Association (ICLA), a member of the International Academy of Construction Lawyers (IACL), founder of the International Construction Practice and Law MBE program at the University of Stuttgart, and a founding member of the Leading Construction Lawyers International Alliance (LCL).

FOREWORD

International Construction Law

Wolfgang Breyer

This book is an attempt to provide a comprehensive overview of construction law globally. While it may be impossible to give a full and complete analysis of all the legal issues which may be encountered around the world, we have sought to illustrate this to the greatest degree possible through comparing and contrasting various families of law and jurisdictions. The families of law are evaluated not only in legal terms and their histories, but also through consideration of their economic and cultural importance and influence worldwide.

What makes a construction contract international? Major projects, which involve international calls to tender are easily identified and certainly would be considered international. However, at the most elemental level, a construction contract is international, where there is at least some degree of cross-border contracting. Therefore, even where a project seems entirely domestic in nature, the involvement of foreign contractors or sub-contractors will give an otherwise purely domestic construction contract a distinctly international character. This may affect the parties' approaches to contractual deadlines, notice periods, time-bar provisions, liquidated damages provisions, and so on, especially to the extent that such provisions are not common or even legally enforceable in the foreign domestic market. This can often lead to significant misunderstandings, communication problems, and disputes, which of course all add to the cost of the project and harm the relationship between the contract participants.

In this book, we take a comparative look at the history and background of contracts, and in particular construction contracts, across various jurisdictions. We then look at how certain key milestones and provisions in the construction contract, such as "acceptance" or "taking-over", "time-bars", the interaction between statutory warranty provisions vs. contractual defects liability periods, and how the applicable law is crucial in contract drafting and interpretation. For example, the concept of acceptance is codified in many civil law jurisdictions and clearly defines what is meant by the term, whereas under common law jurisdictions such as in England or the USA, there is no such codified definition, and it is incumbent on the parties to define the term. Also, acceptance triggers the beginning of the statutory warranty period in many civil law jurisdictions, but what happens when there is a contractual defects liability period and acceptance occurs at the end of that contractual period?

Finally, we look at the interaction between the contract and its background, the applicable law chosen by the parties and the mandatory law of the site location. How do different cultures and jurisdictions approach contract interpretation? Should the subjective intent of the parties be considered, or is an objective approach preferable? Should extrinsic evidence be permitted in order to establish the intent of the parties, or is the four corner's doctrine sufficient? Is it possible to achieve harmonization across cultures, legal families and jurisdictions? How should language barriers be treated? For example, under German law delay damages can be dealt with by means of "*Vertragsstrafen*", which is literally translated as "contractual penalty". In most common law jurisdictions contractual penalties are disfavoured by the courts and generally unenforceable. Liquidated damages provisions, on the other hand, are permissible, provided that they generally represent a genuine pre-estimate of the loss likely to be incurred. Therefore, an otherwise valid liquidated damages provision may face increased scrutiny and risk being held invalid because of a language barrier. We have tried to address these questions and more through the in-depth comparison and discussion of the approach to international construction under major legal families and jurisdictions.

AUTHOR BIOGRAPHIES

Chapter 1

Janet Walker CM

Janet is an independent arbitrator with chambers in London at Atkin Chambers and in Toronto and Sydney. Over the past 20 years, she has served as sole arbitrator, co-arbitrator and chair in ad hoc arbitrations and ICC, ICDR, DIAC, HKIAC, KCAB, PCA and SIAC-administered arbitrations in a variety of seats. Her matters include construction, M&A, shareholder, intellectual property, pharma and environmental. She has a good working knowledge of Spanish and French.

Janet is an officer of the IBA International Construction Projects Committee and a member of the boards of the International Construction Law Association and CIArb Canada. She is a founding member of SCL North America and past chair of the ICC Canada Arbitration Committee.

Janet is a Distinguished Research Professor (past associate dean) at Osgoode Hall Law School, a member of the Ontario Bar, and a licensed legal consultant of the New York State Bar. She authors Canada's main text on conflict of laws, cited in more than 400 judgments, and she is co-author of the third edition of *Commercial Arbitration in Australia.* Since 2017, she has taught in the Stuttgart International Construction Practice and Law Program.

Chapter 2

Erlmest Burns

Erlmest is currently working as an in-house counsel, where he is responsible for advising on construction law related matters, both in Germany and internationally. Prior to starting his current role, Erlmest was a Senior Associate. Erlmest was a Senior Associate at Breyer Rechtsanwälte, based in Stuttgart Germany. He works exclusively on contentious and non-contentious matters in the field of international construction law and private international law. He has vast experience and regularly advises on a wide range of domestic and international standard forms of construction contract, such as JCT, NEC, AIA and FIDIC. In addition to his work as an international construction lawyer, he also was a regular lecturer in the International Construction Practice and Law, MBE program at the University of Stuttgart. Mr. Burns was also a member the International Construction Law Association (ICLA) and assisted the Chairman, Dr. Wolfgang Breyer in its administration.

Mr. Burns earned his Bachelor of Arts Degree from the University of Massachusetts and his Juris Doctor from Suffolk University Law School in Boston.

Leo Grutters

Leo is a Construction Engineer and a Dispute Resolution Expert with over 35 years of professional experience. He holds an MBA and is a Fellow of the Chartered Institute of Arbitrators. As a Member of FIDIC's President's List of Certified Dispute Adjudicators he has been involved as an independent neutral expert in many large prestigious international engineering projects involving such wide-ranging sectors as general building, roads, railways, power generation & distribution, off-shore, marine, renewable energies, etc. Due to his extensive participation in international contractual dispute resolution procedures such as Adjudication, Dispute Boards and Arbitration, he is a project-focused expert that understands the interaction between complex engineering methodologies and the unavoidable legal and commercial implications when seen in a contractual environment. He also regularly lectures on Dispute Resolution Methodologies, Proactive Contract Administration Systems & Procedures and he is a regular speaker at related international events. He routinely conducts training and coaching events on the entire FIDIC Rainbow Suite of Contracts, as well as other construction management related topics.

Chapter 3

Christopher Howard

Christopher (Chris) qualified as a non-contentious Construction solicitor with leading London firm Trowers & Hamlins, as part of its award-winning Projects & Construction team. Since 2006 he has worked as a legal Academic and in that time has been a Senior Lecturer at King's College London, delivering the MSc for its renowned Centre of Construction Law and Dispute Resolution. Chris is currently the University Partnerships Director for BARBRI Global and is also the Co-Chair of the International Bar Association's Academic and Professional Development Committee. In addition, Chris also has an ongoing interest in the development of Legal Technology and is an advisory member of the IBA's Future of Legal Services Commission.

Anthony Lavers

Anthony is Visiting Professor of Law at King's College, London and Consultant to the Construction Group at Crown Office Chambers, Inner Temple. He spent 22 years in the London office of global law firm, White & Case, where he was Counsel in the Construction & Engineering Group, providing advice and research on construction and engineering projects and international arbitrations, working on matters in over 20 countries worldwide. His last major role there was as counsel in an international arbitration in Latin America. He also provided English Law training across the firm's network of European offices, and co-authored the text 'FIDIC Contracts; Law and Practice'. A member of Council of the UK's Society of Construction Law for 29 years (Chairman 2004-2006), Prof Lavers has since 2006 given papers to Annual Conferences of the European Society of Construction Law in Stockholm, Prague, Athens, Amsterdam, Liege, Frankfurt, Paris, Milan, Vienna, Fribourg, Bucharest,

Delft, Sofia and Copenhagen, and co-edited 'Studies in European Construction Law', a 12-country comparative study published by ESCL. Anthony Lavers was awarded a D.Litt by the University of Portsmouth 'for published work of high distinction' and was elected a Fellow of the Royal Institution of Chartered Surveyors in 2008.

Phillip Hanna

Phillip is an Australian lawyer currently based in Sydney (Australia) and working for Australia's leading renewable energy and major projects firm, Vision Infrastructure. He has over 18 years' experience in renewable energy, infrastructure, and construction contracts and disputes resolution in both common and civil law jurisdictions.

Phillip has advised and represented clients in all aspects of renewables and major projects, from pre-contractual negotiations through to claims management and disputes resolution. Additionally, Phillip also has experience in all international forms of construction contracts, including FIDIC, NEC, PPC, and ENAA. Phillip has previously worked on some of the largest international arbitration matters for contractor clients, as well as representing a state-owned enterprise in its arbitration disputes.

Phillip previously worked in the United Kingdom and Germany and is admitted as a lawyer in both these jurisdictions. During his time internationally, he worked on some of the world's largest infrastructure projects in both common and civil law jurisdictions.

Phillip has been extensively involved in academia over the last 10 years, which has extended to playing a key role in creating and lecturing at the International Construction Law Masters course for the University of Stuttgart and founding (along with others) the International Construction Law Association (ICLA). Since 2020, he has been continually recognised as a "future leader" in Construction Law, of Who's Who Legal.

Chapter 4

Wolfgang Breyer

Dr. Wolfgang Breyer is founder and managing partner of Breyer Rechtsanwälte, a boutique law firm practicing exclusively in the field of construction and architectural law. In addition, Dr. Breyer is the founder and chairman of the International Construction Law Association (ICLA), a member of the International Academy of Construction Lawyers (IACL), founder of the International Construction Practice and Law MBE program at the University of Stuttgart, and a founding member of the Leading Construction Lawyers International Alliance (LCL).

Chapter 5

François Muller

François assists contractors and industrialists in their projects and disputes, especially in relation to public procurement contracts, JV agreements, construction law, and subcontracting, as well as judicial review of calls for tenders and the filing and litigation of claims in that respect. His clientele encompasses the engineering & construction sectors, the defense and nuclear industries, and railway rolling stock manufacturers.

He has acted as counsel in arbitration procedures, whether administered (ICC, European Development Fund ("EDF") or *ad hoc*.

François Muller is a lecturer at the University of Paris II (Panthéon Assas), LLM *International Construction Contracts*, and a member of the Association Française d'Arbitrage (French Arbitration Association).

Admitted to the Paris bar in 1999, François Muller practiced at Rambaud Martel (1999) and Proskauer Rose (2005) before joining ADVANT Altana as a partner upon its creation in 2009.

Victoria Aquino

Victoria specializes in litigation and dispute resolution processes including arbitration, mediation and dispute board, which involve financial and technical claims relating to major infrastructure and civil engineering projects.

She also assists clients in negotiating and drafting all major construction and consultancy contracts, as well as bespoke contracts. Victoria has a particular knowledge of FIDIC and NEC engineering and construction contracts.

Victoria is a lecturer in international construction contracts at the University of Paris II (Panthéon Assas), Master 2 in Real Estate and Construction Law.

She is member of the International Chapter of the Association Française pour le Droit de la Construction et de l'Immobilier (the AFDCI which includes the French SCL committee) which has launched the French translation of the SCL Delay and Disruption Protocol and is currently working on a harmonised version of the SCL Delay and Disruption Protocol with French law.

Admitted to the Paris bar in 2014, she joined ADVANT Altana the same year.

Victoria holds a Master 2 in Real Estate and Construction Law (University of Paris II Panthéon Assas) and a MSc in Construction Law and Dispute Resolution (King's College London).

Chapter 6

Jinghui Tan

Jinghui is the Director of Beijing Jundu Law Firm. Prior to this, she served as General Counsel for CSCEC International for more than 20 years. She holds Master of Law and Master in Structure Engineering. Besides, she got the training certificate for mediator in Pepperdine University. She holds a number of certificates including the Chartered Institute of Building, Cost Engineer, Level One project manager, Senior economist. Ms.Tan serves as a legal advisor to the Ministry of Housing and Construction and the National Development and Reform Commission, and is currently the Vice Chairman of the Legal Committee of the China Construction Industry Association (CCIA). She also serves as arbitrator for China International Economic and Trade ArbitrationCommission(CIETAC), Beijing Arbitration Commission(BAC)/ Beijing International Arbitration Center(BIAC) and more than 25 other arbitration commissions.

Ms. Tan participates in drafting and discussing a lot of important national legislations,regulations and Model Text in the field of construction. She also provide legal service for the most famous construction projects in China such as Hong Kong-Zhuhai-Macao Bridge (HZMB),Xiongan New Area, subprovincial district of Beijing,Daxing International Airport,China Zun and so on.

Ms. Tan, as one of the country's most renowned experts in construction engineering law, has the most solid professional knowledge and extensive project legal experience in infrastructure development, PPP, domestic and international investment, and complex dispute resolution.

Dongfeng Zhao

Dongfeng is Senior Partner of Beijing ChangAn Law Firm; Board member of International Construction Law Association ("**ICLA**");Executive Director of International Construction Law Program of Peking University (From 2016–2019) ;Expert of China Association of International Engineering Consultants Expert Committee; Expert of China International Contractors Association; Expert of China Society for World Trade Organization Studies and China Association for International Economic Cooperation; Arbitrator of Russian Arbitration Centre; Arbitrator of Shenzhen Court of International Arbitration; Deputy dean of Society of International Trade and Foreign Business Law of Fengtai District of Beijing; Member of China Law Society

Dongfeng worked in a top Chinese international construction company after graduating from Peking University Law School, Beijing, China, then practiced as a counsel for eight years in PinsentMasons LLP, and thereafter practiced at a leading Chinese law firm. Up to now, Mr. Zhao has provided legal services for hundreds of projects in more than 80 countries and has extensive experience in ICC arbitration, UNCITRAL arbitration and local court litigation in China and other countries in the area of construction.

Mr. Zhao has lectured on international construction law and contract at many top universities including Peking University, Tsinghua University, Beijing Foreign Studies University, China University of Political Science and Law, Tianjin University, Tianjin, China, and has also lectured or provided training to numerous construction related academies, institutions, and companies.

Chapter 7

Michael Grose

Michael is well known for conducting complex construction arbitrations pursuant to the DIAC, LCIA, and ICC Rules of Arbitration. He has represented parties in numerous disputes involving variations, extensions of time, early termination and related issues. He has been appointed as a sole arbitrator by the Dubai International Arbitration Centre and is a judge of the Bahrain Court of Cassation assigned to the Bahrain Chamber for Dispute Resolution Court.

In addition to conducting disputes, Michael reviews and drafts conditions of contract and the associated suite of documents for infrastructure and building projects and has extensive experience of the FIDIC Conditions.

Michael is the author of "Construction Law in the United Arab Emirates and the Gulf" (Wiley-Blackwell, 2016), which includes a commentary on the application of the FIDIC Conditions (1999) in the GCC. He has presented papers at various conferences including the Commercial Law Conference in Bahrain for members of the region's judiciary at the invitation of the United States Department of Commerce, the first international conference of the Society of Construction Law as well as the first conference of the Gulf branch of the Society of Construction Law in Dubai.

He is recommended in the top tier of all the leading independent legal directories including Who's Who Legal, Chambers Global and Legal 500.

Aymen Masadeh

Aymen received his education in both the Civil and Common legal systems. He completed his LLB degree at the University of Jordan, LLM at Aberdeen University in the UK, and obtained his PhD from Bristol University, also in the UK. Throughout his career, he has worked in various countries, including the UK, Jordan, and Qatar. In 2011, he made the decision to move to Dubai with his family to embark on an exciting new chapter in their lives. Currently, Professor Masadeh holds multiple esteemed positions at the British University in Dubai. He serves as a professor of law, as well as the Head of the PhD program in Business Law and Dean of the Faculty of Business & Law. Alongside his academic responsibilities, he has made notable contributions to his field. He has published extensively in reputable journals and has been invited to speak at numerous international conferences and events. His research primarily focuses on contract law, construction law, business law, arbitration, and dispute resolution. Additionally, he frequently conducts training sessions on matters related to arbitration and contract law

Professor Masadeh is actively involved in arbitration proceedings. He takes on various roles, including serving as a sole arbitrator, chairman of a tribunal, and co-arbitrator. He is a member of the Chartered Institute of Arbitrators and a board member of the International Construction Law Association. His expertise has led him to be part of the panel of arbitrators at several esteemed arbitration centers, such as the Dubai International Arbitration Centre (DIAC), Abu Dhabi Global Market Arbitration Centre (ADGMAC), London Court of International Arbitration (LCIA), Hong-Kong International Arbitration Centre (HKIAC), Saudi Center for Commercial Arbitration (SCCA), and Asian International Arbitration Centre (AIAC)

Chapter 8

John B. Tieder, Jr. †2017

John concentrated his practice in major construction matters with a particular emphasis on international projects. He was involved in advising clients on a broad range of issues related to the construction of major infrastructure and energy projects throughout the world. He represented foreign governments, utilities, oil companies and U.S. and international contractors in a variety of venues, including federal and state courts and international and domestic arbitration associations. He advised clients in all phases of construction from advising on the most effective procurement process to coordinating financing with U.S. and European credit agencies to resolving complex disputes. He is recognized for his exceptional negotiating and litigation skills.

John was a member of the following associations: the American College of Construction Lawyers (Charter Member); International Center for Disputes Resolution (Panel Arbitrator); American Bar Association; International Bar Association; Federal Bar Association; Inter-Pacific Bar Association; Virginia Bar Association; District of Columbia Bar Association; New York State Bar Association

He was also regularly recognized for his legal prowess in industry publications such as: Martindale-Hubbell AV Preeminent Rating; "2013 Top Rated Lawyer" in International Law & International Trade (American Lawyer Media & Martindale-Hubbell); Super Lawyers, Corporate Counsel Edition, Construction/Surety Law 2009 – 2013; Best Lawyers in America, Construction Law (International) and Construction Litigation Categories - 2003 – 2014; Chambers USA – list of Top Construction Lawyers in Virginia – 2004–2014; Washington

D.C. Super Lawyers, Construction Law – 2007–2013; Legal 500 US – 2009–2010, 2012–2013; International Who's Who of Construction Lawyers - 2005–2013; International Who's Who of Business Lawyers – 2006–2013; Virginia Super Lawyers, Construction Law – 2006–2014.

David F. McPherson

David is the managing partner of the Firm's Irvine office. For 30 years, David has concentrated his practice in major, high stakes construction matters. He is involved in advising clients on a broad range of issues related to the complex construction disputes and litigation. He has a broad range of experience in representing clients on virtually every type of major construction project and provides legal representation to some of the world's largest contractors and engineering firms as well as prominent general contractors, developers owners, and subcontractors in the western United States.

David has handled contract negotiations and disputes involving all types of public and private construction projects throughout the Western United States including, power plants, water treatment plants, wastewater treatment plants, military base construction, libraries, highways, mass transit systems, high-rise apartments, parking structures, hospitals, high-rise buildings, commercial complexes, universities, five-star resorts, international resorts, and high-end luxury homes.

For the past 15 years, David has been an arbitrator with the American Arbitration Association on its Construction Panel and was elected to join AAA's Mega Projects Construction Panel in 2020. Mr. McPherson has served as lead arbitrator (individually and on panels) for over 40 matters and has written awards on relating to disputes with claim values from $1 million to in excess of $12 million.

In addition, David is also a member of the following associations: American Arbitration Association – Arbitrator – Mega Projects Construction Panel and Construction Panel; Associated General Contractors Legal Advisory Committee; Construction Lawyers Society of America – Fellow; American Bar Association; Orange County Bar Association.

Chapter 9

Federico Allendes

Federico received his degree as Bachelor of Legal and Social Sciences from Universidad Diego Portales, Santiago, Chile, in November 1993. In October 1994 he received his law degree from the Chilean Supreme Court. He holds a Master's degree in Business Law from the Pontificia Universidad Católica de Chile. Since 1999 he has practiced professionally in the field of construction law, partaking as an on-site lawyer in infrastructure projects and advising important construction and mining companies present in the Chilean market and abroad, especially in the Latin American forum - Ecuador, Costa Rica. He has participated as speaker and attendee in construction law meetings and congresses. He was Chairman of the Pro Acceso Foundation, which is dedicated to matters of right of access to public information, transparency, and personal data protection law. He has also been director of a non-governmental organization on urban planning and sustainable transportation systems. He is an active member of the Chilean Bar Association (Colegio de Abogados de Chile). He is founder of Chilean law firm Infante Valenzuela

Molina Abogados Limitada, and as a partner of said firm he is the head of the Litigation, Arbitration, and Construction Law practice area.

Alexandre Aroeira Salles

Alexandre is founding and managing partner of Aroeira Salles advising on a range of contentious and non-contentious matters in particular in the infrastructure and energy sectors. His areas of expertise include dispute resolution, procurement, PPPs and concessions, administrative and regulatory law, and the legal management of construction and energy contracts.

Alexandre has advised on some of the most important projects in Brazil, including significant projects for the 2014 World Cup and 2016 Olympic Games. Alexandre is ranked as a leading lawyer in international directories including Chambers & Partners.

Alexandre is currently a board member of the International Construction Law Association (ICLA), director of the Brazilian Institute of Construction Law (IBDiC), and founding member of the Brazil Infrastructure Institute and the Brazilian Institute of Law and Control of the Public Administration (IBDCAP).

Alexandre is a Fellow of the Chartered Institute of Arbitrators (CIArb) and has a PhD in Law from the Pontifical Catholic University of São Paulo.

Francisco Ferreira

Francisco is a senior partner of Aroeira Salles and his areas of expertise include construction law, civil procedure and contract law. Francisco has a strong disputes practice and as a head of the dispute resolution team he oversees many of the firm's most high-profile cases.

Francisco acts closely on high value contractual disputes, mainly in the infrastructure sector, frequently representing clients in hearings including before appeal courts, the Supreme Federal Court (STF) and Superior Court of Justice (STJ) in Brazil. He also advises on the judicial review of acts of regulatory bodies such as the Federal Court of Accounts (TCU) as well as representing clients in relation to proceedings overseas together with local counsel.

Francisco has a significant non-contentious practice, advising Brazilian and international companies on investment and business ventures in Brazil.

Francisco has a post-graduate degree in Public Law from PUC-MG and a master's degree in Dispute Resolution from University College London.

Mariana Miraglia

Mariana is a partner at Aroeira Salles and acts for domestic and overseas clients in relation to major projects in Brazil, advising on the drafting and negotiation of contracts, procurement, contract management, and regulatory law.

Mariana advises clients from various industries, in particular the infrastructure and construction, energy, oil and gas, and naval sectors. She has extensive experience advising on public and private contracts as well as working on significant projects such as roads, railroads, airports, renewable energy projects, urban and industrial infrastructure, and naval construction in Brazil.

Mariana has a particularly strong international practice and assists clients on matters worldwide including the United Kingdom, the United States, and Africa.

Mariana is recognised as a leading lawyer and has been featured among the most admired lawyers in the Análise 500 legal directory.

She has a specialist degree in Public Law from PUC-MG and an L.L.M. in Business Law and in Energy Law and Clean Technology from the University of California, Berkeley.

Chapter 10

Herman Bruserud

Herman Bruserud, PhD, is an associate professor at the Department of Private Law at the University of Oslo. He specializes in the law obligations, sales law and construction contract law. He has previously worked as a lawyer and in the Norwegian Ministry of Justice. For the last ten years, Bruserud has frequently acted as an arbitrator and mediator in commercial disputes, with a special focus on construction projects.

Sylvie Cécile Cavaleri

Sylvie Cécile Cavaleri, PhD, is an Associate professor at the Centre for Private Governance at the Faculty of Law of Copenhagen University. She is a Swiss and Danish qualified attorney, specialized in international contract law and international commercial dispute resolution, with a special focus on construction law. Prior to starting her academic career in 2009, Sylvie worked as a practicing attorney at two top-tier business law firms in Switzerland, as an in-house counsel with a bank in Denmark, and, after the completion of her PhD degree, as a senior legal counsel with a large Danish contractor active on international markets. Sylvie's research and teaching focus on her areas of practice, i.e. international and comparative contract law and international dispute resolution, with a special emphasis in construction law. In parallel to her academic career, Sylvie regularly advises clients and authors legal opinions on various aspects of international contract law and dispute resolution.

Chapter 11

Nikolay Scherbakov

Nikolay is a founding Partner of the "Legal Solutions" Law Firm.

He is also chairman of the Construction Club (constructionclub.ru), a discussion platform on Russian and comparative construction law, as well as a center for the study and training of construction law. Member of the Board of the International Construction Law Association (ICLA).

In addition, Mr. Scherbakov is a lecturer at the Department of Civil Law, Faculty of Law, Lomonosov Moscow State University - the general course of civil law, the course on construction law at the magistracy.

Rounding out Mr. Scherbakov's profile is his work as an arbitrator of the Russian Arbitration Center at the Institute of Modern Arbitration, as well as its branch for dispute resolution in the nuclear industry; a permanent member of the working groups of the Supreme Court of the Russian Federation on the development of resolutions of the Plenum of the Supreme Court on the application of civil legislation by the courts; editor-in-chief and co-author of Russia's only commentary on construction contract (Chapter 37 of the Russian Civil Code), published in 2019; a member of the editorial board of the main

Russian journal on civil law "Civil Law Review"; and author of the adaptation to Russian law FAC-1, published in Russia in 2020.

Chapter 12

Philip L. Bruner

Phillip is a full-time arbitrator, mediator and resolver of disputes and claims arising out of construction, engineering, energy, infrastructure and development projects and other commercial endeavors in the United States and internationally. He is a Member of the JAMS national and international Panels of Neutrals, and is Director of JAMS Global Engineering and Construction panel of neutrals. (See "neutrals" and "practices" at www.jamsadr.com).

Mr. Bruner is co-author with Patrick J. O'Connor, Jr. of *BRUNER & O'CONNOR ON CONSTRUCTION LAW* (ThomsonReuters/West 2002, supplemented annually). Since its publication in 2002, the treatise has been cited as legal authority in more than 550 Westlaw reported judicial opinions.

Mr. Bruner's professional honors include Founding Fellow and past President of The American College of Construction Lawyers; Honourary Fellow of The Canadian College of Construction Lawyers; Fellow of The International Academy of Construction Lawyers; Chartered Arbitrator and Fellow of the Chartered Institute of Arbitrators (London); Arbitrator Member of Britain's Society of Construction Arbitrators; Certified Mediator, International Mediation Institute; and Member of The National Academy of Distinguished Neutrals. Mr. Bruner is a recipient of the 2005 Cornerstone Award presented by the ABA Forum on Construction Law for "exceptional service to the construction industry, to the public and to the legal profession", as well as the 2011 Norman Royce Prize presented by Britain's Society of Construction Arbitrators.

Mr. Bruner earned his Bachelor of Arts Degree from Princeton University, Juris Doctor Degree from the University of Michigan Law School, and Master of Business Administration Degree from Syracuse University.

CHAPTER 1

Applicable Law

Janet Walker CM

Contents

DOI: 10.4324/9781315671376-1

Introduction

1.1 To place the effect of mandatory law on international construction projects into context, it is helpful to begin by examining how the laws governing the contracts in the project are determined. Just as the interplay between party autonomy and local laws and regulations form the basis for the rules of domestic systems of contract law, so too does this interplay shape the means by which the applicable systems of contract law are determined in international projects. This chapter examines the way in which the systems of law governing international construction contracts are determined and the extent to which other laws, including mandatory rules of laws relating to the parties' agreement may apply notwithstanding the governing law.

1.2 The policy issues affecting international construction contracts have been addressed in two ways. First, harmonized regimes, such as the FIDIC forms of contract and the Convention on Contracts for the International Sale of Goods,[1] have been developed to strike a balance between party autonomy and regulation. Second, uniform choice of law rules have been developed to clarify which national law applies in various situations to the many aspects of contractual relations between the parties. One such codified uniform regime is the European Regulation on the law applicable to contractual obligations ("Rome I Regulation"), which applies in the European Union.[2] Another is the Inter-American Convention on the Law Applicable to International Contracts ("OAS Convention"), which was adopted in 1994 by the Organization of American States.[3] A third is the draft set of model "principles" on contract choice of law developed by The Hague Conference on Private International Law that may be adopted by courts and arbitral tribunals.[4]

1.3 Finally, where uniform choice of law rules do not apply, there are common law doctrines that reflect a general consensus on the approach taken to determining the applicable law in common law countries, and there are widely adopted civil code provisions that determine the governing law in civil law jurisdictions.

1.4 Before looking in greater detail at the various ways in which the applicable law is determined, it is worth pausing to note the logistical aspects of ascertaining the content of the applicable law, once that law has been determined. This might seem like a subsequent consideration, but it is anything but that. In the common law, much of the "law" on choice of law is developed by judges who seek to identify and explain, after a dispute has arisen, which law the parties' intended to govern their agreement or which law governs if the parties have not clearly demonstrated a choice. The reasoning process is even more complex than this would suggest because this judicial analysis is based on submissions made by counsel in the course of an adversarial proceeding in which the parties have advanced conflicting positions that they have developed after the dispute has arisen – positions that

1 United Nations Convention on Contracts for the International Sale of Goods (Vienna, 1980) ("CISG").

2 Council Regulation (EC) No. 593/2008 of the European Parliament and of the Council of 17 June 2008 on the law applicable to contractual obligations. The Regulation replaced the European Community Convention on the Law Applicable to Contractual Obligations of 19 June 1980 (80/934/EEC) ("Rome Convention").

3 OAS Treaty Series No. 78 adopted at the OAS's Fifth Inter-American <www.oas.org/juridico/english/treaties/b-56.html> accessed on February 3, 2018.

4 Hague Conference on Private International Law, Draft Hague Principles as Approved by the November 2012 Special Commission Meeting on Choice of Law in International Contracts and Recommendations for the Commentary (2012), available online, Hague Conference on Private International Law <www.hcch.net/upload/wop/contracts2012principles_e.pdf> accessed on February 10, 2018.

they may seek to support with expert evidence that they have commissioned on these points of law.[5] To civil lawyers, it must be difficult to see how such partisan hindsight could reliably inform a sound approach to establishing reliable rules on which to negotiate a contract and from which to seek guidance in its performance. Indeed, in arbitration, where it may be argued that no law is 'foreign', the parties and the tribunal may agree that experts are not needed and that counsel should explain their perspective on the applicable law in their submissions to the tribunal.

1.5 In the civil law, the process is more straightforward. Many civil codes contain the rules for determining the governing law and its content. Once the case is assigned to the judge will determine the contents of the relevant foreign legal system. To do so, the judge may be assisted by a tribunal-appointed expert or by a professional service retained to provide an independent explanation of the content of the governing law if it is not local law. The rules contained in the civil code for determining the applicable law and its contents are available to commercial parties for negotiating and drafting their contracts at the outset of the business relationship.

1.6 In international construction projects, where the number and variety of interrelated contracts often exceeds that in other business relationships, there are often parties from two or more legal traditions. It is helpful, therefore, for each party to be aware of the way in which the law that shapes their contract might be identified and its contents ascertained in the event of a dispute. In many situations, this will be yet another reason why the parties will plan for their disputes to be resolved through a means that does not involve a national court. For example, where the parties choose arbitration, the process of determining the legal rules of the governing law may be more informal, and it may rely more upon the expertise of counsel and the tribunal members themselves.[6]

The Law Governing the Parties' Agreement

1.7 The rules for determining which law governs the interpretation of the parties' agreement arise in two different situations:[7] where the parties' have expressly chosen a law to govern their agreement, and where the parties have not chosen a law to govern their agreement.

Expressly Chosen Law

1.8 The rules in the common law and the civil law traditions for identifying the law that governs the interpretation of the parties' agreement seek to promote party autonomy.[8] For example, the first operative provision of the Rome I Regulation states, "A contract shall be governed by the law chosen by the parties".[9] Similarly, in the leading common

5 Richard Fentiman, *Foreign Law in English Courts* (Oxford University Press 1998).

6 International Law Association, "International Commercial Arbitration Committee's Report and Recommendations on 'Ascertaining the Contents of the Applicable Law in International Commercial Arbitration'" (2010) 26 ArbIntl 193.

7 *Amin Rasheed Shipping Corp v Kuwait Insurance Co* [1984] AC 50 (HL), 61 (Lord Diplock) (Amin Rasheed case).

8 Peter Nygh, *Autonomy in International Contracts* (Clarendon Press Oxford 1999).

9 Rome I Regulation (n 3) Art. 3(1).

law decision, the Privy Council said, "where there is an express statement by the parties of their intention to select the law of the contract, it is difficult to see what qualifications are possible".[10]

1.9 In some situations, it is not clear whether the parties have chosen a governing law or which law they have chosen. For example, if the parties have referred to different laws in different parts of their agreement, it may not be clear whether one of the references to a governing law was unintended or whether the parties intended the two different laws to apply.[11] Similarly, if the choice of law is found in the fine print, or in one of the parties' standard terms, it may be necessary to determine whether the parties intended this provision to form part of the instant agreement.[12] Finally, the parties might have referred to a governing law indirectly, such as by indicating a forum for the resolution of disputes, thereby making it necessary to consider further the circumstances surrounding their agreement to determine whether they also intended the law of that forum to govern their rights and obligations under the contract.

1.10 The Rome I Regulation addresses these situations by providing that "[t]he choice shall be made expressly or clearly demonstrated by the terms of the contract or the circumstances of the case".[13]

1.11 Finally, in some rare situations where there is uncertainty about whether the parties have made an effective choice of a governing law, it may be necessary to identify the law that governs the making of the choice. One approach has been to apply the law chosen by the parties to determine whether their choice is a valid one.[14] However, where there is an issue about whether the parties have chosen a governing law at all, courts have applied either the law the parties appear to have chosen (the "putative proper law"), or the law of the forum.[15]

Choosing Combined Governing Laws

1.12 In certain special situations, the parties may choose to have their contract governed by more than one national law.[16] This is the practice under the Washington Convention for the resolution of disputes between states and commercial parties.[17] Where the par-

10 *Vita Food Products Inc v Unus Shipping Company Limited in liquidation* [1939] UKPC 7, [1939] AC 277 (PC), (1939) 63 Ll L Rep 21 (30 January 1939) (PC on appeal from Nova Scotia) (*Vita Food* case); *The Hollandia* [1983] 1 AC 565, 576; *Amin Rasheed* case (n 8).

11 *St John Shipbuilding & Dry Dock Co v Kingsland Maritime Corp* [1981] FCJ No. 603 (CA) (clauses in purchase order and in subsequently issued bill of lading).

12 *Re Modern Fashions Ltd.* [1969] MJ No. 69, 8 DLR (3d) 590 (QB).

13 Rome I Regulation (n 3) Art. 3(1).

14 *Drew Brown Ltd. v "Orient Trader"* [1972] SCJ No. 143, [1974] SCR 1286 (whether deviation voided choice of law clause to be decided according to the chosen law); *Mackender v Feldia AG* [1967] 2 QB 590 (CA) (effect of illegal purpose or misrepresentation on the validity of a contract was a matter for the proper law).

15 *Egon Oldendorff v Liberia Corporation* [1995] 2 Lloyd's Rep 64, (No. 2) [1996] 2 Lloyd's Rep 380 (*Egon Oldendorff* case).

16 *Montreal Trust Co v Stanrock Uranium Mines Ltd.* [1965] OJ No. 1170 (HCJ) (bondholders' rights could not be governed by a different system of law from the issuing company's obligations).

17 The 1965 Convention on the Settlement of Investment Disputes between States and Nationals of Other States (also referred to as the "Washington Convention"). The purpose of the ICSID Convention is to encourage cross-border investment in developing states by providing an effective means of enforcing contractual rights. To this end, the Convention established the International Centre for Settlement of Investment Disputes.

ties have not chosen a governing law, the laws of the states where the parties are based apply concurrently with such rules of international law as may be applicable.[18] This *tronc commun* approach has been applied in some commercial contracts, perhaps the most notable of which was the Channel Tunnel project[19] in which the parties agreed to apply rules common to both English law and French law and, failing that, general principles of international trade. This generated considerable work for lawyers in interpreting the agreement,[20] and it provoked considerable criticism from the courts resolving the disputes that arose because it was very cumbersome and complex.[21]

1.13 This is not to suggest that the parties cannot choose different laws to govern different parts of their agreement.[22] This could be a practical way, for example, to deal with situations in which the contract contemplates performance in two different places. The need for this could arise when there are two different phases of performance in two different places; or it could occur where the payment obligation must be performed in accordance with local rules that are different from the place where the substantive performance occurs. The Rome I Regulation endorses this possibility, "By their choice the parties can select the law applicable to the whole or to part only of the contract".[23] In the common law, this is described as the technique of "*depeçage*".

Choosing a Non-National Law

1.14 The governing law in matters subject to litigation has generally been restricted to national laws.[24] Even harmonized regimes, such as the CISG for the supply of goods, operate in the context of a national law of the country that has adopted when it comes to resolving interpretive issues and filling gaps in the provisions of the CISG.[25]

1.15 Where the parties have chosen to arbitrate their disputes, they may have more freedom to choose to have their contract governed by a legal regime other than a national

18 Klöckner Industrie-Anlagen v Republic of Cameroon ICSID Case No. ARB/81/2, 03 May 1995.

19 *Channel Tunnel Group Ltd. v Balfour Beatty Construction Ltd.* [1993] AC 334 The contract provided that it would "in all respects be governed by and interpreted in accordance with the principles common to both English law and French law, and in the absence of such common principles by such general principles of international trade law as have been applied by national and international tribunals".

20 Pierre Raoul-Duval, "English and French Law: The Search for Common Principles" (1997) 25 Int'l Bus Law 181.

21 *Centrax Ltd. v Citibank NA* [1999] 1 All ER (Comm) 557, 562 (CA).

22 *Re United Railways of the Havana and Regla Warehouses Ltd.* [1961] AC 1007, [1084] (HL) (*United Railways* case); *Club Mediterranée NZ v Wendell* [1989] 1 NZLR 216; *Re Pope & Talbot Ltd.* [2010] 6 WWR 449 (BC).

23 Rome I Regulation (n 3) Art. 3(1); OAS Convention (n 3) Art. 8.

24 *Amin Rasheed* (n 8) (Lord Diplock); Frédérique Sabourin, "Le contrat sans loi en droit international privé canadien" (2006) 19 RQDI 35 ; Paul Lagarde, "Le nouveau droit international privé des contracts après l'entrée en vigueur de la Convention du 19 juin 1980", in : *Rev.crit.dr.int.pr.* 1991, pp. 300–1. ; Hague Conference on Private International Law, Draft Hague Principles as Approved by the November 2012 Special Commission Meeting on Choice of Law in International Contracts and Recommendations for the Commentary (2012) <www.hcch.net/upload/wop/contracts2012principles_e.pdf> accessed on February 10, 2018.

25 CISG (n 1) Art. 7 provides: (1) In the interpretation of this convention, regard is to be had to its international character and to the need to promote uniformity in its application and the observance of good faith in international trade. (2) Questions concerning matters governed by this convention which are not expressly settled in it are to be settled in conformity with the general principles on which it is based or, in the absence of such principles, in conformity with the law applicable by virtue of the rules of private international law.

law, provided that the arbitral law of the seat permits this. In the case of matters with seats that have adopted the UNCITRAL Model Law, the parties may choose to have their contract governed by a non-national law, but in the absence of choice, a tribunal must identify a national law to govern the parties' contract.[26] In addition, there are many specialized regimes operating in particular sectors, some of them formally codified and others remaining a matter of soft law and trade usages. In the case of trade usages, these are specifically to be taken into account under the UNCITRAL Model Law[27] and the rules of some institutions, such as the International Chamber of Commerce.[28]

1.16 However, in a more general way, in matters subject to arbitration, the *lex mercatoria* may be selected to govern the contract by the parties or the tribunal. Where the *lex mercatoria* is chosen, reference may be made to one of various instruments for its elaboration. One such example is the UNIDROIT Principles of International Commercial Contracts,[29] which codifies general principles of contract. Even where the parties have not chosen to be governed by the *lex mercatoria,* tribunals may resort to the UNIDROIT Principles for the purposes of interpreting the terms of the contract where there is no clear interpretation discernible from a governing national law.

1.17 In rare circumstances, the tribunal may depart from legal rules to decide issues *ex aequo et bono* (on the basis of equity and good conscience) or as an *amiable compositeur.* Under the Model Law, this can occur only where the parties have expressly authorized it.[30]

Incorporating a Law or Legal Regime

1.18 In addition to choosing a law to govern the interpretation of the terms of their contract, the parties are free to incorporate *as a term of their contract,* a particular feature of a national law, such as a specified statutory regime.[31] This is different from *depeçage.* When the parties have incorporated a law for a particular purpose as a term of their contract, the interpretation of their contract as whole continues to be governed by the governing law.

The Version of the Governing Law that Applies

1.19 There is one significant difference in the application of a governing law and a law incorporated into the parties' agreement. In general, the law governing the contract will

26 The Model Law on International Commercial Arbitration ("Model Law") provides, Art. 28 (1) The arbitral tribunal shall decide the dispute in accordance with such rules of law as are chosen by the parties as applicable to the substance of the dispute. Any designation of the law or legal system of a given State shall be construed, unless otherwise expressed, as directly referring to the substantive law of that State and not to its conflict of laws rules. (2) Failing any designation by the parties, the arbitral tribunal shall apply the law determined by the conflict of laws rules which it considers applicable. (3) The arbitral tribunal shall decide *ex aequo et bono* or as *amiable compositeur* only if the parties have expressly authorized it to do so. (4) In all cases, the arbitral tribunal shall decide in accordance with the terms of the contract and shall take into account the usages of the trade applicable to the transaction.

27 Ibid., Art. 28(4).

28 International Chamber of Commerce 2017 Arbitration Rules ("ICC Rules") Art. 21(2).

29 International Institute for the Unification of Private Law, UNIDROIT Principles of International Commercial Contracts 2016 ("UNIDROIT Principles") <www.unidroit.org> accessed on August 30, 2018.

30 Model Law (n 27), Art. 28(3); ICC Rules (n 29) Art. 21(3).

31 *Vita Food* case (n 11) 286, 291–2; *GE Dobell & Co v SS Rossmore Co Ltd.* [1895] 2 QB 408, 412 (CA) (original says "as if they were written").

be the law as at the time the parties seek to apply it,[32] such as when a dispute arises, and not the law as at the time when they entered into the contract. In contrast, a law that is incorporated into their contract will apply unchanged from the time it was incorporated.[33]

1.20 Of course, changes in the governing law could make the contract impossible to perform, thereby giving rise to doctrines that excuse performance. However, short of this, where the parties wish to be insulated against changes in the governing law, particularly in long-term agreements with State parties, they may seek to include stabilization clauses in their agreement. In some situations, this has been held to make some changes to the governing law wrongful, such as the nationalization of the subject matter of the contract,[34] but in other situations it has served merely as the basis for creating an obligation to provide adequate compensation.[35]

1.21 The effect of changes in the law of the country where the permanent works are located is addressed by Sub-Clause 13.7 [*Adjustment for Changes in Legislation*] of FIDIC which contemplates the possibility of extensions of time for completion or payment of the additional resulting cost.

Restrictions on Party Choice

1.22 In the leading common law decision on express choices of a governing law, the Privy Council noted that the parties' choice would be respected "provided the intention expressed is *bona fide* and legal, and provided there is no reason for avoiding the choice on the ground of public policy".[36] This restriction raises the questions of when a choice will be regarded as not *bona fide* and when a choice will be considered illegal.

1.23 A choice of law unconnected with the parties or the contract may, nevertheless, be *bona fide*; for example, where the parties have chosen it because they wish to have their contract governed by a neutral law.[37] However, where the parties choose a law for the purpose of evading mandatory provisions of the law that would, but for their choice, apply to their contract, their choice might be disregarded.[38] It may seem unlikely that the parties would make a sham choice of governing law. It is more likely, therefore, that this situation should be explained differently, that is, as a situation in which the mandatory provisions of

32 Kahler v Midland Bank Ltd. [1950] AC 24 (HL) (Kahler v Midland Bank case) (litigation); Rossano v Manufacturers' Life Ins Co [1963] 2 QB 352 (Rossano case); Sapphire International Petroleum Ltd. v The National Iranian Oil Company (1964) 13 ICLQ 1011, 1012 (arbitration, commercial contracts with government will regime in transition).

33 *Vita Food* case (n 11).

34 *Texaco* and *BP* arbitrations (1981) VI Yearbook Commercial Arbitration 89.

35 *Liamco* arbitration (1981) VI Yearbook Commercial Arbitration 89 lt 104, 113; *Aminoil v Kuwait* [1982] 21 ILM 976.

36 *Vita Food* case (n 11) 290, [1939] 2 DLR 1, 8 (PC).

37 *Boissevain v Weil* [1949] 1 KB 482, 490–1 (CA) (Denning L.J.), affd [1950] AC 327 (HL); *Re Helbert Wagg & Co Ltd.'s Claim* [1956] Ch 323, 341; *Queensland Estates Pty Ltd. v Collas* [1971] Qd R 75 80, 81 (Full Ct); *Hunter Engineering Co v Syncrude Canada Ltd.* [1989] SCJ No. 23, [1989] 1 SCR 426, 57 DLR (4th) 321 (contract between Alberta-based and American-based companies expressly governed by Ontario law).

38 James J. Fawcett, "Evasion of Law and Mandatory Rules in Private International Law" (1990) 49 Camb LJ 44; *Golden Acres Ltd. v Queensland Estates Pty Ltd.* [1969] Qd R 378 (SC) so held, but on appeal the regulatory rule, which was in a statute of the *lex fori*, was simply applied on its own terms: *Freehold Land Investments Ltd. v Queensland Estates Pty Ltd.* (1970) 123 CLR 418 (HC); *Eco Swiss China Ltd. v Benetton International NV* [1999] ECR I- 3055 (ECJ).

applicable laws will apply despite the parties' choice of a different governing law.[39] This is the formulation found in Article 3(3) of the Rome I Regulation, which provides,

> Where all other elements relevant to the situation at the time of the choice are located in a country other than the country whose law has been chosen, the choice of the parties shall not prejudice the application of provisions of the law of that other country which cannot be derogated from by agreement.
>
> [40]

1.24 However, a choice of law will be illegal if it contravenes a statutory prohibition.[41] For example, the Warsaw Convention and the Montreal Convention concerning carriage of goods by air, prohibit the evasion of their provisions by, *inter alia*, choosing a governing law that will have that effect.[42]

Impliedly Chosen Law

1.25 Where the parties have not designated explicitly the law that they wish to govern their contract, common law courts have held that they may nevertheless have implied a choice in the terms of the contract.[43] Such a choice can be ascertained in the same way as any other term of a contract.[44] Examples of this have included contracts with foreign contractors partly directed by foreign governments;[45] contracts of carriage drafted in the style of a particular legal system and conforming with both the local regulations and the regulations of that legal system;[46] contracts for financing insurance premiums payable by an insured workforce in one place to an insurer in another incorporating unique provisions of the insurer's law;[47] oral agreements following written agreements of the same

39 Ibid.

40 Rome I Regulation (n 3) Art. 3(3).

41 *Agro Co of Canada v "Regal Scout"* [1983] FCJ No. 424, 148 DLR (3d) 412 (TD), following *"Morviken"*, [1983] 1 AC 565 (*sub nom "Hollandia"*), [1983] 1 Lloyd's LR 1 (HL); *Akai Pty Ltd. v The People's Insurance Co Ltd.* [1996] HCA 39, 188 CLR 418, (the statute nullified any choice of a foreign governing law where, in the absence of choice, the contract would be governed the law of an Australian jurisdiction); *Soleimany v Soleimany* [1999] QB 785 (CA) (arbitral award denied enforcement in claim arising from contract made in connection with smuggling rugs from Iran).

42 Convention for the Unification of Certain Rules Relating to International Carriage by Air, Signed at Warsaw on 12 October 1929 (Warsaw Convention 1929) Art. 32; Convention for the Unification of Certain Rules for International Carriage by Air (Montreal Convention) Official Journal L 194, 18/07/2001 p. 0039–0049, Art. 49.

43 *Whitworth Street Estates (Manchester) Ltd. v James Miller and Partners Ltd.* [1970] AC 583 (Whitworth Street Estates case); Amin Rasheed (n 8); *The Kominos S* [1991] 1 Lloyd's Rep 370 (CA).

44 *Akai Pty Ltd. v The People's Insurance Co Ltd.* [1996] HCA 39, 188 CLR 418, 440 (express choice and implied choice of a governing law "are but species of the one genus, that concerned with giving effect to the intention of the parties").

45 *Wilson v Metcalfe Construction Co* [1947] AJ No. 68, [1947] 3 DLR 491 (SC), affd [1947] AJ No. 69, [1947] 4 DLR 472 (CA) (construction of the Alaska Highway in Canada).

46 *George C Anspach Co Ltd. v Canadian National Railway* [1950] OJ No. 445, [1950] OR 317, [1950] 3 DLR 26 (SC) (contract of carriage of goods from Washington State to Toronto); *Bunge North American Grain Corp v "Skarp"* [1933] Ex CR 75 (*Skarp* case) (carriage by water from the United States to Canada).

47 *Re Ivaco Inc* [2003] OJ No. 6041, 1 CBR (5th) 204 (SCJ).

sort that include express choice of law provisions;[48] bills of lading incorporating terms of a charter party expressly governed by a particular law.[49]

1.26 A choice of the place for arbitrating disputes may imply a governing law for the substantive terms of the contract itself in the absence of other indications,[50] but this may vary with a consideration of the circumstances of the contract as a whole.[51] A choice of forum for litigating disputes is more likely to be interpreted as implying a governing law than a choice of the place of arbitration.[52] The Rome I Regulation notes that a choice of forum may be a factor in determining whether a choice of law has been clearly demonstrated[53] but the OAS Convention provides that it does not necessarily entail selection of the applicable law.[54]

Objectively Determined Governing Law

1.27 Where the parties have not agreed on the law governing their contract, the governing law will be determined by an objective assessment of all the circumstances[55] at the time the contract is made.[56] The leading common law decision described this as "the system of law by reference to which the contract was made or that with which the transaction has its closest and most real connection".[57] The Rome I Regulation similarly provides for means of identifying a governing law to the extent that the law applicable to the contract has not been chosen expressly or clearly demonstrated by the terms of the contract or the circumstances of the case.[58] The OAS Convention describes the choice made on this basis as the law with which the contract has the closest ties.[59]

1.28 Although this is an objective test that is made in the absence of a discernible choice by the parties, the analysis is guided by an interest in supporting the parties' intentions for the operation of their contract. This militates in favor of a governing law that facilitates

48 Thod Investment Ltd. (cob Jeff Parry Promotions) v André-Philippe Gagnon Inc [2005] AJ No. 1105, 2005 ABQB 601, 385 AR 199 (Master).

49 *"Njegos"* [1936] p. 90, 155 L.T.R. 109.

50 *"Star Texas"* [1993] 2 Lloyd's Rep 445 (CA) (no inference possible where place of arbitration left to be determined by respondent); *Richardson International Ltd. v "Mys Chikhacheva"* [2002] FCJ No. 425, 2002 FCA 97, [2002] 4 FC 80 (financing contract for refitting Russian fishing vessels, arbitration in State of Washington); *NV Kwik Hoo Tong Handel Maatschappij v James Finlay & Co Ltd.* [1927] AC 604 (HL) (*NV Kwik Hoo* case) (Bombay buyers purchasing Java sugar from Hong Kong sellers through Java brokers, with London arbitration clause); *Spurrier v La Cloche* [1902] AC 446 (PC) (*Spurrier* case) (arbitration under the English Arbitration Acts); *Egon Oldendorff* (n 16).

51 *Compagnie Tunisienne de Navigation SA v Compagnie d'Armement Maritime SA* [1971] AC 572 (HL) (*Compagnie Tunisienne* case) (French ship owners contracting with Tunisian company to carry cargo between two Tunisian ports; French law applied despite the provision for arbitration in England).

52 *Hamlyn & Co v Talisker Distillery* [1984] AC 202, 212–13 (HL); *Royal Exchange Assurance Corp v Sjoforsakrings Aktiebolaget Vega* [1902] 2 KB 384, 394 (CA); *NV Kwik Hoo* (n 51) (agreement that arbitration award should be enforceable as a judgment of the English court).

53 Rome I Regulation (n 3) preamble.

54 OAS Convention Art. 7, para 2.

55 Compagnie Tunisienne (n 52); Coast Lines Ltd. v Hudig and Veder Chartering NV [1972] 2 QB 34, 44 (CA) (Coast Lines case); Monterosso Shipping Ltd. v International Transport Workers Federation [1982] ICR 675 (CA); X AG v A Bank [1983] 2 All ER 464.

56 *Whitworth Street Estates* (n 44) 603, 606, 611, 615 (HL) (parties' post-contract conduct irrelevant to establishing proper law).

57 *Bonython v Commonwealth of Australia* [1951] AC 201 (PC) (*Bonython* case).

58 Rome I Regulation (n 3) Art. 4.

59 OAS Convention (n 4) Art. 9.

the performance of the contract[60] and against one that might invalidate its terms,[61] unless that law is a mandatory law that would prohibit agreeing to the terms in question.

The common law has been slow to establish a hierarchy of factors for determining the law with which the contract has its closest and most real connection. It was once thought that the place of contracting met the reasonable expectations of the parties,[62] but the place of contracting has waned in significance with the increasing practice of contracting remotely by electronic means. Other relevant factors in determining the law with the "closest and most real connection" have included: The form of the contract and the legal concepts on which it is based;[63] the language of the contract;[64] the place where the contract was negotiated;[65] the law governing related contracts;[66] the location of the subject matter of the contract;[67] the location of property securing a debt;[68] the place where an insurer accepts the risk;[69] the place where the employee works;[70] the law of the country of the party sought out to perform the contract;[71] the location of the office at which an account is to be operated;[72] the place of the delivery of goods or provision of services;[73] the place of payment;[74] or of the currency required for payment.[75]

---

60 *Sayers v International Drilling Co NV* [1971] 1 WLR 1176 (CA) (*Sayers* case); (accepting the parties' explicit rejection of a particular governing law).

61 *Sharn Importing Ltd. v Babchuk* [1971] BCJ No. 477, 21 DLR (3d) 349 (SC) (*Sharn Importing* case) (formal validity of guarantee); *Cloyes v Chapman* [1876] OJ No. 54, 27 UCCP 22 (CA) (legality of rate of interest on promissory note); *Coast Lines* (n 52) (validity of exemption clause).

62 Peninsular and Oriental Steam Navigation Co v Shand (1865) 3 Moo PCC (NS) 272, 16 ER 103, 110.

63 *Skarp* (n 47) (contract of carriage); *Whitworth Street Estates* (n 44) (construction contract); *Spurrier* (n 51) (insurance policy); *Amin Rasheed* (n 8) (marine insurance policy); *"Industrie"* [1984] P 58 (CA) (charter party); *Chatenay v Brazilian Submarine Telegraph Co Ltd.* [1891] 1 QB 79, 82 (CA) (power of attorney); *"Leon XIII"* (1883) 8 PD 121 (CA) (seaman's employment contract).

64 Eastern Power Ltd. v Azienda Communale Energia and Ambiente [1999] OJ No. 3275, 178 DLR (4th) 409 (CA).

65 *243930 Alberta Ltd. v Wickham* [1990] OJ No. 1781, 73 DLR (4th) 474 (CA).

66 *American Home Assurance Co v Temple Insurance Co.* [2009] OJ No. 249, 94 OR (3d) 534 (SCJ).

67 But see *Whitworth Street Estates* (n 44) (English law governed construction contract for a building in Scotland).

68 *Bonython* (n 58) (bonds secured on revenues of colony); *Mount Albert Borough Council v Australasian Temperance and General Mutual Life Assurance Society Ltd.* [1938] AC 324 (PC) (bonds secured on revenues of municipality).

69 *Rossano* (n 33) (life insurance); *Imperial Life Assurance Co of Canada v Colmenares* [1967] SCJ No. 30, [1967] SCR 443 (*Imperial Life* case).

70 *Caglar v Moore* [2005] OJ No. 4606, [2005] OTC 935 (SCJ) (employment connected with franchise outlets); *Baranowski v Binks Manufacturing Co* [2000] OJ No. 49, 49 CCEL (2d) 170 (SCJ).

71 United Railways (n 23).

72 *Canaccord Capital Corp v 884003 Alberta Inc* [2005] BCJ No. 413, 2005 BCCA 124, 46 BCLR (4th) 64; *Greenshields Inc v Johnston* [1981] AJ No. 946, 119 DLR (3d) 714 (QB), affd [1981] AJ No. 695, 131 DLR (3d) 234 (CA).

73 *Mansonville Plastics (BC) Ltd. v Kurtz GmbH* [2003] BCJ No. 1958, 2003 BCSC 1298 (sale and installation of industrial equipment); *Block Bros Realty Ltd. v Mollard* [1981] BCJ No. 4, 122 DLR (3d) 323 (CA) (real estate agency services); *Rôtisserie May's Ltée v Stoel-Tek Inc* [1990] NBJ No. 1160, 104 NBR (2d) 255 (QB) (delivery and installation of equipment); *Re George Beck Ltd.* [1982] OJ No. 2466, 42 CBR (NS) 307 (SC) (delivery of goods); *Re Viscount Supply Ltd.* [1963] OJ No. 863, 40 DLR (2d) 501 (SC) (delivery of goods); *Deco Automotive Inc v GPA Gesellschaft für Pressenautomation mbH* [1989] OJ No. 1805 (Dist Ct) (delivery and installation of production system).

74 *Rosencrantz v Union Contractors Ltd.* [1960] BCJ No. 91, 23 DLR (2d) 473 (SC) (*Rosencrantz* case) (loan); *United Railways* (n 23) (lease of rolling stock).

75 *R v International Trustee for Protection of Bondholders AG* [1937] AC 500 (HL) (British government bonds issued in US dollars); *"Assunzione"* [1954] P 150 (CA).

1.33 As discussed above, the choice of a place of arbitration may, absent other indications, suggest a governing law. However, it would be wrong to suggest that an international arbitral tribunal has a *lex fori* in the same way as a national court. This raises special considerations for the means by which a governing law is identified by an arbitral tribunal: just as the laws of one legal system differ from the laws of another so too do the rules for determining the governing law. Accordingly, in the case of international arbitration, a question has arisen as to whether an arbitral tribunal should arrive at its determination of the governing law by way of the choice of law rules of a particular legal system (*voie indirecte*) or whether it should do so or simply by applying the law that it regards appropriate (*voie directe*).[76] In some cases, this question is answered either by the *lex fori*, or the arbitration rules under which the arbitration is commenced. For example, under the European Convention on International Commercial Arbitration[77] and the Model Law,[78] the tribunal is required to apply the law determined by the conflict of laws rules that the tribunal considers applicable.

1.34 The Rome I Regulation takes a more direct approach to this question by establishing a clear presumption in favor of the "law of the country where the party required to effect the characteristic performance of the contract has his habitual residence".[79] The Regulation specifies these places in the case of contracts for the sale of goods (seller), the provision of services (provider), franchises (franchisee), and distribution (distributor), and the Regulation specifies that where the contract relates to rights *in rem* or tenancies of immovable property it is the place where the property is situated, and where it is a sale by auction it is the place where the auction is held.[80] Only where the contract is manifestly more closely connected with a different country or where the applicable law cannot be determined by the first two rules is a law other than the law specified applied.[81] The OAS Convention follows the general approach of the common law and the Rome I Regulation by providing for the application of the law chosen by the parties[82] or the law with which the contract has its closest ties.[83] However, the OAS Convention then adds that "the guidelines, customs, and principles of international commercial law as well as commercial usage and practices generally accepted shall apply in order to discharge the requirements of justice and equity in the particular case".[84]

Renvoi

1.35 Sometimes, it happens that the courts of the place of the governing law would apply a different law to determine the rights and obligations of the parties on the point in question. Where the court deciding the case is prepared to apply that other law instead

76 D. Jones "Choosing the Law or Rules of Law to Govern the Substantive Rights of the Parties" (2014) 26 SAcLJ 911.

77 European Convention on International Commercial Arbitration, Geneva, 21 April 1961, Art. VII.

78 Model Law (n 27) Art. 28(2).

79 Rome I Regulation (n 3) Art. 4(2).

80 Rome I Regulation (n 3) Art. 4(1).

81 Rome I Regulation (n 3) Arts. 4(3)–(4).

82 OAS Convention (n 4) Art. 7.

83 OAS Convention (n 4) Art. 9.

84 OAS Convention (n 4) Art. 10.

of the governing law, the process is known as *renvoi*. It is said that *renvoi* has no place in the law of contract[85] because it is presumed that the parties have intended to have their contract governed by the law of the place that they have designated and not by some other law.[86] However, this rationale operates in tension with the question of whether a particular legal rule of the chosen law was intended to apply to purely local dealings or to dealings of an international nature such as those in issue. In other words, it might also be presumed that the parties intended to have the issues in their case resolved in the way that these particular issues would be resolved under the governing law, which may involve the application of a different law.

Non-Contractual Liability

1.36 In some situations in a business relationship governed by contract a claimant may wish to seek recovery for harms arising from negligence or some other wrongful conduct that is not a breach of the contract *per se*. The common law has long recognized the possibility of concurrently liability in contract and tort[87] and has permitted plaintiffs to elect which form of civil wrong to rely upon in framing their claims[88] or, indeed, to rely upon both contract and tort in the alternative in bringing the claim. The question arises as to whether the potential for the application of different choice of law rules would give rise to the possibility of different applicable laws.

1.37 In Europe, under the Rome II Regulation non-contractual obligations arising in a contractual relationship is normally governed by the law governing the contract.[89] This approach has been taken in the common law as well.[90]

Laws Governing Other Aspects of the Agreement

1.38 The "governing law" governs many of the issues that might arise in the business relationship, including those relating to the validity, interpretation, performance, and discharge of the contract, as well as its effect on third parties.[91] However, there are some important questions that may be governed by other laws. It is helpful, therefore, to identify the range of issues that might arise in a contractual dispute and to consider whether they are subject to the governing law or to some other law.

85 United Railways (n 23); Amin Rasheed (n 8).

86 *Rosencrantz v Union Contractors Ltd.* (n 75).

87 Lister v Romford Ice and Cold Storage Co. Ltd. [1957] A.C. 555, 573; Henderson v Merrett Syndicates Ltd. [1995] 2 A.C. 145.

88 *Matthews v Kuwait Bechtel Corp* [1959] 2 Q.B. 57 (C.A.); *Coupland v Arabian Gulf Oil Co.* [1983] 1 W.L.R. 1136, affd [1983] 1 W.L.R. 1151 (C.A.); *Johnson v Coventry Churchill International Ltd.* [1992] 3 All E.R. 14 [hereinafter "Johnson"].

89 Regulation (EC) 864/2007 of the European Parliament and of the Council of 11 July 2007 on the law applicable to non-contractual obligations ("Rome II Regulation"), Art. 4(3); *Samcrete Egypt Engineers and Contractors Sae v Land Rover Exports Ltd.* [2001] EWCA Civ 2019, [2002] CLC 533 [41]–[43].

90 *Johnson* (n 89).

91 *Compagnie Tunisienne* (n 52); Rome I Regulation (n 3) Art. 12.

Capacity

1.39 The capacity of the parties to enter into the contract is generally governed by their personal laws (i.e., the laws of their respective domiciles or residences) in addition to the law governing the contract.[92] Where the contract is with a legal person, the counterparty is able to identify the corporate seat and inquire into the capacity of the corporation or other entity to enter into the contract. Where the contract is with a natural person, it may be less reasonable to require a counterparty to be aware of restrictions on the person's capacity under a foreign law of the person's domicile. Accordingly, the rule seeks to prevent such persons from relying upon "lurking foreign incapacities".[93] The Rome I Regulation formulates this principle as follows:

> [A] natural person ... may invoke his incapacity resulting from the law of another country only if the other party to the contract was aware of that incapacity at the time of the conclusion of the contract or was not aware thereof as a result of negligence.[94]

Formation

1.40 Questions of formation, such as those relating to offer and acceptance and consideration, are typically governed by the law that would apply if the agreement was determined to be valid.[95] Similarly, the Rome I Regulation provides that "[t]he existence and validity of a contract, or of any term of a contract, shall be determined by the law which would govern it under this Regulation if the contract or term were valid".[96]

1.41 Where the existence or validity of the governing clause itself is disputed, the way to determine the governing law may be less straightforward. Where the parties have reached agreement, but there is an issue with the validity of the contract; for example, because it lacks consideration or it is subject to rescission or avoidance for one reason or another, the governing law clause will apply,[97] unless the contract has been obtained by fraud or duress and the governing law displaces the otherwise applicable law.[98] However, in cases where there is a dispute over whether the parties agreed to the applicable law, various options have been considered including applying the objectively determined proper law[99] or, where it is not reasonable to assess the consent of the objecting party on this basis, to apply that person's law to determine whether there was consent.[100]

---

92 L Collins, et al., Dicey, Morris and Collins: The Conflict of Laws (16th edn, Sweeet & Maxwell 2022) (Dicey, Morris and Collins) 1884 et seq.

93 *Charron v Montreal Trust Co.* [1958] OJ No. 640, [1958] OR 597, 15 DLR (2d) 240 (CA); *Bondholders Securities Corp. v Manville*, [1933] S.J. No. 75, [1933] 4 D.L.R. 699 (C.A.).

94 Rome I Regulation (n 3) Art. 13.

95 Sharn Importing (n 62).

96 Rome I Regulation (n 3) Art. 10(1).

97 *Re Bonacina* [1912] 2 Ch 394 (CA) (*Re Bonacina* case) (agreement to pay a sum already owing held binding because governed by Italian law).

98 *Blanchard v Jacobi* [1918] OJ No. 149, 43 OLR 442 (HC).

99 Albeko Schuhmaschinen AG v Kamborian Shoe Machine Co. Ltd. (1961), 111 LJ 519 (QBD).

100 The Rome I Regulation (n 3) Art. 10, para 2 provides "Nevertheless, a party, in order to establish that he did not consent, may rely upon the law of the country in which he has his habitual residence if it appears from the circumstances that it would not be reasonable to determine the effect of his conduct in accordance with the law specified in paragraph 1". The OAS Convention (n 4) Art. 12, para 2 provides: "to establish that one of the

Formal Validity

In many legal systems, the choice of law rule for formal validity operates differently from most choice of law rules in that it does not provide for the application of one law to the exclusion of others. Rather, to support the parties' intentions, the rule permits the application of the law of the place of contracting *or* the governing law (and perhaps also other laws) to be relied upon to validate the contract. The reason is that compliance with the formal requirements of the governing law may not be feasible in the place of contracting, and yet it would be unreasonable to apply the law of the place of contracting to invalidate the contract. This has been described as a permissive approach to the principle of *locus regit actum*.[101]

The Rome I Regulation provides that, if the parties or their agents are in the same country when the contract is made, the contract is valid as to form if it complies with the law of that place or the law that governs the contract.[102] If the parties or their agents are in different countries, the Rome I Regulation permits the contract to be validated by the law of either of the countries, or the law of the country of either party's habitual residence.[103]

Where the contract concerns the transfer of an immovable, such as real property, the conveyance of that property must conform to the requirements of the place where the land is situated.[104]

Essential Validity

1.42 All other issues of validity are considered to be questions of *essential* validity and they are subject to the law governing the contract. These include issues such as whether there has been consideration;[105] whether the contract is for an illegal purpose,[106] whether particular parts of the contract are valid such as limitation or exclusion of liability clauses;[107] or clauses limiting extra-contractual liability, such as liability in tort.[108]

1.43 Further issues that are regarded as matters of essential validity include: Issues of waiver and estoppel;[109] statutory rules barring claims for the balance of the debt after

parties has not duly consented, the judge shall determine the applicable law, taking into account the habitual residence or place of business".

101 *Ross v Ross* [1894] 2 SCR 307.

102 Rome I Regulation (n 3) Art. 11, para 1.

103 Rome I Regulation (n 3) Art. 11, para 2.

104 Rome I Regulation (n 3) Art. 11, para 5.

105 *Re Bonacina* (n 98).

106 *Hochberger v Rittenberg* [1916] SCJ No. 68, 54 SCR 480, 36 DLR 450 (fraudulent preference); *Mackender v Feldia AG* [1967] 2 QB 590 (CA) (agreement in furtherance of an illegal scheme).

107 *Vita Food* (n 11) (contractual exclusion of liability); *James Richardson & Sons Ltd. v "Burlington"* [1930] SCJ No. 42, [1931] SCR 76, [1930] 4 DLR 527 (statutory exclusion of liability); *Bunge North American Grain Corp*

v "Skarp", [1933] Ex CR 75 (statutory exclusion of liability); *Sayers* (n 61) (contractual limitation of liability).

108 *Sayers* (n 61).

109 *Sunlite International Inc v Trans-Canada Resources Ltd.*, [1978] AJ No. 798, [1978] 5 WWR 345 (TD) (whether claim was barred by failure to perform condition precedent).

foreclosure and sale of a property,[110] and claims for fees by unlicensed agents or brokers.[111] The governing law also determines the extent of implied obligations,[112] such as liability to pay interest on overdue amounts;[113] and whether the contract has been invalidated in whole or in part by a change in the law.[114]

Interpretation and Effect of the Contract

1.44 The governing law determines the interpretation of the contract,[115] even where a particular term or concept is foreign to that law,[116] or the question is one of the extent to which trade usages and other circumstances surrounding the negotiation of the contract may be considered.[117] Exceptionally, the governing law may permit reference to another legal system for particular terms or concepts.[118] For example, units of measurement[119] and currency[120] are taken to be those found in the governing law, unless it is clear that a different measure or currency was intended.[121]

1.45 Similarly, the nature of the obligations are understood as they would be under the governing law, such the obligations of an insurer[122] or the rights of a seller under a conditional sales agreement,[123] subject, of course, to proprietary stipulations under the law of the place where the property is located.[124]

---

110 *Sigurdson v Farrow*, [1981] AJ No. 996, 121 DLR (3d) 183 (QB) (*Sigurdson* case); *243930 Alberta Ltd. v Wickham* [1990] OJ No. 1781, 73 DLR (4th) 474 (CA).

111 *Ezer v Yorkton Securities Inc* [2005] BCJ No. 30, 2005 BCCA 22 (CA); *Sennett v Tape Estate* [1986] SJ No. 223, 45 Sask R 314 (QB).

112 *Dallas Oilfield Contractors Ltd. v Syroteuk* [1980] SJ No. 832 [1980] 3 WWR 119 (Dist Ct).

113 *Montreal Trust Co. v Stanrock Uranium Mines Ltd.* [1965] OJ No. 1170, 53 DLR (2d) 594 (HCJ); *Fergusson v Fyffe* (1840), 8 Cl & F 121, 8 ER 49 (HL).

114 Mount Albert Borough Council v Australasian Temperance and General Mutual Life Assurance Society Ltd. [1938] AC 224 (PC); F & K Jabbour v Custodian of Israeli Absentee Property [1954] 1 WLR 139 (QBD); Imperial Life (n 33); Etler v Kertesz [1960] OJ No. 568, 26 DLR (2d) 209 (CA); Zivnostenska Banka National Corp v Frankman [1950] AC 57 (HL); R v International Trustee for Protection of Bondholders AG [1937] AC 500 (HL); De Beéche v South American Stores (Gath & Chaves) Ltd. [1935] AC 148 (HL); Rossano (n 33); Re Claim of Helbert Wagg & Co. Ltd. [1956] Ch 323.

115 *Vita Food* (n 11).

116 *Di Sora v Phillips* (1863) 10 HL Cas 624, 638, 11 ER 1168, 1174.

117 Whitworth Street Estates (n 44).

118 *Rowett, Leakey & Co. v Scottish Provident Institution* (1927) 135 LT 558 (CA) (expression in an English insurance contract interpreted according to Scottish law); *Agat Laboratories Ltd. v EnGlobe Corp* [2013] JQ No. 17626, 2013 QCCS 6272 (Alberta law applied to the "interpretation" of a service agreement where Québec law governed the agreement as a whole).

119 *Melady v Jenkins Steamship Co.* [1909] OJ No. 194, 18 OLR 251 (CA) (whether US or Canadian "bushel" was meant).

120 *National Bank of Australasia Ltd. v Scottish Union & National Insurance Co. Ltd.* [1952] AC 493 (PC) (Queensland company's deposit stock issued in "pounds" were redeemable in Australian pounds); *Bonython* (n 58) ("pounds" meaning, when the bonds were issued, Queensland pounds).

121 Pyrmont Ltd. v Schott [1939] AC 145 (PC); Ottoman Bank of Nicosia v Chakarian [1938] AC 260 (PC).

122 Gerling Global Insurance Co. v Canadian Occidental Petroleum Ltd. [1998] AJ No. 918, 1998 ABQB 714.

123 *Hannah v Pearlman and Selchen* [1953] BCJ No. 146, [1954] 1 DLR 282 (SC).

124 *Re Maritime Heating Co.* [1968] NBJ No. 20, 2 DLR (3d) 471 (CA) (local requirement to register the security interest).

Mode of Performance and Laws Affecting the Obligation

1.46 While the governing law determines the nature of the obligation, this may be subject to various aspects of the law of the place of performance, such as those relating to local business hours[125] and licensing requirements,[126] and may also include matters such as the local grace period for payment on a bill of exchange once presented.[127]

1.47 A payment obligation may involve two potentially applicable laws: The *currency of payment*, which is determined by the law of the place where the payment is to be made; and the *currency of account*, which is determined by the law governing the contract. Accordingly, where the place of payment prescribes the local currency as the only legal tender, payment must be made in that currency but in an amount equal to the currency determined by the law governing the contract,[128] or that stipulated by the parties. The exchange rate is based on the amount of the currency of payment required to purchase the amount in the currency of account on the day payment is due. The rate and basis for computing interest on a payment obligation is based on the law governing the contract.[129]

1.48 The law of the place of performance can also affect the nature of the obligation where, for example, illegality under that law either makes performance impossible and, therefore, extinguishes, or alters the obligation,[130] or where illegality renders whole or part of the contract unenforceable. This is different from the application of local rules for enforcing obligations, which may have no effect on the obligation itself.[131]

Discharge

The proper law determines the nature of the obligations arising from a contract and whether those obligations have been discharged by performance, by taking the security,[132] by breach,[133] by insolvency,[134] or by some excusing event such as frustration or *force*

125 *Dallas Oilfield Contractors Ltd. v Syroteuk* [1980] SJ No. 832, [1980] 3 WWR 119 (Dist Ct) (entitlement to overtime).

126 *AV Pound & Co. v MW Hardy & C. Inc* [1956] AC 588 (HL) (which party must obtain the license).

127 *Rouquette v Overmann and Schou* (1875) LR 10 QB 525, 542.

128 *Weiss v State Life Insurance Co.* [1935] SCJ No. 17, [1935] SCR 461, [1935] 4 DLR 5 (Ontario-based insured was to be paid in "dollars" at insurer's head office in Indiana, obligation was denominated in Canadian dollars); *Groner v Lake Ontario Portland Cement Co.* [1960] OJ No. 603, 23 DLR (2d) 602 (CA) (California consultant's fees denominated in US dollars despite employment on Ontario project); *Myers v Union Natural Gas Co.* [1922] OJ No. 16, 53 OLR 88 (HC) (royalties on natural gas extracted from Ontario land and sold in Ontario payable in the US but in Canadian dollars); *Bonython* (n 58) (obligation denominated in Australian currency despite obligation to pay in London); *De Bueger v J Ballantyne & Co. Ltd.* [1938] AC 452 (PC) (English man hired to work in New Zealand for annual compensation stated in "pounds sterling" held entitled to salary computed in UK currency); *Mount Albert Borough Council v Australasian Temperance and General Mutual Life Assurance Society Ltd.* [1938] AC 224 (PC) (obligation denominated in New Zealand currency although payment to be made in Victoria).

129 *Livesley v E Clemens Horst Co.* [1924] SCJ No. 40, [1924] SCR 605, 609, [1925] 1 DLR 159, 162.

130 *Ralli Bros v Compania Naviera Sota y Aznar* [1920] 1 KB 614; [1920] 2 KB 287, 291, 300 (CA) (*Ralli Bros* case).

131 *Khalij Commercial Bank Ltd. v Woods* [1985] OJ No. 2500, 17 DLR (4th) 358, 50 OR (2d) 446 (HCJ).

132 *Sigurdson* (n 111), *Trans Canada Credit Corp Ltd. v Prince* [1965] MJ No. 78, 53 DLR (2d) 92 (CA); *Canadian Acceptance Corp Ltd. v Matte* [1957] SJ No. 41, 9 DLR (2d) 304 (CA).

133 *Drew Brown Ltd. v "Orient Trader"* [1972] SCJ No. 143, [1974] SCR 1286, 34 DLR (3d) 339.

134 *Re Hudson Fashion Shoppe Ltd.* [1925] OJ No. 117, [1926] 1 DLR 199 (C.A.); *Re Ivaco Inc* [2003] OJ No. 6041, 1 CBR (5th) 204 (SCJ).

majeure.[135] Legislation in the place of the governing law can affect the nature of the obligation itself,[136] but not legislation elsewhere, such as in the place of performance. Whether a new agreement between the parties under the same governing law has changed the obligations is a question of the validity of the second agreement.[137] The effect of a subsequent agreement on the parties' obligations is a question of whether this is possible under the law governing the first agreement and a question of whether this has occurred under the law of the second agreement.[138] A similar principle applies to whether one party has been replaced by another party.[139]

Assignment, the Rights of Third Parties, and Effects on Property

1.53 The assignment of rights under a contract is a transfer of intangible movable property but certain aspects of the assignment relate to the laws governing the contract in question. Whether a benefit under the contract may be assigned is a matter for the governing law of the original contract,[140] but the validity and effect of the assignment is a matter for the law governing the assignment agreement.[141] The assigned obligations continue to be determined by the law governing the original contract. Notice to the debtor and other steps needed to make the assignment effective are matters for the law governing the assignment agreement.[142]

1.54 Third party rights other than those arising from an agency relationship are a matter for the law governing the contract, including the right to rely on an agreed limitation of liability against the third parties in question.[143] In insurance matters, the law governing a life insurance policy determines who are the validly designated beneficiaries,[144] and the law governing an automobile insurance policy determines whether an insured can claim directly against the insurer.[145] The ability of heirs to claim against a person with

135 *Newfoundland (Attorney General) v Churchill Falls (Labrador) Corp* [1983] NJ No. 142, 49 Nfld & PEIR 181, affd [1985] NJ No. 80, 56 Nfld & PEIR 91 (CA), affd [1988] SCJ No. 53, [1988] 1 SCR 1085; *Jacobs, Marcus & Co. v Crédit Lyonnais* (1884), 12 QBD 589.

136 Kahler v Midland Bank Ltd. (n 33); R v International Trustee for Protection of Bondholders AG [1937] AC 500 (HL); Re Helbert Wagg & Co. Ltd..'s Claim [1956] Ch 323 (debt moratorium characterized as affecting the contractual obligation, and not confiscation of property invoking the lex situs of the debt).

137 *Instrument Concepts-Sensor Software Inc v Geokinetics Acquisition Co.* [2012] NSJ No. 69, 2012 NSSC 62, 313 NSR (2d) 200 (whether settlement agreement implicitly included choice of forum clause in previous contract).

138 *Rosencrantz v Union Contractors Ltd.* (n 75), 476–7.

139 *Re United Railways of the Havana and Regla Warehouses Ltd.* [1960] Ch 52, 84–6 (CA), revd in part on other grounds [1961] AC 1007 (HL).

140 *Plastyle Inc v CKF Inc* [1992] OJ No. 3889, 8 BLR (2d) 210 (Gen Div), affd [1993] OJ No. 3542, 8 BLR (2d) 210n (CA) (whether assignment champertous).

141 *Raiffeisen Zentralbank Osterreich v Five Star Trading LLC* [2000] 1 All ER (Comm) 897, varied [2001] QB 825 (CA).

142 *Laîné v Viking Helicopters Ltd.* [1999] JQ No. 1462, [1999] RJQ 1472 (SC); *Regas Ltd. v Plotkins* [1961] SCJ No. 34, [1961] SCR 566, 29 DLR (2d) 282 (right to sue the debtor in assignees name is a procedural issue governed by the *lex fori*).

143 St John Shipbuilding & Dry Dock Co. v Kingsland Marine Corp [1981] FCJ No. 603, 126 DLR (3d) 322 (CA).

144 *Gray v Kerslake* [1957] SCJ No. 62, [1958] SCR 3, 11 DLR (2d) 225 (New York law governed whether Ontario-resident beneficiary of an annuity had to consent to insured's designating a different beneficiary).

145 Eg., *Insurance (Vehicle) Act*, RSBC 1996, c. 231, s 76.

contractual liability in respect of the death of the victim is governed by the fatal accidents legislation of the law governing the contract.[146]

1.55 The law of the place where property is situated usually determines whether and when title is passed in a sales contract, even where the contract of sale is governed by a different law.[147]

Laws that Apply in Addition to or Notwithstanding the Governing Law

Rules that Cannot be Derogated From by Agreement

1.56 The Rome I Regulation provides that:

> [w]here all other elements relevant to the situation at the time of the choice are located in a country other than the country whose law has been chosen, the choice of the parties shall not prejudice the application of provisions of the law of that other country which cannot be derogated from by agreement.[148]

1.57 Under this rule, rules of law, typically statutory rules, apply despite the parties' choice of some other law to govern their contract. This consideration is bound to arise with frequency in international construction projects where the law governing the contract may be different from the law of the place where the project is being undertaken. A host of laws, such as labour laws and building codes, will apply even if the agreement between owner and contractor is governed by a different law. In a sense, these laws apply within their scope in tandem with the law chosen by the parties and, in the event of inconsistency between the two, the statutory provisions prevail. However, this principle is not directed merely (or, perhaps, primarily) at rules at the place of performance, but operates "where all other elements relevant to the situation at the time of the choice are located in a country other than the country whose law has been chosen".

1.58 There are many laws that apply at the place of the works that can have important implications for the contract and that cannot be derogated from. Among these are labour laws, regulatory standards, and statutory adjudication. For example, under the *Housing Grants, Construction and Regeneration Act 1996*, the parties to a construction contract in England are required to submit disputes, such as those over interim payments, delay and disruption, extensions of time for completion, and the final account, to a process of adjudication that creates a decision that is binding until the dispute is finally determined by legal proceedings, arbitration, or by agreement.[149] Similar adjudication schemes exist

146 *Herman v Alberta (Public Trustee)* [2002] AJ No. 308, 2002 ABQB 255, [2002] 7 WWR 177, 2 Alta LR (4th) 132.

147 Air Foyle Ltd. v Center Capital Ltd. [2002] EWHC 2535 (Comm); Dicey, Morris and Collins (n 93) 1393 et seq.

148 Rome I Regulation (n 3) Art. 3(3).

149 Scheme for Construction Contracts (England and Wales) Regulations 1998 (SI 1998/649). In *Yuanda (UK) Co. Ltd. v WW Gear Construction Ltd.* [2010] EWHC 720 (TCC), the plaintiff, a UK subsidiary of a Chinese curtain walling contractor was engaged by the defendant to on the construction of Plaza Hotel, Westminster Bridge Park under a JCT Trade Contract with amendments, which included changes to adjudication and the interest on late payment. The adjudication clause required the plaintiff to pay the legal fees of both parties and the adjudicator should it make a referral to adjudication, irrespective of whether it won or lost in the adjudication, and the interest on late payments was amended by the defendant from the JCT standard of 5% to just 0.5% above the base rate. Edwards-Stuart J held that the adjudication provision was not compliant

in a number of other common law countries, such as Malaysia, Singapore, New Zealand, Hong Kong and some of the Australian states and Canadian provinces. A choice of law other than a law where the contract is being performed will not affect the obligation to participate in such a scheme.

1.59 Similarly, the law in a number of civil law countries includes a concept of decennial liability, which in some countries includes an obligation to obtain decennial liability insurance (latent defect insurance) to cover the costs associated with the fix serious defects that appear in a building in the ten years following completion.[150] The cost, which may amount to 1.5% of the value of the works can increase the construction costs significantly. A choice of law other than a law of the place where the contract is being performed will not affect these obligations.

Overriding Mandatory Provisions

1.60 In relation to the essential validity of the contract, it was noted above that a contract may be regarded as invalid and unenforceable if it is for a purpose that is illegal under the law of performance (*lex loci solutionis*).[151] There is some debate over whether this is a choice of law rule that operates as an expression of public policy or whether it is merely an expression of the doctrine of frustration or force majeure under which performance of a contract governed by the law of the forum would be excused if performance were illegal under the law of the place of performance.[152] Under the Rome I Regulation, a court may give effect:

> to the overriding mandatory provisions of the law of the country where the obligations arising out of the contract have to be or have been performed, in so far as those overriding mandatory provisions render the performance of the contract unlawful.[153]

1.61 The application of the mandatory provisions of the place of performance is a matter of discretion for the court. The Regulation goes on to provide, "[i]n considering whether to give effect to those provisions, regard shall be had to their nature and purpose and to the consequences of their application or non-application".[154] In the common law, where the parties' contract is not itself the product of a conspiracy to engage in illegality,[155] the

---

with HGCRA 1996 and set them aside in favour of Part 1 of the Scheme (i.e., the entire statutory adjudication rules were applicable rather than the contractual rules); and held that the contractual interest rate was not a substantial remedy. The statutory rate was 8% above the base rate; and 0.5% above the base rate was clearly not a substantial remedy, and so the Late Payment of Commercial Debts (Interest) Act 1998 rate of 8% applied. The judge held that the practical effect of the amended adjudication clause was that the plaintiff would be deprived of the benefit of adjudication up to the amount of WW's costs which were, technically unlimited, and this would fetter the right to adjudicate in contravention of s108 of HGCRA.

150 French Civil Code, *Art.* 1792 *et seq.*

151 *Ralli Bros* (n 131).

152 See *Dicey, Morris and Collins* (n 93) 1906-1910.

153 Rome I Regulation (n 3) Art. 9(3).

154 Rome I Regulation (n 3) Art. 9(3).

155 *Foster v Driscoll* [1929] 1 KB 470, 518 (CA).

illegality under the law of the place of performance may not operate to extinguish entirely the rights under the contract.[156]

Rome Regulations and Contracts in Construction

1.62 Some salient issues of the application of the Rome I Regulation to contracts in construction projects[157] are considered in this section based on the limited jurisprudence on contracts in construction projects under the Rome I Regulation.[158] The Rome I Regulation seeks to establish the applicable law as follows:

a) Stage 1 – Party autonomy is paramount. The contract is governed to the extent possible by the law chosen by the parties provided that their choice is made expressly or clearly demonstrated by the terms of the contract or the circumstances of the case.[159] The issue that parties may encounter is the extent to which the applicable law may be implied. For instance, if the sub-contract for works does not mention the applicable law, does the applicable law of the main construction contract for works apply to the sub-contract for works? In *JMJ Contractors Ltd v Marples Ridgway*,[160] the parties agreed to the FCEC subcontract, which was silent on the applicable law. The main contract was based on the FIDIC construction contract (2nd edn), and it identified the laws of Iraq as its governing law. The court held that the law of Iraq also applied to the subcontract because it had to operate in conjunction with the main FIDIC contract and was compatible with the main contract.
b) Stage 2 – If the parties' choice is not clearly demonstrated, then the governing law is determined in accordance with Art. 4(1). The four categories potentially relevant to construction contracts include:
contracts for the sale of goods[161] – law of the country where seller has habitual residence.[162] This may apply to suppliers of goods in construction but is unlikely to apply to construction works as a whole unless the "goods" are central to the contract and are supplied pre-fabricated, as may occur, for example, in some wind and hydro power projects;
contracts for the supply of services[163] – law of the country in which the service provider has his habitual residence. In common law jurisdictions this might apply to contracts with architects, engineers, project managers, and other construction-related consultant agreements. However, in some civil

156 *Re Courtney Ex p Pollard* (1830) Mont & Ch 239, 250; *Frischke v Royal Bank of Canada* 919770 80 DLR (3d) 393 (Ont CA).

157 This includes construction contracts, consultancy agreements, supply agreements, concession agreements, and other agreements related to construction projects.

158 English cases dealing with the applicable law in construction projects under the Rome Convention, include *Ennstone Building Products Ltd. v Stranger Ltd.* [2002] EWCA Civ 916 (negligent provision of consultancy work) but these were decided under a previous version of the Rome I Regulation.

159 Rome I Regulation (n XX) Art. 3(1).

160 (1985) 31 BLR 100.

161 Rome I Regulation (n 3) Art. 4(1)(a).

162 "*Habitual residence*" is defined under Art. 19 of Rome I Regulation.

163 Rome I Regulation (n 3) Art. 4(1)(b).

jurisdictions such as Germany, contracts such as those with architects are considered "work contracts" and not "services contracts". There may also be uncertainty if the parties do not state the applicable law in contracts for procurement routes in EPCM or construction management, where these may be regarded "services contracts" because the contractors are merely providing services that facilitate the construction;

contracts relating to rights *in rem* or tenancy (i.e., right in use) of immovable property[164] – law of country in which property is situated. It is unlikely that this will apply to construction contracts but could be relevant to a concession holder (generally a contractor consortium) under a PPP construction model where the government authority transfers/leases land and/or assets to the contractor for operation and/or construction to be transferred back to the government authority at the end of the contract period;[165]

distribution contracts[166] – law of country where distributor has his habitual residence.

c) Stage 3 – If the contact does not fall with the list described above under Art. 4(1), the contract will be governed by the law of the habitual residence of the party required to effect its characteristic performance.[167] This is likely to be the case for construction contracts, subject to the escape clause and default rule.

To apply this rule, it must be determined which party is required to perform the "*characteristic performance*" and also what this includes. The Recitals explain that the characteristic performance is determined "*having regard to its centre of gravity*".[168] In simple transactions, this is typically the party other than the party who has the payment obligation. However, in large construction projects, where parties from different legal systems provide the goods and services contributing to the building works, it can be complicated. Even where the provision of goods or services is limited to the construction, design, or supply of material, it is increasingly supplied from offices globally with multiple parties located in different countries. This can prove challenging in determining the characteristic performance and the centre of gravity of the contract.[169]

d) Stage 4A (escape clause) – If the contract is "*manifestly more closely connected*" with a country other than the country identified in the previous rules, then that other country's law applies.[170] This would have to be clearly evident,[171] as indicated in *Danzas & Westra v Tapiola*[172] where the French Supreme Court

164 Rome I Regulation (n 3) Art. 4(1)(c).

165 This is not limited to the described PPP model and can include BOT, BOOT and PFI models in their many variant forms.

166 Rome I Regulation (n 3) Art. 4(1)(f).

167 Rome I Regulation (n 3) Art. 4(2).

168 Rome I Regulation (n 3) Recital 19.

169 Art. 19 of the Rome I Regulations does provide guidance with a definition for "*habitual residence*" however this is not without its own complexities. Note that it is unlikely courts will hold that counter performance, usually taking on the form of money (i.e., payment), is the characteristic performance in a contract.

170 Rome I Regulation (n 3) Art. 4(3).

171 R Pender and M Wilderspin, *The European Private International Law of Obligations* (3rd edn, Sweet & Maxwell 2009), p 196.

172 Ibid., [2007] Rev. Crit. DIP 592.

emphasized that the court needed to compare the connections between presumptive applicable law and the law contended to apply, and in *Caledonia Subsea v Microperi*,[173] where a clear preponderance of factors favoured the other law.[174]

Factors such as performance taking place in a country other than the law determined by Arts. 4(1) and (2) may not be sufficient to trigger the escape clause. For instance, the German Supreme Court stated (in obiter) that in a construction contract the location of the construction site was not a sufficient factor in applying Art. 4(5) of the Rome Convention (being equivalent to the current Art. 4(3) of the Rome I Regulation).[175] In *Ferguson Shipbuilders Ltd v Voith Hydro GmbH & Co. KG*,[176] Voith (based in Germany) entered into a construction and delivery contract with Ferguson (based in Scotland) for propeller systems to be incorporated into ships being built in Scotland for Scottish buyers. The propeller systems were tailor-made for the vessels being built in Scotland. The court determined that Scottish law applied because the contract had a real connection only with Scotland. Performance was in Scotland and construction and delivery of the propellers were closely and unambiguously connected to the construction works in Scotland.[177]

e) Stage 4B (default rule) – If the applicable law cannot be identified by using any of these provisions, then the contract is governed by the law of the country which is most closely connected.[178]

173 Ibid., S.C. 70, Inner House, Court of Session.
174 Ibid., p 197.
175 BGH, February 25, 1999, VII Z.R. 408/97.
176 [2000] S.L.T. 229.
177 R Pender and M Wilderspin (n 172), p 198.
178 Rome I Regulation (n 3) Art. 4(4).

CHAPTER 2

International Construction Contracts

FIDIC

Leo Grutters and Erlmest Burns

Contents

 DOI: 10.4324/9781315671376-2

Introduction

2.1 This chapter introduces the reader to the fundamentals of the FIDIC (Fédération International des Ingénieur Conseils) Standard Forms of Major Works Contracts.[1] FIDIC publishes a large variety of documents supporting the international construction industry, but there are a few that are considered to be the foundations for the rest.

History of the FIDIC Organization

2.2 In order to facilitate a thorough understanding of the principles underpinning these publications, it is imperative that FIDIC as an organization is briefly explained. The very existence of FIDIC as an organization is in fact a coincidental consequence of a general requirement for services of independent expert consultants in relation to the 1913 World Fair Exhibitions. The exhibition was held in Ghent (Belgium) from 26 April to 3 November 1913.

2.3 An important driving force behind the fair was Paul Marie Ghislain Otlet (1868–1944), who was an early proponent of international cooperation promoting the formation of associations enabling knowledge to become available on a global scale. He is famous for having co-founded the Union of International Associations in 1907 together with Henri La Fontaine (1854–1943), a Nobel Peace Prize winner (1913). Both Otlet and La Fontaine were instrumental in bringing together every international association existing in the world.

2.4 Consequently, on 22 July 1913, the initial discussion led to the creation of the Fédération Internationale des Ingénieurs Conseils (FIDIC) or later the International Federation of Consulting Engineers. The formal founding members were Belgium, France and Switzerland. FIDIC's first elected President was Louis Prangey from France (1913–1937). Over the years other countries joined the federation, but it was not until the 1950s that a true international identity was achieved when South Africa, the USA, Canada and Australia joined as the first non-European bloc. As of 2022, the organization has some 100 member states,[2] all contributing to an effective umbrella for the consulting engineering profession around the globe.

The FIDIC Code of Ethics

2.5 When FIDIC was founded in 1913, it was done so with the objective of promoting the professional interests of the member associations, and to enable broadcasting of information of interest to its members. Its founding principles were quality, integrity, and sustainability. Principles that remain fundamental pillars of the organization today. Overall, these principles are defined in the FIDIC Code of Ethics. These were developed as a result of FIDIC's belief that the work of the consulting engineering industry is critical to the achievement of sustainable development of society and the environment, whereby engineers should strive to continuously improve their knowledge and skills, but where

1 Unless otherwise stated, all clause references in this chapter are to the First Edition 1999 version of the respective FIDIC Contract. Where appropriate, differences between the various books and editions are noted.

2 For a full listing of member states refer www.fidic.org under FIDIC Member Associations & Associates (www.fidic.org/members).

society must be able to trust and respect the integrity and judgement of the members of the engineering profession. All member associations subscribe to and believe in the following fundamental principles:[3]

Responsibility to Society and The Consulting Industry

2.6 The Consulting Engineer shall:

- Accept the responsibility of the consulting industry to society;
- Seek solutions that are compatible with the principles of sustainable development;
- At all times uphold the dignity, standing and reputation of the consulting industry.

Competence

2.7 The Consulting Engineer shall:

- Maintain knowledge and skills at levels consistent with development in technology, legislation and management, and apply due skill, care and diligence in the services rendered to the client;
- Perform services only when competent to perform them.

Integrity

2.8 The Consulting Engineer shall:

- Act at all times in the legitimate interest of the client and provide all services with integrity and faithfulness.

Impartiality

2.9 The Consulting Engineer shall:

- Be impartial in the provision of professional advice, judgement, or decision;
- Inform the client of any potential conflict of interest that might arise in the performance of its services to the client;
- Not accept remuneration which prejudices its independent judgement.

Fairness to others

2.10 The Consulting Engineer shall:

- Promote the concept of "Quality-Based Selection" (QBS);
- Neither carelessly nor intentionally do anything to injure the reputation or business of others;
- Neither directly nor indirectly attempt to take the place of another Consulting Engineer, already appointed for a specific work;
- Not take over the work of another consulting Engineer before notifying the Consulting Engineer in question, and without being advised in writing by the client of the termination of the prior appointment for that work;

3 www.fidic.org/about-fidic/fidic-policies/fidic-code-ethics.

- In the event of being asked to review the work of another, behave in accordance with appropriate conduct and courtesy.

CORRUPTION

2.11 The Consulting Engineer shall:

- Neither offer nor accept remuneration of any kind which in perception or effect either a) seeks to influence the process of selection or compensation of consulting engineers and/or their clients, or b) seeks to affect the Consulting Engineer's impartial judgement;
- Co-operate fully with any legitimately constituted investigative body which makes inquiry into the administration of any Contract for services or construction.

FIDIC's Organizational Structure

2.12 As stated before, FIDIC is a global umbrella organization representing the consulting engineering industry at large. At the core of the FIDIC organization are the member associations. Each member state is represented through its local engineering organization (only one per member state). For example, for Germany that is the "Vereinigung Beratender Ingenieure", or VBI, or for the UK it would be the "Association for Consultancy and Engineering", or ACE. Each member association itself has national memberships, mostly companies (or individuals) involved in the engineering and construction industries.

Executive Committee

2.13 Decision making within FIDIC is vested within the Executive Committee, which is made up of representatives of nine Member Associations. The Executive Committee is responsible for the administration and management of all matters concerning the organization, and in particular the strategic planning of such matters as continuous assessment of developments affecting the consulting industry at large; planning of actions to reposition FIDIC; and review and update, or prepare, new FIDIC policies.

2.14 The strategic decisions made by the Executive Committee are in principle carried out by specialist committees and the Secretariat.

Secretariat

2.15 At present the Secretariat is located at the FIDIC Headquarters, World Trade Centre II, Geneva (Switzerland). It is responsible for the day-to-day management of all necessary operational matters concerning the organization.

Specialist Committees

2.16 The Executive Committee and the Secretariat are supported by Specialist Committees, staffed by volunteers globally.

2.17 The most important committee is the "Contracts Committee". The Contracts Committee recommends to the Executive Committee which Conditions of Contract and related documents should be prepared or updated by FIDIC. It assists the Secretariat in establishing task groups as required, to monitor their work at agreed intervals and to conduct a final review of the documents for submission to the Executive Committee.

2.18 The Contracts Committee also liaises with organizations interested in FIDIC Conditions of Contract and documents. The Contracts Committee is supported at various times by different task groups as needed.

Task Groups

2.19 The Task Groups are staffed by selected experts from around the globe. Typically, a task group would be composed of a number of people with a variety of backgrounds suited to the tasks mandated. Their principal mandate is to carry out the objectives of the responsible committee. For the Contract Committee, this would be the research and development of appropriate wording and structure to either revisions for existing or, alternatively, new documents that the Executive Committee has decided upon.

FIDIC Standard Forms of Contract

Evolution of the FIDIC Contracts

2.20 In 1957, FIDIC published its "*Conditions of Contract (International) for Works of Civil Engineering Construction 1st Edition 1957*".[4] This was very much based on the "*Overseas (Civil) Conditions of Contract*" published by ACE (UK's Association for Consultancy and Engineering), also often referred to as the "*ACE Contract*".[5] The ACE Contract being an adaptation of the version of the ICE Contract in use primarily as a domestic standard form civil engineering Contract in the UK.[6]

2.21 Over the years, FIDIC was aware of the rival Contracts published by the Institute for Civil Engineers (ICE), and the subsequent updates to the 1st Edition kept remarkably close to those rival forms. The FIDIC Red Book 3rd Edition (1977) was close enough to the 1973 ICE 5th Edition, for some industry users to express concern about the stand-alone position of the FIDIC effort. It was not until FIDIC published its acclaimed 4th Edition in 1987, that a role-reversal could be identified. As per Edward Corbett[7] on the development of the FIDIC 4th Edition, one could identify a symmetry with the ICE 6th Edition 1991 – an obvious hint that this time around the ICE was "borrowing" from the FIDIC achievement in 1987.

2.22 FIDIC's aim had always been to produce a Standard Form of Contract that could be used throughout the international world, but due to its initial development being so close to the UK's ACE and ICE forms, it was difficult not to notice the influences inherited from the Common Law system (discussed below). What was required was a more general style that could be implemented in various jurisdictions independent of the underlying legal system. This proved to be a challenge, as it was not only the independence from a certain legal system that needed to be achieved, but also independence from the Laws of a country within which a construction project was being executed (this does not extend

4 As a matter of interest, it is believed that because of the rather lengthy title of that 1957 1st Edition, the construction industry preferred to refer to it as the "Red" Book because of its distinct red cover, and it has kept its "nickname" ever since.

5 Nael G. Bunni, *The FIDIC Forms of Contract* (3rd edn, Blackwell Publishing 2005), giving a useful guide on the actual development of the Red Book.

6 Ibid.

7 Edward Corbett, *FIDIC 4th – A Practical Legal Guide* (Sweet & Maxwell 1991).

to the overriding mandatory laws of the country). The solution was to publish a set of general terms and conditions and allow or even encourage the Parties to amend them through particular conditions, and to supplement this with a set of various other relevant documents which set out and define the scope of the Parties' obligations and the basis of their Contracted terms. Also, all this to suit any local legal peculiarities to which the project may be subjected. This has been the concept of the FIDIC forms of Contract for many years, and it has proven largely successful.

The FIDIC Rainbow Suite of Contracts

2.23 Red Book – The Red Book represents a traditional re-measurement Contract, where the Employer provides all or most of the design and the Contractor constructs the works in accordance therewith. Under the Red Book, the Contractor has very limited if any design obligations. The Contract management is undertaken by the Engineer, who is not a Party to the Contract, but rather a Third-Party engaged by the Employer.

2.24 Yellow Book – The original Red Book was in effect a form of Contract specifically written for civil engineering projects, and consequently FIDIC decided at the time that the industry was in need of additional forms of Contract to cater for other types of projects. The first such alternative Contract was the "*Conditions of Contract for Electrical & Mechanical Works*", commonly referred to as the Yellow Book.

2.25 Orange Book – This was followed in 1995 by the "Conditions of Contract for Design Build and Turn-Key", or the Orange Book. As is evident, these forms of Contract differentiated on the basis of what type of construction project was contemplated. For example, power plants could easily be split into a civil engineering section and an electrical and mechanical section.

2.26 It would seem that the FIDIC split into Red and Yellow Books was a logical alternative for use on such complex projects. But times were changing, and the construction industry moved from a sectional project execution to a more holistic model where the entire works would be carried out by one Contractor, that is, the civil as well as the electrical and mechanical parts. In addition, the technological revolution would enable Contractors to develop new modern methodologies to facilitate quicker and cheaper solutions to erstwhile complex engineering problems. The result was that project owners developed a realisation that the design, as a traditional "Employer task", in certain projects, would be better realized by the Contractor. This was in essence the reason for the development of the Orange Book. So, it was not unexpected that FIDIC realized it had to react to this change in market requirements. This realisation culminated into the, what is now known as, 1st Edition 1999 Rainbow Suite of Contracts.

2.27 This new set of Contracts differed remarkably from the widely accepted 1987 Red (4th) and Yellow (3rd) Books. Basically, FIDIC had decided that the market was better served by a set of Contracts that were based on who ultimately would provide the design for the works to be executed. The current Rainbow Suite of Contracts (1999–2017) comprises the four Contracts for major works, that is, (i) Red Book for designs by the Employer,[8]

8 *FIDIC Conditions of Contract for Construction*, First Edition. FIDIC, 1999 ("Red Book").

(ii) Yellow Book for designs by the Contractor,[9] (iii) Silver Book for Turn-Key/EPC projects (design by Contractor),[10] (iv) the Gold Book (2008)[11] and the Emerald Book (2019):[12] for projects designed by the Contractor but with an additional component to cater for the commercial operation by the Contractor after completing the build-phase. There are additional Contracts for smaller projects (Green Book – 2021), dredging and reclamation works (Blue Book – 2006), the Sub-Contract for use with the Red Book (2011), and others.

Structure of the Contract

2.28 One of the Characteristics of the FIDIC Suite of Contracts is its structure and layout across the various forms. In particular, the General Conditions, which will be discussed later are structured in a very similar way, with minor changes to accommodate the particularities of the types of projects for which they were drafted. The documents forming the basis of a FIDIC Contract are also largely consistent across the various forms with slight variations depending on the specific needs of the various books.

Conditions of Contract (General and Particular)

2.29 The conditions of Contract comprise the General and Particular Conditions. Together, these form the central element of the Contract and are the principal source of the rights, obligations and responsibilities of the Parties dealing with the design and construction of the Works. The Particular Conditions modify and/or supplement the General Conditions in order to tailor the Contract to the specific needs of the project and expectations of the Parties.

Contract Agreement

2.30 The Contract Agreement is the formal record of the agreement between Parties. It sets forth basic information such as the Parties, a description of the Works, and the documents forming part of the Contract. The Contract Price or Accepted Contract Amount is generally included in the Letters of Tender and Acceptance, which are two of the documents that make up the Contract.[13]

Letter of Acceptance

2.31 The Letter of Acceptance, signed by Employer, is the Employer's formal acceptance of the Contractor's offer (Letter of Tender/Tender), which may include any annexed memoranda comprising agreements between and signed by both Parties.[14]

Tender/Letter of Tender – Appendix to Tender

2.32 The Tender/Letter of Tender is the Contractor's offer submitted in response to the Employer's invitation to tender. In the Red and Yellow Books this includes the complete

9 *FIDIC Conditions of Contract for Plant and Design-Build for Electrical and Mechanical Works and for Building and Engineering Works Designed by the Contractor*, First Edition. FIDIC, 1999 ("Yellow Book").

10 *FIDIC Conditions of Contract for EPC/Turnkey Projects*. FIDIC, 1999 ("Silver Book").

11 *FIDIC Conditions of Contract for Design, Build and Operate Projects*. FIDIC, 2008.

12 FIDIC Conditions of Contract for Underground Works 2019.

13 See Red, Yellow, and Silver Books, Sub-Clauses 1.1.1.2 and 1.6.

14 See Red, and Yellow Books, Sub-Clause 1.1.1.3.

Appendix to Tender. The Appendix to Tender is a critical document identifying many key terms of the Contract, such as the names and addresses of the Parties and the Engineer, the Time for Completion, the Defects Notification Period, amount of Performance Security and Advance Payment (if any), delay damages, etc.[15]

Other Key Documents Making up the Contract

2.33 In addition to the foregoing, there are a variety of documents, which address in large part the performance of the works. Such documents include the Specification, which describes the Works in detail;[16] Drawings, which are Drawings of the Works that are issued by the Employer and may be added to or modified from time to time;[17] the Employer's Requirements, which describe in detail, among other things the purpose, scope, technical and design requirements, and other information necessary for the Works;[18][19] the Contractor's Proposal, which describes the Contractor's plan for carrying out the Works in accordance with the Employer's Requirements;[20] Schedules, which are documents prepared and submitted by Contractor along with the Letter of Tender such as Bill of Quantities, rates and/or prices.[21]

Risk Distribution

2.34 Construction projects are vulnerable to a host of risks, but in its most basic concept these risks can be categorized as:

- The risk of not completing on time;
- The risk of not completing within budget;
- The risk of not completing in accordance with the envisaged quality.

What is of importance here, is the way FIDIC has opted to deal with these various risks as a fundamental concept that recurs in all the Standard Forms of Contract it publishes.

2.35 It is first necessary to understand some core principles of risks in construction projects (or, for that matter, in general). Once a project is conceived by its owner, and the owner has initiated a process of procurement to get the project on its next stage of development, it is by definition subjected to the full array of risks that may or may not eventuate during its life cycle. It is logical that the project owner, in the very first instance, also owns all these risks. He will continue to do so, until he decides to transfer some of these risks to other Parties with whom he opts to Contract in order to have the project executed. Since the formation of a Contract by definition aims to identify and apportion the rights and obligations of the Parties to such Contract, it is not difficult to see that such apportionment can only be done effectively if the underlying risks associated with any identified

15 See Red, Yellow, and Silver Books, Sub-Clauses 1.1.1.4. See also Red and Yellow Books Sub-Clauses 1.1.1.8 and 1.1.1.9.

16 See Red Book, Sub-Clause 1.1.1.5.

17 See Red Book, Sub-Clause 1.1.1.6.

18 See Yellow and Silver Books, Sub-Clauses 1.1.1.5 and 1.1.1.3, respectively.

19 The Employer's Requirements replace the Specification and Drawings from the Red Book.

20 See Yellow Book, Sub-Clause 1.1.1.7.

21 See Red and Yellow Books, Sub-Clauses 1.1.1.7 and 1.1.1.6, respectively.

obligation or right are properly assessed. This applies without a doubt to any construction project and its associated Contract(s).

2.36 It is incumbent on the project owner, as good and prudent project strategies require, to identify and assess the numerous risks that his project may or may not be exposed to. It is at this juncture that he has to decide on whether these identified risks are acceptable or not. This is in fact the first "Go/No-Go" decision that has to be made. Assuming that the risks are at first evaluation acceptable, the next step would be to assess if and how these risks could be eliminated or at the least mitigated. Typically for a construction project this assessment is at the highest level divided into the elementary construction project phases, that is, (i) conception and pre-tender, (ii) construction, and (iii) warranty and post-construction.

2.37 What follows is fundamental for any Construction Contract: The owner must now decide to what extent he wishes to transfer the identified and assessed risks to other persons. These other persons are typically either insurers or Contractors to a part (or the whole) of the project execution stages. The owner must be aware that if he does not manage these risks properly at this stage, the viability and/or success of the project could be placed in serious jeopardy.

2.38 Transferring risks is not without problems either. It would seem logical that if all risks, no matter what, could be disposed of to some other Party, the project owner would be without exposure, other than the monetary premium to be paid to the Party actually taking on the transferred risk. History has proven this to be wrong! The concept of transferring risks, or also called "risk allocation" must by definition be based on the principle of it being fair and balanced. There are numerous historic legal cases that have dealt with this sometimes-contentious issue, and an evaluation of some of the leading ones will provide a useful set of criteria when determining proper risk allocation:[22]

I. Which Party can best control the risk, and/or its associate consequences? (***McCook v Lobo & Others***[23] and ***Yarm Road Ltd. & Anor v Hewden Tower Cranes Ltd.***);[24]
II. Which Party can best foresee the risk? (***Eckersly & Others v Binny & Others***[25] and ***Sandhu Menswear Company Ltd. v Woolworths plc***);[26]
III. Which Party can best bear that risk? (***Eckersly & Others v Binny & Others***);[27]
IV. Which Party ultimately most suffers or benefits when the risk actually eventuates? (***Davis v Fareham UCD***).[28]

2.39 It is fair to say that FIDIC, under the guidance of Prof. Dr. Nael G. Bunni,[29] its special advisor on risk and insurance issues (among others), has incorporated those criteria in all its publications.

22 Lydia B. Bunni, Risk and Insurance in Construction, Construction Bar Association of Ireland, 2015.

23 *McCook v Lobo & Others* [2003] 1 ICR 89.

24 *Yarm Road Ltd. & Anor v Hewden Tower Cranes Ltd.* [2002] EWHC 2265 (TCC) (4th November 2002).

25 *Eckersly & Others v Binny & Others* [1988] 18 ConLR 1.

26 *Sandhu Menswear Company Ltd. V. Woolworths plc* [2006] EWHC 1299 (TCC) (5th June 2006).

27 op. cit. n. 20.

28 *Davis v Fareham UCD* [1956] AC 696.

29 Prof. Dr. Bunni is a Chartered Engineer, Chartered Arbitrator, Conciliator/Mediator and Visiting Professor in Construction Law and Contract Administration, Trinity College Dublin. Past President of the

A comparison of risk allocation between the various FIDIC Contracts

2.40 Generally speaking, across the FIDIC Rainbow Suite, the more control the Contractor has over the execution of the project, the more risk it will ultimately bear. This is consistent with a fair and balanced approach to risk allocation, since ultimately the more control a Party has, the better the position it will be in to foresee, control, and manage such risks. However, as the risk profile for the Contractor increases the Contract Price inevitably increases with it. Below are a few examples of differing risk allocations based on the chosen Contract.

DESIGN RISK

2.41 In the Red Book all (or at least the vast majority) of the design is to be undertaken and provided by the Employer. As such, the Contractor has no liability for design errors, except to the extent that it was required to provide certain design under the Contract.[30] This is in stark contrast to the Yellow Book, where the Contractor takes on a much greater design obligation, and the Silver Book where the Contractor has full design liability, including for design and other documents provided to it by the Employer.

GROUND RISK

2.42 The ground risk, specifically with regard to Unforeseeable conditions, remains with the Employer and unchanged across the Red and Yellow Books.[31] In contrast, under the Silver Book the Contractor is "*deemed to have obtained all necessary information as to risks, contingencies and other circumstances which may influence or affect the Works*" and "*accepts total responsibility for having foreseen all difficulties and costs of successfully completing the Works*" and therefore has no entitlement to an adjustment of the Contract Price for any unforeseen difficulties or costs.[32]

RISK OF QUANTITIES

2.43 In the Red Book, being a traditional design-bid-build remeasurement Contract, the risk of quantities lies with the Employer. All quantities in the Bill of Quantities or any Schedule are considered estimated values.[33] While the same is true under the Yellow and Silver Books, the risk shifts to the Contractor, except where, under the Yellow Book, remuneration is to be based on actual quantities supplied or work done.[34] No such provision exists under the Silver Book, such that the lump sum Contract Price is meant to cover all the works to be performed under the Contract.

EMPLOYER'S RISKS AND FORCE MAJEURE

2.44 Clauses 17 and 19 address the Employer's Risks and *Force Majeure.* These two clauses largely mirror each other with respect to the risks which are covered. Those risks

Chartered Institute of Arbitrators; Past President of the Association of Consulting Engineers of Ireland. Past Member of the LCIA Board of Directors.

30 Red Book, Sub-Clause 4.1.

31 See Red and Yellow Books, Sub-Clause 4.12.

32 Silver Book, Sub-Clause 4.12.

33 Red Book, Sub-Clause 14.1 (c).

34 Yellow Book, Sub-Clause 14.1.

are generally outside of the influence or control of either Party, difficult to insure against, and normally not attributable to the other Party. However, there are several key differences between the two clauses which are worth addressing. With the exception of natural catastrophes, Employer's Design, and use or occupation of the Works by the Employer, which are risks to be borne by the Contractor under Clause 17 of the Silver Book,[35] these two clauses are largely identical across the Red, Yellow, and Silver Books.

2.45 Clause 17 addresses risks and indemnities and in particular the Contractor's Care for the Works.[36] Where an Employer's Risk[37] event occurs resulting in loss or damage to the Works, the Contractor is entitled to an extension of the Time for Completion and/or costs to the extent that the Employer requires that such loss or damage be rectified.[38] Clause 19 deals with *Force Majeure*,[39] where the Contractor may be entitled to an extension of the Time for Completion and in some cases costs to the extent that its performance was prevented as a result of the occurrence of a *Force Majeure* event.[40] FIDIC has provided some guidance as to the meaning of "prevented" in the *Force Majeure* context and clarified that prevention requires that performance was "*insurmountable*" such that performance became "*impossible ... with no alternative method of performance to avoid the problem*" and not merely more difficult or costly.[41]

FIDIC General Conditions[42]

2.46 The General Conditions under FIDIC were overhauled for the 1999 Rainbow Suite. The total number of clauses in the Red Book, for example, were reduced from 72 to 20 and were also reorganized in a more thematic and logical way.

2.47 Generally speaking, the clauses have been organized according to the following general themes:

- General provisions – Clause 1;
- Contract participants and their respective duties – Clauses 2–4;
- Design and resources – Clauses 5–7;
- Time – Clause 8;
- Testing, taking-over, and defects liability – Clauses 9–11(RB)/12(YB/SB);
- Payment and variations – Clauses 12–14;
- Termination – Clauses 15–16;
- Risk, insurance, and *Force Majeure* – Clauses 17–19;
- Claims and disputes – Clause 20.

35 Compare Sub-Clause 17.3 in the Red, Yellow, and Silver Books.
36 See Red, Yellow, and Silver Books, Sub-Clause 17.2.
37 See Red, Yellow, and Silver Books, Sub-Clause 17.3.
38 See Red, Yellow, and Silver Books, Sub-Clause 17.4.
39 *Force Majeure* has been replaced by Exceptional Events in the 2017 Versions of the Red, Yellow, and Silver Books; however, there is little difference with regard to content.
40 See Red, Yellow, and Silver Books, Sub-Clause 19.4.
41 FIDIC COVID-19 Update, Issue 1: 27 March 2020 (https://fidic.org/node/29210).
42 For this section, see generally the Red, Yellow, and Silver Books.

General Provisions – Clause 1

2.48 Under Clause 1, all significant terms are defined. In addition, all other general terms are addressed relating to the interpretation of the Contract, including the language for communications, form of notice, applicable law and language, and priority of documents.

Contract Participants and their Duties – Clauses 2–4

2.49 Clauses 2 through 4 address the roles, responsibilities and obligations of the Contract participants. Here the term Contract participants (as opposed to Parties) is used since the Engineer, who plays a key role in the administration of the Contract but is not a Party, is addressed in Clause 3 (RB/YB/GB).

Design and Resources – Clauses 5–7

2.50 Clauses 5 through 7 deal with resources and design. Under the Red Book, where the Contractor has no or very limited design obligations, Clause 5 addresses Sub-Contractors, whereas under the Yellow and Silver Books, the design obligations of the Contractor are addressed. Under Clause 6 Staff and Labour are dealt with, which includes among other things working conditions, adherence to any applicable labour laws, health and safety, and supervision. Clause 7 is primarily concerned with ensuring that the quality of the Plant, Materials, and Workmanship meet the contractual requirements and the Employer's entitlements, should those standards not be met.

Time – Clause 8

2.51 Clause 8 focuses on time related provisions including among other things the Commencement Date, the time for Completion of the Works and extensions thereto, delay damages, and suspension of the Works by the Employer and its consequences.

Testing, Taking-Over, and Defects Liability – Clauses 9–11(RB)/12 (YB/SB).

2.52 Clauses 9 through 11 govern issues surrounding Taking-Over and post Taking-Over defects liability. Under the Yellow and Silver Books Clause 12 deals with the performance of tests after Taking-Over and thus fits thematically here.

Payment and Variations – Clauses 12 (RB)/13 (YB/SB)–14

2.53 Clauses 12 (RB) through 14 address Payments and Variations. Clause 12 in the Red Book provides the method of measurement and evaluation of the works performed by the Contractor. Clauses 13 covers Variations as well as other mechanisms for adjusting the Contract Price with regard to changes in legislation or price escalations. Clause 14 addresses the general terms regarding and the procedure for payment.

Termination – Clauses 15–16

2.54 Clauses 15 and 16 cover the grounds for and consequences of Termination by the Employer and Contractor, respectively. Clause 16 also addresses the Contractor's suspension rights.

Risk, Insurance, and Force Majeure – Clauses 17–19[43]

2.55 Under Clauses 17 and 19 Risks which are generally outside the control of either of the Parties are addressed. Clause 17 deals with the Contractor's entitlement to claim

43 In the Second Edition (2017) Version of the Red, Yellow, and Silver Books ("Second Edition"), Clause 17 has been renamed "Care of the Works and Indemnities"; Clause 18 now addresses what was formerly referred

for additional time and/or costs arising out of damage to the works for certain enumerated risks, which largely mirror those found in Clause 19 *Force Majeure*, whereby Clause 19 regulates the situation where a Party is prevented from performing any or all of its obligations as a result of the occurrence of a *Force Majeure* event. Clause 18 covers the insurance obligations of the Parties. Clause 18 addresses the insurance obligations of the Parties.

Claims and Disputes – Clause 20[44]

2.56 Under Clause 20 the notice obligations of the Contractor are addressed with regard to claims, which include a time bar mechanism, should the Contractor fail to meet its notice obligations within the timescales set forth therein. Furthermore, the tiered dispute resolution mechanism is set forth, providing for a DAB in the first instance followed then by arbitration.

The Role of the Engineer

2.57 The FIDIC Engineer is another vestige of the common law roots of the FIDIC Suite. The Engineer's role very much reflects the common law approach of having an impartial (or fair or neutral)[45] Contract administrator, who is not only responsible for issuing determinations with regard to claims, but also for the day-to-day management of the Contract on behalf of the Employer. The Contract administration/project management duties of the FIDIC Engineer are a foreign concept in many Civil law jurisdictions, where a project manager with no engineering background may be engaged to perform many of these administrative duties.[46]

2.58 The Engineer's authority and duties are described in Clause 3 of the Rainbow Suite.[47] Therein the Engineer is tasked with the administration of the Contract, which includes acting on behalf of the Employer. Nevertheless, except as set forth in the Particular Conditions, the Employer shall not place any further restrictions on the Engineer's authority under the Contract.[48]

2.59 The Engineer is further authorized to delegate certain duties and authority to others and to revoke such delegation. Such delegation does not require the approval of the Parties; however, the Engineer is not empowered to delegate its authority to determine any matters pursuant to Sub-Clause 3.5. Those delegees must be suitably qualified for the tasks delegated to them and shall enjoy only such authority which is expressly assigned to them in the delegation.[49]

---

to as *Force Majeure* (Clause 19 of the First Edition 1999) under the heading "Exceptional Events"; Clause 19 now regulates Insurance (formerly Clause 18 in the First Edition 1999).

44 In the Second Edition claims and disputes were separated out into their own individual Clauses (20 and 21, respectively). In addition, Employer's Claims are treated identically to Contractor's Claims, most notably with respect to the notice requirements.

45 Compare FIDIC Red Book 4th edn (1987), Sub-Clause 2.6; Red Book, Sub-Clause 3.5; and FIDIC Red Book 2nd edn (2017) Sub-Clause 3.7.

46 See also German Law Chapter 4.42.

47 But see FIDIC Silver Book, where Clause 3 deals with the Employer's Administration and the role of the Engineer is subsumed by the Employer's Representative.

48 See Red and Yellow Books, Sub-Clause 3.1.

49 See Red and Yellow Books, Sub-Clause 3.2.

2.60 Furthermore, the Engineer is entitled to issue instructions (in accordance with the Contract) to the Contractor or modify certain Drawings as may be necessary for the completion of the Works or remedying of defects. Such instructions must be given in writing whenever practicable; however, oral instructions may be confirmed in writing (by the Contractor), whereby such written confirmation shall be deemed the written instruction, if the Engineer or its delegate does not reply in writing within two days rejecting the confirmation or issuing the instruction itself.[50]

2.61 Finally, the Engineer is responsible under the Contract for seeking agreement between the Parties or determining certain matters. In the absence of agreement, the Engineer is required make a fair determination.[51]

2.62 This dual role as a neutral Third-Party for the purposes of determining claims and as an employee of the Employer for the purposes of Contract management can lead to controversy and dissatisfaction on both the Employer and Contractor sides, and for similar reasons. The Contractor may often see the Engineer as an agent or employee of the Employer and as such any determinations or decisions to the detriment of the Contractor must be biased; whereas on the other hand, the Employer may see the Engineer as its employee and expect that the Engineer's determinations reflect that, such that the determinations are made in the Employer's favour.[52]

Claims and Dispute Resolution under FIDIC

2.63 It is said that Construction Contracts are written with claims and disputes in mind, as the very essence of a construction project dictates their occurrence. This stems in principle from the fact that such projects are almost always subject to variations and changes as they develop. But this is not the only reason contracting Parties find themselves in a position of having to pursue claims or disputes. They originate from a variety of reasons, for example:

- Technical changes/variations;
- Weather impact;
- Coordination with Third-Parties within the overall project;
- Legislative changes;
- Ambiguous or incomplete contractual wording;
- Etc.

2.64 These are all project risks that should have been identified, assessed/evaluated and allocated by the owner at the early stages of the project. Depending on the required allocation, the responsibility for these risks should be regulated within the terms and conditions of the Contract.

2.65 FIDIC has always promoted a multi-tiered dispute management and resolution procedure. This effectively means that for any issue between the Parties, the Contract will

50 See Red and Yellow Books, Sub-Clause 3.3.

51 See Red and Yellow Books, Sub-Clause 3.5.

52 FIDIC has attempted to address this issue in the Red and Yellow Books Second Edition, where "*[w]hen carrying out his/her duties under this Sub-Clause [3.7], the Engineer shall act neutrally between the Parties and shall not be deemed to act for the Employer*".

always direct those involved towards the following (in order of precedence) sequential procedures:

(i) Amicable settlement;
(ii) Engineer's determination;[53]
(iii) Dispute Adjudication Board's (DAB) decision;
(iv) Arbitration/Litigation.

2.66 Note, that the word "claim" is not present in this list, as it is often misconstrued that a claim is something contentious. A claim is nothing more than a contractual right accruing to a Party to the Contract. It is only if and when a claim is submitted, and the other Party is not in agreement with the stated reasoning for such claim that the issue may become contentious and thus may evolve into a dispute. It was not until 2008, when FIDIC published its "Gold" Book, that an attempt was made to define the word dispute (Sub-Clause 1.1.31):

> *"**Dispute**" means any situation where (a) one Party makes a claim against the other Party; (b) the other Party rejects the claim in whole or in part; and (c) the first Party does not acquiesce, provided, however, that a failure by the other Party to oppose or respond to the claim, in whole or in part, may constitute a rejection, if in the circumstances, the DAB or the arbitrator(s), as the case may be, deem it reasonable for it to do so.*

2.67 Prior to this, a dispute was often informally defined as "a rejection of a rejection", something that proved to be contentious in its own right. In summary, and as per FIDIC's vision, an attempt should always be made to resolve issues between the Parties amicably, failing this the Engineer is tasked with deciding the matter fairly, considering all the relevant facts and circumstances.[54] Dissatisfaction which such an Engineer's determination allows either Party to give a notice of dissatisfaction and thus declare the existence of a dispute, and to take the matter to the next stage (DAB).

Claims

2.68 For all of the FIDIC Major Works Contracts, the claim procedures are essentially split into two top categories: (i) Employer's Claims, and (ii) Contractor's Claims. But before embarking on a summary discussion of these two alternatives, it is imperative to deal with a significant principle incorporated into the FIDIC Standard Forms of Construction Contracts: The Time-Bar! This principle has been the cause of many disputes, and it is found within Sub-Clause 20.1 [*Contractor's Claims*].

The Time-Bar

2.69 Sub-Clause § 20.1 paragraph 1 opens with the following statement:

53 By convention all defined words in the FIDIC series of Standard Contracts are capitalized in the various sub-clause wordings. The Engineer is by definition the project's administrator employed by the Employer, and acts as his agent. in situations of apparent discord between the Parties, the Engineer is also tasked with deciding the matter fairly by taking due regard of all the relevant facts and circumstances.

54 Op. cit. n. 50.

> *If the Contractor considers himself to be entitled to any extension of the Time for Completion and/or any additional payment, under any Clause of these Conditions or otherwise in connection with the Contract, the Contractor shall give notice to the Engineer, describing the event or circumstance giving rise to the claim.* ***The notice shall be given as soon as practicable, and not later than 28 days after the Contractor became aware, or should have become aware, of the event or circumstance***. [emphasis added.]

2.70 It is clear that a notice shall be given and it must be within a specified time (28 days). When compared to the Employer's equivalent requirement ("whenever practicable"), the mentioned leniency towards the Employer is apparent. However, the issue becomes even more contentious when taking into account the second paragraph of Sub-Clause 20.1:

> ***If the Contractor fails to give notice of a claim within such period of 28 days****, the Time for Completion shall not be extended, the Contractor shall not be entitled to additional payment, and* ***the Employer shall be discharged from all liability in connection with the claim***. [emphasis added.]

2.71 The above has been the cause of many disputes in the construction world. It has also been debated at length by legal practitioners in most of the world's legal jurisdictions. Before embarking on a rudimentary discussion of the time-bar under a Common law or Civil law system, it must be stated that the doctrine of "freedom of Contract" determines that Parties may in fact agree on any term of a Contract they may deem fit, as long as the Contract does not violate any mandatory laws in operation. Whenever the Contractor is late with his notice under Sub-Clause 20.1, and the reason for his claim cannot be attributed to the Employer, the time-bar is in effect valid. It becomes contentious if and when the reason for the Contractor's Claim is in fact an act or omission by the Employer of any of his obligations under the terms of the Contract (e.g., possession of the site Sub-Clause 2.1).

2.72 In many Common Law jurisdictions, the issue of the time-bar is often discussed and evaluated in connection with the "Prevention Principle": *A Party to a Contract cannot benefit from its own wrong, or insist on the performance of an obligation by its contractual partner, if it prevents that obligation from being performed.*[55]

2.73 It has, however, nevertheless been determined that in principle, and whenever a Construction Contract contains a sub-clause under which a Party can claim recourse for the fact that the other Party has prevented an obligation from being performed, the prevention principle does not serve to protect the aggrieved Party. This is most visible in situations of delay by the Contractor: For example, if the Employer delays the Contractor, but the Contract incorporates a mechanism for the Contractor to claim an extension to the time for completion (EoT), then the Employer is entitled to recover any agreed liquidated damages on the grounds that the Contractor had the opportunity to claim EoT but elected not (or forgot or otherwise failed) to do so.[56] All FIDIC Contracts incorporate such a sub-clause under which the Contractor can claim EoT, and as such the time-bar would normally apply. There is thus good reason for any Party faced with a time-bar condition precedent in their Contract (such as a FIDIC Contract) to strictly follow the time-bar

55 *Amalgamated Building Contractors v Waltham Holy cross UDC* [1952] 2 All ER 452, 455 (Denning LJ).

56 *Adyard Abu Dhabi v SD Marine Services* [2011] EWHC 848 (Comm).

(FIDIC: Sub-Clause 20.1) procedure, and not to rely on the prevention principle to save them from any negative consequences.

2.74 However, there may well be circumstances where the condition precedent (the time-bar which, if not complied with, results in the loss of entitlement) can be circumvented. The Scottish case *City Inn v Shepherd Construction*[57] gives an example of how this could happen. The case was decided on the principle that, even though there was a condition precedent, and the Contractor did have an option to claim EoT, his late notice was not submitted immediately as a reason for rejection of the entitlement. The Employer in fact allowed detailed discussions on the merit of the case, and only when it became obvious that there was a case to defend against, did they elect to invoke the time-bar. The judge in case ruled that the time-bar does provide for immunity, but only if actually invoked, as it is always an option for the Employer to waive this immunity clause. In general, time-bars have the effect of providing immediate relief to any claim for damages and should be used as such. Not invoking the consequences immediately may be construed as a waiver of that clause's effects.

2.75 In Civil law jurisdictions, the issue is often raised in conjunction with the so-called "principles of good faith" and/or "Unjust Enrichment", all with the same outcome in mind, that is, recourse from the damages to be suffered for failing to comply with the time-bar provisions. For example, the UAE Civil Code, under Art 246(1) states that:

> "*The Contract must be performed in accordance with its contents, and in a manner consistent with the requirements of good faith*".

2.76 The most basic and frequent interpretation being that a time-bar provision may not be relied upon by an Employer in circumstances where he is in breach, and he was fully aware that his breach would cause damage (e.g., delay to the project) to the Contractor.

2.77 Under the German Civil law, the courts usually take a slightly different approach, in that they view the time-bar is not a condition precedent upon the claimant, but that it is actually an obligation to be performed under the terms of the Contract. The effect is that a late notice does not necessarily result in a loss of entitlement, but that the claimant has a higher duty to demonstrate that his claims are valid and, most importantly, are not affected by the fact that his notice was late. In other words, a valid meritorious claim cannot be defeated by the time-bar if it is shown that the late notice did not in fact increase the claimant's entitlements.

2.78 As shown above it is possible under both Civil as well as Common Law jurisdictions to successfully defend against the onerous effect of a contractually agreed time-bar. Since FIDIC made it known that the rainbow suite of Contracts was developed to be used independently of any legal system or jurisdiction, the wave of disputes coming from the time-bar provision prompted corrective action. In the "Gold" Book, Sub-Clause 20.1(a) states:

> *However, if the Contractor considers there are circumstances which justify the late submission, he may submit the details to the DAB for a ruling. If the DAB considers the circumstances are*

57 *City Inn Ltd. v Shepherd Construction Ltd.* [2007] CSOH 190 & on appeal [2010] ScotCS CSIH 68.

such that the late submission was acceptable, the DAB shall have the authority under this sub-clause to override the given 28-day limit and advise both the Parties accordingly.[58]

2.79 Thus, a Contractor is able to submit to the DAB, the details of any circumstances which may justify the late submission of a claim. The clause empowers the DAB to consider all these circumstances and, in the event it decides them to be "acceptable", it may override the condition precedent, effectively doing away with the loss of entitlement effect. It must be stressed that this power of the DAB will never create a general effect, and it must be invoked on a case-by-case basis.

Employer's Claims

2.80 Even though the FIDIC Contracts (1999 series) dedicate a special Clause (20) to the concepts of claims and dispute resolution, the procedure for Employer's Claims is found under Sub-Clause § 2.5 [Employer's Claims]. Previous versions of the FIDIC Contracts did not have a dedicated sub-clause for Employer's Claims, resulting in frequent arbitrary deductions to the Contractor's payments,[59] with the resulting problems hence.

2.81 From a contractual perspective, the Employer's Claim procedure is fairly simple and straightforward; whenever there is a perception of a right to claim, a corresponding notice shall be given to the Contractor whenever reasonably practical. Interestingly, the notice shall "*specify the Clause or other basis of the claim, and shall include substantiation of the amount and/or extension to which the Employer considers himself to be entitled in connection with the Contract*". In other words, it seemingly suffices to specify the respective Contract clause on which the alleged entitlement is based, that is, no other reasoning required! When compared to the Contractor's obligations to successfully pursue a claim, this seems unreasonably lenient.

2.82 In addition, the Employer's Claims are not subject to the time-bar provisions of Sub-Clause 20.1, again an issue not necessarily seen as fair and balanced towards the contracting world.

2.83 This perceived leniency towards the Employer has been the subject of discussions since their first publication in 1999. FIDIC likes to state that the rainbow series is written by engineers for engineers. Considering that the Engineer (capital "E") under the Contracts is de facto an agent for the Employer, is seen by some as an explanation in that it ostensibly eliminates the contentiousness of any Employer's issues the Engineer may have to face. On the other hand, giving the Contractor a hard time for his issues, may make him/her look better, and it is no surprise that the Contractor's Claim procedure is thus not as simple.

Contractor's Claims

2.84 As stated, the contractual procedure for Contractor's Claims is found in Sub-Clause 20.1 [*Contractor's Claims*]. Assuming that the notice provision discussed above

58 Similarly in the Second Edition, the Party whose claim was time-barred has the opportunity to provide justification for the late submission of its claim in order to overcome the time bar. See Second Edition, Sub-Clause 20.2.4.

59 Barr/Grutters, FIDIC Users' Guide 3rd Edition, ICE Publishing 2013.

in relation to the time-bar, has either been complied with or is otherwise not an issue, the following specific scenario is activated:

a) *Within 42 days after the Contractor became aware (or should have become aware) of the event or circumstance giving rise to the claim, or within such other period as may be proposed by the Contractor and approved by the Engineer, the Contractor shall send to the Engineer a fully detailed claim which includes full supporting particulars of the basis of the claim and of the extension of time and/ or additional payment claimed.*

b) *Within 42 days after receiving a claim or any further particulars supporting a previous claim, or within such other period as may be proposed by the Engineer and approved by the Contractor, the Engineer shall respond with approval, or with disapproval and detailed comments. He may also request any necessary further particulars, but shall nevertheless give his response on the principles of the claim within such time.*

c) *The Engineer shall proceed in accordance with Sub-Clause 3.5 [Determinations] to agree or determine (i) the extension (if any) of the Time for Completion (before or after its expiry) in accordance with Sub-Clause 8.4 [Extension of Time for Completion], and/or (ii) the additional payment (if any) to which the Contractor is entitled under the Contract.*

Dispute Resolution

2.85 Already the 1st Edition of the FIDIC Red Book (1957) incorporated in clause 66 a (then) two staged dispute resolution process: (i) The Engineer was to make a decision on a matter, followed by a straight route to (ii) arbitration. Is goes without saying that FIDIC already at these early days recognized the necessity of creating opportunities for the contracting Parties to resolve their differences as early as possible in the project through the Engineer's decision. That Engineer's decision was stated as "final and binding" for the Parties until the completion of the work. The 1969 2nd Edition and the 1977 3rd Edition maintained this concept. It was at the launch of the 1987 4th Edition that FIDIC introduced the concept of "amicable settlement" to be attempted before arbitration could be commenced.

2.86 All this was considered commendable but at the same time the construction industry grappled with the role of the FIDIC Engineer. Although his prime role was that of a neutral Contract administrator, and even though Sub-Clause 2.6 in the 4th Edition called for the Engineer to be independent and impartial, he was still regarded as being an extension of the Employer because of the simple fact that he was appointed and paid by that very Employer. FIDIC reacted through the 1995 introduction of the Orange Book, where for the 1st time the concept of a Dispute Board was introduced. These had been promoted by the World Bank for use on other mega-projects like the new Hong Kong airport or the Honduras El Cajon project as early as 1980.

2.87 The 1999 Rainbow Suite of Contracts finally incorporated the DAB concept in total, making it a mandatory process before arbitration could be initiated.[60] It also marked the start of the FIDIC multi-tiered dispute resolution process.

60 See Sub-Clause 20.6 [*Arbitration*], where the Arbitral tribunal would only have jurisdiction to hear cases for which there had been a "Notice of Dissatisfaction" to a DAB decision.

2.88 What follows is a discussion on the individual FIDIC multi-tiered dispute resolution steps to be followed by the Parties in their pursuit of recourse to a rejected claim or other perceived damage incurred under the terms of the Contract.

Determinations

2.89 As per Sub-Clause 20.1 the Engineer must act in accordance with Sub-Clause 3.5 [*Determinations*] whenever he receives a claim from either Party. This sub-clause states that

> Whenever these Conditions provide that the Engineer shall proceed in accordance with this Sub-Clause 3.5 to agree or determine any matter, the Engineer shall consult with each Party in an endeavour to reach agreement. If agreement is not achieved, the Engineer shall make a fair determination in accordance with the Contract, taking due regard of all relevant circumstances.

As per Barr/Grutters[61] this means that the Engineer shall first consult with each Party in an endeavour to reach agreement. To comply with this requirement the Engineer must act as a mediator and try to help the Parties towards agreement. If agreement is not achieved the Engineer must make "*a fair determination in accordance with the Contract, taking due regard of all relevant circumstances*". The key phrase here is "*in accordance with the Contract*". The determination must express the rights and obligations of the Parties, in accordance with the Contract and the applicable law, regardless of the preferences of either Party. It is said that this is the one instance where the Engineer, as being employed by the Employer and acting as his agent, shall take the role of a neutral. Under Sub-Clause 3.2 [*Delegation by the Engineer*] the Engineer cannot delegate this task without the agreement of both Parties.

2.90 FIDIC does not impose a strict time-limit on the Engineer to make a determination under Sub-Clause 3.5, but the situation would be covered by the requirement of Sub-Clause 1.3 [Communications] where it is held that a determination "shall not be unreasonably withheld".

2.91 Obviously, whenever the Engineer makes a determination, he would express his own views and opinions (albeit within the limits of the Contract and all relevant circumstances) on a matter. If either Party is not in agreement with or expresses a dissatisfaction with the determination, they have the option of declaring the matter in dispute. The latter is important in that it is closely related to the next step of the FIDIC multi-tiered dispute management/resolution process.

The Dispute Adjudication Board or DAB

2.92 If a dispute arises between the Employer and the Contractor then it may be referred to the DAB, under Clause 20.4 [*Obtaining Dispute Board's decision*]. The wording of Sub-Clause 20.4 includes disputes of any kind whatsoever, in connection with or arising out of the Contract or the execution of the Works. However, the DAB only has jurisdiction to decide actual "disputes". It is thus imperative for either Party that contemplates going

61 Op. cit. n. 57

to the DAB for a decision, to make certain that the issue is a declared dispute, and that the other Party is aware of that fact.

2.93 At Sub-Clauses 20.2 to 20.4, the Appendix "*General Conditions of Dispute Adjudication Agreement/General Conditions of Dispute Board Agreement*" and the Annex: "*Procedural Rules*" give detailed provisions regarding the powers of the DAB and the way the process is to be conducted.

2.94 Although the FIDIC 1999 suite of Contracts provide for either a "Standing DAB" (Red Book) or an "Ad-Hoc" DAB (Yellow and Silver Book), the industry consensus is that the Standing Board is preferable in terms of costs and effectiveness. The latter in that the Standing DAB will be in a position to actively pursue dispute avoidance techniques, and in doing so can assist the Parties in their attempts to manage their differences at the earliest stage possible, often before they become fully fledged disputes.

2.95 The Standing DAB comprises either one or three people and is chosen by agreement at the start of the project. For the three-person board each side proposes one person for the other side's agreement and the chairman is chosen by agreement. This is also sometimes referred to as the "bottom-up" procedure, as opposed to the Parties appointing a chairman, who in turn selects his wingmen ("top-down"). Failing agreement by the Parties, the selection is made by an independent organization, such as, for example, FIDIC, the ICC, the Dispute Board Federation (DBF) or The Institution of Civil Engineers (ICE), named in the appendix to tender, all as stated in Sub-Clause 20.3.

2.96 In contrast, an Ad-Hoc DAB is only appointed if and when an actual dispute has arisen, and a Party wishes for this dispute to be decided by that DAB. Once the decision is made, the DAB appointment comes to an end, and any future disputes necessarily involves the appointment of another (not necessarily different DAB).

2.97 Much has been said about the lack of legal enforcement potential for Dispute Board Decisions, or adjudication decisions in general. Unlike arbitration, there is no widespread international agreement on the legal status of a DAB decision. The UK has been a front-runner in this regard, in that it provided for the adjudication process to become mandatory through the Construction Act.[62] There is also some secondary legislation affecting the adjudication process in the UK through The Scheme for Construction Contracts (England and Wales) Regulations 1998 and The Scheme for Construction Contracts (England and Wales) Regulations 1998 (Amendment) (England) Regulations 2011. Those Schemes provide "model terms" which are incorporated into a Construction Contract when required by the primary legislation. The Acts require every Construction Contract to contain certain provisions regarding Adjudication and, if the Contract fails to provide such provisions or provides contrary provisions, then the Act prescribes that those provisions are removed and replaced, in their entirety, by those in the Scheme.

2.98 But also in the UK, any adjudication decision is still binding in the interim, meaning it will only be enforceable if confirmed through either an arbitral award or court decision.

62 The term "Construction Act" refers originally to the Housing Grants, Construction and Regeneration Act 1996 (now called the old Act) and recently to the Local Democracy, Economic Development and Construction Act 2009 (now called the new Act).

Arbitration

2.99 Arbitration is perhaps the better-known process for resolving disputes in construction projects. Its proper functioning and detailed processes are discussed elsewhere. It suffices to state here that FIDIC also incorporates this method, albeit at the end of their multi-tiered process. It is considered expensive and time consuming, and therefore correctly positioned as a last resort for the Parties. There are no real issues concerning the enforceability of arbitral awards, as this aspect has been cleared through the "New York Convention".[63] The Convention's principal aim being that foreign and non-domestic arbitral awards will not be discriminated against, and it obliges Parties to the Convention to ensure such awards are recognized and generally capable of enforcement in their jurisdiction in the same way as domestic awards. An ancillary aim of the Convention is to require courts to give full effect to arbitration agreements by requiring courts to deny the Parties access to court in contravention of their agreement to refer the matter to an arbitral tribunal.[64]

Dispute Avoidance under FIDIC

2.100 It is accepted by almost all involved in the construction industry, that disputes are an irritating, costly and stress-inducing "necessity". The development of the contracting world did not help to alleviate this fact; the involvement of the legal fraternity in drafting and interpreting Construction Contracts was, for many years, entirely focussed on how to deal with a dispute once arisen. Contracts were drafted such that Parties knew how to deal with a situation where one Party was alleged or perceived to be in violation of that Contract's conditions and terms. Clever Contract drafting was attempted to preserve the rights of individual Parties, depending on who was paying the legal fees.

2.101 If the existence of disputes in construction projects is something considered "normal", and that they will occur to some extent in all projects, it is even more remarkable that the very players in these projects, that is, Employers and Contractors, still have an inherent reluctance to provide for these disputes in their project pricing. Contractors know they will incur costs and expenses in dealing with disputes but will not allow for these costs in their bid prices for fear of being too expensive and hence not being awarded the job. Equally, Employers will not include these costs in their budgeting, mostly under the false belief that the world's lending institutions will not cover these in the respective loan agreements. In addition, there are still people naively convinced that "*their projects will not have any disputes, as they know the other Party too well*". This myth has been proven wrong on too many occasions for it to be believable. In summary, there is an underlying notion of ignoring the negative aspects of the true existence of disputes in the hope that "*they will go away*".

2.102 It is only when the disputes actually do arise, that the people involved start realizing they now have to deal with it, often with disastrous consequences as the process is initiated far too late.

63 Convention on the Recognition and Enforcement of Foreign Arbitral Awards (New York, 1958)
64 https://uncitral.un.org/en/texts/arbitration/conventions/foreign_arbitral_awards.

2.103 Dispute resolution by definition implies the very existence of a dispute! These disputes will always have a negative effect on the project's (i) execution, (ii) costs, (iii) timing, and (iv) relationships. They will also impact through additional risks to the project as well as consequential effects on, for example, follow-on projects. Centuries ago, expressions like "*Prevention is better than cure*"[65] or "*An ounce of prevention is worth a pound of cure*"[66] were coined to warn against the negative effects of ignoring signs of danger. But, to effectively prevent negative things from happening, we necessarily need to understand how they come to exist in the first place. For construction projects, disputes almost always find their origins in the underlying Contracts. A badly written Contract will have an exponential propensity to develop disputes through, for example, ambiguities, incompleteness or language issues. The latter is certainly true for international projects.

2.104 FIDIC's approach to dealing with disputes has been heavily influenced by the industry's increasing concerns of the rising costs of dispute resolution, especially arbitration. FIDIC realized that the industry is in need of a different approach to disputes: Avoid them altogether.

2.105 The 1999 series of FIDIC Contracts have all been drafted with dispute avoidance in mind. This is accomplished through some basic principles:

Fixed Contractual Procedures

2.106 FIDIC does not encourage deviations from its General Conditions (GCs). As such, FIDIC has developed their "Golden Principles", being those mechanisms within their Contracts that, if deviated from, excludes the Parties from stating that their project is in fact a "FIDIC Contract". This could prove to be a problem for those Parties, especially if they have to rely on International Funding Institutions such as the World Bank, EBRD,[67] ADB,[68] and others that encourage or require their borrowers to use the FIDIC forms as a basis for their projects.

2.107 Task Group 15 was charged with developing the Golden Principles, which were formally published in 2019 as the "FIDIC Golden Principles, First Edition 2019". The publication not only lays out the Golden Principles, but also gives guidance on appropriate Contract drafting in accordance therewith. The Golden Principles are:

> *GP1: The duties, rights, obligations, roles and responsibilities of all the Contract Participants must be generally as implied in the General Conditions, and appropriate to the requirements of the project.*
>
> *GP2: The Particular Conditions must be drafted clearly and unambiguously.*
>
> *GP3: The Particular Conditions must not change the balance of risk/reward allocation provided for in the General Conditions.*
>
> *GP4: All time periods specified in the Contract for Contract Participants to perform their obligations must be of reasonable duration.*

65 Desiderius Erasmus (1466–1536).
66 Benjamin Franklin (1706–1790).
67 European Bank for Reconstruction and Development.
68 Asian Development Bank.

GP5: Unless there is a conflict with the governing law of the Contract, all formal disputes must be referred to a Dispute Avoidance/Adjudication Board (or a Dispute Adjudication Board, if applicable) for a provisionally binding decision as a condition precedent to arbitration.

2.108 The Engineer has a function to mediate an issue between the Parties, before unilaterally making a determination under Sub-Clause 3.5 [*Determinations*]. In doing so he has the opportunity, and by implication a contractual duty (GP 01), to try and avoid conflicts from becoming full-fledged disputes.

2.109 Under Sub-Clause 4.6 [*Co-operation*], the various stakeholders in the project are obligated to co-operate with each other, and to allow the other to carry out his duties and responsibilities.

2.110 It is exactly these fixed contractual procedures that allow the Parties to know in advance what is and can be expected from the other in terms of working together to achieve a successful project. Without these fixed principles, the Parties would have no means of knowing and anticipating the reactions and actions of their contractual partners in situations that otherwise would quickly develop into contentiousness and stress.

Transparency and Early Communication

2.111 There are various sub-clauses in the FIDIC rainbow Suite of Contracts that obligate the Parties to act with transparency in mind. Again, this transparency enables the Parties to better understand the other, and to anticipate certain reactions and behaviour before issues become contentious. Examples include Sub-Clause 1.12 [*Confidential Details*] where the Contractor is required to disclose all such information that may reasonably be required by the other Party to evaluate compliance with the Contract. Similarly, under Sub-Clause 2.4 [*Employer's Financial Arrangements*] it is incumbent on the Employer to submit reasonable evidence to the Contractor that he has the means to fund the project. Sub-Clause § 8.3 [*Programme*] is in fact an early warning mechanism whereby "*the Contractor shall promptly give notice to the Engineer of specific probable future events or circumstances which may adversely affect the work, increase the Contract Price or delay the execution of the Works*". Other early warning obligations stem from, for example, Sub-Clause 1.9 [*Delayed Drawings or Instructions*] enabling both Parties to anticipate potential issues before they become an actual problem. In addition, there are numerous sub-clauses that require prompt notifications to be submitted if and when a certain issue or situation arises or may arise.

2.112 There is no doubt that any potential argument between two or more Parties is most effectively dealt with through a compelling and persuasive argument backed up by sustainable evidence. FIDIC recognizes this principle in that it encourages the Parties to become expert Contract administrators. Next to the Engineer, who is specifically appointed to administer the Contract (i.e., initiate, develop, and track important project executional data), the Parties are obligated to do the same. This is most notably seen through the extensive record keeping activities in relation to progress; Sub-Clause 4.21 [*Progress Reports*] spells out in great detail what records the Contractor is to keep on a regular basis. Last but not least, Sub-Clause 20.1 [*Contractor's Claims*] empowers the Engineer to instruct the Contractor what records, evidence or other information to keep or collect so as to be able to properly and professionally evaluate a notified claim, and in doing so minimize the potential for disputes in relation to the outcome of that evaluation.

The Role of the Dispute Adjudication Board in Dispute Avoidance

2.113 As an Ad-Hoc Board is only appointed if and when an actual dispute has arisen, we can limit our discussion here to Standing Boards. Standing Boards have a unique opportunity to get involved in positive and active dispute avoidance strategies due to the fact that they are appointed at the onset of the project's execution. The DAB is also obligated to visit the project (site) at regular intervals (70 < × < 140 days). The combination of an early appointment and in-depth interaction with the Parties at the regular site visits ensures that the DAB is always highly informed about issues and matters that play at any time between the Parties. It is this level of information that the DAB uses to implement a healthy dispute avoidance strategy.

2.114 Obviously, if the DAB has access to that level of information, it will be easy to keep pace with developments if and when they occur. They will be able to discuss these developments with the Parties ad hoc, without significant preparation time. This in turn will give the Parties a sense of security, in that the DAB is seen as competent and effective in their provision of services. This is significant, as the Parties are less likely to object to any formal decision or informal opinion given by the DAB, which in turn has a positive effect on the further potential for disputes.

2.115 In accordance with Sub-Clause 20.4 [Obtaining Dispute Adjudication Board's Decision], it is agreed that

> *within 84 days after receiving such reference, or within such other period as may be proposed by the DAB and approved by both Parties, the DAB shall give its decision, which shall be reasoned and shall state that it is given under this Sub-Clause.*

This means that the Parties will have a decision on their disputes within a relatively short period of time (compare 84 days with 2–3 years arbitration). These short periods have a positive effect on the impact any dispute undoubtedly has on the project's day-to-day execution. The project is minimally affected, and the Parties can continue the execution with maximum planning certainty.

2.116 FIDIC, when developing the DAB concept, had in mind that the process could be used for all disputes whatsoever, but that the most effective use would stem from the fact that the Parties have an opportunity to refer relatively small issues for immediate resolution before they develop into full-blown large contentious fights. If used in this manner, the Parties will obtain decisions on small issues that may re-occur many times thereafter. However, any such future re-occurrence will no longer be a problem in that it was decided already.

2.117 Without a doubt, the costs of a DAB process are significantly lower than a formal arbitration procedure. The DAB process does not necessarily require a team of legal counsel to represent a Party, and the overall duration (per dispute) is only a fraction of the time an arbitration would take. But the real cost saving is not in the evaluation of a dispute resolved, but rather in the number of issues that never developed into disputes and in consequence did not require expenses to be incurred.

2.118 There is another profound difference between a DAB process and arbitration procedures in the way the DAB members are empowered to execute their services. Sub-Clause 20.2 [*Appointment of the Dispute Adjudication Board*], 5th paragraph states that

> *The agreement between the Parties and either the sole member ("adjudicator") or each of the three members shall incorporate by reference the General Conditions of Dispute Adjudication Agreement contained in the Appendix to these General Conditions, with such amendments as are agreed between them.*

In other words, any agreement between the Parties and the DAB (so-called Dispute Adjudication Agreement or DAA), shall make it obligatory for the DAB to act in accordance with the General Conditions of Dispute Adjudication Agreement (GCDAA). Within these GCDAA, under Art. § 4(e) it is stated that the DAB shall "*comply with the annexed procedural rules and with Sub-Clause 20.4 of the Conditions of Contract*". The reference to the Procedural Rules (PR) links to PR 7, where it is stated that inter alia: "*Except as otherwise agreed in writing by the Employer and the Contractor, the DAB shall have power to adopt an inquisitorial procedure* ...). thus, the DAB is empowered to be inquisitorial whenever executing their services, giving them a practical licence to embark on a quest for the truth without having to solely rely on legal presentations by the Parties' respective counsel. It is often rumoured that the DAB has a licence to seek the actual truth as opposed to deciding which of the Parties' representatives was telling most of the truth. This is also reflected in PR 8(d) where it is confirmed that the DAB is empowered to "*take the initiative in ascertaining the facts and matters required for a decision*". This ability to be inquisitorial has the effect that the DAB, without a formal dispute having been referred, can ask questions of the Parties (no leading) that would enable it to better understand a potential issue before it becomes a major issue. In turn, this knowledge will allow the DAB to pursue a route in dealing with the as yet minor issue towards convincing the Parties to sort it out amicably between themselves. This is also further confirmed in GCDAA Art. § 4(k) where it is held that the DAB shall "*be available to give advice and opinions, on any matter relevant to the Contract when requested by both the Employer and the Contractor, subject to the agreement of the Other Members (if any)*".

2.119 In summary, the DAB plays a significant role in the process of dispute avoidance, and if performed pro-actively the Parties will benefit in many ways. The following is a listing of some of the more profound advantages:

- If the Board is introduced at tender stage, both Parties will have trust in the other's intentions as to fairness and honesty;
- The Parties' Staff will maintain amicable relationships, rather than entrenching themselves in dispute battles;
- The Board will act as a policing entity encouraging the Parties to abstain from frivolous claims or subjective rejections;
- The Board's ability to give opinions and advice may resolve a potential dispute before it arises.

The Future

2.120 When originally drafting this chapter, FIDIC had just published its 2nd Edition to the Rainbow Suite (Red, Yellow, and Silver Books only). It had already been dubbed as the "2017 Version" as opposed to the "2nd Edition".

2.121 There has been much controversy surrounding this new version, in that it took FIDIC nearly eight years to complete the set. The following gives an idea of the thinking of the Contracts Committee and the corresponding task group (UTG 6 a & b) and a brief overview of some of the major changes in the 2017 version:

a) The notion that claims are not disputes has been given credence; the old Clause § 20 [*Claims, Disputes and Arbitration*], has now been renamed "*Employer's and Contractor's Claims*". The old Sub-Clause 2.5 [*Employer's Claims*] has logically been moved to this new clause;
b) There is new Clause § 21 under the heading "*Disputes and Arbitration*", a dedicated clause to dealing with disputes by both Parties;
c) The old DAB has been renamed "*Dispute Avoidance/Adjudication Board*" or DAAB, further emphasizing its role in dispute avoidance as encouraged by FIDIC for all projects, as opposed to a merely it has a function in the dispute avoidance activities;
d) The Standing Board is now incorporated into all three new books. The 1999 version incorporated a Standing board only for the Red Book, and Ad-Hoc boards for the Yellow and Silver Books. There is a new Sub-Clause 21.3 [*Avoidance of Disputes*] highlighting the increased importance placed on the DAAB as a dispute avoidance tool;
e) The 1999 version intended for any DAB decision to be complied with immediately, but reality has shown that many "losers" of such DAB decision simply ignored this and relied upon the law to protect them from enforcement of such a decision. This loophole has now been closed through new Sub-Clause 21.7 [*Failure to comply with DAAB's Decision*];
f) There is an increased importance placed on the Contractor to prove compliance with the Contract. The most notable requirement being the development and management of an elaborate "*Quality Management and Compliance Verification System*" (refer Sub-Clause 4.9);
g) The old Clause § 17 [*Risk and Responsibilities*] has been replaced by "*Care of the Works and Indemnities*". The content is similar but given clearer structure;
h) The old Clause § 18 [*Insurance*] has been moved towards the end of the document. This in response to the historical idea that the FIDIC Contracts should be structured such that the sequence of clauses follows the events within a project;
i) The concept of "*Force Majeure*" (old clause § 19) has been removed as it was proven to be a contentious issue when seen under different legal jurisdictions and legal systems. It has now been included within new Clause § 18 [*Exceptional Events*], where the actual wording was carefully drafted so as to make the issue more independently usable within various legal systems and jurisdictions;
j) The infamous time-bar on claims notification has been maintained, but there is now a mechanism whereby the DAAB, when requested to do so, has the power to waive the time-bar restriction;
k) There is an enhanced role for the Engineer, in that he is to become more involved in the day-to-day resolution of issues between the Parties. His function now also includes providing services in anticipation of a matter going to the DAAB. But, on the other side, he is now much more controlled in terms of when he should

do certain things. There is an increase in the "deemed" provisions where the Engineer does not act in a timely manner;

l) There is an increase in prescriptiveness towards the Parties. Many sub-clauses have been textually enhanced to provide more clarity. Unfortunately, this increase resulted in the word-count and overall thickness of the document to increase as well. What used to be some 30.000 words has blown up to > 50.000, and the actual document now weighs in at a healthy 1.1 kg.

CHAPTER 3

English Common Law

Christopher Howard, Anthony Lavers, and Phillip Hanna

Contents

 DOI: 10.4324/9781315671376-3

History of English Common Law

Sources of Law

3.1 English common law underwent a lengthy gestation before it emerged into the nuanced system which exists today. Its genesis can be traced back to the Norman Conquest of England. Prior to that point, England was made up of a number of separate kingdoms, each with its own local legal system. William the Conqueror's innovation was to unite these disparate systems so as to create a "law common to all", thus giving rise to the term "common law". This common law was administered by regional courts and was sanctioned by the ruling monarch. It drew on local customary law and was gradually fused into a set of nationwide precedents. These precedents created a body of governing formulations which could be applied in lower courts as fixed principles, subject to further development of precedent as novel situations arose.

3.2 From this piecemeal beginning, the system of common law in England became a sophisticated, multi-faceted institution. That said, however, common law does not exist in a void and is part of an overall framework of different sources of law governing the jurisdiction of England and Wales. These sources may be classified as follows:

EU Law

3.3 Upon joining the European Economic Community in 1973 and subsequent integration with European Union institutions and treaties, the UK became subject to the full range of EU Law, both in terms of statutory law such as Regulations and Directives, but also judicially in terms of the supremacy of the European Court of Justice and the European Court of Human Rights. While the UK was a member of the EU, all relevant statutes and judgments were required to be integrated into UK law, superseding domestic law as appropriate. This ceased to be the case when the UK formally withdrew from the EU in 2021. A significant residue of EU influenced legislation remained after withdrawal, as well as some amended and some abolished.

Statute

3.4 Domestic statute takes priority over what may be described as judge-made law (i.e., the common law as embodied in judicial precedent). Domestic statute may take a variety of forms, from primary legislation such as Acts of Parliament through to secondary (delegated) legislation such as statutory instruments. It must be noted, however, that the *interpretation* of statute, in terms of its application to real life instances, is the sole province of the judiciary in the courts of common law.

Common Law

3.5 As described above, the courts, operating in a hierarchical structure, effect law through the creation and maintenance of judicial precedent. This process is captured in the Latin phrase "*stare decisis*" – "let the decision stand". The declaratory theory would suggest that the pronouncements of the courts do not represent the judges *making* law; instead, they are merely *declaring* the law as it already exists, based on previous precedent. The law to be applied consists in the "*ratio decidendi*" – the reason for the decision, that is, the legal principle which informed the previous judgment in this area. However, it is for later courts to discern the *ratio* and continually to refine it to meet the needs of ever-changing sets of facts. Some commentators have queried the whole notion of the declaratory principle, which rests on the notion that all principles of common law already exist, and need only be discovered and reiterated by judges in the future. A more controversial analysis, as proposed by the famous jurist Lord Denning, is that in fact common law judges do make law, through their creative powers in the manipulation and extension of existing precedent.

3.6 A final important note before leaving the general notion of common law is that the system of precedent works under strict rules regarding the hierarchy of the courts and the limited ability of the courts to diverge from existing precedent. The Supreme Court and the Court of Appeal currently represent the top tiers of decision-making in England and Wales.

Equity

3.7 Arguably, it is inappropriate to treat Equity as a separate source of law, it being in essence a subset of the wider category of common law. However, it is often described as a separate jurisdiction, a concept dating back to its historical roots. Rigid rules regarding the administration of the common law courts, coupled with arbitrary application of existing principles, led to a demand for a more flexible, responsive form of justice. This led to the formation of a royally-sanctioned parallel jurisdiction, where claimants could seek remedies unavailable under the common law, based in a broader concept of fairness and justice. This system itself gradually became formalized and subject to strict rules of application and its own precedents. After a time, it became clear that having two separate, competing systems of justice was inefficient and costly, at which point the legislature brought the two systems together, to be administered by the same judges in the same courts.[1] Today, the notion of equity still exists and it is still treated as a separate judicial power. Its main application lies in the form of more flexible remedies, such as specific performance and the injunction. It also governs the law of trusts.

Customary

3.8 Local customary law is still a source of law in England and Wales, although its influence is now highly limited, given that most such principles have been subsumed in general common law and statute. To rely on customary law, the claimant will need to satisfy a number of requirements to demonstrate the extent of its local recognition and longevity.[2] Customary law is perhaps of greater importance in the context of international trade, where it can be a significant factor in the creation of commercial contracts.

International Law

3.9 To some extent, international law should perhaps be at the head of this list, in that, where applicable, it takes precedence over all domestic rules. However, in many cases it is binding on the State only and does not take effect at domestic level until enacted in domestic statute, albeit there is a presumption that domestic law is to be interpreted in the light of international treaty obligations.[3]

---

1 See the Supreme Court of Judicature Acts of 1873 and 1875.

2 *Egerton v Harding* [1975] Q.B. 62.

3 *Sidhu v British Airways Plc* [1997] 1 All E.R. 193.

Countries/Jurisdictions Deriving from English Common Law

3.10 The worldwide spread of English common law can be largely connected to the establishment and development of the British Empire in the 18th, 19th, and 20th centuries. As such, diverse countries across a range of continents, such as Ireland, Australia, Hong Kong, South Africa, India, and Canada all derive their law from the English common law system. While some, such as South Africa and Canada, may have adopted aspects of Civil law, again due to historic connections to European empires, the system of English common law remains a popular and successful form of justice across a large part of the globe.

Australia

3.11 The Australian legal system was, initially, completely based on English common law, Australia having been established as an English colony in the late 18th century. Australia's English founders determined that Australia was "*terra nullius*",[4] thus claiming possession of the land. Therefore, it followed that English law immediately applied to the new settled lands.[5]

3.12 Naturally, being an English colony, the Australian states turned to England for legal direction. For instance, the Australian Courts Act (1828)[6] stated that all laws and statutes in force in England at the date of enactment should be applied in the courts of New South Wales and Van Diemen's Land (Tasmania), so far as those laws and statutes were applicable.[7] Other laws were implemented, further cementing the application of English law. For instance, the New South Wales Act (1923) gave the Chief Justice the right to review legislation; no bill would be enacted unless the Chief Justice certified it was "not repugnant to the Laws of England, but consistent with such Laws as far as the circumstances of the said Colony will admit".

3.13 Gradual independence from English laws occurred with the introduction of Colonial Laws Validity Act (1865), confirming that colonial legislation would apply to the extent such legislation did not contradict any English Act of Parliament extending to the said colony. This was followed by the Statute of Westminster (1931),[8] where the British Parliament could no longer make laws for the "Dominions",[9] other than by the request and

4 The English proclaimed Australia "*terra nullius*", that is, "land belonging to no-one". This meant that there was no sovereign, law, social order, and customs, and no recognisable tenure in land (the native Australian Aborigines were not recognized as having any native title related to land).

5 The English understanding of international law at the time was that unsettled lands inhabited by English subjects meant English law applied by default. This was confirmed by the Privy Council in *Cooper v Stuart* (1889) 14 App Cas 286 and affirmed in *Milirripum and Ors. v Nabulco Pty Ltd and the Commonwealth of Australia* (1971) 17 FLR 141). However, in 1993 the High Court of Australia issued its landmark decision in *Mabo and others v Queensland* (No. 2) [1992] HCA 23; (1992) 175 CLR 1 F.C. 92/014 (3 June 1992) determining that a form of native title existed in Murray Island (off the tip of east coast in Queensland) at the time of settlement. The decision overturned the longstanding notion of terra nullius and recognized Aboriginal and Torres Strait Island people as having rights to the land they traditionally owned.

6 25 July 1828.

7 UK Acts would not apply unless they specifically referred to the colonies. Note, Queensland and Victoria were originally part of New South Wales, thus the same date applies for the reception of English law. South Australia and Western Australia adopted different (and later) dates and Acts.

8 11 December 1931.

9 "Dominion status" was a constitutional term of art used to signify an independent Commonwealth realm. This included: Canada, Australia, New Zealand, Newfoundland, South Africa, and the Irish Free State, and then from the late 1940s also India, Pakistan, and Sri Lanka.

consent of the government of the Dominion in question. The Australia Act of 1986 finally removed any power of the British Parliament to create legislation for Australia and its States and Territories .

3.14 English common law principles and decisions from the English Privy Council were strictly binding on all Australian courts.[10] It wasn't until the Australian cases of *Viro v R*[11] and *National Employers' Mutual General Association Ltd v Waind*[12] that judicial attitudes of the Australian courts towards the authority of the Privy Council changed; the High Court of Australia determined that Australian courts were no longer bound by decisions of the Privy Council.

3.15 Appeals to the Privy Council from the High Court were abolished through the combined effect of the Privy Council (Limitation of Appeals) Act 1968 (Cth) and the Privy Council (Appeals from the High Court) Act 1975 (Cth). The Privy Council Act also abolished appeals to the Privy Council from decisions of the Federal Courts and Supreme Courts of the Territories, and the Judiciary Act 1968 ensured it was not possible to appeal to the Privy Council from decisions of State Courts exercising Federal jurisdiction. However, a right of appeal remained from State courts, in matters governed by State law. The Australia Act 1986 (Cth) finally removed any avenue of appeal by any Australian courts.

3.16 Doctrines of English common law applied to the new Australian colonies. There were very few cases in which a principle of English common law was held inapplicable.[13] New doctrines of English common law continued to be treated as representing the common law of Australia. For instance, the doctrine establishing the modern negligence law in *Donoghue v Stevenson*,[14] was determined as being latent within the Australian common law at the time of its reception.[15] That is, "parts of the common law which are suitable to a more advanced state, lie dormant until occasion arises for enforcing them".[16]

3.17 The Australian judiciary traditionally placed great weight on the authority of decisions handed down by the higher English courts. Decisions from the High Court of Australia, such as *Sexton v Horton*[17] and *Piro v Foster*,[18] demonstrate the persuasive authority of English judicial decisions. For instance, in *Sexton v Horton*, Chief Justice Knox and Starke J commented that the High Court rendered an "abiding service to the community" if it accepted decisions of the English Court of Appeal, "particularly in relation to such subjects as the law of property, the law of contract and mercantile law".[19]

10 In *Bruce v Waldron* [1963] V.R. 3, the court was required to determine whether it ought to follow the House of Lords' decision in *Duncan v Cammell, Laird & Co.* [1942] A.C. 624 or the Privy Council's decision in *Robinson v State of South Australia (No. 2)* [1931] A.C. 704. The court held that the Privy Council's decisions had a direct binding authority on the Australian courts.

11 (1978) 18 A.L.R. 257.

12 [1979] HCA 11; 141 CLR 648.

13 *State Government Insurance Commission v Trigwell* [1979] HCA 40; (1979) 142 CLR 617.

14 [1932] UKHL 100.

15 *State Government Insurance Commission v Trigwell* (n 13).

16 Mason J, *State Government Insurance Commission v Trigwell* (n 13); *Dugan v Mirror Newspapers* [1978] HCA 54; (1978) 142 CLR 583.

17 (1926) 38 C.L.R. 240.

18 (1943) 68 C.L.R. 313.

19 *Sexton* (n 17) 244.

3.18 Despite these previous positions taken by the Australian judiciary, Australian courts in the latter half of the 20th century were more readily inclined not to find English court decisions persuasive. For instance, Australian courts have departed from the English court position on implying good faith in contract.[20]

Singapore

3.19 The foundation of Singapore's legal system is based on English law, especially in contracts, torts and restitution.[21] Singapore was founded by Sir Thomas Stamford Raffles of the British East India Company in 1819 as a strategic centre for English mercantile trade in the region. In 1824, the Sultan of Johore and Temenggong ceded Singapore to the English, who thus acquired full sovereignty over Singapore.

3.20 In 1826, the English Parliament issued the Second Charter of Justice, which created a new court to serve Penang, Malacca and Singapore and was vested with the jurisdiction and powers of the English courts.[22] Although the Second Charter did not expressly state that the laws of England would apply as the laws of Singapore, this was confirmed by local case law adopting the legal position that English law (both common law and equity as it stood in 1826 and pre-1826 English legislation) was introduced to Singapore via the Second Charter.[23] The Privy Council established caveats on the application of the Second Charter, namely: 1) Only English law of general policy and application was to be implemented; and 2) English law implementation was subject to local religions, manners, and customs.[24]

3.21 In 1867, Singapore was separated from the colony of India and became accountable directly to England. This remained the case through to 1963 when, following a brief period of being part of the Malaysian Federation, Singapore achieved republic status in 1965.

3.22 Despite becoming independent from England, the common law connection remains significant. The Civil Act 1988 directed the courts to apply the current English law to mercantile, or commercial, issues unless there was local legislation governing the matter.[25] Due to conflicts in interpretation of this section, there were on-going issues whether certain English statutes applied in various matters. This was finally settled with

20 The Australian case *BP Refinery (Westernport) Pty Ltd v President, Councillors and Ratepayers of the Shire of Hastings* (1977) 180 CLR 266 accepted as a general concept implied duty of good faith, subject to a number of caveats, whereas the English Court of Appeal in *MSC Mediterranean Shipping Company S.A. v Cottonex Anstalt* [2016] EWCA Civ 789 made it clear that there is no "general organizing principle" of good faith under English law.

21 Helena H M Chan, "Legal History" in *The Legal System of Singapore* (Butterworths Asia 1995) 2.

22 The Second Charter of Justice created the Court of Judicature of Prince of Wales Island, Singapore, and Malacca, with civil and criminal jurisdictions on a par with the courts in England. Although not explicitly stated, it was assumed to provide the legal basis for the general reception of English law in Singapore.

23 In *R v Willans* (1858) 3 *Kyshe's Reports* 16 (Supreme Court, Straits Settlements), the Recorder, Sir Benson Maxwell, held that "a direction in an English Charter to decide according to justice and right, without expressly stating by what known body of law they shall be dispensed and so to decide in a country which has not already an established body of law, is plainly a direction to decide according to the law of England".

24 *Choa Choon Neo v Spottiswoode* (1869) 12 Ky 216, 221 (Supreme Court, Straits Settlements) and *Yeap Cheah Neo v Ong Cheng Neo* (1875) LR 6 PC 381 (Privy Council on appeal from the Straits Settlements)

25 Sec 5, Cap 43, 1988 Rev. Edn.

the Application of English Law Act,[26] ("AELA") which clearly stipulated which English statutes apply, or continue to apply, subject to modifications.[27] The continued application of English case law (including equity) is subject to caveats of suitability to the circumstances of Singapore.[28]

3.23 In the same year the AELA was enacted, appeals to the Privy Council were abolished.[29] The move towards greater development of Singapore's local jurisprudence was further encouraged by Singapore's previous Chief Justice, issuing a practice direction where existence of local judgments directly relevant to the issue should be cited in preference to foreign judgments.[30]

Hong Kong

3.24 Hong Kong was a colony ceded to the British Empire from China from 1841/1842 until 1997. The English common law has prevailed since its colonization and even through its accession to the People's Republic of China (PRC).[31] The legal system of the Hong Kong Special Administrative Region (HKSAR) is based on the rule of law and independence of the judiciary with its constitutional framework provided by the Basic Law.[32]

3.25 The continuance of English common law in Hong Kong is confirmed under the Basic Law, which states that the laws previously in force in Hong Kong prior to enacting of the Basic Law (that is, the common law, rules of equity, ordinances, subordinate legislation, and customary law, all having been derived from England) shall be maintained.[33] National laws of the PRC are not applicable to the HKSAR, unless provided for in the Basic Law.

3.26 The doctrine of precedent, forming the backbone of English common law, applies to judicial decisions generated in Hong Kong. The Basic Law provides that Hong Kong courts may refer to case precedents from other countries under common law jurisdiction.[34]

---

26 Chapter 7A, 1994 Rev. Edn.

27 Ibid., s 6(1).

28 Ibid., s 3(2), this section provides that the common law of England already a part of Singapore law shall continue to be part of Singapore law, so long as it is applicable to local circumstances and its inhabitants, subject to such modifications as may be required.

29 Judicial Committee (Repeal) Act 1994.

30 Practice Direction 1 of 2008, available at <www.supremecourt.gov.sg/docs/default-source/default-document-library/legislation-and-directions/practice-direction-no-1.pdf> (accessed 5 March 2019).

31 The transfer of sovereignty, the future administration of Hong Kong, and the preservation of Hong Kong's economic, political, and legal systems, are governed by the Sino-British Joint Declaration signed in December 1984, a binding international treaty registered with the United Nations. For fifty years beyond 1997 it guarantees "one country, two systems". Except in respect of defence and foreign affairs, which are the responsibilities of the Central People's Government, the HKSAR has a high degree of autonomy with its own government and legislature composed of local inhabitants.

32 The Basic Law was enacted by the National People's Republic Congress and is equivalent to a mini-constitution for the HKSAR promulgated on 4 April 1990 and taking effect on 1 July 1997 on the establishment of the HKSAR. All the systems and policies practised in the HKSAR must be based on the provisions of the Basic Law. These include the social and economic systems; safeguarding the fundamental rights and freedoms of its residents; the executive, legislative and judicial systems; and the relevant policies. Furthermore, no law enacted by the legislature of the HKSAR may contravene the Basic Law.

33 Basic Law, Art. 8.

34 Ibid., Art. 84.

Additionally, foreign judges from England and Wales, Australia, New Zealand, and Canada may be appointed to the highest court in Hong Kong, the Court of Final Appeals.[35]

3.27 Despite the influence of the English common law in Hong Kong, changes following accession were introduced which have slightly shifted the legal system towards PRC. For instance, appeals to the Privy Council from the Court of Final Appeals were abolished with the handover. Additionally, questions in relation to interpretation of the Basic Law are vested not in the courts of Hong Kong, but the Standing Committee.[36]

3.28 English common law principles, or more specifically English construction contract principles, run directly through Hong Kong construction contracts. For instance, the English JCT 1963 standard form of contract, under which the majority of English construction case law has evolved, was the basis for the HKIS Standard Form of Building Contract Private Edition (1986).[37]

3.29 Like many other courts from former English colonies, the Hong Kong courts have not entirely followed the English judgments. For instance, in *Maeda Corporation v Government of the Hong Kong* SAR,[38] the Hong Kong Court of Appeals decided not to follow the position of the English Court of Appeal's decision in *Henry Boot Construction Ltd v Alstom Combined Cycles Ltd*[39] on the immutability of contract rates. The Hong Kong Court of Appeal favoured fairness and identified circumstances where it would be appropriate not to follow the contractually incorrect rates and to apply reasonable rates in lieu.

Impact of English Common Law on other Countries/Jurisdictions

3.30 This can be taken in two senses. Taking the term "English common law" in its narrowest sense as common law derived solely from the jurisprudence of England and Wales, it should first be noted that English decisions remain binding on some Commonwealth jurisdictions, and the Privy Council, an appellate court separate from the Supreme Court but made up of certain of its judges, retains jurisdiction as the highest appellate court for certain overseas states.

3.31 As well as limited direct jurisdiction, English courts' decisions also impact on other common law jurisdictions as highly persuasive authority. Equally, the existing body of historical English precedents has been imported as binding authority by many of the former states of the British Empire which retain common law systems.

3.32 In addition, the decisions of other common law states are also persuasive authority both on England and Wales and on other equivalent states. A good example of the interaction of international English common law precedents from different states can be

35 Ibid., Art. 92, Judges from other common law jurisdictions can be recruited to serve in the judiciary as non-permanent judges. A bench comprises four local judges and one overseas judge; the overseas judges rotate through the court on a monthly basis; See Sir Anthony Mason, "The Hong Kong Court of Final Appeal", Melbourne Journal of International Law, v2 (2001), for an overview of Hong Kong Court of Final Appeal.

36 Ibid., Art. 158.

37 This version has been updated with Standard Form of Building Contract for use in the HKSAR, 2005 Edition ("SFBC2005"); however, commentary suggests the latest version of the contract has not been widely used by the industry.

38 HKSAR [2012] HKCA 587.

39 [2005] EWCA Civ 814.

found in the seminal volume "Construction Law"[40] by Julian Bailey, which considers UK, Australian, Hong Kong, and Singapore construction law principles law as a collection of relative and intersecting *rationes*.

3.33 The extent to which English common law impacts upon countries/jurisdictions outside its scope is more uncertain. Clearly, parties in many non-common law jurisdictions will make English common law their default law of choice, due to its perceived robustness and flexibility.

3.34 Equally, in the discussion of international construction law, the historical depth and sophistication of English common law marks it out as an inspiration for the establishment of new legal principles in less-developed legal systems.

3.35 The English common law has had a direct influence on construction contracts globally used in both Common and Civil jurisdictions. Most standard forms of Construction contracts have their genesis in the standard forms originating from England or were written by English lawyers. Naturally, common law principles, terminologies, concepts, and attitudes have found their way into construction contracts that are also being used in Civil law jurisdictions.

3.36 The FIDIC contract form is the most prominent international standard construction contract form having originated entirely from England. The first FIDIC Red Book released in 1957 was based on the Association of Consulting Engineers (ACE) Form 1st Edition, which itself was the international version the Institution of Civil of Engineers (ICE) 4th Edition – the principal UK domestic engineering contract of that time.[41] Of the 2nd Edition of the FIDIC Red Book, [the late] Ian Duncan Wallace QC noted:

> As a general comment, it is difficult to escape the conclusion that at least one primary object in preparing the present international contract was to depart as little as humanly possible from the English conditions.[42]

3.37 The influence of English common law principles and concepts (and even words used) in the FIDIC contract forms is undeniable. Some examples include:

3.38 Impartial Contract Administrator ("Engineer" in FIDIC Forms): It is the common law position that the contract administrator has an implied duty to act impartially in administration of the contract or decision-making between the parties, that is, he must act in a "fair and unbiased manner".[43] The FIDIC Code of Ethics also requires the Engineer to "[b]e impartial in the provision of professional advice, judgment or decision".[44] This was previously implied in the FIDIC forms and expressly introduced in the 1987 4th Edition form.[45] The Engineer's requirement to act "impartially" was removed from the 1999 5th Edition form and replaced with a requirement to make a "fair determination".[46]

40 2nd Edition, Informa 2016.

41 Baker. E et al., *FIDIC Contracts: Law and Practice* (1st Edn, 2009, Informa) [1.17]; see also Nael G. Bunni, *The FIDIC Forms of Contract* (3rd Edn, 2005, Blackwell Publishing).

42 I.N. Duncan Wallace QC, *The International Engineering Contract*, 1974; Glover. J and Hughes. S, *Understanding the New FIDIC Book: A Clause-by-Clause Commentary* (2006, Sweet & Maxwell) xiii.

43 *Sutcliffe v Thackrah* [1974] AC 727.

44 Statutes and By-Laws, FIDIC, October 1996.

45 FIDIC Red Book, 4th Edn, sub-clause 2.6.

46 FIDIC Red Book, 5th Edn, sub-clause 3.5; English courts in *Semco Salvage & Marine Pty Ltd v Lancer Navigation* [1997] UKHL 2 held "fair" means "fair to both Parties". The distinction of "fairness" and

The typical position of an Engineer acting impartially under most Civil law jurisdictions does not exist. For instance, in Germany the Engineer is engaged by the employer and there is no implied requirement to act as an intermediary or independent person.

3.39 Time bar clause: Under English law, time bar clauses are a mechanism which states that if one party fails to perform an act within a specified time period, that party loses certain rights and benefits provided under the contract. The FIDIC forms contain a time-bar clause stating that if the contractor fails to issue the requisite notice within 28 days, he will be time barred from claiming extension of time and/or additional payment. This sub-clause follows the common law approach to time bars and, although generally acceptable in common law jurisdictions, may sometimes be unenforceable as contrary to public policy in civil law jurisdictions. For instance, in Germany time bar clauses similar to the FIDIC form will be held void; the German Supreme Court (*Bundesgerichtshof*) determined that changes to the VOB/B General Terms and Conditions (German standard form of construction contract), prohibiting the right to claim additional payment if notice was not given within a certain time period, was void.[47]

3.40 Defects notification period: The FIDIC forms provide for a defects notification period where the contractor is obliged to return to site during this period and rectify any defective works.[48] English law does not have a statutory defects liability period specifically for construction works, and there are no statutory obligations on contractors to rectify defective works during the general statutory limitation period, unlike Civil law jurisdictions such as Germany[49] or Russia[50] being five years and in France[51] and the UAE,[52] being decennial liability (ten years). Failing to include an express obligation under the contract means that the employer must commence legal proceedings for damages under contracts law and/or torts law. The defects liability period or defects rectification period was largely conceived to regulate the obligation to remedy defects where no statutory requirement to do so existed. .

3.41 Another international standard form of construction contract used in both common and Civil law jurisdictions is the New Engineering and Construction Contract (NEC Contract). UK Project Management Consultant, Prof. Martin Barnes, was commissioned in 1986 by the Institution of Civil Engineers (ICE), a professional association of civil engineers for the United Kingdom, to draft the NEC contract. The NEC contract was first released in 1993 and originally entirely prepared for the English market. Sir Michael Latham noted in his report "Constructing the Team" (1994), a report dedicated to reviewing the English construction industry and recommendations for improvement, that: "[a] set of basic principles is required on which modern contracts can be based. A complete family

"impartiality" is not simple for English speakers from non-common law backgrounds, as the term "fair" has many connotations and includes "impartial".

47 BGH 20 December 1990, the rationale of the court was that the employer ought not be allowed to have the benefit of work done without payment.

48 FIDIC Red Book, sub-clause 11.1

49 German Civil Code, arts 634a (1) 2 and 634(1)–(4).

50 Russian Civil Code, arts 723 and 756.

51 French Civil Code, Art. 1792.

52 UAE Civil Code, art 880(1).

of interlocking documents is also required. The NEC fulfils many of these principles".[53] Eleven out of Latham's thirteen principles for an effective and modern contract were incorporated with the second Latham-compliant edition of the NEC Contract released in 1995.[54] The NEC contract is now in its 4th edition (2017) and is also used in some jurisdictions outside the UK, as well as extensively in the British public sector.

3.42 The Project Partnering Contract 2000 (PPC2000) was a standard form of partnering contract drafted in response to Sir John Egan's, Rethinking Construction (1998) report. Like the NEC Contract, PPC2000 was drafted for the English construction industry, its lead author being Prof. David Mosey.[55] It follows that the contract reflects English common law principles and concepts. In 2007, the PPC2000 International version[56] was released to accommodate the growing demand for a partnering contract to be used in construction projects globally. A comprehensive review of the PPC2000 International version is beyond the remit of this chapter; however, translation and adaptation of the PPC2000 contract into other languages to accommodate for jurisdictions outside the United Kingdom is a notable feature.[57]

3.43 The only international contract which is not English common law influenced is the Engineering Advancement Association of Japan (ENAA) model forms. The two main forms are the ENAA Model Form-International Contract for Process Plant Construction (Turnkey Lump-sum Basis) (3rd Edition, 2010), first published in 1986, and the ENAA Model Form-International Contract for Power Plant Construction (Turnkey Lump-sum Basis), published in 1996. In preparing these model forms, the ENAA extensively referred to and considered recommendations, advice and suggestions of various stakeholders such as the World Bank, major financing institutions, employer and contractors, and other relevant organizations in the US and Europe. The model forms were reviewed by UK law firms and a certified quantity surveyor.[58]

3.44 In Singapore, the Singapore Institute of Architects Building Contract (Lump Sum) 2016 Edition (SIA Building Contract) was originally drafted by the English lawyer Ian Duncan Wallace QC in 1980. Prior to this, parties in construction works were using either JCT, RIBA,[59] FIDIC or a bespoke form of building contract. The Real Estate Developers' Association of Singapore (REDAS) produced its own REDAS Design and Build Conditions of Contract (3rd Edition) first released in 2001. Prior to the introduction of the REDAS Design and Build Contract, most private sector employers in Singapore adopted, with modifications, the English JCT Design and Build Conditions of Contract 1998 or

---

53 NEC: Evolving to be the World's Favourite Procurement Suite available at <www.neccontract.com/getmedia/a83e3c69-bfab-48d0-b9cb-ae479425c0b0/The-History-of-NEC-Whitepaper> (access on 5 March 2019).

54 ibid.

55 The PPC2000 was formulated by the Construction Industry Council (CIC) in collaboration with the Association of Consultant Architects (ACA). It was published by the ACA, and is a joint venture with the Association of Consulting Engineers (ACE).

56 PPC2000 available at <http://ppc2000.co.uk/ppc2000/> (accessed on 5 March 2019).

57 The PPC2000 contract has been translated into German.

58 ENAA Model Form available at <www.enaa.or.jp/EN/activities/model.html> (accessed on 5 March 2019).

59 Dr Philip Chan, "The Export Potential of the NEC: Destination – Singapore" [2006] ICLR 2006 118–26; until 1987, the RIBA contract form was still being used by architects in consultancy, and parties were still using the amended versions of the JCT contract for construction works.

bespoke contracts. The REDAS Design and Build Contract was based on the FIDIC Orange Book and JCT Conditions of Building Contract with Contractor's Design (JCT 1981). With respect to public sector works, the Building and Construction Authority published the Public Sector Standard Conditions of Contract in 1995 (PSSCOC), now in its 2006 edition. The PSSCOC was based on a number of contract forms used by Government Departments, with influences from both FIDIC and the UK ICE forms.[60]

Contract Law

3.45 As an important caveat, it must be noted that what follows is a summary of contract law from the perspective of English common law as articulated in the courts of England and Wales, as opposed to a broader picture of the contract law in other similar jurisdictions, which is beyond the scope of this Chapter. However, as noted above, the lasting influence of England and Wales precedents on other common law jurisdictions, makes the study of this jurisdiction genuinely representative of the core principles of the wider realm.

The Formation of a Contract

3.46 Although, as is detailed below, English contract law has in general terms taken a rigid view of the fundamental requirements of a contract, in terms of offer, acceptance etc., equally there has always been a body of judicial opinion which has seen these formal requirements more as tools for the judiciary than absolute rules. Given that it is the court which ultimately adjudicates on the existence or otherwise of a contract under the common law system, this more nuanced view is perhaps explicable. A good example of the conflicting views on the strictness of the requirements can be found in two statements from the Court of Appeal and House of Lords judgments in *Gibson v Manchester City Council* respectively:

To my mind it is a mistake to think that all contracts can be analysed into the form of offer and acceptance. I know in some of the text books it has been the custom to do so: but, as I understand the law, there is no need to look for a strict offer and acceptance. You should look at the correspondence as a whole and at the conduct of the parties and see therefrom whether the parties have come to an agreement on everything that was material.[61]

3.47 Contrasted with:

> My Lords, there may be certain types of contract, though I think they are exceptional, which do not fit easily into the normal analysis of a contract as being constituted by offer and acceptance; but a contract alleged to have been made by an exchange of correspondence between the parties in which the successive communications other than the first are in reply to one another, is not one of these. I can see no reason in the instant case for departing from the conventional approach.[62]

60 Drs Phillip Chan and Asanga Gunawarra, 'Is it the Correct time for an ASEAN Standard form of building and construction contract?' [2010] 448–62.

61 Lord Denning MR, in *Gibson v Manchester City Council* [1978] 1 W.L.R. 520, at para 523.

62 Lord Diplock, in *Gibson v Manchester City Council* [1979] 1 W.L.R. 294, at para 297.

3.48 Notwithstanding the more radical views expressed by some, however, the latter view, that is, that offer and acceptance need to be evident in the formation of a contract, still represents the orthodox position, even if the identification of agreement in this way represents a forensic challenge to the court.

Offer and Acceptance

3.49 Beginning with the requirement for an offer, there must be an offer which is specific enough to be accepted and which, at the time of acceptance, has not been revoked. Offers are to be distinguished from other statements/representations such as invitations to treat (i.e., invitations to make an offer),[63] advertisements;[64] or the display of goods in a shop.[65]

3.50 Offers can be unilateral, that is, an offer can be made to the world at large/a group of people, rather than to a single individual, provided it is sufficiently clear how the offer may be accepted.[66]

3.51 The offer must be communicated to the offeree[67] and may be revoked at any time up to the point of acceptance.[68] Revocation of a unilateral offer presents greater difficulties with regard to revocation, as acceptance may comprise the commission of an action which makes it difficult to discern at what point it would no longer be possible to revoke.[69]

3.52 An offer may also be terminated by other means, such as lapse of time,[70] rejection,[71] counter-offer,[72] occurrence of a condition, or possibly the death or incapacity of the offeror.[73]

3.53 Acceptance must be final and unequivocal.[74] If it is qualified in any way, it may only serve as a counter-offer.[75] A particular creation of English contract law is what is known as "the battle of the forms".[76] This issue illustrates well the difficulties of confining a complex negotiation into the strict "offer and acceptance" format. The "battle of the forms" represents the situation where one party asserts its own standard terms in an offer, only to be "accepted" by the assertion of the other party's standard terms. This may then be followed by a series of exchanges where each party thinks its bespoke terms have been accepted. The court must then unravel the position to decide whose terms were actually the basis of the deal. In general terms, the courts apply the "last shot" doctrine, the notion being that the last party to assert their standard terms wins the battle. However, some

63 The final analysis of the letter in *Gibson*, above represents a good example of an ITT.
64 *Partridge v Crittenden* [1968] 2 All E.R. 421.
65 *Fisher v Bell* [1960] 3 All E.R. 731.
66 *Carlill v Carbolic Smoke Ball Co* [1893] 1 Q.B. 256.
67 *Taylor v Allon* [1965] 1 All E.R. 557.
68 *Routledge v Grant* (1828) 3 Car. & P. 267.
69 *Errington v Errington and Woods* [1952] 1 K.B. 290.
70 *Ramsgate Victoria Hotel Co Ltd v Montefiore* (1865-66) L.R. 1 Ex. 109.
71 *Stevenson, Jaques & Co v McLean* (1880) 5 QBD 346.
72 *Hyde v Wrench* (1840) 3 Beav. 334.
73 *Bradbury v Morgan* (1862) 1 Hurl. & C. 249.
74 *Rees v Warwick* (1818) 2 B. & Ald. 113.
75 *Stevenson, Jaques & Co v McLean* (n 74).
76 *Butler Machine Tool Co v Ex-cell-o Corp (England)* [1979] 1 All E.R. 965.

judges have applied a more nuanced approach, sifting through the documentation and deciding whose terms were accepted on each individual point.[77]

3.54 An interesting and developing area of English contract law is the status of electronic communication of acceptance. The contract is only formed when the acceptance is communicated to the offeror, but the timing of such communication may be uncertain when electronic means such as fax or email are used. The rule currently being developed seems to be that electronic communication is only received at the point where it would be reasonable to assume that the offeror would be available to receive it. As such, the moment of contract formation may be the point at which the receiver of the message is in appropriate "office hours" (for example, 9am–5pm), but this may depend on the nature and timing of ongoing dealings between the parties.[78]

Intention to Create Legal Relations

3.55 An intention to create legal relations is, as in other jurisdictions, a prerequisite to the formation of a legally binding contract. Provided the other prerequisites exist, English common law will generally assume an intention to create legal relations, particularly between commercial parties.[79] However, there are some exceptions to this general rule. For example, in domestic relationships, such as husband and wife, there is a presumption against intention to be legally bound by an agreement[80] and similarly in social relationships.[81] However, even these relationships may not be a bar where there is sufficient certainty/formality about the arrangement.[82]

3.56 It is commonplace for parties to a construction contract to attempt to reserve their rights and limit their exposure to entering into formal contractual relations by means of the use of "letters of intent" and other rather vague agreements. Such terminology may not, however, be sufficient to exclude the creation of a formal contract. More formal exclusion terminology such as an "honour pledge" may be sufficient to avoid legal relations,[83] but precedents do exist where even "subject to contract" wording was not sufficient to avoid entering into a binding agreement.[84]

Capacity

3.57 With regard to the capacity of persons to enter into a contract, the basic premise is that only a legal person can do so. Broadly speaking, persons may be categorized for these purposes as individual human beings or properly registered companies, although a variety of other entities may also contract.[85] Minors and persons incapacitated through mental illness or intoxication are more limited in their ability to contract, although even

77 *Aries Powerplant Ltd v ECE Systems Ltd* (1995) 45 Con. L.R. 111.

78 *Entores Ltd v Miles Far East Corp* [1955] 2 Q.B. 327; *University of Plymouth v European Language Centre Ltd* [2009] EWCA Civ 784; for a recent case on email communication see *Thomas v BPE Solicitors (A Firm)* [2010] EWHC 306 (Ch).

79 *Esso Petroleum Ltd v Comrs of Customs and Excise* [1976] 1 WLR.

80 *Balfour v Balfour* [1919] 2 K.B. 571.

81 *Coward v Motor Insurers Bureau* [1963] 1 Q.B. 259.

82 *Merritt v Merritt* [1970] 2 All E.R. 760.

83 *Rose & Frank Co v JR Crompton & Bros Ltd* (1924) 20 Ll. L. Rep. 249.

84 *Alpenstow Ltd v Regalian Properties Plc* [1985] 2 All E.R. 545.

85 Such as cooperative societies registered under the Co-operative and Community Benefit Societies Act 2014

these persons may in some instances be deemed to enter into binding legal relations, for example, for contracts for "necessaries".[86]

3.58 Historically, there were some limitations on the ability of companies to enter into contracts where such contracts were ultra vires, that is, outside the scope of the company's constitution.[87] However, the effects of this common law doctrine have been vitiated latterly by the latest iteration of the Companies Act, which renders all contracts by companies binding as against a good faith third party purchaser.[88]

Formalities

3.59 In general terms, English contract law does not impose any particular formalities on the creation of contracts – most contracts can be made orally. However, a lack of formality does, obviously, impose a heavy evidential burden on the party seeking to enforce the terms of the contract.

3.60 Some specific types of contract do require formalities, however, such as contracts for the sale or other disposition of an interest in land, which requires a written contract signed by both parties.[89] Similarly, a deed (see later) requires compliance with a specific set of statutory formalities.[90]

Consideration

3.61 English common Law has held on tightly to the doctrine of consideration as a basic requirement for the existence of a contract. This orthodoxy has not been without its critics,[91] not least in the face of some strained examples of court-created detriment, where only through supreme judicial creativity has some consideration been identified in order to justify the existence of a contract.[92]

3.62 The classical English definition of consideration may be found in *Currie v Misa*[93] and runs as follows:

> A valuable consideration, in the sense of the law, may consist either in some right, interest, profit, or benefit accruing to the one party, or some forbearance, detriment, loss, or responsibility, given, suffered, or undertaken by the other.[94]

3.63 Contractual consideration needs to be *sufficient*, but does not need to be adequate.[95] As such, for example, collateral warranties, are a form of construction contract where nominal sums are used to satisfy the consideration requirement. Some restrictions

86 Defined as: "goods suitable to the condition in life of the person concerned and to his actual requirements at the time of the sale and delivery" in the Sale of Goods Act 1979, s3.
87 *Ashbury Railway Carriage and Iron Co v Riche* (1874-75) L.R. 7 H.L. 653.
88 Companies Act 2006 ss 39(1) and 40(4) & (5).
89 Law of Property (Miscellaneous Provisions) Act 1989, sec 2.
90 Ibid., sec 1.
91 See, e.g., Atiyah "Consideration: A Restatement" in Essays on Contract, Clarendon Paperbacks, 1990.
92 *Edmonds v Lawson* [2000] Q.B. 501.
93 (1874–1875) L.R. 10 Ex. 153.
94 Lush, J at para 162.
95 For an example of nominal consideration see *Chappell & Co Ltd v Nestle Co Ltd* [1960] A.C. 87.

do exist, however, such as the disqualification of past actions[96] and existing legal obligations[97] as forms of consideration.

3.64 The greatest interest, and the greatest difficulties, have surrounded attempts to use existing contractual obligations as consideration for further promises. This has arisen in two key contexts – promises to pay *more* for the satisfaction of an existing obligation, and promises to accept less in respect of a debt obligation.

3.65 In respect of debt obligations, the courts have maintained a strong line that a promise to accept less in respect of an existing debt will not constitute sufficient consideration.[98] The only significant exceptions to this principle are where the debt is satisfied by alternative consideration[99] or where the party enforcing the debt is estopped from doing so by the application of the doctrine of promissory estoppel.[100]

3.66 With regard to the satisfaction of the consideration requirement through existing consideration, the picture is more uncertain. While it is clear that the parties may terminate their contract and then re-forge it as a varied contract, or add new mutual obligations, problems emerge when the parties try to add additional, unsupported consideration to an existing contract. Generally, the position is that such additional consideration is not enforceable.[101] However, the courts will on occasion find a creative solution to the "no consideration" problem in such instances. This approach emerged in the case of *Williams v Roffey*,[102] which involved the not unfamiliar situation of a subcontractor unable to perform due to workforce pressures, and a main contractor desperate for the subcontractor to complete. The subcontractor was incentivised by the promise of additional payment for his works, and, when the works were completed on time, the subcontractor asked for the bonus payment. The main contractor refused to fulfil this additional obligation, arguing that it represented gratuitous payment for work already promised. The court took the view that the additional payment was supported by new consideration in the form of the practical benefit which the main contractor received by dint of the timely completion of the sub-contractor. This decision remains controversial, however, and it is clear that the same outcome would not apply had the additional consideration been obtained through the application of economic duress.[103]

Agency

3.67 As in many legal systems, it is possible for an agent to enter into contracts on behalf of his/her principal. The agreement creates legally binding obligations between the contracting party and the principal, with the agent having no direct personal liability.

3.68 The authority of the agent may derive from the express terms of their appointment, as the basis of "actual authority".[104] Equally, even if the express terms of the appoint-

96 *Roscorla v Thomas* (1842) 3 Q.B. 234.
97 *Collins v Godefroy* (1831) 1 B. & Ad. 950.
98 *Re Selectmove Ltd* [1995] 2 All E.R. 531.
99 *Foakes v Beer* (1884) 9 App. Cas. 605.
100 *Central London Property Trust Ltd v High Trees House Ltd* [1947] K.B. 130.
101 *Stilk v Myrick* (1809) 2 Camp. 317.
102 *Williams v Roffey Bros & Nicholls (Contractors) Ltd* [1991] 1 Q.B. 1.
103 For an example, albeit in slightly different circumstances, see *D&C Builders Ltd v Rees* [1966] 2 Q.B. 617.
104 *Frederick Betts Ltd v Pickfords Ltd* [1906] 2 Ch. 87.

ment are silent on the issue, the agent may have "implied actual authority" based on the circumstances.[105] Equally, even where no authority exists, the principal may be bound by the agent's actions if the principal has allowed the agent to give the impression of being authorised,[106] or has represented that the agent is authorised,[107] which may be categorised as "usual" or "ostensible" authority.

3.69 Where an agent has acted entirely without authority in creating a contract, it is open to the principal to ratify the contract nonetheless.[108] Equally, if a contract is formed which ultimately turns out to be invalid due to lack of authority, the party suffering the loss may be able to bring a claim against the unauthorised agent for breach of warranty of authority.[109] Finally, if the agent does not disclose his/her agency, they may find themselves personally liable for the contract in question.[110]

The Contents of a Contract

Terms of a Contract (Express and Implied Terms)

3.70 At the outset, it must be noted that one of the prevailing themes of English contract law is the need for certainty. A lack of clarity and/or significant omissions can mean that no contract will be found to exist, see the words of Maugham J in *Foley v Classique Coaches Ltd*:

> It is indisputable that unless all the material terms of the contract are agreed there is no binding obligation. An agreement to agree in the future is not a contract; nor is there a contract if a material term is neither settled nor implied by law and the document contains no machinery for ascertaining it.[111]

3.71 As such, although in some instances the courts have been willing to fill in the gaps in a contract by reference to the wider machinery of the agreement,[112] they will not do so if the position is too vague,[113] and in particular will not support "agreements to agree".[114]

3.72 Even where the terms of a contract are largely clear, it may be difficult to differentiate the terms of a contract from mere pre-contractual representations which were not intended to have contractual effect. Considerations in this regard include the timing of the statement,[115] whether an oral statement is later put in writing,[116] and the knowledge or skill of the person making the representation.[117]

3.73 The English courts have maintained the "parol evidence rule" which dictates that if a contract is in written form, the starting presumption is that it comprises the entirety of

105 *Scrivener v Pask* (1865-66) L.R. 1 C.P. 715; *Hely-Hutchinson v Brayhead Ltd* [1968] 1 Q.B. 549.
106 *Watteau v Fenwick* [1893] 1 Q.B. 346.
107 *Freeman & Lockyer v Buckhurst Park Properties (Mangal) Ltd* [1964] 2 Q.B. 480.
108 *Keighley Maxsted & Co v Durant (t/a Bryan Durant & Co)* [1901] A.C. 240.
109 *Yonge v Toynbee* [1910] 1 K.B. 215.
110 *Sika Contracts Ltd v BL Gill and Closeglen Properties Ltd* (1978) 9 B.L.R. 11.
111 Maugham L.J., *Foley v Classique Coaches Ltd* [1934] 2 K.B. 1 at para 13.
112 *WN Hillas & Co Ltd v Arcos Ltd* (1932) 43 Ll. L. Rep. 359.
113 *Baird Textile Holdings Ltd v Marks & Spencer Plc* [2001] EWCA Civ 274.
114 *May & Butcher Ltd v King, The* [1934] 2 K.B. 17.
115 *Bannerman v White* 142 E.R. 685; (1861).
116 *Birch v Paramount Estates Ltd* (1956) 167 EG.
117 *Harling v Eddy* [1951] 2 K.B. 739.

the agreement. However, it is relatively straightforward to dis-apply the rule if the contract was demonstrably intended to comprise both written and oral elements.[118] Equally, the existence of a written contract does not preclude the implication of terms by the courts or through statute. On a connected point, "entire agreement" clauses have been supported by the courts to an extent,[119] but once again will not have the effect of automatically precluding implied terms.

3.74 While the basic principles should make the identification of express terms a relatively straightforward process, particular problems emerge when both parties assert that the contract was made on their own conflicting standard terms, a situation known as the "battle of the forms". This is not least a problem in the construction industry where fragmented exchanges of correspondence may leave the parties uncertain as to which set of terms represent the agreed contract. The courts have adopted a policy known as the "last shot doctrine", whereby the concluding assertion of terms, if unchallenged, represents the final word. However, the application of this doctrine is not simple, and the courts have sometimes had to adopt a nuanced approach to this process.[120]

3.75 Implied terms in English law may broadly be placed in two categories: Standard implied terms and specific implied terms. Put another way, these may be described as those implied terms common to all contracts of the type in question, and those which are only implied on the particular facts of an individual case. Implied terms in the former category, that is, standard implied terms, may be broken down into three further sub-categories: Statutory implied terms,[121] customary implied terms,[122] and common law implied terms.

3.76 Statutory implied terms are most prevalent in the area of consumer contracts, which has recently been consolidated in the Consumer Rights Act 2015. However, a significant collection of statutory implied terms may also be applied to business to business contracts, with the Sale of Goods Act 1979 and the Supply of Goods and Services Act 1982 as key examples. Key implied terms include the obligation to use reasonable care and skill[123] in the provision of services, and the obligation to provide goods of satisfactory quality in goods contracts.[124]

3.77 Customary implied terms may be industry specific or locality-specific[125] and require evidence of the existence of the customary practice.[126] Finally, standard common law implied terms are those which are implied into all contracts of a particular type. For example, construction law cases have given rise to a number of standard implied terms, such as an employer's obligation to provide access to the site.[127]

118 *J Evans & Son (Portsmouth) Ltd v Andrea Merzario Ltd* [1976] 1 W.L.R. 1078.

119 *Inntrepreneur Pub Co Ltd v East Crown Ltd* [2000] 2 Lloyd's Rep. 611.

120 For an example of an incremental approach of this kind, see *Aries Powerplant Ltd v ECE Systems Ltd* (1995) 45 Con. L.R. 111. See also *McCutcheon v David MacBrayne Ltd* [1964] 1 W.L.R. 125 for a discussion of the relevance of a course of dealing.

121 See for example the terms implied into consumer contracts under the Consumer Rights Act 2015.

122 For an example, see *Hutton v Warren, Clerk* (1836) 1 M. & W. 466.

123 Supply of Goods and Services Act 1983, s13.

124 Sale of Goods Act 1979, s14(2).

125 *J Evans & Son (Portsmouth) Ltd v Andrea Merzario Ltd* (n 120); *Hutton v Warren* (1836) 1 M&W 466.

126 *Kum v Wah Tat Bank Ltd* [1971] 1 Lloyd's Rep. 439.

127 *LB Merton v Leach* (1985) 32 BLR 51.

3.78 More interesting perhaps is the challenge of specific implied terms. As stated above, these are terms particular to a specific situation and will thus be entirely bespoke. Given that English common law has long been committed to the basic principle of freedom of contract,[128] it requires fairly extreme circumstances for the courts to be willing to impose an additional term on the parties in this way. The courts have developed various tests to determine the appropriateness of implying a term, which were summarised in the leading case of *BP Refinery v Shire of Hastings*[129] as follows: It must be reasonable and equitable to do so; it must be necessary for business efficacy; it [the implied term] must be so obvious that it "goes without saying" (otherwise known as the officious bystander test);[130] it must be capable of clear expression; and it must not contradict any express terms of the contract. Finally, it must be noted that, while these tests are well-known and well established, there is some dispute as to whether they serve as a definitive list, or merely as alternative approaches to the same problem.[131]

Unfair Contract Terms

3.79 As in many jurisdictions, the discussion of unfair contract terms has centred on the field of exclusion clauses. Exclusion clauses (and other potential unfair terms) are subject to three levels of scrutiny: Incorporation, construction, and statutory control.

3.80 With regard to incorporation, the abiding question is whether the clause in question has become part of the contract or not, a process governed by the courts. Common law applies different tests such as the potential requirement for notice of a clause buried in one party's standard terms which will have a particularly detrimental effect on the other party's rights.[132]

3.81 In respect of interpretation, the courts will, in general terms, apply a "*contra proferentem*" approach. This requires the court to view the clause narrowly, interpreting it against the party asserting it. For example, when trying to achieve an exclusion of negligent performance, the clause will need to be drafted in such a way that there can be no doubt of this effect.[133]

3.82 Finally, even where the contractual effect of the clause can be substantiated, it may still be nullified by the application of statute. In recent times, the law in this area in England and Wales has been subdivided into two jurisdictions: Consumer Law, and Business to Business Law. The consumer protections for unfair contract terms are now largely to be found in the Consumer Rights Act 2015, whereas the business to business principles remain in the Unfair Contract Terms Act 1977 (UCTA). Space does not permit a detailed consideration of the provisions, but the position for B2B contracts may be broadly summarised as follows.

---

128 For the classic articulation of this principle, see Jessell MR's famous statement in *Printing and Numerical Registering Co v Sampson* (1874–1875) L.R. 19 Eq. 462, at para 465.

129 *BP Refinery (Westernport) Pty Ltd v Shire of Hastings* 180 C.L.R. 266.

130 *Southern Foundries (1926) Ltd v Shirlaw* [1940] A.C. 701.

131 See Lord Hoffmann's comments in *Attorney General of Belize v Belize Telecom Ltd* [2009] UKPC 10 at para 27; for the latest discussion of this issue, see *Marks & Spencer Plc v BNP Paribas Securities Services Trust Co (Jersey) Ltd* [2015] UKSC 72.

132 See the famous "red hand" test from *J Spurling Ltd v Bradshaw* [1956] 2 All E.R. 121 at [35].

133 See the guidelines for interpreting such exclusion clauses in the *Canada Steamship* case [1952] A.C. 192.

3.83 UCTA applies to unfair terms contained in "standard" terms of business.[134] Certain forms of exclusion are always unlawful, such as clauses seeking to exclude liability for death or personal injury.[135] Similarly, exclusion of liability for key implied terms, such as those relating to title in goods being sold, is not permissible.[136] However, other exclusions of liability, such as for negligence/breach of contract, may be acceptable, but will be subject to a defined test of reasonableness.[137]

Vitiating Factors under Contract Law

3.84 Before embarking on a brief overview of vitiating factors in English common law, it is worth once again bearing in mind the overriding principle of freedom of contract. As famously stated by Lord Jessell MR:

> Therefore, you have this paramount public policy to consider—that you are not lightly to interfere with this freedom of contract.[138]

3.85 Accordingly, while remedies are available for so-called vitiating factors, it has to be borne in mind throughout that such remedies will not be awarded lightly.

Misrepresentation and Mistake

3.86 As in other jurisdictions, the categories of misrepresentation and mistake to some extent overlap, albeit they are separate principles. The distinguishing factor, in as much as it is possible to separate them, is that misrepresentation involves a statement made by one party, indicating a state of affairs as being true, which later turns out to be false. Mistake will involve one, or both of the parties assuming that a state of affairs exists, without reliance on an indication by the other.

3.87 As identified above, the first part of any analysis of misrepresentation is to ask whether a representation has been made at all. A representation, for these purposes, is defined as a statement confirming existing facts or law.[139] It will not have become a term of the contract (which would create the possibility of an action for breach) but will have been an inducement to enter into the contract or at least a statement upon which the other party has relied.[140] It need not, however, have been the only inducement,[141] provided it is a substantial cause.[142]

3.88 As may be imagined, many discussions have focused on borderline cases such as statements of opinion,[143] misleading conduct,[144] "blind-eye knowledge",[145] and failure to disclose information or a changing state of affairs.[146]

---

134 UCTA s3(1), note that the definition of 'standard terms' has been debated in several cases.

135 Ibid., s2(1).

136 Ibid., s6(1).

137 Ibid., s11. For an example of the application of the reasonableness test in a construction context, see *Phillips Products v Hyland* (1988) 4 Const. L.J. 53.

138 Jessell MR in *Printing and Numerical Registering Co v Sampson* (1874-75) L.R. 19 Eq. 462, at [465].

139 *Pankhania v Hackney LBC* [2002] EWHC 2441 (Ch).

140 *MCI WorldCom International Inc v Primus Telecommunications Inc* [2004] EWCA Civ 957.

141 *Edgington v Fitzmaurice* (1885) 29 Ch. D. 459.

142 *Raiffeisen Zentralbank Osterreich AG v Royal Bank of Scotland plc* [2010] EWHC 1392 (Comm).

143 *Bisset v Wilkinson* [1927] A.C. 177.

144 *Gordon v Selico Ltd* (1986) 18 H.L.R. 219.

145 *Manifest Shipping Co Ltd v Uni-Polaris Insurance Co Ltd (The Star Sea)* [2001] UKHL 1.

146 While there is not general obligation of "good faith" in English contract law, some industries, such as the insurance industry, do have specific implied obligations of disclosure (*uberrimae fidei*). Equally, a changed

3.89 Once it is established that a misrepresentation has occurred, there are four possible categories it may fall into, the difference for the claimant being the remedies which are applicable. It must be noted at this point that the Consumer Rights Act 2015[147] now classifies a range of statements made in relation to specific types of consumer contract as contractual terms, regardless of whether they were simply intended as representations. Equally, the new consumer legislation also enshrines a number of new, more efficient remedies for cases of misrepresentation in consumer contracts.[148] The details of the new regime which follow only cover the existing regime for business to business contracts.

3.90 The most severe form of misrepresentation is fraudulent misrepresentation. Grounded in the tort of deceit, this category of misrepresentation involves a statement made with knowledge that it is false, or recklessly as to its potential falsehood.[149] As may be imagined, this category is notoriously difficult to prove, relying on a demonstration of deliberate deceit. However, if established, the benefit is that a successful claim allows both for the innocent party to elect rescission,[150] that is, treating the contract as void,[151] restoring the parties to their original position,[152] and/or to seek damages on the tortious measure (given that the action is extra-contractual), again with a view to restoring the innocent party to the position it would have been in had the tort not occurred. The particular benefit of fraudulent misrepresentation in this respect is that there is no requirement that the losses should have been reasonably foreseeable – *all* losses are claimable, regardless of their remoteness.

3.91 The second type of misrepresentation is negligent misrepresentation at common law. This action has the advantage that it does not require proof of fraud or deliberately reckless behaviour, only that there has been an assumption of responsibility by the person making the statement and that they have been negligent as to its truth.[153] Rescission is again available here, as are damages, albeit that damages in this case are limited to those which are reasonably foreseeable.[154]

3.92 The most common form of misrepresentation claim is statutory misrepresentation under the Misrepresentation Act 1967.[155] This has several advantages – it is based in negligence, but it puts the onus on the defending party to prove that he had reasonable grounds for believing the statement to be true. Also, and perhaps more significantly, it provides for damages on the same, more generous, scale as fraudulent misrepresentation,[156] as well as allowing for rescission.

---

state of affairs prior to the formation of a contract could create an obligation to update the other party – *With v O'Flanagan* [1936] Ch. 575; *Spice Girls Ltd v Aprilia World Service BV* [2002] EWCA Civ 15.

147 ss 12 and 50.

148 See the Consumer Protection from Unfair Trading Regulations 2008 as amended by the Consumer Protection from Unfair Trading (Amendment) Regulations 2014.

149 For the most recent formulation of the test, see *Ludsin Overseas Ltd v Eco3 Capital Ltd* [2013] EWCA Civ 413.

150 Although rescission may be barred in some cases, such as where too much time has elapsed, or where innocent third party rights may be affected.

151 Note that in this context the contract is to be treated as 'voidable' rather than void *ab initio*.

152 Including, as necessary, restitutionary awards.

153 More generally, this type of claim may be described as negligent misstatement and arises originally from the landmark case of *Hedley Byrne & Co Ltd v Heller & Partners Ltd* [1964] A.C. 465.

154 *Overseas Tankship (UK) Ltd v Miller Steamship Co Pty Ltd (The Wagon Mound)* [1967] 1 A.C. 617.

155 s 2(1).

156 See the interpretation of s 2(1) in *Royscot Trust Ltd v Rogerson* [1991] 2 Q.B. 297.

3.93 Finally, there is also a residual category of innocent misrepresentation. In this case, the only available remedy in general terms will be rescission, albeit the Misrepresentation Act does allow for the court to award damages in lieu of rescission in exceptional cases.[157]

3.94 A contract formed on the basis of a mistake will be treated as void *ab initio*. However, this formulation is rarely applied and does not, therefore, represent an easy escape route for a party who has entered into a contract on the basis of a misapprehension.[158]

3.95 Broadly speaking, English common law recognizes three forms of mistake, unilateral mistake, mutual mistake, and common mistake, each based on different types of contractual problem.

3.96 Unilateral mistake involves a mistaken apprehension by one party to the contract. In general terms, provided there has been no misrepresentation by the other party, the mistake of just one party is his/her own risk, based in a general notion of "*caveat emptor*". However, where the other party is aware of the mistaken view of the "innocent" party and is complicit in that state of affairs, it may be possible for the mistaken party to claim a remedy,[159] either that the contract is declared void, or possibly for rectification.[160]

3.97 Mutual mistake represents the situation when both parties were unknowingly at cross-purposes as to the basis of the contract, for example in a shipping contract when the parties both thought that a different ship of the same name was under discussion.[161]

3.98 Finally, common mistake consists of situations where both parties are under a shared misapprehension as to a factual situation which undermines the whole basis of the contract. This may include, for example, situations where the goods to be sold have ceased to exist,[162] or a mistake as to the possibility of legal performance.[163]

3.99 However, it must be noted that there is no general equitable jurisdiction for the courts to find common mistake for reasons of justice alone,[164] and equally, at common law, the courts may often reject an argument for common mistake on the basis that such circumstances are merely part of the risk profile of any commercial contract.[165]

3.100 Finally, it must be noted that while common mistake is infrequently applied, the remedy of rectification is more easily adopted by the courts and may be a more obvious remedy in many cases of this nature.[166]

---

157 See s 2(2) of the Misrepresentation Act. Questions nonetheless remain about the measure of such damages, and whether such damages may be available where the right to rescission has been lost: *Floods of Queensferry v Shand Construction Ltd* [2000] BLR 81; *William Sindall Plc v Cambridgeshire CC* [1994] 1 W.L.R. 1016.

158 For an example of a failed attempt at its application, see *William Sindall Plc v Cambridgeshire CC* [1994] 1 W.L.R. 1016.

159 *Hartog v Colin and Shields* [1939] 3 All ER 566.

160 For the criteria for rectification in such instances, see *Thomas Bates & Son Ltd v Wyndham's (Lingerie) Ltd* [1981] 1 W.L.R. 505.

161 *Raffles v Wichelhaus* (1864) 2 Hurl. & C. 906.

162 *Couturier v Hastie* (1856) 5 H.L. Cas. 673 (now also covered by the Sale of Goods Act 1979 s6).

163 *Cooper v Phibbs* (1867) L.R. 2 H.L. 149.

164 See the failed attempt by Lord Denning to establish such a jurisdiction in *Solle v Butcher* [1950] 1 K.B. 671.

165 For two striking examples of such rejection, see *Bell v Lever Bros Ltd* [1932] AC 161; and *McRae v Commonwealth Disposals Commission* (1951) 84 CLR 377.

166 See the promotion of this equitable remedy in *Chartbrook v Persimmon Homes Ltd* [2009] UKHL 38.

Illegality

3.101 The English principle of illegality as a vitiating factor for a contract finds its origins in the notion of *ex turpi causa non oritur actio*, that is, that a civil action cannot be based on a dishonest cause. Illegality renders a contract void and unenforceable. Illegality in this context may include breach of public policy, such as the general prohibition on restraint of trade.[167] It is clear, however, that the contract must be criminal/quasi criminal – problems with civil liability alone will not suffice as the basis for such an understanding.[168]

3.102 Illegality will be most straightforwardly found in instances when the object of the contract itself is illegal, for example a contract to commit a violent crime.[169] Greater problems emerge when the object of the contract is not criminal, but the method of performance is. In such instances, while collusion by both parties in illegal performance may render the contract unenforceable,[170] if one party has performed in a criminal manner, but has nonetheless rendered effective performance, the contract may stand.[171]

3.103 While the general effect of illegality is that the contract is void and unenforceable, the court does also have the option of rendering part of the contract ineffective, while maintaining the force of another part, sometimes called the "blue-pencil test".[172] Where the entire contract has been declared unenforceable, it may still be open to a party who has suffered loss to claim a restitutionary remedy in limited circumstances.[173]

Duress and Undue Influence

3.104 The extent to which a common law doctrine of duress exists remains uncertain. It is clear that certain types of specific duress will vitiate the existence of a contract by the fundamentally illegitimate nature of the pressure applied. Thus, contracts made in the context of threats of violence to the person,[174] or to goods,[175] will be void.

3.105 The more difficult area lies with the issue of economic duress and whether simple commercial pressure applied in the context of commercial bargaining could constitute duress sufficient to vitiate a contract.

3.106 The possibility of such a doctrine of economic duress has been confirmed in cases such as *R v A-G for England and Wales*.[176] However, its scope, and the appropriate test to be applied, remains in doubt. The problem lies in the fact that, under the general common law doctrine of freedom of contract, parties are entitled to enter into whatever agreements they wish, even if an agreement is manifestly to the disadvantage of one party. This is particularly the case in the context of business to business transactions, where

---

167 *Proactive Sports Management Ltd v Rooney* [2011] EWCA Civ 1444.

168 *Les Laboratoires Servier v Apotex Inc* [2014] UKSC 55.

169 See, for example, *Allen v Rescous* (1675) 2 Levinz 174.

170 *Ashmore Benson Pease & Co Ltd v AV Dawson Ltd* [1973] 1 W.L.R. 828; see also *Archbolds (Freightage) Ltd v S Spanglett Ltd* [1961] 1 All E.R. 417.

171 *St John Shipping Corp v Joseph Rank Ltd* [1957] 1 Q.B. 267.

172 *Frank W Clifford Ltd v Garth* [1956] 1 W.L.R. 570.

173 *Mohamed v Alaga & Co. (a firm)* [2000] 1 W.L.R. 1815.

174 *Barton (Alexander) v Armstrong (Alexander Ewan)* [1976] A.C. 104.

175 Although there was some doubt over this due to an early decision in *Skeate v Beale* (1840) 11 Ad & E 983, it is now thought that this will definitely be a form of duress, see *Occidental Worldwide Investment Corp v Skibs A/S Avanti (The Siboen and The Sibotre)* [1976] 1 Lloyd's Rep. 293.

176 [2003] UKPC22.

courts accept that bad deals may be struck in the "*the rough and tumble of the pressures of normal commercial bargaining*".[177]

3.107 While initially focusing on the issue of "coercion of the will",[178] English common law has moved the test to the issue of the legitimacy of the pressure being applied, in acknowledgment of the fact that consent will be real, even if coerced through economic pressure; a decision to enter into a contract is nonetheless consent. The question then arises as to what would constitute *illegitimate* pressure. It seems to be confirmed that a threat to carry out an unlawful act, for example, a breach of contract, would be a form of illegitimate pressure.[179] However, a more interesting question arises of whether it is possible to assert economic pressure such as to vitiate a contract by the threat of a lawful action (such as a right to terminate a contract). Some UK judgments have indicated that such a threat could, in the right circumstances, amount to illegitimate pressure, even indicating that to an extent this is an issue of "bad faith".[180]

3.108 Finally, it is of interest to contrast the possibility of bad faith with the willingness in other decisions of the court to recognize "practical benefit" consideration in circumstances which could alternatively be characterised as economic duress by the party unwilling or unable to perform for the agreed contract price.[181]

3.109 Undue influence is an equitable doctrine which in some ways shares features with duress, in that it centres on the notion that the claimant's consent to the transaction was procured through the imposition of inappropriate pressure or coercion.

3.110 In its simplest form, sometimes described as "actual undue influence", it will involve the application of threats, for example, threats of personal violence or other punitive activity.[182] In such cases, the undue influence will be obvious to the observer and, therefore, more straightforward for the courts to apply a remedy.

3.111 More difficult is a category known as "presumed undue influence". This consists of a situation where an individual is deemed, simply by the context of the transaction, to have entered into the arrangement under illegitimate pressure. This is most common in domestic relationships, or other similar relationships of trust between individuals. The largest volume of cases in this area has arisen from situations where a husband and wife enter into a mortgage over jointly owned property, but the husband has coerced the wife into entering into the mortgage, against her best financial interests. As may quickly be seen, a counter-argument may always exist that a mortgage generating monies for the husband, could, in effect, be seen as an advantage for the wife, given the nature of the relationship. Nonetheless, the courts have, in some cases, been willing to dis-apply the mortgage from the wife's share of the property on the basis that a relationship of trust and confidence existed between the couple, that the husband took advantage of this to coerce

177 The Hon Mr Justice Dyson in *DSND Subsea Ltd (formerly DSND Oceantech Ltd) v Petroleum Geo Services ASA* [2000] B.L.R. 530 at para 131.

178 *Occidental Worldwide Investment Corp v Skibs A/S Avanti (The Siboen and The Sibotre)* [1976] 1 Lloyd's Rep. 293.

179 See Lord Hoffman *in R v Attorney General of England and Wales* [2003] UKPC22 at [507].

180 See obiter in *CTN Cash and Carry Ltd v Gallaher Ltd* [1994] 4 All E.R. 714; and *Huyton SA v Peter Cremer GmbH & Co* [1999] 1 Lloyd's Rep. 620 to that effect.

181 *Williams v Roffey Bros & Nicholls (Contractors) Ltd* [1991] 1 Q.B. 1.

182 *Williams v Bayley* (1866) L.R. 1 H.L. 200.

the wife into the mortgage, and that the resulting arrangement was manifestly disadvantageous to the wife.[183]

3.112 As may be anticipated, such a situation leaves the mortgage lender in a precarious position. It may be unaware of the situation giving rise to the mortgage and thus, if undue influence is found, runs the risk of losing a part of the mortgage security. To offset this risk, the courts have introduced a final check and balance. If the lender can take sufficient steps to ensure that it has done everything it can to prevent the risk of undue influence, then such a situation will not reduce its right to claim the security in the event of default. Such steps may include, inter alia, requiring both of the mortagees to separately seek legal advice, so as to ensure that they are fully aware of the nature of the transaction and the associated risks.[184]

The Rights and Liabilities of Third Parties

3.113 English contract law starts with an orthodox position on privity, that is, that the burdens and benefits of a contract rest with the parties to the contract alone. In the words of Lord Haldane: "*only a person who is a party to a contract can sue on it*".[185]

3.114 However, that overarching proposition is subject to a number of exceptions which can be used to displace the basic proposition.

3.115 First, it is well-established that the benefit of a contract can be assigned to a third party as a "chose in action", that is, a right to demand and receive performance. The formalities for assignment will depend on the nature of the rights being assigned – legal assignment (i.e., assignment in law rather than at equity) is governed by s136 of the Law of Property Act 1925 (LPA)and basically requires a written statement, signed by the assignor and notified to the person with the burden. Equitable assignment has a slightly less formal requirement, as set out in s53(1)(a) of the LPA.

3.116 Of course, it must be noted that the original parties to the contract can agree to limit the assignability of a contract, as is commonplace in building contracts. Equally, some benefits may not be assignable as a matter of statute law, or by the nature of the obligation; for example, where the benefit is personal to a particular individual.[186]

3.117 The next key exception is the introduction of the Contracts (Rights of Third Parties) Act 1999. This statute was introduced to make it easier for parties to a contract to intentionally confer a benefit on third parties without the necessity of a specially crafted collateral contract.[187] The Act allows for this in two ways, either through specifically naming a third party, or by allowing for the benefit to accrue to a specific class of person(s).[188]

183 The two most significant cases in this area are *Barclays Bank Plc v O'Brien* [1994] 1 A.C. 180; and *Royal Bank of Scotland Plc v Etridge (No.2)* [2001] UKHL 44, albeit the latter should be seen as the leading authority, superseding *Barclays*.

184 Lord Bingham of Cornhill in *Royal Bank of Scotland Plc v Etridge (No.2)* [2001] UKHL 44 at para 50.

185 *Dunlop Pneumatic Tyre Co. v Selfridge* [1915] AC 847 at para 853.

186 See for example *Tolhurst v Associated Portland Cement Manufacturers (1900) Limited* [1902] 2 KB 660.

187 In construction law, collateral warranties remain a popular means of conferring the benefit of a building contract on specified third parties such as tenants, end-users, funders, etc.

188 See the Contracts (Rights of Third Parties) Act 1999, ss1(1)–(3).

3.118 Finally, in terms of the burden, while this cannot be assigned in the same manner as a benefit, it can be formally transferred by means of a contractual novation. A contractual novation consists of an agreement by the parties to the contract and a new third party that the existing contract will be discharged and thereby come to an end, to be replaced with a new contract with the new part taking on this original promisor's obligations. Such "novation agreements" are commonly used in the construction industry, for example in order to novate the services of a designer. In general terms, care needs to be taken to ensure clarity on the extent of those obligations being discharged and the new obligations being entered into.

3.119 It should be added here that performance of one's own obligations by a third party, that is, subcontracting, is accepted by the UK courts and does not constitute another exception to the rules regarding privity. Performance via a subcontractor is known as "vicarious performance" and is an implied right unless there is a specific reason why performance has to be personal.[189] Given that the contracting party will still be liable for the obligation if the subcontractor fails, vicarious performance does not offend the rules of privity.

3.120 As a final note, the courts in the UK have been troubled on several occasions by the "no loss" problem in connection with the assignment of contractual rights. In essence, this problem emerges where there is an assignment of the benefit of contractual rights, but where it also becomes apparent that the original party would never have been able to bring an action. As will be discussed later, the primary remedy in English contract law is damages, and in order to claim damages a party needs to be able to demonstrate loss. The general principle goes that the assignee cannot inherit greater rights than the assignor originally had, and so cannot sue if that would not have been a possibility for the original party. However, a series of decisions has established an exception to this rule, where it is clear that it would not be in the spirit of the original contractual arrangement not to allow such a claim.[190] However, there may still be problems for the assignee if they already had a contractual route for a claim in their own name via a separate collateral agreement.[191]

Performance of a Contract

Performance

3.121 English common law begins with "*Pacta Sunt Servanda*", that is, performance must be complete and must match the promises made. As such, failure to perform *prima facie* provides an opportunity for a remedy in favour of the innocent party, a remedy which may be extreme in nature.[192]

3.122 However, exceptions to the "complete performance" principle outlined above do exist. As alluded to below, there is the right to terminate the contract, thus avoiding all

189 *British Waggon Co v Lea & Co* (1880) 5 Q.B.D. 149; *Southway Group Ltd v Wolff* (1991) 57 B.L.R. 33.

190 For an example, see *Darlington BC v Wiltshier Northern Ltd* [1995] 1 W.L.R. 68.

191 See *Alfred McAlpine Construction Ltd v Panatown Ltd* (No.1) [2001] 1 A.C. 518.

192 For a famous example of an arguably disproportionate remedy for a minor breach, see *Arcos Ltd v EA Ronaasen & Son* [1933] A.C. 470, albeit such an outcome would today be unlikely under the modern Sale of Goods legislation.

future obligations and still maintaining a right to damages for losses accrued.[193] This remedy relies, however, on breach of condition, that is, a substantial failure to perform.[194] In some cases, the courts have made an exception and disallowed termination where there has been "substantial performance" of the obligation, albeit not complete performance (but not that this does not remove a right to damages for losses resulting from the minor breach).[195] Other exceptions include divisible contracts, where non-performance of a stage does not remove the right to payment for previous stages,[196] and, in a sense, the availability of *quantum meruit*.

Frustration

3.123 The doctrine of frustration consists of a proposition that where performance of the contract is rendered impossible or illegal by an intervening external event subsequent to formation of the contract, both parties will be relieved from any further obligations to perform under the contract.

3.124 However, the identification and isolation of such circumstances, and the uncertain definition of "impossibility" have made the doctrine difficult to apply. In addition, the courts are reluctant to invoke the principle too easily, given that it has the potential to relieve a party of their agreed obligations.[197]

3.125 The main thrust of many of the key decisions in this area has been the extent to which the parties could have foreseen the possibility of such an event occurring and whether failure to account for it in the express contractual terms should simply be treated as a risk for which one party must bear the cost. Lord Justice Rix in *The Sea Angel*[198] stated that the decision on whether a frustrating event has occurred required a "multifactorial approach"[199] which should include the parties' objective knowledge and understanding at the time the contract was formed.

3.126 The effect of frustration is to make void all future obligations, but not those which have already accrued.[200] Where monies have been paid in respect of obligations which are no longer possible for the other party to perform, these may be recoverable, as may, to a more limited extent, the value of goods or services provided to the other party.[201]

3.127 Finally, it must be noted that frustration will not be applied where the frustrating event is self-induced.[202]

Breach

3.128 Breach of contract consists in a failure by one party to perform one of more of their obligations under the contract. Such failure will provide the innocent party with an

193 See paras 3.131-3.133.

194 See, for example, *Bolton v Mahadeva* [1972] 1 W.L.R. 1009.

195 See, for example, *Hoenig v Isaacs* [1952] 2 All E.R. 176.

196 *Roberts v Havelock* (1832) 3 B. & Ad. 404.

197 See *Davis Contractors v Fareham Urban District Council* [1956] AC 696.

198 *Edwinton Commercial Corp v Tsavliris Russ (Worldwide Salvage & Towage) Ltd (The Sea Angel)* [2007] EWCA Civ 547.

199 ibid. [111].

200 *Hirji Mulji v Cheong Yue Steamship Co Ltd* [1926] A.C. 497.

201 See the effects of s1 Law Reform (Frustrated Conracts) Act 1943.

202 *Maritime National Fish Ltd v Ocean Trawlers Ltd* [1935] A.C. 524.

opportunity to seek a remedy. The nature of the remedy depends on the seriousness of the breach. For more detail, see the following sections.

Termination, Rescission, and Repudiation

3.129 In the normal course of events, a contract will be terminated through performance – once performed, the contract is discharged and ceases to exist. Equally, the contract may have in-built mechanisms for automatic termination, such as termination clauses[203] or conditional performance provisions. As we have seen above, the contract may also be frustrated, which represents termination of the contract due to external factors.

3.130 However, perhaps of greatest concern to contract lawyers is the ability of the parties arbitrarily to terminate the contract due to repudiatory breach by the other. Although this remedy is sometimes described as "rescission", many prefer to call this remedy simply "termination", as true "rescission" has a different meaning as a remedy for misrepresentation, as outlined above.

3.131 For the purpose of termination, obligations are broken down into three categories – conditions, warranties, and innominate terms. Breach of condition will entitle the innocent party to terminate the contract with immediate effect and thus be relieved of any future obligations, notwithstanding that obligations already accrued will still be enforceable as will certain pervasive provisions such as confidentiality and dispute resolution. The innocent party will also be entitled to damages to the extent of any loss sustained. A condition is defined by reference to the severity of the impact of any breach, not the parties' intentions,[204] and is thus a classification for the court to apply on an objective basis. Equally, some statutory implied obligations are automatically classified as conditions.[205]

3.132 Warranties, by comparison, comprise those obligations which are not so significant as to trigger a right to terminate.

3.133 Finally, innominate terms are those which can, at least initially, neither be classed as conditions nor warranties. Their ultimate classification will depend on the effect of the breach which may vary depending on the circumstances, unlike breach of a straightforward condition which will always be sufficiently serious. It is for the court to determine whether, on the facts, breach of the innominate term entitles the innocent party to terminate.[206]

3.134 Breach of a condition in this manner is known as "repudiatory breach". Where a party indicates, ahead of the proposed time for performance that it is not going to perform, it may also be called "anticipatory breach".[207] From the point of the repudiatory breach, the innocent party has two options. It may *accept* the breach, by which we mean accepting that the other party has repudiated the contract, with the effect of terminating the contract forthwith, or *affirm* the contract, by which we mean that the innocent party is treating the

203 Albeit these must be exercised with caution, see *Woodar Investment Development Ltd v Wimpey Construction UK Ltd* [1980] 1 W.L.R. 277.

204 *L Schuler AG v Wickman Machine Tool Sales* Ltd [1974] A.C. 235.

205 See ss12-15 Sale of Goods Act 1979.

206 *Hong Kong Fir* Shipping *v Kawasaki Kisen Kaisha* [1962] 2 QB 26.

207 *Hochster v De La Tour* (1853) 118 E.R. 922.

contract as continuing notwithstanding the breach and will, therefore, only seek a remedy in damages.

3.135 The innocent party needs to be aware that, although they may take time before making their election (i.e., either to terminate or affirm),[208] in some circumstances too great a delay may render the right to terminate redundant.[209] Equally, in cases of affirmation, the court may refuse to accept the viability of affirmation where the innocent party has no legitimate interest in continuing to perform their side of the bargain (on a similar basis to the "duty" to mitigate).[210]

Remedies

3.136 The primary remedy in contract law is damages, as detailed below. However, in some circumstances, alternative remedies may be applicable and more effective, such as termination,[211] rescission,[212] rejection of the goods,[213] injunction, rectification, *quantum meruit*, or set-off. Discussion will focus on the common law as applied to business to business contracts. Further remedies are now available to consumers under the scope of the new Consumer Rights Act 2015.

Common Law Remedies

3.137 As stated above, the main Contractual Remedy at common law is that of damages. The contractual measure of damages may be best summarised in the famous *dicta* of Parke, B in *Robinson v Harman*:[214]

> [w]here a party sustains a loss by reason of a breach of contract, he is, so far as money can do it, to be placed in the same situation, with respect to damages, as if the contract had been performed.[215]

3.138 In order to demonstrate the extent of damages which should be awarded, the injured party must demonstrate that the losses being claimed were caused by the failure of the other party to perform. In contract law, such losses may include "pure economic loss", for example, loss of business, but the extent of such losses may be difficult to quantify and/or justify. Causation itself is a hugely complex and difficult issue in pleadings. The underlying test is the "balance of probabilities" test, that is, a likelihood of more than 50%.[216] However, given the limitations of this test, the courts have been willing to apply a variety of more nuanced tests such as the "but for" test,[217] the "dominant/effective cause" test and the "loss of chance" test.[218] Equally, causation arguments may be undermined

208 *Stocznia Gdanska SA v Latvian Shipping Co* (Repudiation) [2002] EWCA Civ 889.
209 See for example *Avery v Bowden* 119 E.R. 647; see also s35 Sale of Goods Act 1979.
210 *Clea Shipping Corp v Bulk Oil International (The Alaskan Trader)* (No.1) [1983] 1 Lloyd's Rep. 315.
211 See para 3.135 on repudiatory breach.
212 See para 3.131 on rescission.
213 See the range of remedies provided under the new Consumer Rights Act 2015.
214 (1848) 1 Exchequer Reports (Welsby, Hurlstone and Gordon) 850.
215 Parke, B [855].
216 *Nulty v Milton Keynes BC* [2013] EWCA Civ 15.
217 Albeit see the criticism of this rather blunt instrument in *Galoo Ltd v Bright Grahame Murray* [1994] 1 W.L.R. 1360 in the context of tortious claims.
218 *Chaplin v Hicks* [1911] 2 K.B. 786.

by "*novus actus interveniens*", that is, third party events which break the chain of causation.[219] Where multiple parties contributed to the loss, there may be a possibility of claims between the parties for contribution[220] and, in limited circumstances, reduction in respect of contributory negligence by the claimant.[221]

3.139 Even where causation can be demonstrated, the parties have the further problem of demonstrating that the losses may not be considered too remote. The basic test for remoteness is the extent to which such losses could have reasonably been within the contemplation of the parties at the time when they entered into the contract.[222] This ultimately will come down to a conjectural analysis which will be challenging for the court and the claimant.[223]

3.140 Finally, with regard to damages, the last difficulty rests in terms of measure. The usual measure which the courts will apply is expectation loss, that is, what the claimant expected to receive as a result of the contract and/or the position the claimant expected to be in. However, in many cases this will be difficult for the court to apply. For a good example of this difficulty, see the application of "loss of amenity" as an alternative to expectation loss in the famous case of *Ruxley v Forsyth*.[224] Other cases provide examples of reliance losses[225] (i.e., incidental costs in preparation for the other party's performance), and even, on rare occasions, restitutionary losses[226] (reclaiming profits made by the breaching party as a result of the breach).

3.141 There is a limited duty to mitigate one's losses in a contractual claim, and the defendant can seek to have the damages reduced if there is a failure to do so. Equally, if actions in mitigation bring unexpected benefits to the claimant, damages may be reduced in light of such betterment.[227]

Equitable Remedies

3.142 As stated at the outset, equity can provide remedies where the common law remedy of damages proves insufficient to provide effective relief.[228] However, it must be noted that equitable remedies are at the discretion of the court and are thus not available as of right. In addition, equitable remedies will not be available where there has been undue delay in bringing the claim[229] or where the party seeking relief has acted inequitably.[230]

3.143 A primary equitable remedy in contract is the remedy of specific performance where the promisor is required to fulfil his/her promise, rather than being allowed to escape performance through the payment of damages. However, in many cases, not least

219 *Quinn v Burch Bros (Builders) Ltd* [1966] 2 Q.B. 370.
220 Civil Liability (Contribution) Act 1978.
221 Law Reform (Contributory Negligence) Act 1945.
222 *Victoria Laundry (Windsor) v Newman Industries* [1949] 2 K.B. 528.
223 *Koufos v C Czarnikow Ltd (The Heron II)* [1969] 1 A.C. 350.
224 *Ruxley Electronics & Construction Ltd v Forsyth* [1996] A.C. 344.
225 *Anglia Television v Reed* [1972] 1 Q.B. 60.
226 *Attorney General v Blake* [2001] 1 A.C. 268.
227 *British Westinghouse Electric & Manufacturing Co Ltd v Underground Electric Railways Co of London Ltd* (No.2) [1912] A.C. 673 where damages were wiped out by the success of the reparative measure.
228 See for example, *Evans Marshall & Co v Bertola SA (No.1)* [1973] 1 All E.R. 992.
229 The equitable doctrine of "laches".
230 The equitable doctrine of "clean hands".

in construction, the court may be unwilling to award such a remedy due to the difficulties of enforcement.[231]

3.144 Another important equitable remedy is the use of an injunction to prohibit the doing of something, or, in some cases, to require action (mandatory injunction). This may be relevant in a contractual context to stop the defendant from reducing its assets ahead of a successful claim.

3.145 Set-off, that is, the reduction of damages in the light of mutual debts, is also available as an equitable remedy.[232] This principle of counter-claim can be complex, however, in the context of construction operations subject to payment provisions of the Housing Grants Construction and Regeneration Act 1996 (HGCR Act).

3.146 *Quantum meruit* may be applied in cases where work has been carried out, but no contract was ultimately concluded, as a means of requiring the party who has received the benefit to pay a reasonable sum for work undertaken. Calculation of the value of the work can, in some cases, be based on the contractual negotiations which preceded.[233]

3.147 Finally, another equitable remedy which is worth noting is that of rectification by which the court will amend a contract so that it represents the actual agreement of the parties. This is a means of clarifying an ambiguity or omission in order that the agreed term may be enforced. In this context, the court may use the prior negotiations of the parties as evidence of their intentions, as an exception to the normal position on contractual interpretation as per the exclusionary rule.[234]

Remedies Agreed by the Parties

3.148 The courts will generally be supportive of the parties' agreed remedies under express contractual terms. However, if it is the intention of the parties that alternative common law remedies are to be excluded, the words of the contract will need to be sufficiently clear for this to be the case, as the courts take a restrictive view of attempts to usurp their authority[235] (discussed further below).

3.149 Equally, to a certain extent the courts provide a limit on the ability of the parties to create unbounded contractual remedies. In the context of construction, liquidated and ascertained damages clauses are commonplace, setting agreed sums for events such as delay. While the courts are happy for these agreed remedies to be imposed, they could, in theory, be nullified if the court was to view the sum imposed as a "penalty". The doctrine of penalties has a long history in common law and, in effect, outlaws any agreed remedy which is so excessive as to constitute an undue punishment, exerted in a deliberately penal fashion. However, this limit is to be balanced against the overriding principle of freedom of contract, allowing the parties to enter into any bargain they choose, provided they fully consent to do so. The latest and most authoritative examination of the doctrine of penalties can be found in the Supreme Court judgment in *Cavendish Square Holdings*

231 *North East Lincolnshire BC v Millennium Park (Grimsby) Ltd* (Specific Performance) [2002] EWHC 365 (Ch).

232 *Hanak v Green* [1958] 2 All E.R.

233 *Way v Latilla* [1937] 3 All ER 759.

234 *Chartbrook v Persimmon Homes Ltd* (n 169).

235 See for example *Stocznia Gdanska SA v Latvian Shipping Co* (Repudiation) [2002] EWCA Civ 889; *Gilbert Ash (Northern) Ltd v Modern Engineering (Bristol) Ltd* [1974] A.C. 689.

v Makdessi.[236] In that case, Lord Neuberger stated that, while the basic test for the legitimacy of an agreed remedy clause was the extent to which it could be justified on the basis of reasonably foreseeable losses,[237] such a clause could still be justified if in excess of this, provided there was some demonstrable "legitimate interest",[238] which was satisfied by the higher figure. While this case has been helpful in clarifying the position to some extent, uncertainty still remains as to the scope of the new test.

Remedies (Exclusion of Remedies): Limitation

3.150 In English contract law, the limitation period generally begins from the breach. The period will be 6 years for a simple contract, and 12 years where a deed[239] has been used.[240] In construction contracts, the contractual limitation period usually starts from the date of practical completion under the building contract, to avoid any confusion about the precise date of the breach. Legal action for a contractual claim must be started within the relevant limitation period.

3.151 Under the common law, the party in breach of contract will be required to pay damages to the innocent party for the damage suffered, putting the innocent party back into the position he would have been in had the breach not occurred. However, parties may also agree to specific "contractual remedies" either in addition to, or in lieu of, common law remedies. For instance, any advance payments or deposits paid maybe forfeited to the innocent party upon breach by the defaulting party, or payment of a pre-agreed sum (liquidated damages), maybe payable to the innocent party upon a certain breach.

3.152 Where the parties are unable to rely upon the contractual remedies agreed between parties because the mechanism governing the contractual remedies is unenforceable, the innocent party can still rely on common law remedies, provided these have not been excluded. If parties have surrendered their rights to common law damages by consent or a contractual remedies mechanism is unenforceable, this may have serious consequences for the innocent party, who may be unable to claim any damages at all.

3.153 In *Scottish Power UK Plc v BP Exploration Operating Co Ltd & Ors* [2016][241], the parties entered into a long-term gas supply contract containing a comprehensive provision as to the remedy available to the purchaser (Scottish Power) for under-deliveries of gas by the seller (BP) (a 70% discount for any gas shortfall). This payment mechanism stated: "in *full satisfaction and discharge of all rights, remedies and claims howsoever arising ... in respect of under-deliveries by the Seller [BP]*". BP defaulted in its gas deliveries and Scottish Power claimed the discount and common law damages. BP argued that the clause was a complete remedy for all losses from any gas shortfalls. The court rejected Scottish Power's argument, that it shouldn't be presumed parties intended to deprive themselves of the common law right to damages, in absence of clear language to the contrary. The court

---

236 [2015] UKSC 67.

237 See the earlier test in *Dunlop Pneumatic Tyre Co Ltd v New Garage and Motor Co Ltd* [1915] AC 79.

238 Lord Neuberger at [1203].

239 For the formalities for the completion of a Deed see the Law of Property (Miscellaneous Provisions) Act 1989, s1.

240 Full details of the limitation periods in both Tort and Contract can be found in the Limitation Act 1980, as amended.

241 EWCA Civ 1043, 1 November 2016.

held that parties were experienced operators in the industry, knowing the intention of their contract, and thus would be bound by its provisions.

3.154 In *Temloc Ltd v Errill Properties Ltd*[242], the parties inserted a rate of "£Nil" in the Appendix of the construction contract for liquidated damages payable.[243] The Court of Appeal held that inserting "£Nil" had the effect of excluding both unliquidated, and liquidated, damages for delay.This was because the contract contained a valid and enforceable liquidated damages provision noting the amount of "£Nil" in the Appendix and, as a matter of interpretation, if the parties completed this part, it constituted an exhaustive agreement as to damages. That is, the parties' agreement in relation to liquidated damages for delay (even at a "nil" rate) replaced the remedy of unliquidated (common law) damages; exclusion of common law damages did not require an express clause stating so.[244]

Contractual Interpretation

3.155 The starting point for contractual interpretation in English common law is the literal rule. Words in a contract are to be given their natural and ordinary meaning and the court is not to be tempted to impose a preferred meaning arbitrarily.[245]

3.156 However, this "rule" is subject to the jurisdiction of the courts to intervene where it appears that there is a problem with the strict application of the terms. In the words of Lord Hoffmann:

> The "rule" that words should be given their "natural and ordinary meaning" reflects the common sense proposition that we do not easily accept that people have made linguistic mistakes, particularly in formal documents. On the other hand, if one would nevertheless conclude from the background that something must have gone wrong with the language, the law does not require judges to attribute to the parties an intention which they plainly could not have had.[246]

3.157 The question remains as to in what circumstances and in what ways a court can apply its own interpretation of the contract, and upon what basis. Lord Hoffmann's views in a series of key cases[247] represent the high watermark of what may be described as an "interventionist" mindset. The general principle of contractual interpretation is that the court may intervene when the terms of a contract are ambiguous and require further analysis in order to ascertain the nature and application of the obligation. In the *Chartbrook* case, Lord Hoffmann stated:

> All that is required is that it should be clear that something has gone wrong with the language and that it should be clear what a reasonable person would have understood the parties to have meant.[248]

242 39 BLR 30 (1 January 1988).

243 JCT Standard Form of Building Contract (1980 edition), clause 24.2.

244 The evidence established that the employer conceded the sum "£nil" was entered as a "bonus" in order to incentivise timely completion thereby adding confirmation to the proper interpretation of the contract.

245 *Lovell Ltd & Christmas Ltd v Wall* (1911) 104 LT 85, CA.

246 Lord Hoffmann in *Investors Compensation Scheme LTD. v West Bromwich Building Society* (No. 1) [1998] 1 All E.R. 98 at p. 913.

247 *Chartbrook v Persimmon Homes Ltd* (n 169); *Attorney General of Belize v Belize Telecom Ltd* [2009] UKPC 10.

248 Ibid., Lord Hoffmann in *Chartbrook v Persimmon Homes Ltd* (n 169) [1114].

3.158 With regard to the evidence which can be used to inform a decision on the correct interpretation of a term, it is clear that pre-contractual negotiation cannot be used for such a purpose, given that it did not find its way into the final contract. This is known as the exclusionary rule. However, the court is entitled to consider the "matrix of facts"[249] at the time the contract was formed, albeit there remains uncertainty as to the extent of this so-called "matrix".

3.159 When considering the correct interpretation of the contract, the court is seeking to ascertain, objectively, the intention of the parties when forming the contract. The court may apply "business common sense" to construe the meaning, preferring a commercially sensible meaning to a meaning which would otherwise be absurd.[250] The court may also consider evidence pertaining to market practice in the area concerned.[251]

3.160 However, notwithstanding the above points, it has been reiterated several times that the court is not engaged in an analysis of the parties' subjective intentions, nor is it open to the court to assert a view purely on the basis of an inequality arising from the natural interpretation of the contract. In a recent judgment, Lord Neuberger reasserted this orthodoxy, confirming that if there is a clear natural reading of the relevant clause, there is no question of interpreting it in a business-common sense fashion, even if the natural reading is greatly disadvantageous to the party which is challenging it.[252]

3.161 The latest authoritative decision in this area has sought to bring together many of the approaches applied in the past and to demonstrate the consistency and continuity between them. In *Wood v Capita Insurance Services Ltd*,[253] the Supreme Court expressed a view that both the "business common sense" approach and the literalist approach could be applied to contractual interpretation and that ultimately it depended on the context. In a tightly drafted written contract between experienced parties, a literal reading may be appropriate, even if it represents poor judgement by the losing contracting party. Equally, in oral contracts between less experienced parties, where there may be real ambiguity, a more contextual analysis may be necessary.

3.162 Finally, it should be noted that the processes and approaches to implied terms (as detailed above), while in some ways similar to the process of contractual interpretation, are not to be confused and do not overlap.[254]

National Standard Forms of Contracts

3.163 This chapter is limited to construction law in England and Wales. Although many aspects of the subject are the same or similar in Scotland (and even more so in Northern Ireland), there are significant differences which make generalization impossible. Scottish standard form building contracts are not identical to their English counterparts. The principal statute, the HGCR Act (as amended) also applies generally to Scotland and Northern

249 As per Lord Wilberforce in *Reardon Smith Line Ltd v Hansen-Tangen (The Diana Prosperity)* [1976] 1 W.L.R. 989.

250 *Rainy Sky SA v Kookmin Bank* [2011] UKSC 50.

251 *Crema v Cenkos Securities Plc* [2010] EWCA Civ 1444.

252 *Arnold v Britton* [2015] UKSC 36 at [19].

253 [2017] UKSC 24.

254 See Lord Neuberger in *Marks & Spencer Plc v BNP Paribas Securities Services Trust Co (Jersey) Ltd* [2015] UKSC 72 at para 26.

Ireland, respectively, but there are certain provisions of the Act which only apply to one of these jurisdictions and the Scottish courts interpret some of the provisions differently from the courts of England and Wales.

Forms of Contract

3.164 The most prevalent form of building contract is the suite produced by the Joint Contracts Tribunal (JCT). The predecessors to JCT contracts, those produced by the Royal Institute of British Architects (RIBA), date back to before 1903 and JCT was set up in 1931. It is not actually a tribunal in the normal sense of the word but a body representing the major participants in the construction process: the employers through the British Property Federation and the Local Government Association, contractors and sub-contractors through the Contractors Legal Group and the National Specialist Contractors Council and consultants, through the RIBA and the Royal Institution of Chartered Surveyors (RICS). The first JCT standard form of building contract was issued in 1931 (although the forms were not referred to as JCT until 1977). Editions of the contract were revised and published in 1939, 1963, 1980, 2005, 2011, and 1998 with the most recent versions published in 2016.

3.165 The extensive JCT range of contracts covers all levels from major projects, standard, intermediate to minor works and many different procurement types. The JCT forms are suitable for use by both private and public authority employers: Employer design, design and build (contractor design) and management contracts, with term contracts, subcontracts, repair and maintenance contracts and associated agreements and warranties.[255] Although earlier editions of JCT were much criticised for the quality of their drafting,[256] the modern versions are widely accepted by the industry as providing reasonably fair risk allocation and the latest edition, JCT 2016, continues to be heavily used in residential and commercial projects in the UK. The JCT contract continues to be the most widely used standard form of contract in the UK in over 60% of all projects.[257]

3.166 The New Engineering Contract (NEC) form is produced by the Institution of Civil Engineers (ICE), though it is intended for use in both construction and engineering projects; its official title is the Engineering and Construction Contract. It was introduced in 1993 and the third edition, widely known as NEC3, was introduced in 2005. It was published simultaneously with the traditional ICE form, which was controversially discontinued in 2011. NEC3 was replaced by NEC4 during 2017. The traditional ICE form has been revived and revised as the Infrastructure Conditions of Contract.[258] NEC3 was particularly successful in public sector work, most noticeably for the London Olympics 2012, where recent studies have shown that the NEC forms follow the JCT forms as the

255 Practice Note – Deciding on the appropriate JCT contract (2016), Joint Contracts Tribunal. This practice note provides a thorough overview of Project Strategy, Range of Main JCT Contracts and Sub-contract and comparison of contract provisions as a mean of assisting potential users which contract may be suitable for their construction works.

256 A "farrago of obscurities" per Lord Justice Davies in *English Industrial Estates v George Wimpey* [1972] 7 BLR 122.

257 National Construction Contracts and Law Report 2018 (RIBA, NBS 2018) p. 18.

258 Known as ICC and not to be confused with the EPC Turnkey Contract produced by the International Chamber of Commerce.

most widely used construction forms in the UK.[259] It takes a modular approach, with pricing and other options "bolted on" to the main "core clauses". The simple English and unique "narrative" style of drafting is attractive to some users, although it has been criticised in the English High Court (the Technology and Construction Court): "*No doubt this approach to drafting has its adherents within the industry but ... from the point of view of a lawyer it seems to me to represent a triumph of form over substance*".[260] Beyond JCT and NEC, there are other major standard form contracts. The Institution of Mechanical Engineers publishes the MF/1 and MF/2 contracts for mechanical and electrical works and the Institution of Chemical Engineers publishes the IChemE forms for use in process plans and notably in the water industry.

3.167 The Association of Consultant Architects produces the specialist partnering forms PPC 2000 and TPC and the Chartered Institute of Building produced its Contract for Complex Projects in 2013. PPC2000 is the first standard form of partnering contract drafted in response to the Egan Report, Rethinking Construction. It can be used on any type or value of partnered project .[261] Its principal features include: A multi-party contract comprising a "partnering team" primarily between the "client", "constructor", and the "client representative"; specialist contractors and consultants may join the contract as part of the partnering team, that is, a single contractual hub allowing all team members to "contract as a team" on identical terms;[262] integration of design, supply and construction process from the inception of the project with "early involvement" of contractor/s and specialist/s; early warning and painshare/gainshare mechanisms, clauses dealing with continuous improvements, key performance indicators; and an open-book exchange of information, all of which are directed to fostering a partnering relationship between parties.

3.168 The Institution of Chemical Engineers (IChemE), an organization of chemical engineers founded in the UK in 1922, has a range of standard contract forms for use on complex process plant projects. These were first published in 1968 and initially used in the petrochemical industry in the UK. They are now used for a range of process plant works, which includes manufacturing plant for pharmaceuticals, water treatment or desalination plant and other chemical processes.[263] The latest versions of IChemE contracts were released in 2013 providing for the standard procurement types (lump sum, reimbursable and target price contract). Additionally, there are contracts for minor works, sub-contract and professional services agreements (short and long form).[264] Commentators have noted that the IChemE contracts' underlying philosophy is "performance based" rather than

259 Practice Note – Deciding on the appropriate JCT contract (2016), Joint Contracts Tribunal (n 258) 18.

260 Mr Justice Edwards Stuart in *Anglian Water Services v Laing O'Rourke Utilities Ltd* [2010] EWHC 1529 (TCC).

261 Benefits of PPC at <http://ppc2000.co.uk/benefits-of-ppc2000/> (accessed on 5 March 2019), PPC2000 has been used on a wide variety of projects and programmes in the public and private sectors ranging in value from £250,000 to £700 million.

262 Ibid.

263 Practical Law Construction, IChemE Contracts at <https://uk.practicallaw.thomsonreuters.com/0-383-5696?transitionType=Default&contextData=(sc.Default)&firstPage=true&comp=pluk> (accessed on 5 March 2019). IChemE has noted that their standard forms are also used outside the processing industry sector and have been used on all types of projects, which includes Tunnelling (underground power line on London 2012 Olympics site, Railway signalling works, Port cargo handling plant and LNG plants.

264 IChemE has also issued an international suite of standard forms of contracts, last suite issued in 2007.

"works based", that is, the value of a process plant is in its ability to process and produce; thus the standard forms have a greater emphasis on testing and completion and protection of intellectual property rights.

3.169 The FIDIC forms of contract have historically not been used much for projects in the UK, partly because of the existence of the well-established domestic forms described above. There are indications of some increase in FIDIC usage in recent years, particularly in the field of renewable energy.[265] However, there are legal issues to be overcome in using a FIDIC contract for a project governed by the UK's HGCR Act, since the FIDIC dispute resolution provisions, for example, do not comply with the requirements of the Act .

Construction Law Principles

Procurement and Tendering

3.170 Traditionally, English law gave little protection to tenderers, whether contractors or consultants. The employer/client had virtually complete discretion as to what information was given to tenderers, as to procedure for submission, as to criteria and procedure for evaluation of tenders, as to equality of treatment for tenderers and as to procedure for award of the contract, including feedback.

3.171 This position began to change in the 1990s. In the public sector, this was principally as a result of EU-derived legislation,[266] which created a regulatory regime for the advertisement and conduct of tendering exercises in the award of public contracts, including the provision and application of criteria for evaluation and award of contracts. The current version of this legislation[267] provides for a much-amended version of the regulatory regime, especially insofar as it concerns challenges to awards by unsuccessful tenderers alleging breach of the regulations. It is currently uncertain whether this system will survive the UK's exit from the EU in the longer term, but it will govern until replaced.

3.172 In parallel, the courts developed the common law concept of the tender contract.[268] The concept here is that every tender which complies with the invitation to tender forms a contractual relationship between the tenderer and the employer. These tender contracts do not relate to the principal contract which is the subject of the tendering exercise. They bind the employer to conduct the process properly. This includes the duty to act fairly and equally.[269] Although the early cases were in the public sector, where constraints on the process continue to be tighter, tender contracts have also been held to exist in the private sector.[270] However, there is much more scope to limit and control the contents of the tender contract through express provision in the invitation to tender in the private sector, where there is no statutory regime.

3.173 A degree of uncertainty in English procurement law makes advice on tendering strategy and choice of contract a hazardous task. Architects have been held to be negligent

265 See for example *Peterborough City Council v Enterprise Managed Services Ltd* on which the FIDIC Yellow Book 1999 was used for a solar energy plant.

266 Notably the Public Works Contracts Regulations 1991.

267 Public Contracts Regulations 2015.

268 Beginning with *Blackpool and Fylde Aero Club v Blackpool Borough Council* [1990] EWCA Civ 13.

269 *Harmon CFEM Facades v Corporate Officer of the House of Commons* [1999] EWHC 199.

270 *J & A Developments v Edina Manufacturing* [2006] NIQB 85.

in failing to discuss with clients alternatives to a two-stage tendering process to meet the client's strict budgetary constraints.[271] Project managers have also been held negligent in failing to advise clients of the dangers of proceeding with a project under a series of letters of intent, rather than a properly executed construction contract.[272] Letters of intent were formerly drafted so as to have no legal effect[273] and merely informed a contractor or consultant of a future intention to enter into a contract. However, modern letters of intent may be "expressly designed to give rise to some albeit limited, reciprocal rights and liabilities"[274] in order to induce the contractor to mobilize and commence preliminary work before the construction contract is ready for signature. This can create great uncertainty as to legal effect and whether the construction contract governs the preliminary agreement under the letter of intent.[275] A preferable solution is to execute a separate agreement for the early stages of the project – an early works contract. The contractor is sometimes asked to enter into a FEED contract[276] for a different purpose, namely to assist in the formulation of a design and project strategy. Early contractor involvement is an important modern trend in English procurement practice.[277]

Different Types of Contract (Unit Price, Lump Sum, etc.)

3.174 Construction projects in the UK are executed under a number of different types of contracts generally linked to pricing models, and the contracts which contain them are often referred to by those names.

3.175 The most commonly used is the traditional lump sum contract. In theory, this model gives a fixed price for the project which the employer will pay for completion of the works described in the contract. In reality, the lump sum method rarely provides the certainty of outcome which this would imply. The "fixed" price will only be what is paid by the employer if no changes are requested during construction and if none of the events occur which would entitle the contractor to claim additional payment. Some contracts additionally contain fluctuation clauses, allowing the contractor to claim increased costs of materials or labour.[278] Furthermore, the lump sum method does not mean that the price is only paid on completion. Such an agreement would be very unusual and indeed difficult to achieve. A contract where the lump sum price would only be payable on completion of entire performance is known as an "entire contract" in English law. For any contract with a duration of more than 45 days, the contractor has a statutory entitlement to payment by instalments, stage payments or other forms of periodic payment.[279] Even if the contract was outside the provisions of the Act, it would require very clear words to make it into an entire contract.

271 *Plymouth & Southwest Cooperative Society v Architecture Structure and Management* [2006] EWHC 5 (TCC).

272 *Ampleforth Abbey Trust v Turner & Townsend Project Management Ltd* (2012) 144 ConLR 115.

273 *Turriff Construction Ltd v Regalia Knitting Mills Ltd* (1974) 9 BLR 20.

274 *Cunningham v Collett and Farmer* [2008] EWHC 1771 (TCC).

275 *RTS Flexible Systems Ltd v Molkerei Alois Muller* [2010] UKSC 14.

276 Front End Engineering Design.

277 See David Mosey, "Early Contractor Involvement in Building Procurement" (Wiley 2009).

278 JCT Fluctuations Option A, Schedule 7 of the JCT Standard Building Contract 2016.

279 HGCR Act, s.109.

3.176 A guaranteed maximum price contract, as its name suggests is, the closest of any price mechanism to providing certainty of financial outcome. The employer will not pay more than the guaranteed maximum price unless the contractor is ordered to carry out additional work. If the contractor requested a variation, the employer would pay no more than the actual cost to the contractor of making the change.

3.177 Apart from the lump sum method, the most commonly-used form of contract pricing is measurement. Under this model, the work is valued at the outset on the basis of expected quantities of work to be carried out. The amount to be paid is calculated on the basis of items of work contained in a schedule of rates or bill of quantities.

3.178 At specific stages in the project, the employer's professional consultants, notably quantity surveyors, will measure the amount of work which has been completed by the contractor then value it in accordance with the prices in the schedule of rates/bill of quantities, to ascertain what interim payments should be made to the contractor.

3.179 In addition to the main types of contract pricing, there are more specialized alternatives, all of which are used to some extent in the UK, though they will not be suitable for all types of project. Under the "cost plus" concept, the contractor is paid the actual cost of executing the work plus an amount for agreed profit, usually in the form of a percentage, which may include an element of overhead expenses.[280] This transfers a large part of the financial risk to the employer and can be seen as very beneficial to the contractor. In management contracting, where the contractor's role is not construction itself but the management of trade contractors, this is often expressed as a "management fee". Under a "target cost contract", the parties agree a "target cost" for a defined scope of work. The contractor carries out the work and is paid based on the cost of doing so. Crucially, the total payment to the contractor will typically be subject to a pain share/gain share mechanism. If the cost is above the target cost, the contractor will have to contribute to meeting the excess. In both cases, this is done according to an agreed formula. The New Engineering Contract has a Target Cost Option and another example is found in the Institution of Chemical Engineers Burgundy Book.

3.180 Pain share/gain share mechanisms of this kind are commonly used in partnering contracts, where the concept is of team-working between employer, contractor, consultants and supply chain. The ACA publishes specialist standard form agreements for partnering projects of which PPC 2000[281] is the best known (see para 3.168).[282]

Nature of Construction Contracts

3.181 In the literal sense, construction contracts in the UK are very similar to those in other developed countries. They are agreements for goods and services to be provided by a contractor for the purchaser of the building or facility, referred to as the employer or owner. They are usually in writing and may be either in standard form, such as JCT or NEC, or bespoke, meaning prepared specially for the individual project.

280 There are many combinations of Cost Plus contracts with respect to the agreed profit, the main types included: Cost Plus Fixed Percentage, Cost Plus Fixed Fee, Cost Plus with Guaranteed Maximum Price, Cost Plus Fixed Fee with Bonus Contract and Cost Plus with Guaranteed Maximum Price and Bonus Contract.

281 Amended in 2013.

282 See also the Framework Alliance Contract (FAC-1) 2016.

3.182 However, in the statutory sense, "construction contract" has a specific meaning under the HGCR Act.[283] That is, a "construction contract" means an agreement with a person for any of the following:

3.183 An agreement by one party to:

- Carry out construction operations;
- Arrange for the carrying out of construction operations by others, whether under subcontract to him or otherwise;
- Provide his own labour or the labour of others for the carrying out of construction operations;
- Do architectural design or surveying work;
- Provide advice on building, engineering, interior or exterior decoration or on the lay-out or landscape.[284]

3.184 This definition depends greatly on the meaning of "construction operations" which are very widely defined[285] to include:

- Construction, alteration, repair, maintenance, extensions, demolition or dismantling of buildings or structures forming part of the land (permanent or not);
- Walls, road works, power-lines, telecommunication apparatus, aircraft runways, docks and harbours, railways, inland waterways, pipe-lines, reservoirs, water-mains, wells, sewers, industrial plant, drainage installations, coastal protection or defence installations;
- Site clearance, earthmoving, excavation, tunnelling and boring, laying of foundations, erection, maintenance or dismantling of scaffolding, site restoration, landscaping and the provision of roadways and other access works.

3.185 Expressly *excluded* from the definition of "construction operations" are:

- Drilling for or extraction of oil and natural gas;
- Extraction of minerals or tunnelling or boring for that purpose;
- Assembly, installation or demolition of plant or machinery or erection or demolition of steelwork for support or access to machinery where the primary activity is nuclear processing, power generation or water/effluent treatment, production, transmission, processing or bulk storage of chemicals, pharmaceuticals, oil, gas, steel, food or drink.

3.186 Also excluded are manufacture or delivery to site of:

- Building/engineering components or equipment, materials, plant or machinery, components for systems of heating, lighting, ventilation, air-conditioners, power-supply, drainage, sanitation, water supply, fire protection, security, or communication systems, *unless* the contract also provides for their installation.

283 As amended by the Local Democracy Economic Development and Construction Act 2009.
284 HGCR Act, s 104.
285 Ibid., s 105.

3.187 The HGCR Act only applies to contracts for the carrying out of construction operations in the United Kingdom.[286] A contract in another country is not governed by these statutory rules even if it is stated to be under English law. By contrast, the Act applies to the carrying out of construction operations in the UK even if they are stated to be subject to a different jurisdiction. In *Comsite Projects v Andritz AG*,[287] a waste water treatment plant contract in England was stated to be under Austrian law, but the HGCR Act still governed it.

3.188 It is a crucial question as to whether a contract for the construction of a building in the UK is a "construction contract" within the meaning of the Act. If it is, the contract must comply with the Act's mandatory requirements as to payment and dispute resolution (adjudication), see paras 3.367–3.374.

Employer and Contractor

3.189 The employer and the contractor enter into the building contract or construction contract. These terms are interchangeable, though "construction" is more modern and "building contract" would not today normally be used in relation to a sophisticated complex project. The contract may be referred to as the "main contract" and the contractor as the "main contractor" for purposes of differentiation from sub-contractors.

3.190 The term "employer" is widely used, though it is neither universal nor legally accurate. It is used in the JCT contracts, as it is internationally in the FIDIC forms. In the NEC forms, the term "client" is used, and this is also in common use in a professional services context, where a consultant will often be said to supply a service to its client.

3.191 Other commonly used synonyms for "employer" are "owner" and "developer", the latter only if the contract concerns a development project, rather than just the construction of a building.[288]

3.192 The most logical and legally accurate term is that used in the IChem E forms of contract[289] much favoured in the water and process industries, namely "Purchaser", describing a party who purchases the construction of the plant or building from the contractor in the form of a product of goods and services.

3.193 To summarise, the main contract under traditional forms of procurement will be between the employer/owner/client/developer/purchaser, and the contractor.

3.194 The nature of the relationship depends upon the contents of the contract and the identity of the parties. The employer may be a business or an individual. If the employer is a business, the contract will be governed by the Supply of Goods and Services Act 1982,

---

286 Scotland and Northern Ireland have separate but comparable statutory regimes to that of England and Wales.

287 [2003] All ER (D) 64.

288 None of these terms is ideal, because of their legal imprecision. "Employer" may be the official JCT term, but a construction contract is not an employment contract, which is a contract of service. The contractor is not at all in a similar position to employees under an employment contract. "Owner" or "developer" are only accurate if used in the correct context: projects may be commissioned by parties who are not themselves the legal owner of the site and they will not be considered "developers" merely because they are doing so. "Client" can be confusing in the legal profession, since contractors, sub-contractors and consultants can all be clients of the lawyer's firm; to say that the "client" is a client self-evidently sounds strange, especially as the traditional meaning of "client" was a dependent, rather than a master.

289 Institution of Chemical Engineers.

whereas if the employer is a private individual consumer, the contract will be subject to the Consumer Rights Act 2015. Both have some similar provisions in relation to implied terms, though unsurprisingly there are further protections where the employer is a consumer. While the Unfair Contract Terms Act 1977, which restricts the ability of parties to exclude or limit their liability, is not solely applicable to consumers, nevertheless the English courts are much less willing to intervene by declaring that an exclusion is unreasonable where the contracting parties are both businesses.[290]

3.195 The primary obligations of the employer and contractor are generally expressly stated in the contract.[291] The overarching employer's obligations include: Defining the scope of works, determining the programme and budget, monitoring progress of the works and making interim payments. In JCT contracts, the employer's duty is generally prefaced by the term "shall"; however, there are also other duties which by implication may apply: The appointment and replacement of consultants and the contractor, giving possession of the site,[292] ensuring that the CDM Co-ordinator and principal contractor perform their duties under the CDM Regulations,[293] paying interim and final payment certificate amounts,[294] holding retention as fiduciary trustee,[295] not assigning rights under the contact,[296] and, where applicable, taking out the requisite insurance.[297]

3.196 As stated above in para 5.38, the contract administrator/engineer has an implied duty to act fairly and impartially. There is an implied duty on the employer not to interfere unlawfully with the contract administrator/engineer in performing his obligation to act independently. In *Hickman & Co. v Roberts*[298] the architect notified the employer that he intended to issue an interim payment certificate in response to the contractor's request. The employer instructed the architect to withhold the certificate until the contractor provided an account of all extras.[299] The architect informed the contractor of the employer's instruction and failed to issue the certificate. The House of Lords held that the architect had improperly allowed the employer to influence his decision; the employer's act amounted to wrongful interference. There may also be limited circumstances where the employer may be liable for the faults of his contract administrator/engineer (generally an employer will not be liable for the faults of his contract administrator/engineer, **unless** being aware of the contract administrator's/engineer's error, the employer does nothing).[300]

3.197 The contractor's primary obligation is to carry out and complete the construction of the works.[301] The JCT contract outlines the contractor's obligations more

290 *Watford Electronics Ltd v Sanderson CFL Ltd* [2001] EWCA Civ 317.

291 In the UK, there will also be implied obligations/duties under common law or statute.

292 JCT SBC/Q, clause 2.4.

293 Ibid., clause 3.23.

294 Ibid., clause 4.11.

295 Ibid., clause 4.17.1.

296 Ibid., clauses 7.1 and 7.2.

297 Ibid., clause 6.7, Option C.

298 (1913) AC 229.

299 The evidence established that the employer was experiencing financial difficulties hence instructing architect to cut down the claim for interim payment.

300 *Panamena Europea Navigacion v Leyland*[1943] 76 Lloyd's Reports 113; *Penwith District Council v VP Development Ltd* (1999) (unreported).

301 JCT SBC/Q, Art. 1; there is also an obligation of "design" under the D&B Contract.

comprehensively as to the required quality of material and standard of workmanship,[302] designing the works,[303] making good defects,[304] sub-contracting,[305] complying with employer's or architect's instructions,[306] providing and updating master programme[307] and giving notices on various matters and events to ensure that the employer is informed and can act in a timely manner. Other contracts such as the FIDIC contract have a very helpful and detailed clause dedicated to the contractor's work obligations,[308] and where applicable, procurement of design.[309]

3.198 In respect to carrying out works, the obligation of the contractor to the employer will usually be one of "fitness for purpose", whether by express or implied terms[310]. In a design and build contract, design obligations might expressly be limited to "reasonable care and skill"[311] but it would be rare for the contractor to have a lesser duty than fitness for purpose for workmanship or materials; it is almost always a strict obligation to achieve the employer's purpose. If the building is a "dwelling", under the Defective Premises Act 1972, the contractor's obligation is to produce a building which is "fit for human habitation". More specific obligations are a matter of express contractual provision.

Design Obligations

3.199 The basic obligation of a designer under English law is to exercise reasonable care and skill in undertaking the design. It has long been true of professionals, which covers architects, engineers and quantity surveyors, that they are expected to work to the standard of reasonable care and skill, as measured against the notional "ordinary competent practitioner".[312] This basic standard is applied in the law of tort and is the default position in the law of contract:

> *In a relevant contract for the supply of a service where the supplier is acting in the course of a business, there is an implied term that the supplier will carry out the service with reasonable care and skill.*[313]

This statutory provision applies to all suppliers of services, not only to professionals. Where fire had destroyed a factory, it was held by the Court of Appeal that the standard to be expected of the company designing, installing and commissioning the fire safety

302 Ibid., clauses 2.1 and 2.3.

303 Ibid., clause 2.2.

304 Ibid., clauses 2.38–2.39.

305 Ibid., clauses 3.7–3.9.

306 Ibid., clauses 3.10.

307 Ibid., clause 2.9; NEC and PPC contracts place a positive duty on the contractor also warn which is discussed below; FIDIC Contract are noteworthy for the emphasis on updating the construction programme.

308 FIDIC Red Book, clause 4 [The Contractor].

309 FIDIC Red Book, clause 5 [Design].

310 *Young & Marten Ltd v McManus Childs Ltd* (1969) 9 BLR 77; *Gloucestershire C.C . v Richardson* [1968] 1 AC 480.

311 This is the standard position in the UK and is either expressly made as an amendment or noted in the Employer's Requirements.

312 This is often called the "Bolam standard" after the medical negligence case of *Bolam v Friern Hospital Management Committee* [1957] 1 WLR 582.

313 Supply of Goods and Services Act (n 126), s13. There is an equivalent provision for consumer contracts in the Consumer Rights Act 2015, s 49.

system was reasonable care and skill, not fitness for purpose: "*it was inappropriate and implausible to read the specification as a guarantee of the success of the system, very clear words would have been required for that*".[314]

3.200 However, although designers could not provide a lower standard than reasonable care and skill, there are many exceptions to this where a higher standard of fitness for purpose would apply (that is, an absolute obligation with no need to establish negligence normally required under tort law). In the residential sector, a person "*taking on work for or in connection with the provision of a dwelling*", which includes design work, has an obligation "*so that as regards that work the dwelling will be fit for human habitation*".[315] In the commercial sector, the position can be much more complex, especially in the case of design and build projects. Following the collapse of a television mast, the appellate court put the design obligation of the contractor at its highest:

> [*i*]*n the absence of a clear, contractual indication to the contrary, I see no reason why one who in the course of his business contracts to design, supply and erect a television aerial mast is not under an obligation to ensure that it is reasonably fit for the purpose for which he knows it is intended to be used.*[316]

3.201 The courts have shown little willingness to separate a design and build contractor's obligations into different categories, unless forced to do so by clear express contractual wording. The preferred route is for "*an implied term of fitness for purpose of the entire product irrespective of considerations of fault and of whether its unfitness derives from the quality of work or materials or design*".[317]

3.202 It is possible that a professional designer may also be subject to the higher fitness for purpose duty.

3.203 This could occur by express contractual provision. Where an employer required its architects to ensure that the design of a computer suite complied with an installation manual published by the manufacturer, the architects were held to have "*failed to ensure that the raised access flooring conformed to the standards that their clients required and thus failed to discharge their duties to (their clients) as architects*".[318] In design and build agreements, there is a significant possibility that such a term will be implied in the absence of express agreement. Where design and build contractors retained a firm of consulting engineers to provide a structural design for a warehouse where loaded trucks would operate, the design failed. The Court of Appeal held that a term would be implied in the contract for professional services "that if the work was completed in accordance with the design it would be reasonably fit for the use of loaded stacker trucks. The engineers failed to make such a design and are therefore liable".[319] Implication of a fitness for purpose obligation can be excluded by express provision.

---

314 *Trebor Bassett Holdings Ltd v ADT Fire & Security* [2012] EWCA Civ 1158.

315 Defective Premises Act 1972.

316 *Independent Broadcasting Authority v BICC Construction* (1980) 14 BLR 1.

317 *Viking Grain Storage v TH White Installations* (1985) 33 BLR 108.

318 *Thomas Saunders Partnership v Harvey* (1989) 30 Con LR 103.

319 *Greaves & Co (Contractors) Ltd v Baynham Meikle and Partners* [1975] 3 All ER 99; 1 WLR 1095.

3.204 In *MT Højgaard AS v E.ON Climate and Renewables UK Robin Rigg East Ltd & Anor*,[320] there was conflict in the contract, with references to both the contractor using reasonable skill and care and completing the works fit for purpose. The court held:

> where two provisions ... impose different or inconsistent standards or requirements ... the correct analysis ... is that the more rigorous or demanding of the two standards or requirements must prevail, as the less rigorous can properly be treated as a minimum requirement.

Duty to Warn

3.205 Where the method of procurement is traditional employer design and not design and build, contractors obviously do not have extensive responsibilities for the design. In the JCT Standard Building Contract there is the so-called duty of notification of discrepancies[321] by which a contractor who identified any discrepancy or divergence in the design drawings, bills of quantities, instructions and statutory requirements (such as building regulations) is under a duty to give written notice to the contract administrator. Under NEC3;[322] the contractor and project manager have a duty to notify each other of any ambiguities or discrepancies of which they become aware.

3.206 The courts have developed a common law duty to warn through the use of implied terms in certain circumstances. In *Equitable Debenture Asset Corporation v William Moss*[323] main contractors were held partly responsible for failing to warn of the deficiency of a curtain walling design: "they must have come to know of the lack of buildability in the design ... by failing to warn [the architects] of that defect Moss became in breach of the implied term requiring them to give such warning". The duty to warn should not be construed as a general implied term under common law. In this case, and in others, the term was implied in the circumstances, to give efficacy to the contract.

3.207 The duty to warn was considered in *University of Glasgow v William Whitfield and John Laing Construction Limited.*[324] The court held the contractor's duty to warn the employer of design defects and/or the duty of care owed to the architect to inform of defects in designs (of which he knew or should have known) did not exist because the JCT contract was comprehensive enough to rule out any implied duty and the architect did not rely on the contractor reviewing the design (it was submitted there was a breach of duty of care in tort because there was no contract binding architect and contractor), respectively.

3.208 The most extreme version to date of the duty to warn was in the Court of Appeal's decision of *Plant Construction Ltd v Clive Adams Associates (No2)*,[325] where a sub-contractor was held liable to the main contractor for failure to warn sufficiently of the inadequacy of the temporary works design. This was so even though the sub-contractor had raised queries which had been overruled by the employer's engineer. Knowing the design to be defective and dangerous, the sub-contractor should have "protested more vigorously".

---

320 [2017] UKSC 59.
321 JCT SBC/Q, clause 2.15.
322 Ibid., clause 17.
323 [1984] 2 Con LR 43 (OR).
324 (1988) 42 BLR 66: (1988) 19 CLR 111.
325 [2000] BLR 137.

3.209 So far as professional designers are concerned, obviously they have a responsibility to advise their clients of the risks inherent in particular designs. Generally speaking, the extent of this duty is limited by the scope of services. However, this can be expanded by particular circumstances. For example, in *Hart Investments v Fidler*[326] an engineer whose agreement for services only covered design of permanent works was nevertheless held to be under a duty to warn the employer of inadequacies in the contractor's temporary design, once the engineer had become aware of them.[327] Where the express duties undertaken include a project management responsibility, there will be an obligation to warn the employer of deficient performance by other participants in the project, including designers.[328]

3.210 General guidance on the duty to warn particularly on the part of professionals, such as engineers or architects, was outlined in *Goldswain & Anor v Beltec Ltd (t/a BCS Consulting) & Anor*[329] as follows:

- Where professionals (engineers in this case) are engaged, the court must initially determine the scope of the contractual duties, that is, is there a contractual duty to warn?
- It is possible to view the duty to warn as an aspect/extension of the duty of a professional to act with reasonable skill and care;
- Whether, when, and to what extent the duty will arise will depend on all the circumstances;
- A duty to warn will often arise when there is an obvious and significant danger either to life and limb or to property.;
- Where the consultant should have known of the danger, there may still not be a duty to warn, if it merely derives from the possibility that the contractor may not do the works properly.

Consultants' Roles and Liability

3.211 In a construction contract in the UK, there may be participation by consultants, principally architect, engineer and quantity surveyor. Their roles come under two main headings:

- Design;
- Contract administration.

Consultants' Design Responsibility

3.212 Responsibility for carrying out design work will depend upon the type of procurement model used. In the traditional employer design model, the design is carried

326 [2007] BLR 526.

327 The Recorder in this case emphasized on the necessity to warn considering the temporary works being dangerous and causing immediate peril: "It would appear strange if he is under a duty to take such steps as he can to see that they survive for say, the next 25 years, or whatever the design life for the building is, but is not obliged to take any steps to warn of an immediate danger to those works caused by an imperilling act by the contractor", at [22].

328 *Chesham Properties Ltd v Bucknall Auction Project Managers Services* (1996) 82 BLR 92.

329 [2015] BLR 300, [2015] EWHC 556 (TCC) at [47].

out on behalf of the employer. The designer could be an employee, working under an employment contract (a contract of service) or an independent consultant working under a consultancy agreement (a contract for services). Under the design and build model, the designer could be working as an employee of the design and build contractor, or, again, as an independent consultant supplying services to the design and build contractor.

3.213 The nature of design obligations is dealt with above.[330] In short, the basic obligation of the supplier of design services is to use reasonable care and skill, which may be increased to fitness for purpose in certain circumstances, especially in design and build projects. Potential liability for breach of the design obligations, that is, negligent design, is principally to the client,[331] under the law of contract and to a third party, such as a future purchaser or occupier, under the law of tort or under a collateral warranty.

3.214 The designer will be expected to be pro-active in protecting the client's interests:

> if the client has expressed his instructions in terms which leave the architect in doubt as to what his purpose is, the architect has a duty to ascertain the purpose he is instructed to achieve. In making his design, an architect has a duty to exercise due care to ensure that the design should be reasonably effective to achieve the client's purpose.[332]

Having accepted responsibility for design, the architect or engineer cannot simply pass it to someone else, such as the employer[333] or the contractor,[334] although it may be necessary to obtain additional specialist assistance where part of the design task is beyond the designer's expertise. The Contractor's Designed Portion[335] found in JCT and other contracts expressly permits specialist design work to be allocated to the contractor, but there is no general power to do so.

3.215 A designer also owes a duty of care to third parties in the tort of negligence. These would include future purchasers, tenants, occupiers, and lawful users of the building or facility. The duty is more limited than the contractual duty to the client, in that it does not include pure economic loss, such as the cost of repair of defects covering death, personal injury and physical damage to property. In *Eckersley v Binnie*,[336] it was held that consulting engineers owed a duty of care in the design of water works to protect visitors to the plant, who were killed and injured by an explosion partly caused by faulty design.

3.216 Because designers do not generally have a duty in tort to protect third parties against pure economic loss, it has become common practice for developers to seek to persuade designers, and other parties engaged in the project, to execute collateral warranties in favour of third parties. This has the effect of creating a contractual relationship between the designer and the third party, for example, a prospective tenant, so that in principle damages for pure economic loss could be recovered from the designer, if the loss can be proved to have been caused by negligent design.

330 See Design Obligations, paras REF _Ref419048992 \r \h 0– REF _Ref419049006 \r \h 0

331 The client would be the employer under traditional procurement and the contractor under design and build.

332 *Stormont Main Working Men's Club v J Roscoe Milne Partnership* (1988) 13 ConLR 187.

333 *Richard Roberts Holdings v Douglas Smith Stimson Partnership* (1990) 46 BLR 50.

334 *Moresk Cleaners v Hicks* [1966] 2 Lloyds Rep 338.

335 JCT 2016 SBC, clause 2.19.

336 (1988) 18 Con LR 1.

3.217 Another change that can take place in the liability exposure of designers is as a result of novation, by which they move from working for the employer to preparing designs for the design and build contractor. If the novation is successful, the effect is to render the designer liable to the design and build contractor even for defects in preliminary work carried out for the employer.

3.218 The other area of work where consultants have a major role in a UK construction contract is in contract administration. Not all contracts have a third party "neutral" as contract administrator; it is not uncommon for the employer to undertake the contract administration role; this is especially true of smaller projects.

Consultants' Contract Administration Liability

3.219 The contract administrator could be an engineer, architect or quantity surveyor. Some contracts contain provision for more than one role, for example the JCT 2016 SBC provides for both an Architect/Contract Administrator[337] and a Quantity Surveyor.[338] The NEC contracts are administered by the Project Manager. Project Management could be carried out by professionals of any discipline, or none, but usually engineers, quantity surveyors, or architects are appointed.

3.220 Although express contractual provision to the contrary is possible, the default position is that contract administrators will be expected to hold the scales evenly as between employer and contractor, so that decision-making is fair and impartial.[339]

3.221 In carrying out a decision-making function such as certification, the contract administrator will owe a contractual duty to the employer to use reasonable care and skill in avoiding over-certification,[340] which would either be corrected by a subsequent interim certificate or resolved as a dispute in adjudication or arbitration. The contract administrator would have no liability to the contractor, except in the extreme case where it could be proved that the contract administrator had fraudulently colluded with the employer to under-certify.[341]

3.222 Generally speaking, the liability of the consultant in both design and contract administration is governed by the contents of the contract with the employer/client and by the duties and functions set out in the construction contract; the contract administrator is not a party to the latter, but is appointed under it. Therefore, if the consultant adheres to the scope of the works, this restricts his/her liability exposure. However, if the consultant becomes aware of a danger to the works or the client, it would be under a duty to give a warning.[342] Under the modern RIBA[343] standard form consultancy agreements, an architect would not routinely undertake to supervise the contractor's work,[344] although both architects and engineers can agree expressly to do so, and can be liable for failure to inspect the completed work with reasonable care and skill.[345]

337 Article 3.
338 Article 4.
339 *Costain Ltd v Bechtel Ltd* [2005] EWHC 1019.
340 *Pacific Associates v Baxter* [1990] 1QB 993.
341 *Stevenson v Watson* (1879) 4 CPD 148.
342 *Hart Investments Ltd v Fidler* [2007] BLR 526.
343 Royal Institute of British Architects.
344 *Consarc v Hutch Investments* [2002] 84 ConLR 36.
345 *West v Ian Finlay Associates* [2014] EWCA Civ 316.

Sub-Contracting

3.223 In English law, no differentiation is made between a contract and a sub-contract. Thus, in construction law, both the main contract, between employer and main contractor, and the sub-contract, between main contractor and sub-contractor, are capable of being "construction contracts" for the purposes of the HGCR Act. There may be some difference as to how the provisions of the Act and other principles of law affect sub-contractors and contractors respectively, but this is because of their differing situations and not from any distinction in law.

3.224 Contractors in the UK frequently sub-contract parts of the project, both specialist and non-specialist. Sub-contracts may be for the provision of services of work and materials. If they are for the supply of goods which will be installed by someone else, they would often be referred to as "supply contracts", though in the legal sense they have the same status as sub-contracts. There is no absolute entitlement for a main contractor to sub-contract work. The JCT forms of contract require the main contractor to obtain the employer's consent to sub-contracting.[346]

3.225 Sub-contracts for consultancy services, for example to the architect, may be described as sub-consultancies. The contractor remains responsible to the employer for any defects in the performance of the sub-contractor. This even applies in the case of "nominated sub-contractors". Under this procedure, the main contract provides that the employer may "nominate" a specific sub-contractor, with whom the main contractor must then enter into a sub-contract. Nomination of sub-contractors is less common in the UK than was previously the case, for two main reasons. First, the employer is exposed to a degree of risk not otherwise present. It is still entitled to hold the contractor responsible for any error by the nominated sub-contractor, but in the event of a complete failure, where the nominated sub-contractor becomes insolvent or otherwise unable to proceed, the employer becomes under a duty to re-nominate and delay or omission to act will usually give the contractor the basis for a claim for additional time and additional cost. Second, the contractor is exposed to the risk of being forced to accept a sub-contractor whom it would not choose, instead of its own preference.[347] This inevitably affects tender prices. However, the degree of control which nomination gives to an employer has always been an attraction: The JCT contracts make provision for "Named Specialists"[348] which retains some of this advantage.

3.226 There is no requirement that the terms of a sub-contract should exactly reflect the terms of the main contract. It is open to a main contractor to seek to impose more onerous duties on the sub-contractor than it owes to the employer, or conversely to accept a greater burden itself than it requires of the sub-contractor. More logically, the obligations in both the main contract and sub-contract will be "back to back" and it makes sense to use standard forms from the same suite or bespoke contracts prepared together to achieve this.

3.227 Because the employer is not in a relationship of privity of contract with the sub-contractor, the basic legal position is that it will have no right of action against the sub-contractor. It might have a right of action in tort if the sub-contractor has caused death,

346 JCT SBC/Q, sub-clause 3.7.

347 The contractor's chosen sub-contractor is referred to as a "domestic sub-contractor".

348 Supplemental Provision 9.

personal injury or physical damage to the property, though such cases are relatively rare, of course. At one time, it appeared that the courts would allow direct recourse for defective work by an employer against a nominated sub-contractor,[349] on the grounds of reliance on its expertise, but this is now doubted and would never apply to a domestic sub-contractor in any event. To overcome this gap in the employer's rights of recourse, it has become common for sub-contractors to be required to enter into a "collateral warranty", being a subsidiary contractual relationship formed directly with the owner. Such warranties can cover the cost of repair of defects and other economic loss which would be normally irrecoverable against the responsible sub-contractor in tort. These are important, for example, where the main contractor goes into liquidation. They can, unless restricted, be assigned to future purchasers/tenants who acquire the building from the employer.

3.228 Payment of sub-contractors has been a problematic area. Basically, they have no entitlement to claim payment from the employer directly, though in certain limited circumstances such an arrangement can be expressly agreed, provided it does not offend against the rules on insolvency.[350] The HGCR Act sought to assist in cash-flow, primarily to sub-contractors (though not limited to them), by prohibiting "pay-when-paid" clauses,[351] by which the sub-contractor would not be paid until the main contractor had received payment. This has been extended[352] to most situations where a contract purports to make payment conditional on some event involving a third party and some improvement has been achieved by these measures in ensuring that contractors pay their sub-contractors.

Unforeseen Physical Conditions

3.229 English law has no doctrinal equivalent of *imprévision* or *rebus sic stantibus*, and of course, no civil code to give effect to such concepts. There is not even a fundamental concept of *force majeure*. Insofar as there is an English law of *force majeure*, it derives from the interpretation of contractual provisions.

3.230 The law of frustration rarely aids a non-performing party under a construction contract because the test is so rigorous, fulfilled only when "a contractual obligation has become incapable of being performed because the circumstances in which performance is called for would render it a thing radically different from that which was undertaken by the contract".[353] Because English law rarely offers any relief where a party finds that performance is more onerous than anticipated, it has become routine practice for construction contracts to make express contractual provision. Force Majeure clauses govern, amongst other things, natural disasters, such as floods and earthquakes and human disasters such as riots and revolutions. Under a JCT contract a contractor could claim an extension of time, if it gives notification of circumstances giving rise to a Relevant Event.[354] Additional payment can be obtained for loss and expense caused by a Relevant Event.[355]

349 *Junior Books Ltd v Veitchi Co Ltd* [1983] 1 AC 520.
350 *Mullan v Ross and London* (1996) 86 BLR 1.
351 s 113 (i).
352 Local Democracy Economic Development and Construction Act 2009.
353 *Davis Contractors v Fareham Urban District Council* [1956] AC 696.
354 JCT SBC/Q, sub-clauses 2.27 and 2.29.
355 Ibid., sub-clauses 4.20 and 4.22.

Under NEC4[356] a contractor can claim additional time and money if it notifies the Project Manager of a compensation event.[357]

3.231 Compensation events can include the contractor encountering "physical conditions which are within the site, are not weather conditions and: an experienced contractor would have judged at the Contract Date to have such a small chance of occurring that it would have been unreasonable for him to have allowed for them".[358] However, this possibility of relief is restricted by the provision that "In judging the physical conditions for the purpose of assessing a compensation event, the Contractor is assumed to have taken into account

- The Site Information;
- Publicly available information referred to in the Site Information, the Site;
- Other information which any experienced contractor could reasonably be expected to have or to obtain".[359]

3.232 These contractual provisions are a limited modification of the strict English law position, that "It is no excuse for late performance or non-performance that the site conditions which the contractor encountered were worse than it anticipated … the risk of adverse site conditions, whether they be known or latent, is with the contractor".[360]

Contract Pricing and Payment

3.233 The English approach to contract pricing is outlined under the paras 5.175–5.181, Types of Contracts. This section will cover the JCT contract's pricing models and also the payment mechanisms.

3.234 Under the JCT Standard Building Contract with Quantities (JCT SBC/Q), the contract price is based on a lump sum with interim or scheduled payment. The contractor must supply the employer with a fully priced copy of the bills of quantities (Contract Bills) prepared in accordance with the RICS New Rules of Measurement (Measurement Rules),[361] unless otherwise stated in the contract. The Contract Bill outlines the price for each unit item necessary for valuation including valuation of variations. The risk in relation to quantities is the employer's responsibility,[362] and the contract provides for the correction of errors with appropriate adjustment of the Contract Sum.[363] The contract price (Contract Sum) is the total arrived at in the fully priced copy of the itemized Contract Bills.

3.235 Where the employer intends only to provide drawings with either a specification or works schedule (without any bill of quantities), the parties can use the JCT Standard Building Contract without Quantities. The contractor prices the contract according to the Specification and Work Schedules to determine the Contract Sum. Similar to JCT SBC/Q, the contract price is based on a lump sum with interim or scheduled payments. The contractor also has the option to ascertain the Contract Sum by way of Contract Sum Analysis

356 NEC4 was released in late June 2017.

357 NEC4, clause 61.

358 Ibid., sub-clause 60.1.12

359 Ibid., sub-clause 60.2.

360 Julian Bailey "What lies beneath: site conditions and contract risk" Society of Construction Law Paper No. 137 (2007).

361 JCT SBC/Q, Rec. 2 and sub-clause 2.13.1.

362 Ibid., sub-clause 2.14.1–2.

363 Ibid., sub-clause 4.2.

or Schedule of Rates, which becomes the Priced Document – this document is used for valuation of variations. The Practice Note correctly states that the risk of error is largely placed on the contractor where tender amounts are generally increased to cover preparation costs and disputes regarding quantity of work implied in the Contract Documents.

3.236 In construction projects where there are incomplete drawings (i.e., no detailed drawings) and work cannot be accurately measured because the employer only has an approximate bill of quantities, the JCT Standard Build Contract with Approximate Quantities is appropriate (design is reasonably complete and quality substantiated). This is otherwise known as a "re-measurement" contract where the contract price is initially submitted on an indicative basis at tender stage and converted to an Ascertained Final Sum on re-measurement and valuation of all the works after completion. As with the other JCT contracts, interim payment is monthly.

3.237 There are many contractual mechanisms which may change the contract price, such as variations, fluctuations (change in material and labour cost, levy and taxes, increase in head office and administrative costs), liquidated damages, loss and/or expenses, price adjustments, and the like.[364] There is no general common law right to change the contract price. This differs to many civil law jurisdictions which provide for increases to take account of "economic hardship" arising out of unforeseen event/s.

3.238 Payment by the employer to the contractor is usually made through some form of certification by the contract administrator, who may be an architect, quantity surveyor or engineer.[365] There is no general right under common law afforded to the contractor to claim progress payments; this can only be supported by contract or under statute (under the HGCR Act stage payments are mandatory under most contracts)..

3.239 JCT contracts have introduced Interim Valuation Dates, being "common" valuation dates also intended to apply down the supply chain to sub-contracts and sub-sub-contracts. The intention is to deliver a fairer payment mechanism by having a common assessment date, thereby synchronizing payment through all the tiers of contracts.[366] If the payment provisions are unamended, payment will be made from the top to the bottom of the chain within thirty days.

3.240 The Interim Valuation Date is the date chosen by the parties. The contractor is permitted to make an application for payment any time before the Interim Valuation Date. The due date for payment is 7 days, with the final date for payment 14 days following the due date (applies to both interim and final payments).[367] Should the employer fail to issue a Payment Notice in time, the contractor's Payment Application[368] operates as the Payment Notice.[369] Any Pay Less Notice is due no later than 5 days before the final date for payment.[370]

364 Ibid., sub-clause 4.13, this sub-clause is a list of items which allow for adjustment to the Contract Sum.

365 JCT SBC/Q, clauses 4.7–4.11.

366 This has been introduced in order to comply with the Government's Fair Payment campaign aimed at achieving standard industry payment terms by 2025.

367 JCT SBC/Q sub-clauses 4.8 and 4.11.1.

368 A Payment Application is an application to the Quantity Surveyor stating the sum the contractor considers due to him at the relevant due date, and the basis on which that sum has been calculated.

369 JCT SBC/Q, sub-clause 4.10.

370 Ibid., sub-clause 4.11.5.

3.241 These notice provisions reflect the payment procedure under the HGCR Act and the spirit of promoting "cash flow" through the supply chain. In *Melville Dundas Ltd (In Receivership) v George Wimpey UK Ltd*[371] the House of Lords noted that the purpose of such notices in construction contracts is to reduce the incidence of set off abuse by formalizing the payment process, so that the contractor is aware immediately what payment needs to be made and the reasons for any amounts being withheld.

3.242 Under the JCT forms, the architect/contract administrator must issue, no later than 5 days after the due date, an Interim Certificate (irrespective of whether a Payment Application has been submitted the valuation date). If no Interim Certificate has been issued by the architect/contract administrator and the contractor has failed to make a Payment Application by the valuation date, the contractor may issue a Payment Notice, at any time after the last date for issue of the Interim Certificate, stating the amount due at the relevant due date and the basis on which this sum has been calculated.

3.243 Failure by a party to pay a notified sum by the final payment date means that the sum will be automatically recoverable as a debt.[372] This may prove more effective through an application for summary judgment than pursuing payment under the adjudication mechanism.

3.244 The contractor is entitled to claim direct loss and/or expense which he incurs or is likely to incur for any Relevant Event.[373] This includes: Variations, architect instructions relating to discrepancies or opening up and inspection, inaccurate approximate quantities and impediments caused by the employer.[374] The contract administrator must assess a claim for loss and/or expense within 28 days of receipt (or, should an update to the initial claim be made, 14 days following this).[375] To ensure that the architect/contract administrator observes these time limits, there is a reciprocal requirement on the contractor to submit its supporting information with the notice, or as soon as reasonably practicable thereafter, rather than "on request". The JCT Guidance confirms that it is not intended to create a condition precedent with this requirement.

3.245 The Scheme for Construction Contracts (England and Wales) Regulations 1998, known as "the Scheme", supplements the HGCR Act in England and Wales and provides fall-back provisions where the contract itself does not include the necessary payment (and adjudication) provisions. The payment provisions under the Scheme are further outlined in para 5.375.

3.246 The contractor is required to provide to the architect/contract administrator within six months after the practical completion certificate has been issued documentation necessary for the architect/contract administrator to calculate the adjusted Contract Sum.[376] If the contractor does not supply the necessary documentation within this time period, and does not respond within one month of the architect/contractor administrator's notice to do so, the architect/contract administrator may rely on the documents already in its

371 [2007] BLR, 257.
372 JCT SBC/Q, sub-clause 4.11.7
373 Ibid., sub-clause 4.20.1
374 Ibid., sub-clause 4.22,
375 Ibid., sub-clause 4.21.4.
376 Ibid., sub-clause 4.25.1.

possession in ascertaining the adjusted Contract Sum.[377] The architect/contractor administrator has three months from this date to review and respond with the final adjustment figure, which must also take into account any loss and/or expense notified by the contractor.[378] Normally, the final certificate will be issued within two months after the end of the rectification period, with payment being made within two months from issuing the final certificate.[379] The final certificate is conclusive evidence of all computations regarding the Contract Sum (excluding any fraud or error).[380]

Materials and Workmanship

3.247 The common law will imply into a construction contract an obligation that the contractor will do his work in a good and workmanlike manner, will supply good and proper materials and that a residentialbuilding will be reasonably fit for human habitation.[381] In traditional procurement, the basic obligation of the contractor is as to method of construction, since most of all the design is provided by the employer and its consultants.

3.248 Where the contract is for the supply of materials, a warranty will be implied that the materials are of good quality and, if the principal has made known the purpose for which the materials are to be supplied, that they are reasonably fit for the purpose for which they will be used (that is, the circumstances indicate that the employer relied on the skill and judgment of the contractor in determining the suitability of material used). Either or both warranties may be excluded where the express terms and context reveal an intention to do so.

3.249 In *Young & Marten Ltd v McManus Childs Ltd*[382] the contractor (McManus Childs) was appointed by the employer for the construction of dwelling homes. The contractor sub-contracted roof works to the sub-contractor (Young & Marten). The sub-contract directed using a specific type of tile available only from one manufacturer. Within 12 months, the tiles began to disintegrate; the problem was caused by a defective batch of tiles not detectable even upon "reasonable inspection". The contractor claimed damages from the sub-contractor for breach of implied warranty that the tiles would be fit for their intended purpose. The House of Lords held that there would be an implied term that materials were of good quality and also reasonably fit for the purpose for which they were used. In this instance, there was no fitness for purpose obligation; however, there was still a duty to ensure that materials were of good quality. The contractor did not rely on the sub-contractor's skill and judgment in selecting the materials, as the tiles were chosen by the contractor and from only one available supplier. The contractor took on himself the responsibility of selecting tiles suitable for his purpose; thus there was no implied warranty.

3.250 If the employer makes known to the contractor (expressly or impliedly) the purpose for which materials and goods are being supplied and that he relies upon the skill and judgment of the contractor, it will be an implied condition that the materials and goods are

377 Ibid., sub-clause 4.25.3.

378 Ibid., sub-clause 4.25.2.

379 Ibid., sub-clause 4.26.1 and 3.

380 Ibid., sub-clause 1.9.2.

381 *Greaves & Co (Contractors) Ltd v Baynham Meikle and Partners* (n 321).

382 (1969) 9 BLR 77

fit for purpose. However, if there is no reliance on the skill and care of the contractor with respect to quality or indication of purpose, the contractor can avoid liability.

3.251 Warranties that materials are of satisfactory quality and fit for purpose are also covered by statute law as implied conditions under Section 14 of the Sale of Goods Act 1979.[383]

3.252 The JCT contract position on materials and workmanship is relatively straightforward:

3.253 The Contractor is obliged to carry out and complete the works in a proper and workmanlike manner and in compliance with the Contract Documents, the Construction Phase Plan, and the Statutory Requirements.[384] This is an absolute obligation and the contractor cannot raise as a defence to liability for non-compliance that the Architect approved or included the works in a payment certificate.

3.254 All materials and goods for the works (excluding design works), must, so far as procurable, be of the kinds and standards described in the Contract (whether this is the Employer's Requirements, Contractor Proposals or others) and no substitutions are permitted without the Architect's consent.[385]

3.255 Workmanship for the works, excluding design works, must reflect standards outlined in the Contract Bills. Workmanship for any design works must be carried out as per the Employer's Requirements (or Contractor's Proposal if not mentioned there).[386]

3.256 To the extent that quality of materials and goods and standards of workmanship are neither described in the contract nor left to the reasonable satisfaction of the architect/contract administrator as already explained, a JCT contract normally requires such quality and standards to be "appropriate" to the works. This may be different from the "good and workmanlike manner" standard normally implied at common law – the term "appropriate" to the work may even be construed as 'fitness for purpose'.

3.257 The Final Certificate is conclusive evidence that materials, goods and workmanship are to the Contract Administrator/Architects' reasonable satisfaction provided the particular quality of materials, goods or standard of workmanship were expressly described in the Contract Documents, instructed by Contractor Administrator/Architect or any drawings/documents issued by the contractor for his approval.[387]

Labour Law Considerations

3.258 Under English common law, the employer owes a duty to its employees to take reasonable care for their physical safety, that is, to take all reasonable steps to ensure a safe

383 s14(3): "Where the seller sells goods in the course of a business and the buyer, expressly or by implication, makes known: (a) to the seller, or (b) where the purchase price or part of it is payable by installments and the goods were previously sold by a credit-broker to the seller, to that credit-broker, any particular purpose for which the goods are being bought, there is an implied term that the goods supplied under the contract are reasonably fit for that purpose, whether or not that is a purpose for which such goods are commonly supplied, except where the circumstances show that the buyer does not rely, or that it is unreasonable for him to rely, on the skill or judgment of the seller".

384 JCT SBC/Q, sub-clause 2.1.

385 Ibid., sub-clause 2.2.

386 Ibid., sub-clause 2.3.

387 Ibid., sub-clause 1.9.1.

system of work (this applies to both contract and tort).[388] The duty to provide a safe system of work may extend beyond the employer-employee relationship to protect an independent contractor.[389]

3.259 The employer must provide its employees with proper and adequate means of carrying out their work without any unnecessary risk, whether by warning or giving instructions.[390] The obligation extends to taking reasonable steps to provide safe plant and equipment.[391] However, if the employer obtains plant or equipment from a reputable supplier, and there is nothing to suggest the plant or equipment is unsafe, the employer may escape liability.[392]

3.260 There is a general tortious principle that the employer is not responsible for the negligent conduct of the contractor (or the main contractor for the sub-contractor). There are some exceptions which include: Where the main contractor had actual knowledge that a sub-contractor's work was done in a foreseeably dangerous way and approved it; and, where the the main-contractor owes a "non-delegable duty", that is, that the main-contractor will procure careful performance of the works carried out by its sub-contractor.[393]

3.261 In England, there are many statutes covering labour considerations such as the Health and Safety at Work Act 1974, dealing with regulation of health and safety and the Employers' Liability (Compulsory Insurance) Act 1969, where the employer is obliged to take out compulsory insurance for liability in respect of bodily injury or disease to its employees. The most relevant to construction are the Construction (Design and Management) Regulations 2015 ("CDM Regulations") which cover the management of health, safety and welfare when carrying out construction works in the United Kingdom, the aim being to reduce the risk of those who build, use and maintain structures.

Performance and Taking-Over

3.262 Taking-over (or "practical completion" as it is known in England) is a term which has no authoritative definition; English common law does not have a doctrine of "practical completion", which is determined by the project's purpose and any contractual definition requirements (that is, the physical building and engineering work required, testing and commissioning procedure and results, and/or procuring of documents).

3.263 Interestingly, neither the JCT contract nor leading international standard forms provide a definition for practical completion.[394] The JCT contract procedure for practical completion is quite short, stating that when in the architect/contract administrator's opinion practical completion of the works is achieved then he will issue the practical

388 Bailey J, Construction Law (Informa 2016) at [21.04], *Quinn v JW Green (Painters) Ltd* [1966] 1 QB 509.

389 Ibid., *Wheeler v Copas* [1981] 3 All ER 405.

390 Ibid., *Hopps v Mott Macdonald Ltd* [2009] EWCH 1881 (QB); *O'Connell v Commissioner for Government Transport* (1954) 100 CLR 225.

391 Ibid., *Andar Transport Pty Ltd v Brambles Ltd* (2004) 217 CLR 424.

392 Ibid., *Davie v New Merton Board Mills Ltd* [1959] AC 604.

393 *Willmott Dixon Construction Ltd v Robert West Consulting Ltd* [2016] EWHC 3291 (TCC).

394 See the Australian Standard AS4000-1997 General Conditions of Contract, unlike the JCT contract, it has a very comprehensive definition of "practical completion".

completion certificate and practical completion is deemed to have occurred on the date stated in the certificate.[395]

3.264 Guidance is found in the two leading House of Lords decisions (and two decisions of courts of first instance) limited to dicta and construction law literature which define practical completion as follows:[396]

- Practical completion means the completion of all the construction work that has to be done;
- Completion for all practical purposes, that is to say for the purpose of allowing the employer to take possession of the works and use them as intended;[397]
- A certificate of practical completion may not be issued if there are patent defects;
- The works can be practically complete notwithstanding that there are latent defects;
- The architect/contract administrator has discretion to certify practical completion where there are very minor items of work left incomplete, on "*de minimis*" principles.[398]

3.265 In summary, practical completion occurs when works are physically complete or certified complete save for minor defects or omissions, and are reasonably capable of their intended purpose. However, if there are patent defects (i.e., known defects) not *de minimis* in nature, then practical completion is not effected. The English courts have not defined the meaning of "patent" defects.

3.266 It is possible that a building is physically complete, allowing for practical completion even though not functioning as it should.[399] For instance, *Bovis Lend Lease Ltd v Saillard Fuller & Partners* entailed the construction of new office building with the pressurization system working only at 80% of its efficiency or capacity; this did not preclude practical completion occurring. With respect to construction of a house, it must at least be in a state fit for human habitation.[400] For instance, in a contract for a new build house where there is a requirement for a porch constructed over a front door, the house may be certified practically complete even if the porch remains unconstructed because the house is complete and habitable. Conversely, a house will not be considered complete if significant aspects of the dwelling are missing.[401]

---

395 JCT SBC/Q, sub-clause 2.30.

396 Furst S and Ramsey V, *Keating on Construction Contracts*, 9th Edn, Sweet & Maxwell (2012), 894. Note this definition is given in the context of practical completion under the JCT contract form. The two House of Lords cases cited as obiter are *Jarvis & Sons v Westminister Corp* [1970] 1 W.L.R 637 and *P&M Kaye v Hosier & Dickinson* [1972] 1 W.L.R 146; The other, and more recent, decision providing guidance on "practical completion" is found in the judgment of Akenhead J in *Walter Lilly & Co Ltd v Mackay [2012] EWHC 1773 (TCC)*.

397 *Murphy Corporation Ltd v Acumen Design & Development (Queensland) Pty and Anor* [1995] 11 BCL 274.

398 *Nevill v William Press* [1981] 20 BLR 78.

399 *Bovis Lend Lease Ltd (formerly Bovis Construction Ltd) v Saillard Fuller & Partners* [2001] 77 Con. L.R. 134.

400 *Perry v Sharon Development Co Ltd* [1937] 4 All ER 390.

401 Ibid.

3.267 Practical completion means "complete for all practical purposes" rather than completion down to the last detail. The existence of defects need not mean that practical completion has not been achieved.[402]

3.268 Failure to define practical completion may be construed as completion of all the contractor's work obligations under the contract, and this may not necessarily be substantial or practical completion.[403] Actually achieving practical completion is a question of fact; one must examine what the contractor promised, the contractual definition of practical completion (if any) and whether what is built corresponds with the contract.

3.269 The consequences of refusing practical completion may be serious. In *Elmbid Ltd v Burgess* the buyer was required to complete on the purchase of residential premises from a barn conversion following the architect issuing the practical completion certificate. The certificate was issued and the buyer asserted it was not valid and the seller (and contractor) was unable to complete the contract, entitling her to rescind. The seller considered this to be repudiatory breach of contract and rescinded the contract. The court determined that the buyer had breached the contract by wrongfully repudiating and allowing the seller to forfeit the deposit and claim damages.[404]

3.270 Practical completion is crucial to both parties, triggering a number of contractual and legal implications which include: End of contractor's liability to pay liquidated damages; contractor entitlement to retention monies; commencement of defects notification period; risk of loss and damage passes to employer; contractor's work insurance obligation ends; and contract administrator/architect can no longer issue variation instructions.

3.271 Most contracts are silent on the issue of occupation before practical completion and many include a deemed practical completion provision.

3.272 The JCT contract allows "partial possession" by the employer, with the contractor's consent, according to the specific contractual mechanism for partial possession; it does not refer to "possession" generally.[405] The distinction is to be made between early use of the works and partial possession. In *Impressa Castelli SpA v Cola Holdings Ltd*,[406] the court determined that the contractor granting the employer early use of the works (construction of a hotel) was not partial possession for the purpose of ending the contractor's liability for liquidated damages. Partial possession would mean exclusive possession by the employer, other than for the contractor accessing works for rectifying defects. In this case, the contractor still had on-going and incomplete works, despite the employer accessing and making use of the hotel.

3.273 There is also a distinction to be made between partial possession of "parts" of the work and the "whole" works, where the latter may mean that practical completion has occurred.[407] Additionally, use and occupation by the building owner of his flat does not

---

402 *Elmbid Ltd v Burgess* [2013] EWHC 1489 (Ch); [2013] 24 E.G. 101 (C.S.), *Menolly Investments Sarl v Cerep Sarl* [2009] EWHC 516 (Ch), 125 Con. L.R. 75 applied.

403 *Cordon Investments Pty Ltd v Lesdor Properties Pty Ltd* [2012] NSWCA 184.

404 *Elmbid* (n 406), the court held that if there were still defects in the works at the practical completion stage, the purchaser's remedies were those for breach of contract and did not entitle her to refuse to complete.

405 JCT SBC/Q, sub-clause 2.33.

406 [2002] EWHC 1363 (TCC).

407 *Skanska Construction (Regions) Ltd v Anglo Amsterdam Corp Ltd* [2002] 84 Con. L.R. 100.

imply acceptance of works, waiver of defects, nor stop the building owner from contending that works have not been performed in accordance with contract.[408]

Defects Liability

3.274 Where the defects occur during the construction and before a practical completion certificate is issued, the works are generally considered to be incomplete. The method of dealing with these types of defects is wholly different to defects that occur after issuing of a practical completion certificate. The review in this section is limited to defects that occur during this period, which is otherwise known as the defects notification period (or "Rectification Period," under the JCT contract).

3.275 "Defect" is not a legal term of art; the English courts have provided helpful (and varying) definitions, such as anything rendering plant and equipment unfit for its intended purpose,[409] failure to meet a particular specification or a lack, or absence, of something essential to completeness.[410]

3.276 However, it is essential to make the distinction between patent and latent defects, because practical completion hinges on whether there are patent defects not *de minimis* in nature. A patent defect is "detectable" and the test for determining this is objective.[411]

3.277 Incorporating a defects notification period in a contract is primarily a device arising out of English contract law to provide for the contractor returning to site and remedying any defects. Unless the contract expressly provides for a contractor to remedy defects post practical completion, the contractor is not permitted or required to carry out any rectification works. The employer is entitled to claim damages against the contractor for breach of contract. Given that this is not the most economically viable or practical solution, English contracts (and virtually all international forms) will have a dedicated defects liability clause.

3.278 The Rectification Period in the JCT contract is stated in the Contract Particulars. Parties are free to select the period which commences from the date of the practical completion certificate (the default period is six months). If there are any defects or faults during the Rectification Period, the architect/contract administrator may issue instructions for the defects to be made good.[412] The architect/contract administrator must specify in a schedule of defects (otherwise known as a "snagging list") all those defects requiring remediation.[413] Failing this, the employer cannot request the contractor to remedy defects not noted in the schedule.

3.279 The contractor must remedy the defects within a reasonable time after notice at no cost to the employer. There is an option, requiring the Employer's consent, to leave the defect unremedied, and to make an appropriate deduction from the Contract Sum.[414] There

408 *Hall and Shivers v Van Der Heiden* [2010] EWHC 586 (TCC).

409 *Yarmouth v France* (1887) QBD 647.

410 *Tate v Latham* [1897] 1 QB 502.

411 *Sanderson v National Coal Board* [1961] 2 QB 244.

412 JCT SBC/Q, sub-clause 2.38.

413 This must be done no later than 14 days after expiry of the Rectification Period, Sub-clause 2.38.1, JCT SBC/Q.

414 JCT SBC/Q, sub-clause 2.38.

is no requirement for the contractor's consent to the amount of deduction. However the deduction must be "appropriate", permitting the contractor to dispute if it is otherwise.[415]

3.280 Where an employer refuses to allow the contractor to return and repair defects or the contractor does not respond to a defects notice and the employer uses an alternative contractor, the employer may be prevented from claiming more than it would have cost had he used the original contractor.[416] However, the employer may be allowed to use an alternative contractor where the contractor has acted fraudulently, where the defects were so extensive that no reasonable person would agree to the contractor returning or the contractor refuses to repair any defects.[417]

3.281 Latent defects which become patent following expiry of the Rectification Period, will only entitle the employer to have a cause of action against the contractor for negligent work (unless excluded from the contract). However, the architect/contract administrator issuing the final certificate may provide evidence of the adequacy of the contractor's works, thereby prejudicing the employer's right.

3.282 The JCT contract states that the final certificate once issued provides conclusive evidence of compliance by the contractor on all matters of quality not objectively specified (that is, that such work was to the reasonable satisfaction of the architect/contract administrator).[418] This means that the contractor is not liable for defects relating to the architect/contract administrator's opinion; however, liability for all other defects in quality still remains with the contractor and is governed by statutory limitation periods (generally being latent defects becoming patent defects post issuing of final certificate).

3.283 Where there is defective work, this gives rise to a cause of action for breach of contract by the contractor. However, this avenue is only available to the employer as a party to the contract, whereas subsequent purchasers do not have this recourse unless the benefits under the building contract are validly assigned or there are collateral warranties in place.[419] The only route available to the purchaser would be under tort. However, pure economic loss for the repair of a defect is not generally available under English law: there must be damage to give rise to a cause of action.[420]

3.284 The limitation periods noted in para 5.151 are extended by the Latent Damage Act 1986. The extension applies to claims in negligence for latent defects being the later of 6 years from the date the damage occurred and 3 years from the date which the claimant

415 Ibid.

416 *Pearce and High Ltd v Baxter and Baxter* [1999] EWCA Civ 789; *Persimmon Homes (South Coast) Ltd v (1) Hall Aggregates (South Coast) Ltd (2) Cemex UK Properties Ltd* [2008] EWHC 2379 (TCC).

417 *Mul v Hutton Construction Ltd [2014] EWHC 1797 (TCC)*, see Akenhead J's obiter comments; In *SSE Generation Ltd v Hochtief Solutions AG and anor* [2016] ScotCS CSOH 177 the contractor refused to return to site and repair defects, claiming it had not caused the defects. The court found that the contractor was not responsible for causing the defects; however, he was still in breach of contract because the contract required the contractor to return and repair defects irrespective of fault.

418 JCT SBC/Q, sub-clause 1.9.1.1, this is subject to the employer not disputing the final certificate within 28 days (sub-clause 1.9.2).

419 The purchaser of a dwelling may have recourse under the *Defective Premises Act 1972*, but only if the works were done "in the course of a business", such as by a property developer, not a home owner, and the defects render the property unfit for habitation.

420 *D&F Estates v Church Commissioners for England and others* [1988] UKHL 4; *Murphy v Brentwood* (n 398).

had requisite knowledge of the right to bring an action. This is subject to a maximum period of 15 years from the last possible negligent act or omission.

Restriction or Exclusion of Liability

3.285 Inherent in the nature of construction works are "risks", and attached to each risk is potential for liability. Thus, in the event of the risk materializing, it must be determined which party (or parties) will be liable for the consequences of the risk (in this instance, the financial consequences). Under construction related agreements, the employer, contractor, sub-contractor, or consultant will tend towards restriction of their liability because unchecked and onerous exposure to risk can have severe financial consequences. Thus in every construction related agreement there will exist a limitation or exclusion of liability clause (sometimes multiple clauses or indirect mechanisms for limiting liability).

3.286 Even if the contract contains a mechanism for purporting to limit or restrict liabilitz, provisions of statute may affect the permissibility of limiting (and/or excluding) certain types of liabilities. These include the Unfair Contract Terms Act 1977, Sale of Goods Act 1979, Supply of Goods and Services Act 1982 and Consumer Rights Act 2015. For instance under the UCTA, a contractual term cannot limit or exclude liability for death or personal injury from negligence.[421]

3.287 In the absence of such a clause, there is no financial limit on the loss or damages a party can claim. There are practical limits, and legal limits under the general law of damages; however, beyond these, no limits are normally implied. A party wishing to reduce its exposure must insert an express exclusion or restriction of limitation of liability.

3.288 A distinction is to be made between limitation of liability and exclusion of liability. Exclusion clauses operate to exclude the liability of a party under a contract or at law for default, unlawful act or omission by the breaching party. Limitation clauses operate to reduce, limit or otherwise qualify liability for loss or damages by the breach party.

3.289 A "blanket" exclusion preventing recovery of damages is not automatically unenforceable. The broader the exclusion, the clearer the wording must be for it to be effective.[422] Limiting liability with a reasonable cap will more likely be upheld than a blanket exclusion seeking to exclude it altogether.[423]

3.290 Normally, construction contracts will contain a cap on liability, thereby limiting either the total liability under the contract to a certain sum or liability for different heads of loss or damage. There are no standard rules on cap amounts; they can be a percentage of the contract value or a fixed money amount unrelated to the contract sum. The contractor may also link a cap on liability to the amount recoverable under an insurance claim. The JCT contract does not have a clause allowing parties to place a cap on liability to a specific sum, unlike the FIDIC or NEC4 contracts.

3.291 A liquidated damages clause allows the employer to claim a pre-determined amount for contractor delays. The rate, whether daily, weekly or monthly, is agreed between the parties and is often capped at a percentage of the contract value.

421 UCTA 1977, ss 2(1) and (11).

422 *Trident Turboprop (Dublin) Ltd v First Flight Couriers* [2008] 2 Lloyd's Rep 581.

423 *Photo Production Ltd v Securicor Transport Ltd* [1980] AC 827; [1980] 2 WLR 283.

3.292 Another contractual mechanism used in English contracts to limit liability is the "net contribution clause". There is no concept of proportionate liability in English law. If more than one party is responsible for the same damage, they can be jointly and severally liable for 100% of the loss. For instance, if an engineer and contractor are both liable for the same defective work, the employer can elect to recover all its damages from only the engineer. The engineer would need to pursue the contractor at his own cost and expense to recover the contractor's contribution under the Civil Liability (Contribution) Act 1978.

3.293 A net contribution clause (otherwise known as a proportionate liability clause), limits the liability of each stakeholder to an amount that is agreed to be proportionate to the contribution of that party to the enterprise.[424] The employer must commence proceedings against all stakeholders responsible for the damage to recoup all his losses. Thus, from the previous example, if the court finds the engineer 75% liable for damages, the employer must pursue the contractor for the remaining 25%.

3.294 In *Hadley v Baxendale*[425] the longstanding principle in English common law was established limiting the damages recoverable in the event of a breach of contract to damages which:

> [m]ay fairly and reasonably be considered either arising naturally, that is, according to the usual course of things from such breach of contract itself [direct losses], or such as may be supposed to have been in the contemplation of both parties at the time they made the contract, as the probable result of the breach of it [indirect losses].

3.295 Construction contracts will commonly include a provision excluding the right to claim indirect or consequential losses because such losses are difficult to predict and to price and parties will not wish to expose themselves to unlimited damages. When a contract excludes "indirect losses" (also known as "consequential losses"), as a matter of law, it only excludes the second limb of *Hadley v Baxendale*.[426] What constitutes direct and indirect losses has been dealt with extensively in the English courts. For instance, loss of profit, while commonly regarded as indirect loss, will often be held to be direct losses. Additionally, fixed costs and overheads may also be considered direct losses and thus recoverable.[427]

3.296 The JCT contract provides for parties agreeing to a cap limiting the contractor's liability for loss of use, loss of profit or other consequential losses arising from negligent design.[428] The cap does not limit the contractor's responsibility for all direct losses (for example, damage caused to adjacent property).

---

424 In *West and another v Ian Finlay & Associates (a firm)* [2014] EWCA Civ 316, the Court of Appeal reversed the finding of the court at first instance and held a net contribution clause to be valid and binding, enabling the defendant architect to exclude losses for which an insolvent contractor party was responsible.

425 (1854) 9 Ex 341.

426 Irrespective of whether losses are direct or indirect, if such losses are too remote then they will not be claimable.

427 *Deepak Fertilisers & Petrochemical Corporation Limited v Davy McKee (London) Ltd* [1999] 1 All ER (Comm) 69.

428 JCT SBC/Q, sub-clause 2.19.3, the cap only applies to non-dwellings, it does not not apply to construction works for residential dwellings under the Defective Premises Act 1972.

Variations

3.297 A variation is defined in the JCT form of contract[429] as "the alteration or modification of the design, quality or quantity of the Works". It can include omission of work, that is, deletion, as well as additions or substitution. Such a variation will be ordered by the architect/Contract administrator on behalf of the employer, and may result from a realization that a change or modification is necessary, for example, to meet new demands or constraints. Variations can, however, also derive from changes in the way in which the contractor is required to undertake the work: alteration of standards of materials, removal of materials from site, restrictions in access to site or working hours or sequencing work. Although these will still have to be ordered by the architect/contract administrator, they will actually originate with the contractor, who will, in effect, claim a variation, by reason of the changes required. The issue of a variation as a result of the instructions of the architect/contract administrator may entitle the contractor to an additional payment[430] or additional time, as a Relevant Event.[431]

3.298 However, it is not the case under English law that all variations would entitle a contractor to claim additional time or money.

3.299 One recurring contention between parties is the extent to which bill of quantities rates are applicable to the value of work, particularly to variations. In *Henry Boot Construction v Alstom*[432] the court decided on the use of incorrect contract rates for valuing a variation and held that whether rates are "appropriate" or "applicable" is not dependent on whether they are "fair" or comparable to market rates:

> It is in any event a basic principle of the law of contract that a party cannot avoid the effect of a unilateral mistake made prior to the making of the contract (subject to exceptions such as where the mistake was in fact known to the other contracting party). A mistake in a rate or price or in its application binds both parties … The fact that the rate or price otherwise applicable may appear to be "too high" or "too low" is immaterial: The parties have agreed that such a rate or price is to be used to value variations or, if clause 55 is applicable, the correction of an error or omission.

3.300 Anything expressly included in the specification would not, obviously, be a variation, but something not expressly stated which would nevertheless be understood to be part of the task would not create any additional entitlement. An important threshold question is whether what is requested can be achieved within the operation of the variation clause at all. A high volume of instructions or other documents issued is not proof that they cannot all be treated as variations,[433] but ordering something different in nature may not be capable of being treated as a variation. Where a contractor was asked to perform a dredging contract in such a way as to create an artificial island in a lake, the court held this was not a variation but the creation of a new agreement.[434] The method of working

429 Ibid., clause 5.
430 Ibid., clauses 5.2 and 5.5.
431 Ibid., clause 2.29.1.
432 [2000] BLR 247.
433 *McAlpine Humberoak v McDermott International* [1992] 58 BLR1.
434 *Blue Circle Industries v Holland Dredging Co (UK) Ltd* [1987] 37 BLR 40.

requested for a particular purpose may not have been in the parties' contemplation under the original contract.[435]

3.301 Under US law, the sheer volume of changes is capable of taking the parties outside the operation of the variation provisions: This is known as the "cardinal change" doctrine. It does not apply as such to English law, where there is no equivalent expression, though in one extreme case, a 100% increase in contract sum through variations in building a power station was held to take the parties outside their original agreement.[436]

3.302 As indicated above, deletion of works can constitute a variation, and this is expressly contemplated by JCT and other contracts. However, the deletion of part of the works by variation in order to give it to another contractor is not normally permitted. Unless there are very clear words in the contract allowing omission of items for this purpose, it cannot be done: "the approach to variation clauses must be one which respects a contractor's right to complete the works which it has undertaken to do".[437] At the very least "an arbitrary withdrawal of work … and the giving of it to a third party" would entitle the contractor to financial compensation.[438] Even though there is no over-arching duty of good faith in English construction law, the courts would be prepared to review how certain powers had been exercised under the contract, and variation clauses fall into this category; they cannot be utilized arbitrarily and clear express words are required to confer wide discretion.

Delay and Disruption

3.303 One of the most common types of contractor claim is the "delay and disruption" claim. The contractor seeks additional payment for loss alleged to be caused by an event for which the contractor is not responsible. There may be a further claim for extension of time as a result of the same event.

3.304 Delay and disruption claims and extension of time claims create significant practical and legal difficulties for all concerned: Initially the contract administrator, the parties respectively advancing and defending the claim, and their advisors and ultimately any tribunal required to make a decision on a dispute arising from the claim. The problems derive from the need to prove causation and to quantify loss, in order to make good the claim. Contractors, and their advisors, who may be lawyers or "claims consultants", frequently try to overcome the evidential and legal difficulties of proving causal link between breach and loss, and quantifying the loss accruing from each breach, by submitting "global claims". These comprise a collection of alleged breaches or other claims events and a total amount of money and/or time claimed without detailed particularization of the relationship between each event and the cost/time said to result from it. Such global claims were traditionally regarded with extreme suspicion by the judiciary[439] but more recently the

435 *Costain Civil Engineering v Zanen Dredging* [1996] 85 BLR 77.

436 *Sir Lindsay Parkinson v Commissioners of His Majesty's Works* [1950] 1 All ER 208.

437 *Abbey Development Ltd v PP Brickwork Ltd* [2003] Ad; LR 07/04.

438 *Amec Building Ltd v Cadmus Investment Co* [1996] 51 Con LR 105.

439 *Wharf Properties v Eric Cumine Associates (No 2)* (1991) 52 BLR 8.

Scottish courts[440] and English courts[441] have conceded that they will be acceptable in certain circumstances and subject to appropriate protections for the defendant/respondent.

3.305 Complex claims are especially problematic where they are alleged to include concurrent causes or where the resulting delay/loss runs concurrently, that is, simultaneously.

3.306 Concurrent delay is treated by English law quite differently from most major jurisdictions, including Scotland. The principle is that where contractor delay to completion occurs concurrently with delay for which the employer is responsible, the contractor should nevertheless receive full extension of time with no deduction, although this would not extend to entitlement to financial compensation.[442] In other jurisdictions, more pragmatic approaches are adopted, based usually on apportionment[443] as between the respective causes.

3.307 A major source of reference for delay and disruption claims is the Society of Construction Law Delay and Disruption Protocol ("Protocol"),[444] which usefully collects definitions and methodologies of delay analysis, although it should be noted that it does not have any binding legal status.

3.308 The Protocol comprises 22 "Core Principles" which address the following:

- the utility of a properly prepared programme, the preparation of updated programmes and the maintenance of site records;
- the purpose, entitlement and procedure for extensions of time;
- the effect of delay;
- the impact of float and concurrency in the context of delay, extensions of time and compensation;
- delay analysis, both contemporaneously when delay events occur and after completion of the works (or substantially later in time);
- the basis for calculating compensation for prolongation;
- global claims, acceleration and disruption – details as to the nature of making these claims.

3.309 The Protocol is internationally used in supporting delay and disruption claims. For example, the Queensland Supreme Court approved the use of the Protocol in determining the sufficiency of a plaintiff's pleaded claim for delay and disruption.[445] The Protocol was developed with a focus on the UK construction market. However, it is also used in civil law jurisdictions and will also be available in French.[446]

440 *John Doyle Construction v Laing Management* (2004) SLT B78.

441 *Walter Lilly & Co Ltd v Mackay* (n 397).

442 *Henry Boot Construction Ltd v Malmaison Hotel (Manchester) Ltd* (1999) 70 ConLR 32.

443 In Scotland, *City Inn v Shepherd Construction* [2010] BLR 473.

444 2nd Edition 2017.

445 *Santos Ltd v Fluor Australia Pty Ltd* [2017] QSC 153.

446 Frederic Gillion, "French version of protocol will help with international construction disputes" at www.out-law.com/en/articles/2018/september/french-version-of-protocol-will-help-with-international-construction-disputes/ (accessed on 5 March 2019).

Liquidated Damages

3.310 Liquidated damages are known colloquially as "LDs" in the UK industry. Their purpose is to provide the employer[447] with a pre-agreed remedy for breach by the contractor of the completion obligation. Under English law, to claim liquidated damages the employer does not need to prove that it has suffered any loss at all, and it does not need to prove quantum of loss nor mitigation. If liquidated damages are the exclusive remedy for delay under the contract, the contractor has the benefit of knowing its maximum risk exposure. This is especially so if the liquidated damages are capped, for example, at 10% of the contract sum. If the employer agrees such a cap, it will be bound by it, even if the effect is to deny recovery for loss actually suffered.[448]

3.311 The English law of liquidated damages has recently undergone a major re-evaluation by the Supreme Court. Traditionally, in order to be valid, a liquidated damages clause had to constitute a "genuine pre-estimate of loss" at the time the contract was agreed; if the purpose was to put the contractor *in terrorem*, the clause would be unenforceable as a penalty.[449] The new position is that a liquidated damages clause will only be an unenforceable penalty if it "imposes a detriment on the contract-breaker out of all proportion to any legitimate interest of the innocent party in the enforcement of the primary obligation".[450] If the contract had no liquidated damages clause, which is unlikely in the UK, or it was not expressed to be the exclusive remedy for delay, damages would in principle be recoverable under the normal rules of contract law.

Insurance

3.312 There are certain construction risks which are managed by way of insurance arrangements to absorb financial losses that may arise from these risks. Provided the risk is insurable, the insurer generally agrees to indemnify against loss or to make good the loss suffered.[451]

3.313 In construction works, there are typically two types of insurance. The first, insurance taken out by the stakeholders, that is, contractor, sub-contractors and consultants (or sometimes the employer); and second, often found in larger projects, is project insurance. The former entails each party individually obtaining insurance to cover their own works and/or services and the latter involves all parties participating jointly in insurance covering the project, which may involve them contributing collectively to the insurance premium.

3.314 In the UK, construction contracts will normally impose an obligation on the contractor to obtain insurance throughout the duration of the works, as "possession" of the site is given to the contractor (insurance will generally extend up to the point of practical completion, where site risk is transferred back to the employer). The contractor will be

447 Or main contractor under a sub-contract.

448 *Decoma Ltd v Haden Drysys International* [2005] EWHC B12 (TCC).

449 *Dunlop Pneumatic Tyre Co* (n 188).

450 *Cavendish Square Holdings v Makdessi* [2015] UKSC 67.

451 In Art. 1 and sub-clause 2.1 of the JCT contract the Contractor agrees to carry out and complete the Works, he must reinstate (at his own cost and expense) any loss or damage to the Works and Site Materials.

obliged to obtain insurance in the joint names of the employer, and possibly nominated sub-contractors.

3.315 The insurance policy agreed will determine the risks covered; for instance, negligent conduct of parties (the extent of the negligence and consequences arising out of it is variable), physical loss or damage to the works (permanent or temporary), damage to property arising out of events such as fire or inclement weather, delay caused by non-calculable events such as labour strikes or damage to adjoining property causing damage to the works. The value of construction works will generally drive the type of insurance and level/amount of cover expected.

3.316 There is a distinction to be made between an allocation of risk clause and an insurance clause. A risk clause governs liability for the risk occurring, whereas an insurance clause identifies the party responsible for taking out insurance against the risk occurring.

3.317 There are 4 main types of insurance in construction projects, these include: Contractor's all risks insurance, professional indemnity insurance, third party liability insurance (this extends to both person and property) and defects liability insurance (there may also be product liability insurance, required under provisions of supply contracts).

3.318 It is noted that "contractor's all risks" insurance (also known as CARs) does not mean that each and every risk eventuating is covered. The policy will determine the extent of risks covered and this does not include, for example, payment for remediation of defective works or designs errors or materials supplied.[452]

3.319 In the JCT contracts, there are three alternative options for the insurance of Works and Existing Structures, these are: Options A, New Buildings Works – All Risks Insurance of the Works by the Contractor), Option B, New Buildings Works – All Risks Insurance of the Works by the Contract, and Option C, Joint Names Insurance by the Employer of Existing Structures and Works in or extensions to them.[453] All these options require the same "All Risk Insurance"; however, there are differences regarding responsibility for taking out, maintaining and administrative procedure.

3.320 Insurance Option A is intended for new work where the intention of the parties is that the contractor is the Insuring Party. Likewise, insurance Option B is also intended for new work but the Employer is responsible for obtaining the cover. Option C, which usually applies where there are existing structures, allows alternative (non JCT prescribed) solutions for existing structures and contents cover to be adopted through a Replacement Schedule (this provides flexibility where works are being undertaken in only part of a multiple occupancy building). Although the contractor normally takes out insurance, the employer may be better placed, for example, if the Employer is business as a developer and is thereby able to obtain cheaper insurance premiums.

Suspension and Termination

3.321 As a general proposition, contractors are not entitled to suspend performance of their contractual obligations in order to enforce entitlements or pursue grievances. The

452 Bailey J (n 389), para 17.04.
453 JCT SBQ/Q, sub-clause 6.7.

English law position is that stated by the New Zealand Court of Appeal:[454] "*if he chooses to rescind, his own obligations continue. He is bound to go on with the work*". However, a construction contract can contain express provision permitting suspension and under the HGCR Act (as amended), a right must be given to suspend performance for non-payment of interim sums due:[455]

> the person to whom the sum is due has the right (without prejudice to any other right or remedy) to suspend performance of any or all of his obligations under the contract to the party by whom payment ought to have been paid.

3.322 Termination is available to either party under general principles of contract law for a fundamental repudiatory breach which deprives a party substantially of the benefit of the contract. Construction contracts typically contain express provision for termination, which can be of two kinds.

3.323 First, termination for cause. The JCT contracts contain certain grounds permitting termination by the Employer, subject to following the stated procedure. For example, failure to proceed regularly and diligently with the Works, or acts of insolvency or corruption by the contractor, would create such an entitlement. There are equivalent, though not identical, rights for the contractor to terminate, for example, in the event of non-payment by the employer or interference with the issue of certificates. Termination for *force majeure* is normally available to both parties.

3.324 Second, termination for convenience. This not uniformly available in the English standard forms, but it is in the New Engineering Contract[456] where the employer "may terminate for any reason". Such a power is invariably only available to the employer, not the contractor. The courts have shown themselves willing to review how this power is exercised, so that it can only be used "in good faith". Specifically, it would not usually be permissible to terminate for convenience in order to give the work to another contractor; very clear words would be required to give such a power, and its exercise could be submitted to judicial scrutiny by an aggrieved contractor.

3.325 There is a common law principle that a termination clause does not prohibit a party from terminating at common law for repudiation, unless expressly or impliedly stated by the contract.[457] Under the JCT contract, the right to terminate under common law is expressly preserved.[458] Unlike the JCT contract, there is no elaborate procedure under the common law, other than issuing a notice, followed by the terminating party claiming any damages applicable.

Forms of Security – Bonds and Guarantees

3.326 In projects carried out under English law, as in other jurisdictions, it is usual for securities to be put in place by way of protection, particularly of the employer's interest. As well as practical measures, such as the taking of retentions, a cash deduction from

454 *Canterbury Pipelines v Christchurch Drainage Board* [1979] 2 NZLR 347.
455 s 112.
456 NEC4, sub-clause 90.2.
457 *Lockland Builders Ltd v John Kim Rickwood* (1995) 77 BLR 38.
458 JCT SBC/Q, sub-clause 8.3.1.

payments of certified sums, these securities will take the form of bonds and guarantees. These terms are used loosely and sometimes interchangeably, as if they were identical, as in "on-demand bonds" and "on-demand guarantees"; English law distinguishes between them, however.

3.327 A bond is an obligation by the issuer, such as a bank, to pay the beneficiary; for example, the employer, a sum of money if a specified event occurs. This is a primary obligation, which does not depend upon the performance of the underlying construction contract, except to the extent that the event which triggers the call on the bond may be related to a breach or alleged breach by the contractor. By contrast, a guarantee is an undertaking by the guarantor, such as a bank, which supports the obligations of the principal, for example, the contractor, under the underlying construction contract. The obligation of the guarantor to the beneficiary, for example, the employer, is thus in the nature of a surety and is secondary to the principal's liability to the beneficiary.

3.328 In UK construction projects, there are several types of bonds/guarantees, performing different functions. The most common are the bid bond,[459] the advance payment bond, performance bond guarantee, retention bond, defects liability bond and parent company guarantee.

3.329 The bid bond will be required from a contractor as a pre-condition to acceptance of a tender, to deal with the situation where the tenderer is successful but refuses or fails to enter into the contract with the employer. The advance payment bond protects the employer's release of funds to the contractor before work has started. An advance payment is often made to enable the contractor to order long-lead items and to mobilize more generally, but would only be given after the contractor had procured the bond, to provide repayment to the employer in the event of default by the contractor. Retention bonds are less common in the UK than in some continental European countries. Their purpose is to protect the employer in releasing to the contractor the retention moneys which are deducted[460] from the certified sums payable to provide a security fund for the employer to be used in the event of defective performance by the contractor. In the UK, cash retention, rather than bond retention, is still very common, despite the objections of contractors and sub-contractors. A defects liability or "warranty" bond may be required from the contractor as a pre-condition to the issue of a certificate of practical completion; its purpose is to fund the remedy of defects in the event of the contractor's failure to do so.

3.330 A parent company guarantee has a similar purpose to a performance bond, but is not a liquid instrument, being given by the parent company of a contractor or sub-contractor rather than by a bank. Note the guarantor's (parent company's) obligation is to ensure that the principal (the contractor) performs the obligations being guaranteed. If the principal fails to perform its obligations, the guarantor is liable to the beneficiary (employer). The parent company's primary duty is to ensure that the contractor performs its obligations; the secondary duty is to pay damages. Generally, employers require the parent company to act as "primary obligor", which means that the guarantor's obligation stands alone and is not contingent upon liability being established by employer against the contractor.

459 Sometimes known as "tender" bond

460 Typically 5% of certified sums.

3.331 A frequent concern, especially for the employer, is the extent to which the instrument is "on-demand" or "conditional". Pure unconditional on-demand bonds are less common than more qualified products, where a bank will require certain conditions to be met before making payment, such as a signed statement providing evidence of the contractor's breach and supporting documentation for the amount claimed. Most bonds are conditional in some way.

3.332 Failure to comply with these procedural requirements would entitle the bank to refuse to honour the bond. A pure "on-demand" bond, however, must be paid. Most attempts by the contractor to prevent payment could only succeed if the call on the bond could be shown to be fraudulent,[461] although in exceptional cases, an injunction might be granted against the employer to prevent the call[462] or against the bank to prevent the payment, where the call was in breach of contract or in some other way ineffective.

Claims

3.333 A claim is an assertion of an entitlement or right, in this context, under a construction contract. Most construction contracts contain detailed procedural mechanisms for dealing with claims, as part of the contract administration process. Claims can be made by employer or contractor, though contractors' claims tend to be a more prominent feature of most construction projects.

3.334 Claims in construction contracts are often for both time and money and must be based on either the contract (express or implied provisions) and/or as provided by law, provided this has not been excluded under the contract. If there is a contractual procedure for making a claim, it must be followed. However, English courts may interpret this procedure as broadly as possible to avoid legitimate claims being lost, particularly if it is a condition precedent clause.[463] For example, in *Walter Lilly & Company Limited v Mackay*,[464] Akenhead J confirmed that if the contractor wanted to claim losses, then two conditions precedent under the contract were to be fulfilled: first, making timely application to the architect; and second, providing details of loss or expense to enable ascertainment of quantum.

3.335 The claiming party must also substantiate the claim and establish that the loss or expense directly results from the defaulting party responsible under law or as provided by the contract. Finally, there may exist rules established by the courts that the claiming party must follow for the particular type of claims. For instance, referring again to *Walter Lilly & Company Limited v Mackay*, in relation to the delay and disruption claim, the court ruled that losses and expenses must be proved as a matter of fact. The contractor needed to demonstrate on a balance of probabilities that, first, events occurred which entitled it to loss and expense, second, that those events caused delay and/or disruption and third, that such delay or disruption caused it to incur loss and/or expense.

3.336 Categories of claim by the employer are relatively few. An employer can recover liquidated damages for delayed completion for which it is responsible (see para 3.310 on

461 *Balfour Beatty Civil Engineering v Technical & General Guarantee Co Ltd* [1999] 68 Con LR 180.

462 *Doosan Babcock v Commercializadora de Equipos y Materiales Mabe Lda* [2014] BLR 33.

463 *Obrascon Huarte Lain SA v Her Majesty's Attorney General for Gibraltar* (n 48).

464 *Walter Lilly & Company Limited v Mackay* (n 397).

Liquidated Damages) but in practical terms there is no need for the employer to make a "claim" against the contractor. Since the employer routinely makes payments to the contractor, as a matter of English language it is more usual to speak of the employer "deducting" liquidated damages than "claiming" for them. There will still be a procedure to follow in making the deduction, and the entitlement must be soundly based under the contract, but it is still not really a "claim" by the employer.

3.337 One of the relatively few situations where an employer makes a claim under a construction contract is in respect of a breach of indemnity. Contractors usually indemnify the employer against losses arising in respect of death, personal injury or damage to property and the employer would be entitled to claim against the contractor under such indemnity.[465] In principle, of course, an employer can sue either a contractor or a consultant for any default, but this would be characterized as a claim for damages for *breach* of the contract, rather than a claim for some relief by *operation* of the contract.

3.338 Contractors' claims are more numerous usually, both in volume and types of category. Many are not contentious. A routine application for payment for work done may be described as a claim. It is perhaps unfortunate that the same word should be used for such an uncontroversial procedure and also for an aggressive assertion of an entitlement by the contractor which will be denied or resisted by the contract administrator. JCT uses the term "Payment Application"[466] as an alternative to claim.

3.339 A contractor, like the employer, can also usually claim under a contractual indemnity, but the most prevalent types of contractor claim are for extension of time and additional cost. It is also common to speak of variation claims, but this is usually related to a claim for extension of time or additional cost, or both.

3.340 A variation is an alteration or modification of design, quality or quantity of work, or of the method of work. It may be simply instructed by the contract administrator on behalf of the employer. But if an instruction is alleged to have implications for the contractor, it may be the subject of a "variation claim". In either case, the contractor will seek relief in the form of additional payment and additional time.

Time-Bar Provisions

3.341 Contractual mechanisms for claims, for example, for extensions of time or additional payment, are often made subject to time-limits within which the claim must be brought. Under English law, if these time limits are mandatory, they are likely to operate as time-bars, meaning that, in the event of non-compliance with them, the right to claim will be barred, or lost. The NEC4 contract provides that

> if the Contractor does not notify a compensation event within eight weeks of becoming aware of the event, he is not entitled to a change in the Prices, the Completion Date or a Key Date unless the event arises from the Project Manager or the Supervisor giving an instruction, issuing a certificate, changing an earlier decision or correcting an assumption.
>
> [467]

465 JCT SBC/Q, sub-clauses 6.1 and 6.2.
466 Ibid., sub-clause 4.10.1
467 NEC 4, sub-clause 61.3.

Not all standard forms contain such time limits: The JCT Standard Building Contract merely refers to the need to bring the claim "forthwith", but others do, for example, the Institution of Chemical Engineers (I Chem E) forms of contract,[468] which provide that "If the Contractor intends to claim any additional cost element, rate or charge ... he shall notify the Project Manager of such intention within fourteen days of becoming aware of the event which gives rise to the claim".[469] If these time limits are to be construed as time-bars, preventing the claim, they must be interpreted as conditions precedent.

3.342 The English courts have developed certain guidelines to decide this question:

> Whether this clause is a condition precedent or a contractual term of some other character must depend on the form of the clause itself, the relationship of the clause to the contract as a whole and general considerations of law.[470]

This approach derives from a commercial case and has been developed in more detail in construction contract case-law. The leading case is still *CJ Sims Ltd v Shaftesbury plc*,[471] which sets out a number of factors operating respectively in favour of or against the interpretation of a time-limit as a condition precedent to a claim.

3.343 Generally, English courts are supportive of time-bars and are willing to enforce them as providing useful discipline in contract administration: "Contractual terms requiring a contractor to give prompt notice of delay serve a valuable purpose; such notice enables matters to be investigated while they are still current".[472] The rigour of this approach is well illustrated by a statement of the Scottish Court of Session, which would closely reflect an English court's position:

> The same factors which point to the clause being a condition precedent also point to the need for any notice served in accordance with the clause to comply strictly with its terms. Where parties have laid down in clear terms what has to be done by one of them if he is to claim certain relief, the court should be slow to seek to relieve that party from the consequence of failure.[473]

3.344 A somewhat more flexible approach was taken by the Technology and Construction Court in one of the rare considerations by an English court of the FIDIC provisions,[474] where the judge could "see no reason why this clause should be construed strictly against the contractor and can see reason why it should be construed reasonably broadly". His interpretation of sub-clause 20.1 was that an extension of time could be claimed either *prospectively* when it became clear that there would be a delay or *retrospectively* when the delay has begun, and the time-limit would be construed accordingly.[475]

3.345 It is possible to argue that a time limit has been waived by the conduct of a party or of the contract administrator in allowing a claim out of time, but notwithstanding the

468 For example, Target Cost Contract 2nd ed 2013.

469 I Chem E sub-clause 18.1.

470 *Bremer Handelsgesellschaft v Vanden Avenne-Izegem* (1978) 2 Lloyds' Reports 109.

471 [1991] 60 BLR 94.

472 *Multiplex Construction (UK) Ltd v Honeywell Control Systems Ltd* [2007] BLR 167 TCC.

473 *Education 4 Ayrshire Ltd v South Ayrshire Council* [2009] CSOH 146.

474 *Obrascon Huarte Lain SA v Her Majesty's Attorney General for Gibraltar* (n 48).

475 The decision was upheld on other grounds by the Court of Appeal at [2015] BLR 521.

flexibility shown in *Obrascon*, English law is rigorous in its enforcement of time-bar provisions, even to the extent that an entire claim is lost.

Dispute Resolution

3.346 Most properly drafted construction contracts, including all the major UK standard forms, contain procedural mechanisms for the resolution of disputes.

3.347 These dispute resolution mechanisms do not, by definition, operate until there is a dispute between the parties. It is, therefore, an important preliminary question under English law as to when a dispute comes into existence; when it is said to "crystallize". The courts have developed guiding principles[476] to help decide the point in time at which the dispute crystallizes. The existence or notification of a claim, for example, will not automatically give rise to a dispute until it is clear that the claim is not accepted, which could be by express rejection, implication, silence or inaction.

3.348 Once a dispute has arisen, if the parties cannot resolve it by themselves, they may seek the involvement of a third party neutral. Mediation has become a major component of construction dispute resolution in the UK. It is included as a preliminary stage of settlement of Disputes in the JCT contracts,[477] which obliges each Party to "give serious consideration to any request by the other to refer the matter to mediation". There is little benefit in making mediation mandatory, which this does not, because mediation requires a co-operative approach to have any chance of succeeding. Having said that, if the parties end up by proceeding to litigation, they will be expected by the court to have explored the possibility of early resolution of the dispute.

3.349 The specialist Technology and Construction Court,[478] which is part of the High Court in England and Wales, strongly encourages this in its Pre-Action Protocol, applicable to "all construction and engineering disputes (including professional negligence claims against architects, engineers, and quantity surveyors)" which states[479] that a major objective is "to make appropriate attempts to resolve the matter without starting proceedings and, in particular, to consider the use of an appropriate form of ADR in order to do so". Mediation can be attempted at any time up to and even during litigation or arbitration, but it is especially associated with early opportunities to avoid the expansion of the dispute and associated expenditure.

3.350 While mediation, though strongly encouraged, is ultimately a matter of choice for the parties, adjudication is not. Under the HGCR Act,[480] most construction contracts must give all parties the right to refer a dispute to adjudication and the other party/parties are taken to have consented. If a contract did not contain provision for adjudication, its dispute

---

476 *Amec Civil Engineering Ltd v Secretary of State for Transport* [2005] EWCA Civ 291.

477 JCT SBC/Q, Section 9.1.

478 The Technology and Construction Court ("TCC") was established in 1873 and originally known as the office of the Official Referee. The Referee's task was to hear cases involving technical and detailed issues that could not be tried competently by a judge and/or jury. By the 1920s, most of the Referees matters entailed construction and engineering disputes. The Referees, most of whom were King's or Queen's Counsel, sat in the High Court, albeit as circuit judges. In 2004 it was decided that all cases in the TCC in London should be heard exclusively by High Court judges, though that is not always possible.

479 Alternative Dispute Resolution, such as mediation.

480 As amended by the Local Democracy Economic Development and Construction Act 2009.

resolution provisions would be replaced in their entirety[481] by what are, in effect, statutory implied terms. The adjudicator, unlike a mediator, is appointed to give a decision, not to produce a settlement, which is binding on the parties on an interim basis, that is, unless and until overturned by the decision of an arbitrator or a court.

3.351 The contract provisions must enable reference of a dispute to adjudication by a party at any time. Appointment and referral must take place within 7 days of notice being given and the adjudicator must reach a decision with 28 days (or extended period by agreement). The adjudicator will/must act fairly, but will have the power to act inquisitorially in ascertaining facts and law. To a large extent, the courts have been willing to give summary enforcement to adjudicators' decisions, meaning that they have to be complied with by the parties pending any further reference to an arbitration or litigation. Attempts have been made by parties to challenge adjudicators' decisions or resist enforcement on a number of grounds, including error as to law, facts or calculations, or procedural failings. Almost all have been unsuccessful, except where there have been serious breaches of the rules of natural justice, or a lack of jurisdiction of some kind. Statutory adjudication is seen by most commentators as having had some success in making dispute resolution in construction swifter and more efficient, despite ongoing concerns about the quality of some adjudicators and about certain procedural flaws, which the Local Democracy Economic Development and Construction Act 2009 partially addressed.

3.352 One of the principal effects of having statutory adjudication since 1998[482] has been a perceived reduction in the volume of construction arbitration, which is very likely, although impossible to prove statistically. Nevertheless, arbitration is still utilized by the construction industry; even where statutory adjudication applies, there is still the need for a final process of decision-making. Under the JCT contracts, for example, arbitrations in relation to termination[483] "shall be conducted in accordance with the JCT 2016 edition of the Construction Industry Model Arbitration Rules (CIMAR)". Arbitration is also often specified in bespoke construction contracts as the final method of dispute resolution, usually after earlier stages, which may include ADR and which must include adjudication where the HGCR Act applies. Arbitration under English law is governed by the Arbitration Act 1996 and construction arbitrators are appointed by professional bodies such as the Chartered Institute of Arbitrators or the Royal Institution of Chartered Surveyors, or by agreement between the parties.

Construction Law Issues Specific to English Law

The Construction (Design and Management) Regulations and Related Legislation

3.353 Historically, few English statutes have been exclusively concerned with construction law. Most of the substance of English construction law consists of decisions of the courts and statutes which apply to all contracts. Construction contracts may be affected by the Sale of Goods Act 1979, the Supply of Goods and Services Act 1982 (for

481 See *Spring Ltd v London Borough of Camden* [2012] BLR 83 and Sir Peter Coulson, *Coulson on Construction Adjudication* (3rd ed 2015) para 4.12.

482 The HGCR Act 1996 came into force on 1 April 1998.

483 JCT SBC/Q, Section 8.

business to business contracts), the Consumer Rights Act 2015 (for consumer contracts) the Unfair Contract Terms Act 1977, the Contracts (Rights of Third Parties) Act 1999 and the Limitation Act 1980: The last named governs tort actions also. None of these are construction-specific; the same applies to procurement in the public sector and utilities under the Public Contracts Regulations 2015 and the Utilities Regulations 2015.

3.354 The few exceptions are, of course, very significant. The Building Regulations 2010 (known widely as the "Building Regulations"), delegated legislation made under the Building Act 1984, constitute a regime for the control of construction standards, especially in relation to health and safety of those occupying and using buildings. Approval must be obtained from a local government authority (or from a private inspector acting in its place) for the design drawings and calculations and then for the implementation of the design by the construction of the building. The local authority has extensive powers to ensure the removal of non-compliant work or dangerous structures.

3.355 The Construction (Design and Management) Regulations 2015 ("CDM Regulations"), known in the industry as the CDM Regulations, are important in the execution of construction work in two main respects:

- The creation of statutory roles with specific responsibilities;
- The imposition of standards to protect health and safety during the construction process.

3.356 The CDM Regulations identify certain key participants in the design and construction processes such as "principal designer" and "principal contractor" and allocate to them significant obligations in planning, management, monitoring and co-ordination of matters relating to health and safety. The CDM Regulations also set out general standards relating to safety and a range of construction site risks. The client, principal designer, principal contractor, designers and contractors all have responsibilities to maintain these standards. Liability under the Building Regulations and CDM Regulations is statutory; the purpose is regulatory and the sanctions are punitive, such as fines.

3.357 The CDM Co-ordinator (under the previous regime) is replaced by "Principal Designer" for the identification, planning, managing, monitoring and co-ordination of pre-construction health and safety[484] – the primary responsibility being managing health and safety on site. The client is required to appoint a principal designer (and principal contractor) for any project where more than one contractor is involved[485] before the construction phase.[486] The principal designer duty extends to liaising with the principal contractor through the construction phase and ensuring that all designers comply with their general duties under the CDM 2015 Regulations.[487] If the client fails to appoint a principal designer or principal contractor in these circumstances, statutory liability for the performance of the principal designer's obligations falls upon the client.[488]

3.358 The CDM Regulations have shifted greater responsibility onto the client which includes: notification of the project particulars and confirming that they are aware of

484 CDM Regulations, reg 11(1).
485 Ibid., reg 5(1).
486 Ibid., reg 5(2).
487 Ibid., reg 11(5).
488 Ibid., reg 5(3) and (4).

their duties;[489] appointing a principal designer and principal contractor;[490] ensuring duty holders comply with their duties under the CDM 2015 Regulations;[491] providing the pre-construction information;[492] ensuring that the minimum health and safety standards are maintained on site throughout the works;[493] ensuring that the construction phase health and safety plan is drawn up by the principal contractor;[494] and ensuring that a health and safety file is produced by the principal designer.[495] The client is permitted to delegate this responsibility, but still remains liable for compliance.

3.359 The primary duty of the principal contractor is to plan, manage and monitor the construction phase and coordinate matters relating to health and safety during the construction phase to ensure that, so far as is reasonably practicable, construction work is carried out without risks to health or safety.[496] Additionally, all contractors are required to plan, manage and monitor construction work, to ensure that their works are carried out without risk to health and safety.[497]

3.360 The JCT contracts have provisions covering the mandatory obligations required under the CDM Regulation wherein each party undertakes to the other, in relation to the Works and site, to comply with the applicable CDM Regulations.[498]

3.361 Commercial responsibility for construction standards is normally a matter of contract, governed by the common law principles set out above and by general statutes. An exception is the Defective Premises Act 1972, which imposes duties upon designers and builders to achieve minimum standards, but these are strictly limited to dwellings (i.e., houses and flats). The duty is to ensure that construction is carried out in a workman-like manner with proper materials and that design work is done in a professional manner, so that the completed dwelling will be fit for human habitation. This provides a remedy to the employer and to any person who acquires a legal or equitable interest in the dwelling against contractors, sub-contractors, developers and construction professionals, including architects and engineers.

Housing Grant, Construction and Regeneration Act ("HGCR Act") and The Scheme for Construction Contract (England and Wales) Regulation 1998 ("Construction Scheme")

3.362 The most important construction-specific statute in the English legal system is the Housing Grants Construction and Regeneration Act 1996 (the HGCR Act), as amended by the Local Democracy Economic Development and Construction Act 2009. This statute, known in the industry as the HGCR Act, was passed as a result of Sir Michael Latham's landmark report "Constructing the Team" (1994), which identified lengthy disputes and

489 Ibid., reg 6(2).
490 Ibid., reg 5.
491 Ibid., reg 4(6).
492 Ibid., reg 4(4).
493 Ibid., reg 4(3).
494 Ibid., reg 4(5)(a).
495 Ibid., reg 4(5)(b).
496 Ibid., reg 13(1).
497 Ibid., reg 15(2).
498 JCT SBC/Q, sub-clause 3.23.

obstacles to cash-flow as major problems in the UK construction industry. The HGCR Act was passed, therefore, to deal more efficiently with disputes and to improve payment practices.

3.363 The HGCR Act applies to a wide range of agreements within the definition of a "construction contract"[499] for the carrying out of "construction operations", itself covering a wide range of activities,[500] including construction, alteration, repair, maintenance, extension, demolition, but subject to a number of exclusions (see para 3.181 and infra on application of the Act).

3.364 A construction contract is required to comply with the HGCR Act. If it does not do so, the Scheme for Construction Contracts (England and Wales) Regulations 1998 ("Construction Scheme")[501] applies and its provisions prevail over the parties' non-compliant agreement. Thus, if there are no provisions in the contract, the provisions of the Construction Scheme will be implied into the contract.

3.365 The effect of deploying this default scheme varies according to the non-compliance of payment provisions or adjudication provisions. If part of the payment provision fails to comply with the HGCR Act, then the complying part remains in effect and the non-compliant part is replaced by the relevant part under the Construction Scheme. If a payment provision is missing in part then the relevant part of the Construction Scheme will be implied into the contract. By contrast, non-compliance of a particular adjudication provision in a contract will cause all adjudication provisions to be replaced with the full set of HGCR Act adjudication provisions.

3.366 Since the HGCR Act came into force in 1998 in the UK, a number of comparable legislative schemes have been introduced in other common law countries. The Australian states and territories, starting with New South Wales,[502] have all enacted controls over payment and adjudication of construction disputes. The scope of adjudication is narrower in Australia, being restricted to payment disputes. New Zealand,[503] Singapore,[504] and Malaysia[505] have all taken an approach similar, though not identical, to that in Australia. More recently, Ireland's statute came into force[506] and in South Africa amendments to existing legislation[507] are being used to introduce similar payment controls and adjudication provisions.

Statutory Adjudication

3.367 Under the HGCR Act's adjudication requirements, any party must have the right to refer any dispute under the construction contract for decision by an adjudicator, who must reach a decision within 28 days.[508] The adjudicator's decision is binding on the parties and must be immediately complied with, being enforceable by summary judgment in the courts. The decision remains binding unless successfully challenged in arbitration or litigation.

499 HGCR Act s104.
500 Ibid., s105.
501 The Construction Scheme is secondary legislation made under the HGCR Act.
502 The Building and Construction Industry Security of Payment Act 1999.
503 Construction Contracts Act 2002.
504 Building and Construction Industry Security of Payment Act 2005.
505 Construction Industry Payment and Adjudication Act.
506 Construction Contracts Act 2013.
507 Construction Industry Board Development Act 2000.
508 Or 42, if extended.

Payment Terms

3.368 The payment provisions of the HGCR Act are primarily to assist cash-flow of contractors (under main contracts) and sub-contractors (under sub-contracts). There is a right to stage payments (instalments) even if the price is expressed as a lump sum.[509] There must be an adequate contractual mechanism for determining what payments become due and when.[510] There are strict controls on withholding of payment and procedures for doing so.[511] If payment is not made, there is a right to suspend performance.[512] Clauses by which payment is made conditional on the paying party receiving funds (pay when paid clauses) are invalid.[513]

3.369 The procedure for payment under the Construction Scheme is as follows:

(a) the payee may claim interim instalments every 28 days ("relevant period");[514] (on most contracts)
(b) interim payments are to be made within 7 days following the relevant period or when claim is submitted;[515]
(c) final payment is to be made 30 days following completion of the works or when claim is submitted;[516]
(d) the final date for making any payment is a maximum of 17 days;[517]
(e) payer must give payment notice within 5 days before payment date specifying payment they propose to make, what payment relates to and basis of calculation;[518]
(f) any intention to withhold payment must be notified within 7 days of the final date for payment.[519]

3.370 The Construction Scheme prohibits any conditional payment provision ("pay-when-paid") under a contract and, unless parties have agreed other payment terms, the payment provisions in the Construction Scheme will apply in lieu of all existing payment provisions.[520]

Constructing the Team (1994) – The Latham Report

3.371 In 1994 the final report by Sir Michael Latham, Constructing the Team, was published[521] ("Latham Report"). The Latham Report was commissioned by the UK government and industry stakeholders following the recession of 1989 which had a significant impact on the construction industry.

509 HGCR Act, s109.
510 Ibid., s110.
511 Ibid., s111.
512 Ibid., s112.
513 Ibid., s113.
514 Construction Scheme, regs 2 and 12.
515 Ibid., reg 4.
516 Ibid., reg 5.
517 Ibid., reg 8.
518 Ibid., reg 9.
519 Ibid., reg 10.
520 Ibid., reg 11.
521 Joint Review of Procurement and Contractual Arrangements in the United Kingdom Construction Industry, Final Report. Published by HMSO (1994).

3.372 The Latham Report made 30 recommendations to change industry practices and increase efficiency. The report emphasized removal of the adversarial ethos prevalent in the industry by moving towards adjudication for expedient resolution of disputes and implementing partnering arrangements between parties in construction. The Latham Report paved the way for a mandatory right to refer disputes to adjudication in English construction contracts with Parliament passing the HGCR Act.

3.373 The Latham Report favoured partnering between contractual parties and also went on to suggest that the (then recent) 1st Edition of the NEC contract was the standard form of contract closest to fulfilling many of the principles and requirements of best practice.

3.374 Recommendations arising out of the Latham Report included:

(a) partnering should be used more, to encourage establishment of long-term contracting arrangement;
(b) the NEC contract ought to be adopted more widely in the industry as a less adversarial form of contract;
(c) greater standardization and better interlocking of construction documents;
(d) legislation should be introduced, preventing set-off and requiring compulsory latent defects insurance;
(e) avoidance of conflict and quicker dispute resolution with adjudication as the normal method of dispute resolution;
(f) parties in the supply chain fairly dealing with each other and encouraging an atmosphere of mutual co-operation with allocation of risk to the party best able to carry it.

National Construction Law and International Forms

3.375 The FIDIC contract forms in particular and other international forms have historic English common law influence. However, some adjustment will usually be necessary to cpmply with current legislation before they can be used on a project in the UK.

3.376 The adjudication procedure under the HGCR Act is mandatory on any project in England and Wales. If parties are using FIDIC, the disputes resolution procedure will not comply with the HGCR Act and where parties have not included any particular conditions changing this, the procedure in the Construction Scheme will replace the whole adjudication sub-clause. FIDIC provides that if an engineer determination is disputed, that dispute may be referred to the Disputes Adjudication Board (now DAAB in the 2017 contract) for deciding upon and issuing a decision within 84 days. This is inconsistent with the adjudication procedure under the HGCR Act requiring the adjudicator to decide within 28 days of the referral notice.

3.377 The FIDIC subcontract contains a pay-when-paid provision which conflicts with the HGCR Act. Under the FIDIC subcontract the contractor can defer payment to a subcontractor if the engineer has not certified the amount or, if so, has not been paid by the employer. This is a condition payment provision prohibited under the HGCR Act.

3.378 Where English law is the governing law, design is subject to the lower standard of reasonable skill and care, not fitness for purpose. Under English common law, if the contractor is also performing design, a fit for purpose obligation might be implied unless expressly excluded in the contract. The contractor performing design under a FIDIC contract would have to try to remove the fitness for purpose obligation, stating that design would be subject to reasonable skill and care, in order to confirm this.

3.379 Under the FIDIC contract, both parties exclude liability for loss of profits and loss of contract. As stated above in para 5.296, loss of profit is considered by the English courts as a direct loss recoverable for breach of contract. If the employer decided to omit parts of the works, the contractor will be unable to claim loss of profits because of the limitation of liability clause.

Disclaimer

The material for this chapter was originally prepared in the period 2017–2019.

CHAPTER 4

German Law

Wolfgang Breyer

Contents

DOI: 10.4324/9781315671376-4

Procurement and Tendering

4.1 Similar to many other countries Germany does not have specific laws dedicated to procurement and tendering for private construction works,[1] any issues in relation to procurement and tendering are purely governed between the parties and subject to contract law. For procurement and tendering of public construction works in Germany, substantial laws and regulations exist; not only does German law apply, but also European public procurement law. The hierarchy of public procurement law in Germany is as follows:

i. EU Directives – both EU Directives and decisions of the European Court of Justice ("EU Laws") apply and are incorporated into German law;
ii. German Act Against Restraints on Competition (GWB) – governs who qualifies as a public entity and the legal recourse available in case of award infringement for contracts with a value above the relevant threshold;[2]
iii. the Ordinance on the Award of Public Contracts (VgV) – applies for contracts where the threshold values provided for in the GWB are exceeded and outlines applicable sections national contracting rules (i.e., Award of Public Works Contracts Rules: VOB/A, VOL/A and VOF). In particular, the VOB/A is applicable through §113 sentence 1 GWB and §2 VgV for such contracts over the stated thresholds.

Which procurement rule(s) and to what extent it/they apply, depends on the contracting entity, the contract values and if any exceptional circumstances allow otherwise.

4.2 Public contracting entities are divided as follows: State contracting entities; state-controlled entities; contracting entities performing state functions; and sector entities. State contracting entities have the most restrictive application of procurement law by virtue of being part of the state, for example federal and state governments or municipalities.[3] State-controlled entities are legal entities, both public and private, which perform non-commercial functions and are financed or managed under state control.[4]

4.3 The contract value will determine whether calls for tender are required to be pan-European, domestic, or if no call for tenders must take place at all. All work forming the contract (or intended) must be included in calculating the contract value.[5]

4.4 Under certain exceptional circumstances, even contracts above the threshold may not be required to be submitted for tender even though they may be public contracts.[6]

---

1 That is to say, consumer to business or business-to-business construction works which do not involve a public entity.

2 See §97 et. seq. GWB.

3 BVerfG, NJW 2006, 3701 para 4, 64 et seq. Note that contract value threshold determines which rules apply, i.e., for values above the threshold Contracting Rules for the Award of Public Works Contracts (VOB/A) and the Contracting Rules for the Award of Contracts for Freelance Services (VOF) apply whereas contract values below the threshold are governed by German budget law.

4 For contracts with a value above the threshold VOB/A and VOL/A apply, whereas contracts with a value below the threshold are not subject to public procurement laws.

5 GWB §§106 (1), (2), 97 et seq.; *M. Kau*, "§106 GWB", in Burgi, M. and Dreher, M. (eds.), *Beck'scher Vergaberechtskommentar*, vol. 1, 3rd edition, Munich, C.H. Beck Verlag, 2017, GWB §106, margin 1.

6 Exceptional circumstances include international organization contracts, contracts related to state secrets, awarding contracts to public contracting entities having state monopoly and land purchase or lease contracts, GWB §§107–109.

Nature of the Construction Contract

4.5 The German BGB does not contain any *numerus clausus* (imposed limit) regarding the nature of contracts. There is reference to special forms of contracts such as contracts for the sale of goods, gift contracts or leases;[7] however, these forms are not mandatory, and parties can enter into any form, which may be entirely different from those or they may combine parts from the various types if contracts. For instance, a construction contract may contain elements of both a works contract (*Werkvertrag*)[8] and sales contract regarding materials (*Kaufvertrag*).[9]

4.6 Construction contracts in Germany are considered contracts for works ("*Werkvertrag*"). Under a Werkvertrag the contractor is obliged to perform the agreed works free from defects and in turn is paid the agreed remuneration[10] upon the employer's acceptance of the works. Unlike the common law, the contractor is obliged to produce a particular result/success of the constructed works (i.e., the works are fit for purpose).[11] It is also important to note that professional consultant agreements (i.e., engineering and architect services) are considered contracts for works as well, thus the consultant is required to perform its "works" fit for purpose; this being completely contrary to common law (English Common Law (4.199)) understanding of engineers and architects performing their services with reasonable skill and care.[12]

4.7 One other form of contract worthy of mention is the services contract ("*Dienstvertrag*"), where the service provider is only obliged to perform the agreed service, rather than being obliged to produce a particular success.[13] Liability is incurred if the services provided are not in accordance with the contract and the failure of the service provider was based on, at a minimum, negligence.[14] This is more typical to the common law understanding of engineering and architect services and covered in detail at Section 5.199, Consultant's Role and Liability and closer to the concept of reasonable skill and care in its result.

4.8 Aside from the construction contract, typical examples of a Werkvertrag include supply and installation contracts, repair and furnishing contracts and transportation contracts.[15] Making the distinction between a *Werkvertrag* and *Dienstvertrag* is particularly important because this will determine duty of care the contractor owes to employer and consequently defects liability and limitation periods.[16] Where parties are in dispute as

---

7 Section VII, Book Two, §§433-853 BGB, Particular Obligations (*Einzelne Schulderverhaeltnisse*).

8 BGB §§631 et seq.

9 BGB §§433 et seq.

10 The customers obligation to pay the remuneration is set forth in BGB §632.

11 BGB §631 (1).

12 The issue of whether architects providing services fall under a Werkvertrag have been thoroughly debated and decided on, refer to BGH, NJW 1960, 431 (431 et seq); BGH, NJW 1982, 438 (439 et seq); in contrast to Supreme Court of the German Reich [86] RGZ 75 (76 et seq).

13 BGB §611 (1).

14 Reflecting the general requirements for damages, BGB §§280, 276: Negligence, deliberate, and gross negligence.

15 W. Voit, 631 BGB in Bamberger, G., Roth, H., Hau, W., and Poseck, R. (eds.), *BeckOK BGB*, 49th edition, Munich, C.H. Beck Verlag, 2019, BGB §631, margin 21, 22, 44.

16 Defects liability period of two to five years for a Werkvertrag against limitation period of three years to claim for negligent services under a Dienstvertrag (BGB §634a and BGB §§611, 195 (1) respectively).

to the nature of the contract, the standard rules for contract interpretation will apply.[17] Making the distinction is often not without difficulty and has been the subject of numerous court decisions and scholarly debate. Certain positions or rules have been determined by the courts in drawing the distinction between the nature of contracts, for instance, evaluating the likelihood of achieving the desired results/success of the work or service, that is to say, the higher the risk of failure the more likely it is a contract for services.[18] Scholars have also provided commentary on making the distinction, for instance, if any collateral duty to maintain safety is shifted to another party in order to secure the achievement of result/success then presumably the parties intended to enter into a works contract.[19]

4.9 There is also a third form of contract relevant to construction dealing with the supply of movable goods to be produced or manufactured and incorporated in the works ("*Werklieferungsvertrag*"). In this instance, generally the laws relating to sale of goods apply.[20]

4.10 Due to the systematic interpretation of the German Civil Code, all general provisions (BGB §§1–432) apply to a contract for labor and work accordingly, if there is no special provision in BGB §§631–650v. Additionally, assuming the parties validly agree to incorporate the provisions of the VOB/B into the contract, they will apply as standard terms in major construction contracts, since the provisions of the BGB, which equally apply to a contract between a tailor and its customer, cannot satisfy the interests of parties to a complex construction contract.

Procurement and Contract Regulations for Construction Services Parts B and C (VOB/B And VOB/C)

4.11 The procurement and contract regulations for construction services (VOB) are divided into three parts. Part A concerns itself with procurement, whereas parts B and C are concerned with the construction contract and the focus of this section.

4.12 The first edition of the VOB, published in 1926, was a result of the significant population growth and technological advancement of the 19th century. The intent of the national procurement committee (*Reichsverdingungsausschuss* now *Verdingungsausschuss*) in establishing the VOB was to provide for a more balanced[21] and harmonized[22] system of awarding and drafting contracts in order to give weight to the peculiarities of construction contracts.[23] This was done in particular, to bridge the gaps in the German law for work and

17 BGH, NJW 2013, 3022 (3023).

18 BGH, NJW 2002, 3323 (3324).

19 *A.C. Wietfeld*, Die Rolle von Verkehrssicherungspflichten bei der Abgrenzung von Dienst- und Werkverträgen, Neue Juristische Wochenschrift, vol. 67, no. 17, 2014, p. 1206 (1207 et seq.); contrary: BGH, NJW 2013, 3022 (3023).

20 BGB §433 et seq., BGB §650 Sentences 1 and 3 BGB; *J. Busche*, §650 BGB, in Henssler, J. (ed.), *Münchener Kommentar zum BGB*, vol. 5/1, 7th edition, Munich, C.H. Beck Verlag, 2018, BGB §650, margin 1. For the supply of building materials see: *S. Leupertz*, Baustofflieferung und Baustoffhandel: Im juristischen Niemandsland, Baurecht, vol. 37, no. 10, 2006, p. 1648.

21 *C. von Rintelen*, Einleitung, in Kapellmann, K., and Messerschmidt, B. (eds.), *VOB-Kommentar*, 6th edition, Munich, C.H. Beck Verlag, 2018, VOB/B, margin 1; *T. Schneider*, "Einleitung", in Kapellmann/ Messerschmidt (2018), VOB/A, margin 5.

22 *S. Leupertz and M. von Wietersheim*, Einleitung, in Leupertz, S., and von Wietersheim, M. (eds.), VOB Teile A und B, 20th edition, Cologne, Werner Verlag, 2017, Einleitung margin 7.

23 *Leupertz* and *von Wietersheim* (2017) margin 53.

service contracts (*Werkvertragsrecht*), which were often either unsuitable or inchoate for the purposes of construction law.[24]

4.13 The VOB/B and VOB/C have been drafted to be used in conjunction with one another. This is plainly evident by VOB/B §1 (1) Sentence 2, where it states that "the General Technical Terms and Conditions for Construction Services (VOB/C) also apply as part of the contract". The VOB/B deals with general contractual terms such as payment, liability of the parties, deadlines, acceptance, termination and the like. The VOB/C on the other hand focuses on the contractor's performance obligations with regard to technical aspects of the contract.

4.14 In 2018, the German legislature, recognizing the need for regulations specific to the construction industry, enacted a new construction law which was designed to more precisely and effectively deal with the issues particular to the construction industry[25] than it had under the German BGB at that time. Additionally, for the first time under German law there was a clear definition of what a construction contract is.[26] The new law, however, strays from the widely used and accepted VOB/B in several areas.[27] The VOB/B, it must be noted, is not law, but rather a set of general terms and conditions for construction contracts,[28] which may also lead to issues of compliance with the General Terms and Conditions Act (GTCA).[29]

4.15 Given that the new law regarding construction contracts under the BGB diverges from the VOB/B in several aspects; for example, remuneration under VOB/B §2 building on the original basis of calculation in contrast to BGB §650 c (1), which only entitles the contractor to remuneration for actually incurred costs,[30] it begs the question if the VOB/B can survive, and if so, in what form, or if it will be supplanted entirely the new law. So far, there have been no concrete answers to these questions. However, when given the opportunity, the national procurement committee, which is the body responsible for amending and modifying the VOB, has declined to act and has taken a more cautious approach. Whether the VOB/B will endure in its current form or require a wholesale overhaul, will likely be left for the courts to decide.[31]

Different Types of Contract (Unit Price, Lump Sum, etc.)

4.16 There are a number of different types of construction contracts in Germany can be usefully divided on the basis of categories of payment and procurement.

---

24 Ibid at 7.

25 Bundestag Drucksache 18/11437, 08.03.2017.

26 BGB §650a.

27 For example, compare the right to order changes: BGB §650b vs. VOB/B §1 (3) and 1 (4) Sentence 1.

28 *von Rintelen* (2018), Einleitung, margin 38.

29 For more on the GTCA see 4.140 et. seq. below.

30 *S. Althaus* and *M. Kattenbusch*, §650c Vergütungsanpassung bei Anordnungen nach §650b Absatz 2 in Leupertz, S., Preussner, M., and Sienz, C. (eds.), BeckOK Bauvertragsrecht, 2018, Munich, C.H. Beck Verlag, BGB §650c, margin 159. More cf. *W. Langen*, "Guter Preis bleibt gut, schlechter Preis wird gut": Folgen der AGB-Unwirksamkeit der VOB/B nach neuem Recht, Neue Zeitschrift für Baurecht und Vergaberecht, vol. 20 no. 1, 2019, pp. 10 et seq.; *I.* Oberhauser, §650 b I BGB – Änderungen des Vertrags durch Einvernehmen der Parteien, Neue Zeitschrift für Baurecht und Vergaberecht, vol. 20 no. 1, 2019, pp. 3 et seq.

31 See BGH, NJW 2020, 337.

Unit Price Contract (Einheitspreisvertrag)[32]

4.17 The unit price contract in Germany is similar to the FIDIC Red Book contract (i.e., remeasurement contract). The employer prepares the bill of quantities itemising and describing the individual works. The contractor then submits unit prices for each item in the bill of quantities with the total taken as the contract price. After completion, the actual works performed are measured and multiplied by the unit price. The parties are free to stipulate how the contractor must perform the measurement (*Aufmaß*) of actual works. If the contract fails to stipulate this procedure, the relevant provision outlined in the VOB/C for the type of works will apply.

Lump Sum Contract (Pauschalpreisvertrag)

4.18 Generally, turnkey construction projects in Germany are undertaken on the basis of lump sum contracts.[33] In German practice, lump sum contracts are further categorized as detailed lump sum contracts (*Detailpauschalvertrag*) or global lump sum contracts (*Globalpauschalpreisvertrag*).[34]

Detailed Lump Sum Contract (Detailpauschalvertrag)

4.19 In a detailed lump sum contract, the component works of the building contract are conclusively itemized in great detail in the specifications, drawings and progress plans.[35] The employer also specifies assumptions about the quantities to be provided for each of the items in a bill of quantities. The contractor, therefore, bears the risk for the accuracy of the measurement of the pre-estimated quantities. However, should the quantities necessary for the completion of the project vary from those pre-estimates by more than 10% they may be subject to a price adjustment.[36] Generally, however, and subject to the foregoing, the contractor will bear the risk of an increase in the quantities, and will not be entitled to compensation[37] for those additional amounts required for the fulfilment of the contract.[38] However, should the actual quantities necessary for the completion of the works be less than those originally calculated as the basis of the lump sum, the contractor receives the benefit. Any additional work, required by the employer for the completion of the works in accordance with the contract, but not included in the bill of quantities, is not covered by the lump sum and must be compensated separately according to BGB §650b, even if the definition of functional completion remains unchanged.

4.20 A distinction should, therefore, be made between variation in quantities from what was planned and what was actually required, and fluctuations in quantities resulting from

32 Cf. *Busche* (2018), BGB §631, margin 91.

33 *J. Glöckner*, Der Bauträgervertrag, in Kleine-Möller, N., Merl, H., and Glöckner, J. (eds.), *Handbuch des privaten Baurechts*, 5th edition, Munich, C.H. Beck Verlag, 2014, Part I, Chapter 1, §4, margin 139; *R. Schröder*, Die statistische Realität des Bauprozesses, Neue Zeitschrift für Baurecht und Vergaberecht, vol. 9, no. 1, 2008, p. 1 (2).

34 *Kapellmann*(2018), VOB/A §4, margin 28; *S. Leupertz*, Grundfragen der Vergütung, in Messerschmidt, B., and Voit, W. (eds.), *Privates Baurecht*, 3rd edition, Munich, C.H. Beck Verlag, 2018, Chap. K, margin 18.

35 Ibid., Para 140.

36 VOB/B §2 (3).

37 *Glöckner* (2014) margins. 140 et seq.; *Kapellmann*_(2018), VOB/A §4, margin 34.

38 *Glöckner* (2014) margins. 140 et seq.; *Kapellmann* (2018), VOB/A §4, margin 34.

variations or change orders from the employer, and whether such change orders were within the scope of the contract.

Global Lump Sum Contract (Globalpauschalpreisvertrag)

4.21 In a global lump sum contract, the contractor prepares his bid based on his estimation of the total cost of performing the works. The contractor, therefore, bears all the risk of not only of quantities, but also of ensuring that the works achieve the function/purpose desired by the employer. Should the contractor err in his estimation, he will receive no additional remuneration beyond the agreed lump sum as long as the employer does not request or order a modification to the definition of the functional completion of the works.[39] Therefore, the contractor assumes the risk of quantities, but also may have to undertake work not originally specified by the employer and not included in his global lump sum calculation. This risk can generally be managed in either a basic or complex global lump sum contract.

4.22 A basic global lump sum contract is created by adding an individually agreed and thus effective "clause of completeness" to a detailed lump sum contract.[40] By virtue of this legal agreement, the contractor assumes the calculation of design risk, but only to the extent that it would reasonably agree to it, taking into account the monetary consequences of divergences between the specification of the works and what is actually required for fully functional works.[41]This does not apply to works, which, outside the recognisable design specifications, result from individual user or site-specific requirements. Also, in accordance with general principles of German contract law, the contractor is generally not liable for evident errors in the design provided by the employer. The additional works required as a result of such errors are, therefore, not covered by the scope of works any more than additional expenses arising from change orders of the employer.[42]

4.23 In a complex global lump sum contract, the employer outlines only the function/purpose of the works and does not devise a detailed bill of quantities. The specifications consist merely of an explanation of the objectives of the project and a basic description of the works tendered for.[43] Quantities, detailed specifications of the works, and designs of any kind are not provided by the employer. The contractor takes on full design responsibility and it, therefore, has to ensure the functional completion of the works and undertake all that is necessary to achieve those ends without receiving any extra remuneration.[44]

---

39 *Busche* (2018), BGB §631, margin 94.

40 *Kapellmann* (2018), VOB/B §2, margin 246.

41 This method of contracting has been seen to be vulnerable to exploitation by employers, who on occasion will use a bill of quantities as a basis for a global lump sum contract, allocating all risks related to quantities and incomplete Employer's Requirements (including defective design) to the contractor by referring to the detailed description of the works provided by the bill of quantities. As might be expected, this approach has been a source of many disputes.

42 *Kapellmann* (2018), VOB/B §2, margin 265.

43 Ibid., at margin 267.

44 BeckOK VOB/B, 20. Ed. 1.7.2015. §2 para 7, margins. 23, 25.

Partnering Contracts (Partnering Vertrag)

4.24 Thus far, partnering contracts have seen relatively little uptake in Germany.[45] However, the collapse of several large German construction companies resulted in the first movements in the German construction market towards alliance contracts. In recent years, the success and increasing acceptance in the UK of alternative contracting forms such as PPC2000 and FAC-1 and in the US of Integrated Project Delivery (IPD) has led to a renewed push in Germany to develop alliance contracting models. These initiatives have come predominantly from four different directions: Contractors' initiatives, Initiative Teambuilding,[46] research undertaken by the Federal Ministry for the Environment, Nature Conservation, Building and Nuclear Safety,[47] and the Deutscher Baugerichtstag.[48] As a result of this research several pilot projects based on IPD have been initiated including Kongresshotel Hafencity in Hamburg and Spring Park Valley in Frankfurt. Additionally, an edition of FAC-1 has been developed for use in Germany.[49]

4.25 The collapse of construction companies in the 1980s resulted from a phenomenon similar to what took place in England prior to the release of the Latham Report, variously described as "cut-throat bidding" and "suicidal practices".[50] As a result, some of the largest German contractors recognized the need for reform with regard to the existing contracting models for large and complex projects and took it upon themselves to design alternative contracting methods in order to minimize conflict at the development and management stages of these projects and to implement these projects more effectively and more amicably; for example, PreFair by Hochtief,[51] established in 2002, teamconcept by Züblin,[52] established in 1994, i.volution by Bilfinger SE,[53] established in 2000, Smart Construction by Zech Bau,[54] renamed in 2018, Bauteam by Kondor Wessels Bouw Berlin,[55] date of establishment not discernible.

Other Contracts

4.26 In addition to the contracts discussed above, there are certain contracts or pricing schemes which are seen less often in Germany.[56] These include guaranteed maximum price (GMP) and cost-plus contracts.[57]

---

45 *T. Richter*, in Messerschmidt/Voit (2018), I. Chap. D, margin 258.

46 See www.initiative-teambuilding.de/ (accessed 12 July 2019).

47 See www.bundesbaublatt.de/news/bbb_Reform_Bundesbau_Bessere_Kosten-_Termin-_und_Qualitaetssicherheit_bei_2551595.html (accessed 12 July 2019).

48 See Thesenpapier 7. Deutscher Baugerichtstag, 4./5. Mai 2018, pp. 64 et seq.

49 The German version of FAC-1 is available at: https://shop.reguvis.de/bau-und-architektenrecht-hoai/fac-1-e-book/.

50 *J. Gardiner*, "*Latham's Report: Did it change us?*", www.building.co.uk/focus/lathams-report-did-it-change-us/5069333.article (accessed 12 July 2019). For the discussion of the current situation in Germany, see *G. Bosch* and *K. Zühlke-Robinet*, "*Der Bauarbeitsmarkt: Soziologie und Ökonomie einer Branche*", Frankfurt, Campus Verlag, 2000, pp. 49–57.

51 *W. Breyer* and *S. Leupertz*, How Does Collaborative Procurement Operate in Germany?, in Mosey, D. (ed), Collaborative Construction Procurement and Improved Value, 2019, Chichester, Wiley Blackwell, p. 437.

52 www.zueblin-teamconcept.de/ (accessed 12 July 2019).

53 *Breyer* and *Leupertz* (2019), p. 438.

54 www.smart-construction.de/ (accessed 12 July 2019).

55 *M. Becker*, "Das Bauteamverfahren – erfolgreich und kostengünstig Bauen", 2018, www.dabkon.de/application/files/5715/3682/0219/DaB_II_Becker_Kondor_Wessels.pdf (accessed 12 July 2019).

56 *Leupertz* (2018) margin 32; *Breyer* and *Leupertz* (2019), p. 438.

57 E.g. *teamconcept* by Züblin.

GMP contracts generally reflects the nature of a Global Lump Sum Contract (see above). In a GMP contract the employer usually sets a target budget and the contractor evaluates the project and submits his GMP. Once agreed, barring any change of scope, this amount cannot be exceeded, irrespective of the actual costs incurred. Under such a contract the contractor will get paid based on the actual costs incurred plus a fee. Additionally, there will typically be a mechanism in the contract which incentivizes the contractor to come in under the GMP.[58] For example, the contractor may be entitled to 50% of any savings.

4.27 Cost-plus contracts are generally good options where the project is not clearly defined or designed. With the appropriate mechanisms this can be a good option for the employer, as he will pay only the actual costs incurred plus an agreed fee. This is additionally beneficial to the employer because any cost savings over the course of the project are enjoyed by him.[59] For the contractor it requires only an estimate of the cost of the project and he will not be punished for underbidding. However, such a contract requires openness and transparency between the parties, particularly with regard to the employer's right to inspect the books of the contractor regarding the actual costs.

Design Obligations

4.28 Under German law the contractor is obliged to provide the construction works free from defects and fit for its intended purpose.[60] The same also applies to any design provided by an architect or engineer, that is, the design must be defect free and fit for purpose (this is covered in detail under Consultant Liability).[61] Thus, if the contract is a design and build contract or turnkey contract, such as the FIDIC Yellow and Silver books (respectively) the contractor is responsible for the design. However, for a traditional build, such as the FIDIC Red book, although the contractor is not responsible for procuring the design, he is still obliged to provide the construction works defect free and fit for purpose. As such, if faulty designs have been prepared by the employer's architect and the contractor builds according to those faulty designs, the contractor may still be liable to the employer unless he notifies the employer of his concerns about the plans.[62] The employer may nonetheless be held partly liable for delivering faulty plans to the contractor, thereby relieving the contractor from bearing the full responsibility of the defect(s).[63]

Duty to Warn/Check/Review

4.29 In long-term contractual relationships, parties to the contract gain access to the others legally protected rights. Therefore, the BGB has implemented a general clause for

58 *B. Merkle*, §631, in Reiter, H. et al. (eds.), *beck-online. GROSSKOMMENTAR*, Munich, C.H. Beck Verlag, 01.03.2019, BGB §631, margin 405.

59 *Busche* (2018), BGB §631, margin 98.

60 BGB §633, see above 4.2.

61 BGH NJW 1960, 431 (431).

62 VOB/B §§13 (4); 4 (3); BGB §242 (Treu und Glauben). See also: BGH, NJW 1987, 643; BGH, NJW 1996, 2372; OLG München, NJW-RR 1987, 854; OLG Düsseldorf, NJW-RR 1993, 405; OLG Koblenz, IBR 2005, 13; *H. C. Schwenker* and *F. Heinze*, Die VOB/B 2002, Baurecht, vol. 33, no. 8, 2002, p. 1143 (1149).

63 BGB §645.

all contractual relationships obliging parties to perform under the principle of good faith.[64] Given the potentially long duration of construction contracts, it follows that the legal relationship between the contractor and employer may create obligations to warn contractual partners, check and/or review the works and ensure works are free from any adverse risks (for both parties).[65] The duty to warn is primarily based on the general duty of good faith[66] and other statutory provisions under the BGB,[67] various VOB/B contractual provisions[68] and on any specifically agreed contractual terms. The duty to warn carries on throughout the duration of the contract[69] and may remain in force even after termination or completion.[70]

4.30 The duty to warn may oblige the contractor to inform the employer of any doubt with respect to inspection of services by a third-party.[71] The duty also applies to the employer and may include providing the necessary planning,[72] coordinating numerous contractors,[73] renegotiating in case of a change of circumstances[74] or cooperating and taking such steps as may be necessary for achieving success of works.[75]

4.31 A breach of the duty to warn may lead to liability for the ensuing damages or a reduced claim in accordance with BGB §254 (2) (i.e., apportioning liability). Additionally, this is also true under the VOB/B §13 (3), where a contractor can be liable for defects relating to the description of the Works or to instructions of the owner, or in the materials or components supplied or required by the contract, or to the quality of the performance of another contractor.[76] Whether a party owes such a duty is determined on a case-by-case basis, for instance the duty may exist if there is expert knowledge proffered, negligence at the time of taking-over, or past dangerous behavior.

Employer and Contractor

General Contractors (Generalunternehmer) and Management Contractor (Generalübernehmer)

4.32 General contractors and management contractors in the German context are in one sense, similar, in that both the *Generalunternehmer* (general contractor) and the *Generalübernehmer* (management contractor) are the only party in privity of contract with the employer (i.e., the *Hauptauftraggeber*).

4.33 The difference between the general contractor and management contractor is that a general contractor generally performs at least some of the construction works that are required to make the project ready for use in the manner specified in the terms of the

64 BGB §242.
65 For construction contracts see: BGH, NJW 1996, 2158; BGH, NJW 2000, 807.
66 See, NZBau 2008, 609 (610), BGB §§241 para 2, 242.
67 For example, BGB §681 Sentence 1.
68 VOB/B §§3 (3) Sentence 2, 4 (3), (4), 6 (1), 13 (3).
69 BGB §§311 (2), 241 (2).
70 BGH, NJW-RR 1990, 141 (142); BGH, NJW 1983, 998; BGH, NJW 1978, 260.
71 OLG Hamm, BeckRS 2007, 05292.
72 VOB/B §3 (1).
73 VOB/B §4 (1) No. 1.
74 BGH, NJW 1996, 2158; BGH, NJW 2000, 807.
75 For example, to provide necessary material: OLG Koeln, NJW-RR 1993, 1528, or grant access to the site; Note, BGB §278 must also be considered, being employers vicariously liable for the conduct of its employees.
76 See VOB/B §13 (3) and VOB/B §4 (3) VOB/B.

contract (i.e., he performs most of the works himself). The management contractor does not complete any of the construction work himself; rather the work is completed entirely by sub-contractors.[77] However, as mentioned above, although the work is subcontracted, the management contractor remains fully liable to the employer for carrying out the work in accordance within specified timescales and quality requirements.[78]

Architect Engineer (Generalplaner) and General Contractor/ Architect Engineer and Management Contractor

4.34 There is a distinction in German practice between construction and management works. An architect engineer is tasked with all architectural, engineering and technical planning and design works.[79] Here it is important to distinguish between design and planning. While the design process takes the employer's concept and develops specifications for bringing that concept to life, the planning process determines the means by which the design is implemented. The architect engineer bears sole legal responsibility for the design services vis-à-vis the client. The construction works are generally carried out by either a general or management contractor (see above, 4.32 and 4.33).

4.35 While the employer generally first undertakes HOAI phases 1–4 (See 4.38 et. Seq. below) on his own, usually by engaging architect engineers, under a design and build contract (*Totalübernehmervertrag*) the employer seeks to have all of the design and construction works done by a single contractor. In such an arrangement, the role of the architect engineer will be absorbed by either the general or management contractor.[80]

4.36 The advantages of this type of arrangement for the employer are as follows:

(a) Employer receives the entire work from one source, and only one party is in privity of contract with the employer. The general or management contractor then engages all sub-contractors.[81] Hence, the employer does not need to coordinate the performance of the individual works, as this is undertaken by the general or management contractor;
(b) Furthermore, when it comes to warranties, the contractor is the sole person obliged to provide the employer with a warranty for all defects that are discovered after completion;[82]
(c) Finally, the employer does not need to negotiate and place different orders for all the works to be performed. His negotiations and contract awards are restricted to the placement of the order with the contractor for the performance of the entire construction works.

Consortium

4.37 Consortiums (*ARGE*) are generally used on large infrastructure projects in Germany; however, an ARGE is not limited to any particular type of project. A consortium

77 *T. Thierau*, in Kapellmann/Messerschmidt (2018), VOB/B C. II. margin 9.
78 Ibid.
79 *Richter* (2018), I. Chap. D, margin 318.
80 *Richter* (2018), I. Chap. D, margin 251.
81 Ibid., margin 318.
82 Ibid., margin 319.

is an association of multiple contractors (and/or consultant firms) that come together to perform the construction works and are governed by a consortium contract (*ARGE-Vertrag*). Generally speaking, an ARGE is not tied to any particular legal form of company. As such, an ARGE could be a registered co-operative (eG) or a limited liability company (GmbH). While an ARGE largely shields its members from personal liability, practice shuns the expense associated with these corporate legal forms. Therefore, ARGEs are, as a general rule, and according to the ARGE model contract, almost always partnerships (Gesellschaft bürgerlichen Rechts).

Consultant's Role and Liability

4.38 The role performed by a FIDIC Engineer outlined in the English Common Law Chapter (4.38), does not exist either under the BGB or VOB. The VOB/B refers only to the Employer and Contractor without any special allocation of responsibilities to an engineer, architect or third-party consultant. Certification, administration, instructions and the like performed by a FIDIC Engineer are all performed directly between the Employer and Contractor under a VOB/B contract. A German engineer will generally not understand the role of a FIDIC Engineer nor normally commit to performing this role as it does not follow the traditional function of a German engineer in construction works.[83] The consultant best resembling the role performed by a FIDIC Engineer is the architect ("Architekten"). The Architect is responsible for producing the design and acting as the Employer's agent during the construction process. However, unlike the FIDIC Engineer, the Architect does not act as the Employer's neutral certifier, administrator or valuer, thus the Architect's role is limited and differs substantially to the traditional role of a FIDIC Engineer. The FIDIC Engineer is tasked with directing the project. He has broad authority under the contract to act, except to the extent that he may not amend the contract or relieve the Parties of their duties under the contract. The Engineer acts as an adjudicator of first instance for disputes between the Employer and Contractor. It is the Engineer's duty, despite the fact that he is paid by the Employer, to make fair determinations, when called upon to do so.[84]

4.39 There is considerable legal literature and cases dealing with consultant contracts; however, this has largely focused on consultant fees. In Germany there is legislation particular to German architects and engineers called German Fee Structure for Architects and Engineers (*Honorarordnung für Architekten und Ingenieure,* HOAI). The HOAI only governs the statutorily determined fee amount architects and engineers must be paid for performing their services. There are no statutory requirements under the HOAI governing the content or scope of the architect's or engineer's contract with the Employer, that is, there are no general terms and conditions. Thus, obligations on whether orders are issued, what services are required to be performed, claiming payment or damages is exclusively governed by the terms of the consultant contract; that is to say, contract law principles of the BGB shall apply. Consultant contracts may be construed either as a services contract

83 Contrary to German practice the FIDIC Engineer is also expected to act as an adjudicator between the Employer and Contractor in settling disputes, the confusion further compounded if a dispute relates to the FIDIC Engineer's own designs, specifications or instructions.

84 See Generally FIDIC Red Book, First Edition 1999, Clause 3.

(*Dienstvertrag*)[85] or works contract (*Werkvertrag*).[86] As previously noted, the difference between the forms of contract are extensive, particularly with respect to the scope and character of the contractual duties and default in performance. German courts have held, however, that an architect or engineer contract is a contract for works rather than a contract for services.[87] There are a number of consequences that flow from this determination , such as the consultant has an obligation to achieve a desired outcome/result rather than merely providing services. The most obvious and pertinent consequence being that consultants are obliged to provide their services free from defects, that is, the design and plans must be without fault and geared towards the construction of a building, which is also free from any defects free on the basis on these plans.[88] This corresponds with a contractor's strict obligation to build "fit for purpose" rather than the Common law standard to provide services with reasonable skill and care.[89]

4.40 In Germany architect services are performed in phases outlined in the HOAI. This law provides 9 phases of services and the permissible fees, these being as follows:

(a) Phase 1 – Pre-design;
(b) Phase 2 – Schematic design;
(c) Phase 3 – Design development;
(d) Phase 4 – Approval planning;
(e) Phase 5 – Construction documents and detail drawings;
(f) Phase 6 – Tender documents and bill of quantities;
(g) Phase 7 – Negotiations;
(h) Phase 8 – Construction managing;
(i) Phase 9 – Documentation, controlling.

4.41 The HOAI applies to architects and engineers based in Germany, provided the services performed are listed in the HOAI and for construction works in Germany.[90] Foreign architects and engineers are also required to comply with the provision of HOAI when they are based in Germany, however, merely performing services in Germany does not trigger the application of the HOAI. Additionally, if the foreign architect is engaged to perform various services normally expected from a German architect then he must follow the procedure for formally registering as an architect.[91] The HOAI can also be applied to services of German consultants if parties have agreed to German law as the law governing the contract. The HOAI tables the mandatory minimum and maximum fees and their

85 Contract for Services, BGB §611.

86 Contract for Works, BGB §631.

87 BGH, NJW 1960, 431 (431); BGH, NJW 1974, 898 (899); KG, IBR 2008, 1165, the courts determined that the architect's contract is a combination of works and services contract, however the predominant aspect being a contract for works. This ruling has been also applied to all engineering disciplines (geotechnical, structural, mechanical, electrical, etc.).

88 According to BGB §633, work is defective when (a) it is not of agreed quality; or (b) if quality has not been agreed, the work is not suitable for use presumed by contract or its intended purpose.

89 It is noted that the obligation is not to ensure building works are defects free; the obligation is to ensure that consultant's services are provided (for instance provision of designs plans) are without fault so that building works are done defects free based on these services.

90 HOAI §1.

91 Registering as an architect is governed on state-by-state basis in Germany.

character that Employer must pay. Up until 2019, even if parties have agreed to a different fee the mandatory fee structure would have overridden their agreement.[92]

4.42 As seen from above, the role of the Engineer in FIDIC Contracts is not the norm for services performed by Engineers in the German construction industry. The role of an architect or engineer in Germany is very distinct from that of the FIDIC Engineer, with the services performed by the FIDIC Engineer being generally allotted to a project manager (which may not necessarily be a qualified engineer). Thus, German architects or engineers will often resist any appointment as the FIDIC Engineer.

Sub-Contracting (Subunternehmer)

4.43 Under German law (and similar to English common law, English Common Law Chapter (3.221)), the employer has no direct contractual claims against subcontractors engaged by the *Generalunternehmer*; the employer may only claim directly against the contractor and the contractor against the sub-contractor. Similar to the FIDIC contracts the employer can prevent subcontracting of works and/or allow only nominated sub-contractors to perform specified parts of works.[93]

Unforeseeable Physical Conditions

4.44 The issue of "unforeseeable physical conditions" ("*Baugrundrisiko*") is a topic of interest in the German legal fraternity, even to the extent that an entire text dedicated to the law of the building site and ground conditions has been published.[94] *Baugrundrisiko* is best defined as follows:

> *The building ground risk [unforeseeable physical conditions] and specifically in the area of tunnel construction, the mountain risk is any deviation of the building ground, mountain and water situation from the composition of the ground water layers to be expected and described in more detail in the performance specifications which arises unexpectedly during the execution of the works. Such deviations include unknown ground water flow, stratum water, crevasses, intercalculations, underground building remains, underground tanks, supply pipes, but also areas of the ground contaminated due to former industrial activities or for other reasons.*[95]

4.45 While there is no accepted general definition for *Baugrundrisiko*, the Courts have contributed to developing a working definition, in particular:

---

92 There are circumstance where the HOAI won't apply, for instance various works where services fees are greater than €25,000,000; basic services for outdoor facilities; and planning and supervision of pre-fabricated components. Furthermore, in 2019 the European Court of Justice struck down the minimum and maximum fee provisions of the HOAI (Judgment of 4 July 2019, C-377/17) as violative of Article 15(1), (2)(g) and (3) of Directive 2006/123/EC of the European Parliament and of the Council of 12 December 2006 on services in the internal market.

93 VOB/B §4 (8).

94 The authoritative text in Germany on the law of building site and ground conditions is "*Handbuch des Baugrund- und Tiefbaurechts*", Prof. Dr. Klaus Englert, Josef Grauvogl and Michael Maurer (2011, Werner Verlag).

95 *M. Marbach*, Nachtragsforderung bei mangelnder Leistungsbeschreibung der Baugrundverhältnisse im VOB-Bauvertrag und bei Verwirklichung des [Baugrundrisikos], Baurecht, vol. 25, no. 2, 1994, p. 168 (178). Note, although this definition starts in the context of tunnel boring through a mountain, the latter part deals with general building ground risk.

"The risk of unforeseen difficulties caused by the condition of the ground on site",[96] or "the risk of performance becoming more onerous due to the given geological condition".[97]

4.46 Although the BGB does not contain any explicit reference to *Baugrundrisiko*, §§644 and 645 of the BGB have been traditionally construed by the Courts to place the risk of any unforeseeable ground conditions on the Employer. The latter, BGB §645 (1), states that if the works, prior to acceptance, is destroyed or deteriorates or becomes impracticable as the result of a defect in the materials supplied by the Customer [Employer] or as the result of an instruction given by the Customer [Employer] for the carrying out of the works, subject to no circumstances contributed by the Contractor, then the Contractor may demand payment that corresponds to the works performed and reimbursement of those expenses not included in the original remuneration (i.e., contract price). Thus, the leading view of Courts was that any contractual term(s), to the extent that it falls under the GTCA, which aims to shift the building ground risk onto the Contractor would be deemed void. However, a term which is freely negotiated between the parties and outside the scope of the GTCA may still be enforced by the courts.[98]

4.47 A contractor may argue frustration (*Störung der Geschäftsgrundlage*) under §313 (1) of the BGB to potentially realign the risk of unforeseeable site conditions allocated under a contract back onto the Employer. This section states that if terms being the basis of the contract (i.e., essential terms) have significantly changed from when the contract was first entered into by the parties and the parties would not have entered into the contract under the same terms, or at all had they foreseen such circumstances (in the current instance unforeseen site conditions), a party may seek revision of the contract.[99] The BGB also provides for parties to terminate the contract if changing it is not possible or a party cannot be reasonably expected to accept the change.[100] The position under the BGB contrasts remarkably with the English common law that, without an express provision to the contrary, ground condition risk rests with the Contractor like any other physical condition or buildability issue.[101]

4.48 FIDIC Contracts provide that the Contractor is responsible for interpreting site data and the Employer warranting the accuracy of such site data. If the Contractor discovers any potential errors or discrepancies then this must be reported to the Employer before submitting its tender where the risk then shifts to the Employer, failing this, the Contractor remains responsible for the risk.[102] Unlike the other forms, the Silver Book places this risk wholly on the Contractor, that is, the Contractor is required to verify the accuracy and completeness of the data with the Employer explicitly taking no responsibility for the

96 OLG Brandenburg, NZBau 2009, 181 (182).

97 OLG Muenchen, BeckRS 2015, 10192.

98 BGB §305.

99 Changing the contract is qualified by taking into account all the circumstances of the individual case and in particular contractual or statutory division of risk. The section is followed by Sub-Section (2) which continues to define change of circumstances as essential preconceptions being the basis of the contract turning out incorrect.

100 See, NZBau 2006, 241 (244), where the contractor sought revision of the contract under BGB §313; however, was denied because he failed to show that it would be unreasonable for him to adhere to the terms of the contract as agreed.

101 *Thorn v Mayor and Commonality of London* (1876) 1 App Cas 120; English Common Law (3.232).

102 Sub-Clause 4.10 [Site Data], Red Book and Yellow Book.

accuracy, sufficiency or completeness of such data.[103] FIDIC Contracts dedicate a clause specifically to unforeseeable physical conditions, where depending on the form used, this will determine which party bears the risk. Under the Red and Yellow Books the Employer bears the risk whereas under the Silver Book the risk of unforeseeable physical conditions rests with the Contractor.[104] How would these conditions be treated under the BGB? As stated previously the FIDIC Contracts will be classified as standard terms, therefore, the protective regime applicable to standard terms and conditions will apply. The GTCA will not affect the Red and Yellow Books position on site data; however, with respect to unforeseeable physical conditions (or difficulties) being shifted wholly onto the Contractor under the Silver Book without any recourse will be found void.[105]

4.49 However, this review is not complete without also examining how the VOB/B deals with this risk. First, unlike the FIDIC Contracts, the VOB/B does not contain an explicit clause dealing with "building ground risk". In contrast, FIDIC Contracts do explicitly deal with this risk by either allocating it onto the Employer subject to the main caveat of the physical conditions being adverse and unforeseeable or completely on the Contractor.[106] Although not covered in the VOB/B, ground risks are clearly addressed under the VOB/A, tendering procedure, which states in VOB/A §7 (1) Nr. 6:

> *The conditions at the building site which are crucial to the execution of the works, e.g., ground and water conditions, must be described in such a way that the bidder can adequately assess their effects on the construction project and on the execution of the construction work.*

Material and Workmanship

4.50 Under German law the contractor must use materials of the same quality agreed to in the contract. In the absence of a quality agreement, the materials must be of the usual quality for a works of the same or similar type.[107]

4.51 The quality obligation of the contractor is to provide a building, which is fit for its intended purpose. This means it must provide a building free from any material and legal defects.[108] A building is free from material defects if it is of the quality agreed to in the contract, or, if no quality standard has been agreed to, if it is fit for the purpose envisaged by the contract.[109]

Labour Law Considerations

4.52 For the employment of workers from the EU, there are no limitations. For non-EU citizens, a residency permit as well as a work visa is required for employment. Such permits are usually limited in time and scope.

---

103 Sub-Clause 4.10 [Site Data], Silver Book.

104 Sub-Clause 4.12 [Unforeseeable Physical Conditions] Red and Yellow Books, Sub-Clause 4.12 [Unforeseeable Difficulties] Silver Book.

105 KG, IBR 2012, p. 695; *G.-S. Hök*, FIDIC Verträge im deutschen Umfeld – Theorie und Praxis, Zeitschrift für deutsches und internationales Bau- und Vergaberecht, vol. 37, no. 7, 2014, p. 627 (632).

106 The former being the Yellow and Red Books and the latter Silver Book allocates.

107 BGB §633 (2) No. 2.

108 BGB §633 (1).

109 BGB §633 (2).

4.53 Employers must also adhere to certain employee-protection regulations, most importantly being the German Occupational Health and Safety Act (*Arbeitsschutzgesetz*), the Working Hours Act (*Arbeitszeitgesetz*), the Federal Leave Act (*Bundesurlaubsgesetz*), and the Temporary Employment Act (*Arbeitnehmerüberlassungsgesetz*).

4.54 Particularly applicable to work on the construction site are the Construction Site Ordinance (*Baustellenverordnung*), the Workplace Ordinance (*Arbeitsstättenverordnung*), the Industrial Safety Ordinance (*Betriebssicherheitsverordnung*), the Industrial Equipment Act (*Gerätesicherheitsgesetz*), the Noise and Vibration Occupational Safety Ordinance (*Lärm- und Vibrations-Arbeitsschutzverordnung*), and amendments made by worker's compensation boards, which stipulate additional safety measures to be undertaken.

4.55 Employment contracts can – if so agreed – be limited to a specific project or period of time (TzBfG §§15, 14). Absent such an agreement, either party may only terminate the contract in compliance with the law concerning termination of labour contracts.

Performance and Taking-Over (Abnahme)

4.56 Under BGB §631, the contractor agrees to perform the construction works and the employer is obliged to pay the agreed remuneration (i.e., contract price), which becomes due and payable after completion of the works and its acceptance by the employer. Thus, performance is pre-requisite for payment.

Acceptance (*Abnahme*) means the express or tacit declaration of the employer that he acknowledges the contractor has performed the works being substantially in compliance with the contract.[110] It is also to be considered as a confirmation that the performance period has been completed.[111]

4.57 Under BGB §640:

"the employer is obliged to accept the [ready] work produced in conformity with the contract … Acceptance may not be refused by reason of trivial defects".

This is reflected in the VOB/B where the employer is obliged to accept the work if free from defects and the contractor demands acceptance[112] – the employer may not refuse acceptance on account of de minimis defects. The German Supreme Court has held that if the defect is so trivial relative to the interests of both parties, then it is fair for the employer to accept the work and not inhibit the performance of the contract[113] (this being similar to the concept of "minor defects" in English common law) (see English Common Law Chapter (3.263)). Where there are minor outstanding works yet to be completed, but altogether the works meet the contract requirements, the contractor can still demand acceptance.[114]

110 RG [110] RGZ 404, 406.

111 *Busche* (2018), BGB §640, margin 17; *M. Havers*, in Kapellmann/ Messerschmidt (2018), VOB/B §12 margin 19.

112 VOB/B §12 (1).

113 BGH, NJW 1981, 1448 (1448 et seq); The purpose of the works is very important because if the Works cannot be used in accordance with its purpose then it is not trivial. However, if there are many "trivial" defects then when collated this could be considered a serious defect and grounds for not accepting the works.

114 BGH, judgement from 15.6.2000 – VII ZR 30/99.

4.58 One problem encountered with Common law contracts is when does acceptance occur? By reference to the FIDIC forms, issuing the Taking-Over Certificate might indicate *Abnahme*, since this signals the beginning of the defects notification period, in the same way acceptance would trigger the statutory period under German law. However what effect does the issuance of the Performance certificate have? On the one hand it signals the end of the Defects Notification Period, but is it the end of the performance period too? Its name would indicate yes. If the performance certificate implies acceptance under German law and no changes are made to the contract then the employer may obtain the benefit of an additional defects notification period provided by the mandatory law beginning with the issuance of the Performance certificate (discussed further below).

4.59 Where the employer is aware of a defect and nevertheless accepts the works despite that defect, the employer waives the rights enshrined in BGB §§634 (1–3) (i.e., employer's right for defective works) unless upon accepting the work, he reserves his rights with respect to the defect.[115] Upon acceptance of the works, the burden of proof regarding defects shifts from the contractor to the employer.

4.60 Acceptance has very important consequences and is a defining moment in the relationship between the contractor and the employer, including the following:

(a) Acceptance marks the start of the warranty period for all parts of the contract to which the acceptance relates and which have been accepted without defect;[116]

(b) The declaration of acceptance reverses the burden of proof with regards to contractual defects and proof of the contractual performance of the work insofar as the work is free from defects (latent). Note that the contractor bears the burden of proof for performance of the work in compliance with the contract. If the employer reports aspects of the work as being defective at the time of acceptance the contractor must perform this work in compliance with the contract as outstanding works and must establish compliance with the contract as the works are being performed.[117] Nevertheless, the defects warranty period for the defective parts of the works begins with acceptance as well;[118]

(c) Defects that the principal is aware of at the time of the acceptance, but which he does not report during the acceptance (*Abnahme*), are not required to subsequently be remedied by the contractor in accordance with the contract either as remaining work to be completed or to remedy them as part of the warranty given;

(d) The remuneration of the contractor becomes due;[119]

(e) The contractor's obligation to carry out the works ends and the risk transfers from the contractor to the employer (for instance, the risk for accidental damage to the works shifts to the employer).[120]

115 BGB §640 (2), "*If the customer accepts a defective work ... even though he knows of the defect, he only has the rights designated in §634 nos. 1 to 3 if he reserves his rights with regard to the defect when he accepts the work*".

116 BGB §643a, note there is no distinction between latent and patent defects and structural defects.

117 BGB §640 (2).

118 *Busche* (2018), BGB §640, margins. 15, 19.

119 BGB §641.

120 BGB §644.

4.61 German law and the VOB/B provide for different types of acceptance (*Abnahme*), these are as follows:

Express acceptance: This is a formal statement issued by the employer acknowledging acceptance (*Abnahme*).

Acceptance on demand: The contractor may, upon completion, demand acceptance from the employer, whether or not the contractually agreed time for completion has expired. Upon receiving a demand for acceptance, the employer must inspect the works within 12 working days of notification by the contractor that works are complete and ready for acceptance.[121]

Formal acceptance: This entails the contractor and employer examining the works and issuing an acceptance report on acceptance.[122] The acceptance report contains the scope of acceptance, the declaration as to whether acceptance has been granted, the declaration as to whether claims or liquidated damages are reserved and the time of the start of the warranty period and in general also its term. Generally, in construction contracts for complex construction projects, acceptance must occur formally with the contractor and the Employer examining the site and confirming taking-over.[123]

4.62 Similar to the BGB, under the VOB/B acceptance can be refused if material defects are determined on inspection.[124] Formal acceptance may occur without the contractor present if a date for acceptance was agreed or reasonable notice was provided and the contractor failed to attend.[125]

Constructive acceptance:

In addition to acceptance implied by conduct, discussed below, there are two main ways in which acceptance may be deemed to have been declared without an express declaration by the employer.

(a) Under the VOB/B, if the contractor has notified the employer in writing of the completion of the work and following 12 working days neither party has demanded acceptance of the work, or the employer refuses to accept the work, then such work shall be deemed to have been accepted.[126] In order for a constructive acceptance to take place, the contractor's work must be free from material defects and in substantial compliance with the contract.

If no acceptance is demanded and the employer has started to use the works, or part of the works, then acceptance will be deemed to have been granted on expiry of six working days after the start of use, unless otherwise agreed;[127]

(b) Under the BGB, acceptance will be implied if the Employer fails to respond within a reasonable time to the Contractor's request for *Abnahme*.[128] Note, this may be explicitly excluded by the parties. If the time given by the Contractor is

121 VOB/B §12 (1).

122 VOB/B §12 (4).

123 *Messerschmidt* (2018), BGB §640, margins. 118, 122.

124 VOB/B §12 (3).

125 VOB/B §12 (4), No. 2.

126 VOB/B §12 (5), No. 1.

127 VOB/B §12 (5), No. 2; note that using of parts of a building structure to continue the work is not deemed to be acceptance, *Havers* (2018), VOB/B §12 margin 17.

128 BGB §640 (1) Sentence 3.

too short, then the "reasonable period" provision will apply, which will be determined on a case by case basis.[129]

Implied acceptance: *Abnahme* can be implied from the conduct of the parties and the surrounding circumstances; this is viewed from the perspective of the "objective observer" and whether he would have questioned or rejected *Abnahme* due to defective or incomplete works. Examples of implied *Abnahme* include, the employer taking possession and commencing operation the works, or the employer not declaring acceptance but having made full payment for the works.[130]

Acceptance under the new BGB: Constructive acceptance under the BGB discussed above changed under the construction law reform in 2018. Now, the works shall be deemed accepted if the employer does not respond by refusing acceptance (rejecting the works) by stating at least one defect.[131] If the employer is a consumer, such a constructive acceptance will only be valid if the contractor also provides the employer with a written explanation of the consequences of failing to reply within a reasonable time or failing to site specific defects in the works.[132]

Contract Price and Payment

Fundamental Principles

4.63 The German Civil Code explicitly provides that in a contract for works, the Employer is obligated to pay to the Contractor the price agreed to in the contract and the Contractor is obliged to carry out the promised works.[133] The obligation of the employer to pay the contractor arises at the point in time at which the acceptance (*Abnahme*) of the works takes place.[134] Where payment amount isn't specified in the contract, payment for the works is deemed to have been tacitly agreed if performance of the works could only have been expected to have been agreed upon in exchange for payment.[135] In such circumstances the applicable statutory fee (if any) will determine the price of the works.[136] If no statutory fee is applicable, the usual price for the works will apply.[137]

4.64 If the parties have agreed to undertake separate acceptances (i.e., sectional completion) for separate parts of the works and agreed to a price for each of those parts, payment becomes due at the point in at which acceptance of that part of the works takes place, provided remuneration for each part is specified in the contract.[138] The contractor's entitlement for partial payment is expressly provided for in the BGB[139] and the contractor can demand payment by instalments in proportion to the contractual value of the works

129 *Busche* (2018), BGB §640, margin 28; the VOB/B provides for a 12-day period.

130 BGH, BauR 1994, 103; Possessing and using the works will not automatically mean "implied" *Abnahme*, especially if possession and use is due to the employer wanting to avoid damages (BGH, BauR 1975, 344).

131 BGB §640 (2) Sentence 1.

132 BGB §640 (2) Sentence 2.

133 BGB §631 (1).

134 BGB §641 (1) Sentence 1.

135 BGB §632 (1).

136 BGB §632 (2); *A. Boldt*, in Messerschmidt/Voit (2018), BGB §632 margins. 31 et seq.

137 BGB §632 (2).

138 BGB §641 (1) Sentence 2.

139 BGB §632a (1).

produced under the contract.[140] The contractor bears the onus of proving the works it produced are in accordance with the contract.[141]

VOB/B Regulations

4.65 Under the VOB/B, the contract amount has to renumerate the contractor for all works the contractor owes under the contract according to the specification of works, special conditions of the contract, supplementary conditions of the contract, general technical specifications of construction contracts (VOB/C)[142] and usual business practice.[143] The amount of remuneration payable is to be calculated on the basis of unit prices specified in the contract and works actually executed if no other method of calculation has been agreed (i.e., parties have not agreed to lump sum, hourly wage rates or cost reimbursement).[144]

Special Provisions for Unit-Price Contracts

4.66 Under the VOB/B unit prices agreed under contract may change if this exceed the stipulated amount as follows:

(a) Where the quantity of works (or a part thereof) differs on completion from the quantity provided for in the contract by less than 10%, then the unit price agreed to shall determine the remuneration amount and remain unchanged;[145]
(b) If on completion the quantity of works (or a part of) exceeds the quantity that was originally estimated by greater than 10%, a new price must be agreed upon by the parties on request of either party that takes into account the increase or reduction of the cost of the works;[146]
(c) If on completion the quantity of works (or a part thereof) is more than 10% lower than originally estimated, the unit price for the quantity of the actual amount of work completed must be increased on the contractor's request unless the contractor can be compensated by an increase in the quantities of other parts of the works or in some other way.[147] The increase in the unit price must correspond approximately to the additional costs that arise out of reapportioning the site facilities' costs, site overheads, and general business costs to the reduced quantity of work.[148]

Special Provisions for Lump Sum Contracts

4.67 Under the VOB/B where a lump sum amount has been agreed this must remain unchanged.[149] If the works executed differ from the contractually agreed works to such

140 BGB §632a (1).
141 BGB §632a (1) Sentence 3.
142 The General Technical Conditions of Contracts for Construction Works.
143 VOB/B §2 (1).
144 VOB/B §2 (2).
145 VOB/B §2 (3) No. 1.
146 VOB/B §2 (3) No. 2, however, only for the quantities exceeding 110%.
147 VOB/B §2 (3) No. 3 Sentence 1.
148 VOB/B §2 (3) No. 3 Sentence 2.
149 VOB/B §2 (7) No. 1 Sentence 1.

an extent that the employer or contractor cannot be reasonably expected to be bound by the stipulated lump sum, then compensation will be granted on the disadvantaged party's request to allow for an increase or decrease in costs (the original price calculations are used as basis for determining compensation).[150] Where parts of the works to which a lump sum applies are contingent upon the execution of works for which unit price apply, an appropriate adjustment of the lump sum can be demanded if the unit price is changed.[151]

Other Provisions

4.68 If the Employer requires the Contractor to submit drawings, calculations or other documents which the Contractor did not agree to submit under the contract, the Employer must accordingly provide additional payment in addition to the contractually agreed payment,[152] and if the Employer requires the Contractor to inspect technical calculations made by third-parties, the Employer must reimburse the Contractor's costs.[153]

4.69 Works are only renumerated on the basis of an hourly wage if this was expressly agreed to before the works commenced.[154]

Defects Liability (Gewaehrleistung)

4.70 The German BGB is prescriptive in dealing with defects liability and requires the Contractor to produce the works free from defects.[155] Works will be considered defect free if procured in accordance with the agreed quality[156] or where this has not been agreed, then fit for purpose under the Contract.[157](failing this, the Works are suitable for its ordinary use and of a quality ordinarily expected for such Works[158]). This principle is reflected in the VOB/B §13 where the Contractor is required to provide the Works free from defects on "acceptance" (*Abnahme*)[159] with Works considered free from defects if in accordance with generally accepted engineering principles. This differs from English law where there is no statutory obligation to produce the Works "fit for purpose" (see English Common Law Chapter (3.249)), instead the parties must contractually stipulate such Works will be fit for its intended purpose.[160] However, Contractors are required under statute to supply goods and materials that are fit for their intended purpose.[161]

---

150 VOB/B §2 (7) No. 1 Sentence 1.
151 VOB/B §2 (7) No. 3, (3) No. 4.
152 VOB/B §2 (9) No. 1.
153 VOB/B §2 (9) No. 2.
154 VOB/B §2 (10).
155 BGB §633 (1).
156 BGB §633 (2) Sentence 1.
157 BGB §633 (2) Sentence 2 No. 1.
158 BGB §633 (2) Sentence 2 No. 2.
159 VOB/B §13 (1) Sentence 1.
160 There may be an implied obligation to procure Works "fit for purpose" under Common law, in the absence of a clause negating such an obligation in Contract, where the Contractor provides both design and build services, see *IBA v EMI and BICC* [1980] 14 BLR 1.
161 Sale of Goods Act 1979 which imposes implied terms on any seller acting in the course of business that the goods supplied will be of satisfactory quality and, where the purchaser makes known any particular purpose, are reasonably fit for their intended purpose.

4.71 German law prescribes the defects liability period (*Gewaehrleistungsfrist*) which commences on "acceptance" (*Abnahme*) of the works[162] for the duration of five years for construction works[163] and two years for other works whose outcome consist of manufacture, maintenance or alteration of an item.[164] Parties are free to change the defects liability period under the BGB in their contracts provided such periods are not endless or unreasonably long.[165] Under the VOB/B, the default defects liability period is four years for construction works; two years for other works whose outcome consist of manufacture, maintenance or alteration of an item; two years for heating; and two years for machinery parts and electrical and electronic equipment.[166]

4.72 There are three distinct differences between the BGB and common law jurisdictions regarding defects liability periods: The first, defects liability periods are prescribed by the BGB and not just a creature of contract;[167] second, the legal consequences of failing to remedy a defect are explicitly outlined in the BGB; and last, under the BGB the contractor must be given the opportunity to remedy the defect (that is, the doctrine of specific performance as a form of equitable relief is not an optional recourse against the contractor, but rather it is the standard rule under the BGB). This is important, as the failure of a contractor to remedy the defect after being given a reasonable opportunity to do so (including a being given a reasonable deadline for completion) is a prerequisite for employer's entitlement to termination of the contract,[168] claims for damages[169][170] and the entitlement for remuneration in case the defect is remedied by a third-party.[171] The first needs no explanation, under Common law there is no implied defects liability period, parties must expressly provide for a defects liability period in their contract (see English Common Law Chapter (3.40)). The second difference is covered under BGB §634, which itemises the rights of customers (i.e., Employer) in case of defects as follows:

(a) Demand rectification – the Contractor bears all expenditure in rectifying[172] but may also refuse rectification if the cost of the remedy is disproportionate to the defect;[173]

(b) Self-help rectification works and claim reimbursement of expenses – upon giving the Contractor reasonable notice to remedy, the Employer may rectify defects itself and claim reimbursement.[174] The Employer may even demand advance payment from the Contractor;[175]

---

162 BGB §634a (2).

163 BGB §634a (1) No. 2.

164 BGB §634a (1) No. 1.

165 BGH, IBR 1999, 307, however, note an indefinite warranty or unreasonably long warranty period will be held void.

166 VOB/B §13 (4) Nos. 1, 2.

167 Common law jurisdictions generally provide under Contract a defects liability period of 12 months after the time for completion for which the Contractor is required to return and remedy any defect.

168 BGB §§634 No. 3, 323.

169 BGB §§634 No. 4, 281.

170 *Busche* (2018), BGB §636, margin 1.

171 VOB/B §13 (5) No. 2.

172 BGB §635 (2).

173 BGB §635 (3).

174 BGB §637 (1).

175 BGB §637 (3).

(c) Revocation of contract and reduced payment;[176]
(d) Claim for damages or expenses.[177]

4.73 The final key difference is the Contractor's right to either remedy the defect or reproduce the (affected) works anew.[178] That is, German law explicitly provides for the Contractor to remedy defects during the warranty period. Under Common law there is no equivalent statutory provision, the Contractor's rights and obligations with respect to remedying defects must be specifically conferred upon it under the defects liability provisions or otherwise in the Contract (for JCT mechanisms cf. English Common Law (3.277 et seq.)). The general position found in Common law is to allow the Contractor 12 months to return onsite and remedy any defects, failing this the contractual provisions will normally allow the Employer to obtain the services of another to carry out the remediation works.[179] If not provided for in the contract, the contractor generally has no obligation (or right) to remedy any defects and the employer may remedy the defects himself or by a third-party and seek damages (see the chapter on English Common Law (3.277)).

Limitation of Liability

4.74 A contractual limitation of liability is generally valid under the auspices of freedom of contract; however, it has its limits and in evaluating these limits one must differentiate between individually negotiated contract terms and general terms and conditions. Parties to a construction contract under German law may, for example, limit their liability for negligent, but not wilful (mis-)conduct.[180] Similarly to the extent that the obligor would be vicariously liable for the actions of his agent, he may not limit his liability for the wilful conduct of his agent, to the extent that the agent is acting within the scope of his agency. However, even as far as a limitation of liability would be valid under BGB §276, it may still be deemed void under the GTCA.

Variations

Provisions of the VOB/B on Variations

4.75 Similar to other construction contracts, the VOB/B provides that the employer can order modifications to the design of the works.[181] If the design modification or other instructions change the basis of the price calculation provided in the contract, the parties must try to agree to a new price allowing for the increase or reduction in the costs of works before commencing such works.[182] Failure to agree on the price of a variation entitles the contractor to refuse to execute said variation, only if the employer refuses to agree on an

176 BGB §634 No. 3.
177 BGB §634 No. 4.
178 BGB §635 (1).
179 FIDIC, Sub-clause 11.4 [*Failure to Remedy Defects*].
180 BGB §276.
181 VOB/B §1 (3).
182 VOB/B §2 (5).

adjusted price.[183] If, however, the parties are unable to agree only as to the amount of the price of the variation, the employer must name his "minimum price" and must agree to pay at least that minimum amount and difference must be agreed or otherwise determined later on.[184] The contractor may not refuse execution if the variation results in an insignificant increase in the costs of execution.[185] Furthermore, performance cannot be refused if no agreement can be reached due to the contractor's failure to negotiate in good faith.[186]

4.76 The employer may also order works that were not originally agreed in the contract but which have become necessary for its completion. The contractor is then obliged to execute such works unless it is lacks the ability or capacity to do so. Additional works which are not necessary for completion can only be instructed by agreement.[187] If the employer instructs the contractor to execute additional works, the contractor is entitled to remuneration for such work.[188] The amount of remuneration is calculated using prices for the original works and any extra costs in carrying out the additional works.[189] The contractor must inform the employer of its claim for remuneration[190] prior to beginning the execution of the additional works[191] (i.e., the employer's knowledge is required before works are commenced).

4.77 Generally, the contractor will not be entitled to additional or revised remuneration if undertaking works not instructed by the employer; the contractor can be required by the employer to remove such works within a reasonable time period and failing this the contractor may be liable for the costs of the removal of such works (and any ensuing damages) incurred by the employer.[192] The contractor will be entitled to remuneration for uninstructed works if these were necessary for the full performance of the contract, presumed to have been in accordance with the employer's intention and if the employer was given immediate notice of the works.[193] If this exception applies, the contractor's remuneration will be calculated in accordance with §2 Section 5 VOB/B or §2 Section 6 VOB/B.[194]

Variations Relating to Success of the Works

4.78 Until January 1, 2018 the BGB did not provide employers with any right to instruct variations in construction contracts. Since the BGB Reform Act new provisions on variations in construction contracts (*Anordnungsrechte*) have been ushered in. The objective of the lawmakers in enacting these provisions was to end the controversy between

183 *Kapellmann* (2018), VOB/B §2, margin 205; *R. Kandel*, VOB/B §2 Abs. 5 in Jansen, G., Kandel, R., and Preussner, M. (eds.), *BeckOK VOB/B*, 34th edition, Munich, C.H. Beck Verlag, 2019, VOB/B §2 (5), margin 104; BGH, NZBau 2004, 437 (440); BGH, NZBau 2004, 612 (613).

184 *Kapellmann* (2018), VOB/B §2, margin 206; *Kandel* (2019), VOB/B §2 (5), margin 107.

185 BGH, NZBau 2004, 437 (440).

186 OLG Dresden, NJW-RR 1998, 672 (673); *Kandel* (2019), VOB/B §2 (5), margin 105.

187 VOB/B §1 (4) Sentence 2.

188 VOB/B §2 (6) No. 1.

189 VOB/B §2 (6) No. 2.

190 Despite the notice requirement of VOB/B §2 (6) No. 1, failure to give such notice does not act as a time bar precluding payment for services rendered.

191 VOB/B §2 (6) No. 1 Sentence 2.

192 VOB/B §2 (8) No. 1.

193 VOB/B §2 (8) No. 2 Sentence 2.

194 VOB/B §2 (8) No. 2 Sentence 3.

contractors and employers on how contractual prices should be adjusted in the event that additional works or variations are agreed to. Furthermore, the lawmakers intended to incentivize the lodging of more plausible and realistic tenders.

4.79 Under the new law, if the employer requests either a variation to the definition of the "success" of the works[195] or a variation necessary to achieving success of the works, then the parties are obliged to "strive" to reach an agreement on the content and price of the variation,[196] and the contractor must offer a quote for the carrying out of the variation.[197] The contractor can request up to 80% of the remuneration quoted in the offer pursuant to §650b Section 1 BGB to be paid in instalments.[198] In the case of a variation of the definition of the success of the works, the contractor only has to submit such a quote if reasonable in the circumstances for that variation to be carried out, however the burden of proof on unreasonableness is borne by the contractor.[199] If the parties cannot reach agreement on the variation and the price for the variation within two weeks of the employer's request, the employer can unilaterally instruct the variation in writing.[200] However, if the employer instructs a variation of the contractually stipulated definition of the success of the works in those circumstances, the contractor is only obliged to execute those works if the variation is reasonable.[201]

4.80 The compensation owed by the employer due to a variation ordered under BGB §650b (2) will be determined by:

(a) Adding the actual necessary costs incurred in carrying out the variations and a surcharge for overheads, risk and profit;[202]

(b) At the discretion of the Employer, the contractor's original breakdown of prices for the works.[203] However, there is a presumption that prices will correspond with the price that would be arrived at by using method (a).[204]

Delay and Disruption

4.81 A contractor will be entitled to an extension of time in the case of delays which are caused by circumstances for which the employer bears the risk, a strike or lockout within the contractor's company (or a direct sub-contractor of the contractor), or for *Force Majeure* or other circumstances which are unavoidable for the contractor.[205] The circumstances for which the employer bears the risk are not defined in the VOB/B or the BGB.

195 "Success" in the sense of BGB §631 (2), which states that the subject of a contract for works can be either the production or alteration of something or another result to be achieved through the execution of a work or service.

196 New BGB Act §650b (1) Sentence 1.

197 New BGB Act §650b (1) Sentence 2.

198 New BGB Act §650c (3) Sentence 1.

199 New BGB Act §650b (1) Sentences 2, 3.

200 New BGB Act §650b (2) Sentence 1.

201 New BGB Act §650b (2) Sentence 2.

202 New BGB Act §650c (1).

203 New BGB Act §650c (2) Sentence 1.

204 New BGB Act §650c (2) Sentence 2.

205 VOB/B §6 (2) No. 1 VOB/B.

4.82 A condition precedent for the contractor's entitlement to an extension of time under the VOB/B is that the contractor notifies the employer without undue delay if he thinks he may be hindered in his performance.[206] This notice requirement is waived, however, if the circumstance and its delaying effect were both obvious to the employer.[207] Contractors are, by contrast, not generally entitled to an extension of time under the BGB. However, German courts have held that contractors do have a right to an extension of time even when the VOB/B has not been incorporated into the contract.[208]

4.83 In determining the length of the extension of time, the actual time of the delay plus allowances for the re-start of the works and for the postponement of the works to a less favourable time of year will be taken into account.[209]

4.84 Regarding entitlements to claims for compensation, each party can claim compensation for losses which occurred as a result of the delaying events, which were wilfully or negligently caused by the other party. An entitlement to lost profits exists only in the case of wilful (mis)conduct or gross negligence. Similar to extension of time claims, a condition precedent for a compensation claim is that the contractor immediately notify the employer of its entitlement, unless the disruption was obvious (*offenkundig*).[210]

4.85 The VOB/B provides yet another mechanism to claim compensation for delays. VOB/B §2 (5) and (6) entitle the contractor to claim for additional money in the event of a variation order by the employer. While this generally only entitles the contractor to claim for the higher costs as a result of the variation, if the variation leads to the delay of other work and the contractor reserves the right to make such a claim in the future, then the contractor my claim the costs of those delays as well.[211] The BGB provides the contractor with an entitlement to claim reasonable compensation if the employer fails to perform a necessary act, and as a result is in default of acceptance of the contractor's performance.[212] This entitlement requires that the contractor be ready and willing to perform the works (since the employer would otherwise not be in "default of acceptance"). Furthermore, like under the VOB/B, it is a condition precedent to an entitlement to compensation that the contractor immediately notify the employer of the disruption, unless that disruption was obvious. §642 BGB is also advantageous for the contractor because it does not require fault on behalf of the employer. Additionally, it applies whether or not the VOB/B is incorporated into the contract.[213]

206 VOB/B §6 (1).

207 Ibid.

208 The jurisprudential reasoning for this result is not entirely clear. According to some commentators, §6 (2) and §6 (4) of the VOB/B apply "indirectly" or "by analogy" even without incorporation of the VOB/B. They justify this approach by reference to §242 of the BGB, the German good faith obligation, H Ganten, W Jagenburg, and G Motzke, *Beck'scher VOB-Kommentar. Verdingungsordnung für Bauleistungen Teil B – Allgemeine Vertragsbedingungen für die Ausführung von Bauleistungen* (C H Beck Verlag, Munich, 1997), vor §6 VOB/B, margin 2. Against such an "indirect" or "analogue" application of the VOB/B clauses, but arriving at the same result, see A Roquette, M Viering, and S Leupertz, *Handbuch Bauzeit* (2nd edition, Werner Verlag, Cologne, 2013), margin 493.

209 VOB/B §6 (4).

210 VOB/B §6 (1).

211 VOB/B §6 (6). See also, OLG Brandenburg, Beschluss vom 18 August 2009 – 11 W 25/08.

212 BGB §642.

213 VOB/B §6 (6).

Liquidated Damages and Other Damages

4.86 The fact that a party does not perform on time does not, in itself, constitute delayed performance (*Verzug*). The following is required:

(a) Unless there is a fixed date, or the party refused to perform, then a warning must be given that performance is due (*Mahnung*);[214]
(b) The breaching party must be responsible for the delay, for instance if *Force Majeure* occurs the party is excused from performance and thus not responsible for the delay.[215]

4.87 Where the breaching party is responsible for delay, subject to the caveats above, then monetary compensation is payable for all damages attributed to the delayed performance. The other party is entitled to compensation in addition to having performance completed.[216] Thus, from a construction law perspective, the right to claim damages for delayed performance is available to both the contractor and employer.

4.88 Following on from the above, both liquidated damages and contractual penalties (*pauschalierter Schadensersatz or Vertragsstrafe*) are allowed under German law; however, there are severe restrictions imposed on such provisions under the GTCA in the BGB. Whether the clause refers to *pauschalisierter Schadensersatz*[217] or *Vertragsstrafen*[218] is determined with an eye to the parties' common intent, indicated trough the wording of the clause and the surrounding circumstances. *Pauschalisierter Schadensersatz* is meant to ease enforcement of damage claims; however, it is a prerequisite for a claim under a *Pauschalisierter Schadensersatz* clause that the employer actually incur damages.[219] *Vertragsstrafen* on the other hand serve an additional dual role meant to deter a party from breaching its contractual duties. The parties may only agree on a *Vertragsstrafe* in general terms and conditions for the breach of duties mentioned in BGB §309 no. 6. *Pauschalisierter Schadensersatz* can be agreed upon in general terms and conditions if the lump-sum stipulated therein is not excessively high in comparison to what the expected damage would have been in the normal course of affairs and if the other party is not precluded from proving that damages were not incurred or the lump-sum in the present dispute is actually significantly lower than the actual damages incurred.[220] In particular, a liquidated damages provision must not be contrary to the principle of good faith[221] and the amount claimed should not exceed the amount typically incurred as a consequence of comparable events.[222] Although there is no generally accepted level for liquidated damages for construction contract, where the liquidated damages clause in question triggers

214 Note, no warning is required if a fixed time period specified, time period can be calculated, starting from a specified event, the breaching party explicitly refuses performance for exceptional reasons, the immediate commencement of default is justified considering the interest of both parties (BGB §286 (2) Nos. 1–4).

215 BGB §280 (1) Sentence 2.

216 *S. Lorenz*, 280 BGB in Bamberger, G., Roth, H., Hau, W., and Poseck, R. (eds.), *BeckOK BGB*, 49th edition, Munich, C.H. Beck Verlag, 2019, BGB §280, margin 45.

217 BGB §309 No. 5.

218 BGB §309 No. 6.

219 BGB §309 No. 5 (b).

220 BGB §309 No. 5.

221 BGB §307 (1) Sentence 1.

222 BGB §309 (1) No. 5.

application of the GTCA, German courts have held *Verstragsstrafen* of more than 5% of the total contract price[223] or greater than 0.3% per day are void under the BGB,[224] whereas *pauschalisierter Schadensersatz* of 10% in turnkey contracts[225] and modular homes[226] were held to be valid. If milestones apply to the contract and there is a delay to a milestone, the employer can only claim liquidated damages once for the same delay and not liquidated damages for delay caused by each successive milestone.[227]

4.89 German law allows for the imposition of contractual penalties (*Vertragstrafen*)[228] in addition to liquidated damages for delayed performance.[229] This tolerance of penalty clauses is in stark contrast to the position in common law countries (see English Common Law (3.315)), where the highest authorities have deemed penalty clauses to be unenforceable.[230] Penalty clauses can be both monetary and non-monetary[231] and can be mitigated if they are "*disproportionate or exorbitantly high*".[232] One of the most important distinctions between penalties and liquidated damages is that a penalty may be claimed by the innocent party, even though the innocent party suffered no injury, provided that the breaching party is responsible for the non-, delayed-, or improper performance. Hence, where the breaching party does not perform in a timely or proper manner, the innocent party is entitled to the penalty in addition to proper or timely performance.[233]

4.90 The VOB/B provides for damages if the contractor does not complete the works on time.[234] Similar to the BGB, the employer is entitled to indemnification for any damages which have been demonstrably sustained; however, this does not extend to loss of profit.[235] In addition to liquidated damages, the VOB/B allows for the employer to impose penalties on the contractor (as prescribed by BGB §§339–45).[236] The contractor is required to pay the penalty "*agreed for the case where the contractor fails to complete the works within the period set for its execution*".[237]

---

223 BGH, NJW 2003, 1805 (1808).

224 BGH, NZBau 2013, 222 (223).

225 BGH, NJW 2006, 2551.

226 OLG Duesseldorf, BeckRS 2017, 117301 para 50.

227 BGH, Judgement from 6.12.2012 – VII ZR 133/11.

228 BGB §§339–445, however penalties only apply business to business, penalties imposed business to consumer are prohibited under BGB §309 No. 6.

229 BGB §§340 and 341; BGB §341 (1) states : "*If the obligor has promised the penalty in the event that he fails to perform his obligation properly, including without limitation performance at the specified time, the obligee may demand the payable penalty in addition to performance*".

230 Leading cases on penalties under UK Common law, *Dunlop Pneumatic Tyre Co Ltd v New Garage and Motor Co Ltd* [1915] AC 79, 86-87, where the House of Lords established the principles on how to determine whether a damage clause actually is a penalty and thereby unenforceable. This case was cited by the High Court of Australia in *Ringrow Pty Ltd v BP Australia Pty Ltd* [2005] HCA 71, Section 12, and by the Supreme Court of Ireland in *O'Donnell v Truck and Machinery Sales Limited* 1998 4 IR 191. The Supreme Court of Canada has adapted a similar approach in *Elsley v. J.G. Collins Ins Agencies*, [1978] 2 S.C.R. 916, 946, and does not allow for any recovery of an amount exceeding the actual damage.

231 BGB §342 (1).

232 BGB §343 (1).

233 BGB §341 (1).

234 VOB/B §5 (4).

235 VOB/B §6 (6), loss of profit can be claimed in cases of wilful conduct or gross negligence.

236 VOB/B §11 (1).

237 VOB/B §11 (2).

Insurance

Mandatory Insurance

4.91 Generally speaking, architects and engineers need to be members of a regional professional chamber, which impose the requirement on its members to have professional indemnity insurance as part of their membership rules. In addition, all parties in construction projects are required to have third-party liability insurance for damages or injuries to third parties.

Third-Party Liability Insurance (Haftpflichtversicherung)

4.92 Third-party liability insurance, like its name suggests, is an insurance policy which is taken out to cover injury to third-parties. In Germany, there are a multitude of third-party liability insurances, each covering different circumstances surrounding the loss or damage. Personal liability insurance will cover one if he causes damage to another. However, if that damage is caused while he is driving, he will need an automobile liability insurance. The same can be expected with respect to a construction site.

Building Owner's Liability Insurance (Bauherrenhaftpflichtversicherung)

4.93 Building owner's liability insurance offers insurance protection against claims stemming from unsafe conditions on the construction site (e.g., poor signage, insufficient safety measures on site, etc.) when carrying out one's own building projects.[238] Generally, the building owner is jointly and severally liable with the contractor and perhaps the architect as well for such claims for injuries to third-parties.[239]

4.94 Among other things, the owner is obligated to ensure the safety of those on his construction site so as to avoid injury. It is customary for the owner to delegate these duties to a site manager or contractor. Nonetheless, the owner remains liable for the safety of the property even if the day-to-day duties are delegated to others and he will be held liable in the event of a breach of this obligation.[240]

4.95 Private and business liability insurances regularly cover the owner's risk within the scope of the home- and landowner's liability insurance, but often these are limited to a certain amount. If those amounts are exceeded, a separate building owner's liability insurance policy must be taken out.[241]

Contractor's All-Risk Insurance (Bauleistungversicherung, formerly Bauwesenversicherung)[242]

4.96 Contractor's all-risk insurance is a required insurance policy for new buildings and protects ***contractors*** and builders from damage that is unforeseeable and occurs during

238 Krause-Allenstein, *Handbuch Bauversicherungsrecht*, 1. Auflage 2013, Ch. 2, margin 126.
239 Ibid.
240 Ibid.
241 Ibid., at margin 132.
242 Krause-Allenstein, at Ch. 3, margins 5–6.

the construction period.[243] In particular, this includes damage due to *Force Majeure* such as floods or storms, acts of war, terrorism and the like. Damage caused by vandalism, unknown subsoil conditions, defects, and negligence are also covered. While billed as an all-risk policy for the construction project there are several common exclusions from coverage, which include: Damage caused by fire, lightning, explosion, impact or rebound of manned and unmanned missiles.[244] The fire risk is usually insured via a so-called fire construction insurance policy, which is generally offered free of charge by the insurers during the construction period.

4.97 The term of the contractor's all-risk insurance policy usually extends over the entire construction period (including any contractually agreed to warranty period). Also, under such a policy, the contractor can obtain compensation for repeated performance, which may be not compensable by the owner under the contract.[245] Furthermore, the owner will be covered in the event of *Force Majeure* or another unavoidable event for which he bears the risk.[246]

Suspension

4.98 Under a VOB/B contract suspension is dealt with under §6 (5) and (6). The BGB also has its say regarding the consequences of suspension under §642, which is specifically referenced in the VOB/B.[247] The consequences under the VOB/B and BGB largely mirror FIDIC. The Contractor is entitled to an extension of time for the delay, although the VOB/B provides for additional time for the restart of works and taking into account that the time of year that the work resumes may be less favourable and, therefore, the work may be more time consuming and expensive than before the suspension.[248] Furthermore, under FIDIC and the VOB/B the Contractor may seek compensation for any additional costs incurred as a result of the suspension of the works. Under the VOB/B the Contractor may also seek any lost profits in the case of wilful misconduct or gross negligence on behalf of the employer.[249] BGB §642 (2) allows for the amount of compensation to be determined by the length of the delay and the value of the contract less any savings as a result of the delay.

4.99 Another interesting problem arises under German law with regard to the Employer's right to order a change to the time for completion. VOB/B §1 (3) and (4) provide the Employer with a right to order changes. The question, therefore, arises if this also extends to ordering a change to the time for completion. In fact, the first draft of the 2006 revision of the VOB/B contained a provision for just that, but was ultimately not included in the final version.[250] Some scholars take the position that VOB/B §1 (3) provides a very broad right of the Employer to order changes regardless of whether they are neces-

243 Ibid., at margin 84.
244 Ibid., at margin 66.
245 Ibid., at margin 86.
246 Ibid., at margin 2.
247 VOB/B §6 (6) Sentence 2.
248 VOB/B §6 (4).
249 VOB/B §6 (6) Sentence 1.
250 *J. Markus*, VOB/B-Novelle 2006 – Es bleibt dabei: Keine Anordnungsbefugnis des Auftraggebers zur Bauzeit, Neue Zeitschrift für Baurecht und Vergaberecht, vol. 7, no. 9, 2006, p. 537 (537).

sary for the success of the project or merely economically advantageous to the Employer, as the Contractors rights to remuneration are protected by VOB/B §2 (5).[251] Whereas the opposite position is equally supported, that while the right to order changes to the contract exists, such a right extends merely to the construction planning, but not to the progress or time for completion.[252] Such a right, therefore, must, in this case, must be separately agreed and explicitly included in order to exist.[253]

4.100 Despite the various legal opinions on this, it may be largely irrelevant in light of the new construction law. Under the new construction contract law, the Employer's rights to order changes have now been incorporated into the law, which is conspicuously silent on the issue of changes with regard to the time for completion.[254] This is shown in BGB §650b (1), "the parties shall seek agreement on the amendment (...)". Only after the failure of the attempt to reach an agreement can orders of the Employer be made effectively under narrow conditions. This requirement of the law that the parties come together to talk or negotiate is intended to avoid the parties to the construction contract postponing disputes to a later point in time.[255] Even if the parties fail to reach an agreement, the right to issue an order under BGB §650b (1) nos. 1 and 2 does not extend to the agreed execution periods.[256] Through the deliberate non-regulation, the legislature has clearly expressed that the instructing party's right to issue instructions relates exclusively to the success of the work itself and not to the type of construction and the agreed execution deadlines.[257]

4.101 However, while the prevailing opinion is that the Employer may not instruct changes with regard to the time for completion under BGB §650b, it is still quite controversial whether this right has been completely taken away. Under BGB §271; the rules of supplementary contract interpretation; the principles of good faith; changed circumstances; and frustration the Employer may be able to issue an instruction with regard to the time for completion without running afoul of BGB §650b.[258]

Termination

Termination by Employer

4.102 The reasons for termination under the new construction law are found in §§643, 648 and 648a of the BGB, the following analysis will be limited to the grounds for

251 *C. Zanner and N. Keller*, Das einseitige Anordnungsrecht des Auftraggebers zu Bauzeit und Bauablauf und seine Vergütungsfolgen, Neue Zeitschrift für Baurecht und Vergaberecht, vol. 5, no. 7, 2004, p. 353. See also, Breyer, *Bauzeitliche Folgen aus geänderten und zusätzlichen Leistungen gemäß §§2 Abs. 5 und 2 Abs. 6 VOB/B*, BauR 2013, 1924.

252 Ibid., See also, *R. Thode*, Nachträge wegen gestörten Bauablaufs im VOB/B-Vertrag Eine kritische Bestandsaufnahme, Zeitschrift für deutsches und internationales Bau- und Vergaberecht, vol. 27, no. 7, 2004, p. 214 (225).

253 Ibid.

254 BGB §650b.

255 *R. Leinemann* and *J.-H. Kues*, §650b, in: Leinemann, R. and Kues, J.-H. (eds.), *BGB Bauvertragsrecht*, Munich, C.H. Beck Verlag, 1st ed., 2018, BGB §650b, margin 11.

256 Ibid., at margin 60.

257 Ibid., at margin 61.

258 See, Kniffka/Koeble/Jurgeleit/Sacher, 5. Aufl. 2020, Kompendium des Baurechts, Teil 4 Der Werklohnanspruch des Auftragnehmers, Marginal 245, 246; Messerschmidt/Voit/von Rintelen, 3. Aufl. 2018, BGB §650b Rn. 27, 28.

termination found under a VOB/B contract. Once a contract is terminated, parties may refuse any further performance and claim for any performance rendered according to the rules of restitution.[259]

4.103 The preconditions for termination are frequently regulated by the contract in supplement or replacement of the terms of the VOB/B. Caution is required when it comes to termination, because unjustified termination of the contract without notice represents per se a reason for termination without notice by the counter-party who received the ineffective termination.[260] Hence a careful legal examination and preparation of the reasons for the termination must be made prior to the termination of a contract, particularly without notice, since a notification of termination cannot be revoked, contested or otherwise retracted.[261]

4.104 The Employer's termination rights are governed by §8 VOB/B, which gives the Employer, among others, the right to freely terminate the contract at any time up to the completion of the work.[262] This stems from the freedom of the Employer to be able to decide at any time not to proceed further the performance of the construction contract.[263] If the Employer exercises this right, the Contractor has the right to demand the contractually agreed remuneration, less any savings the Contractor realized through the Employer's termination and any sums earned through the re-appropriation of its staff and business operations (similar to the principles of set off under English common law).[264]

4.105 The Employer also has the right to terminate with or, under certain circumstances, without notice.[265] Reasons that justify termination without notice are also listed in §8, VOB/B. They are as follows:

1. Application for or initiation of insolvency proceedings or comparable legal proceedings on the assets of the Contractor or cessation of payments by the Contractor;[266]
2. Outstanding defects despite the Employer having granted the contractor a grace period for the remedying of said defects prior to acceptance (taking-over);[267]
3. Delay in the execution of the works by the Contractor following a prior request of the employer to expedite the works and the setting of a deadline for the expedited works;[268]
4. Agreements on the part of the contractor which constitute improper restraints on competition during the awarding of contracts for construction work;[269]

259 BGB §§346 et seq.

260 BGH, NJW 1969, 419 (420); BGH, NJW 1996, 3270 (3271).

261 BGB §130 para 1 Sentence 2.

262 VOB/B §8 (1) No. 1.

263 *M. Lederer*, in Kapellmann/Messerschmidt (2018), VOB/B §8, margin 11.

264 VOB/B §8 (1) Sentence 2, this runs in similar vein to BGB §649; however, the reference to presumed 5% remuneration for parts of the works not yet performed is included.

265 VOB/B §8 (2) No. 1.

266 VOB/B §8 (2) No. 1.

267 VOB/B §8 (3) No. 1 Sentence 1 in conjunction with VOB/B §5 (4).

268 Ibid.

269 VOB/B §8 (4) Sentence 1.

5. Any behaviour of the Contractor which makes the continuance of the contract unreasonable for the Employer (e.g., irretrievable loss of trust in the contract).[270]

Notice of termination must be given in writing[271] and the Contractor is required to submit, without undue delay, an verifiable invoice for the cost of the works performed up to the date of termination.[272]

Termination by Contractor

4.106 The preconditions under which the Contractor may terminate the contract without notice are covered briefly under VOB/B §9 as follows:

1. The Employer fails to perform an action for which he is responsible and as a result prevents the Contractor from performing the works;[273]
2. The Employer does not make a due payment or otherwise defaults on payment.[274]

4.107 Both these reasons for termination require the Contractor to set the Employer a reasonable deadline for subsequent performance of the action or for making payment, and for that deadline to pass.[275] The threat of termination as a result of a default of payment carries great risk. The Employer must have defaulted on a substantial part of the claim up to total remuneration.[276]

4.108 If the Contractor's termination without notice is legally valid, the work previously performed is to be invoiced according to the contract prices. Moreover, the contractor has a right to reasonable compensation in accordance with BGB §642 where any claims above and beyond this remain unaffected.[277]

4.109 A noteworthy feature of German law is the Employer's right to terminate the contract for convenience.[278] Under English law (English Common Law (4.129 et seq.)) the concept of repudiation allows the non-breaching party to terminate the contract if the other party refuses to perform the contract, breaches a condition (as opposed to a warranty) or breaches an intermediate term which affects the purpose of the contract. Anticipatory repudiation occurs when a party treats an act or declaration of the other party, which indicates the party will not perform its obligations under the contract even though performance is not yet due, as a breach and terminate the contract. Under German law the Employer is not in breach of contract if he terminates the contract prematurely. In that case, however, according to BGB a.F. §649, the Contractor will be entitled to claim for the agreed fee subject to a set-off of the amount saved as a result of the premature termination. In practice the fee will often be pre-estimated and fixed in the contract. Unlike the English law (cf. English Common Law (4.137 et seq.)), the BGB prescribes for the

270 BGH NJW-RR 1996, 1108, BGH, NJW 2000, 202.
271 VOB/B §8 (6).
272 VOB/B §8 (7).
273 VOB/B §9 (1) No. 1.
274 VOB/B §9 (1) No. 2.
275 VOB/B §9 (2) Sentence 2, note that the contractor must declare its intent to terminate if the obligation remains unfulfilled by the deadline.
276 MüKoBGB/Gaier, 8. Aufl. 2019, BGB §314 margin 18.
277 VOB/B §9 (3) Sentence 2.
278 BGB a.F. §649.

contractor a "presumed" entitlement to 5% of remuneration owing for unperformed works on the date of effective notice, baring evidence of a higher loss of profit.[279]

Forms of Security – Bonds and Guarantees

Bonds (Bürgschaften)

4.110 Under a *Bürgschaft*, the *Bürge* (guarantor) assumes responsibility for the discharge of a third party's obligation to the creditor.[280] Hence, in payment bonds under construction contracts, the guarantor promises to pay the employer's debt to the contractor if the employer does not fulfil its payment obligations.

4.111 The two key features of a *Bürgschaft* are:

(a) A *Bürgschaft* is conditional, and thus payment will only be made once the loss has been established;
(b) The obligation of the *Bürge* is strictly "accessory". Hence, if the primary obligation does not exist (or is not actual) then there is no claim arising out of the *Bürgschaft*.

4.112 The same types of bonds that are found in common law jurisdictions (English Common Law (4.334 et seq.)) are also found in Germany, including:

(a) Bid bond/tender bond – not particularly common in Germany;
(b) Advance payment bond – "*Vorauszahlungsbürgschaft*";
(c) Performance bond – "*Vertragserfüllungsbürgschaft*";
(d) Payment bond – "*Zahlungsbürgschaft*";
(e) Defects liability period – "*Gewährleistungsbürgschaft*" oder "Bürgschaft für Mängelansprüche".

On-Demand On-demand Bonds(Bürgschaft auf erstes Anforden)

4.113 On-demand On-demand bonds are not native to Germany because of the accessory nature of *Bürgschaften*; they were introduced into the German market to accommodate for the demands of international stakeholders. On-demand bonds are only valid under German law if their terms have been explicitly and individually negotiated by the parties and the parties are sufficiently sophisticated,[281] otherwise they will be held void if included in the general terms and conditions of a contract.[282]

279 BGB a.F. §649 (1) Sentence 3; *J. Busche*, §650 BGB, in Henssler, J. (ed.), *Münchener Kommentar zum BGB*, vol. 4, 6th edition, Munich, C.H. Beck Verlag, 2012, BGB §649, margin 29.

280 BGB §765 (1).

281 See, BGH NJW 1992, 1446 (1447), where an on-demand bond was held invalid between a commercially inexperienced married couple. But see, BGH, NJW 1997, 1435, BGH, NJW 1998, 2280 (2281), where the employer was a French company; BGH NJW 1998, 2280 (2281), where the affected party was regularly engaged in construction activities.

282 BGH, NJW 2002, 2388 (2389).

Latest Reform of German Construction Law

4.114 The latest reforms have introduced considerable changes to the operation of bonds and guarantees, in particular, the former §648 and §648a BGB, dealing with contractor's security for payment. The key changes include:

(a) With regard to change orders by the employer, the parties must strive to agree to contract amendments reflecting the change.[283] To the extent that an agreement is not reached within 30 days, the employer may unilaterally order the change.[284] The contractor is then required to perform the ordered change, unless it would be unreasonable for the contractor to do so;[285]

(b) Compensation for changes pursuant to §650b (2) is to be calculated based on costs actually incurred plus reasonable allowances for overheads and profit and taking into account additional risk.[286] The contractor may also use the original calculation (of the contract price) as a basis for an estimate of the additional costs;[287]

(c) Regarding instalment payments, the basis of calculation has changed from being based on the increased value to the employer resulting from the contractor's services, to now being calculated based on the value of the services rendered by the contractor under the contract.[288] To the extent that the invoiced services were not performed in accordance with the contract, the employer is now able to refuse to make payment on a reasonable amount of the invoiced amount.[289] Furthermore, the contractor may charge 80% of the quoted amount as an instalment, if the parties are unable to come to terms on the amount of compensation for changes according to §650b;[290]

(d) The contractor's ability to seek payment security from the employer remained largely unchanged with one significant exception, where the employer is a consumer.[291] The provisions of §650f (1)–(5) BGB are not applicable if the contract is a consumer construction contract according to §650i, or if the consumer employer is conducting certain property development such as constructing a multi-family house, where the contractor is required to transfer ownership of the land, as contemplated by §650u.

Defences

4.115 As in English law, the surety may assert the defences to which the debtor is entitled under the principal agreement, but in addition, the surety can still assert the same defences that the debtor is allowed under the principal agreement, even if the debtor has

283 BGB §650b (1).
284 BGB §650b (2) Sentence 1.
285 BGB §650b (2) Sentence 2. See also, Section 4.16 above.
286 BGB §650c (1).
287 BGB §650f 2.
288 BGB 632a (1) Sentence 1.
289 BGB 632a (1) Sentence 2.
290 BGB §650c (3).
291 BGB §650f (6).

waived those defences.[292] Furthermore, the bondsman may refuse to "satisfy" the creditor as long as the principal debtor is entitled to avoid the legal transaction upon which the obligation is based or as long as the creditor can obtain "satisfaction" by setting-off against a claim of the principal debtor.[293]

Guarantees (Garantie)

4.116 In Germany there are 2 forms of *Garantie*:

1. (a) Regular guarantee (*Garantie*) – the (bondsman) agrees to return the beneficiary to a position as if the triggering event (*materialler Garantiefall*) had not occurred; and
2. (b) Guarantee on First Demand (*Garantie auf erstes Anfordern*)[294] – the beneficiary is not obliged to prove that the *materialler Garantiefall* occurred when calling on the *Garantie*, rather a mere written declaration from the beneficiary that the underlying contract has been breached suffices for recovery. However, unlike an on-demand bond, where the alleged breach of contract did not take place or cannot have taken place, the bondsman it entitled to refuse satisfaction.

4.117 Unlike a *Bürgschaft*, a *Garantie* is not an "accessory" obligation. Hence, if the underlying contract becomes void, the *Garantie* survives and remains enforceable. Another difference is that the *Garantie* does not require any particular form or even writing.

Parent Company Guarantees (Patronatserklärung)

4.118 There are two forms in Germany:

(a) Non-binding parent company guarantee (*Weiche Patronatserklärung*) is a mere declaration of goodwill (or recommendation) by the parent company. It does not impose any obligations on the parent company to fulfil the obligations of the subsidiary;[295]
(b) Binding parent company guarantee (*Harte Patronatserklärung*), the parent company agrees to provide its subsidiary with adequate funds to facilitate satisfaction of its obligations to the beneficiary. This type of *Patronatserklärung* is an accessory obligation, as with a *Bürgschaft*, and in fact, the sections of the BGB that relate to *Bürgschaften* also apply to *Harte Patronatserklärungen*.[296]

292 BGB §768 (2).
293 BGB §770.
294 The validity of such guarantees on first demand are similar to on demand bonds. See, BGH NJW 2002, 3627 (3268), where the court held that the managing member of a limited liability company (GmbH) was inexperienced and the guarantee was, therefore, invalid. But see, OLG Frankfurt (Main) BeckRS 2004, 14947 para 14, where the court held that there is a lower threshold for guarantees on first demand in international commerce.
295 BGH, IBRRS 2011, 2119.
296 OLG Nuernberg, IPRax 1999, 464.

Retention (Sicherheitseinbehalt)

4.119 For retention before the taking-over (*Abnahme*) of the works, the retention amount allowed under a retention, under the GTCA, is similar to that in England, being 10% of the contract price.[297] However, if there are other forms of security, these must not exceed 10% of the contract price in the aggregate.

4.120 The VOB/B contains special terms and conditions related to retention,[298] as follows:

(a) Maximum retention amount permissible is 10% of payments;
(b) Payment of retention is made to a separate 'blocked' (escrow) account (*Sperrkonto*) – a joint bank account between the contractor and employer. The contractor is entitled to any interest accrued on the account;
(c) The employer is required to notify the contractor of the retention amount – there is an obligation to transfer retention money within 18 days;
(d) The employer must cause the bank to notify the contractor of the amount being deposited;
(e) If the employer fails to deposit the retention amount, the contractor must notify the employer and allow the employer a reasonable period of time to cure the situation. Otherwise, the consequences are:
    (i) Immediate release of the retention money to the contractor;
    (ii) the employer will lose each and every kind of security issued under the contract.

4.121 Unlike under the German VOB/B terms and conditions where retention money must be held in escrow, under the JCT the contractor may ask for the retention to be placed in a separate and properly designated bank account (so the retention moneys may be readily traced and identified). Thus, the separate bank account will only be set up if the Contractor requests it. Other important differences are the drastic nature of the consequences of the employer failing to deposit the retention money under the VOB/B terms and conditions and the fact that the interest earned from this account goes to the employer.

Claims

4.122 Whereas the VOB/B §1 (3) and (4) grant the employer the possibility to modify the works without stipulating consequences as to the compensation of the contractor for said works, VOB/B §2 (5) (variations) and (6) (additional works) set forth the consequences in that regard. Both, however, require that the work as planned (*Bausoll*) deviates from the work as built (*Bauist*).[299]

4.123 The distinction between variations and additional work is made by looking to the parties' original agreement and the scope of work. If these works were agreed upon but in a *qualitatively* different way, they are, if later instructed to be performed, variations

297 BGH, IBR 2016, 342, BGH, IBR 2011, 139.
298 §17 Absatz 6 VOB/B.
299 *J. Markus*, in Kapellmann/Messerschmidt (2018), VOB/B §2, margin 175.

(VOB/B §2 (5)). However, if these works fall outside of the original scope of works or vary significantly in *quantity*, they are considered additional works (VOB/B §2 (6)).[300] Furthermore, VOB/B §2 (6) will apply if, after a fundamental variation of the works, the contract no longer contains a point of reference so as to calculate the adjusted price.[301]

4.124 What follows from the distinction between additional and modified work is that under VOB/B §2 (6), the contractor is obliged to notify the employer before the execution of the additional work and may, absent such notification, lose its claim. Recognizing that these consequences disproportionately burden the contractor, the German Federal Supreme Court has crafted an exception to the rule[302] that no notification must be given if:

- If the employer expected or should have expected that the work would be performed only against payment (which applies in almost every case);
- No alternative to the contractor's immediate performance was given;
- If the failure to give notice does not arise from the contractor's own default.

4.125 Generally speaking, however, the VOB/B §2 (5) and (6) have almost identical requirements and a distinction between variations and additional work is rarely relevant. Whether §2 (5) or (6) applies, the parties must agree as to the additional remuneration. If such an agreement cannot be reached, the contractor may make use of its right to refuse executing the variation or additional work under the aforementioned circumstances (see 4.75–4.77).

4.126 As to the question to what extent variations and additional works affect the contract price, courts generally have held that the originally agreed contract price should give guidance in calculating any variation or additional work ("vorkalkulatorische Preisfortschreibung").[303]

4.127 The contractor's damages from delay of the employer are addressed in BGB §§280, 281, 282, 283, 286. If the employer has given an instruction from which a deterioration of the works results, the contractor can still demand part of the agreed price as far as it undertook the work. BGB §§677, 681, 670 may grant the contractor a right to claim for unauthorized work, see also VOB/B §2 (8) VOB/B. In case of a null contract, BGB §§812, 818 (2) will grant the contractor an averaged remuneration.[304]

4.128 Main claims of the employer regarding defects are governed by VOB/B §13 as discussed above. For contracts not governed by the VOB/B, according provisions are stated in BGB §634. Both are applicable from the time of acceptance.[305] Prior to acceptance, the employer can either terminate the contract or claim damages in accordance with the general provisions, BGB §§280, 281, 282, 283, 286.

300 *W. Voit*, in: Messerschmidt/Voit (2018), VOB/B §6, margins. 17, 20; *Markus* (2018), VOB/B §2, margin 183.

301 *Markus* (2018), VOB/B §2, margin 184.

302 BGH, BauR 1996, 542 (543).

303 BGH, BauR 2013, 943 para 15; OLG Hamm, IBR 2017, 123.

304 BGH, NJW 1962, 807; BGH, NJW 1962, 2010; BGH, NJW 1990, 2542.

305 BGH, NJW 2017, 1604 also classifying exceptional cases; *C. Schwenker*, Keine Mängelrechte vor Abnahme, Neue Juristische Wochenschrift, vol. 70, no. 22, 2017, p. 1579 (1581); OLG Koblenz BeckRS 2007, 19699; *E. Joussen*, Mängelansprüche vor der Abnahme, Baurecht, vol. 40, no. 2a, 2009, p. 319; *C. Sienz*, Die Neuregelungen im Werkvertragsrecht nach dem Schuldrechtsmodernisierungsgesetz, Baurecht, vol. 33, no. 1a, 2002, p. 181 (184).

4.129 The VOB/B provides for the contractor to suspend the works due to "hindrance and interruption" of works.[306] "Hindrance" is considered any type of negative effect on the time programme of the contractor's working process.[307] Thereby the contractor is free in drawing up the timetable; for example, if work is undertaken step by step or parallel.[308] The contractor is obliged to inform the employer without undue delay. Unlike the English common law position (English Common Law (4.304)), failing to give notice to the employer is not fatal to the contractor's claim; the contractor can still claim for hindrance if its cause and effect are obvious to the employer.[309]

4.130 Examples of circumstances constituting hindrances are:

4.1.1. **Circumstances within the employer's sphere of responsibility**; for example (if the parties did not agree differently)[310] provision of the site (including work to be undertaken by third parties in advance),[311] procurement of necessary building permits and licenses (§4 para. 1 no. 1 sentence 2 VOB/B), required documents (§3 para. 1 VOB/B), infrastructure on site (§4 para. 4 VOB/B), precise specification of service and schedule for tenders, modification of service (§1 para. 3, para. 4)[312] and financing;

4.1.2. **Strike action or by a lock-out** initiated by an employer's trade association and imposed on the contractor's firm or on a firm working directly for him. Strike is every systematic stoppage of multiple workers to put pressure on the employer in order to make it willing to negotiate.[313] Accordingly a lock-out is the exclusion of multiple workers to put pressure on them in order to make them willing to negotiate.[314] The wording does not allow for an extension of time as far as a supplier's workers strike or are locked out; under special circumstances, however, also this can affect the deadline;[315]

4.1.3. ***Force Majeure*** or other circumstances beyond the control of the contractor; however, not weather conditions that are normal for the time of the year and should thus have been allowed for when preparing the tender.

4.131 According to the German Federal Supreme Court, *Force Majeure* is any external event initiated by third-parties or natural forces that is not predictable and avoidable for the claiming party[316] even when exercising the highest duty of care.[317] Any form of fault

---

306 VOB/B §6.

307 *Markus* (2018), VOB/B §6, margin 1.

308 *Markus* (2018), VOB/B §6, margin 1.

309 VOB/B §6 (1).

310 *I. Oberhauser*, in BeckOK VOB/B (2019), VOB/B §6 (2) margin 3; *Markus* (2018), VOB/B §6, margin 21.

311 OLG Dresden, BauR 2015, 1488; OLG Duesseldorf, IBRRS 2009, 3322; *Markus* (2018), VOB/B §6, margin 18; BGH, NJW 2004, 2373 in a different way from BGH, NJW 1985, 2475. However, not to shield the site from weather conditions, BGH, NJW 2017, 2025 (2026).

312 *Markus* (2018), VOB/B §6, margin 20.

313 BAG, NJW 1955, 882; *B. Waas*, in Rolfs, C., Giesen, R., Kreikebohm, R., and Udsching, P. (eds.), *BeckOK Arbeitsreicht*, 51st edition, Munich, C.H. Beck Verlag, 2019, GG Art. 9 margin 90.

314 BAG, NJW 1955, 882.

315 *Oberhauser* (2019), VOB/B §6 (2), margin 9; *Markus* (2018), VOB/B §6, margin 23.

316 BGH, NJW 1997, 3018.

317 BGH, NJW 1953, 184; concerning the provability BGH, NJW 1997, 3018.

on the part of the claiming party excludes forces majeure.[318] Theft and criminal damage are not necessarily unpredictable.[319]

4.132 Atypical weather conditions which may give rise to a claim of *Force Majeure* are long lasting frost periods[320] or exceptional increases in precipitation.[321] As a reference, the circumstances of the past 10[322] to 20[323] years can be adduced.

Disputes – Adjudication and Arbitration

4.133 State court proceedings in Germany are long-winded. On average, proceedings at the regional courts take 15 months,[324] construction proceedings, on the other hand, average 44 months.[325] In case of appeal to the higher regional courts, proceedings can go on for an additional 10 months or longer,[326] plus another 6 to 24 months, if the case is brought before the German Federal Supreme Court.[327] It goes without saying that the costs increase significantly in such a drawn-out proceeding.

4.134 In Germany, disputes arising from construction contracts are resolved by civil courts. According to GVG §23 no. 1 (*Gerichsverfassungsgesetz*), districts courts have jurisdiction over cases up to maximum amount in controversy of €5,000.00. If the disputed amount exceeds €5,000.00, regional courts exercise jurisdiction, GVG §71 (1).

4.135 In determining the proper venue, there are several options from which the claimant can choose, ZPO §35 (German Civil Procedure Code):

- ZPO §§13, 17 set the court at the domicile of the defendant (its registered seat) as the general venue;
- ZPO §21 adds the court at the place of business of the responsible branch office as a possible venue;
- In case of a contractual dispute, according to ZPO §29, also the court of the location of performance (where the work is to be done) shall have jurisdiction;
- If the contracting parties are both merchants in the sense of BGB §14, they can grant any other court local jurisdiction by agreement, ZPO §38 (1). Regarding the validity of such agreement, substantive law (BGB) applies.[328] Note: VOB/B

318 BGH, NJW 1997, 3018.
319 Cf. VOB/B §4 (5).
320 BGH, NJW 2017, 2025.
321 BGH, NJW 1973, 1698.
322 *Markus* (2018), VOB/B §6, margin 26.
323 *Oberhauser* (2019), VOB/B §6 (2) margin 14.
324 Federal Statistical Office, Zivilgerichte Fachserie 2016, p.56: www.destatis.de/GPStatistik/servlets/MCRFileNodeServlet/DEHeft_derivate_00032941/2100210167004.pdf;jsessionid=80917E4CD735695DCEFE3EEB83CFF596 (accessed 12 July 2019).
325 Press Release ARGE Baurecht, 29.06.2015: https://arge-baurecht.com/fileadmin/user_upload/artikel/pressemitteilungen/2015-07-02/PM-AG-BauR_Mehr-Baukammern_weniger-Insolvenzen.pdf (accessed 12 July 2019).
326 Federal Statistical Office, Zivilgerichte Fachserie 2016, p. 102: www.destatis.de/GPStatistik/servlets/MCRFileNodeServlet/DEHeft_derivate_00032941/2100210167004.pdf;jsessionid=80917E4CD735695DCEFE3EEB83CFF596 (*accessed 12 July 2019*).
327 German Federal Supreme Court, "Übersicht über den GESCHÄFTSGANG bei den ZIVILSENATEN des Bundesgerichtshofs im Jahre 2016", 2016, p. 32: www.bundesgerichtshof.de/SharedDocs/Downloads/DE/Service/StatistikZivil/jahresstatistikZivilsenate2016.pdf?__blob=publicationFile (accessed 12 July 2019).
328 BGH, NJW 1968, 1233 (1233); BGH, NJW 1972, 391 (393).

§18 contains such agreement, modifying the provisions of the ZPO by stating an explicit jurisdiction in favor of the employer;

- Also, if the defendant does not object the venue, venue will be deemed proper through waiver, ZPO §39.

4.136 Important to note: Extrajudicial mediation proceedings are not mandatory in Germany before bringing a dispute to court, unless the parties agree otherwise, ZPO §278a. Frequently the parties agree[329] to have disputes solved by an independent board of experts in adjudication proceedings. Adjudication proceedings are not governed by German law, however, several institutions have developed adjudication rules, namely the DIS (*DIS-Verfahrensordnung für Adjudikation* 10, 2010), Deutsche *Gesellschaft für Baurecht* (*SL-Bau*, 2016) or the DBGT (*AO-Bau*, 2009). What distinguishes adjudication from mediation is that the parties want to have the dispute resolved and not necessarily make an agreement. What distinguishes adjudication from arbitration is the binding effect of the final decision, which in the case of adjudication is only preliminary.[330]

4.137 The parties can agree on arbitration proceedings, ZPO §1029, which in turn forces state courts to dismiss claims raised as inadmissible if the defendant objects. However, the agreement must be concluded in accordance with ZPO §1031 and must state which matters shall be governed by arbitration and that state court proceedings in these matters shall be excluded,[331] the responsible arbitral tribunal must also be named.[332] Arbitration rules can be drafted or simply be applied.[333] Common rules of arbitration in Germany are the SGOBau, the SOBau, SL-Bau, or DIS-Rules.

Construction Law Issues Specific to German Law

4.138 Under the BGB there are several issues worth mentioning specifically under the German law relating to construction. Particularly noteworthy are the means by which a contractor is able to secure payment for his services. A contractor is entitled to demand an equitable mortgage (*Sicherungshypothek*) be taken out in its favour on the building plot in order to satisfy claims he has against the employer.[334] If the construction is not yet completed, he may also demand that an equitable mortgage be granted in its favour for the portion of the payment corresponding to the work performed and for expenses not included in the remuneration.[335]

4.139 The contractor may otherwise choose to seek security amounting to 10% of the remuneration sought to be secured for additional works and/or ancillary claims

329 *Boldt* (2018), Chap. T, margin 98.

330 *J. Münch*,Vorbemerkung zu §1025, in Rauscher, T. and Krüger, W. (eds.), *Münchener Kommentar zur ZPO*, vol. 3, 5th edition, Munich, C.H. Beck Verlag, 2017, Preliminary Remarks concerning ZPO §1025, margin 72; *A. Aldinger* and *V. Mahnken*, Adjudikation, in: Roquette, A. and Otto, A., *Vertragsbuch Privates Baurecht*, 2nd edition, Munich, C.H. Beck Verlag (2011), Chap. D, IV margin 2; *Boldt* (2018), Chap. T, margin 96.

331 *C. Wolf* and *N. Eslami*, "§1029" in Vorwerk, V. and Wolf, C. (eds.), *BeckOK ZPO*, 32nd edition, Munich, C.H. Beck Verlag, 2019, ZPO §1029, margins. 10, 11.

332 BGH, NJW 1983, 1267; BGH, BeckRS 2017, 132724.

333 *I. Saenger*, in Saenger, I. (ed.), *Zivilprozessordnung*, 8th edition, Baden-Baden, Nomos Verlag (2019), ZPO §1029, margin 13.

334 BGB §650e (BGB §648 prior to 1.1.2018).

335 Ibid.

(*Nebenforderungen*). Insofar as the contractor has procured security for his claims for remuneration, he will be precluded from obtaining an equitable mortgage according to BGB §650e as well.[336]

National Construction Law and International Forms (Emphasis FIDIC) – How Do FIDIC and Other International Forms Operate?

4.140 Where standard form contracts such as FIDIC are used, the German GTCA regularly comes into play. When a contract or contract term is drafted in such a way as to be used on more than one occasion the GTCA will be triggered.[337] German courts have gone so far as to say that if a clause *could* be used on more than one occasion even if it that the GTCA applies.[338] This gives courts a very wide berth in the application of GTCA. Thus, unless it can be shown that each clause was individually negotiated, the application of the GTCA is nearly unavoidable. BGB §307 states that

> provisions in standard business terms are ineffective if, contrary to the requirements of good faith, they unreasonably disadvantage the other party to the contract with the user. Courts in Germany have broad scope in determining what terms should be held void. The consequences can be severe. Liquidated damages clauses, for example, which are generally permissible under German law, but do not meet the criteria set forth under the GTCA will be held void.
>
> [339]

Furthermore, since German law does not have any "gap filling" provisions, in the case of a liquidated damages clause being held void, the employer's recourse would be limited to the standard measure of damages, and would require the time and cost intensive process of establishing the actual damages resulting from the delay.

4.141 Another key aspect of international standard form contracts which will be held void under German law are time bar clauses.[340] The German Supreme Court has held that a clause in which a party loses its entitlement to make a claim because it failed to meet a deadline for notice runs afoul of the GTCA, as it is violative of the principles of good faith.[341]

4.142 The GTCA had been originally intended as a consumer protection statute,[342] but in practice has been extended by the courts to cover all manner of contracts, including business to business transactions.[343] Whereas in most jurisdictions business to business transactions are generally considered to be concluded by sophisticated parties with the benefit of counsel and, therefore, without the need for additional legislative protections.[344]

336 BGB §650f para 4 (§648a para 4 prior to 1.1.2018) (4).
337 BGB §305.
338 BGH, NZBau 2001, 682 (682).
339 See: BGH, NJW 2003, 1805 (1808).
340 BGH, NJW-RR 1991, 534 (535).
341 Ibid.
342 See, BT-Drs 7/3919 (1975), p. 1.
343 BGH Urt. v. 19.9.2007 – VIII ZR 141/06.
344 Ingeborg Schwenzer and Claudio Marti Whitebread, *International B2B Contracts – Freedom Unchained?*, 4 Penn. St. J.L. & Int'lAff.33 (2015).

CHAPTER 5

French Law (Napoleonic)

François Muller and Victoria Aquino

DOI: 10.4324/9781315671376-5

History of French Law

5.1 Construction law in France stemmed from the large construction projects that have marked its history, from the great cathedrals to the Palace of Versailles. Notably, it was during the construction of the Palace of Versailles that the rules specific to public procurement were formalized, the principles of which later inspired the successive editions of the French Public Procurement Code (*Code des Marchés Publics*).

5.2 The contracting rules were formalized under the reign of Henri IV, in a Royal Declaration of 7 February 1608, that sets clear rules for royal public procurement contracts. Notably, it required the publication of said contracts and the settlement of the final account for the completed works after their formal acceptance, the "*réception*".

5.3 At the time, contracts could be established for a fixed price and, more common for masonry and carpentry contracts, on an *unité d'oeuvre* basis (i.e., a price per unit of work or bill of quantities basis). They were awarded after a tendering procedure, to the lowest bidder according to the established procedures for the acquisition of buildings.

5.4 Under the impulsion of Louis XIV, the practice of public procurement gave rise to fundamental concepts that still exist in the 21st Century Public Procurement Code: Thus, the Royal Declaration of 12 May 1708 organised the pre-selection of suppliers according to criteria of technical and financial capacity; the consultation, that may be open or restricted; the derogation from preliminary publication procedures in case of emergency; the withholding, or the security required from the contractor until the formal acceptance ("*réception*") of the works and the expiration of the performance guarantees for the works which, in time, are organized into one and ten-year periods and are still in effect, integrated in Articles 1792 et seq. of the French Civil Code (referred to not only by judicial courts, but also administrative courts).

5.5 These provisions specific to public procurement contracts, their payment, the settlement of the final account, and the guarantees attached thereto apply in addition to the general provisions of French contract law.

5.6 By the 19th century, a distinction appears between private and public construction contracts, the regimes of which differ not only in the manner they are awarded, but also in their performance.

5.7 Private law contracts are subject to the strict application of the *pacta sunt servanda* principle. In contrast, public procurement contracts are governed by administrative law that recognizes the contractor's right to compensation in the event of unforeseeable circumstances ("*imprévision*"), that stems from the imperative requirements of mutability and adaptability to the evolving constraints of public service.

5.8 Since the latest reform of French Private Contract law of 10 February 2016[1] and recent judicial and administrative developments, the difference between private and public construction contracts is even greater. For example:

- The formation of the contract is governed by mutual consent in private law contracts; whilst the award of an administrative contract falls under a jurisdiction;

1 Ordinnance N° 2016-131 of 10 February 2016 reforming contracts law, further modified by Law n° 2018-287 of 20 April 2018.

- During the pre-contractual phase, the private employer (*Maître d'Ouvrage*) is bound by a reporting obligation derived from a principle of fairness in contractual relations, principle that does not apply in the pre-contractual phase of public law contracts;[2]
- During the performance of the contract, a right to the revision of a private law contract is now recognized if an unforeseeable event overturning the economy of the contract occurs, unless otherwise agreed between the parties, whilst administrative law tends to distance itself from this principle although it largely contributed to creating it;
- In terms of liability, traditionally, the employer in a private contract is contractually liable for the acts of third-parties, that is, for the third parties he or she involves in the performance of his or her own obligations (e.g., consultants, engineers, etc.). By contrast, in administrative law the public employer is now exonerated from the faults of other participants, consultants, engineers, chief engineers, etc. Nevertheless, one ought to remain cautious about the evolution of private case law on third party liability insofar as private case law has recently issued decisions inspired by the administrative solution;
- Late or performance penalties may be reduced or increased by the judge when they are manifestly excessive or derisory with respect to the damages suffered in private law contracts. In administrative contracts, in turn, the judge considers that such penalties are applicable, even if the Administration did not suffer any damages. They may only be exceptionally be reduced if they are proved to be manifestly excessive compared with penalties usually provided for in similar contracts;[3]
- As regards the termination clause, finally: The Administration's co-contractor cannot "*invoke the Administration's violations or failures in order to avoid its own contractual obligations or to take the initiative to unilaterally terminate the contract*". Moreover, the Administration can refuse to abide by a termination clause on grounds of general interest.[4]

Contract Law

5.9 French Contract Law was mostly crafted under Napoleon Bonaparte's reign. Between 1804 and 2016, only four articles of the Civil Code pertaining to contract law were amended, leaving the remainder untouched.

5.10 A significant reform of contract law was passed on 10 February 2016, and came into force on 1 October 2016, and applicable to contracts entered into as from that date. Another reform was then passed on 20 April 2018, and is applicable to contracts entered into after 1 October 2018.

5.11 As a result, three sets of rules may apply to contracts in France. As a principle (subject to various exceptions):

2 *Conseil d'Etat*, Decision of 11 April 2014, No. 375051.
3 *Conseil d'Etat*, Decision of 19 July 2017, No. 392707.
4 *Conseil d'Etat*, Decision of 8 October 2014, No. 370644.

- Contracts entered into before 1 October 2016 remain submitted to the "old" law of contract, mostly defined in the 1804 Civil Code;
- Contracts entered into between 1 October 2016 and 1 October 2018 are submitted to the 2016 Law reform;
- Contracts entered into after 1 October 2018 are submitted to the 2018 Law reform.

5.12 To date, the application by the French Supreme Court (*la Cour de cassation*) of the new rules of contract law has not led to any significant developments..

5.13 The new contract law, in force since October 2016 and sometimes modified by the 2018 Law reform, is addressed below, unless otherwise expressly stated.

Preliminary Rules

5.14 The French Civil Code first provides for a series of preliminary rules applicable to all contracts,[5] including:

- **The notion of contract**: A contract is defined as an agreement between two or more people, aimed at creating, modifying, transferring or extinguishing obligations;[6]
- **Contractual freedom**: Parties are free to enter into any agreement, to choose their co-contractor and to determine the content of the contract, provided that they remain within the limits of *ordre public* (public policy);[7]
- ***Pacta sunt servanda***;[8]
- **Good faith**: Contracts must be negotiated, entered into and performed in good faith. This general duty pertains to public policy; consequently, the parties cannot agree to limit or exclude their duty of good faith.[9]

The Formation of a Contract

- **General Features of All Contracts**

5.15 This section addresses the general principles applicable to the formation of all contracts under French law, namely: (i) The validity of the contract; (ii) offer, and acceptance; (iii) the intention to create Legal Relations; (iv) capacity to enter into a contract; (v) formalities for the conclusion of the contract.

5.16 In addition, French law provides for specific rules regarding negotiations and preliminary agreements, and expressly puts on the parties a duty to inform the other party of elements that could be of "*decisive importance*" (*importance déterminante*) to the other party.

5.17 These features are addressed in turn below.

5 French Civil Code, Articles 1101 to 1111-1.
6 French Civil Code, Article 1101.
7 French Civil Code, Article 1102.
8 French Civil Code, Article 1103.
9 French Civil Code, Article 1104.

Contract Validity

5.18 French law is guided by the principle of "*consensualisme*", which means that a contract is valid as soon as the parties reach an agreement. Unless specifically provided for by law, no form, and especially no writing, is in principle required.[10] Verbal or tacit consent suffices.

5.19 However, consent alone is not enough to form a contract. Rather, three conditions need to be met for a contract to be validly made: (i) The parties consent to the contract; (ii) they have the capacity to conclude a contract, and (iii) the content of the contract is valid and lawful.[11]

5.20 In other words, the parties' consent is not enough to bind them. They must be legally capable and draft a contract that is lawful in its content.

Offer and Acceptance

5.21 Since French contract law is based on the principle of "*consensualisme*", a contract is formed where an offer is met by an acceptance. As an exception, certain contracts are formed not by offer and acceptance, but by the delivery of a thing ("real contracts") or by the accomplishment of formalities ("solemn contracts").

5.22 An offer is defined as a proposition to enter into a contract.[12] To be valid, it must contain the essential elements of the contemplated contract that depend on the type of the transaction. For example, in the case of a sales contract, the essential elements are (i) the object of the sale and (ii) the price.

5.23 Once it reaches its beneficiary, the offer cannot be retracted until the timeframe defined therein expires or, in the absence of such a timeframe, for a reasonable time period. Should the offer be retracted by the offeror before the specified timeframe or a reasonable time period has passed, as the case may be, the beneficiary may be entitled to damages.

5.24 An offer can be accepted explicitly or tacitly, being clarified that silence may only be characterized as acceptance unless specified otherwise "*by law, usages, business relationships or specific circumstances*".[13]

Intention to Create a Legal Relationship

5.25 Intention to create a legal relationship is not expressly required by the Civil Code for a contract to be valid under French law.

5.26 However, it can be argued that, since the parties' *consent* is required,[14] they must have had the intention to create a legal relationship. In particular, a proposal to contract is not binding where it is meant as a joke (e.g., "*my kingdom for a horse*"), or where the parties did not understand the nature or the extent of their commitment.

Capacity

5.27 Valid consent to a contract requires a party to be of sound mind.[15]

---

10 French Civil Code, Article 1172.
11 French Civil Code, Article 1128.
12 French Civil Code, Article 1114.
13 French Civil Code, Article 1120.
14 French Civil Code, Article 1128.
15 French Civil Code, Article 1129.

5.28 In addition, people lacking legal capacity cannot enter into a contract. As a principle, minors under 18 of age cannot enter into a contract. As regards adults, those who suffer from restriction of their legal capacity cannot freely conclude contracts. Thus, a *majeur sous curatelle* (adult under curatorship) cannot enter into certain contracts without the assistance of his or her curator. Similarly, a *majeur sous tutelle* (adult under guardianship) cannot act on his or her own. Such adults must be assisted or represented by their guardians.

Representation

5.29 Article 1161 of the Civil code, created by the 2016 Law reform and modified by the 2018 Law Reform, provides that, regarding physical personals, an agent cannot represent two people who are in a conflict of interest (e.g. a seller and a buyer). Such a rule does not apply to legal entities, since the 2018 Law reform.

Formalities

5.30 Apart from specific contracts (e.g., lease agreements or guarantees), French law does not require any formality for a contract to be valid.[16]

Negotiations

5.31 Offer and acceptance can be preceded by a negotiation period, governed under French law by a number of principles, including:

- Freedom of negotiations: The parties remain free to put an end to the negotiations and not conclude the contemplated agreement;
- Good faith: Negotiations must be initiated, conducted and concluded in good faith. A party in breach of its duty to act in good faith would be liable to pay damages to the other party, the amount of which cannot, however, correspond to the sums the aggrieved party would have received had the contract been concluded;
- Confidentiality: No information obtained during the negotiations can be used or divulged.

Preliminary Agreements (Avant-Contrats)

5.32 Following the 2016 Reform of Contract Law, the French Civil Code now recognizes two types of preliminary agreements (*avant-contrats*): (i) The *pacte de preference*,[17] and (ii) the *promesse unilatérale*.[18]

5.33 The *pacte de préférence* (preemption agreement) is a contract by which a party, the promisor, undertakes to propose by priority to the other party, the beneficiary, to deal with him or her should the promisor decide to enter into a contract. Should the promisor breach the *pacte de préférence*, the beneficiary may obtain damages to compensate its losses. In addition, if the third party with whom the promisor contracted was aware of the existence of the *pacte de preference* and of the beneficiary's intent to benefit from the

16 French Civil Code, Article 1112.
17 French Civil Code, Article 1123.
18 French Civil Code, Article 1124.

pacte de préférence, the beneficiary may apply to have the contract annulled or request the judge to substitute him to the third party in the contract concluded.[19]

5.34 The *promesse unilatérale* (unilateral promise), next, is the contract by which a party, the promisor, grants another, the beneficiary, a right to have the option to conclude a contract which essential elements are specified, and for the formation of which only the beneficiary's consent is missing. The promisor's refusal to conclude the contemplated contract does not prevent its conclusion: A judge may compel the parties to conclude the contract.[20]

Duty to Inform

5.35 The 2016 Reform of Contract Law has introduced a major change: Pursuant to Article 1112-1 of the French Civil Code, the parties are now mutually obliged to disclose any information they are aware of that is of decisive importance to the other, regardless of whether they are professionals or consumers, or of their role in the contract.

5.36 Should a party fail to disclose such a piece of information, the other party could either claim damages, or request the annulment of the contract, depending on whether the defaulting party's silence was intentional or not.

5.37 However, this duty does not apply to the price of the contract: No information has to be given as to whether it is adequate or not.[21]

Particular Features of Public Contracts

5.38 As explained in the "History of French law" section of this Chapter, France has a long tradition of strongly regulated public procurement, which has inspired the European Union and simultaneously spread to a large variety of different public contracts. Statutory law is predominant, as a *Code des marchés publics* has existed since the 1960s and has rapidly evolved to adapt to the European Directives.

5.39 The public procurements regulation and various other applicable legislation stem from constitutional principles and laws and are complemented by case law. For example, the French *Conseil Constitutionnel* has decided that the principles consecrated at Article 1 of the former *Code des marchés publics*[22] (namely: Freedom of access to public procurement, equality of treatment, transparency of procurement procedures, efficiency of public procurement, and good management of public monies), derive from Articles 6 and 14 of the 1789 Declaration of Human Rights.[23] Similarly, the European Court of Justice ("**ECJ**") has laid down basic principles applicable to all public procurement contracts, even those that are not subject to a specific regime under the EU Directives (e.g., public procurement contracts, the amount of which is below the thresholds provided for by such Directives, or works concessions).[24] The ECJ applies to public procurement the principles

19 French Civil Code, Article 1123.

20 French Civil Code, Article 1124.

21 Article 1137 of the French Civil Code was modified in 2018 in accordance with this rule. Not disclosing one's assessment of the value of an obligation is not reprehensible.

22 CCP, Article L. 3.

23 *Conseil Constitutionnel*, Decision of 26 June 2003, No. 2003-473 D.C., A.J.D.A 2003, at p. 2348.

24 Commission Interpretative Communication on Concessions under Community Law of 29 April 2000, *Official Journal*, C-121/2.

of non-discrimination, equality of treatment, transparency, proportionality, and mutual recognition.

5.40 Public procurement is a public contract under French law, the formation of which differs from the general rules addressed above on key points. For example, the negotiation of a public contract following a formal procedure calling for tenders is prohibited. Exceptions to this prohibition are very rare, and strictly limited to cases where negotiations are expressly allowed. Moreover, the vast majority of public contracts, and *all* public procurement contracts, are to be made in writing.

5.41 This section will address, in turn: (i) The various procedures for awarding public procurement contracts; (ii) the mechanisms for the solicitation and submission of tenders or proposals; (iii) the evaluation and comparison of tenders or proposals; (iv) the acceptance of the tender or proposal and the entry into force of the contract, and (v) the control of the award of the contract by judicial review proceedings.

Procedures for Awarding Public Procurement Contracts

- Legal Framework

5.42 The various mandatory procedures for awarding public procurement contracts are contained in a complex legal framework:

- The *Code des marchés publics* of 1 September 2006 and Ordinance No. 2005-649 of 6 June 2005 on procurement contracts concluded by certain public or private entities not subject to the *Code des marchés publics*, were amended to implement new EU Directives Nos. 2014/24[25] and 2014/25.[26] The previous regulation was replaced by (i) Ordinance No. 2015-899 of 23 July 2015 on public procurement contracts, and (ii) Decrees Nos. 2016-360 on public procurement contracts and 2016-361 on defence or security public procurement contracts, of 25 March 2015.
- In addition, Ordinance No. 2016-65 of 29 January 2016 and Decree No. 2016-86 of 1 February 2016 on concession contracts implement EU Directive 2014/23.[27] They have entered into force on 1 April 2016 and apply to procedures commenced as from that date.

5.43 The above regulation (i.e., 2015 and 2016 Ordinances as well as 2016 Decrees) has been codified in 2019 in a new code entitled "*Code de la commande publique*" (hereinafter CCP).

5.44 The mandatory procedures for awarding public procurement contracts detailed in the above legislation are to be followed in specific circumstances that depend on (i) the definition of the purchaser involved, and (ii) the purpose of the contract.

Scope of Application Rationae Personae of the Mandatory Procedures

25 Directive 2014/24/EU of the European Parliament and of the Council of 26 February 2014 on public procurement and repealing Directive 2004/18/EC.

26 Directive 2014/25/EU of the European Parliament and of the Council of 26 February 2014 on procurement by entities operating in the water, energy, transport and postal services sectors and repealing Directive 2004/17/EC.

27 Directive 2014/23/EU of the European Parliament and of the Council of 26 February 2014 on the award of concession contracts.

5.45 The scope of application *rationae personae* of the mandatory procedures stems from the definition of public procurement contracts.

5.46 According to the law, public procurement contracts are defined as "*contracts concluded for pecuniary interest by one or more purchasers [...], with one or more economic operators in order to meet their requirements in relation to works, supplies, or services*".[28]

5.47 It exists two types of "*purchasers*":

1. Contracting *authorities*,[29] that comprise: (i) Legal persons subject to public law; (ii) legal persons subject to private law but established for the specific purpose of meeting needs of general interest, and that do not have an industrial or commercial purpose; and (iii) bodies or other entities subject to private law, established by contracting authorities, that enjoy legal personality for the purpose of performing some activities;
2. Contracting *entities*,[30] that comprise: (i) Certain contracting authorities operating a network in water, energy, transport, and postal services sectors;[31] if they are not contracting authorities, state-owned companies which pursue one of the activities of network operator; and (iii) private law bodies or other entities that enjoy special or exclusive rights in operating a network pursuant to a legally enacted provision, in order to pursue one of the activities of a network operator.
    - Scope of Application *Rationae Materiae* of the Mandatory Procedures

5.48 The definition of public procurement works contracts are defined as contracts having for object the construction, or both the design and build, by any means, of works fulfilling to the requirements set by the contracting authority has a decisive influence on their nature or design.[32]

5.49 However, a number of contracts are expressly excluded[33] from the mandatory awarding procedures, notably: (i) In-house contracts,[34] (ii) contracts entered into exclusively between two or more contracting authorities or contracting entities in the context of cooperation to perform public services with common purposes in general interest; (iii) contracts entered into between a contracting entity and a "related" company in order to pursue one of the activities of network operator, a "related" company being defined as a company under or with dominant influence or presenting consolidated accounts with

28 CCP, Article L. 1111-1.

29 CCP, Article L. 1211-1.

30 CCP, Article L.1212-1.

31 As listed in Article L. 1212-3 of CCP.

32 CCP, Article L. 1111-2. It should be noted that the definition of "works" is aligned with that contained in Directive 2014/24/EU of the European Parliament and of the Council of 26 February 2014 on public procurement and repealing Directive 2004/18/EC, and thus refers to the outcome of building or civil engineering works taken as a whole which is sufficient by itself to fulfil an economic or technical function.

33 CCP, Article L. 2511-1.

34 A contract is deemed "in-house" when the contracting authority exercises over the person concerned a control which is similar to that which it exercises over its own departments and, at the same time, that person carries out the essential part of its activities with the controlling local authority or authorities (ECJ, 18 November 1999, C 107/98, *Teckal*, ECLI:EU:C:1999:562). Ordinance No. 2015-899 allows the direct participation of private capital without monitoring or blocking capacity. The in-house exemption is now incorporated in Article 12 of Directive 2014/24/EU of the European Parliament and of the Council of 26 February 2014 on public procurement and repealing Directive 2004/18/EC, CCP, Article L. 2511-1.

the contracting entity; (iv) certain contracts involving defence or security aspects;[35] (v) contracts requiring secrecy or which cannot be performed without special security measures in accordance with laws, regulations or administrative provisions in force or that the protection of the State's essential interests require, provided that such security and this protection cannot be guaranteed by alternative means; (vi) contracts relating to the acquisition or rental of land, existing buildings, or other real property, whatever the financial terms; (vii) supply, works, or services contracts concluded pursuant to an international agreement concerning the stationing of troops; (viii) supply, works, or services contracts concluded pursuant to an international agreement binding France and one or more third countries to perform or implement a project jointly, the agreement being transmitted to the European Commission, or pursuant to procedures established by an international organization, or (ix) services contracts in relation to arbitration and conciliation.

Presentation of the Various Procedures

5.50 Is regulated through formal procedures, the award of:[36]

- Supply and services contracts, in excess of (i) €135,000, excluding VAT, for State contracts; (ii) €209,000, excluding VAT, for local authorities contracts, and (iii) €418,000, excluding VAT, for public purchasers operating a network,
- Works contracts in the amount of €5,225,000, excluding VAT.

5.51 Those contracts below the thresholds may be subject to an adapted procedure.[37]

5.52 The public purchaser may elect to apply various procedures, subject to specific conditions such as the value and the nature of the contract, namely:

1. A negotiated procedure, without prior publicity nor competition;[38]
2. An open or restricted call for tenders;[39]
3. A "*competitive procedure with negotiation*";[40]
4. A "*negotiated procedure with prior competition*";[41]
5. A *procedure* with competitive dialogue;[42]
6. A design contest.[43]

5.53 All these procedures are addressed, in turn, below, as well as the procedure relative to partnership contracts.

The Negotiated Procedure Without Prior Publicity or Competition[44]

5.54 A negotiated procedure without prior publicity nor competition may be followed in a strictly limited number of cases, some of which are encountered from time to time in

---

35 As listed in Article L. 2515-1 of CCP.

36 Figures may vary, as a result of regulatory adjustments.

37 CCP, Articles R. 2123-1 – R. 2123-3.

38 CCP, Article R. 2122-1.

39 CCP, Article R. 2124-2, Articles R. 2161-2 – R. 2161-11.

40 CCP, Articles R. 2161-12 – R. 2161-20.

41 CCP, Articles R. 2161-21, R. 2161-22, R. 2161-23, R. 2362-14, R. 2362-15, R. 2362-16, R. 2362-17, R. 2362-18.

42 CCP, Article R. 2161-24 – R. 2161-31.

43 CCP, Articles R. 2162-15 – R. 2162-21.

44 CCP, Article R. 2122-1.

the construction field. However, it should be stressed that this "*freedom to negotiate*" is itself strictly construed.[45]

5.55 The cases in which such a procedure may be applied are notably, but not exclusively, the following:

- An imperative urgency resulting from circumstances unforeseeable for the public entity that are not attributable to it, and that require the contract to be concluded in such a timeframe that a formal procedure cannot be followed. In such a case, the public procurement contract is limited to the works strictly necessary to resolve the urgent situation;[46]
- A call for tenders, or a formal procedure, as the case may be, is unsuccessful (for example, absence of candidates or tenders, or absence of appropriate or compliant tenders);[47]
- Only one determined operator is able to perform the works, for intellectual property rights or technical reasons (for example, the acquisition or loan of a minor and non-separable part of a building to be built by the operator);[48]
- Works contracts which purpose is exactly the same as that of a previous contract awarded after formal procedure, provided this possibility had been expressly mentioned in the rules for tenders of the first contract.[49]

The Open or Restricted Call for Tenders[50]

5.56 The call for tenders is the procedure by which the public purchaser selects the economically most advantageous tender, without prior negotiation, on the basis of objective criteria laid down in the contract notice.

5.57 Calls for tenders may either be open or restricted. The choice of the type of call for tenders belongs to the public purchaser, and depends on who may tender: In open calls for tender, any economic operator may do so, whereas restricted calls for tenders are only open to candidates selected by the public purchaser for their technical and/or professional abilities.

5.58 The call for tenders procedure is the default procedure: The public purchaser must follow it for all of its contracts, unless the conditions for the application of any of the other procedures are fulfilled.

The Negotiated Procedures with Competition[51]

5.59 There are two types of negotiated procedures with competition:

- The "*competitive procedure with negotiation*", that is led by the contracting authority;[52]

45 As explained above, the negotiation of a public contract following a formal procedure calling for tenders is prohibited. Exceptions to this prohibition are very rare, and strictly limited to cases where negotiations are expressly allowed.

46 CCP, Article R. 2122-1.

47 CCP, Article R. 2122-2.

48 CCP, Article R. 2122-3.

49 CCP, R. 2122-4.

50 CCP, Article R. 2124-2, Articles R. 2161-2 – R. 2161-11.

51 CCP, Articles R. 2161-12 – R. 2161-23.

52 CCP Articles 2161-12 – R. 2161-20.

- The "*negotiated procedure with prior competition*", that is led by the contracting entity.[53]

5.60 Those two types do not appear in the new CCP.

5.61 In a negotiated procedure, the contracting authority or entity, as the case may be, may negotiate with the candidates selected to have the tenders suited to its needs, provided that (i) the "*minimal requirements*" and selection criteria stipulated are not amended, and (ii) amendments resulting from negotiations are noticed to every competitor in order to respect their equality of treatment.

5.62 If so indicated in the contract notice or invitation to confirm interest, the negotiation may proceed through successive steps and the public purchaser may, at each stage, discard proposals which do not appear appropriate to satisfy its needs, based on the criteria specified in the contract notice or consultation rules.

5.63 The negotiated procedure is available only in the following limited circumstances that are strictly enumerated by law:[54]

1. When the public purchaser's need cannot be satisfied without adapting readily available solutions;[55]
2. When satisfying the public purchaser's need requires an innovative solution. Are expressly considered innovative new or significantly improved works, supplies or services, including but not limited to production, building or construction processes, a new marketing method, or a new organizational method in business practices, workplace organization or external relations of the company;[56]
3. When the tender includes design services;[57]
4. When the tender cannot be awarded without prior negotiations, because of specific circumstances related to the nature, the complexity, or the legal and financial arrangements, or because of the risks attached thereto;[58]
5. If the public purchaser cannot establish with sufficient precision the contract's technical specifications by referring to a standard, a European technical assessment, common technical specification, or a technical reference;[59]
6. Contracts for which, after a call for tenders, the only tenders received are irregular or unacceptable,[60] provided that the contract's initial conditions are not substantially amended.[61]

Competitive Dialogue[62]

5.64 The procedure of competitive dialogue enables the finalization of the contract terms and specifications after discussions with the candidates. Competitive dialogue is

53 CCP Articles R. 2161-21 – R. 2161-23.
54 CCP Article R. 2124-3.
55 CCP, Article R. 2124-3, 1°.
56 CCP, Article R. 2124-3, 2°.
57 CCP, Article R. 2124-3, 3°.
58 CCP, Article R. 2124-3, 4°.
59 CCP, Article R. 2124-3, 5°.
60 The regularity and/or acceptability of a tender is governed by Articles R. 2152-1 – R. 2152-5 of CCP.
61 CCP, Article R. 2124-3, 6°.
62 CCP, Article R. 2161-24 – R. 2161-31.

only available in the limited circumstances set out above for negotiated procedures with competition.[63]

5.65 In this procedure, candidates establish their tender on the basis of the consultation documents, in order to clarify the public purchaser's needs and requirements.[64] Tenders submitted by the selected candidates are developed and amended during negotiation phase with the public purchaser. This allows: (i) The candidates, to obtain additional information for their tender, and (ii) the public purchaser, to request clarifications on the candidates' tenders in order to identify the solution that best fits its needs.[65]

5.66 The negotiation may, here again, take place through successive steps.[66]

5.67 In any event, the public purchaser must ensure an equal treatment of the candidates and their equal access to information at all stages of the negotiation.[67]

Design Contest[68]

5.68 Design contests are, under French law,[69] similar to that of Directive 2014/24/EU of the European Parliament and of the Council of 26 February 2014 on public procurement and repealing Directive 2004/18/EC.

5.69 This procedure enables the public purchaser to choose a plan or a design, mainly in the fields of town and regional planning, architecture and engineering, or data processing. It takes place after competition between the candidates. The regulation of the contest may provide for an open or restricted procedure and/or the award of premiums to candidates. A jury then selects one of the candidates.[70]

5.70 Design contests are generally used for contracts relating to the direction and supervision of public works.

5.71 As an exception, however, they may not be used when the contract has the following objects:[71]

- Infrastructures, renovations, or rehabilitation of existing structures;
- The implementation of urban or landscaped projects;
- Works for the purpose of research testing or implementation;
- Contracts where the contractor is not entrusted with any design assignment.

5.72 In such cases, the public purchaser may adopt the call for tenders or the negotiated procedures, if the conditions for such procedures are met.[72]

Mechanisms for Call for Competition and Submission of Tenders

Call for Tenders

5.73 Call for tenders from economic operators requires the public purchaser to publish a contract notice and, in specific circumstances, a prior information notice.[73]

---

63 CCP, Article R. 2124-3 – R. 2124-5.
64 CCP, Article R. 2161-24.
65 CCP, Article R. 2161-26.
66 CCP, Article R. 2161-27.
67 CCP, Article L. 3.
68 CCP, Articles R. 2162-15 – R. 2162-26.
69 CCP, Article L. 2125-1.
70 CCP, Articles R. 2162-18 – R. 2162-19.
71 CCP, Article R. 2172-2.
72 CCP, Article R. 2171-3.
73 CCP, Articles R. 2331-5 – R. 2331-8.

Transparency Requirements

5.74 These publication requirements are essential to ensure transparency, equality of access to public contracts, and equality of treatment between economic operators,[74] key principles guiding the attribution of public contracts. Failure to comply with these "material" requirements renders the resulting contract unlawful.

5.75 It should be noted that publication is only required for contracts exceeding a certain monetary value, as set out in the table below. However, it should be noted that appropriate publicity may need to be arranged even for contracts below the following thresholds, or subject to informal procedures, in line with the ECJ's case law on the issue.[75]

	Calls for competition not required	Publication according to the value and purpose of the contract, by means freely chosen	Compulsory publication in the BOAMP[a] *or* in the Journal for legal notices	Compulsory publication in the: OJEU[b] *and* in the BOAMP
Works	Below €25,000	From €25,000 to €89,999.99	From €90,000 to €5,224,999.99	Above €5,225,000

[a] *Bulletin officiel d'annonces des marchés publics.*
[b] Official Journal of the European Union.

Contents of the Contract Notice

5.76 The contract notice provides operators with relevant information related to the bid, and the applicable legal requirements. The standard is that the information published must be: (i) *Useful*, describing the scope of works in all necessary details for the potential candidates to bid, and (ii) *efficient*, ensuring that the time period between the publication and the award of the contract is adequate.[76]

Clarifications and Modifications to Call for Tenders Documents

5.77 The competitors may at any time – provided it complies with the relevant rules for tenders obligations (i.e., usually fixing a deadline in order to submit such request) – ask the contracting authority some clarification or any further detail. The contracting authority, to fulfil with the equality of treatment of the competitors, has to circulate its answers to such questions to every of them.

Time-Limits for the Submission of Tenders or Bids

5.78 The time limits for the submission of tenders[77] must be strictly complied with.

5.79 Non-compliance may lead to the tender being declared inadmissible or, if admitted, having the procedure set aside for breach of equality of treatment.

74 CCP, Article L. 3.
75 ECJ, 7 December 2000, *Telaustria* (C-324/98), ECLI:EU:C:2000:669.
76 CPP, Article R. 2342-1 and R. 2162-42.
77 CCP, Article R. 2143-1.

Evaluation and Comparison of Tenders

Opening of Tenders

5.80 The opening of the tenders/bids is not public, and candidates are not allowed to attend.[78]

5.81 Tenders received later than the final date and time set forth are eliminated.[79]

5.82 As regards contracts to be concluded with local authorities, and which price is equal or superior to the thresholds beyond which procedures are compulsory, the economic operator is to be selected by a tendering committee.[80]

Requests for Clarifications of Tender

5.83 Subject to the prohibition of negotiation of public procurement contracts, the public purchaser may request clarifications on the tenders, provided such clarifications do not amend the specifications and do not breach the principle of equality of treatment between the candidates. (e.g., the public purchaser may require all candidates to complete or provide missing documents, as the case may be, within an adequate time limit that is the same for all).[81]

5.84 In case of formal procedures conducted by contracting authorities, variation proposals are forbidden unless expressly authorized in the contract notice or the invitation to confirm interest, whereas they are authorized in formal procedures conducted by contracting entities or in adapted procedures. The public purchaser may also impose variation procedures.[82] At the contrary, when applicable, the competitive dialogue procedure allows candidates to amend their bids at each stage of the dialogue, until the best and final offer is requested.

5.85 In any event, the negotiation cannot deal with the main features of the procedure, such as the subject-matter of the envisaged contract, or the criteria for the selection of candidates or tenders. It may only concern issues such as the price of the envisaged contract and any aspect thereof, including storage or transformation costs, options, replacement parts, warranties maintenance, insurance, and transportation costs, quantities and discounts, quality, time for completion, or provisions in relation to warranties, penalties, or the termination of the contract.

5.86 Irregular,[83] inappropriate,[84] or unacceptable[85] tenders, in all procedures without negotiation, are eliminated. In other procedures with negotiation, inappropriate tenders

78 CCP, Article R. 2144-1.

79 CCP, Article R. 2143-2.

80 Code général des collectivités territoriales (Locals Authorities Code), Article L. 1414-2.

81 CCP, Article R. 2144-2.

82 CCP, Article R. 2151-8.

83 Is irregular, the offer that does not meet the requirements set out in the tender documents, in particular when the offer is incomplete, or which disregards the applicable legislation, notably in social and environmental matters (CCP, Article L. 2152-1).

84 Is inappropriate, the offer with no relation to the contract because, without substantial modifications, it does not meet the public purchaser's needs and requirements as set out in the tender documents (CCP, Article L. 2152-3).

85 Is unacceptable, the offer whose price exceeds the budget allocated to the project, as determined and established before the start of the procedure (CCP, Article L. 2152-3).

are eliminated whereas irregular tenders and unacceptable tenders may be discussed, unless the offer is "abnormally low".[86]

Evaluation Criteria

5.87 The contract is awarded to the candidate having submitted the economically most advantageous tender, selected on the basis of several criteria,[87] including: (i) Quality; (ii) price; (iii) technical merit; (iv) aesthetical and functional characteristics; (v) cultural value of the tender; (vi) environmental performances; (vii) performances in relation to professional insertion of people in difficult situations; (viii) global running costs; (ix) cost-effectiveness; (x) innovative characteristics; (xi) after-sales service and technical assistance; (xii) time for completion, etc.

5.88 When several criteria are provided for the award of the contract, their respective weight and rank is specified in the contract notice or the application file or, in the event of a competitive dialogue, in the descriptive documents. Tenders are graded in decreasing order, and the contract is awarded to the best ranked. If an offer or proposal appears to be abnormally low, it may be rejected by reasoned decision taken after the candidate has been requested to provide explanations.[88]

Acceptance of Tender and Entry into Force of the Contract

Notice of Acceptance of Tender

5.89 In formal procedures, once the tender is selected, the successful candidate must file certain required *affidavits* and certified documents.[89] The public purchaser then informs unsuccessful candidates that they have not been selected, and observes a "stand still" period before signing the contract of at least 11 days, or 16 days if the notification is not made electronically.[90]

5.90 The notifications to the unsuccessful candidates include the reasons for the rejection of their tenders, and, if the contract has already been awarded, the name of the successful bidder and the reasons for which the contract has been awarded to him. Upon request by an unsuccessful candidate, the public purchaser has the obligation to provide, within 15 days, information regarding the conduct and progress of the negotiations and competitive dialogue, and the characteristics and relevant advantages of the tender selected.[91] The rationale of this information is to allow an effective access to judicial review of the decision.

5.91 A number of time periods for the accomplishment of various formalities start running from the notification of the contract. For example, the award of any contract subject to the publication of a contract notice must be announced in an "award notice" within 30 days after the signature of the contract.[92] Such a publication ensures that unsuccessful

86 CCP, Article R. 2152-1.
87 CCP, Article L. 2152-7 and CCP, Article R. 2152-6.
88 CCP, Article L. 2152-6 and CCP, Article R. 2352-2.
89 CCP, Article L. 2142-1 and CCP, Article R. 2142-1 – R. 2142-14.
90 CCP, Article R. 2182-1.
91 CCP, Article R. 2181-1 – R.2181-4.
92 CCP, Article R. 2183-1.

candidates are aware of the price of the tender, and, eventually, to challenge the award of the contract.

5.92 In addition, local authorities or entities must inform the state representative in the relevant district of the signature of the contract within 15 days from the date of such signature.[93]

Judicial Review Proceedings

5.93 The call for tenders, the award and the contract itself may be challenged by way of a number of actions brought by third parties, competitors, and/or the local Government representative ("*Préfet*").

The Référé Pré-Contractuel (Pre-Contractual Summary Proceedings).[94]

5.94 The *référé précontractuel* is a pre-contractual summary proceeding dedicated to disputes relating to the award of public contracts for the performance of works, the supply of products, or the provision of services, with (i) an economic counterpart (i.e., a price or exploitation right); (ii) the delegation of a public service, or (iii) the selection of an economic operator shareholder of a single-purpose mixed owned company.[95]

5.95 The procedure may only be brought prior to the conclusion of the contract: Economic operators having an interest in entering into the contract[96] may obtain a wide range of measures, interim or not,[97] without, however, having to demonstrate that the urgency of the situation.

5.96 A claim is only admissible if grounded on alleged infringement(s) of publicity and/or procurement rules.[98] Additionally, the claimant must demonstrate that he suffered a loss from the alleged infringement (e.g., it has directly prevented it to submit a tender, or obviously violates a key principle of public procurement law to its detriment).[99]

5.97 The judge must rule within 20 days maximum from its referral.[100] The order cannot be appealed, and can only be challenged on issues of law before the *Conseil d'Etat*.[101]

5.98 Remedies may vary, depending on the nature of the involved public entity. If the matter involves a contracting *authority*, the remedies are the broadest: The judge may quash any administrative decision, and/or issue an injunction to resume the awarding process up to a prior step allowing compliance with procurement rules. If a contracting entity is involved, only an injunction can be sought.

5.99 Once the contract is signed, the *référé pré-contractuel* is no longer admissible.[102]

93 Locals authorities Code, Articles L. 2131-1 – L. 2131-2.
94 Administrative Justice Code, Articles L551-1-L551-12.
95 Administrative Justice Code, Articles L551-1 and L551-5.
96 Administrative Justice Code, Article L551-10.
97 Administrative Justice Code, Articles L551-2 and L551-6.
98 Administrative Justice Code, Article L.551-1 and *Conseil d'Etat*, Decision of 21 June 2000, No. 209319.
99 *Conseil d'Etat*, Decision of 3 October 2008, No. 305420, SMIRGEOMES.
100 *Code de justice administrative* (Administrative Justice Code), Article R. 551-5.
101 *Code de justice administrative* (Administrative Justice Code), Article R. 551-6.
102 *Conseil d'Etat*, Decision of 3 November 1995, No. 157304.

The Référé Contractuel (Contractual Summary Proceedings)[103]

5.100 The *référé contractuel* is a summary proceedings procedure that is opened after the signature of the contract, based on an infringement of public procurement rules.

5.101 Since its purpose is similar to that of the *référé pré-contractuel*, it is not opened when the latter could have been initiated.

5.102 The *référé contractuel* may be submitted no later than:

- 31 days after the publication of the award notice in the Official Journal of the European Union, or from the notification of the signature of the contract;
- 6 months after the day following the signature of the contract, in the absence of publication of the award notice, or of notification of the contract's signature.

5.103 The judge may suspend the performance of the contract during the proceeding, except if such suspension entails more disadvantages than advantages in view of the interests at stake.

5.104 The judge has the obligation to rule on the petition within 1 month from its referral, and may declare the contract void if the irregularities are serious.

The Recours De Pleine Juridiction (Full Recourse)

5.105 The validity of the contract, or of any of its provisions if severable, may be challenged by a *recours de pleine juridiction*.[104]

5.106 This procedure is open to any third party whose interests might be damaged in a sufficiently direct and certain way by the award procedure of the contract or its provisions.

5.107 Two categories of third parties may file such an action:[105]

- All third parties (including associations, local taxpayers, public service users, unsuccessful candidates or candidates having an interest to conclude the contract even though they decided not to submit a tender), if they demonstrate (i) its direct and personal interest, and (ii) that the grounds it relies on are directly related to allegedly suffered damages;
- The *Préfet* and the members of the local authority's deliberate organ ("*assemblée délibérante*"): They are deemed to have an interest in bringing an action, and may invoke any argument related to the contract. It should be noted that before the conclusion of the contract, the *Préfet* also controls its legality, as well as that of related administrative acts, which may be brought before the Administrative Court by the way of "*déféré préfectoral*".

5.108 The action must be filed no later than two months after the publication of the contract award notice. If the appropriate publication measures have not been performed, the contract can be challenged at any time.[106]

103 Administrative Justice Code, Articles L551-13-L551-23.

104 Administrative Justice Code, Articles L551-1-L551-12, and *Conseil d'Etat*, Ass., Decision of 4 April 2014, *Tarn et Garonne*, No. 358994.

105 *Conseil d'Etat*, Ass., Decision of 4 April 2014, *Tarn et Garonne*, No. 358994.

106 Administrative Court of Appeal of Lyon, Decision of 30 October 2013, No. 13LY00721.

5.109 If the validity of the contract cannot be remedied and prevents the performance of the contract, the Court may order its termination or, for the most serious infringements of the law, partial or total avoidance of the contract.

The Référé Suspension[107]

5.110 The *référé suspension* is a summary proceeding procedure by which a decision taken by the public purchaser unlawfully may be suspended.

5.111 In its application, the claimant must demonstrate that (i) there is a serious doubt as to the legality of the decision, and (ii) that it is urgent for the decision not to be given effect.[108]

5.112 It should be noted that this proceeding may be brought in addition to a *recours de pleine jurisdiction*, but has to be submitted separately (i.e., through a separate submission).

Content of Contracts

- ***General features to all contracts***

5.113 As a principle, French law provides for the parties' freedom to determine the content of their contract.[109]

5.114 However, this freedom is limited in two ways that are addressed in turn below.

Express and Implied Terms

5.115 The first limit to the parties' freedom to determine the content of their contract is the judge's power to add to the parties' express obligations.

5.116 Indeed, under French contract law, the parties undertake to abide not only by the express terms of their agreements, but also by all of the consequences which derive from equity, usage or legislation.[110]

5.117 Courts can thus infer implied terms, such as a duty to ensure the safety of the other party.

Unfair Contract Terms

5.118 The second limit to the parties' freedom to determine the content of their contract is that courts can subtract from the parties' agreement, by ruling out contractual provisions. For example, between a professional and a consumer, *clauses abusives* (unfair terms) are deemed void.[111]

5.119 Moreover, as of 1 October 2016, are deemed not-written:

- A provision pursuant to which a party is exonerated from performing its principal ("essential") obligation.[112] As a result, a limitation clause can be deemed

107 Administrative Justice Code, Articles L521-1 et seq.

108 Administrative Justice Code, Article L521-1.

109 French Civil Code, Article 1102.

110 French Civil Code, Article 1194.

111 A list of *unfair terms* can be found on the website of the *Commission des clauses abusives*: www.clauses-abusives.fr/textes-de-reference/.

112 French Civil Code, Article 1170.

inexistent if it has for effect of providing a remedy that is considered too low compared to the obligation breached;

- Standard terms creating a "significant imbalance" (*déséquilibre significatif*) in the rights and obligations of the parties.[113] This new provision could be interpreted extensively, thus creating legal uncertainty. It is thus highly recommended to carefully negotiate agreements instead of imposing standard terms, and to document such negotiations.

Particular Features to Public Contracts

5.120 With respect to its performance, two series of consequences derives from a contract being governed by public law.

Impact of Public Law on Contract Terms

5.121 French courts have erected some rules applicable to administrative contracts, and particularly to public procurement, to principles that take precedence, even if the contract does not contain any provision in this regard. Such principle has been very recently codified in the above mentioned CCP.

5.122 Among such principles are:

- Contractual freedom;
- The principle of financial balance, which prescribes the stabilization of the financial conditions of the contract in the event of circumstances affecting the performance of contract (e.g., hardship, unforeseen circumstances, additional works, unilateral modifications, termination for reasons of public interest);
- The public purchaser may always terminate or modify the contract unilaterally by reason of public interest, even in the absence of express provision to that effect. From this principle also derives the right for the public purchaser to substitute the contractor to ensure the performance of th8e contract.

Limited Grounds for Substantial Modification of Contract

5.123 Irrespective the traditional case law grounds for modification of a public contract under the French law, a set of limitations come mainly from European statute law (Directives), by prohibiting any substantial modification (in order not to jeopardize the initial competition result). A substantial modification, therefore, may only be implemented in the following cases:[114]

- Modification is provided for in the initial procurement documents in clear, precise and unequivocal review clauses, which may include price revision clauses, or options. To be valid, such clauses must clarify the scope and nature of possible modifications or options;

113 French Civil Code, Article 1171.

114 Decree No. 2016-360 of 25 March 2016 on public procurement contracts, Articles 139 and 140 and CCP, Articles R. 2194-1 – R. 2194-9. It should be noted that these cases comply with those set out in Directive 2014/24/EU of the European Parliament and of the Council of 26 February 2014, Article 72.

- Additional works have become necessary and a change of contractor (i) is inappropriate for economic or technical reasons; and (ii) would cause significant inconvenience, or substantially increase the costs. In any event, increases in price may not exceed 50 % of the original contract's value;
- The following conditions are fulfilled: (i) Circumstances arise that a diligent public purchaser could not foresee; (ii) the modification does not alter the overall nature of the contract, and (iii) the price increase does not 50 %, being clarified that subsequent modifications should not aim at circumventing this limitation;
- A new contractor is appointed, as a consequence of either: (i) A review clause; (ii) a succession into the position of the initial contractor, following corporate restructuring; (including takeover, merger, acquisition or insolvency, provided it fulfils the initial qualitative selection criteria); or (iii) the public purchaser performs the contractor's obligations itself;
- The modifications, irrespective of their value, are not substantial. A substantial modification is defined as one that: (i) Introduces conditions which, had they been part of the initial procurement procedure, would have allowed other candidates or additional participants to submit tenders; (ii) changes the economical balance of the contract in a manner not provided for in the initial contract; (iii) extends the scope of the contract considerably; or (iv) consists in substituting a new contractor in other cases than those provided for above.

5.124 This set of rules may impacts the flexibility of construction projects. Particularly, the validity of change orders is always controlled, and the overall limit of 50% can in practice be a serious obstacle in the performance of the more complex operations.

5.125 In addition, one should bear in mind that in some cases, since the public purchaser should have entered into a new contract instead of modifying the initial contract, it could be logical to apply the judicial review mechanisms addressed above to amendments or variations.

Vitiating Factors Under Contract Law

5.126 A contract may be annulled for various reasons pertaining to: (i) The parties' consent to the contract; (ii) the parties' lack of capacity to enter into the contract; (iii) the contract's content; and (iv) the contract's form.

Focus on Consent to the Contract as a Vitiating Factor

5.127 The parties' consent is only binding where it was enlightened and freely given.

5.128 Error (mistake), misrepresentation and duress vitiate consent where they are of such a nature that, without them, one of the parties would not have contracted or would have contracted on substantially different terms.[115]

5.129 An *error* is a ground for nullity only where it bears on the "essential qualities" (*qualités essentielles*) of the contract,[116] that are defined as those "*expressly or tacitly*

115 French Civil Code, Article 1130.

116 French Civil Code, Article 1132.

agreed and in consideration of which the parties contracted".[117] By contrast, an error on the economic value of the object of the contract, or an "*inexcusable error*", are not a ground for nullity.

5.130 *Misrepresentation* is defined under French law as an act (e.g., schemes, lies, etc.) by one party which purpose is to obtain the other party's consent to the contract. Misrepresentation is also characterized when a party intentionally conceals a piece of information, knowing that it is of decisive importance to the other party.[118] The aggrieved party then has the choice to apply for either the annulment of the contract, or the award of damages.

5.131 *Duress* (*violence*) can take various forms. Along with physical or psychological violence, the 2016 Reform of Contract Law introduced a new type of duress. Sometimes referred to as economic duress, its scope is, however, much wider to encompass the exploitation, by one party, of the other party's state of dependence to (i) obtain an undertaking to which the latter would not have agreed in the absence of such constraint, and (ii) gain from this undertaking a advantage that is manifestly excessive.[119] It should be noted, however, that, at the time of writing, an uncertainty remains as to whether duress is restricted to economic aspects.[120]

Sanction

5.132 It should be noted that annulment of a contract can only be sought during 5 years once the aggrieved party has gained knowledge of the grounds for annulment. French law knows of two types of nullity:

- *Relative* nullity, is ordered where a mere private interest is at stake. The proceedings can in this case only be initiated by the aggrieved party;
- Where public order is at stake, the nullity is *absolue* ("absolute"), meaning that anyone with sufficient interest can apply for it.

5.133 Nullity is retroactive. Consequently, the contract is deemed never to have existed. As a consequence, the parties must return to another, what they have received pursuant to the contract.

5.134 In public contracts, vitiating factors are very rare due to the complexity and *formalisme* of the procurement rules. Nevertheless, case law has recognized misrepresentation in limited circumstances. The *Conseil d'Etat* has admitted misrepresentation for the benefit of a public purchaser due to anti-competitive agreement of competitors.[121]

5.135 Misrepresentation offers few options to the public authority; he can either ask for indemnity, nullity of contract, or both.

117 French Civil Code, Article 1133.

118 But not the adequateness of the price: French Civil Code, Article 1137, as modified by the 2018 Law reform.

119 French Civil Code, Article 1143.

120 Law 2018-237 has precised that, in order for duress to be a ground for nullity, the state of dependance must have existed between the parties prior to the contract.

121 *Conseil d'Etat*, Decision of 19 December 2007, *Campenon Bernard*, No. 268918.

Rights and Liabilities of Third Parties

5.136 French law recognizes, as a principle, the privity of contracts.

5.137 Prior to the 2016 Reform of Contract Law, the Civil Code expressly stated that contracts had no effect on third parties. However, this contention was judged excessive: Contracts produce a series of consequences for third parties, especially for the creditors of the parties to the contract. It is thus more exact to state that a contract is not binding on third parties, and only creates obligations between the parties:[122] A and B have no power to impose a duty on C.

5.138 By contrast, a contract has an impact on third parties that they must respect. Two sets of consequences arise from this principle:

- Third parties cannot participate in a breach of contract. For example, if a third party encourages a party to breach a non-disclosure agreement, said third party would be liable to pay damages to the aggrieved party;
- Third parties can invoke the breach of a contract where they suffer from such a breach. This solution was crafted by the French Supreme Court.[123] The 2016 Reform of Contract Law does not uphold nor condemn such a solution. A prospective reform of the law of torts, which may be passed in 2019 or 2020, aims at modifying the situation. Third parties would only be able to sue in torts, thus being forced to demonstrate a specific tort towards them, and not a mere breach of contractual obligations.[124]

5.139 In terms of liability, the employer in a private contract is, contractually, liable for the acts of third-parties, that is, for the third parties he or she involves in the performance of his or her own obligations (e.g., consultants, engineers, etc.).

5.140 By contrast, in administrative law the public employer is now exonerated from the faults of other participants, consultants, engineers, chief engineers, etc.[125]

Performance of a Contract

5.141 *Pacta sunt servanda*, said the Romans: Contracts must be performed. French law does not differ. Article 1103 of the Civil Code, which ranks among the Preliminary Rules, states that "*Contracts which are lawfully formed have the binding force of legislation for those who have made them*".

5.142 Such an assertion should not, however, be taken literally: A contract does not have the binding force of a law, since contracts must abide by the law. However, parties have a duty to perform their obligations under the contract.

Force Majeure and Other Excuses for Non-Performance

5.143 As a principle, a party is liable when it fails to perform its obligations. However, a defaulting party may invoke three types of excuses:

122 French Civil Code, Article 1199.
123 Cass. Ass. Plén., decision of 6 October 2006, no 05-13255.
124 Avant-projet de réforme de la responsabilité civile, 13 mars 2017, Article 1234.
125 Conseil d'Etat decision of 11 April 2014 no 375051.

- Non-performance is caused by the other party provided that the non-performance is serious enough (*exceptio non adimpleti contractus*);[126]
- Non-performance is due to *Force Majeure*; that is, an event beyond the control of the defaulting party, that could not reasonably have been foreseen at the time of the conclusion of the contract and whose effects could not be avoided by appropriate measures, and that prevents performance of its obligation by the defaulting party;[127]
- Since the 2016 Reform of Contract Law, when non-performance is caused by hardship;[128] that is, in the event of an unforeseeable change of circumstances rendering the performance of the contract excessively onerous for one party, it can ask the other party to renegotiate the contract. If the negotiations do not take place or are unsuccessful, the parties can agree to terminate the contract or to apply to courts for the revision the contract. In the absence of such an agreement between the parties, any party can apply to courts to have the contract either revised, or terminated. This remedy is not mandatory, so the parties may waive it.

5.144 Performance in public contracts:

- Administrative law strictly prohibits the *exceptio non adimpleti contractus*;[129]
- In case of *Force majeure*, contractors can terminate the contract by introducing a request before the competent jurisdiction;[130]
- The *clausula rebus sic stantibus* is recognized in public contracts. The administration's contractor can ask for a temporary financial compensation when an unanticipated and external event appears causing a disruption of the contract's economy.[131] This principle permits the continuation of public services.

Different Natures of Contracts and Consequences on Performance

5.145 French scholars distinguish *obligations de moyens* ("obligations of means") from *obligations de résultat* ("obligations of result").

5.146 In an *obligation de moyens*, the party does not undertake to reach a certain result, but to provide its best efforts to achieve a result. This is, for example, the case of a doctor: He does not commit to heal a patient, but to do his or her best to do so.

5.147 On the contrary, where the obligation is "*de résultat*", the defaulting party undertakes to achieve a certain result (e.g., a mechanic who commits to repair a car).

5.148 This distinction leads to consequences as to the characterization of a breach of contract. Where the obligation is "*de moyens*", the aggrieved party must establish that the defaulting party failed to provide its best efforts to perform its obligations. Where the obligation is "*de résultat*", the aggrieved party only has to demonstrate that the promised result was not achieved.

126 French Civil Code, Article 1219.
127 French Civil Code, Article 1218.
128 French Civil Code, Article 1195.
129 Exception: Conseil d'Etat, Decision of 8 October 2014, No. 370644.
130 *Conseil d'Etat*, Decision of 2 December 1932, *Compagnie des tramways de Cherbourg, No. 89655.*
131 *Conseil d'Etat*, Decision of 30 March 1916, *Compagnie générale d'éclairage de Bordeaux, No. 59928.*

Breach

5.149 Breach of contract can take various forms under French law:

- Full or total breach, where the defaulting party failed entirely to perform its obligations;
- Partial breach, where the defaulting party performed part of its obligations, or where performance thereof is deficient;
- Belated performance of the contract.

5.150 Any breach may be remedied. However, benign breaches cannot lead to the termination of the contract.

5.151 French law also underlines some specific breaches:

- *Faute lourde* avails to a gross negligence. It does not require the intent to harm the aggrieved party;[132]
- *Faute dolosive* is a voluntary breach of contract. It does not require the intent to harm the aggrieved party.[133]

5.152 These types of breach have specific consequences, including the setting aside of any limitation of liability.

Termination

Overview

5.153 Until the 2016 Reform of Contract Law, termination of a contract was essentially judicial: Except in contracts containing express termination clauses, an aggrieved party was obliged to apply to a judge to have a contract terminated in case of material breaches.[134] The length of the proceedings, added to the risk of the judge finding the breach is not severe enough to justify termination of the contract, led to the creation of alternatives to the judicial termination of the contract.

5.154 With the entry into force of the Reform, termination may now result either from a termination clause, or, where the non-performance is sufficiently serious, from (i) a notice by the aggrieved party to the defaulting party, or (ii) a judicial decision.[135] The order is significant: Judicial termination is neither the exclusive nor the norm, but a last resort.

Termination Clause

5.155 Termination can result from a clause to that effect (*clause résolutoire*). Drafting such a clause is delicate: Under French law, such a clause must specify which obligations are likely to lead to termination if breached.[136] The clause must also expressly state that termination shall be of right (*de plein droit*).[137]

132 *Cour de cassation*, Cass. com., Decision of 29 June 2010, *Faurecia*, No. 09-11841.
133 *Cour de cassation*, Cass. com., Decision of 13 September 2017, No. 16-10.596.
134 French Civil Code, former Article 1184.
135 French Civil Code, Article 1224.
136 French Civil Code, Article 1225.
137 French Civil Code, Article 1225.

5.156 Unless otherwise provided for in the clause, termination can only occur after formal notice (*mise en demeure*), granting a reasonable amount of time to remedy the breach.[138] The formal notice must expressly refer to the termination clause.[139]

5.157 In case of challenge of the termination, the judge only has the power to control (i) the existence of a breach, and (ii) that the breach is attributable to the defaulting party. He is not empowered to assess the gravity of the breach, as the termination clause expresses the parties' intention to terminate the agreement in the event of a breach of the specified obligations.[140]

Unilateral Termination

5.158 Prior to the 2016 Reform of Contract Law, the Civil Code did not expressly provide for unilateral termination of contracts. However, the French *Cour de cassation* remedied this absence by deciding that a party's behaviour may justify the unilateral termination of the contract by the other party in certain circumstances.[141]

5.159 Unilateral termination is an attractive alternative to judicial termination, as it is quicker and cheaper. However, its codification by the 2016 Reform of Contract Law has rendered the process more complex. In addition, a significant change has been made: It is no longer the behaviour of the party that justifies the termination, but the breach of its obligations.

5.160 Indeed, unilateral termination may now only occur after the defaulting party has been served a formal notice expressly stating that, should the defaulting party not resume performance of its obligations within a reasonable timeframe, the contract will be terminated.[142] Then, if the defaulting party still fails to comply, the aggrieved party notifies the defaulting party of the termination and states the reasons for such termination.

Judicial Termination

5.161 Despite its cost and length, judicial termination remains a possibility. The aggrieved party may apply to the court to have the contract terminated. There is a strong risk that the court finds the breach not severe enough to justify terminating the contract and decide instead to award the aggrieved party damages.

5.162 Termination in public contracts:

5.163 Public authority can unilaterally terminate the contract for a public interest reason.[143] In this case of unilateral termination by the public authority, the contractor will receive indemnity.

5.164 At the contrary, the contractor's entitlement to terminate is very restricted. Firstly, termination clauses can't be introduced in public services contracts. Secondly, before applying such a clause in other contracts, the contractor has to inform the public authority of his wish to apply the clause and the public authority can reject the termination

138 French Civil Code, Article 1225.
139 French Civil Code, Article 1225.
140 French Civil Code, Article 1224.
141 *Cour de cassation*, Cass. civ. 1, 13 October 1998, No. 96-21485.
142 French Civil Code, Article 1226.
143 *Conseil d'Etat*, Decision of 2 may 1958, *Distillerie de Magnac Laval, No. 32401.*

for general interest reason, notably continuation of public service. In this case, the contractor has to continue to execute the contract.[144]

Remedies

General

5.165 The remedies available to the aggrieved party are the following:[145]

- *Exceptio non adimpleti contractus*;
- Specific performance in kind of the undertaking;
- Reduction in price;
- Termination of the contract;
- Reparation (damages) for the consequences of non-performance.

5.166 Sanctions which are not incompatible may be combined; damages may always be added to any of the sanctions. The *Cour de cassation* recently held that, where the contract provides for specific sanctions (liquidated damages), it does not prevent the creditor from seeking alternatives remedies set forth at Article 1217 of the French Civil Code. Specifically, the Court ruled that, even if the employer was entitled to liquidated damages because the Contractor was late, the employer could also invoke *exceptio non adimpleti contractus* to refuse to pay until performance was restored.[146]

Public Contracts

5.167 In principle the same remedies apply to public contracts except *exceptio non adimpleti*. However, except for the allocation of damages, the contractor's entitlement to other remedies is restricted (see above).

Interpretation of Contract

5.168 Interpretation of contracts is a complex matter, involving various rules.

5.169 First, it must be stressed that there is no room for interpretation where the contractual terms are clear and unambiguous:[147] No court can "interpret" such terms.

5.170 When interpretation is needed, the general principle is that it must be done in accordance with the common intention of the parties, rather than stopping at the literal meaning of its terms.[148]

5.171 If the common intention of the parties cannot be discerned, the contract is to be interpreted in the sense that a reasonable person placed in the same situation would give to it.[149]

144 *Conseil d'Etat*, Decision of 8 october 2014, *Grenke Location*, No. 370644.
145 French Civil Code, Article 1217.
146 *Cour de cassation*, Cass. civ. 3, 14 February 2019, No. 17-31665.
147 French Civil Code, Article 1192.
148 French Civil Code, Article 1188.
149 French Civil Code, Article 1188.

5.172 In case of ambiguity, a bespoke contract is interpreted against the aggrieved party and in favour of the defaulting party,[150] and a contract of adhesion (*contrat d'adhésion*)[151] is interpreted against the party who proposed it.[152]

5.173 Finally, when a provision is susceptible of being interpreted in two meanings, the meaning giving it some effect is to be preferred over the one which makes it produce no effect (*principe d'effet utile*).[153]

5.174 The administrative law doesn't set forth specific set of interpretation rules of the public contracts. Practically it will rely on the above private law principles, although it must be emphasized that the administrative courts are never bound to apply the Civil Code provisions.

National Standard Forms of Contracts

5.175 Several models of construction contracts are routinely used in France, for private contracts on the one hand, and public procurement contracts on the other.

5.176 It should be noted that although not prohibited, the use of a public standard form of contract for a contract subject to private law, or conversely, that of a private standard form of contract for a contract subject to public law, is obviously not recommended.

5.177 In any event, the nature of the contract is not in principle affected by the use of a standard form, and its legal regime, of private law or public law, remains irrespective of the provisions of the form used.

5.178 For example, a contract for construction works carried out for the benefit of a public authority to pursue a goal of general interest is an administrative contract,[154] even if it is not subject to a public procurement standard form: (i) The rules applicable to all public contracts explained above will be given effect, and (ii) the contract remains of the administrative courts' jurisdiction.

Standard Form for Private Contracts (CCAG Privé)

5.179 The most common standard form was established under the authority of the *Agence française de normalisation* ("AFNOR" – the French Agency for Standardization), whose standard norm "NFP 03 001" is called "*Cahier des Clauses Administratives Générales – Privé*" (CCAG "*privé*"). It results from a consultation of all private construction industry stakeholders. Its current version is dated 20 October 2017.

5.180 The CCAG "*privé*" was designed as a standard form of contract for building works governed by private law. Consequently, it contains express references to the French Civil Code, particularly the fixed-price regime and the regime for post-acceptance guarantees and insurance, expressly referring to the mandatory regime of constructors' decennial liability and its required insurance. It allows for modifications to be made in the course

150 French Civil Code, Article 1190.
151 French Civil Code, Article 1110.
152 French Civil Code, Article 1190.
153 French Civil Code, Article 1191.
154 *Conseil d'Etat*, Decision of 10 June 1921, No. 45681.

of the works. If the employer expressly undertakes to refrain from modifying the works during their performance ("*ne varietur*" contract), a specific annex applies (Annex D).

5.181 The standard is adapted for a pure construction contract, without responsibility for the design or the financing. In general, it is considered balanced as regards the rights and obligations of the two parties.

5.182 Professional practice is also at the origin of standard forms of contracts for:

- Architects, established notably by the *Ordre des architectes* (French Order of Architects);
- Subcontracts, established by various professional federations (e.g., the *Fédération nationale des travaux publics* "FNTP" – the National Federation of Public Works, or the *Fédération Nationale du Bâtiment et des Travaux publics* ("FNBTP" – the National Federation of Building and Public Works). These forms are relatively simplified, and the major construction companies, with large flow of subcontractor contracts, often use their own standard templates.

5.183 Again, the use, or not, of these standard forms does not affect the nature of the contract. This is particularly important as regards to subcontracts, that is governed in large part by public policy. Thus, if a contract, irrespective of its denomination, corresponds to the legal definition of a contract for the subcontracting of works, it will be subject to Law No. 75-1334 of 31 December 1975 on subcontracting, that contains a number of mandatory rules pertaining to public policy (obligations to "declare" the subcontractor to the owner, and to issue a bank guarantee, or to establish a direct payment by the employer – *see below*, Sub-contracting), that are thus to be complied with notwithstanding (i) any provision to the contrary in the contract, or (ii) the absence of provision to that effect.

Standard Forms for Public Contracts (CCAG)

5.184 The public purchaser also uses a standard form of contract, the *Cahier des clauses administratives générales* ("CCAG"), that is approved and published by ministerial order for each main category of service covered by the public procurement: (i) Regular supply, or services (*fourniture courante ou services – FCS*); (ii) industrial procurements (*marchés industriels – MI*); (iii) intellectual services (*prestation intellectuelles – PI*), that are especially used for architecture and *maîtrise d'œuvre* (engineering) services; (iv) Information and Communication Technologies (*Technologies de l'information et de la communication – TIC*); and; (v) finally, construction works (*Travaux – TX*). Both PI and TX CCAG are routinely used in the construction industry.

5.185 The use of these standard forms is optional for local authorities that have a constitutional right to govern freely.[155] In practice, however, local authorities overwhelmingly rely on these standards, which the purchasers and managers of public projects are familiar with.

5.186 The various CCAGs were modified between 2009 and 2021; the previous versions dated from 1976 to 1980.

155 French Constitution of 4 October 1958, Article 72.

5.187 The two most common CCAGs, are the CCAG Travaux and CCAG PI.[156] They represent a very substantial portion of the public construction contracts in France. They both contain time bar clauses if formal "service orders" ("*ordres de service*") are not challenged within 15 days from the day they are noticed,[157] or in case of any dispute[158] or dispute following the reconciliation of the final account.[159] Finally, some public companies or large public purchasers have developed their own standard forms of contracts. For example, the *Société Nationale des Chemins de Fer* ("SNCF" – national company of French railways) uses particular specifications and general conditions for its 2003 CCCG Travaux. The RATP (*Régie Autonome des Transports Parisiens*, the public operator of the Parisian metro) also uses its own CCAG, different from the regular one. Similarly, Commission on Atomic and Alternative Energy (CEA) uses General Conditions of Purchase (*conditions générales d'achat (CGA)*) that include a common base applicable to all types of services, then three sub-sections A, B, and C, the latter relating to construction contracts.

5.188 It is not possible to detail here the content of all these standard forms, or to compare them in detail with the standard CCAG Travaux. However, it is stressed that, like the CCAG Travaux, they are basic construction contracts, without responsibility for design or financing. If the general balance (risk allocation) of these forms does not profoundly differ from that of the CCAG Travaux, the administrative processes and procedures differ in the details (e.g., time limits, forms of notices, dispute resolution procedure, etc.).

Common Points Between Different Forms of Construction Contracts

5.189 A few key points are similar in both administrative CCAG Travaux and the CCAG Privé standard forms of contract:

- Same structure: General conditions, complemented by specific conditions;
- Monthly interim payments;
- 5% retainer on amounts paid to cover potential defects, possibly substituted by a bank guarantee;[160]
- Interests payable to the contractor for failure by the employer to make payments in time;

---

156 The CCAG PI is concluded with an architect, or with an engineering consortium regrouping, around a commissioned architect, specialized consulting firms (e.g., for calculation notes, acoustics, HVAC, etc.) depending on the nature and the complexity of the project. The contract is determined, usually, by reference to standard engineering missions defined by law. **In practice, these missions are detailed in a table annexed to the particular conditions, which (i) state the elements of the mission conferred to the consortium; (ii) identifies the member(s) in charge of carrying them out, and (iii) if necessary, allocates a percentage the mission's elements to each different member.** These particular conditions routinely set forth a sanction mechanism, very specific to engineering contracts: The provider commits to an estimated amount of the works which results in the provision of a "tolerance threshold" (in practice, this threshold is (i) 5–8% at tender, and (ii) 3–5% during the final accounts reconciliation). At tender, if no offer is within the tolerance threshold, then the provider must re-establish, at no charge, all or part of the tender documents in order to obtain tenders within the threshold. During the final accounts reconciliation, the provider incurs a penalty if the threshold is exceeded, in a proportional amount set in the contract.

157 CCAG Travaux 3.8.2; CCAG PI 3.8.

158 CCAG PI 37.

159 CCAG Travaux 50.2.

160 The CCP introduced a lower retainer (3%) for public contracts awarded by the state to a small business corporate.

- Performance bonds are not mandatory, subject to the employer's will, to be eventually included in the specific conditions;
- No cap on liability or liquidated damages for delay;
- Time bar clauses relating to challenging service orders (CCAG Privé sets out time bar provisions relating to "change orders" only whereas the CCAG Travaux provisions concern all "service orders").

International Standard Forms Derived from French Standard Forms

5.190 French public procurement contracts have inspired a significant number of similar standard forms in other countries: Several North African (Tunisia, Algeria, Morocco) and sub-Saharan (Senegal, Ivory Coast, Cameroon, etc.) countries have adopted CCAG Travaux inspired by the French CCAG, that generally are compulsory for works ordered by the public purchaser.

5.191 Despite some occasionally obsolete pieces of wording (e.g., references to the "*Minister's representative*", or the "*engineer*" may need to be interpreted during the performance of the contract), these standard forms have the advantage of being sufficiently close to the French forms to enable interpretation and difficulties solving by reference, in the absence of applicable local case law, to the French public one, that is also commonly admitted as a relevant reference in these systems of laws.

Construction Law Principles

Procurement and Tendering

5.192 See Section "*The Formation of a Contract*" above.

Different Types of Contract (Unit Price, Lump Sum, Etc.)

5.193 The different types of construction contracts are not defined by price considerations under French law. Rather: (i) Under private law, the determination of the price is not a condition for the validity of the contract;[161] (ii) on the contrary, under public law, the price must be determined or determinable.[162]

5.194 As explained above, **private construction contracts** are consensual. Their content is freely negotiated between the parties. Different types of construction contracts exist depending on their purpose, the most common are the contracts for construction, the design and build contracts and the engineering, procurement and construction contracts. However, some construction contracts are subject to specific regulation, mainly to protect the purchaser in specific situations. For example:

- VEFA contracts ("*vente en l'état futur d'achèvement*"),[163] for the off-plan property sale by a developer;

161 See para. [5.19] above.
162 CCP, Articles R. 2112-7 – R. 2112-18.
163 French Civil Code, Article 1601-3.

- VIR (*"vente d'immeuble à rénover"*) contracts,[164] for the sale and refurbishment of a building;
- These are sales contracts between the developer and the purchaser. The developer is considered as (i) an employer towards the contractor and as (ii) a contractor towards the purchaser pursuant to Article 1792-1 of the French Civil Code;
- CCMI (*"contrat de construction de maison individuelle"*) contracts,[165] for the construction of individual houses;
- This contract is a of lease of works between the contractor and the purchaser. The contractor is considered as (i) an employer towards the contractor who will perform the works and as (ii) a contractor towards the purchaser pursuant to Article 1792-1 of the French Civil Code;
- CPI (*"contrat de promotion immobilière"*) contracts,[166] for construction programs construction of one or more buildings, where the property developer hires the contractor(s) and undertakes legal, administrative and financial related operations, for an agreed price. This contract is a mandate of common interest between the developer and the purchaser;
- The developer is considered as (i) an employer towards the contractor and as (ii) a contractor towards the purchaser pursuant to Article 1792-1 of the French Civil Code.

5.195 Public construction contracts, in contrast, are traditionally organized around at least four categories of contracts: (i) Public procurements contracts,[167] (ii) Public service delegation contracts,[168] (iii) Concession contracts,[169] (iv) PPP.[170]

5.196 French public authorities have taken the opportunity of the transposition of European Directives Nos. 2014/24 and 2014/25 of 26 February 2014 to simplify public contracts law, re-organizing it in two categories of contracts: Public procurement contracts, and concession contracts.

5.197 Within these two types of contracts, sub-categories of contracts are available to the parties.

5.198 Contracts that do not provide for deferred payment include:

- Public procurement contracts for design and build (*marchés publics de conception-réalisation*),[171] that allow the public purchaser to entrust an economic operator with a task relating to both the preparation of studies and the performance of the works;

164 Construction and habitation code, Article L. 262-1.

165 Construction and habitation code, Article L. 231-1.

166 French Civil Code, Article 1831-1.

167 *Code des marchés publics*, former Article 1 and CCP, Article L.1.

168 Law No. 2001-1168 of 11 December 2001 on urgent reform economical and financial measures, Article 3.

169 Ordinnance No. 2009-864 of 15 July 2009 relative to contracts for the concession of public works, Article 1.

170 Ordinnance No. 2004-559 of 17 June 2004 relative to partnership contracts, Article 1.

171 CCP, Article L. 2171-2.

- Global performance public markets (*marchés globaux de performance*),[172] that associates the operation or maintenance of the project with the construction or the design and build of services to fulfil defined performance objectives defined in particular in terms of level of activity, quality of service, energy efficiency or environmental impact;
- Global sector public contracts (*marchés publics globaux sectoriels*),[173] whose aim is to entrust an economic operator with a global mission in certain sectors (e.g., buildings assigned to the *gendarmerie*, national police, fire brigades in Paris, etc.).

5.199 Contracts that provide for deferred payment include:

- Partnership contracts (*marchés de partenariat*)[174] by which the economic operator or group of economics operators is entrusted with a global mission consisting of building, transforming, renovating, dismantling or destructing construction works, devices, intangible goods necessary for public services or the exercise of mission of general interest and for partial or global funding;
- Concessions contracts,[175] by which the contractor is entrusted with the financing, building and operating of the project. The public purchaser is allowed to finance such a contract in part, but the risk relating to the operation of the project must be borne by the contractor.

Nature of Construction Contract

5.200 The term "construction contract" is not defined under French law. It is encompassed in a larger category of contracts, referred to as "contract for services" (*contrat d'entreprise*).

5.201 The contract for services is a form of lease of works (*louage d'ouvrage*), a contract by which one of the parties undertakes to do a certain thing for the other, for a price agreed upon between them.[176] There are three types of leases of works, depending on their object:[177] (i) Services; (ii) transportation (whether by land or by water, for the conveyance either of persons or goods); and (iii) architects, contractors and technicians as a result of studies, specifications or contracts.

5.202 From a legal perspective, the design contract is considered as a construction contract.

5.203 Since there is no legislation specific to construction contracts, it is to the parties to determine their respective obligations, within the limits of mandatory provisions relating to the construction industry such as the contractor's statutory liability,[178] or the contractor's guarantee of payment,[179] which cannot be derogated from by contract.

172 CCP, Article L. 2171-3.
173 CCP, Article L. 2171-4.
174 CCP, Articles L. 1112-1.
175 CCP, Article L. 1121-1.
176 French Civil Code, Article 1710.
177 French Civil Code, Article 1779.
178 French Civil Code, Articles 1792 et seq.
179 French Civil Code, Articles 1799-1.

Design Obligations

5.204 Design activities are carried out by "*Maîtres d'oeuvres de conception*"; that is, architects or engineering consultants concentrating on design ("*Bureaux d'études de conception*"). It should be noted that under French law, design activities performed to obtain a building permit are the monopoly of architects.[180]

5.205 The design process is conducted in three phases:[181]

- Assessment of the feasibility of the architectural project, and obtention of the required authorizations: The designer carries out sketch studies ("*ESQ*"), and preliminary project studies ("*AVP*"). The sketch studies are based on the designer's first feasibility studies and allow a first visualization of the project inserted in the site. The preliminary project studies, in turn, consist in (i) the preliminary design studies ("*APS*"), in which the designer provides an accurate description of the various options selected for the project, and (ii) the final design studies ("*APD*") where the latest adjustments are made according to the options selected for the project;
- Detailed project design: The designer carries out project studies ("*PRO*"), which are detailed plans of all the levels of the project, elevations, facades and possibly additional perspectives that ensure a good understanding of the whole project down to the smallest details;
- Technical realization of the project ("*EXE*"): The designer carries out shop drawings at the appropriate scales, calculation notes and specifications of use for the site which allow the performance of the works. Unlike the first two phases which can only be entrusted to *Maîtres d'oeuvres*, this phase can be entrusted to contractors.

5.206 The liability of the designer is based on the standard of the *reasonable skill and care* ("*obligation de moyens*") to be expected of an appropriately qualified professional of the specified discipline, that gives the appearance of having the competence and resources to perform the services and who is experienced in providing services in connection with works of a similar size, scope, nature, complexity, and value, to the project. The designer's failure to uphold this standard must be proved for him to be held liable for breach during the design process.

Duty to Warn/Check/Review

5.207 French law imposes on parties to a contract a duty to warn the other party.[182] The *rationale* is that the party appearing as the most competent or the best informed has an obligation to inform the other party of elements it has knowledge of, and to advise it on how to treat this information.

180 Law No. 77-2 of 3 January 1977 on architecture.

181 These phases result from the Decree No. 93-1268 of 29 November 1993 relative to missions of "*maîtrise d'oeuvre*" entrusted by public authorities to private providers that defines the activities of the "*maîtres d'oeuvre*" in the context of public procurement. However, this practice has been extended to private contracts.

182 This duty was developed by courts from the 1970s (*Cour de cassation*, Commercial Chamber, Decision of 14 November 1997, No. 75-15185) and is applicable to French construction contracts.

5.208 The duty to warn is not aimed at any party in particular. In fact, it is extended to all stakeholders in the construction process, even those not bound by contract (e.g., the contractor who detects a design defect must inform the designer thereof).[183] Examples of this duty for stakeholders include:

- The contractor has a duty to warn at all the stages of the construction process, by notably notifying errors and defects of which he is aware, or if an instruction unreasonable. If he considers that the instruction is dangerous or exceeds his capacity, he must refuse to implement it;[184]
- The *maître d'oeuvre*[185] is also under a duty to warn at all the stages of the construction process. If the *maître d'oeu*vre has been entrusted with both the design and the construction process, his duty to warn is of key importance as he has the obligation to supervise the entire performance of the works. Manifestations of this duty include notably (i) holding construction meetings ("*réunions de chantier*") throughout the project, and (ii) notifying the employer of a contractor's failure to perform his obligations or use of any dangerous method. If the *maître d'oeuvre* has only been entrusted with the design process, he his duty to warn in relation is restricted to his own activities, the employer entrusting responsibility for the construction process to a different *maître d'oeuvre*, referred to as the "*maître d'oeuvre d'exécution*";
- The employer may also have a duty to warn, because of his specific knowledge of the project.

Employer and Contractor

5.209 Under French law, the *employer* is the person on whose behalf the works are carried out, including the purchaser of a construction project.

5.210 The employer has a certain number of obligations *vis-à-vis* the contractor, at different stages of the construction process:

- During the design process, the employer has the obligation to obtain all necessary administrative and civil permits, and must supply the contractor with the design;
- During the construction phase, the employer must give the contractors access to the site, and ensure that hygiene and safety rules are respected thereon. He also has an obligation to refrain from interfering with the construction operations: Interference is at his own risk (notably, in terms of resulting delay to the completion of the works), and he may lose the benefit of the contractor's decennial liability;
- More generally, the employer has to issue to the contractor a payment guarantee, thus securing his payment obligation.[186] This obligation pertains to public policy, it thus cannot be derogated from by contract.

---

183 Cour de cassation, 3rd Civil Chamber, Decision of 31 January 2007, No. 05-18.311.

184 *Cour de cassation*, 3rd Civil Chamber, Decision of 15 December 1993, No. 92-14.001.

185 As explained below (para. [7.216]), the *maître d'oeuvre* is in charge of the direction and/or supervision of the performance of the works, at the design and/or construction phase(s).

186 French Civil Code, Article 1799-1.

5.211 The *contractor ("entrepreneur")*, next, is a person (whether physical or legal) deemed to be *"builder of a work"*.[187]

5.212 The contractor has to perform all the obligations required by law and the contract, notably in accordance with the United Technical Documents (DTU), which are established by the General Commission on Standardization in Construction and Civil Works (*"Commission Générale de Normalisation du Bâtiment"*). These obligations are collectively referred to as *les règles de l'art*. In addition, after taking over,[188] the contractor has a number of mandatory obligations to perform.

5.213 Prior to taking over, the standard for the contractor's responsibility is that of "fitness for purpose": The contractor has the obligation to perform works that are appropriate, strictly compliant with the design and necessary for the works' intended use. This implies a strict liability and an *obligation de résultat*.[189] Consequently, liability of the contractor does not require the demonstration of a fault on his part.[190]

5.214 It should be stressed that after taking over, the contractor's liability becomes statutory, as is further explained below.

Consultant's Role and Liability

5.215 Under French law, the employer's consultants encompass a wide range of professionals.

5.216 The *maître d'oeuvre*, first, is the main consultant. His mission may be restricted to the design process, or the construction process, or both. In any case, he is entrusted with the direction and/or supervision of the performance of the works.

5.217 His tasks include:

- Drawing up the service orders;
- Issuing instructions to the contractor to ensure compliance with the contract;
- Assessing progress of the construction works and holding construction meetings;
- However, the maître d'oeuvre does not determine the contractor's payments.

5.218 The *maître d'oeuvre* also assists the employer at taking over. He draws the employer's attention to the defects and snags to be remedied and warns him of the consequences of a taking over without drafting a punch list attached to the taking over certificate.

5.219 The *maître d'oeuvre*'s level of liability varies depending on taking over:

- **Before taking over**, the standard for his liability is that of reasonable skill and care. As a consequence, the proof of a fault is required to hold him liable in case of breach of his obligations;
- **After taking over**, the standard is that of fitness for purpose. Proof of a fault, whether by the *maître d'oeuvre* or another consultant under his supervision is thus not necessary to hold him liable in case of breach. Again, this standard of

187 French Civil Code, Article 1792-1.
188 See para [5.248] for a definition.
189 See above, para. [5.147].
190 French Civil Code, Article 1231-1.

liability results from the contractor's statutory liability regime,[191] which applies after taking over to all "*builder[s] of works*",[192] notion that encompasses architects, engineers, technicians, technical controllers, any building contractor ("*locateur d'ouvrage*"), as well as real estate developers ("*promoteurs immobiliers*").

5.220 Other consultants include:

- "*Bureaux d'études*": They assist the employer and/or the *maître d'oeuvre* in the technical aspects of his competence. There exist as many types of "*bureaux d'études*" as there are engineering specialties;
- "*OPC*": The Organization, Steering, and Coordination bodies, that are in charge of (i) analyzing the basic tasks relating to the execution studies and the works, determining their sequence and their critical path through graphic documents; (ii) harmonizing in time and space the various stakeholders' actions during the construction phase; and (iii) during the construction and until all the punch list items listed in annex to the taking over certificate are remedied, implementing the various organizational measures set out. The OPC's mission may be entrusted to the *maître d'oeuvre*;
- "*Bureau de contrôle*": Technical controllers, it ensures the consistency of the project with regard to technical issues related to building structure, electricity, plumbing, fire and ventilation standards, among others. It is also responsible for the inspection of works during the construction. The intervention of a "*bureau de contrôle*" is compulsory for the construction of "*ERP*" (Establishments Receiving Public), "*IGH*" (Buildings of High Height), particular buildings and buildings in seismic zones.

Sub-Contracting

5.221 Sub-contracting is governed under French law by Law No. 75-1334 of 31 December 1975, that is in large part mandatory and very protective of subcontractors, notably in relation to the risk of not being paid for their works should the main contractor be in default.

5.222 In the meaning of this law, sub-contracting is the fact for a contractor to entrust part of the performance of the works in its scope with another contractor.[193] The right to subcontract is not limited, and does not depend on the type of works to be performed: Subcontracting is thus possible even for design works (i.e., the engineer and the architect are entitled to subcontract their obligations). By exception, however, in public construction contracts the main contractor cannot sub-contract the whole works and must remain directly in charge of at least a part of it.[194]

5.223 Again, a distinction between private and public contracts must be made.

191 French Civil Code, Articles 1792 et seq.
192 French Civil Code, Article 1792-1.
193 Law No. 75-1334 of 31 December 1975 on sub-contracting, Article 1.
194 Law No. 75-1334 of 31 December 1975 on sub-contracting, Article 1.

Private Construction Contracts

5.224 In private contracts, the protection of the sub-contractor is ensured by two mechanisms.

5.225 First, the contractor must issue to the sub-contractor a joint and several guarantee (*garantie personnelle et solidaire*) by a bank, covering all the amounts due to the sub-contractor under the sub-contract.[195] Alternatively, the main contractor may delegate its obligation to pay the sub-contractor to the employer, subject to the latter's agreement.[196] It is of key important to deliver the guarantee or delegation of payment at the time of signature of the sub-contract: Failure to do so renders the sub-contract null and void,[197] and the sub-contractor's action is time-barred five years after the conclusion of the sub-contract.[198]

5.226 The protection of the sub-contractor is reinforced by the fact that the employer has the obligation to ensure the main contractor abides by its obligations relating to (i) the approval of the sub-contractor by the employer, and (ii) the delivery to the sub-contractor of a bank guarantee or delegation of payment.[199] Thus, if the employer is aware the main contractor has sub-contracted part or whole of its works, the employer has the obligation to put the main contractor on notice to have the sub-contractor approved.[200] Moreover, if the sub-contractor has been approved but does not enjoy the benefit of a delegation of payment, the employer has the obligation to request that the main contractor justifies having delivered the bank guarantee.[201] Failure of the employer to fulfil these obligations renders it liable *vis-à-vis* the subcontractor in tort.[202]

5.227 The second mechanism ensuring the sub-contractor's protection is referred to as "direct action": If the main contractor fails to pay the sub-contractor its works performed under the sub-contract within one month after formal notification to the main contractor with copy to the employer, the sub-contractor may request payment of all sums due under the sub-contract directly from the employer.[203] It is stressed that benefitting from this action:

- Requires to have the sub-contractor, as well as the method of payment, formally approved by the employer;[204]
- Is limited to payments corresponding to the works performed under the sub-contract and which are for the benefit of the employer;[205]
- Payments made by the employer as a result of the direct action are limited to the amount still owed to the main contractor at the date of receipt of the copy of the notice to pay,[206] and do not extend to amounts that could be payable by the employer to the main contractor under other contracts.

195 Law No. 75-1334 of 31 December 1975 on sub-contracting, Article 14.
196 Law No. 75-1334 of 31 December 1975 on sub-contracting, Article 14.
197 Law No. 75-1334 of 31 December 1975 on sub-contracting, Article 14.
198 French Civil Code, Article 2224.
199 Law No. 75-1334 of 31 December 1975 on sub-contracting, Article 14-1.
200 Law No. 75-1334 of 31 December 1975 on sub-contracting, Article 14-1.
201 Law No. 75-1334 of 31 December 1975 on sub-contracting, Article 14-1.
202 French Civil Code, Article 1240.
203 Law No. 75-1334 of 31 December 1975 on sub-contracting, Article 12.
204 Law No. 75-1334 of 31 December 1975 on sub-contracting, Article 6.
205 Law No. 75-1334 of 31 December 1975 on sub-contracting, Article 13.
206 Law No. 75-1334 of 31 December 1975 on sub-contracting, Article 13.

Public Construction Contracts

5.228 The protection of the sub-contractor in public construction contracts is ensured by a mechanism of direct payment.[207]

5.229 This mechanism is reserved to (i) sub-contracts concluded with public legal entities for amount exceeding €600, and (ii) first-tier sub-contractors.[208]

5.230 The main contractor must have indicated, at tender, the nature and amount of each of the services it intends to sub-contract. The notification of the contract then implies approval of the sub-contractor and the conditions of its payment.[209]

5.231 The mechanism of direct payment is as follows:

- The sub-contractor sends his request for payment to the main contractor. After approval by the main contractor, the request is then transmitted to the person designated in the main contract for this purpose;[210]
- If the main contractor (i) has not refused the sub-contractor's request for payment by reasoned decision within 15 days of its receipt, or (ii) has failed to transmit it to the person designated in the main contract to that effect, the sub-contractor may request payment directly from said designated person, by registered letter with acknowledgment of receipt.[211]

Principles Applicable to All Sub-Contracts

5.232 Regardless of the nature of the sub-contract, the main contractor is liable *vis-à-vis* the employer for the sub-contractor's actions (e.g., in case of delay, or damages caused by the subcontractor). Indeed, the main contractor is responsible for all damage, loss or delay, even when evidencing that the subcontractor is at fault.[212]

5.233 If found liable, the main contractor will then seek the sub-contractor's liability for breach of its obligations under the sub-contract. The main contractor may seek compensation for the total amount of damages he paid to the employer: There are no implied terms or legislation limiting the sub-contractor's liability to the amount of the sub-contract. Therefore, parties sometimes include such a limitation clause in the sub-contract.

Unforeseeable Physical Conditions

5.234 Again, a distinction must be made between public and private contracts.

5.235 In case of unforeseeable physical conditions affecting the performance of public construction contracts, courts may adjust the contract to restore its financial balance. The unforeseeable events must be physical, and overturn the general economy of the contract. In addition, their effect must be temporary as opposed to irresistible, which is a condition for *Force Majeure*[213] and which would entail the end of the contract.[214]

---

207 CCP, Article L. 2193-11.
208 Law No. 75-1334 of 31 December 1975 on sub-contracting, Article 6.
209 Law No. 75-1334 of 31 December 1975 on sub-contracting, Articles 5 and 6.
210 CCP, Article R. 2193-11.
211 Law No. 75-1334 of 31 December 1975 on sub-contracting, Article 8.
212 *Cour de cassation*, 3rd Civil Chamber, 13 March 1991, No. 89-13.833.
213 In private contract law, *Force Majeure* is defined at Article 1218 of the Civil Code.
214 *Conseil d'Etat*, Decision of 30 March 1916, *Cie générale d'éclairage de Bordeaux*, No. 59928.

5.236 In private construction contracts, the principle has for a very long time been *pacta sunt servanda*,[215] insofar as courts were denied the power to adjust the contract to restore its financial balance in case of unforeseeable events.[216] Yet, the 2016 Law Reform, applicable to contracts entered into after 1st October 2016, provides that, in case of hardship, the aggrieved party may ask for renegotiations of the contract and, should they fail, for a judicial revision of the contract.[217] This provision, laid by at Article 1195 of the Civil Code, applies to any contract, provided that the parties did not exclude or alter this provision. The applicability of Article 1195 is yet debatable when it comes to lump-sum construction contracts, as Article 1793 of the Civil Code provides that, where a contractor commits to perform an obligation for a lump sum, he cannot claim for additional costs. So far, case-law has not ruled whether Article 1195 shall prevail upon Article 1793 or the opposite. Consequently, the parties would be well advised to specify in their contract whether it should abide by Article 1195 or not.

5.237 Finally, it should be noted that, regardless of the nature of the contract (public or private), there is no legal threshold for the overturn of the general economy of the contract: The courts determine it on a case by case basis, often varying between 20 and 30%.

Material and Workmanship

5.238 The principle under French law is that the choice of material belongs to the contractor.[218]

5.239 In addition, the standard CCAG Privé established by the AFNOR[219] also places responsibility for the quality of the materials supplied and for their implementation on the contractor.[220]

5.240 The contractor is responsible for the materials he has purchased even if they are installed by another contractor, or if the materials are chosen by the employer or the architect: It must indeed refuse to use the materials that do not satisfy all the quality conditions for their intended use.

Labour Law Considerations

5.241 French labour law is governed by a body of normative texts that mainly regulate work relationships, the employment contract, professional union rights, working time, and minimum wages.

5.242 Collective agreements (*conventions collectives*) complete these regulations and are applicable to particular sectors, or a specific profession.

5.243 In case of discrepancy between the Labour Code and a collective agreement, the provisions that are the most favourable to the worker are applied. Each employment contract must refer to the applicable collective agreement. In the construction industry,

215 French Civil Code, Article 1103.
216 Cour de Cassation, Decision of 6 March 1876, *Canal de Craponne*.
217 French Civil Code, Article 1195.
218 *Cour de cassation*, 1st Civil Chamber, Decision of 18 July 1955.
219 See Section "*Standard form for private contracts (CCAG privé)*" above.
220 Article 8.

the main applicable collective agreements are those for property develop$ment, for public works, and regional collective agreements for the building industry.

5.244 One of the main considerations of labour law in the construction industry is health and safety. Article L.4532-2 of the French Labour Code provides:

> *Workers health and safety coordination shall be organised for all building or civil engineering projects involving several self-employed persons or companies, including subcontractors, in order to prevent risks arising from their simultaneous or successive interventions and to provide, where appropriate, the use of common means such as infrastructures, logistical means and collective protections.*

5.245 This coordination is entrusted to a coordinator,[221] as soon as two different companies (including if one is the sub-contractor of the other) intervene concurrently or successively on the same site. In practice, almost all construction sites must thus have a health and safety coordinator.

5.246 Failure to establish a coordinator is a criminal offence under French law.[222]

5.247 The coordinator's liability appears to be contractual: Since he does not seem to be deemed a "*builder of works*" within the meaning of Article 1792-1 of the Civil Code, his liability is only likely to be at stake if one of his decisions has an adverse effect on the works' performance.[223]

Performance and Taking-Over

5.248 Taking over (*réception*) under French law is strictly defined: It corresponds to the employer's unequivocal decision to approve the works by taking over the works, with or without drafting a punch list, at the request of the most diligent party, noted *inter partes*.[224]

5.249 Under French law, taking over has peculiar effects, some extinctive and others creative. The taking over transfers the risks and the duty of care of the works from the contractor to the employer, thus extinguishing the contractor's obligations in this regard. Moreover, it triggers a right for the contractor to payment of work and constitutes the starting point of the contractor's specific warranties, thus creating new rights for the parties.

5.250 There are three types of approval:

1. Express approval:[225] After a site visit, minutes are signed by both the contractor and the employer, clarifying the date of taking over;
2. Approval by judicial order:[226] When the employer refuses to approve the completed works, a judicial order may be issued by the judge, at the contractor's request. The order clarifies the date of approval;

221 The coordinator, whose legal regime is governed by the Labour Code, is a function introduced in French law in 1993 by transposing the Council Directive 92/57/EEC of 24 June 1992 on the implementation of minimum safety and health requirements at temporary or mobile work sites.

222 French Labour Code, Article L. 4744-4.

223 Cour de cassation, Criminal chamber, Decision of 9 June 2009, No. 08-82.847.

224 French Civil Code, Article 1792-6.

225 *Cour de cassation*, 3rd Civil Chamber, Decision of 12 June 1991, No. 90-10.692.

226 *Cour de cassation*, 3rd Civil Chamber, Decision of 8 June 2006, No. 05-15.509.

3. Implied approval:[227] When it is clear that, in the absence of express taking over, there is, however, no doubt that it has occurred, the works may exceptionally be deemed approved. This is notably the case, for example, when the Employer occupies the premises, or the contractor is entirely paid.

5.251 Taking over by judicial order requires the works to be complete. The other two types of approval may be obtained even if the project is not fully completed or if there are minor defects that remain to be remedied.

Contract Price and Payment

Private Construction Contracts

5.252 As explained above, the determination of the price is in principle not a condition for the validity of a contract. However, an exception exists for construction contracts, French law requiring that the price be determinable.[228]

PRICING METHODS

5.253 The construction industry generally uses three pricing methods:

- Lump sum contracts (*marché à forfait*),[229] which are global and definitive: In these contracts, additional works are included in the price, except if agreed otherwise or in case of express, unambiguous acceptance of additional costs by the employer. However, the contractor can claim payment for supplemental work if it leads to disruption of the general economic conditions of the contract;
- Re-measurement contracts (*marché au métré*), in which the parties apply agreed prices to units of executed works;
- Contracts on a "cost plus" basis (*marché aux dépenses réelles*), that is at actual cost, uplifted by a percentage to take into account taxes and profit. This method has arisen from market practice and is applied by judges to determine a price when the contract is silent.

5.254 Payment modalities are not regulated under French law. Thus, it is possible to agree that the total amount of the works will be paid in a single payment after taking over. However, it is common practice to adopt a system of interim payments against milestones. The standard CCAG Privé established by the AFNOR[230] thus provides for monthly payments reflecting the contractor's statement of work.[231]

TIMING OF PAYMENT

5.255 Payments are to be processed within 60 days of performance of the service.[232]

227 *Cour de cassation*, 3rd Civil Chamber, Decision of 12 October 1988, No. 87-11.174.

228 French Civil Code, Article 1165: "*In contracts for the provision of services, if the parties do not agree before the contract is enforced, the price may be fixed by the creditor, who is obliged to justify the amount in the event of dispute. In the event of abuse in the fixing of the price, the judge may be seized of a claim for damages*".

229 French Civil Code, Article 1793.

230 See Section "*Standard form for private contracts (CCAG privé)*" above.

231 Article 19.1.

232 French Commercial Code, Article L.441-10 (as modified by Ordinnance 2019-359 of 24 April 2019).

PAYMENT GUARANTEES

5.256 Payments to the contractor are secured by a mandatory guarantee required by law,[233] that has two applications:

- First, if the employer applies for specific credit to finance the project, the organization providing the credit must pay any sums due under the contract directly to the contractor. In such a case, the guarantee must be specific, and cover the totality of the works' costs;
- If the employer does not apply for such a credit, or does so only for part of the project, payments should be backed by a bank guarantee.

5.257 In the absence of such a guarantee, an unpaid contractor has a right to suspend work after making a final demand for payment.

5.258 The employer, in turn, is entitled to retain an amount not exceeding 5% of the total contract price to guarantee the remediation of any defects arising on the date of taking over (*reception*).[234]

Public Construction Contracts

PRICING METHODS

5.259 Contrary to private construction contracts, the price of public construction contracts must be determined or determinable, and consist either in fixed prices applicable to whole or part of the works, or in unit prices to be applied to the final quantities.[235]

5.260 The CCAG Travaux defines these prices as follows:

- Fixed prices consist in any price that pays the contractor for a work, part of a work, or a specified set of services defined by the contract and that is either explicitly mentioned in the contract as a lump sum, or that applies to a package of services which is not likely to be repeated;[236]
- Unit prices consist in any price which is not fixed as defined above, in particular any price which applies to a type of structure or to a work item whose quantities are indicated in the contract on a provisional basis.[237]

TIMING OF PAYMENT

5.261 The global payment term cannot exceed:[238]

233 French Civil Code, Article 1799-1.

234 French Civil Code, Article 1792-6.

235 Decree No. 2016-360 of 25 March 2016 on public procurement, Article 17:

"*The prices of services covered by a public contract are either* **unit prices** *applied to the quantities actually delivered or executed or* **fixed prices** *applied to all or part of the public contract, irrespective of the quantities delivered or executed.*

Incentives can be introduced in public procurement, particularly to improve the time limit for performance of the work, to seek better quality of services and to reduce production costs.

Subject to the provisions of Article 18, public contracts may provide for price variation clauses".

236 CCAG Travaux, Article 10.2.

237 CCAG Travaux, Article 10.2.

238 CCP, Articles R. 2192-10 – R. 2192-11.; Decree No. 2013-269 of 29 March 2013 on combating late payment in public contracts.

- 30 days for the State and its public establishments and the local authorities and local public institutions;
- 50 days for public health establishments and establishments of the health service of the armed forces;
- 60 days for State-owned companies.

5.262 For contracts exceeding €50,000, the contractor may receive an advance.[239]

Defects Liability

5.263 "*Builders of works*" are subject to a statutory liability relating to defects in the building works they carry out as follows:[240]

- A ten year liability and related insurance obligations ("*garantie /assurance décennale*") in relation to damage (i) affecting the stability of the structure; (ii) causing the work to be unfit for its purpose because one of its constituent parts or elements of equipment has been affected; or (iii) affecting the strength of the elements of equipment of a work, but only if it is an inseparable and integral part of the building structure;[241]
- A 2 year "proper functioning" liability ("*garantie de bon fonctionnement*"), for damages to elements separable from the building (i.e., which can be demounted, dissembled or replaced without damaging);[242]
- A perfect completion warranty ("*garantie de parfait achèvement*") covering the defects listed in the punch list attached to the taking over certificate, as well as those that appear during the first year after taking over.[243] The parties may agree on the period required for remedial work. If the contractor fails to remedy the defects listed in the punch list attached to the taking over certificate, the employer may use the 5% retention money[244] addressed above to pay for the necessary remediation works. The contractor has the right to substitute a joint and several guarantee (*garantie personnelle et solidaire*) of a financial institution to the extent of these 5%.

5.264 The level of liability of builders of work is of fitness for purpose. As a consequence, the fault of the builder is presumed, and does not need to be proven.

5.265 For all other defects outside the scope of the specifically regulated situations above, the employer can bring an action against the contractor based on his ordinary liability for breach of contract. This action is time barred ten years after taking over.[245] In that case, contrary to the situations described above, the fault of the builder of work must be proved to hold him responsible in case of breach.

239 Public procurement and other contracts code, Article 87.

240 French Civil Code, Articles 1792 et seq.

241 French Civil Code, Article 1792. French Civil Code, Article 1792-2.

242 French Civil Code, Article 1792-3.

243 French Civil Code, Article 1792-6.

244 Law No. 71-584 of 16 July 1971 regulating retention guarantees in construction contracts governed by Article 1779-3 of the Civil Code.

245 French Civil Code, Article 1792-4-3.

Limitation of Liability

5.266 Under French law, all liabilities can theoretically be excluded, with the exception of the legal warranties that contractors must provide,[246] since, as part of contractors' statutory liability, they are mandatory.

5.267 Notwithstanding these warranties, the parties are free to limit or exclude contractually their respective liabilities, including indirect or consequential losses, loss of profits, or insufficient economic success. However, these clauses will not be valid in case of gross negligence or willful misconduct, or if the contractual liability provided is insignificant, as a result of a too broad exclusion clause.

5.268 Moreover, parties cannot limit or exclude their liability towards third parties in tort: Limitation and exclusion of liability clauses are only valid in contractual obligations under special conditions.

5.269 Finally, caps on liability are often agreed upon between the parties in their contract, especially in large and complex projects. They are generally expressed as a percentage of the contract price, the exact figure mostly depending on the potential financial costs of delays or other breach of a contractor's obligations leading to termination and retendering of the contract.

Variations

5.270 French construction law allows the employer to change the specifications, design, etc., during the construction works. In turn, the contractor is entitled to additional time and money accordingly.

5.271 The CCAG Privé established by the AFNOR highlights the employer's right to order variations: The contractor may not refuse an increase of his works up to 25%, or a decrease thereof up to 10%.[247]

5.272 Variations of lump sum private construction contracts are regulated: The employer has the obligation to order them in writing, and to negotiate a new price with the contractor.[248] The writing, that encompasses the employer's formal order ("*ordre de service*"), is essential: Without it, all variations are deemed to be included in the initial price, except in case of hardship.

Delay and Disruption

5.273 Contractors are in principle bound to perform the works within the time prescribed in the contract. In the absence of a time for completion, the works are to be performed in such a time as reasonable.[249]

5.274 To avoid responsibility for delay, contractors must demonstrate that it is attributable (i) to the employer, or to another contractor; or (ii) to a case of *Force Majeure*.

5.275 Traditionally, delay is governed by general contracts law.

---

246 French Civil Code, Article 1792-5.

247 CCAG Privé, Articles 11.1.1.1 and 11.1.2.1.

248 French Civil Code, Article 1793.

249 *Cour de cassation*, 3rd Civil Chamber, Decision of 16 March 2011, No. 10-14.051.

5.276 However, when the contract is based on the CCAG Privé, several situations in which the delay is attributable to the employer are provided,[250] namely:

- Delay in completing the administrative formalities the employer is responsible for;
- Instruction leading to a slowdown or suspension of works, except if these instructions derive from the contractor's failure to comply with the contract requirements;
- Failure to provide instructions, if asked to do so in writing by the contractor or after becoming aware of their absence;
- Late payment leading to a suspension of works notified by the contractor to the employer by registered letter at least 15 days before.

5.277 French law does not specifically address the concept of disruption. However, a contractor suffering disruption by an employer may see its loss of productivity compensated as he would for any breach of contract. It should be noted that, once the principle of an entitlement to damages for disruption is established, courts have discretion in awarding damages, even when their quantification is not sufficiently established.

5.278 In case of competing causes of delay, French law does not provide for an established set of rules on concurrent delay. French courts will generally tend to attempt apportioning the delay between the events caused by each party, and consequently, the contractor may receive an extension of time for a part of the delay as apportioned.

Liquidated Damages and Other Damages

5.279 Delay in the performance of contractual obligations may be compensated by damages,[251] that are composed of the loss suffered (*damnum emergens*) and the loss profits (*lucrum cessans*)[252] that were foreseen or foreseeable at the time of conclusion of the contract, save in case of gross negligence ("*faute lourde*") or misrepresentation.[253] In any event, the resulting damages may not compensate indirect losses.[254]

5.280 French law allows, as a matter of public policy, contractual pre-estimations of the *quantum* of damages for delay; being clarified that they may correspond to a penalty contrary to Common law systems.[255] The aim of this agreed penalty is both to compensate damages and ensure the performance of the obligation, thus some part of deterrent nature is implied.

5.281 The purpose of this clause is to provide a remedy in the event of breach by the contractor. They are available for (i) failure to complete the works by completion date (delay damages or delay liquidates damages); and/or (ii) failure to provide a facility or plant capable of achieving the specified performance standard (for example, output – performance damages or performance liquidated damages).

250 Articles 7-5.2.1 and 7-5.2.2.
251 French Civil Code, Article 1231-1.
252 French Civil Code, Article 1231-2.
253 French Civil Code, Article 1231-3.
254 French Civil Code, Article 1231-4.
255 French Civil Code, Article 1231-5.

5.282 In general, liquidated damages are fixed as percentage of the contract sum per day of delay. Nevertheless, there is no rule which prevents fixing a lump sum as a penalty. The CCAG Privé contains a clause fixing a penalty of 1/1000 of the contract sum per day of delay, with 5% of the contract sum as a maximum.

5.283 As a rule, the loss actually suffered by the employer is not taken into consideration in calculating the amount. Also, the employer does not have to prove any loss to claim liquidated damages: The defaulting party cannot avoid paying even if it is proved that the other party did not suffer any loss. Nevertheless, if the contractor considers that the amount of liquidated damages payable is disproportional to the actual loss suffered by the employer, he can apply to the judge to have it adjusted.

5.284 In addition to the payment of damages for delayed performance of the works, it should be noted that French courts may consider that the party to which the delay is attributable must lose the benefit of the clauses governing the contract price that are in its favour. For example, a contractor cannot request the application of a stabilization clause for the period of delay that is attributable to him.[256]

Insurance

5.285 French construction law imposes a compulsory insurance system, to which practice has added a non-compulsory system.

Compulsory Insurance

5.286 French construction law[257] established a system of compulsory insurance binding on both the builder of work and the employer, it is said to be of "double layer":

- The builder of work must subscribe an insurance to cover his decennial liability during ten years following taking over of construction works;
- The employer insures damages to the works, insurance aiming at "pre-financing" within specific deadlines and terms specified in the standard clauses, repair of defects falling within the scope of decennial liability. Subsequently, the insurer files a claim against the builder of work's decennial liability, system that enables a prompt compensation of the employer.

5.287 The compulsory insurance cover concerns in principle all new structures.[258]

256 *Cour de cassation*, 3rd Civil Chamber, Decision of 27 October 1982.

257 Law No. 78-12 on responsibility and insurance in construction.

258 Exceptions are listed at Article L243-1-1 of the French Insurance Code as follows: "*I – Maritime, lake and river works, road, harbour, airport, heliport and railway infrastructure works, municipal, industrial, liquid wastes treatment works as well as parts of the equipment of one of these works shall not be submitted to compulsory insurance provided for in Articles L241-1, L241-2, and L242-1. Roads, pedestrian works, parking lots, various networks, drains, lines or cables and their stands, transport, production, storage and distribution of energy works, telecommunications works, non-insured sporting works as well as parts of their equipment shall also be excluded from compulsory insurance referred to in the first paragraph, except if the work or part of the equipment is incidental to a work submitted to compulsory insurance. II – Compulsory insurance does not apply to the existing works before the commencement of the building works, except for those which are completely incorporated in the new work and become technically inseparable from it*".

Non-Compulsory Insurance

5.288 Several forms of non-mandatory insurance are available relating to construction. Contractors often take out cover complementary to the compulsory decennial insurance. Contractors' All Risk Insurance (*Tous Risques Chantier*) and professional indemnity are the most frequently used non-mandatory insurance coverages.

5.289 Non-compulsory standard form insurance policies that cover the main contractor's liability to the employer (contractual damage) include:

- A two-year "proper operation" insurance, that covers liability, guaranteeing the proper functioning of items of equipment that are not linked to the foundations and main walls of a building (e.g., doors, windows, radiators, etc.) and covers their replacement if there is a manufacturing defect;
- A "perfect completion" warranty;
- General legal liability: Insurers may also cover general legal liability. It is possible to purchase this insurance during the construction process, or after taking over. Liability will be covered, provided that the damage or loss is not serious enough to be within the ten year warranty.

5.290 Cases of *Force Majeure* may also be covered by insurance, as well as the main contractor's liability for torts to third parties (neighbourhood nuisances for instance).

Suspension

Private Construction Contracts

5.291 For private construction contracts, the Roman law maxim of "*Exceptio non adimpleti contractus*" applies.

5.292 This principle stems from the concept of *reciprocity* of obligations whereby a party is not obliged to perform its obligations if the other party has failed to perform its own. As a consequence, a party may withhold performance of its obligations if the other party has failed to perform its own obligations.[259] The failure of the other party may be current,[260] or future if already certain.[261] In any case, the remedy must be proportionate: Courts require the other party's failure be "*serious enough*", in accordance with the good faith principle.

5.293 In the construction industry, the main concern remains payments. Since, in the normal course of events, payment terms may result in payment being due months after the works are performed, the financial risk can be considerable and quickly increase. Therefore, legislation has put in place a specific guarantee that can be relied upon in the absence of or in addition to a contractual right to suspend, as follows:

> *A building owner who enters into a private constructional works contract referred to in Article 1779, 3°, must warrant to the contractor the payment of the sums owed when they exceed a threshold fixed by decree in Conseil d'État* [i.e., €12,000.[262]]

259 The *Cour de cassation* held on 14 February 2019 that, even where the parties have stipulated liquidated damages, they may resort to *exceptio non adimpleti contractus*.

260 French Civil Code, Article 1219.

261 French Civil Code, Article 1120.

262 Decree No. 99-658 of 30 July 1999 for the application of Article 1799-1 of the Civil Code and fixing a guarantee threshold for contractors' payments, Article 1.

Where a building owner does not have recourse to a specific credit or where he has recourse to it only in part, and failing a guarantee resulting from a particular stipulation, payment shall be warranted by a joint and several suretyship agreed to by a credit institution, an insurance company or an institution of collective guarantee, according to terms fixed by decree in Conseil d'État. So long as no guarantee has been given and the contractor is not paid for the works carried out, the latter may suspend performance of the contract after a notice of default remained ineffective at the end of a period of fifteen days.[263]

5.294 In practice, this payment guarantee is far from always being spontaneously implemented, which may give an opportunity to the contractor to stop works at the first non-payment. Generally, the employer implements immediately the guarantee as a result.

Public Construction Contracts

5.295 The principle is that the public legal entity's co-contractor is bound to ensure performance of the contract, except in cases of *Force Majeure*. Thus, the public legal entity's breach or failures do not justify non-performance of the contract, or suspension of the works. "*Exceptio non adimpleti contractus*" thus does not apply, as a matter of principle.

5.296 The CCAG Travaux standard form provides that the Contractor may suspend the performance only in the following circumstances:

- Failure to pay two consecutive monthly interim payments;
- 30 days after application date of the second application, provided (i) the Contractor informed by letter with acknowledgement receipt of its intention to withhold the works within one month, and (ii) the employer does not issue a formal notice to continue performance of the works during this one month time period.

5.297 These restricted circumstances reflect one of the core principles governing public contracts: The imperative continuity of public service (*continuité du service public*) that justifies the very exceptional circumstances in which contractors are restrictively allowed to suspend the works. In principle, it is thus much easier for a contractor to issue claims dealt with at the end of the works.

Termination

5.298 Termination of construction contracts is in principle governed by general contracts law.

5.299 The only exception to this principle concerns private lump sum contracts, wherein the owner has a right to terminate the contract for convenience, provided the contractor is compensated for its expenses, works, and profits.[264]

263 French Civil Code, Article 1799-1.

264 French Civil Code, Article 1794: "*The owner may,* **of his own will,** *terminate* **a contract at a fixed price** *[lump sum], although the work has already begun, by compensating the contractor for all his expenses, for all his works, and for all that he could have earned in that undertaking*".

Forms of Security – Bonds and Guarantees

5.300 As explained throughout this chapter, French construction law requires a number of mandatory guarantees be issued, notably the employer's payment guarantee to the contractor,[265] the subcontractor's guarantees,[266] the retention money or the substituted guarantee of 5%,[267] etc.

5.301 In addition to these guarantees, the parties are free to subscribe to non-compulsory guarantees, defined by Article 2321 of the Civil Code:

> *The self-supporting guarantee is the undertaking by which the guarantor, in consideration of an obligation subscribed by a third party, is obliged to pay an amount either on first demand or on agreed terms.*
>
> *The guarantor is not bound in case of manifest abuse or fraud of the beneficiary or of collusion with the client.*
>
> *The guarantor cannot object to the secured obligation.*
>
> *Unless otherwise agreed, this security does not comply with the secured obligation.*

5.302 Examples of non-mandatory security-bonds and guarantees subscribed in construction projects include:

- *Tender Bond* or *Bid Bond Guarantee*, to guarantee the owner of the works against the withdrawal of the company between the time it submits an offer and the signature of the contract;
- *Down Payment Guarantee*, guarantee the employer a refund of the deposit paid to the tenderer if the latter fails to perform the services corresponding to the amount of the interim payment so received in application of the contract;
- *Performance Guarantees*, to guarantee the customer in case of non-performance or poor performance of the contract.

Claims

5.303 Under French construction law, claims may be issued either before, or after taking over (*réception*).

Before Taking Over (Réception)

PRIVATE CONSTRUCTION CONTRACTS

5.304 General contract law applies in principle: There is no specific mechanism applicable to construction's claims.

5.305 However, under lump sum contracts, the contractor must keep in mind that all additional works will be considered included in the price, in the absence of prior agreement or of the express, unambiguous acceptance of additional cost by the employer.[268]

265 French Civil Code, Article 1799-1.

266 Law No. 75-1334 of 31 December 1975 on sub-contracting.

267 Law No. 71-584 of 16 July 1971 regulating retention guarantees in construction contracts governed by Article 1779-3 of the Civil Code.

268 French Civil Code, Article 1793.

PUBLIC CONSTRUCTION CONTRACTS

5.306 Contractors claim via statements of claim (*dossier de réclamation*).

5.307 A statement of claim sets out in detail each head of the dispute, indicating, on the one hand, the amounts whose payment is requested and, on the other hand, the reasons for these requests, in particular the bases for calculating the amounts claimed.[269]

5.308 Traditionally, the contractor was entitled to full compensation for the loss suffered as a result of delays in the performance of the contract attributable to the employer (or to its other contractors), and distinct from the extension of time due resulting from the performance of additional works, provided that this prejudice appears certain and presents a direct causal link with these delays.[270]

5.309 Recent decisions of the *Conseil d'Etat* have restricted the legal basis of the contractor's entitlement: The employer's liability is incurred for the benefit of the contractor only because of the economy of the contract's overturn, or a fault by the employer, but not because of the employer's other contractors' fault.[271]

5.310 Finally, it should be noted that, for contracts based on the CCAG Travaux, the contractor must address his statement of claim to the *maître d'oeuvre*.[272] Statements of claim addressed directly to the employer are likely to render inadmissible any request for payment of additional works.[273]

After Taking Over (Réception)

5.311 After taking over the contractor's statutory liability explained above applies; that is, the contractor's decennial liability,[274] the two-year "proper functioning" liability,[275] the perfect completion warranty,[276] and the ten-year liability for all the other defects outside the scope of the specifically regulated situations.[277]

5.312 The subcontractor, in turn, is contractually liable:

- *Vis-à-vis* the contractor, either on the basis of his general liability,[278] or on the basis of the transposition of the ten-year and two-year "proper functioning" liabilities to the relationship contractor/subcontractor.[279]
- *Vis-à-vis* the employer, in tort.[280]

269 *Conseil d'Etat*, Decision of 31 October 2012, *Communauté d'agglomération Reims Métropole*, No. 349281; *Conseil d'Etat*, Decision of 15 February 2012, *Commune de Souclin*, No. 346255.

270 *Conseil d'Etat*, Decision of 1 August 2012, *Company Scarpari*, No. 342337.

271 *Conseil d'Etat*, Decision of 5 June 2013, *Region Haute Normandie*, No. 352917 ; *Conseil d'Etat*, Decision of 12 November 2015, *TONIN*, No. 384716.

272 Article 13-44.

273 *Conseil d'Etat*, Decision of 8 April 2009, *Société DV Construction*, No. 297756.

274 French Civil Code, Articles 1792 and 1792-1.

275 French Civil Code, Article 1792-3.

276 French Civil Code, Article 1792-6.

277 French Civil Code, Article 1792-4-3.

278 French Civil Code, Article 1792-4-3.

279 French Civil Code, Article 1792-4-2.

280 *Cour de cassation*, Plenary Assembly, Decision of 12 July 1991, No. 90-13.602.

5.313 Manufacturers and/or suppliers, finally, are contractually liable *vis-à-vis* both the contractor and the employer.[281] If the supplier is the subcontractor's, he will be liable in tort.[282]

Time-Bar Provisions

5.314 Contractual time-bars provisions are licit under French law,[283] subject to those applicable to the contractor's statutory liability: Any clause of a contract which purports to exclude or limit the statutory liability shall be deemed to be unwritten.[284] However, it should be noted that parties are not prohibited from extending these limitation periods.

Disputes – Adjudication and Arbitration

5.315 French law does not have an adjudication procedure similar to the *1996 Housing Grants, Construction and Regeneration Act*. However, parties to construction disputes may always, prior to bringing an action to court or arbitration, request the judge to order a wide range of interim measures, including judicial expertises (*référé expertise*),[285] or provisional payment of an undisputed amount (*référé provision*),[286] such as, for example, a DAB decision for which no notice of dissatisfaction would have been issued under the FIDIC Red Book.

5.316 Arbitration and other means of alternative dispute resolution mechanisms are well developed, and enforced.

5.317 Multi-tiered dispute resolution clauses providing for a prior amicable settlement process are strictly enforced: Failure to attempt to settle a dispute amicably prior to initiating a court or arbitration procedure renders the action inadmissible ("*fin de non recevoir*"),[287] but would not render a subsequent award rendered without prior amicable discussions invalid.

5.318 When the dispute is settled amicably, the parties may conclude an amicable settlement contract ("*transaction*"), whereby they agree to end a dispute or prevent possible future disputes.[288] The transaction validly made may be referred *ex parte* by any of the parties to the judge for approval ("*homologation*"), which renders the agreement enforceable.[289]

---

281 *Cour de cassation*, Plenary Assembly, Decision of 7 February 1986, No. 83-14.631.

282 *Cour de cassation*, 3rd Civil Chamber, Decision of 28 November 2001, No. 00-13.559, 00-14.450.

283 French Civil Code, Article 2254: "*The limitation period may be shortened or extended by agreement of the parties. It may not, however, be reduced to less than one year or be extended to more than ten years.*

The parties may also, by mutual agreement, add to the causes of suspension or interruption of the limitation period provided by law.

The provisions of the two preceding paragraphs do not apply to actions for payment or recovery of salaries, annuity instalments, alimony payments, rents, sharecropping payments, rental expenses, interest on sums of money loaned, and generally on all actions for payment of sums payable by the year or on shorter periodic terms.

284 French Civil Code, Article 1792-5.

285 French Code of Civil Procedure, Article 145.

286 French Code of Civil Procedure, Article 809.

287 *Cour de cassation*, Mixed Chamber, Decision of 14 February 2003, Nos. 00-19.423 and 00-19.424.

288 French Civil Code, Articles 2044 et seq.

289 French Code of Civil Procedure, Articles 1565 et seq.

5.319 Arbitration is governed by Articles 1442 to 1527 of the French Code of Civil Procedure, Articles 1504 to 1527 being dedicated to international arbitration and are applicable "*when international trade interests are at stake*",[290] that courts interpret as meaning when there is a cross-border movement of funds. The French international arbitration regime is one of the most permissible compared to other jurisdictions, and the grounds to challenge international arbitration awards are strictly limited to the following circumstances:[291]

- The arbitral tribunal wrongly upheld or declined jurisdiction;
- The arbitral tribunal was not properly constituted;
- The arbitral tribunal ruled without complying with the mandate conferred upon it;
- Due process was violated;
- Recognition or enforcement of the award is contrary to international public policy.

5.320 France counts many general and trade-related arbitral institutions, among which the International Chamber of Commerce (ICC), and the *Fédération Nationale des Travaux Publics* (National Federation for Public Works – FNTP) that, contrary to what its denomination would imply, also administers disputes arising out of private construction contracts.

Construction Law Issues Specific to French Law

Contrat d'entreprise: Outcome Based Contract

5.321 There is no legal regime corresponding to the outcome-based contract, although performance contracts are frequent in many industrial sectors, where the contractor, beyond the compliance with the regular taking over requirements, has to reach some figured performances, or performance indicators.

5.322 Under public procurement rules, a performance contract is amongst the few allowed exceptions to the principle of allotment – public procurement contracts shall be divided into batches ("*lots*"), to favour small companies access to the competition.

Duty to Advise the Employer

5.323 See above.

Role of the Engineer

5.324 See above.

Joint Several and Strict Liability of Ten Years in Case of Serious Default

5.325 As a result of their statutory liability[292] explained above, builders of works are traditionally subject to an "*in solidum*" liability *vis-à-vis* the employer. They are, in fact,

290 French Code of Civil Procedure, Article 1504.
291 French Code of Civil Procedure, Article 1520.
292 French Civil Code, Articles 1792 et seq.

often regarded as having all participated in the damage. Consequently, the employer may trigger any of their liabilities, and claim compensation for the full amount of the damage. Then, the debt will be distributed among the builders with regard to their faults, often determined by an expert report ordered by the judge.

5.326 In this regard, it must be noted that French law establishes a legal joint and several liability for manufacturers of works, part of works or piece of equipment designed and manufactured to satisfy specific requirement determined in advance. Manufacturers are jointly and several liable along with the contractor who has incorporated (without modification and in accordance with the instructions provided by the manufacturer), in the works, part of works or piece of equipment.[293]

Concession Contract: Numerous Contracts Blending Construction Contracts and Long-Term Public Service Delivery

5.327 Concession contracts are governed by articles L. 3000-1 et seq. of the CCP. The procedure for the award of concession contracts is as follows.

Concession Award Notice

5.328 An award notice is provided for:[294] (i) Concession contracts, the value of which exceeds €5,225,000 excl. tax; (ii) concession contracts related to social services, the value of which exceeds €5,225,000 excl. tax, and (iii) concession contracts awarded on the basis of an exclusive right, the value of which exceeds €5,225,000 excl. tax.

Selection of Candidates

5.329 The list of successful candidates is established by a committee chaired by a representative of the contracting authority and three or five members elected among the contacting authority's deliberative assembly. Candidates are selected on the basis of their professional abilities, economic and financial standing, and their ability to ensure the continuity of public service and the equality of treatment of users.[295]

5.330 For appraisals of candidates, the committee may retain experts of its choice. Such experts may not participate in committee deliberations. After the review of candidates' applications, the committee gives its opinion on the candidates and may send a report to the contracting authority, recommending that negotiation be carried on with all, some, or none of the candidates.[296] The committee's opinion is not binding on the contracting authority.[297]

Scope of Negotiation

5.331 The principle is that the contracting authority and the candidates are free to negotiate of the content of the candidates' proposals.[298] There is no time limit for the nego-

293 French Civil Code, Article 1792-4.

294 CCP, Articles L. 3125-1 – L. 3125-2.

295 General Code for Local Authorities, Article L.1411-5 §1.

296 This recommendation is subject to conditions listed at Article 46 of Ordinance No. 2016-65 of 29 January 2016 on concession contracts.

297 General Code for Local Authorities, Article L.1411-5, §2.

298 CCP, Article L. 3124-1.

tiation, which must be carried out for a reasonable period in light of the technical and financial complexity of the project and the local context.[299]

Selection of Proposal and Award of Contract

5.332 Upon completion of the negotiation, the committee opens envelopes that contain the proposals and the final recommendation for selecting the proposal is made by the contracting authority.[300]

5.333 Not less than two months after constitution of the committee, the deliberative assembly awards the contract after having considered the documents, including the final draft contract transmitted to it by the contracting authority at least 15 days before its vote. It may reject the contracting authority's recommendation, or request the renegotiation of certain provisions that are not finalized.[301]

5.334 Delegations of public services contracts entered into by local authorities or their establishments,[302] are transmitted by the concessioning authorities to the State representative in the relevant territorial district within 15 days from their signature, together with other documents specified by Decree.[303]

5.335 A mention of such transmission is affixed on the contract, which is notified to the economic operator, the state representative being duly informed of such notification within 15 days. The contract must contain the following provisions:

- Duration: The duration of concessions limited. The concessioning authority must estimate the duration of the concession on the basis of the nature and value of the contract and the investments, which include initial investments and investments required to perform the works or services (notably, rehabilitation works, costs related to infrastructures, logistics, copyrights, patents, staff recruitment or training). For concessions lasting over five years, the maximum duration of the concession shall not exceed the time that a concessionaire could reasonably be expected to take to recoup the investment made in operating the works or services, together with a return on invested capital, taking into account the investments required to achieve the specific contractual objectives;[304]
- The amount, and the methods for calculating entry fees and fees paid by the concessionaire to the contracting authority, must be justified in the concession contract. The concession contract determines the tariffs incurred by the users and specifies the impact on these tariffs of the parameters or indices that determine their evolution;[305]
- The conditions for the concession contract performance may take into account economy, innovation, environment, social field or employment-related considerations, provided that they are related to the purpose of the concession contract.[306]

299 *Conseil d'Etat*, Decision of 18 June 2010, No. 336120.
300 General Code for Local Authorities, Article L.1411-5.
301 General Code for Local Authorities, Article L.1411-7.
302 General Code for Local Authorities, Articles L.1411-1-L.1411-19.
303 General Code for Local Authorities, Article L.1411-9.
304 CCP, Articles L. 1121-2 – L. 1121-4.
305 CCP, Article L. 3114-6.
306 CCP, Article L. 3114-2.

5.336 It should be noted that in concession contracts relating to water, sewerage or household waste and other waste, the duration of the concession cannot exceed 20 years, and payment of entry fees is prohibited.[307]

Leading Role of Equitable Case Law for Public Contracts

5.337 Non applicable; French judge rules on law and not in equity.

National Construction Law and International Forms (Emphasis FIDIC) – How Do FIDIC and Other International Forms Operate?

5.338 French law abides by the *pacta sunt servanda* principle.[308] As such, international forms, when inspiring or incorporated into a contract, are applicable in principle, subject to the provisions of public policy enumerated above.

5.339 Very few court decisions are available on the implementation of such forms of contract, primarily due to the fact that these model agreements generally contain arbitration clauses, and that arbitration awards are confidential. To our knowledge, no arbitral award rendered in a dispute arising out of a contract based on or incorporating forms of contract has been set-aside in France for a substantive reason. This is probably due to the fact that the only ground that could be invoked in such a case would be the violation of international public policy, ground rarely admitted for substantive (as opposed to procedural) reasons.

5.340 However, when performing such forms of contract, parties' attention should be drawn to the fact that the interpretation of the contract will likely be made in light of (i) the provisions relating the construction of contracts set out by the French Civil code[309] and (ii) the provisions of French construction law that is, as has been explained throughout this chapter, intrinsically marked with considerations of public policy and public law.

307 CCP, L. 3114-8.
308 French Civil Code, Article 1103.
309 French Civil Code, Articles 1188 and seq.

CHAPTER 6

Chinese Law

Dongfeng Zhao[1] and Jinghui Tan

Contents

1 Dongfeng Zhao, Senior Partner of Beijing ChangAn Law Firm.

 DOI: 10.4324/9781315671376-6

The History of Chinese Law

The Characteristics of Ancient Chinese Law

6.1 Chinese culture has more than 5,000 years of history, which has been exerting a far-reaching influence on its ancient Legal System. It had been thus endowed with the following characteristics.

Nationalism Supreme of Emperor Power

6.2 The philosophy of governing the country in ancient China was absolutism. The order of Emperor can be understood as the law, who has the supreme power.[2] Under the autocracy, he is both the supreme legislator and adjudicator. The law only reflects his individual wills. Though the enactment of law is completed by the courtiers, it must be approved first by the Emperor before enforcement. So, it's believed that the Emperor's power stays above the law.

Combination of Etiquette and Laws

6.3 Etiquette plays an important role in ancient Chinese law system. In traditional Chinese culture, etiquette is regarded as the foundation of governing the country. Etiquette does not only mean moral and ethics, but legal norms. After Emperor Wu of the Han Dynasty made Confucianism[3] the imperial doctrine around 200 BC, Confucianism becomes the state philosophy and code of ethics. Based on this, it gradually forms a feudal Legal System with the combination of etiquette and laws as its main characteristics. Among it, "The Three Cardinal Guides and the Five Constant Virtues", the key content of Confucian doctrines, is regarded as the core of feudal law code. And "rule of morality with its priority to penalty" becomes the principle of legality.

No Independent Jurisdiction

6.4 In the feudal absolutism system, Emperor, the supreme ruler and judiciary of the state, directly controls the administration of justice. Local jurisdiction is under the supervision of administrators at different levels. Although central government establishes the special judicial organ, its activities are actually monitored and controlled by the Emperor himself. Not only the state judicial organ but other supervisory and administrative organs are all empowered to hear the cases. There is no independent jurisdiction in feudal society. The order of the Emperor means all. This kind of system has existed in China for several thousand years.

---

2 See Ke Ning, Fuya Jiang. "Imperial power and the concept of loyalty in China's history" [1994] 02 History Research, p. 84.

3 Confucius (孔子), 28 September 551 BC–479 BC, was a Chinese teacher, editor, politician, and philosopher of the spring and autumn period of Chinese history. The philosophy of Confucius emphasized personal and governmental morality, correctness of social relationships, justice, and sincerity. His followers competed successfully with many other schools during the Hundred Schools of Thought era only to be suppressed in favor of the Legalists during the Qin Dynasty. Following the victory of Han over Chu after the collapse of Qin, Confucius' thoughts received official sanction and were further developed into a system known in the West as "*Confucianism*".

The Influence of Foreign Laws on Modern Chinese Laws

6.5 The Opium War of 1840 is always regarded a turning point for Chinese history. For one thing, it introduces the modern Western economic, political, cultural, and military systems to China; for another, it blazes a trail for comparatively advanced Western law to seep into Chinese society and challenge its old oriental counterpart. From then on, China steps into a historical period of filling its long cherished law system with the Western contents. This period can be divided into several phases listed as below.

From Opium War of 1840 to Revolution of 1911

6.6 During this time, many Chinese officials, scholars, and intellectuals spent no efforts to seek changes for the nation's development, from Modernization Movement to Hundred Days' Reform, then to Qing Court's final failed attempt to reform. In the field of Legal System, those early nationalists tried to learn from the Western laws to set a direction for Chinese nation. Lin Zexu and Wei Yuan advocated learning the advanced political and legal philosophy and thoughts from the West. They took charge of foreign law translation works. Zhang Zhidong agreed four main laws adopted in the Western countries should be used for reference. Those are Mining Law, Road Law, Commerce Law, and Criminal Law on the Foreigners. In Qing Court's final efforts to reform, many world famous laws and codes were translated under the supervision of Law Amending Office, which was known as Criminal Law Office before. The translated works included the Criminal Laws of German, Japan, France, and Russia, the Nationality Laws of Britain and the US, as well as Japan's Civil Procedure Law Annotation, Criminal Procedure Law and Supreme Court Organic Law. With reference to those, Qing Court made or amended the New Criminal Law, General Principles of the Civil Law of The People's Republic of China Draft, Criminal Procedure Law Draft, Civil Procedure Law Draft, Court Organic Law, and several other law codes and drafts. Meanwhile, the Qing government invited some Japanese law experts to help make China's modern law codes. Not only the laws of Britain and the US were borrowed then but more from Germany, Japan, Russia, and France were included.

Republic Era (1912–1949)

6.7 In the era of Republic of China, especially during the reign of Kuomintang Government in Nanjing, China has made substantial progress in the process of legal transplantation from her foreign counterparts. Based on this, the Chinese law system has developed into a modern one. First, the Kuomintang Government established relatively complete Six Codes that make up the main body of its Legal System with reference to General Principles of the Civil Law of The People's Republic of China system adopted in France, Germany, Japan, and others. Second, then the national government has consolidated the legal fruit of borrowing during the past decades, and meanwhile, kept the rules and norms in traditional Chinese law systems.

From the Founding of PRC in 1949 to Late 1990s

6.8 The development of law transplantation falls into two periods: The first lasts from 1949 to 1960s, while the second from early 1970s to 1990s.

6.9 In the first phase, the Chinese Legal System borrowed a lot from the former Soviet Union's. It can be traced in several aspects. First, it has an effect on the Legal System. For example, several Civil Code Drafts made between the 1950s and 1960s are the direct results of transplanting the Soviet Union's relevant laws, not only in the basic frame system but the contents and fruits of academic research. The Soviet Union's mode can be seen in civil legislation and science of General Principles of the Civil Law of The People's Republic of China in the very beginning of New China. Another example lies in the Criminal Law-making. Still during this period, many parts in the draft of Criminal Law mirrors the Soviet Union's, such as, the emphasis on its class nature, the specific definition of the law's tasks and aims, the concept of crime, the denial of the principle of legality of crimes and punishments and the retroactivity of analogy system, the emphasis on public-order crime and illegal speculation, etc. Second, China also draws lessons from the Soviet Union in the area of law education. Many professors of main courses were from the Soviet Union with the Soviet textbooks. Third, China set the law views held in Marxism-Leninism as its guideline during the whole process of reconstructing Chinese political and Legal Systems. Even when facing the disputes from Western law viewpoints, the Chinese law experts still stand together with their Soviet counterparts. After Joseph Stalin passed away, Nikita Khrushchev took power and denied all national and personal achievement made by Stalin. With the Sino-Soviet difference in principle sharper and more serious, China began to reconsider the Soviet development modes and experience.

6.10 In the second phase, especially after the Cultural Revolution ended in China in 1976, the nation put more attention on opening up to the outside world and absorbing the advanced essence of laws from the developed Western countries. During this period, there are several features in China's law learning and borrowing process. First, it transplanted a lot more laws than ever before in a wider range. Some Western Law Codes, Securities Act and Trade Secret Protection Law, and others that are not complete in the previous Chinese Legal System are transplanted fully and completely. Second, the sources of law transplantation are more diverse. Those include the developed Western countries like Britain, the US, France, Germany and Japan, the middle-income developing countries like Australia and Canada, as well as the emerging countries like South Korea, Malaysia, and Singapore. Third, many types of foreign education contents and modes are being applied into China. National Judicial Examination held in March 2002 is indiscriminately imitation of Japan's. Fourth, a great deal of the prestigious foreign law works and papers are published in this period. Fifth, some legal concepts that once caused heated disputes and controversies during their integration into Chinese Legal System have been settled and undisputed among the public, such as the principle of legally prescribed punishment, the presumption of innocence and judicial independence. Sixth, there is an increasing number of Chinese students who choose to study abroad in the major of law, which creates the channel for the exchanges between Chinese laws and Western laws. Seventhly, the emergence of foreign enterprises, joint ventures and specific economic zones and the like makes the management technology and relevant regulations and rules imported into China. Last but not least, China's official entry into WTO in November 2001 is of immeasurable significance for China to transplant foreign laws. Its operation rules were made on basis of the main Western countries' laws. It's become the general regulations accepted by its all member nations. China's entry into WTO means it agreed to obey the WTO rules and regulations, which meanwhile becomes part of China's law system.[4]

4 Qinhua He, "the impact of foreign law on China after the Opium War" [2012]. 04 Journal of Henan Administrative Institute of Politics and Law

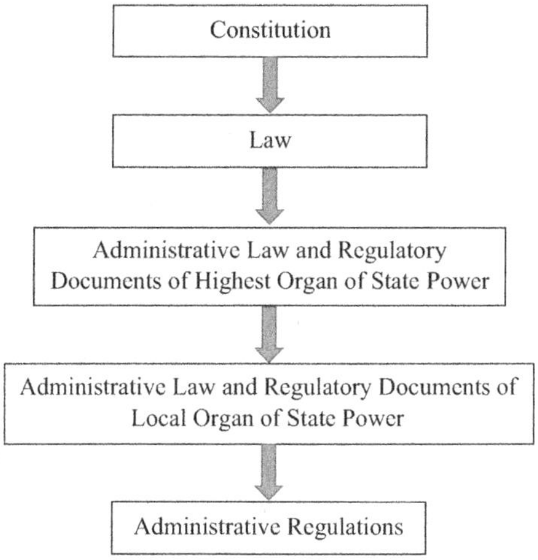

FIGURE 6.1 Hierarchy of Law in China

Modern Chinese Law

6.11 The sources of modern Chinese law, centring on Constitution, can be divided into the following categories.

Constitution

6.12 The Constitution of the People's Republic of China ("PRC") ("Constitution", 中华人民共和国宪法) is enacted by the National People's Congress ("NPC") after the special procedure. The Constitution as the fundamental law of the country is considered with the highest status and effectiveness in China's Legal System.

Law

6.13 Law is a system of rules that are enacted and enforced by NPC and its Standing Committee. Constitutional law provides a framework for the creation of law. The law is only secondary to the Constitution. According to the Legislation Law of PRC,[5] law can be divided into two categories, the basic law (基本法律) and the ordinary law (普通法律). The latter is also known as the non-basic law and the special law. The basic law, enacted by NPC, is the general term for the rules and regulations on the ordinary social relations in people's daily life, such as Criminal Procedure Law, Civil Procedure Law, Administrative Procedure Law and other organic laws etc. The ordinary law, enacted by Standing Committee of NPC, is the general term for regulations on a certain type of specific social

5 Legislation Law of PRC(中华人民共和国立法法) Article 10, reads:

"*The National People's Congress and Standing Committee thereof shall exercise state legislative power.*

The National People's Congress enacts and amends criminal, civil, and state organic laws and other basic laws.

The Standing Committee of National People's Congress enacts and amends laws other than those to be enacted by the National People's Congress; while the National People's Congress is not in session, the Standing Committee thereof partially amends and supplements national law enacted by the National People's Congress, provided that any amendment or supplement may not contravene the basic principles of such national law".

relations or a specific area. It applies in smaller areas than the basic law, but more specifically, such as the Trademark Act, Cultural Relics Protection Law, and so on.

Administrative Law and Regulatory Documents of Highest Organ of State Power

6.14 Administrative Law is the general term of the laws, regulations, and rules made by the State Council, the highest organ of China's state power. Authorized by NPC, they are made according to what are stated in the Constitution and other related laws on how to govern the activities of administrative agencies. They are secondary to the Constitution and law in terms of the legal status and legal validity, but higher than those made by the local government.

Administrative Law and Regulatory Documents of Local Organ of State Power

6.15 Local Administrative Law defines the laws, regulations and rules made by Local People's Congresses and Standing Committees at various levels on how to govern the activities of local administrative agencies based on the specific affairs and situations. The organs empowered to make local laws include People's Congresses and Standing Committees of provinces, autonomous regions, municipalities directly under the Central Government and larger cities. The local laws only have the force and validity in areas within their own jurisdiction.

Administrative Regulations

6.16 The regulatory documents made by the departments under the State Council, the committees, People's Bank of China, National Audit Office and other organizations directly under the Central Government as well as the governments of the provinces, autonomous regions, municipalities directly under the Central Government and larger cities, are known as Administrative Regulations. The contents shall be limited to enforcement of laws, administrative rules, and local laws and other specific administrative management affairs.

Autonomous Decree and Special Decree

6.17 As stated in the Constitution and Law of People's Republic of China on Regional National Autonomy, the People's Congresses of Autonomous Regions shall make their own autonomous decrees and special decrees within the consideration of political, economic and cultural characteristics of local minority nationalities. The decrees shall be limited to the specific autonomous region.

Regulatory Documents of Special Administrative Regions (SAR)

6.18 The Constitution states that "*the country may establish special administrative regions when necessary*".[6] The SAR is authorized to exercise a high degree of autonomy

6 Constitution of PRC Article 31, reads:

> "*Article 31 The state may establish special administrative regions when necessary. The systems to be instituted in special administrative regions shall be prescribed by law enacted by the National People's Congress in the light of specific conditions*".

and enjoy executive, legislative, and independent judicial power. Laws enacted in the SAR also make up the Chinese Legal System.

Treaties and Executive Agreements

6.19 Treaties, or international treaties, are the agreements signed between the China with one or more sovereign states and international organizations under international law. They have the same force and validity as the domestic laws except the country limits its treaty obligations through reservations when signing the treaties.

Informal Law Sources

6.20 Case Law can be understood as that the judges make the judgements based on the important cases that are recorded. They are the accumulated principles of law derived from generations of decisions. A custom is a rule that governs the human conduct in social life, and it's also a practice that can be shown to have existed for a long time. Legal principle means the universal concepts of justice that are upheld by the whole society.

The Influence of Ancient Chinese Law on The Foreign Countries

6.21 Chinese traditional legal culture has exerted profound influence on the Legal System formations in surrounding countries. The past over two thousand years bears witness to how China makes best of its law traditions, passed on with generations of wisdom, to govern the country, compulsorily but effectively. Those law traditions are not only a reflection of Chinese culture, faith, and principles upheld among the whole society, but play a decisive role on the law-making process in China's surrounding countries in feudal times, including but not limited to Japan, Korean Peninsula, Vietnam, and others. Along with the development of the human civilization, the unique Chinese Legal System has gradually come into being.

6.22 Ikeda On, former president of the Institute of Oriental Culture in University of Tokyo, and famous expert on Chinese Legal System history, holds the view that the ancient Japanese laws were made based on the regulations and rules adopted in China's Tang Dynasty era.[7] According to some research results, many old Japanese laws indeed bear similar characteristics of Chinese ones. Among them, The Ōmi code, the Asuka Kiyomihara Code, the Taiho Code, the Yōrō Code, and Engishiki (aka. Procedures of the Engi Era) complied during the seventh century to the tenth century, are the most typical indicators of how the principles and styles of Tang Dynasty laws and the previous ones were written directly in the form of Japanese language.

6.23 With the Taiho Code and the Yōrō Code as its fundamental laws from the 7th to the 10th century, Japan adopted the system of Ritsuryō, also known as Ritsuryō-sei; accordingly, called itself Ritsuryō Nation and marked this three-century era as the Ritsuryō Era. Ritsuryō is the historical law system based on the philosophies of Confucianism and Chinese Legalism. The influence of Chinese laws can also be found in other countries. Korean's Fundamentals of National Construction (경국대전) which came into force

7 Geng Yun, Zhixing Lv, "Chinese elements in premodern Japanese Law" [1992] 02 Journal of Comparative Law, p. 98.

in 1486[8] and Vietnam's record of laws and systems of dynasty compiled in 1843 are both worth-to-mention examples in this regard. To sum up, we can conclude that in the ancient Asia, an East Asian Legal System Sphere centred the Chinese Legal System once was formed just like the East Asian Cultural Sphere in which a group of countries and regions were greatly influenced by the culture of China, sharing a common Chinese characters writing system.

The Chinese Civil Code

The Formation of a Contract

Offer and Acceptance

The Concept of Offer in The Civil Code

6.24 In accordance with the Civil Code of PRC (hereinafter referred to as "Civil Code", 中华人民共和国民法典), offer is an expression of intent to enter into a contract with another party.

Required Elements of Offer

6.25 The required elements of offer include following aspects: The offer shall be made by specific persons; the intent of being bound; contents of contract shall be specific and definite; the offeror shall make an offer to the counterparty with whom the offeror prefers to conclude a contract.[9]

6.26 First, offer is an expression of intent made by specific persons. The specific persons shall be definite irrespective of natural persons or legal persons, the principal or the agent.

6.27 Second, the offeror is willing to be bound by the offer. As mentioned above, offer is an expression of intent to enter into a contract with another person and after acceptance of the offeree, the offeror will be bound by this offer. The offeror's intent to be bound is a feature of the offer.

6.28 Third, the content of offer should be specific and definite. An offer shall contain essential requirements for concluding a contract; in other words, an offer shall satisfy the minimum requirements of a contract. If price or remuneration in the contract is not clearly prescribed, the effectiveness of the contract will not be influenced,[10] as under the Civil Code,[11] the parties are able to make a supplementary agreement and if the supplementary agreement cannot be achieved, the price or remuneration may be determined by relevant provisions in the contract or transaction practices. However, some scholars think that

8 Haoxiu Li, "The influence of ancient Chinese law on the legal history of South Korea" [2012] 28 Legal system and society.

9 Shiyuan Han, The Law of Contract [2011], Law Press China, p. 77.

10 Shiyuan Han, The Law of Contract [2011], Law Press China, p. 80.

11 Article 511, reads:

"*Where certain contents agreed upon by the parties in the contract are ambiguous and cannot be determined in accordance with the provisions in the preceding article, the following provisions shall be applied:*

(2) if price or remuneration is not clear, performance shall be in accordance with the prevailing market price at the place of performance at the time the contract was concluded, and if adoption of a price commissioned by the government or based on government issued pricing guidelines is required by law, such requirement applies".

terms of the contract shall be determined by the nature of the contract or the agreement of parties, for example, because of the nature of sales contracts, the price terms shall be included in the sales contracts.[12]

6.29 Finally, the offeror shall make an offer towards the offeree. Even though the intent of an offer has satisfied three elements mentioned above, it will not be a real offer if such intent is not expressed to any person.

6.30 Under the Civil Code, the invitation for an offer is also stipulated. An invitation for offer is an expression of the intent to invite other parties to make offers thereto. Offer is an expression of intent to make a contract with the offeror's own initiative. In an invitation for an offer, the offeror has the right to decide to accept for the counterparty's intent.[13]

Form of Offer

6.31 There is no particular requirement for the offer's form under the Civil Code. From theoretical and practical perspective, the form of offer can adopt written or oral form. Written form refers to make an offer through letter, telegram exchange, email or other forms that tangibly express the contents contained therein. Oral form refers to make an offer through dialogues or telephone, etc.

Validity of an Offer

6.32 Offer becomes effective when it reaches the offeree. An offer, made in dialogues, will almost become effective at the same time as it is made. An offer, made through other forms other than a dialogue, will become effective when it reaches the offeree. However, there is a time interval between the dispatch and reaching that the offeror should take the risk during this time interval.

6.33 The Civil Code does not stipulate the formal binding force of the offer, but it allows the revocation of the offer. Although the Civil Code makes a certain limit to revoke the offer, it actually acknowledges the formal binding force of an offer to a large extent. Substantial binding force, which actually is a binding force to the offeree, indicates that the offeree gains the right to make an acceptance when the offer becomes effective.

The Withdrawal and Revocation of an Offer

6.34 The withdrawal of an offer is to prevent the effectiveness of an offer before it becomes effective. According to the Article 475 of the Civil Code, the offer may be withdrawn. The notice of withdrawal shall reach the offeree before or at the same time as the offer arrives.

6.35 The revocation of an offer is an expression of the offeror to make the offer lose its efficacy after the offer being effective. Under the Civil Code, when the notice for revoking the offer reaches the offeree, the offer is revoked. However, either the notice of withdrawing or revoking the offer shall reach the offeree before the acceptance comes into force.

12 Liming Wang, Shaokun Fang, Yi Wang, Contract Law 3rd, China Renmin University Press, p. 87.

13 Shiyuan Han, The Law of Contract [2011], *Law Press China*, p. 79.

THE INVALIDITY OF AN OFFER

6.36 Under certain circumstances, the offer will become invalid. For the offeror, the invalidity of offer means to terminate the obligation of the offeror who ought to perform the contract due to the offeree's acceptance. For the offeree, the invalidity of offer is to terminate his capacity for making an acceptance. Subject to the law, the offer will lose its efficacy under any following circumstances. First, the offeree rejects the offer. The rejection of an offer can be express or implied. Especially the extension, limitation, and change of an offer are regarded as a refusal. Second, the offeror revokes the offer in compliance with the law. Third, the offeree fails to dispatch an acceptance prior to the expiration of the time limit for acceptance. Fourth, the offeree makes substantial changes to the contents of the offer. In consistent with the law, the substantial changes to the contents of the offer may include the change of subject matter, quality, quantity, price or remuneration, time or place or method of performance, liabilities for breach of contract and method of dispute resolution, etc.

THE DEFINITION OF ACCEPTANCE

6.37 An acceptance is the intent that the offeree will accept the offer.

REQUIRED ELEMENTS OF ACCEPTANCE

6.38 First, the acceptance is made by the offeree. Only the offeree is eligible to make an acceptance. When the offeree is a specific person, the acceptance should be made by this person. When the offeree is not specific, the acceptance can be made by any person. Besides, the offeree's acceptance can be made by his authorized agents.

6.39 Second, the offeree makes an acceptance towards the offeror. The acceptance is a consensus to the offer so that it will enter into a contract and the offeror shall be a party of the contract.

6.40 Third, the content of acceptance should be consistent with the offer. In accordance with Civil Code, if the offeree substantially modifies the content of the offer, it shall not be an acceptance. It can be regarded as a refusal of the offer and may become a new offer or counteroffer. If the content of offer is not materially modified by the acceptance, the acceptance is valid, unless the offeror rejects it timely or in the offer, it indicates that the content of offer should not be substantially modified by the acceptance. In such case, the content of contract should be in consistent with the acceptance.

6.41 Finally, the acceptance should reach the offeror in the time limit specified in the offer. In Chinese law, the acceptance becomes effective when it reaches offeror. If there is no time limit in the offer, the time limit for making acceptance is stipulated in the Article 481 of Civil Code.[14]

14 Article 481, Civil Code, states:

"An acceptance shall reach the offeror within the time limit prescribed in the offer.

Where no time limit is prescribed in the offer, the acceptance shall reach the offeror in accordance with the following provisions:

if the offer is made in dialogues, the acceptance shall be made immediately unless otherwise agreed upon by the parties;If the offer is made in forms other than a dialogue, the acceptance shall reach the offeror within a reasonable time limit".

THE METHOD TO MAKE AN ACCEPTANCE

6.42 In the Article 480 of Civil Code, "*the acceptance shall be made in the form of a notice, except where acceptance may be made by an act according to the usage of trade or as expressed in the offer*". It is the basic form to make an acceptance, and it does not limit the express method. In some special situations, the acceptance is made by silence or omission.

EFFECTIVE TIME OF ACCEPTANCE

6.43 Subject to the Civil Code, the acceptance becomes effective when the notice of acceptance reaches the offeror no matter the express or implied acceptance.

THE WITHDRAWAL OF ACCEPTANCE

6.44 The withdrawal of acceptance is the intent to impede the effectiveness of the acceptance by the offeree. The acceptance becomes effective when it reaches the offeror and then the contract is established. The offeree should be bound by the contract and cannot revoke the acceptance. Therefore, the withdrawal notice of the acceptance can prevent the effectiveness of the acceptance when it reaches the offeror earlier than or at the same time with the acceptance.

Capacity

6.45 In accordance with Chinese law, civil capacities include the capacities of civil rights and civil act. Based on the civil subject, civil capacities can be divided into the civil capacity of natural persons and legal persons.

THE CAPACITY FOR CIVIL RIGHTS OF NATURAL PERSONS

6.46 The capacity for civil rights of natural persons is the qualification for natural persons to enjoy civil rights and assume civil obligations. In accordance with the Chinese law,[15] citizens have the capacity for civil rights from birth to death. The time for natural persons to have the civil rights begins at birth.

THE CAPACITY FOR CIVIL ACTS OF NATURAL PERSONS

6.47 The capacity for civil acts of natural persons is that nature persons are eligible to obtain civil rights and assume civil obligations by their conducts. On basis of age, civil acts of natural persons are separated into three categories: Persons with full capacity, persons with limited capacity and persons without capacity for civil conduct.

THE CAPACITY FOR CIVIL RIGHTS AND CIVIL CONDUCTS OF LEGAL PERSONS

6.48 In accordance with the Article 57[16] of the Civil Code, the capacity of legal persons for civil rights is accompanied with the capacity for civil acts that both of them

---

15 Article 13, Civil Code, reads

"*A natural person has the capacity for civil rights from the moment of birth to the moment of death, enjoying civil rights and assuming civil obligations in accordance with the law*".

16 Article 57, Civil Code, reads

"*A legal person is an organization with capacity for civil rights and capacity for civil conduct which independently enjoys civil rights and assumes civil obligations in accordance with the law*".

are generated from its establishment and eliminated by its termination. In accordance with Chinese law, business activities, engaged in by an enterprise legal person should not exceed the range approved and registered in the authority department.

Formalities

6.49 In accordance of the Civil Code, a contract can be concluded in written, oral or other forms. However, if the form is specified by law or agreed by parties, the form of contract shall comply with such law or agreement.

Written Form

6.50 The Article 469 of Civil Code stipulates that "*Written form means a written contract, letter, telegram, telex, facsimile, or any other form that can tangibly express the contents thereof*". If the parties fail to comply with the above requirement or agreement, but one party has performed the principal obligation and the other party has accepted it, then the contract is established.[17]

Oral Form

6.51 Oral form means the contract is established by the dialogue based on the mutual intent of parties other than in writing. Obviously, this form is used extensively in the daily life as its simplicity and quick. However, the disadvantage of this form is also apparent that it is difficult to produce evidence when the dispute happens. That does not imply the oral form will not generate any written proof. For example, the literal receipt of oral form is the evidence of the contract, such as the invoice of shopping.[18]

Presumed Form

6.52 The establishment of a contract can be presumed from the civil activities of contract parties that is one of other forms, for instance taking a bus.

Mixed Form

6.53 Mixed form means that a contract may be mixed with other different contract. For example, a travel contract is possible to contain the insurance contract and transport contract.

Agency

6.54 According to the law, the agency is a juristic act performed by agents in the principal's name within the scope of the power of agency.

---

17 Article 490, Civil Code, reads:"*Where the parties enter into a contract in the form of a written contract, the contract is formed when each party affixes its signature, seal, or fingerprint. If a party has performed its principal obligation before the signature, seal or fingerprint is affixed, the contract is formed when the other party accepts the performance.*

If any law or administrative regulation requires that or the parties agrees that a contract should be entered into in written form, but the parties fail to enter into the contract in written form and one party has performed the principal obligation, the contract is formed when the other party accepts the performance".

18 Jianyuan Cui, Contract Law [2014], Perking University Press, p. 75.

6.55 In theory, agency can be divided into narrow agency (狭义代理) and broad agency (广义代理). Narrow agency, known as the direct or named agency, means the agent prefers civil acts in the name of the principal and the principal should take the legal consequences of these civil acts. Broad agency, except including the direct agency, also includes indirect agency or unnamed agency that the agent performs civil acts in his own name while the principal should take the legal consequences of these civil acts. Chapter VII of Book One of the Civil Code adopts the narrow agency; however, the Chapter XXIII of the Book Three of the Civil Code adopts the broad agency to a certain extent. In this chapter, the concept of agency means the unnamed agency.

The Character of Agency

6.56 There are four characters of agency under the laws of China:

First, agency is a civil juristic act that can cause the civil legal consequences. The acts of agency should be only performed by the agent. Second, the agent should be on behalf of the principal to engage in the act of agency and agency cannot exceed the scope of power of agency. Third, agent performs acts of the agency by his independent intent. The act of agency is based on the power of agency. An entrusted agent exercising his power of agency should be within the scope authorized by the principal. A statutory agent or an appointed agent exercising his power of agency should be within the scope prescribed in law or appointed by the relevant organization. Fourth, the legal consequences of the act of agency should belong to the principal directly. The civil acts performed by the agent on the behalf of the principal within the scope are equated with the act of principal. The principal not only enjoys civil rights generated by the act of agency but also bears the relative liabilities and obligations.

The Classification of Agency

6.57 Agency mainly can be classified into two categories. First, based on the grounds of the right of agency, agency can be divided into entrusted agents, statutory agents and appointed agents. In view of transferring the agency, the agency can be separated into original agency and sub-agency.

Entrusted Agency, Statutory Agency, and Appointed Agency

Entrusted Agency

6.58 Entrusted agency is that agents perform acts of agency pursuant to the authorization of the principal. The basis of entrusted agency is the legal relationship between agent and principal, such as commission contract. Principal and agents can choose written form or the oral form as the form of entrusted agency. However, if the written form is requested in the law, principal and agent shall abide by the law.

Statutory Agency

6.59 Statutory agency is directly generated by the law. The guardian of a person without capacity or with limited capacity for civil conducts shall be his statutory agent.

Appointed Agency

6.60 Appointed agency is that agents perform acts of agency subject to the appointment of relevant departments. Without an entrusted agent and a statutory agent, agents are appointed by related departments for the purpose of protecting the rights and interests of persons with limited and without capacity for civil conducts.

Original Agency and Sub-Agency

6.61 Original agency is the agency generated by the entrustment of principal or prescribed in law. Sub-agency is an act of transferring the agency to another person for the benefit of principal. Sub-agent is chosen by the agent in the name of himself other than the principal and the sub-agent is also an agent of principal. Sub-agent exercises the power of agency in name of the principal who should bear the legal consequences of the civil act of the subagent. The power of sub-agency is transferred from the original agent therefore the scope of power of the sub-agency should be limited in the scope of power of original agency, which means it cannot exceed the power of agency of original agent.

The Power of Agency

6.62 The power of agency is a basis for agent to perform the act of agency and its legal consequences should be accepted by the principal.

6.63 The principle of exercising the power of agency includes that it should be within the scope of such power and in general, the agent cannot transfer the agency except for meeting the requirements as referred above. Besides, the agent should perform his obligation in good faith.

Abuse of the Power of Agency

6.64 The abuse of the power of agency means that the agent damages the interests of principal for its own benefit or other party's benefits during performing the act of agency. These following three kinds of the act of agency are considered as the abuse the power of agency:

6.65 First, it indicates that the agent, on behalf of the principal, enters into an agreement with himself. Second, it indicates that in a same civil juristic relation, the agent is not only on the behalf of principal but also the third party. Third, malicious collusion between the agent and third party damages the interests of principal. This behavior is prohibited by law. In accordance with the Civil Code, this act of malicious collusion is invalid and if the principal's interests are damaged by this act, the agent and third party should bear the joint liability for such damage.

Termination of the Power of Agency

6.66 Based on the classification of the power of agency, the termination of it can also be divided into three categories, indicating the termination of entrusted agency, statutory agency and appointed agency.

Termination of Entrusted Agency

6.67 The termination of entrusted agency includes four reasons. First, the period of agency expires and tasks of entrusted agency are completed. Second, principal rescinds the entrustment or the agent resigns from the entrustment. Third, the agent dies. Fourth, the agent becomes incapable or legal person as the principal or agent is terminated.

Termination of Statutory Agency and Appointed Agency

6.68 The reasons for terminating the statutory agency and appointed agency are: The principal becomes capable; the principal dies; the agent becomes incapable or dies; other reasons, such as the cancellation of the guardian; as to the appointed agency, the relevant units rescinds the appointment.

6.69 The statutory agency and appointed agency have a stringent nature of personality that there is a certain personal status relationship between the agent and principal. Once this relationship comes to disappear or the agent becomes incapable, the power of agency will be terminated. However, if the agent does not know the death of principal, the act of agency is still valid.

Unauthorized Agency

6.70 Unauthorized agency is where the agent participates in the civil activities in the name of the principal without the authorization of the principal. Unauthorized agency usually is invalid.

The Validity of Unauthorized Agency

6.71 In the Article 171[19] of the Civil Code, the principal's right of ratification and refusal is stipulated. The right of refusal should be exercised by explicit states and the tacit approval is regarded as a ratification. Through ratifying the authorized agency by the principal, the act of authorized agency will be effective from beginning of the act. If the principal rejects to ratify, the agent should bear the legal consequence of unauthorized agency. The intent of ratification can be expressed to unauthorized agent or the counterparty. It will be effective when the intent of ratification reaches the counterparty.

6.72 The counterparty can urge the principal to ratify as well as the counterparty enjoys the right to withdraw. The notice to urge is an intention of the counterparty to ask for the principal to ratify or refuse the unauthorized agency within a fixed period. The counterparty should make a notice to the principal to express the intention before the principal ratifies. The counterparty may notice the principal to ratify the act of unauthorized agency within 30 days. If the principal fails to ratify it in such period, it shall be regarded as a refusal. Withdrawal is an intention of counterparty to confirm the invalidity the unauthorized agency. A bona fide counterparty has the right to withdraw, which should be expressed prior to ratification of the principal.

---

19 Article 171, Civil Code, reads: "*Where an actor still performs an act of agency without a power of attorney, beyond his or her power of attorney, or after his or her power of attorney terminates, the act shall not be binding on the principal without the principal's ratification.*

The opposite party may, by a notice, urge the principal to ratify within 30 days from the date of receipt of the notice. If the principal fails to respond, ratification shall be deemed denied. Before the ratification of the act, the bona fide opposite party shall be entitled to revoke then act. The revocation shall be made by a notice.

Where ratification of the act is denied, the bona fide opposite party shall be entitled to request that the actor perform obligations or compensate it for any injury suffered by it, but such compensation shall not exceed the interest that could have been obtained by the opposite party if the act were ratified by the principal.

Where the opposite party knows or should have known that the actor has no power of attorney, the opposite party and the actor shall assume liability according to their respective faults.".

Liabilities of Unauthorized Agent

6.73 In German Civil Law,[20] the unauthorized agency is entitled to choose between performing the obligations, which the counterparty would perform on basis of unauthorized agency, and paying compensation for damages if the principal refuses to ratify the contract. Chinese law has no explicit provision; however, a majority of scholars prefer the legalization of Germany on this issue.[21]

6.74 Referring to the liability towards the principal, the unauthorized agent should take the tort liability. Due to the refusal to ratify of the principal, the act of agency is invalid. Therefore, the relationship between the agent and principal is either not based on the real agency relation or the contract relation so that the unauthorized agent does not bear the contract liability. The nature of liability, borne by the unauthorized agent, is the tort liability. If the act makes damages to the principal, the authorized agent should take the liability for paying relevant compensation.

Apparent Agency

6.75 Apparent agency is a Legal System which states that, although the agent has no power of agency, the counterparty has enough reasons to trust that the actor enjoys the power of agency so that performs civil legal activities with the agent. The consequence of this legal act belongs to the principal. In accordance with the Civil Code, the act of apparent agency is effective.

Requirements of Apparent Agency

6.76 Apparent agent requires four following requirements. First, the actor has no power of agency. No power of agency herein means that the actor has no power of agency when performing the act of agency or the actor oversteps the power of agency. Second, the counterparty has reasons to trust the actor enjoys the power of agency which depends on the situation of transaction. Third, the counterparty is in good faith that he does not realize the act of unauthorized agency. Subject to law, if the counterparty knows the act of apparent agency and continues to execute the civil activities so that makes damages to other person, the counterparty and the actor should bear the joint liability. Thus, if the counterparty is malicious, the act shall not be effective. Fourth, the civil activities between the actor and counterparty shall be valid.

The Validity of Apparent Agency

6.77 To the principal, the effectiveness of apparent agency is equated with the act of authorized agency. The principal and counterparty should be bound by the civil act between the actor and counterparty. The principal cannot defend on the ground of unauthorized agency. However, after the establishment of apparent agency, if the principal

20 Section 179(1), German Civil Law reads:

"A person who has entered into a contract as an agent is, if he does not furnish proof of his power of agency, obliged to the other party at the other party's choice either to perform the contract or to pay damages to him, if the principal refuses to ratify the contract".

21 Jianyuan Cui, Civil Law [2013], *Tsinghua University Press* 251; Yongjun Li, General Introduction to Civil Law [2015], *China University of Political Science and Law Press* 267.

suffers damages due to the apparent agency, the principal is entitled to make a claim to the apparent agent.

Consideration

6.78 Under Civil Code, there is no requirement of "consideration" found under Common law. This runs in similar vein to the German position which also does not require the element of "consideration" to form a valid contract.

The Contents of A Contract

Terms of a Contract (Express and Implied Terms)

6.79 The provisions of contract are that parties enter into a contract relying on the procedure. Provisions of contract state and fix the rights and obligation of parties. In accordance with the Civil Code, a contract should contain main clauses; otherwise it will not be established.

6.80 For improving the terms of a contract, the Civil Code lists general provisions as a suggestion when concluding a contract. In accordance with the Article 470 of Civil Code, the content of a contract shall be agreed upon the parities and generally includes the provisions of the name or address of parties, subject matter, quantity, quality, price or remuneration, time limit, place and method of performance, liability for breach of contract, and method to settle the disputes.

6.81 The provision of contract is divided into express provision and implied provision. Express provision is that a contract is concluded by the language. However, the express provision is not limited by the written form; the verbal contract also can be regarded as express provision. Implied provision means that when the relevant content is not clearly stated in the contract by parties, subject to law or transaction practices, the relevant content can be determined as the provision of a contract, this is covered under Article 511, Civil Code.[22]

---

22 Art. 511, Civil Code, reads:

"*Where certain contents agreed upon by the parties in the contract are ambiguous and cannot be determined in accordance with the provisions in the preceding article, the following provisions shall be applied:*

(1) if quality requirement is not clear, performance shall be in accordance with the state mandatory standard; absent any mandatory state standard, performance shall be rendered in accordance with state voluntary standard; absent any state voluntary standard, performance shall be rendered in accordance with the industry voluntary standard; or absent any state or industry standard, performance shall be rendered in accordance with the customary standard or any particular standard consistent with the purpose of the contract;

(2) if price or remuneration is not clear, performance shall be in accordance with the prevailing market price at the place of performance at the time the contract was concluded, and if adoption of a price commissioned by the government or based on government issued pricing guidelines is required by law, such requirement applies;

(3) where the place of performance is not clear, if the obligation is payment of money, performance shall be at the place where the payee is located; if the obligation is delivery of immovable property, performance shall be at the place where the immovable property is located; for any other subject matter, performance shall be effected at the place where the party performing the obligation is located.

(4) if the time of performance is not clear, the obligor may perform, and the obligee may require performance, at any time, provided that the other party shall be given the time required for preparation;

(5) if the method of performance is not clear, performance shall be rendered in a manner which is conducive to realizing the purpose of the contract;

Unfair Contract Terms

6.82 The principle of fairness is the basic rule of the Civil Code.[23] In accordance with the Civil Code, the parties shall adhere to the principle of fairness when deciding their respective rights and obligation. The principle of fairness is emphasized in the Civil Code, which takes the equivalence of contract parties into account. The rule of obvious unfairness in Chinese law reflects the principle of fairness. In conformity to the Civil Code, the party is entitled to request the court or arbitration institution to modify or revoke the contract, which is obvious unfair. If the obvious unfairness is caused by the changed circumstance, the contract would be adjusted in line with the principle of honesty and good faith. In addition, the exception clause in the contract is usually regarded as the unfair contract term that is limited in the Civil Code. In accordance with the Article 506 of the Civil Code, exception clauses will be invalid if they cause the personal injury of counterparty deliberately or property damages to the other party because of the deliberate intent or gross negligence. Furthermore, according to the Article 497 of the Civil Code, the clause will be null and void if standard terms in a contract are under the circumstances prescribed in Section 3 of the Chapter VI of the Book One of the Civil Code, and Article 506 of the Civil Code,[24] or the party which supplies the standard terms exempts itself from its liabilities, increases the liabilities of the other party, and deprives the material rights of the other party.

Vitiating Factors under Civil Code

Gross Misunderstanding and Evident Unfairness

Significant Misconception (Gross Misunderstanding)

6.83 In accordance with Chinese law, the significant misconception or gross misunderstanding is where the actor misunderstands the nature, counterparty, the kind, quality, type and quantity of the subject matter of the act so that intent of the actor is inconsistent with the result of the act and makes a huge loss.

6.84 Gross misunderstanding requires the actor expresses an intention due to the misconception and the misconception should be significant. Gross misunderstanding will vitiate the validity of the contract that leads to a voidable contract. Revocation is that persons with the right of revocation can exercise the right to terminate the effective contract. The voidable contract is effective prior to revocation. However, once the right of revocation is exercised, the contract will be invalid from the very beginning.

(6) if the apportionment of the expenses of performance is not clear, the party performing the obligations shall bear the expenses; and any additional expenses of performance incurred because of the creditor shall be borne by the creditor..

23 Art. 6, Civil Code, reads:

"The parties to civil legal relations shall conduct civil activities under principle of fairness and rationally determine the rights and obligations of each party".

24 Arts. 506, Civil Code, reads:

"*Article 506. The following exception clauses in a contract shall be void:*

(1) those that cause personal injury to the other party;

(2) those that cause property damages to the other party as result of deliberate intent or gross negligence".

EVIDENT UNFAIRNESS

6.85 In accordance with the Chinese Civil Code the evident unfairness is that a party exploits its advantage or the counterparties' lack of experience to conclude a contract, which is contrary to the principle of fairness and the principle of making compensation for equal value. Similar with gross misunderstanding, evident unfairness will vitiate the validity of the contract that leads to a voidable contract.

Malicious Collusion

6.86 In accordance with the Civil Code, malicious collusion indicates that the two parties enter into a contract mutually for the purpose of damaging interests of state, public, and/or the third party. The malicious collusion herein includes subjective and objective elements. The act of malicious collusion will result in the invalidity of the contract.

Fraud and Duress

FRAUD

6.87 In accordance with judicial interpretation by People's Supreme Court of China, fraud means one contractual party intentionally or deliberately releases false information to the counterparty or conceal the facts, with the view to trap or mislead the counterparty to make an incorrect act.

6.88 Fraud should include the deliberate intent of the fraud. The deliberate intent means that, on one hand, the counterparty should make a misunderstanding due to the deliberate intent; on the other hand, the counterparty expresses the intent result from the error.

6.89 An act regarded as fraud requires causality, which means that the counterparty falls into an error due to fraud and then expresses an intent based on the error. The error herein means a cognitive defect on the significant facts of the contract. Notwithstanding it is not stated in the law that counterparty expresses the intent due to the false intention is recognized in theory.

COERCION

6.90 Coercion is where the counterparty is threatened or enforced by the actor to be plunged into fear and then expresses an unreal intention.

6.91 In accordance with the Point 4 of the Article 1 of the General Principles of the Meeting Minutes on the Implementation of the Civil Code by Courts Nationwide, the coercion is where the actor forces the other party to make an unreal declaration by threatening to damage their life, health, honour, reputation, or property of any citizen or his relatives or friends or to damage the credit, repute, and property of any legal person.

6.92 Both fraud and coercion can vitiate the effectiveness of the contract, which will lead the contract to be voidable and modifiable. According to the Civil Code[25], if the contract is concluded based on the fraud or coercion, the defaulted or the coerced party shall be entitled to revoke contract.

25 Article 148 and Article 150, Civil Code, reads: Art. 148. "Where a juridical act is performed by a party against his or her true will as a result of fraud by the other party, the defrauded party shall have the right to request a people's court or an arbitral institution to revoke the act."Art. 150 "Where a juridical act is performed by a party against his or her true will as a result of coercion by the other party or a third party, the coerced party shall have the right to request a people's court or an arbitral institution to revoke the act."

Illegality

6.93 In accordance with the Civil Code these following two illegal acts will lead the contract to be null and void. First, the contract will be invalid that the contract is contrary to public order and good morals. Second, the contract will be invalid that the contract violates the compulsory provisions of laws and administrative regulations.

The Rights and Liabilities of Third Parties

The Contract Performed to the Third Party

6.94 In accordance with the Civil Code, the contract parties conclude a contract that the obligor shall perform its obligations to the third party and if the obligor fails to perform such obligations, it shall be assumed liabilities to the obligee. Based on the agreement between contract parties, the third party is entitled to request the obligor to perform its obligations.

6.95 The obligee can ask for the approval of third party to whom the contract is performed or does not notice the third party. When the obligor performs its obligations to the third party subject to the contract, it shall notice the third party who should express the intention of acceptance when it decides to accept.

The Contract Performed by the Third Party

6.96 In accordance with Chinese law, the obligor shall bear the liabilities if contract party enters into a contract that the third party shall perform the obligations to the obligee and the third party fails to perform such obligations. Such contract is based on the performance of third party, so the contract party shall ask for the approval of third party when concluding the contract.

Performance of a Contract

Performance

6.97 The performance of a contract is the execution of the agreed obligation. The performance of a contract indicates that the obligor should fully and appropriately performs the contract debt and as a result, the obligee can unify the act and result of payment.

The Principle of Performing a Contract

6.98 The principle of performing the contract includes the principle of appropriate performance, the principle of cooperative performance, the principle of economy and rationality and the principle of changed circumstance.

Appropriate Performance

6.99 Appropriate performance, known as full performance, is where the contract shall be performed by the appropriate subject at proper place in proper time limit through appreciate manners and the parties shall fully perform the obligations of contract subject to the subject matter, quality, and quantity of the contract.[26]

---

26 Article509., Civil Code, reads:
"Each party shall fully perform its own obligations as agreed".

THE PRINCIPLE OF COOPERATIVE PERFORMANCE

6.100 The principle of cooperative performance means that during the performance of the contract, the contract parties should cooperatively complete the contract obligations.

THE PRINCIPLE OF ECONOMY AND RATIONALITY

6.101 The principle of economy and rationality means that during the performance of contract, the contract parties should take the economic efficiency into account, meaning that the using the least cost to acquire the best contractual efficiency. In accordance with the Civil Code, besides avoiding wasting resources, the parties shall also avoid polluting the environment, and compromising ecology.

THE PRINCIPLE OF CHANGED CIRCUMSTANCE

6.102 The principle of changed circumstance is that after a contract comes into existence effectively, the basic conditions of a contract has a material variation, which cannot be attributable to the contract parties and if continuing to perform the contract will lead to the obvious unfairness, and then the parties are entitled to change and/ or terminate the contract. Changed circumstance should meet the following requirements. First, there is a fact of changed circumstance. Second, the fact of changed circumstance happens during the period between establishment of contract and completion of performing the contract. Third, the changed circumstance cannot be blamed to the contract parties. Fourth, the changed circumstance cannot be predictable. Fifth, continuing to perform the contract under the changed circumstance will lead to obvious unfairness of the contract.

The Content of Performing a Contract

Obligor or the Agent

6.103 Obligor is the party who bears the liability of performing the debt and includes the agent of the debtor. The agent of obligor, who pays the debt, cannot be determined as the third party. Besides, the obligor should be entitled to perform the obligations.

Third Party

6.104 Clearance of the debt by the third party is that for purpose of eliminating the debts, the third party pays the debt towards the obligee in the name of itself. It should be pointed that the assistant for performance and the agent of obligor cannot be deemed as the clearance of the debt by the third party stated herein. In the principle, clearance of the debt by the third party is effective.

Obligee

6.105 The contract is completed by the acceptance of the obligee. The obligee enjoys the right of claim for payment and the right of acceptance.

The Subject Matter

6.106 The subject matter of performing the contract is a specific act, which has to be performed by the obligor of the contract and it is the core content and the purpose of a contract. The performance should be subject to the nature of the debt and the contract should not be varied randomly, otherwise the interest of a contract will not be fulfilled. When performing the contract, the quality and the quantity should be strictly complied with the contract.

6.107 In accordance with the Civil Code, if the quality of the subject matter is not stated or clearly stated in the contract, the parties can conclude a complementary agreement. If the complementary agreement is not achieved, the quality of the subject matter should be confirmed by the contract provisions and transaction practices. If it still cannot be assured, it should be performed subject to the state mandatory standard. If there is no state mandatory standard, the subject matter should be performed by the state voluntary standard. In absence of the state voluntary standard, the performance shall be rendered in accordance with state voluntary standard. Absent any state voluntary standard the performance shall be complied with the voluntary industry standard; or absent any state or industry standard, the performance shall be in conformity with the customary standard or any particular standard consistent with the purpose of the contract.

6.108 Concerning the quantity of the subject matter, the principle of full performance requires the quantity with full performance other than partial performance. However, if the partial performance is not detrimental to the interests of the party, it shall be allowed. The partial performance should meet the following requirements. First, the debt of the partial performance can be separated. Second, partial performance is not detrimental to the interests of the party. Third, the obligor applies for partial performance.

The Time Limit of Performance

6.109 As the main clause of the contract, the time limit should be agreed in the contract generally and the parties should perform their obligations within such time limit. If the parties fail to comply with the time limit stated in the contract, they may take the responsibility of breach of the contract. If the time limit stated in the contract is not clear, in accordance with the Civil Code, the parties can conclude a complementary agreement. If the complementary agreement is not achieved, the time limit should be confirmed by the contract provisions and transaction practices. If it is still not assured, the obligor can perform it at any time, and the obligee may request to perform at any time, however, the party should give a necessary preparation period to the counterparty.

Place of Performance

6.110 If the place of performance is clearly stated in the contract, the obligor should perform the debt to the obligee at that place. Relatively, the obligee should accept the performance at such place. In accordance with the Civil Code, if the place of performance stated in the contract is not clear, the parties can conclude a complementary agreement. If the complementary agreement is not achieved, the place of performance should be confirmed by the contract provisions and transaction practices. If the place of performance still cannot be assured, it can be confirmed by the subject matter. When the contract is performed by the currency, the place of performance is where the party accepts the currency. When the contract is to deliver the real state, the place of performance is where the real estate is located. Concerning other subject matter, the place of performance is where the party performs the obligation.

Method to Perform

6.111 The method to perform is confirmed by the agreement or law or the nature of the contract. The different nature and content of the contract are performed by different ways. According to the fundamental requirement to perform the contract, as to its measures, the obligor should perform the obligation subject to the contract as priority. If the method stated in the contract is not clear, in accordance with the Civil Code, the parties can conclude a complementary agreement. If the complementary agreement is not achieved, the method should be confirmed by the contract provisions and transaction practices. If it still cannot be assured, the method to perform should be confirmed by a beneficial way to implement the purpose of the contract.

The Expense of Performance

6.112 If it is agreed in the contract, the parties should bear the expense subject to the contract. If the expense is not stated in the contract, in accordance with the Civil Code, the expense should be decided as per the relevant contract provisions or transaction practices. If it cannot still be decided, the party performing the obligations shall bear the expenses, and any additional expenses of performance incurred due to the obligee shall be borne by the obligee.

Right of Defence

6.113 Based on the system of the Civil Code and the practical application, the right of defence in the performance of contract discussed herein includes the counterargument right for simultaneous performance, the counterargument right for security, counterargument right of prior performance. These three counterargument rights exist in the onerous contract.

The Counterargument Right for Simultaneous Performance

6.114 The counterargument right for simultaneous performance is stated in the Article 525 of the Civil Code.[27]

The Required Elements of the Counterargument Right for Simultaneous Performance

6.115 Both parties have obligations towards each other in an onerous contract. The base of the counterargument right for simultaneous performance is the involving relation of the onerous contract, indicating that the payment and reciprocal payment cannot be separated. The payment of parties in the onerous contract is the mutual precondition that if a party fails to perform the payment obligations, the counterparty will not perform the relative obligations either. Meanwhile, the debts between the two parties should be based on the same onerous contract; otherwise the parties shall not claim the counterargument right for simultaneous performance.

27 Article 525, Civil Code, reads:

"*Where both parties have obligations toward one another and there is no order of priority in respect of the performance, the parties shall perform the obligations simultaneously. Each party has the right to reject any request by the other party for performance prior to the performance by the other party. If the performance of the obligations of the party who is to perform first is not in conformity with the agreement, the party who is perform later has the right to reject the other party's request for corresponding performance*".

Exercising the Counterargument Right for Simultaneous Performance

6.116 The counterargument right for simultaneous performance can be exercised by the lawsuit or other forms other than the lawsuit. Notwithstanding a party may claim the counterargument right for simultaneous performance outside lawsuit, the party shall still claim this right during the lawsuit. Under the circumstance of breach of the contract, exercising the right for simultaneous performance by the non-breaching party will not affect a claim to the breaching party to assume the liabilities for breach of contract.

The Counterargument Right of Prior Performance

6.117 The counterargument right of prior performance is a special form of the right for simultaneous performance, which is specifically stated in the Article 526 of Civil Code.[28]

The Counterargument Right for Security

6.118 The counterargument right for security is that after the contract comes into existence, the party who is to perform first has the exact evidence to prove the counterparty has not capacity for performance and the party is entitled to stop the performance of contract before the counterparty recovers its capacity for perforce or provides the guarantee. The circumstances to apply the counterargument right for security are stipulated in the Article 527 of the Civil Code.[29]

Frustration (Changed Circumstance)

6.119 Changed circumstance is that after the establishment of a contract, some reasons, which are not owed to both parties, affect the base of a contract and if the contract is continued to be carried out, it will lead an obvious unfairness. Finally, the contract can be changed or terminated. This principle endows the court to directly intervene the relationship of the contract and balance the conflict of interest between both parties for purpose of keeping a normal economic order. In common law, the principal of changed circumstance is regarded as the principle of frustration.

The Required Elements of Changed Circumstance (情势变更 Qingshibiangeng)

6.120 The required elements of the changed circumstance include first, it needs the fact of the changed basic conditions of a contract and second, the fact should happen after the

---

28 Article 526, Civil Code, reads:

"*Where both parties have obligations toward each other and there is an order of priority in respect of the performance, and the party required to perform the obligation first fails to do, the party who is to perform later has the right to reject the other party's demand for performance. If the performance of the obligations of the party who is to perform first is not in conformity with the agreement, the party who is to perform later has the right to reject the other party's demand for corresponding performance*".

29 Article 527, Civil Code, reads:"*The party required to perform first may suspend its performance if it has conclusive evidence showing that the other party is under any of the following circumstances:*

(1) its business has seriously deteriorated;
(2) it has engaged in transfer of assets or withdrawal of funds for the purpose of evading debts;
(3) it has lost its business creditworthiness;
(4) it is in any other circumstance which will or may cause it to lose its ability to perform.

Where a party suspends performance without conclusive evidence, it shall be liable for breach of contract".

establishment of a contract and prior to the performance completion. It should be noted that if the fact happened before the establishment of the contract or at the same time with the establishment of the contract and both parties do not know such circumstance; the significant misconception should be applied for. Third, the reasons, causing the changed circumstance cannot be attributable to the contract parties. Fourth, the change of circumstance cannot be predictable when concluding a contract. Fifth, continuing to carry out the contract will cause obvious unfairness or the purpose of the contract cannot be implemented.

The Validity of the Changed Circumstance

6.121 The changed circumstance can lead the modification or termination of a contract. Traditionally, the court should modify or terminate a contract through its authority due to the changed circumstance.

Changed Circumstance and Force Majeure

6.122 The provision of Changed Circumstances stipulated in the Article 533 of Civil Code. [30]. The statutory exemption from liability only indicates the *Force Majeure* and except for *Force Majeure*, the party should bear liabilities for breach of the contract. Actually, the changed circumstance is a situation between the *Force Majeure* and liabilities for breach of the contract. The difference between the *Force Majeure* and changed circumstance is that under the *Force Majeure* events, the contract cannot be performed and in case of the changed circumstance, it is difficult to continue to perform but there still is a possibility to perform although continuing to perform will lead the obvious unfairness.

6.123 There are other causes to affect to perform the contract, such as rejection to perform, delay in perform, etc., which will be stated in the Chapter VII of the Termination of Contractual Rights and Obligations of the Title One of the Book Three of the Civil Code.

Breach

6.124 In normal circumstance, the relation of contract will be eliminated if the purpose of contract is fulfilled through the performance. However, if the party fails to perform its obligations subject to the contract, the performance is defective mainly including refusing to perform, delay in performance and incomplete performance.

Refusing to Perform

6.125 Refusing to perform is that a contract party rejects to execute obligations under the contract so that the purpose of the contract cannot be fulfilled. The party can reject to perform the main obligations of the contract through a clear expression or its acts. Refusing to perform should meet two requirements, including that the obligor has capacity to perform but fails to perform and the act of rejecting to perform is illegal. In compliance

---

30 Article 533, Civil Code, reads:"*Where the basic conditions of a contract undergoes a material change unforeseeable by the parties at the time of contracting which is not a commercial risk after the formation of the contract, rendering the continuation of the performance of the contract unconscionable for either party, the adversely affected party may renegotiate with the other party; and if the renegotiation fails within a reasonable time limit, the party may request the people's court or an arbitration institution to modify or rescind the contract.*"

with the Civil Code, the other party is entitled to terminate the contract if the party fails to perform the main obligations of the contract through a clear expression or its acts before the expiration of the contract.

Delay in Performance

6.126 Delay in performance means at the time of expiration of a contract, the obligor who is able to perform obligations fails to perform. Delay in performance requires three factors: i) The obligor has ability to perform; ii) the period for performing expires; iii) failure to perform is illegal.

Incomplete Performance

6.127 Incomplete performance means the obligor's performance fails to comply with the agreement or the law. Incomplete performance also terminates the contract in case of that the purpose of the contract cannot be completed.

Termination

6.128 The cause of terminating a contract is stated expressly in the Article 557 of the Civil Code, mainly including discharge, rescinding, offset, escrow, release, and confusion.

Discharge

6.129 Discharge means that the obligor has performed the obligation subject to the contract and the purpose of the contract has been achieved. Discharge is one of reasons to lead the termination of the rights and obligations of a contract.

Rescinding

6.130 A contract can be rescinded by the unilateral covenant or legal regulation or mutual intent. Rescinding a contract by the unilateral covenant or unilateral legal regulation is based on the right of rescinding. Unilateral right of rescinding a contract is that due to the intent of a contract party, the contract can be rescinded without an approval of the counterparty. Mutual intent for rescinding a contract is due to the intent of mutual parties.

Rescinding a Contract by a Covenant

6.131 Subject to the Chinese law, contract parities can reach a consensus for either party to rescind the contract. On basis of the satisfaction of the conditions, the party with right to rescind a contract can terminate the contract.

Legal Rescission

6.132 In accordance with the Article 563 of the Civil Law, a contract can be terminated under any following circumstances: i) The purpose of a contract cannot be completed due to the *Force Majeure*; ii) prior to the time limit of performance, a party will not perform the main obligations of the contract through an explicitly expression or its acts; iii) a party fails to execute its obligation promptly and after a notice to urge to perform, the party still fails to perform; iv) due to a party delay in performance or other acts of breach of the contract, the purpose of the contract cannot be completed; v) other circumstance as provided by the law.

Exercising the Right to Rescission of a Contract

6.133 According to the nature of the right of formation, exercising the right to rescission of a contract is unnecessary to obtain the consent of counterparty. The party with this right is entitled to terminate the contract by the unilateral intent. Any contract party enjoys the right to terminate if the terminated contract is owed to the objective reason, *Force Majeure* specifically. While the terminated contract is due to the act of breach of the contract, the non-breaching party has the right to terminate.

6.134 When the intent reaches the counterparty, the contract will be terminated. The contract can be terminated by lawsuit or other method outside the lawsuit. However, when the contract is terminated by the lawsuit based on the right to rescission, the court has no power to terminate the contract with the authority and the contract will be terminated only by the application of the contract party with the right to terminate.

Terminating a Contract by Consensus

6.135 Terminating a contract by consensus is where the contract is terminated based on the mutual intent of both parties and it does not require the right to terminate the contract. Under the circumstances of the legal termination and terminating a contract by a covenant, the contract can be unilaterally terminated by a contract party on basis of the right to terminate. Under the circumstances of terminating a contract by the covenant and by the consensus, the contract will be terminated by the intent of the parties.

Offset

6.136 Offset means that when parties have obligations towards one another, they utilize their credits to discharge the debts and their debts offset equally against each other. Offset can be divided into statutory offset and offset by mutual intent.

Statutory Offset

6.137 In accordance with the law, the required elements of the statutory offset include the following requirements. First, the parties should have obligations towards one another. Second, the kind and quality of these two debts are same. Third, the credit of the party with the right to offset has expired. Fourth, the debts of both parties are applicable to offset. The debt can be offset in generally unless otherwise stipulation in the law and the nature of the debt do not permit to offset. Besides, if the parties agree that the debt cannot be offset, it should be effective.

Offset by Mutual Intent

6.138 Offset by mutual intent is regulated in the Article 569 of the Civil Code of the PRC.

Escrow

6.139 Escrow means that the obligor fails to deliver the subject matter due to the reason of obligee and the debt can be eliminated by delivering the subject matter to the relevant organization.

6.140 In accordance with Article 570 of the Civil Code, under any following circumstances, the obligor can escrow the subject matter: i) The obligee has no reason to reject to take the delivery; ii) the whereabouts of the obligee are unknown; iii) when the obligee dies, the successor is uncertain or when the obligee loses civil capacity and a guardian is uncertain. It can be concluded that when the obligee rejects to accept the delivery, or the obligee fails to accept, or the obligee is uncertain, the obligor has right to escrow the subject matter.

Release

6.141 In accordance with the Article 575 of the Civil Code, if the blige releases the entire or partial debt of the obligor, the rights and obligations of the contract will be entirely or partially terminated unless the obligor refuses such release within a reasonable time.

Confusion

6.142 Confusion is regulated in the Article 576 of the Civil Code, indicating that in general, if the rights and obligations under a contract vest in one party, such rights and obligations thereunder shall be terminated. Confusion is a kind of legal fact other than an act. The collateral right will be terminated accompanied under the confusion of rights and obligations. Under the confusion of the claims and guaranteed debts, the guaranteed debts will be released, however, the main obligations still exist.

Remedies

6.143 Remedies mean that if a contract party breaks the contract or the law, the other party is entitled to remedy subject to the contract or the law for the purpose of its legal interest.

Remedies under a Contract

6.144 In practice, the contract parties always reach a consensus in the contract about the remedies when a party breaches the contract. The usual measures of remedies prescribed in the contract include continuing to performance, compensation for losses, termination and liquidated damages. Continuing to performance, compensation for losses and liquidated damages are regulated in the law, which will be specifically introduced hereunder.

6.145 Subject to the principle of voluntariness, the contract party enjoys the right to terminate a contract voluntarily within the scope regulated by law as a measure of remedy. Terminating a contract by a consensus include terminating a contract under a contract and agreed by parties. Terminating a contract under a contract means that a right to terminate is stipulated in a contract by a consensus of parties. When a certain circumstance is incurred during the performance, a contract party or parties has right to terminate the contract. When the conditions of termination in the contract happen, the party with right to terminate is entitled to exercise such right without negotiating with the other party. Terminating a contract agreed by parties means that after entry into force of the contract and prior to the performance of obligations or complete performance of obligations, contract parties enter into an agreement to terminate the original contract for the purpose of termination.

Remedies under Law

6.146 In accordance with the Chinese law, the method to remedy mainly includes continuing to perform the obligations, compensation for losses and payment of liquidated damages.

Continuing to Perform

6.147 Continuing to perform the obligations is referred to as the compulsory performance, meaning that when the party who fails to perform the obligations will be enforced by the court to continue to perform such obligations.

Compensation for Damages

6.148 Compensation for damages is a form of liability of breach of contract that the party who fails to perform obligations or the performance is not consistent with the contract when performing the obligations, compensates the damages for counterparty. Pursuant to the Civil Code, the compensation for damages indicates not only the pecuniary compensation but also the compensation in kind, but limited in the object except from the subject matter of the contract. The required elements of compensation for damages include the act of breach of contract, the damages of counterparty, the causality between the act and damages, no exceptional matter for the defaulting party.

Liquidated Damages

6.149 Liquidated damages are that subject to the contract or the law, the party who fails to perform the obligations shall pay the money to the counterparty. The standard of the liquidated damages is monetary damages but the parties can reach a consensus that the subject matter of liquidated damages is other property instead of money.

6.150 The promissory liquidated damage is agreed by the parties. The Statutory liquidated damage is direct stipulated in the law. The rate of liquidated damages is prescribed in some regulations. It is worthy of emphasizing that the compensation of liquidated damages should be subject to the contract strictly; however, the excessive freedom of contract also is able to give rise to the unfair consequences. Therefore, the amount of liquidated damages is limited in the Civil Code. Specifically, if the agreed liquidated damage is lower than the actual damages, the party is entitled to petition the court or arbitration institution to increase the compensation. If the agreed liquidated damage is much higher than the actual damages, the party is entitled to petition the court or arbitration institution to decrease the compensation.

Limitation on Remedies

6.151 Pertaining to the scope of compensation for damages, the complete compensation for damages is ruled in the Civil Code; however, there are other principles to limit the scope of damages. These principles include the principle of reasonable prediction, the principle of mitigation of damages, the principle of contributory negligence and benefits rule.

6.152 In accordance with the Article 585 of the Civil Code, "*where the amount of liquidated damages agreed upon are significantly higher than the damages incurred, the people's court or arbitration institution may appropriately reduce it at the request of a party*". In the Meeting Minutes on the Implementation of the Civil Code by Courts Nationwide,[31]

31 Meeting Minutes on the Implementation of the Civil Code by Courts Nationwide, enacted by the Supreme People's Court, Interpretation [2021] No.94, date of enforcement: 6Apirl 2021.

the Supreme Court defines the "significantly higher than the damages incurred" as that liquidated damages exceeds the loss incurred by thirty percent.

Interpretation of Contracts

6.153 The provisions of the contract shall be agreed by the contract parities, however, in practice, the contract parties always have disputes on the meaning of some provisions or those provisions, which ought to be stipulated in the contract, not specified in the contract. Under such circumstances, the interpretation of contracts is necessary. In accordance with the Civil Code,[32] the contract interpretation is that when there are some disputes on the contract provisions, the real meaning of those provisions can be ascertained through it subject to the sentence of the contract, the related provision of the contract, the contract purpose, the practice and the principle of good faith.

6.154 "Whether legislatively or jurisprudentially provided, these principles of contractual interpretation are important both to the practitioner and the business person who is called upon to ascertain the meaning and import of a contract".[33] Under Chinese Law, the principles of contractual interpretation can be concluded from five factors.

Semantic Interpretation

6.155 Semantic interpretation is to seek the real intent of contract party through the sentence stated in the contract. Complying with Civil Law, when interpreting the contract, the mutual real intent of the contract party is essential that interpretation shall not limited in the words and expression stated in the contract.[34]

Whole Interpretation

6.156 Whole interpretation regards all provisions in the contract as a whole and the disputes between parties shall be interpreted and analyzed from the interrelation, status of every contract provisions and parts.

Goal Interpretation

6.157 Goal Interpretation is that when there exists two explains of a contract provision, the interpretation, which is the most applicable to the purpose of a contract, shall prevail.[35.]

---

32 Article 125, Contract Law, reads:"*If any disputes arise between the parties over the understanding of any clause of the contract, the true meaning thereof shall be determined according to the words and sentences used in the contract, the relevant provisions in the contract, the purpose of the contract, the transaction practices and the principle of good faith.*

Where a contract is concluded in two or more languages and it is agreed that all versions are equally authentic, the words and sentences in each version are construed to have the same meaning. In case of any discrepancy in the words or sentences used in the different language versions, they shall be interpreted in light of the purpose of the contract".

33 Patrick S. Ottinger, "Principles of Contractual Interpretation", 60 La. L. Rev., p. 766.

34 Huixing Liang, Cases and Legalisations of Civil Law No. 2 [1999], Chinese Academy of Governance Press, pp. 260–1.

35 Huixing Liang, Cases and Legalisations of Civil Law No. 2 [1999], Chinese Academy of Governance Press, p. 262.

Custom Interpretation

6.158 Custom interpretation means that when there are different explanations of a contract provision, the meaning of such provision shall be confirmed by custom and practice and if due to the loophole, the rights and obligations are ambiguous, custom and practice will play a supplementary role to the interpretation of that contract provision.

The Principle of Good Faith

6.159 As a basic principle of the Civil Code,[36] the principle of good faith can be also used to interpret the contract where has a discrepancy.

Overview of the Construction Project Contract Model Text

6.160 On 24 December 1999, based on the practice of Model Text (GF-91-0201) and international precedents, Ministry of Housing and Urban–Rural Development issued the Model Text of Construction Project Contract for Construction Project (GF-1999-0201).

6.161 In the following decade, three major aspects of achievement in this field led to a more advanced Model Text: The improving legislation mechanism, advanced project technology/management system and developed project pricing system. Therefore, on 3 April 2013, the Ministry of Housing and Urban–Rural Development and the State Administration for Industry and Commerce of the Chinese government jointly promulgated a model text for construction project contract. The "Construction project contract for Construction Project" (GF-2013-0201) ("Model Text") introduced new features that were not in the 1999 version of the construction project contract model text. Those new features of system include: Mutual guarantee, reasonable price adjustment, defect liability period, construction series insurance, consultation and determination system, claim period, double compensation, and dispute review system. Besides, the 2013 Model Text also makes the contract structure system more perfect, improves the type of contract price, pays more attention to the guidance, regulation and balance of rights and interests of the employer and the contractor's market behavior, strengthens the connection with the existing laws and other texts to ensure the applicability of the contract, etc.

6.162 The 2013 Model Text was composed of three parts: Contract Agreement, General Provisions, and Customized Provisions. It also includes 11 annexes, such as a list of the contractor's previous work a list of the materials and equipment supplied by the employer, a quality warranty covenant. The Contract Agreement part contains 12 clauses, such as in the FIDIC Contract. The General Provisions contain 20 clauses, which pertain to general stipulations, the employer, the contractor, the supervisor, quality of work, works for safety and environmental protection, project duration and progress, materials and equipment, tests and inspections, variation, price adjustments, contract price, measurements and payments, acceptance and trial, final account on completion, defect liabilities and warranty, breach of contract, *Force Majeure*, insurance, claims, and dispute resolution. These clauses not only address the needs of

36 Article 7 Civil Code, *reads*:

"The parties to civil legal relations shall conduct civil activities under the principle of good faith, adhere to honesty, and fulfill their promises".

construction management, but also provide special arrangements for construction within the constraints of existing law. Further, these clauses strike a good balance on the rights and obligations of the counterparties.

6.163 The Model Text fully considers construction project characteristics and properly arranges the employer's and the contractor's rights and obligations in the contract structure. In the General Provisions, the clauses are devised to direct the contract parties to exercise their rights and fulfill their obligations in conformity with existing laws and regulations. At the same time, considering the special features of these contracts, the Model Text offers leeway to the parties to enhance negotiability. Thus, the parties may form their own terms to meet their specific needs as long as the terms conform to the Customized Provisions of the Model Text.

6.164 On 22 September 2017, considering the ambiguities on timing of guarantee deposit repayment and defects liability period, Ministry of Housing and Urban–Rural Development revised the Model Text and published the 2017 version (GF-2017-0201), which came into effect on 1 October 2016. This version fully considered regulations in Management Measures on Construction Project Quality Deposit ([2017] No. 138), stipulating that the defects liability period is no longer than 24 months, and modified articles on timing of guarantee deposit repayment and defects liability period, other terms remain unchanged.

Eight Mechanisms in the 2013/2017 Model Text

6.165 Inspired by successful contract formation practices in China and abroad, eight mechanisms were incorporated into the Model Text:

6.166 (1) Mutual guarantee mechanism. To address specific performance in construction project contracts, especially the problem with payment defaults, Article 2.5 of the General Provisions sets out the employer's obligation to present a proof of funding source and provide a payment guarantee. Additionally, Article 3.7 of the General Provisions sets out the contractor's obligation to provide a performance guarantee. These clauses mirror clauses in the FIDIC Contract and the U.S. AIA contract. The purpose of these clauses is to promote contract fulfillment through performance guarantees. Similar clauses are required by regulations governing other contract types. These clauses align with state policy that requires investors to act in a reasonable and prudent manner and in conformity with the traditional practice of a contractor providing a performance guarantee. And at the same time, these clauses encourage the employer to fulfill payment obligations to ensure construction is completed on time and up to standards.

6.167 (2) Reasonable price adjustment mechanism. To control the risk caused by fluctuations in market prices, the Model Text incorporates a reasonable price adjustment mechanism, which means the fixed contract price can be adjusted based on price fluctuations in materials, equipment and labour. The rationale behind the price adjustment mechanism is for the contract parties to equitably share market risks. Article 11.1 of the General Provisions stipulates that the price in Lump Sum contracts should be adjusted for any market fluctuation that falls outside the scope of the risk management agreement. This stipulation is consistent with the practice adopted by the local government departments in charge of construction cost controls. The price adjustment mechanism helps settle contract price disputes caused by unanticipated market price fluctuations during contract performance.

6.168 (3) Defect liability period mechanism. In order to further implement the "Management Measures on Construction Project Quality Deposit"[37] on the provisions of the defect liability period, while solving the long-standing dispute between the parties to the contract agreed to "return the deposit after warranty period", the model text of the General Provisions of Contract Article 15 introduces the defect liability and warranty system, clarifying that the defect liability period refers to "the contractor in accordance with contractual obligations to repair defects, and the contractor withhold the quality of the deposit period, calculated from the date of completion and acceptance of the project". It is necessary to point out that defect liability period and warranty period are two different concepts. At present, relevant Chinese legislation stipulates that the warranty period should conform to the life expectancy of the construction, which would be 50 years for residential projects, while the defect liability period is usually two years. In practice, some employers would not return the deposit arguing that the contractor should wait until the warranty period expires. This argument confuses the defect liability period and the warranty period. It is noteworthy that the defect liability period stipulated in Model Text is similar to the defect liability notice period stipulated in the FIDIC Contract.

6.169 (4) Construction insurance mechanism. Article 18 of the General Provisions not only provides for construction insurance, but also incorporates requirements for work-related injury insurance and other insurance, which conforms to the National People's Congress' suggestions for amending the Construction Law. The insurance mechanism improves the construction insurance system in China while maintaining room for the potential implement the construction warranty insurance mechanism, which is the standard in the FIDIC Contract.

6.170 (5) Consultation and determination mechanism. The biggest obstacle in construction project contract performance is the disagreement between the employer and the contractor on performance matters. If such differences cannot be settled in a timely manner, they may endanger the whole project. To address this problem, the Model Text adopts the method utilized by the FIDIC Contract and the "Standard Construction Bidding Document" (2007), which is incorporated in Article 4.4 of the General Provisions as "Consultation and Determination Mechanism", to stipulate that the chief supervising engineer shall assume the responsibility for the organization and implementation of the agreement and determination, and specifying the prerequisites for the activation of the system.

6.171 (6) Claim period mechanism. Claims arising from unforeseen incidents and from variations in contract performance are common, reaching a level where almost every case is claimed. To ensure the timeliness of claims and to facilitate the timely collection and evaluation of claim evidence by both contracting parties, the 2013 Model Text borrows the "claim period" from common international practice and the "Standard Construction Bidding Document" (2007).[38] As such, Article 19 of the 2013 Construction Project Contract stipulates that the claim period is 28 days for both employer and contractor, and any claim is waived if the injured party fails to raise the claim in writing within this period. The

37 "Management Measures on Construction Project Quality Deposit" ([2017] No. 138), jointly promulgated by the Ministry of Housing and Urban–Rural Development and the Ministry of Finance on 20 June 2017.

38 Effective 1 May 2008

stipulation of a claim period is a significant improvement on the 1999 Construction Project Contract, which was silent on the claim period.

6.172 (7) Double compensation mechanism. To solve the problem of the employers defaulting on payments, the 2013 Model Text stipulates double compensation for payments default. The mechanism further requires procedural provisions such as notice and reasonable period for correction. If the employer eventually fails to perform the payment obligation, the employer will incur a default penalty equal to the two times the benchmark interest stipulated by the Central Bank of China for the corresponding period. This mechanism is reflected in all payment phases, including progress payments, construction completion payment and final payment.

6.173 (8) Dispute review mechanism. To improve dispute settlement in long construction projects with complicated elements, Article 20.3 of the General Provisions allows for a Dispute Adjudication Board, which has long been a standard internationally. According to this dispute review mechanism, a group of experts can participate throughout the entire construction process to offer an independent review on any dispute that arises. With this independent review, differences tend to be diminished, contract performance will be improved, and economic outcomes for the project will be enhanced. The dispute evaluation and resolution system belongs to the increased social dispute resolution mechanism, and also provides a new dispute resolution path for administrative supervision and management departments to manage the construction market.

2017 Model Text's Update on the Starting of Defects Liability Period

6.174 With the new practice implemented in Management Measures on Construction Project Quality Deposit the 2017 Model Text Article 15.2.1 was updated in accordance with the new practice in terms of the starting point of defects liability period under special circumstances. "The defects liability period starts from the final acceptance of construction, the parties shall agree to a specific period no longer than 24 months in the special contract. Unit project shall be accepted before the whole project. The defect liability period of such unit starts from the date of delivery after acceptance. If the acceptance and delivery cannot be fulfilled due to subcontractor, the defect liability period starts from the actual day of acceptance. If the acceptance and delivery cannot be fulfilled due to the employer, the defect liability period starts from the date right after a 90-day period upon issuance of a final acceptance report by the subcontractor. If the employer skipped the acceptance and possessed the project without proper procedures, the defect liability period starts from the date of such actual change possession".

Procurement and Tendering

Overview of the Bidding and Procurement System in PRC

6.175 The buyers and suppliers entering into deal transactions through bidding and procurement process has become a common practice of market economy in PRC. According to the current practice, bidding involves a wide range of industry sectors, with numbers of matching rules and regulations. The corresponding Legal System is complex and multi-faceted with different specific requirements and significant features. For instance, bidding of engineering and bidding of service are quite different in bidding conditions and evaluation methods. The "Bidding Law"[39] and the "Government Procurement Law"[40] are key legislation in this field.

6.176 The scope of projects that must conduct bidding process had been a hot issue. In 2018 China's National Development and Reform Commission (hereinafter referred to as the NDRC) issued Decree No. 16 "Regulations on Projects that Must Conduct Bidding Process", clarifying that a large number of private enterprises and other social investment entities invested in engineering projects no longer needed bidding process but rather using a direct procurement or direct subcontracting method to conclude a contract, specifically provided as follows:

> "***Article II*** *wholly or partially using state-owned funds to invest or state-financed projects include:*
>
> *(A) the use of budget funds of more than RMB 2 million, and the funds account for more than 10% of the investment amount of the project.*
>
> *(B) the use of state-owned enterprises and institutions funds, and the funds account for a controlling or dominant position in the project.*
>
> ***Article III*** *use of international organizations or foreign government loans, aid funds for projects including:*
>
> *(A) the use of the World Bank, the Asian Development Bank and other international organizations loans, aid funds for the project.*
>
> *(B) the use of foreign governments and their agencies loans, aid funds for the project*".

6.177 Naturally, bidding process is a must for projects with social public interest, public safety such as coal, railroads, highways, pipelines, water transport, and public aviation projects.

Bidding System Characteristics

6.178 With the implementation of the "Regulation on the Implementation of the Bidding Law",[41] in 2012, the bidding system in China has grown into a more mature one during the past decade. It plays a vital role in the economic and social life of China. Furthermore, with the development of social productivity, economic growth places more demands on

39 Passed at the 11th meeting of the Standing Committee of the Ninth National People's Congress on 30 August 1999, and revised at the 31st Session of the Standing Committee of the 12th National People's Congress on 27 December 2017.

40 Passed at the 28th meeting of the Standing Committee of the Ninth National People's Congress on 29 June 2002, and revised at the 10th Session of the Standing Committee of the 12th National People's Congress on 31 August 2014.

41 Passed at the 183rd executive meeting of the State Council on 30 November 2011, and implemented since the date of 1 February 2012. revised for the first time in accordance with the Decision of the State Council to Amend and Repeal Certain Administrative Regulations on March 1, 2017; revised for the second time in accordance with the Decision of the State Council to Amend and Repeal Certain Administrative Regulations on March 19, 2018; and revised for the third time in accordance with the Decision of the State Council to Amend Certain Administrative Regulations on March 2, 2019.

the Legal System of bidding and tendering. The current Chinese bidding system has following features:

Legal Attributes of the Bidding Law

6.179 Since the implementation of the Bidding Law on 1 January 2000, the legal characterization of the law has been disputed. By analyzing the content of the provisions of the Bidding Law, it is clear that most of the Bidding Law regulates procedural matters in the bidding and procurement process, and part of it regulates the relevant content in the bidding documents and contract formation. Professor Jiang Ping,[42] one of the most respected law professors in China, commented, "The bidding law is mainly a procedural law. I always hold the opinion that the procedural laws protect the economic prosperity and democratic processes".

The Bidding Law Is the Basic Law of the Bidding Legal System

6.180 Among the many legislative norms on bidding and procurement, another issue is the status of the Bidding Law as the basic law of the bidding and tendering Legal System. Given the relatively large scope of adjustment of the Bidding Law and its long period of operation, from the perspective of the overall measure of the legal purpose of bidding and procurement, it can be concluded that the Bidding Law is the basic law in the bidding and tendering Legal System and becomes the rule followed by many procurement activities in PRC practice.

Regulations on Bidding Activities

6.181 In view of the large number of industries involved in bidding and tendering, the National Development and Reform Commission (NDRC) acts as the lead coordinator among the departments that supervise bidding and tendering activities accordingly. At the same time, the Bidding and Tendering Law belongs to the bidding and tendering market subject law, and one of its main purposes is to promote effective and orderly competition in the bidding and tendering market, whether or not to reach the winning bid is also a civil legal consequence of the parties' voluntary participation in the competitive selection.

Characteristics of PPP Bidding and Procurement Laws

6.182 Currently, bidding and procurement in China's PPP (public-private partnerships) sector is in a stable development stage. It is important to pay attention to the arrangement for combined competition, that is, social investors who have multiple qualifications and capabilities for investment, construction and operation can use combined in one tender procurement selection.

6.183 In accordance with the legislative spirit of Article 9 of the "Regulations for the Implementation of the Bidding Law", it is usually considered that for projects using PPP mode for engineering construction, it is stipulated that if the investor is selected by bidding and the investor has construction capability, the construction unit can be selected and exempted from bidding a second time.

42 A respected legal scholar in China, law professor, and advisor for doctoral candidates at the China University of Political Science and Law.

6.184 According to the relevant documents of the Ministry of Finance, the investors can use the following five purchase methods in PPP model: (1) Open tender bidding, (2) competitive negotiation, (3) competitive consultation, (4) single sourcing, and (5) public tender bidding, which is the default method.

Legal Consequences Resulting from the Violation of Bidding Laws and Administrative Regulations

6.185 According to Article 153 of the Civil Code of PRC,[43] "A juridical act violating the imperative provisions of any law or administrative regulation shall be void, unless the imperative provisions do not result in the nullity of the juridical act". Article 52 of the original Contract Law provides that a contract concluded in violation of the mandatory provisions of laws and administrative regulations shall be void ab initio. This mandatory provision, in the original Interpretation (II) to the Contract Law[44] of Supreme Court, refers to the mandatory norms of validity.

6.186 The Bidding Law prescribes several legal consequences for violations of the law on bidding and tendering. The most common consequence is the bidding being deemed invalid. The "Regulation on the Implementation of the Bidding Law" also prescribes liability for many illegal activities. It has 19 clauses addressing the liabilities for illegal activities, with special focus on collusive bidding.

6.187 It is important to note that, Article 81 of the "Regulation on the Implementation of the Bidding Law" stipulates:

> If the bidding activities for a project that is required to adopt a bidding method by law violate the Bidding Law or this current regulation, and exert substantial influence on the bidding result, and it is impossible to take remedial measures, the whole process and the result shall be deemed void, and the whole process shall be restarted by law.

This statute is of great value and significance because it directly addresses validity. It provides three factors to decide whether the bidding process and result is invalid: (1) the project is one that required by law to adopt a bidding process; (2) Whether any statutes or administrative regulations were violated; (3) whether the bidding activities had a substantial influence on the bidding result, that is, impacted the choice of the winning bidder and the winning price; (4) in the foregoing circumstances, the bidding activity cannot take remedial measures to correct.

---

43 The Civil Code of the People's Republic of China, as adopted at the 3rd Session of the Thirteenth National People's Congress of the People's Republic of China on 28 May 2020 came into force on 1 January 2021.

44 The Interpretation (II) of the Supreme People's Court on Several Issues Concerning the Application of the Contract Law of the People's Republic of China was adopted by the 1462nd meeting of the Judicial Committee of the Supreme People's Court on 9 February 2009 and came into effect on 13 May 2009, and the judicial interpretation has expired on 1 January 2021.

Validity of Contract Formed Through Flawed Bidding Process

6.188 If a contract is formed as the fruit of a flawed bidding process, the validity of the contract may be challenged. In practice, validity of a bidding result and a contract formed afterwards will be determined by the objectives of the project, the severity of the flaws, and the possibility of remediation. This issue is analyzed as follows:

Bidding Prerequisites in the Bidding Law

6.189 Article 9 of the Bidding Law stipulates:

> *where a bidding project is subject to examination and approval per the relevant regulations, it shall undergo the examination and approval process and get approval first. A tenderee shall possess sufficient funds for the bidding project; if not yet in possession of sufficient funds, the sources of funds for the project shall have been confirmed, and all these related facts shall be noted in the bidding invitation documents.*

This statute provides two bidding prerequisites: Project examination and approval and proof of funds. If the two prerequisites are not met, such as in the situation where the administrative agency does not approve the project or insufficient funds are available for the project, the bidding result would be considered unreliable because the bidding invitation documents would not have provided reasonable and comprehensive information. It may also lead to further difficulties in investment and financing at a later stage, and lead to a deadlock in contract performance. This behavior would violate the basic legal principles of the Bidding Law.

Analysis of the Illegality of Bidding Activities That Bidding Process That Does Not Meet Prerequisites

6.190 Article 81 of the "Regulation on the Implementation of the Bidding Law" stipulates:

> If the bidding activities for a project that is required to adopt a bidding method by law violate the Bidding Law or this current regulation, and exert substantial influence on the bidding result, and it is impossible to take remedial measures, the whole process and the result shall be deemed void, and the whole process shall be restarted by law.

6.191 This stipulation is in the last section in the chapter on legal liability in the "Regulation on the Implementation of the Bidding Law". It summarizes the legal liability for bidding activities, but also very important adjudicative provisions. This article applies only the following conditions are concurrently fulfilled in deciding a bidding process/result is invalid:

(1) The project is one that required by law to adopt a bidding process;
(2) The Bidding Law and the Regulation on the Implementation of the Bidding Law are violated;
(3) Such violations cannot be corrected through remedial measures;
(4) The legal consequences caused by such violations substantially influenced the result.

6.192 The bid without bidding conditions is obviously illegal, but whether it will cause the legal consequences of invalid bidding or invalid bid-winning, the above four conditions need to be met, otherwise it should not be easily identified.

Different Contract Types

Lump Sum Contract

6.193 The Lump Sum contract is a common construction project contract widely used in engineering construction in China, especially in general contracting and sub-contracting transactions. In current practice, contract parties would often make different interpretations of this type of contract. Chinese national standards documents and contract model texts provide provisions pertaining to Lump Sum contracts:

6.194 Article 7.1.3 of the "Code of Valuation with Bill Quantity of Construction Works"[45] ("Bill Quantity Valuation Code") is specially tailored for the Lump Sum contract. Article 7.1.3 stipulates that a Lump Sum contract can only be used for small-scale and short-period construction with reviewed and approved construction drawing designs.

6.195 In view of the fixed price can easily be understood as no adjustment of the contract price under any circumstances, the Model Text is defined and regulated again on the basis of the national standard. Article 12.1 of the Model Text defines the term "Lump Sum contract" as follows:

> Lump Sum contract is a construction project contract where the contract price is calculated, regulated and confirmed on the basis of the construction drawings, bill of work quantities, budget statement and other relevant factors agreed upon by the parties, and the total price may not be adjusted if a deviation falls within the agreed scope. The parties shall agree on the scope of risks and the method for calculation of risk costs and include them in the contract, and the parties shall agree on the method for adjustment of the contract price if the deviation falls outside the agreed scope of risks. Specifically, contract terms pertaining to an adjustment arising from market price fluctuation shall conform to Article 11.1 (adjustment arising from market price fluctuation), and contract terms pertaining to an adjustment arising from variation of laws shall conform to Article 11.2 (adjustment arising from variation of laws).

6.196 Above definition in the Model Text is very comprehensive and it is obvious that even under Lump Sum price does not mean that the contract price can be never adjustable.

6.197 On 26 June 2015, the Ministry of Transport promulgated the "Administrative Measures for General Contracting in High-way Project Design and Construction".[46] The measures generally prohibit any price adjustments in Lump Sum contracts except for those price adjustments related to the risk costs assumed by the project employer. Furthermore, the measures require that the project employer determine the bidding price limit within the budget approved in the preliminary design. The measures aid in promoting the integration of highway project design and construction and in improving the overall effectiveness of highway project design and construction.

6.198 On 1 March 2020, Notice by the Ministry of Housing and Urban–Rural Development and the National Development and Reform Commission of issue of the Management of General Contracting for Housing Construction and Municipal Infrastructure Projects ([2019] No. 12), similarly stipulated in Article 16 that

45 "Bill Quantity Valuation Code" was approved by the Ministry of Housing and Urban–Rural Development as national standard, code number is GB50500-2013, effective 1 April 2013.

46 Ministry of Transport, (No. 10 [2015]), promulgated on 19 June 2015, activated on 1 August 2015.

general contracting for projects invested by enterprises is appropriate to use fixed price contracts, and general contracting for projects invested by the government shall reasonably determine the form of contract price. If a fixed price contract is adopted, the total contract price shall not be adjusted in general, except for the cases where the contract is agreed to be adjusted.

6.199 In PRC practice, the Lump Sum contract has some legal issues that can easily cause disputes, especially when a Lump Sum contract is prematurely terminated before work completion, the accounting for the uncompleted construction remains a complicated problem.

6.200 The Supreme People's Court addressed this problem in its opinion in "Dispute under the Construction Project Contract between Qinghai Fangsheng Building Engineering Co., Ltd. and Qinghai Longhao Property Co., Ltd.".[47] The Supreme People's Court held that a Lump Sum construction project contract terminated due to the parties' failure to fully perform the contract, it was inappropriate to calculate the payment for the completed work simply by referring to the construction projects quota issued by the government or by using a fixed formula. Instead, the payment calculation should be conducted on case-by-case basis considering the actual performance of both contract parties, especially paying attention to the degree of the parties' fault and the moral impact of the judicial decision for the payment decision.

6.201 The case-by-case method favored by the Supreme People's Court emphasizes equity and attempts to balance both parties' interests. In the author's opinion, however, a more predictable settlement method might be preferable. This predictability could be achieved, for instance, by adopting the "same ratio method of third-party standard" in the Guiding Opinions[48] of the High People's Court of Beijing.

Unit Price Contract

6.202 The unit price contract is also a common construction project contract in China. It is used in construction practice such as in large highway, waterway, railroad and housing construction projects where the process and method are more mature and the unit price is relatively certain, but the volume of work cannot be determined in advance.

6.203 Article 7.1.3 of the "Bill Quantity Valuation Code" stipulates: "a project for valuation with bill quantity shall apply a unit price contract".

6.204 According to Article 12.1 of the Model Text,

the term "unit price contract" means a construction project contract for a construction project where the contract price is calculated, regulated and confirmed by the bill of quantities and an overall unit price agreed by the parties thereto, and the unit contract price may not be regulated within the agreed upon scope. The parties thereto shall agree to the scope of risks contained in the overall unit price and the method for calculation of risk costs agreed in the specific clauses and conditions of the contract, and the parties shall agree to the method for regulation of the

47 See Case No. (2014) 民一终字No. 69, www.court.gov.cn/whenshu/xiangqing-8389.html.

48 According to Article 13 of the "Interpretation of Beijing High People's Court on Several Difficult Problems about Hearing Dispute Cases of Construction Contract", the evaluation institution shall adopt the "proportion calculation" method, which calculates the proportion rate between the completed work and the whole contract work, and multiple the contract price with this rate. The result of the calculation is the payment shall be made to the contractor.

contract price beyond the scope of risks. Specifically, regulation arising from floating of the market price shall be made under Article 11.1 (regulation arising from floating of the market price).

This definition is further explained in the "Guidelines for the use of Construction Project Contract for Construction Projects (Model Text)",[49] promulgated by the Ministry of Housing and Urban–Rural Development.

6.205 When a unit price contract is adopted, the parties should pay particular attention to the definition for the scope of risks, especially for contract price adjustments arising from changes in laws, which is specified in Article 11 of Model Text. Except for small-scale and using simple technology projects, the final payment amount usually differs from the agreed upon contract price. Therefore, all factors that cause the contract price to vary should be recorded during the performance of the contract, and all project documents should be safely maintained to help determine the final price and to control costs.

Cost-Plus Contract

6.206 The cost-plus contract is seldom adopted in China. The author believes that this contract is similar to the project management contract. In China, contract parties often have significant differences in their understanding of their contract rights and obligations and in their understanding of the concept of "consideration". Meanwhile, companies often have internal cost management systems that are underdeveloped; as such, it is often difficult to reach consensus between the counterparties. Therefore, the cost-plus contract rarely applies in practice.

Nature of Construction Project Contract

6.207 Article 269, Chapter 16 of the original Contract Law[50] defines "contract" for construction projects. A contract for a construction project is one formed for the purpose of a contractor to perform project construction and a project employer to pay for the contractor's work. Construction Project Contracts include contracts for survey, design, and construction. This definition is retained in the provisions of Article 788 of the Civil Code, which come into force on 1 January 2021. Article 808 of the Civil Code also stipulates that any issue not discussed in Chapter 18, "Contracts for Construction Projects" shall be governed by the relevant provision governing contracts for hired works in Chapter 17, "Contracts for Work".[51] It is such a feature that determines the similarity between the construction project contract and the contracts for work.

6.208 From a legal perspective, construction project contracts have the following fundamental characteristics:

49 See Pang Zongzhan, Tan Jinghui, Guidelines on the Model Text of the Construction Contract, China City Press, 2015, pp. 191–3.

50 The Contract Law of the People's Republic of China has been adopted at the 2nd Session of the 9th National People's Congress on 15 March 1999, and is hereby promulgated, it will come into force as of 1 October 1999. Now it has been expired since the Civil Code come into effect in 2021.

51 See Tan Jinghui, Focus on Legal Issues in Construction, Law Press, 2016.

(1) The contract for construction is developed from the works contract. In the absence of relevant provisions tailored for the contract for construction projects, the provisions governing works contracts apply. This default application acknowledges the attributes of the of the construction project contract originate in the works contract;
(2) The contractor's obligation is to perform construction work and the employer's obligation is to pay the contract price. These obligations are the basic obligations for the formulation and execution of a construction project contract;
(3) The works contract and the construction project contract share a common characteristic, which is of low additional value and poor anti-risk capacity. However, despite these shared characteristics, the construction project contract provides greater risk protection because: There is no requirement for the legal qualifications as being a contractor in the works contract in China, while there is a much-higher bar for being a contractor in the construction project contract because the requirements for management skills of personnel, procurement capacity of materials and equipment, and organizing ability in the construction projects create a higher threshold for entrants in this field;
(4) The settlement and liquidation of the construction project contract need to meet the basic premise of satisfactory quality, which is also the conformity requirement for the performance of the main obligations of the contract, and also the guarantee for the realization of the contract purpose for the employer.

6.209 Besides these four fundamental characteristics, construction project contracts have five additional characteristics based on Chinese legislation addressing management systems for construction projects.[52]

6.210 First, the policy goals behind legislation governing construction project contracts prioritize both the public interest and the value of order and efficiency.

6.211 Second, the main feature of the construction project contract is that contractor qualifications and practitioner qualifications dictate the validity of the contract.

6.212 Third, the principle of reasonable consideration applies to the whole contract formation and project performance. In other words, the concept of reasonable consideration that takes full account of the obligations under the conditions of performance, includes the pricing principle of reasonable cost and profit.

6.213 Fourth, regardless of the contract pricing mode, all construction project contracts have risk boundaries, including time boundary and spatial boundary. Spatial boundary includes geological conditions, project conditions, climate conditions, blueprint conditions, and so forth.

6.214 Fifth, construction project contracts must adhere to the "currency" principle, which means the contract contents are closely connected with the performance of the contract, including current measurements, current confirmation, and current payment.

52 See Tan Jinghui, Focus on Legal Issues in Construction, Law Press, 2016.

Author's Opinion

6.215 In conclusion, construction project contract originated from the works contract. When we form and execute a construction project contract, we should focus on its legal features, especially risk boundaries, to ensure fairness and efficiency are realized.

Forms of Security – Bonds and Guarantee

6.216 In engineering construction in China, the most common securitization method is the letter of guarantee. The guarantor for a letter of guarantee may be a bank, a financial institution or another institution, such as a guarantee company.

6.217 In 2016, the State Council promulgated the "Circular on Clearing and Standardizing Deposits in the Engineering Construction Field".[53] Subsequently, the Ministry of Housing and Urban–Rural Development entrusted a research group to study problems in construction project security.[54] Based on that research, they promulgated guiding opinions.[55]

6.218 In general, an engineering construction guarantee includes a series of guarantees, including a bid guarantee, an advance payment guarantee, a performance guarantee, a work quality guarantee, and a migrant worker wage guarantee.

6.219 A bid guarantee is a written commitment a guarantor provides to the tenderee to guarantee that the bidder will participate in the bidding activities in conformity with the bidding invitation documents and that the guarantor shall be liable if the bidder fails to do so. In general, the amount of a bid guarantee may not exceed 2% of the estimated project price.

6.220 An advance payment guarantee is a written commitment a guarantor provides to the tenderee to guarantee that the contractor will use the advance payment as stipulated in the contract and that the guarantor shall be liable if the contractor fails to do so.

6.221 A performance guarantee is a written commitment a guarantor provides to the tenderee to guarantee that the contractor will perform the obligations as stipulated in the contract from the date of signing of the contract to the date of completion of the construction project, and that the guarantor shall be liable if the contractor fails to do so. The amount of the performance guarantee may not exceed 10% of the contract price.[56]

6.222 A project quality warranty also called as defects liability warranty, which is a written commitment a guarantor provides to the tenderee to guarantee that the contractor will cure all flaws during the defects liability period and that the guarantor shall be liable if the contractor fails to cure the defects during the defects liability period. Generally, the amount of a project quality warranty guarantee may not exceed 5% of the contract price.

6.223 A migrant worker wage guarantee is a written commitment a guarantor provides to the local worker's rights agency to guarantee that the contractor will pay their workers

53 Promulgated by the General Office of the State Council on 23 June 2016.

54 See "Research Report on Promoting Construction Security System", lead author Tan Jinghui.

55 See "Guidelines on Issuing Bank Guarantees for Construction Projects", which was promulgated by MOHURD in 2016.

56 See Article 58 of the "Regulation on the Implementation of the Bidding Law", which provides "if the bid winner is requested by the bidding invite documents to submit a deposit, the bid winner shall do so. The amount of the deposit shall not exceed 10% of the contract price".

in a sufficient and prompt way and that the guarantor shall be liable if the contractor fails to do so.

Author's Opinion

6.224 Independence is the most important issue regarding the letter of guarantee. According to the first paragraph of Article 682 of the Civil Code, "*The guarantee contract is a subordinate contract to the main debt contract. If the main debt contract is invalid, the guarantee contract is invalid, except as otherwise provided by law*". As well as Article 2 of the Interpretation of the Supreme People's Court on the Application of the Civil Code of the People's Republic of China Concerning the Guarantee System[57], provides that

> *If the parties agree in the guarantee contract that the effectiveness of the guarantee contract is independent of the main contract, or agree that the guarantor is liable for the legal consequences of the invalidity of the main contract, the agreement on the independence of the guarantee is invalid. If the main contract is valid, the agreement on the independence of the guarantee is invalid does not affect the effectiveness of the guarantee contract; if the main contract is invalid, the people's court shall find that the guarantee contract is invalid, except as otherwise provided by law. In case of disputes arising from independent guarantee letters issued by financial institutions, the "Provisions of the Supreme People's Court on Several Issues Concerning the Trial of Disputes on Independent Guarantee.*[58]

shall apply. Currently Chinese judicial practice usually only recognizes the independence of independent guarantee letters.

Design Obligations[59]

6.225 In China, designs must (1) meet mandatory requirements stipulated by laws and administrative rules and (2) fulfill the project employer's demands. If the employer's demands conflict with mandatory laws or regulations, then the design contractor must reject the employer's demands. The main risks of design are usually borne by the designer as an experienced design professional compared to the employer, except when the employer's design specifications conflict with mandatory laws or regulations.

6.226 The engineering construction design in China can be divided into two phases: The engineering survey stage and the engineering design stage. The engineering survey can be further divided into the feasibility study survey, the preliminary design survey and the detailed survey. Thus, engineering design is the activities combined with overall planning, positioning and designing of the functions, layout, structure, landscape, use, environment and aesthetic aspects of the project. Eventually, all of this work is reduced to characters, drawings, and models.

6.227 Article 788 of the Civil Code stipulates that "a contract for a construction project is a contract whereby the contractor performs project construction, and the employer pays

57 (Fa Shi [2020] No. 28), which came into effect on 1 January 2021.

58 Adopted at the 1688th Session of the Judicial Committee of the Supreme People's Court on 11 July 2016, are hereby issued, and shall come into force on 1 December 2016.

59 See Li Qiming, Bidding Procurement Contract Management, China Planning Press, 2014.

for the work. Contracts for construction projects include contracts for survey, design, and construction". In a construction project contract, the employer entrusts the contractor to survey, design, and construct the project, and the contractor accepts such entrustment and completes the survey, design and construction tasks. The employer pays the contractor for these tasks.

6.228 In accordance with the "Model Text of Construction Project Design Contract (Housing Construction Projects)" (GF-2015-0209) and the "Model Text of Construction Project Design Contract (Specialty Construction Projects)" (GF-2015-0210) promulgated by the Ministry of Housing and Urban–Rural Development in 2015, engineering design can be divided into three stages: Conceptual design, preliminary design, and construction drawing design.

6.229 According to the Construction Law and other relevant legislation,[60] the legal provisions regulating engineering design cover qualifications, mandatory design standards and cost management.

6.230 Qualifications. The laws and administrative regulations stipulate that a contract will be deemed invalid[61] if design institutions and design personnel are unqualified according to the mandatory legal requirements fail to comply with mandatory requirements.[62]

6.231 Mandatory design standards. As public policy, engineering design activities should strictly comply with the "Project Construction Compulsory Standard", which stipulates various nationwide and industrywide standards; otherwise, violators will face civil and administrative liability and even criminal liability if aggravating factors are present.[63]

6.232 Cost management. In the past, the Chinese government controlled pricing in engineering design contracts. Now, according to the National Development and Reform Commission,[64] the contract should be subject to market forces, and the contract may include: Pre-construction project consultation fees; engineering survey and design costs; bid agency fee; engineering supervision fee; and environmental impact consultation fee.

---

60 See Article 56 of the Construction Law stipulates: "survey and designing institutions shall be responsible for the survey and design quality of construction projects. Survey and design documents shall conform to the stipulations of relevant laws and administrative regulations, quality and safety standards on construction projects, survey and design technical codes on construction projects, and contract terms".

61 See Article 18 of the "Regulation on the Quality Management of Construction Projects" provides: "an entity engaging in the survey or design of construction projects shall obtain a qualification certificate of the corresponding grade and shall undertake projects within the scope licensed by its qualification grade".

62 See Article 8 of the "Regulation on the Administration of Survey and Design of Construction Projects" provides: "any entity engaging in the survey or design of construction projects shall undertake the survey or design of construction projects within the permitted scope of its qualifications. No entity engaging in the survey or design of construction projects shall undertake the survey or design of construction projects beyond the permitted scope of its qualifications or in the name of another entity engaging in the survey or design of construction projects. No entity engaging in the survey or design of construction projects shall allow another entity or any individual to undertake the survey or design of construction projects in its name".

63 See Article 5 of the "Regulation on the Administration of Survey and Design of Construction Projects" provides: "the units for surveying or designing of construction projects must conduct the surveying or designing of construction projects according to law, strictly implement the compulsory standards for construction projects, and shall be responsible for the surveyor design quality of construction projects".

64 See the "Circular on Further Opening Professional Service Price of Construction Projects" (F.G.J.G. [2015] No. 299), which stipulates: "on the basis of lifting the control over the professional service price of construction projects that are invested and entrusted by non-government organizations, the professional service price for construction projects below would implement market-regulated price and loose the control of the government's guideline price management".

Duty to Warn, Check, Review

6.233 Combined inspection and final acceptance is commonly adopted for inspecting, testing, checking and accepting construction projects in China. The Model Text specifically addresses this combined process in project quality clauses, materials and equipment clauses, test and inspection clauses, and acceptance and project trial clauses. Article 13.1 provides the following for acceptance of divisional and sub-divisional works:

the quality of divisional and sub-divisional works shall comply with the relevant national specifications, standards, and the contract terms on project construction acceptance. The contractor shall complete the entire divisional and sub-divisional works as required by the project design.

6.234 In China, the relationship between the project acceptance system and the project supervisor is of great importance. The Construction Law provides that a supervision system must be adopted for projects that affect public interest and involve state-owned funds. For these projects, a project supervisor with expertise shall represent the employer to in inspection and acceptance work during inspection, test, check and acceptance processes.

6.235 Article 13.1.2 of the Model Text stipulates:

except otherwise provided in specific clauses and conditions, the contractor shall notify the supervisor to make acceptance 48 hours in advance if the divisional and sub-divisional works comply with the acceptance conditions through self-inspection by the contractor. If the supervisor is unable to make acceptance on time, the supervisor shall submit 24 hours before acceptance a written request for extending the period, but the extension shall not exceed 48 hours. If the supervisor neither accepts divisional and sub-divisional works on time nor submits a request for extending the period, the contractor shall have the right to self-accept the divisional and sub-divisional works, and the supervisor shall recognize the subsequent result of the contractor's own acceptance. The project cannot proceed to the next phase without proper acceptance of the previous phase.

Employer and Contractor

6.236 The counterparties in a construction project contract are referred to as the employer and the contractor. The supervisor acts as a professional agent entrusted by the employer.

Employer

6.237 The employer shall perform its rights and obligations per legal provisions and contractual stipulations. Under China's current Legal System, an employer is always the applicant when a state approval is required. An employer is also the investor. The requirements for the employer's performance capacity are subject to the relevant laws. The investor shall have the reasonable cognitive ability in terms of understanding and shall remain informed about the project construction.[65]

65 See Article 15 of the Construction Law, which stipulates: "the contract issuing unit and contracting unit of a construction project shall conclude written covenants, specifying the rights and obligations of each party. The contract issuing unit and contracting unit of a construction project should fulfill their contractual

6.238 For contracts, Article 2 of the General Provisions of the Model Text (2017) provides detailed stipulations for the employer, including permits or approvals, employer's representatives, employer's personnel, provision of construction site, facilitation and necessary information, evidence of source of funds and payment guarantee, payment of contract price, arrangement for completion acceptance, and coordinated site management agreement.

6.239 In practice, many disputes relate to employer's construction site preparation, the completeness of basic data information and the fulfillment of payment obligations. For example, the employer fails to provide geological survey data and design drawings in time resulting in delayed construction and a large number of changes, which will inevitably affect the construction progress and claim.

Contractor

6.240 A general contractor is a contractor responsible for all the groundworks and construction work, whereas a specialized contractor does specialized work, like interior decoration. The general contractor should perform the construction work in accordance with the blueprint and submit construction records and completion drawings.

6.241 Strictly speaking, contractors on construction projects may be deemed as general contractors or specialized contractors. According to Chinese legislation, a contractor is required to, first, have relevant qualifications and a "safety work permit;" second, have the capacity to work as a professional institution, that is, work with focus, prudence, prediction and precaution in construction activities, which are always taken as the contractor's obligations stipulated in a construction project contract.[66]

6.242 In addition, relating to the conduct of the contractor to subcontract, China's construction laws has also regulated correspondingly. Article 29 of the Construction Law[67] prescribes: "the general contractor can subcontract parts of the project to subcontractors with appropriate qualifications. Except for the situation in which the subcontracting activity is specified in the general contract, approval from the project employer shall be obtained. With regard to general contracting, the construction of the main structure of the project shall be completed by the general contractor. The general contractor shall be held responsible to the project employer per the provisions of the general contract; the subcontractors shall be held responsible to the general contractor per the terms of the subcontracting contract. The general contractor and subcontractor shall bear joint responsibilities to the project employer for the subcontracted parts".

obligations. A failure to fulfill contractual obligations will subject the violator to liability for breach of contractor under the law".

66 See Article 26 of the Construction Law, which stipulates: "the project contracting units shall hold legally-obtained certificates of qualifications and contract projects within the business scope as allowed by their level of qualification. Project contracting units are prohibited from contracting projects beyond the business scope as allowed by their level of qualification or in the name of other construction enterprises in any form. Construction enterprises are prohibited from allowing other units or individuals to use their own certificates of qualification, business licenses or their name in any form in order to contract construction projects".

67 Decision on Revising the Construction Law was passed at the 20th meeting of the Standing Committee of the 11th National People's Congress on 22 April 2011 and was implemented on 1 July 2011.

Consultant's Role and Liability[68]

Supervisor's Legal Status and Corresponding Rights

6.243 The term "supervisor" refers to an institutional supervisor in China. According to the needs of the project, the agency will dispatch chief supervisory engineers and other supervisory engineers. The supervisor's legal status and obligations are associated with the legal rights of the supervisor and directly depend on statutory default rules and contractual stipulations. In China, many disputes arise over the supervisor's legal status. These disputes focus on whether the supervisor's role is as a contract third party or as the employer's agent. Under the Construction Law,[69] the dominant view is where the supervisor is the employer's agent.[70]

Supervisor's Legal Obligations[71]

6.244 From the point of view of the legal provisions to study the obligations of the supervisor, according to laws and administrative regulations,[72] a supervisor's legal obligations can be summarized as follows:

(1) Work content and standards. The supervisor shall, on behalf of the employer, supervise the construction quality and progress and the use of construction funds per laws, administrative regulations, industrial standards, design documents, and contract terms.
(2) Practice scope. The supervisor shall only conduct supervisory activities for which the supervisor is qualified. The construction supervisor shall not have control over or a financial interest in the supervised contractor or in the suppliers of building materials, components and equipment.
(3) Supervisory personnel qualifications. Construction companies, prospecting companies, design companies and supervising companies that engage in construction activities must employ specialized professionals possessing state-accreditation pertaining to the activities in which they engage. Meanwhile, as mentioned in the "Regulation on the Quality Management of Construction Projects" provides that

68 See Tan Jinghui, Focus on Legal Issues in Construction, Law Press, 2016.

69 See Article 31 of the Construction Law, which stipulates: "construction projects subject to supervision shall be supervised by appropriately qualified project supervising units entrusted by the project owners. The project owners shall enter into written supervision contracts with the project supervising units".

70 See Article 37 of the "Regulation on the Quality Management of Construction Projects", which stipulates: "a project supervisory entity shall select and assign the qualified chief supervisory engineer and supervisory engineer to supervise the construction site. Without the signature of the supervisory engineer, no construction materials, components, fittings or equipment may be used or installed on the project, and the construction entity may not undertake the construction of the next phase. Without the signature of the chief supervisory engineer, the construction entity may not appropriate the project fund, nor conduct completion-based checks and acceptances".

71 See Tan Jinghui, Focus on Legal Issues in Construction, Law Press, 2016.

72 See Article 12 of the Construction Law, which stipulates: "construction engineering enterprises, prospecting units, design units and project supervisory units that engage in construction activities shall possess the following: (1) registered capital that complies with the state provisions; (2) specialized technical personnel with statutory professional qualifications consistent with the construction activities they engage in; (3) technologies and equipment necessary for the construction activities; (4) other qualifications as stipulated by laws and administrative regulations".

a supervisor shall appoint a qualified chief supervisory engineer and supervisory engineers to supervise the construction work.

(4) Liability. The supervisor or supervising personnel who violate laws and regulations shall bear legal liability, including civil liability, administrative liability and criminal liability.

Supervisor's Contractual Obligations

6.245 In addition to these legal obligations, the supervisor is also bound by the contractual obligations agreed upon in the supervision contract so that the employer can achieve the purpose of the construction project contract. The supervisor's contractual obligations:

(1) Establish a legal relationship of entrustment between the employer and the supervisor. As such, the supervisor shall conduct construction supervision in a manner commonly found in an entrustment relationship, including being bound by the duty of care and the duty of loyalty;
(2) Specify the supervisor's authority and the project's acceptable outcomes. As such, the supervisor shall exercise the supervisory rights on behalf of the employer and in a professional manner, to ensure the project objectives are achieved, and all documents and records are properly maintained.

Sub-Contracting[73]

6.246 Construction subcontracting in China has four main legal characteristics.

(1) First, subcontracting in China can be divided into professional subcontracting and labour subcontracting. Subcontracting corresponds to the subcontracting of works in foreign engineering contracts;
(2) Second, unlike international practice or model text, Chinese law currently prohibits the designation of subcontracting practices;
(3) Third, a subcontractor in China possess relevant qualifications and may not undertake any project beyond those qualifications;
(4) Fourth, when adopting professional subcontracting, the general contractor must observe legal requirements and may not violate prohibitive provisions. Please refer to Part 7.2 of this article for further details.

Material and Workmanship

6.247 In Chinese engineering projects, the quality of construction project materials needs to meet two requirements: First, the production quality is qualified. In addition, in installation and use, engineering materials must meet both national and industry standards for testing and acceptance. Either the employer or the contractor may supply project construction materials and manufacturing equipment for the engineering process.

73 See Tan Jinghui, Focus on Legal Issues in Construction, Law Press, 2016.

Materials and Equipment Supplied by the Employer

6.248 The employer is not prohibited from supplying materials and equipment under the Construction Law. However, if the contract states that the contractor shall provide materials and equipment, the employer may not designate the brand and the supplier of those materials and equipment. Article 25 of the Construction Law states:

> for building materials, components and equipment which shall be purchased by the contractor as specified by the contract, the employer shall not designate the building materials, components, and equipment for the projects to be purchased by the contractor or designate manufacturers and suppliers thereof.

6.249 If the employer will provide materials and equipment, the brand, model, quantity, unit price, quality level, tendering place, and other necessary issues shall be specified in the construction project contract.[74]

Materials and Equipment Supplied by the Contractor

6.250 The contractor shall strictly follow designs and specifications when purchasing materials and equipment. Further, the contractor shall be responsible for the quality of these materials and project equipment.[75]

6.251 In addition, if the employer designates a manufacturer or a supplier for the materials and project equipment, the contractor has the right to decline. If the contractor follows the employer's instruction to purchase the materials and project equipment from a manufacturer designated by the employer, the contractor's liability may not be exempted for any quality or safety defects attributable to the purchased materials and project equipment. However, the employer also shall be jointly liable according to the degree of its own fault.

Labour Law Issues[76]

6.252 Labour law issues in construction arise from labour subcontracts and employment contracts, which are two contractual relations of different nature. The labour

74 See Article 8.1 of the 2017 Model Text, which stipulates: "If the employer supplies materials and project equipment itself, the brand, model, quantity, unit price, quality level, service address and other necessary items of the supplied materials and project equipment shall be specified in the annex "List of Materials and Equipment Supplied by the Employer" when the contract is signed. The contractor shall, 30 days in advance and through the supervisor, notify the employer in written form of delivery of materials and project equipment".

75 See Article 74 of the Construction Law, which stipulates: "a construction enterprise that has been found to have used inferior materials, unqualified construction materials, parts and components and equipment or committed other acts inconsistent with the blueprints or technical standards shall be ordered to correct the nonconforming behavior and be fined. An enterprise found to have serious violations shall be ordered to cease business operations for rectification, shall have its level of qualification reduced, or shall have its certificate of qualification revoked".

76 The laws and regulations relating to labour employment in China include: Construction Law, Civil Code, Law on Tenders and Bids, Labour Law, Labour Contract Law, Work Safety Law, Regulation on the Quality Management of Construction Projects, Administrative Regulations on the Work Safety of Construction Projects, Regulations on Work Safety Permits, Labour Protection and Supervision Regulations, Work-related Injury Insurance Regulations, Regulations on Administration of Enterprise Qualifications of the Construction Industry, Measures for Administration of Recognition and Punishment of Illegal Subcontracting and Illegal

subcontracting contract forms a contractual relationship between entities, whereas the employment contract forms a contractual relationship between the employer and the employee. The labour subcontract is a type of construction project contract governed by the Civil Code, the Construction Law and other relevant laws and regulations, whereas the employment contract is a contract to create an employment relationship between the employer and the employee. The most significant difference between the two contracts is that they form different legal relationships. The labour subcontract forms a contractual relationship between entities and is also subject to the "Labour Contract Law"[77] and the "Work-Related Injury Insurance Regulations".[78]

6.253 In China, the labour subcontract has the following features:

(1) A labour subcontract contract is subordinate to an existing construction project contract. A labour subcontract contract may not exist independent of a construction project contract;
(2) Both parties to a labour subcontract must possess the relevant qualifications as required by law. At present, a labour subcontractor must be qualified to conduct labour operations and get relevant permits. According to the latest opinions and guidance in 2021, however, it will only need registration rather than permit issuance in future practice;
(3) The subject of a labour subcontract is labour instead of project construction. Therefore, in general, the labour subcontractor is not required to provide materials and equipment.

Differences Between the Labour Subcontract and the Professional Services Subcontract

Different Contract Parties

6.254 Professional services subcontracting occurs between a general contracting entity and a professional service contracting entity, while labour subcontracting occurs between a general or professional contracting entity and a labour contracting entity.

Acts in Construction Subcontracting of Construction Projects (Trial) (J.S. [2014] No. 118), Interim Measures for Lifelong Quality Liability Investigation of Five Liability Entities' Project Principals of Construction Projects (J.Z. [2014] No. 124), Ten Provisions for Quality Safety Liability for Construction Project Managers (Trial) (J.Z. [2014] No. 123), Circular on Strictly Implementing Lifelong Liability Commitment System for Quality of Construction Projects (J.B.Z. [2014] No. 44), Interim Measures for Work Safety Standard Appraisal of Construction, Provisions for Safety Supervision of Construction of Houses, Buildings and Municipal Infrastructures Projects, Measures for Administration of Construction Subcontracting of Houses, Buildings and Municipal Infrastructures Projects, Interpretation of the Supreme People's Court on Problems about Application of Laws in Hearing Dispute Cases of Construction Contracts for Construction Projects, Interpretation of the Supreme People's Court on Several Problems about Application of Laws in Hearing Personal Injury Compensation Cases.

77 This law was passed at the 28th meeting of the standing committee of the National People's Congress, and was revised on 28 October 2012.

78 This regulation was promulgated by the 375th Order of the State Council, and was revised on 20 December 2010.

Different Subject Matter

6.255 The subject matter of the professional services subcontract is professional engineering services except for the main structure construction, while the subject matter of the labour subcontract is the labour services of personnel involved in project construction.

Different Legal Consequences

6.256 Both parties to a professional services subcontract contract bear joint and several liability for the quality and safety of the construction work, while the parties to a labour subcontract are not required to bear joint and several liability for the quality of the construction.

Different Standards for Calculating Remuneration.

6.257 In a labour subcontract, remuneration is calculated solely based on labour costs, while in a professional services subcontract, remuneration is calculated based on labour costs, material costs, machinery costs, and other relevant management expenses.

Performance and Take-Over

6.258 In China, to perform a construction project contract, the parties must abide by the requirements stipulated in the law and in the contract.[79] They must also follow other governmental requirements, which are reflected in the blueprint inspection, the construction permit, and the safety inspections.

6.259 The delivery of a completed construction project must comply with procedural and substantive requirements, including subjects, timing, methods, and transition content. It is noteworthy that the regulatory prerequisite for the delivery is the project acceptance.

6.260 Construction activities in China should comply with regulatory requirements and contractual requirements. First, laws and regulatory standards in China stipulate mandatory requirements[80] for project construction, with serious legal consequences to deter violations and the government ensures supervision for contract execution. Second, both parties in a contract may stipulate their obligations in the contract. Once those obligations are agreed upon, the parties must fully perform. Article 509 of the Civil Code provides:

> *each party shall fully perform its obligations as agreed upon. The parties shall abide by the principle of good faith, and perform obligations of notification, assistance, and confidentiality, in line with the nature and purpose of the contract and the transaction practice.*

The Civil Code also stipulates the defences for the party who is accused of breaching the contract, such as the defence of simultaneous performance, the defence of later performance and unsafe right of defence.

---

79 See Gao Yinli, Legal Issues and Analysis in Construction Contracts, China Construction Industry Press, 2012, p. 72.

80 See Article 58 of the Construction Law, which stipulates: "Construction enterprises are responsible for the quality of construction projects. Construction enterprises must carry out construction operation in accordance with design drawings of projects and construction technical standards, and shall not cheat on work and materials. The original designing institution shall bear the responsibility for altering the design of projects. Construction enterprises shall not alter the design of projects without authorization".

6.261 Additionally, in China, the legal provisions for the delivery after project completion also have the following requirements:

(1) The delivery shall be handled only after construction completion and project acceptance. According to the Construction Law, a project shall not be put into use without being inspected and accepted.[81] Therefore, in that situation where inspection and acceptance has not occurred, a delivery would be impossible;
(2) The delivery of projects should comply with the requirements prescribed by law and contracts, including technical standards, quality standards, and use and function standards. It also has to meet the requirements on the submission of completion documents;[82]
(3) All the documents relevant to completion and acceptance shall be submitted to the government agencies for approval or registration. The ownership certificate will be issued only after the completion and acceptance are recorded by the government agency. As Article 49 of the "Regulation on the Quality Management of Construction Projects" states:

> *the employer shall, within 15 days from the day when the construction project passes the completion check, submit the completion check report, the approval documents issued by the government agencies of planning, public security and fire prevention, environmental protection, and so on, to the government agency that is in charge of construction administrative issues, for archival purposes.*

Contract Price

6.262 Contract price provisions are the core clauses of contracts with considerations. For a general contract with consideration, the contract price may not be adjusted once it is confirmed. It is another story for construction project contracts. Due to the long performance period of a construction project contract, the market prices of labour service, materials, project equipment and machines may fluctuate. Meanwhile, the frequent occurrence of variations, claims and breaches also justify the floating the contract price in a construction project contract.

6.263 In the Model Text, the terms related to contract prices include signed contract price, contract price, and settled contract price. The signed contract price is a fixed price indicated in the winning bid and, generally, in the winning notification. Contract price is a dynamic figure, which is determined after the completion of construction. It serves as the basis for the whole compensation.

81 See Article 61 of the Construction Law, which provides: "only after a completed construction project is proved to meet the standards through examination can it be delivered for use. Construction projects having not been examined and accepted or having failed in examination shall not be delivered for use".

82 See Article 6.1.5 of the 2017 Model Text stipulates: "prior to project delivery, the contractor shall clear all its project equipment, surplus materials, waste and all temporary works out of the construction site and keep the construction site tidy and clean."".

6.264 Article 12 of the "Measures for the Administration of Pricing in the Construction project contract-issuing and Contracting of Construction Projects",[83] issued by the Ministry of Housing and Urban–Rural Development, prescribes composition and adjustment of the contract price as:

> The tenderee and the bid winner shall enter into a contract at the winning bid price. Matters concerning the contract price shall be agreed by the employer and the contractor. Those matters generally include payment and settlement of contract price, advance payment, progress payment and final payment, as well as the adjustment of the contract price.

6.265 Article 13 of the same document provides that

> to determine the contract price, the employer and the contractor shall consider the influence from the variation in the market environment and the fluctuation in prices for various production elements. If the bill of quantities is implemented to calculate the price of a construction project, the employer and the contractor should determine the contract price on the basis of unit price. If the construction project is small-scale with low technical difficulty and a short construction period, the employer and the contractor may use the total price method to determine the contract price. If the construction project is undertaken for urgent rescue or disaster relief and involves complicated construction technology, the employer and the contractor may adopt the cost-plus fee method to determine the contract price.

6.266 Article 14 of the same documents provides that "*the employer and the contractor shall agree in the contract on the method for adjusting the contract price under the following circumstances:*

(1) *changes in laws, regulations, rules or relevant national policies affect the contract price;*
(2) *the governmental project management agency promulgates mandatory price adjustment provisions;*
(3) *the project design has been changed and approved;*
(4) *an increase in expenses arises due to the employer's alternation of the initial plans;*
(5) *other situations as agreed upon by the parties*".

6.267 These terms conform to the FIDIC Red Book which states that it is fair and reasonable to adjust the price of the contract when unforeseen variations occur. Standard Method of Measurement for Works encourages the parties to adopt the unit pricing method in general, but in PRC practice the parties tend to adopt the fixed-price method.

Payment

6.268 Payment in a construction project contract includes advance payment, progress payment, and final payment.

83 This regulation was passed at the 9th standing committee meeting of the Ministry of Housing and Urban–Rural Development, and was implemented on 1 February 2014.

6.269 For the advance payment, the "National Standard Code of Valuation with Bill Quantity" provides advance payment guidance. Generally, the advance payment should not be lower than 10% of the contract price but not higher than 30% of the contract price.

6.270 The progress payment generally may be paid in accordance with the milestone events or be calculated and paid in monthly installments.

6.271 As for the final payment, generally, 97% of the final payment should be paid after project completion, with the remaining balance serving as the quality deposit. However, the final payment may be paid in full if quality warranty guarantee is received.

6.272 To determine the priority of construction project payments, Article 807[84] of the Civil Code stipulates that the contractor's payment claim has higher priority than other security rights on the construction project.

Author's Opinion

6.273 On the validity of the contract terms regarding the prerequisites of the employer's payment. In the engineering construction field, general contractors include language in the subcontract's payment clauses that "the payment depends on the employer's payment". This language means that the general contractor only makes payment to the subcontractor when it receives the employer's payment. Similar terms used in contracts in Europe and the US express this idea as "pay if paid".

6.274 In China, experts continue to argue whether "pay if paid" clauses are valid. Article 158 of Civil Code stipulates: "a civil juristic act may have conditions attached to it. Conditional civil juristic acts shall take effect when the relevant conditions are met". The "pay if paid" clause treats the subcontract payment as a conditional civil juristic act, and this act takes effect only when the condition is met. Under the theory of autonomy of will, this clause should be valid. However, some experts argue that this clause is unfair because the general contractor is abusing its dominant contractual power. Due to this abuse and unfairness, these experts believe "pay if paid" clauses should be invalid.

6.275 In the author's opinion, if both parties have a full understanding and are willing to assume the risks, the "pay if paid" clause should be deemed valid. However, the validity should be subject to conditions and have a narrow scope. To ensure the general contractor does not abuse this clause, legislation or judicial guidance could impose notification obligations on the general contractor. In other words, when a dispute between the general contractor and subcontractor occurs, the general contractor should be required to provide evidence to prove that it has fulfilled its *bona fide* obligations allowing it to claim payment from the employer. If the general contractor is unable to provide such evidence, then it may not use the "pay if paid" clause as a defence to the subcontractor's payment claim.

84 See Article 807 of the Civil Code, which stipulates: "If the developer fails to pay the price in accordance with the contract, the contractor may demand payment from the developer within a reasonable period. Where the developer fails to pay the price at the end of such period, the contractor may enter into an agreement with the developer to liquidate the project, and may also petition the People's Court to auction the project in accordance with the law, unless such project is not fit for liquidation or auction in light of its nature. The payment of the construction project price shall have priority in being paid from the proceeds from the liquidation or auction of the project".

Defects Liability and Limitation

6.276 "Quality[85] defect" means that the construction quality does not comply with mandatory statutory or regulatory standards or with the standards in the design documents and the contract.[86] According to the Construction Law and other relevant administrative regulations, if any quality defect is attributable to the contractor, the contractor has the obligation to repair the defect. The obligation to repair includes the obligation to amend, replace and redo. In terms of responsibility, the responsibility for quality defects includes warranty obligations and legal consequences. The former refers to the obligation to repair defects, whereas the latter refers to the obligation to compensate for defects.

6.277 Defects liability in construction in China have has the following characteristics:

(1) The defects liability period is different from the warranty period. Generally, the defects liability period does not exceed 24 months,[87] while the warranty period must comply with the "Regulation on the Quality Management of Construction Projects". Even the minimum statutory quality warranty period is longer than the defect liability period. For example, the quality warranty period of waterproofing project is five years.[88] The defects liability is different from both the warranty period and the FIDIC defects notification period.

(2) During the defects liability period, the contractor becomes liable for a defect when notified of the defect.[89]

(3) The defects liability period may be extended for up to 24 months.[90]

(4) The quality deposit must be refunded or the quality warranty guarantee must be terminated immediately when the defects liability period expires.

85 "Quality" is defined as "the sum of the distinct and indistinct characteristics and features of the functioning subject", Quality and Safety Control on Construction Projects, Mechanic Industrial Press, 2004, p. 1.

86 See Article 2.2 of the "Measures for the Management of Construction Project Quality Deposits", which stipulates: "Defect means that the construction project quality does not comply with the mandatory standard or design document for the construction project, or the agreement in the contracting contract".

87 See Article 15.2.1 of the 2017 Model Text, which stipulates: "the defects liability period shall be calculated from the date of actual completion. The contract parties shall agree to the defects liability period stipulated in the special terms and conditions, which shall not exceed 24 months".

88 See Article 40 of the "Regulation on the Quality Management of Construction Projects", which provides:
"(1) For infrastructure, foundations and main parts of a building, the quality repair guarantee period shall be the number of years of reasonable use as prescribed in the design documents; (2) For the roof waterproofing, and the leak prevention of the toilets, rooms and outside walls that should be waterproofed, the quality repair guarantee period shall be 5 years; (3) For the heat supply and air-conditioning systems, the quality repair guarantee period shall be 2 heating periods and 2 air-conditioning periods; (4) For electric wires, gas, water supply and drainage pipes, equipment installation and decoration, the quality repair guarantee period shall be 2 years.
The quality repair guarantee period for other projects shall be agreed by the employer and the contractor. The warranty period starts from the date of project completion acceptance".

89 See Article 15.4.3 of the 2017 Model Text, which stipulates: "If, during the warranty period, the employer detects any defect or damage in the use of the works received, the employer shall in writing notify the contractor for repair. Where it is necessary to repair the defect or damage immediately in urgent situations, the employer may notify the contractor orally and confirm the oral notice in writing within 48 hours after the oral notice. The contractor shall arrive at the site and repair the defect or damage within the reasonable time limit agreed in the special terms and conditions of the contract".

90 See Article 15.2.2 of the 2017 Model Text, which stipulates: "after the engineering is qualified through completion acceptance, if the works, the unit works or any main equipment cannot be used according to its original designated purpose because of any defect or damage attributable to the contractor, the employer may ask the contractor to extend the defects liability period and to provide an extension notice prior to expiration of the original defects liability period. However, the extended defects liability period shall not exceed 24 months".

Variations[91]

6.278 According to the Civil Code in China, a construction project contract shall be reduced to writing. Disputes frequently occur during the performance of construction project contracts due to variations in terms made orally between the parties. Variations could impact the construction time and the contract price, which would in turn cause disputes. Therefore, parties should pay special attention to procedural and substantive requirements for variation. For variation that leads to claims and price adjustments, the construction laws in China provide the following:

(1) According to the "Code of Valuation with Bill Quantity", "construction variation" means that, during the performance of a construction project contract, and as requested by the employer or requested by the contractor and approved by the employer, there is: (1) An increase, decrease or cancellation of any work on the project; (2) a change of the construction process, sequence or period; (3) an amendment of design drawings; (4) a change of construction conditions; (5) a change of contract conditions or an increase, decrease or change of quantities due to mistakes or omissions in the bill of the quantities.

According to the Model Text, variation during construction includes: Increase or decrease of any work under the contract, or introduction of additional work; cancellation of any work under the contract, except the work delegated to others for performance; change of the quality standards or features of any work under the contract; change of the baseline, elevation, location, and size of the project; or change of the time or the sequence of project performance.

(2) A variation should be conducting according to the proper procedures. Due to the complexity of managing variation, generally speaking, the variation procedures for should be specified in the construction project contract. The "Standard Document" (2007) specifies variation procedures in detail and prescribes requirements for the variation proposals and performance requested by the employer and the supervisor. Of these variation procedures, parties should pay special attention to:

i. Request for variation. No matter which party requests a change, a change order must be issued through the supervisor to the contractor. The change order must indicate the project scope and the contents of the item changes. Such change shall be permitted by the employer;

ii. With respect to evaluating the variation and its impact on the construction period, three principles must be followed. First, when there is an identical item in bill of quantities or budget documents, such price can be used in the evaluation. Second, when there is no identical item but a similar item, such similar item price can be used in the evaluation. Third, when the variation would cause the original price to fluctuate by more than 15%, then the parties should renegotiate a new, fair price. As mentioned before, the variation shall be reduced to writing and contain

91 See *Tan Jinghui*, Bidding Procurement Contract Management, China Planning Press, 2015.

the scope, reasoning, and content of the variation, as well as the impact on the contract price and construction period;

iii. Performance of variation. If the contractor does not agree with the variation order issued by the supervisor, the contractor shall articulate the reasons why it is unable to perform the variation order immediately after receiving the order. The reasons can include the engineering procedures, the work procedures, and the impact on the construction period. The employer shall thoroughly consider the contractor's reasons. If the contractor's reasoning has merits, the employer shall notify the contractor through the supervisor to revoke the variation order.

Delay and Disruption[92]

6.279 "Delay" means an extension in the actual construction period resulting in an increase in construction costs.

6.280 "Disruption" means that the construction is disrupted by strike, shut-down, delayed payment or other unforeseen incidents, resulting in the extension of the construction period and the increase of construction costs. In practice, it is unnecessary to distinguish between a "delay" and a "disruption", but it is necessary to analyze the specific incident to determine if the compensation is merited.

6.281 A construction delay is when the actual project progress lags behind schedule. Generally speaking, a delay during construction can be classified according to its cause and its legal status. In terms of the cause, delays can be classified as events caused by the employer, events caused by the contractor, events resulting from neutral causes, and *Force Majeure*. In terms of the legal status, a delay can be classified as a breach, a variation, a neutral incident or a *Force Majeure* event.

6.282 Article 7.5 of the Model Text provides guidance on construction delay.

6.283 In a dispute over the cause of an extension in the construction period, the contractor always claims that there shall be extension of work period which the employer claims the opposite. Therefore, the contractor bears the burden to prove that the delay was not caused by the contractor. If the contractor fails to meet this burden, then the contractor will be liable for the delay.

Causes for Delay

6.284 Causes for a delay can be classified as the employer, the contractor, and other sources. They can also be classified from the perspective of different conditions of generation as breaches, adverse conditions, bad weather, other *Force Majeure*, and variation. However, not all delays result in an extension of the construction period. Two criteria determine whether the extension is allowable. First, does the delay affect the completion of the key milestones, or whether or not it increases costs due to an extension of the construction period even if it does not affect the key milestones. Second, is the delay caused by

92 See Tan Jinghui, Focus on Legal Issues in Construction, Law Press, 2016.

incidents that cannot be attributed to the contractor? The contractor may claim compensation if the delay cannot be imputed to the contractor.

Extension Caused by the Employer

6.285 Article 803 of the Civil Code stipulates: "when the employer fails to provide raw materials, equipment, construction site, funds, or technical information in accordance with the contractual requirements, the contractor may extend project milestones, and is entitled to claim damages". According to the Model Text and traditional practice, delaying events that can be imputed to the employer include the employer's failure to obtain the construction permit, delay in providing the place for the construction, delay in providing the construction drawings, variation in design and in the engineering progress, delay in delivery of goods, delay in payment, and delay in inspection and acceptance.[93]

6.286 These "delaying events" do not always result in an actual delay in construction progress. Whether the event constitutes an actual delay in construction progress should be analyzed on a case-by-case basis. This analysis should focus on whether the events affect the completion of the milestones in the schedule. An analysis of this kind is often complicated.

6.287 The following guidance usually applies to delays in construction progress caused by the employer:

(1) If a delay is caused by the employer's failure to provide construction conditions, including the lack of drawings, construction site, geological conditions and underground pipelines, which results in work impracticability for the contractor, the commencement date is the date on which the employer meets those required conditions;

(2) The extension of construction period is allowed when there are errors in the technical data, such as construction drawings, engineering geology data, and underground pipeline layout, which are provided by the employer and result in work stoppage, enforced idleness, or work alteration;

---

93 See *Article 7.5.1 of the 2017 Model Text, which stipulates: "if, during the performance of the contract, a delay in the project or an increase in project cost is caused by the following circumstances, the employer shall be obliged to bear the losses due to the delay in the project and the increase in project cost and shall pay a reasonable profit to the contractor.*

(1) The employer fails to provide drawings or the drawings fail to conform to the contract;

(2) The employer fails to provide construction site, construction conditions, basic information, permits, approvals and other conditions of work as agreed upon in the contract;

(3) The base point, reference line, bench mark and other written materials provided by the employer contain any errors due to the employer's negligence;

(4) The employer disputes that the commencement notice was issued within 7 days from the proposed project commencement date;

(5) The employer fails to pay the advance payment, progress payment or completion settlement within the date specified in the contract;

(6) The supervisor fails to give instructions, approvals, and other documents as stipulated in the contract;

(7) Other circumstances specified in the contract.

If the project is not started from the proposed date of commencement due to the employer, the employer should postpone the completion date according to the actual commencement date, to ensure that actual project duration is no less than the total calendar days specified in the contract. Any delay in the construction period due to the employer must be in accordance with Article 7.2.2 (Revision of construction progress schedule)".

(3) If the employer fails to provide the materials and equipment per the contract requirements, including failure to supply materials and equipment on time, or the quality or quantity of materials and equipment provided are not in line with the contract requirements, then the extension of construction period is allowed;
(4) If the employer or the supervisor provides wrongful instructions causing work stoppage, enforced idleness, or work alteration, a construction period is allowed;
(5) According to the Model Text, if the employer delays the advance payment or the progress payment even after the contractor submits a claim for the payment and for any compensation due to a delay in construction progress caused by the late payment, the contractor may stop work and the time for completion shall be extended unless otherwise stipulated in the contract;[94]
(6) The general contractor shall bear joint and several liabilities for the subcontracting; that is to say, the general contractor shall be held responsible for the quality and construction progress in subcontracted work. However, if the subcontractor was selected by the employer rather than the general contractor, Article 13 of the "Judicial Interpretation for Construction Project Contract for Construction Project" shall apply even though ordered-subcontracting[95] and ordered-supplying[96] are prohibited under Chinese law. Article 13 provides that the employer shall be liable for losses arising from delays caused by the subcontractor. The general contractor shall assume no responsibility if the subcontractor was chosen by the employer unless the general contractor was involved in the selection of the subcontractor. In practice, it is difficult to prove that the employer selected the subcontractor since most selections are made off the record.

Delay Caused by Adverse Conditions and Adverse Weather

6.288 Adverse conditions include unforeseen natural conditions, manmade obstacles, subsurface geographic and hydro-logical conditions, contaminants encountered on the construction site, and other circumstances specified in the contract. Weather conditions are not included in this category.[97]

94 See Article 16.1.1 of the 2017 Model Text, which stipulates: "if the contract price is not paid according to the contract due to the employer, the contractor shall notify the employer requiring the employer to take effective measures against the default. If the employer fails to make correction within 28 days after receiving the notice from the contractor, the contractor may suspend the construction of corresponding parts and notify the supervisor."".

95 See Article 66 of the "Construction Projects Bidding Method" stipulates: "the employer may not directly designate contractor". This regulation was implemented on 1 May 2003.

96 See Article 55 of the Construction Law , which stipulates: "For building materials, components and equipment which shall be purchased by the project contracting units as specified by the contracts, the out-contracting units shall not designate the building materials, components and equipment for the projects to be purchased by the contracting units or designate manufacturers and suppliers thereof".

97 See Article 7.6 of the 2017 Model Text, which stipulates: "if the contractor is experiencing unfavourable conditions, the contractor shall continue the work by taking proper measures to overcome the unfavorable conditions, and notify the employer and the supervisor in a timely manner. The notice shall specify physical/ material conditions and the unforeseen reasons considered by the contractor. The supervisor shall promptly provide instructions with the consent of the employer. In case of any change in the instruction, the change must be in accordance with Article 10 [change]. The employer shall be liable for losses caused by any increase in the cost generated from reasonable measures and/or delay in construction period".

6.289 Adverse weather refer to weather conditions less than a *Force Majeure* event but still having a serious effect on ordinary construction activities. Industry insiders have different understandings on whether an extension should be allowed for adverse weather conditions. The 1999 Model Text did not mention the extension issue. According to Article 17.3 of the FIDIC, adverse weather conditions are defined as any unforeseen natural forces that cannot reasonably be expected, despite the fact that an experienced contractor has taken appropriate preventive measures. Under the FIDIC, this risk shall be assumed by the employer. In current market practice in China, considering equity and fairness, adverse weather conditions risks are assumed by the employer. An extension shall be allowed in this situation.

6.290 Normally, it is difficult for an experienced contractor to predict adverse weather conditions and to prevent its effects. We think, considering the principle of fairness, the attributes embodied in engineering construction project contracts, and the risks boundary theory in construction project contracts, the risk of adverse weather conditions shall be assumed by the employer, and an extension shall be allowed in this situation.

Delay Caused by Force Majeure

6.291 *Force Majeure* is a statutory liability exemption situation, referring to exceptional events that cannot be imputed to either party, and are unforeseeable when signing the contract, and cannot be controlled, avoided or overcome by either party. *Force Majeure* results in one or both parties' failure to perform the contract on time or at all. The failing party may be exempted from the liability under the contract if the party cannot perform continually or promptly. *Force Majeure* is defined in the "Civil Code"[98] as objective circumstances that are unforeseeable and cannot be controlled, avoided or overcome.

6.292 *Force Majeure* events are generally classified into two types: Natural incidents (e.g., earthquake, typhoon, flood, tsunami) and social incidents (e.g., war, pirate attack, strike, government action). In China, delay due to *Force Majeure* cannot be imputed to the contractor, just as in the international practice. In this sense, an extension is normally allowed. The rationale is where the employer has the property right over the construction project; therefore, the losses due to *Force Majeure* should be assumed by the owner; in other words, the employer. By the same token, if the material and equipment are supplied by the contractor and are destroyed by a *Force Majeure* event, the contractor cannot claim compensation since the owner assumes the property risk.

6.293 However, according to the Civil Code, the breaching party shall assume responsibility for and bear the consequences of a breach of contract caused by *Force Majeure* unless otherwise provided by law.[99]

98 "Article 180 of the Civil Code", which provides: "A Force Majeure means any objective circumstance that is unforeseeable, inevitable, and insurmountable".

99 See Article 180 of the Civil Code", which provides:"A Force Majeure means any objective circumstance that is unforeseeable, inevitable, and insurmountable".

6.294 The Model Text, as adopted in practice in China's construction market, also stipulates provisions regarding *Force Majeure*.[100]

Liquidated Damages and Other Damages

6.295 Liquidated damages for the delay in construction progress are not specified in construction-related laws, nor in the Model Text. Liquidated damages, including punitive damages, may be stipulated in the contract, per Chinese Civil Code. If the liquidated damages specified in the contract are too high or too low compared to the actual loss, the liquidated damages shall be adjusted accordingly. If the liquidated damages specified in the contract are too low compared to the actual loss, then the awarded damages should be adjusted to the level of actual loss; if the liquidated damages specified in the contract are too high, then it can be reduced to a reasonable level by the people's courts or an arbitration institution requested by the parties.[101]

6.296 According to the original "the Meeting Minutes on the Implementation of the Civil Code by Courts Nationwide"[102] promulgated by the Supreme People's Court, the liquidated damages specified in the contract cannot exceed 30% of the actual loss; however, in practice, it is difficult to calculate liquidated damages as a percentage of the actual loss.

6.297 In construction project contract practice, liquidated damages for delay in construction generally exceed 5% of the contract price.

---

100 See Article 17.3.2 of the 2017 Model Text, which stipulates: "*Force Majeure* causes casualties, property losses, cost increases and/or delay in construction period, etc., the parties concerned shall assume responsibilities according to the following principles:

(1) Damage in permanent works, materials and engineering equipment on the site, as well as third-party casualties and property losses caused by the damage in project, shall be borne by the employer;

(2) Contractor's damage in construction equipment shall be borne by contractor;

(3) Employee casualties and property losses shall be borne by the employer and the contractor respectively;

(4) If the contractor fails to fulfill its contract obligations, and there is a delay in project duration due to the *Force Majeure*, time for completion shall be extended, and losses resulting in the contractor's stoppage of work shall be borne by the employer and the contractor respectively. Wages for employees during the stoppage of work shall be borne by the employer;

(5) If the employer requires work to be expedited due to a delay caused by the *Force Majeure*, the increased fees arising thereof shall be borne by the employer;

(6) During the stoppage of work, costs relating to the contractor's care, cleaning and repair of works according to the requirements of the employer shall be borne by the employer".

101 See Article 585 of the Civil Code, which stipulates: "the parties may agree that if one party breaches the contract, it will pay a certain sum of liquidated damages to the other party in light of the degree of breach, or agree to a method for calculation of damages for the loss resulting from the party's breach. Where the amount of liquidated damages is less than the loss resulting from the breach, a party may petition the people's court or an arbitration institution to increase the amount; where the amount of liquidated damages exceeds the loss resulting from the breach, a party may petition the People's Court or an arbitration institution to decrease the amount as appropriate".

102 See Article 11(3) of the "Notice by the Supreme People's Court regarding Issuing the Meeting Minutes on the Implementation of the Civil Code by Courts Nationwide", which stipulates: "Where a party requests a people's court to reduce liquidated damages, the people's court shall, based on the losses provided for in Article 584 of the Civil Code, take into account such comprehensive factors as the performance of the contract and the degree of fault of the party, and adjudicate under the principles of fairness and good faith. If the agreed liquidated damages exceed 30% of the losses determined in accordance with Article 584 of the Civil Code, it may generally be determined as 'significantly higher than the losses incurred' provided for in paragraph 2 of Article 585 of the Civil Code. If a party claims that the amount of agreed liquidated damages is significantly high and requests an appropriate reduction, it shall bear the burden of proof; if the other party claims that the agreement on liquidated damages is reasonable, it shall also produce corresponding evidence."

6.298 Compensation for poor quality is also commonly seen in construction project contracts. Article 80 of the Construction Law stipulates that if a loss results from inferior construction quality during the reasonable lifespan of the buildings, the damaged party is entitled to make claims against the responsible party. However, it should be noted that the right to claim against poor quality should be distinguished in different phases, such as construction period, defect liability period, warranty period, and post-warranty period, resulting in different responsibilities and legal consequences.

Insurance[103]

6.299 Generally speaking, insurance in construction project contracts includes construction property insurance, work-related injury insurance, third-party liability insurance, and other relevant insurance. The employer is required to purchase all these types of insurance, except construction property insurance, which the parties may stipulate in the contract who will purchase.[104] If the employer authorizes the contractor to purchase the insurance, then the insurance premium and other related expenses incurred shall be accounted to the employer. The contractor shall purchase the property insurance for all the construction equipment.

6.300 In terms of work-related injury insurance, the employer shall purchase work-related injury insurance for all workers on the construction site and pay the premium. The supervisor and the third party, hired by the employer, shall purchase work-related insurance for their workers.[105]

6.301 The regulation of work-related injury insurance in the Construction Law has transitioned from mandatory purchase to voluntary purchase. Current law provides that construction entities can decide by themselves whether to purchase work-related injury insurance for their employees, and in construction involving hazardous operations, the entities are encouraged to purchase personal accident insurance for the employees.

6.302 Article 2 of the "Regulations on Work-related Injury Insurance" provides that:

> enterprises, institutions, social organizations, private non-profit entities, funds, law firms, accounting firms and other organizations and individual proprietors with employees shall participate in work-related injury insurance and pay work-the premiums for all of the staff or hired workers.

---

103 See Tan Jinghui, The Jurisdiction, Cognizance and Commitment of Quality Responsibility After the Expiry of Construction Project Quality Guarantee Period, 2016.

104 See Article 18.1 of the 2017 Model Text, which stipulates: "the employer shall purchase comprehensive construction risk insurance, unless otherwise stipulated by special provisions in the contract. If the employer authorizes the contractor to purchase the insurance, then the insurance premium and other related expenses incurred shall be borne by the employer".

105 See Article 18.2 of the 2017 Model Text, which stipulates: "the employer shall purchase work-related injury insurance according to legal rules, and pay for work-related injury insurance for all employees in the construction site, and for the supervisor and the third party appointed by the employer to perform the contract; the contractor shall purchase work-related injury insurance for its own employees and all other employees working on the project, and also require the subcontractor and the third party appointed by contractor to participate in work-related injury insurance".

6.303 The "Opinions on Promoting the Insurance of Construction Project Quality Construction"[106] (2005 No. 133), promulgated by the Ministry of Housing and Urban–Rural Development, provide the legal basis for supporting insurance markets playing a role in a healthy and stable construction market. In the Opinions, construction project quality insurance is described as a method for the construction project to transfer economic liability caused by potential quality defects. From this definition, it can be deduced that the insured period for the quality insurance spans the whole lifespan of the construction project. The post-warranty quality liability should be addressed by the construction quality liability insurance. In China, unlike in France, the construction laws do not stipulate the insurance period and the insurance scope.

6.304 With joint support from the Ministry of Construction and the China Insurance Regulatory Commission, the People's Insurance Company of China (PICC) initiated construction quality insurance products in 14 cities, including Beijing, Shanghai, Tianjin, Dalian, Qingdao, Xiamen, Shenzhen, and Lanzhou, kicking off the quality insurance practice of construction project in China. This pilot project was designed to implement the mandatory engineering quality insurance system in China and introduced the new insurance system in conformity with the market-oriented economy. The new system will gradually replace the quality deposit system in the construction industry. The construction project quality insurance covers the compensation for accidents and damages to buildings resulting from latent defects of construction quality and occurring during the insurance period, and it can provide as long as a ten-year insurance period for the main structure of buildings. Meanwhile, for leakage problems with construction work, a five-year additional leakage insurance is available for optional purchase.

6.305 Construction insurance is one of the key solutions to address the issue of construction quality responsibility. Future market practice and precedents will help further develop this model.

Suspension

6.306 The contractor's right to suspend work can be justified for two reasons: Employer causes and administrative supervision causes. The relevant legal theories and stipulations addressing the contractor's right to suspend work are discussed as follows.[107]

6.307 The construction project contractor's right to suspend work means that the contractor can suspend all or part of the construction work per legal stipulations and contractual conditions. The contractor's right to suspend work may be prescribed by law or contract, the latter of which manifests as consent between the employer and the contractor. In China, contractors often exercise the right to suspend work when the employer breaches the contract. In this situation, the suspension works as a civil defence. In addition, the contractor may exercise the suspension right when the construction entity fails to meet the necessary requirements set out in laws and administrative regulations. In this situation, the suspension right works as a defence and an obligation.

106 Jointly issued by the Ministry of Housing and Urban–Rural Development and China Insurance Regulatory Commission on 5 August 2005.

107 See Tan Jinghui, Focus on Legal Issues in Construction, Law Press, 2016.

6.308 Civil rights are classified into the right of disposal, the right of claim, the right of defence and the right of formation based on their different functions. The contractor's right to suspend work is a temporary right of defence, that is, where a construction entity breaks laws or breaches the contract, the contractor can use the right to deny the other party's request to resume the work. But once the default or illegal behavior is eliminated, the contractor's right to suspend work terminates too.

6.309 The Civil Code stipulates the right of defence for concurrent performance, the right of defence for first fulfill, and unsafe right of defence. Sometimes, the contractor's suspension right is related to the first fulfil right of defence.[108] The construction progress is usually sequenced as follows: Advance payment, construction, progress payment, construction, final payment, warranty, and payment of deposit. The timing of the progress payment may be paid by monthly, every two months, every three months, or in accordance with project milestones. The Contractor may exercise the suspension right if the employer fails to pay the progress payment as stipulated in the contract, which conforms with Article 526 of the Civil Code: That when the parties' performance is sequential, the party who is to perform second is entitled to decline to perform if the party required to perform first renders non-conforming performance or no performance at all. If the contractor suspends work due to the employer's deteriorating economic situation, such as transfer of assets, withdrawal of funds, evasion of debts, loss of credibility, the contractor may exercise the unsafe right of defence specified in Article 527[109] of the Civil Code. Thus, the contractor's suspension right may be used either as the defence for first fulfill or unsafe right of defence.

6.310 When the employer has violated relevant construction laws and regulations, impeded construction activities, and damaged the interests of society, the contractor has the right to suspend work.

6.311 For example, according to the Construction Law,[110] a construction entity should apply for approval from the related government agencies before it: Temporarily occupies area beyond the approved site area; engages in construction that could damage roads, pipelines, power lines, telecommunications equipment and other public facilities, or cause temporary power blackouts, water supply shutdowns, or traffic disruptions; or engages in an operation where blasting is involved. If the construction entity fails to obtain the approval, the contractor may stop the corresponding work, and only resume work after the

108 Although some scholars argue that it is not necessary to differentiate "defense" from "the defense right of simultaneous performance", the author chose to stick with the Civil Code.

109 See Article 527 of the Civil Code, which stipulates: "the party required to perform first may suspend its performance if it has conclusive evidence establishing that the other party: (1) has had a serious deterioration in its business conditions; (2) has engaged in transferred assets or withdrawn funds for the purpose of evading debts; (3) has lost its business creditworthiness; (4) is experiencing any other circumstance that will or may cause it to lose its ability to perform. Where a party suspends performance without conclusive evidence, it shall be liable for breach of contract".

110 See Article 42 of the Construction Law, which stipulates: "in accordance with relevant state regulations, units undertaking projects shall go through application and approval procedures for: (1) temporary occupation of areas not covered by approved construction programs; (2) actions likely to damage roads, pipes and electric wires, power supply and post and telecommunication equipment and other public facilities; (3) temporary cut-off of water and power supply or suspension of traffic; (4) blasting operations; (5) other matters for which application and approval procedures are required in accordance with the stipulations of laws and regulations".

approval is obtained. Construction activities are conducted in part for the public welfare, and they involve public transportation, health, environment, and other public interests. A contractor's failure to fulfill obligations set out in construction laws and regulations not only infringe employer's rights under the contract but also encroach on public interests. Thus, the contractor's right to suspend work protects its own rights as well as the public. From this perspective, the contractor's failure to suspend work when warranted is not simply a waiver of its own rights, but is also assistance in the employer's infringement of public interests. Thus, when the employer violates construction laws and regulations and impedes construction activities, the contractor not only may but also should exercise the right to suspend work.

Elements for the Contractor's Suspension Right

6.312 According to Article 16.1.1 of the Model Text, the contractor may suspend work if the employer breached its contractual duty under eight kinds of circumstances:

(1) Fails to provide the notice of commencement at least seven days prior to the stipulated starting date;
(2) Fails to pay the progress payment;
(3) Performs by itself or transfers the cancelled work to others in violation of Article 10.1(2) (scope of change);
(4) Provides material and engineering equipment that do not conform to the stipulated specifications, quantity or quality, or delivers it late or to the wrong place;
(5) Breaches the contract to get the construction suspended;
(6) Fails, without justification, to provide instructions for resumption of work;
(7) Indicates that it will not perform primary obligations under the contract;
(8) Fails to perform other obligations under the contract.

6.313 Article 16.1.1 also stipulates:

> except for the breach of the contract set out in Article 7, the contractor may provide notice requiring the employer to take corrective measures effectively. If the employer fails to take corrective measures within 28 days after receiving the notice from the contractor, the contractor has the right to suspend the corresponding parts of the work, and notify the supervisor of it.

Termination

6.314 In China, the termination of a construction project contract can be divided into two categories in practice: Stipulated termination and statutory termination. Statutory termination has two elements: Whether a fundamental breach of contract occurs; and whether the purpose of the contract cannot be realized. Stipulated termination can be invoked unilaterally by either party if the contract's termination conditions of are met. If the employer terminates the contract arbitrarily, then the employer must compensate the contractor, including for the contractor's costs and expected benefits.

6.315 Termination of a construction project contract is a major event in the performance of the construction project contract. Unless the contract purpose cannot be realized, the employer and the contractor normally would not choose to terminate the contract, since the termination of the contract would harm both sides. Normally, termination of the construction project contract is caused by the employer, the contractor, *Force Majeure*, or other incidents that cannot be imputed to either party.

6.316 One issue in the termination of the construction project contract is the payment settlement for unfinished projects.

6.317 Article 24(1) and Article 19(3) of the "Interpretation of the Supreme People's Court on Certain Issues Concerning the Application of Law in the Trial of Cases Involving Project Construction Project Contract Disputes(1)" (2020 No.25) once stipulated:

> After the construction project contract is terminated, if the completed construction project is qualified, the employer shall pay the corresponding project price according to the agreement; If the completed construction work fails inspection due to poor quality, then Article 577 of the Civil Code.

6.318 The 2017 Model Text also contains provisions on contract termination due to breach of contract. According to Article 16.1.4 [Payment after termination due to breach of contract by the employer],

> if the contractor terminates the contract in accordance with the contract's stipulation, the employer shall make the following payments within 28 days after the termination of the contract, and the performance guarantee of the contractor is relieved: (1) Payments for the completed construction work prior to the termination of the contract; (2) payments for the engineering materials, equipment and other goods used for the construction that have been purchased by the contractor; (3) costs for the contractor's evacuation from construction site and dismissal of personnel; (4) liquidated damages occurring before the termination of the contract as stipulated in the contract; (5) other payments to the contractor as stipulated by the contract; (6) any deposit made by the contractor as a guarantee; (7) losses incurred by the contractor due to the termination of the contract.

6.319 If the contracting parties fail to agree on the settlement for the termination of the contract, then the Article 20 of Dispute Settlement applies. Therefore, the contractor shall make arrangements for the preservation and transfer of the completed work, purchased materials and equipment, and relevant documents, and for the removal of equipment and personnel from the construction site. The employer shall provide necessary assistance for the contractor's removal.

6.320 Similarly, if the employer rescinds the contract due to a default by the contractor, Article 16.2.3 of the Model Text [Breach of contract by the contractor] stipulates:

> unless otherwise stipulated in the contract, if any circumstances specified in item (7) of Article 16.2.1 occur, or if the contractor fails to make rectification within reasonable period after the supervisor gives the rectification notice, to the extent that the purposes of the contract are frustrated, then the employer has the right to terminate the contract. After the termination of the contract, in order to complete the construction, the employer has the right to use the materials, equipment, and temporary projects left on the construction site, and the relevant documents prepared by the contractor. The parties to the contract shall stipulate the method of bearing the corresponding expenses in the terms of the special contract. The behavior of the employer to continue to use will not relieve the contractor's liability for the breach of contract.

Claim

6.321 Claim is a frequent event in engineering practice. Both the employer and the contractor have the right to bring claim under the construction project contract. It is the same as the contract liability in the contract conditions and constitutes a strict contract restriction relationship. The claim in construction project contract is mutual, including the employer claim and contractor claim. Normally, the contractor's claim against the employer is called "claim", and vice versa, referred to as "counterclaim". In practice, the contractor's claims can include extension of construction period and compensation for costs. The employer's claims against the contractor can include deduction in payment and extension of the defects liability period.

6.322 In the contract language used in construction project contracts, claims are never defined by Chinese law. Grounds for claims are mentioned in administrative regulations but are not clearly defined. Therefore, the legal nature of claims is often associated with the provisions on liability for breach of contract, which are stipulated in the Civil Code. Therefore, it is necessary to understand the similarities and differences between the claims arising from breach of contract and the liability for breach of contract prescribed by the Civil Code.

6.323 Article 9.13 of the "Bill Quantity Valuation Code" stipulates: "when one party files a claim against the other party of the contract, the claimant shall have grounds and evidence to support its claim, and comply with the stipulations of the contract". This clause specifies the compensation procedures that the contractor believes that the losses caused by events other than contractors.

6.324 According to Article 19 of the Model Text (2017), if the contractor believes that he "has the right to obtain additional payment and (or) an extension for construction period under the contractor", or if the employer believes that he "may get compensation and (or) an extension of defect liability period under the contract", then they have the right to file claims against each other.

6.325 The Model Text (2017) stipulates the procedure, the time limit and the compensation for a contractor claim. The time limit for the contractor to file a claim is 28 days, which is the same as the 2017 version of the FIDIC Contract text.

6.326 As for employer claims, the Model Text provides: "under the contract, if the employer believes that he deserves pecuniary compensation and defects liability extension, the supervisor shall send a notice to the contractor with thorough evidence attached".

6.327 The employer should notify the contractor through the supervisor within 28 days after the employer knows or should have known about the grounds for the claim; otherwise, the employer loses the right to claim pecuniary compensation and defects liability extension.

6.328 In fact, claim has three elements, incidents other than the claimant's cause, existence of losses, and notification of claims.

6.329 Causation is complicated. It has claim arising from the breach of contract, such as failure to deliver the drawings and basic information in time, quality defects, and unqualified materials. And it involves involuntary acts, such as *Force Majeure*, harsh weather conditions, adverse geographic conditions, changes in market prices, changes in law and changes related to the contract.

6.330 Compensation varies depending on the claim. Usually, in a claim arising from one party's breach of contract, the claimant may seek compensation for losses related to increased costs, time extensions, and lost profits. If construction is disrupted due to the employer's unreasonable delay in providing materials and equipment, the contractor may require the employer to compensate for increased costs and lost profits and to extend the construction period. However, for claims arising from involuntary incidents, the claimant may seek compensation for increased costs and time extensions but not for lost profits. For a claim due to adverse weather conditions, the contractor may see compensation for the increased costs and delay in the construction period due to additional work being required.

6.331 Chinese courts rely on the evidence provided by the parties when ruling on a claim. If during the performance of the contract, the parties agree to negotiate and settle the claim in the stage of completion settlement, the court will usually support it.

If the Letter of Intent is not Submitted Within the 28-Day Time Limit, Will the Right to Claim be Lost?

6.332 Under the provisions in the standard construction bidding documents, the contractor must submit the claim to the supervisor, within 28 days after the occurrence of the claim event; otherwise, the contractor loses the right to seek an extension of time for completion and to seek additional payment. If the contractor misses the deadline, the contractor loses the right to claim compensation. At present, the judicial practice and arbitration practice in China basically hold this view.

What Needs To Be Emphasized About the Issue of Claim Evidence Is That Whether It Is Time Claim Or Cost Claim, the Premise Is To Have The Evidence Of The Cause Of The Claim, Followed By The Evidence Of The Cost Of The Claim?

6.333 Both are indispensable. Any deficiency may lead to the loss of the claim.

6.334 In the claim for construction period, the basic documentary evidence of the claim is closely related to the project management documents, including schedule management, alteration management, quality management, and resource management. Other documents include timescale network diagrams, workforce planning, and material and equipment plans. Evidence demonstrating actual performance, alteration, and construction measures is also important. At present, Chinese legal experts are working to establish the rules for an extension claim in order to further standardization.

Disputes – Adjudication and Arbitration[111]

6.335 In construction project contracts, due to the long time periods involved in the contracts, the large contract prices, and the resource-intensive project, disputes are common in the process of contract formation and performance, especially when the construction market is undergoing instability. Disputes usual arise over price settlements, construction delays, and quality defects. For settling disputes, dispute resolution mechanisms are available. These mechanisms are stipulated in the Model Text and other standard contract texts.

Dispute Review Mechanism

6.336 Adjudication has significantly progressed and developed in developed countries. In China, a developing country, promising progress and developments have also

111 See Tan Jinghui, Focus on Legal Issues in Construction, Law Press, 2016.

been made. China International Economic and Trade Arbitration Commission, Beijing Arbitration Commission/Beijing International Arbitration Center and other organizations have established rules for dispute review and mediation. They have advocated for these rules to be implemented in construction project contracts.

6.337 The dispute review mechanism has a number of advantages including whole process, expert referees, timeliness, freedom, and flexibility. For example, in a tunnel construction project for a highway project, disputes may result from the complex geological conditions encountered when tunnelling. The focus of the disputes between the parties lie on whether the complex geological conditions can be foreseen by experienced contractors. If this issue cannot be solved, then suspension of work is inevitable. If the construction project contract includes the dispute review mechanism, then the review team would be on site promptly listen to the arguments from both sides, and provide a timely opinion after conducting on-site investigation. This dispute resolution method minimizes the losses due to a work suspension and mitigates hostility between the two sides.

6.338 Therefore, the most significant function of the dispute review mechanism is avoiding the deterioration in the relationship between parties because of a dispute. However, as the review opinion is not mandatory on parties, it has not been fully utilized in the construction field. Nonetheless, the dispute review mechanism has demonstrated utility in major infrastructure projects with cutting-edge technology, complex geological conditions, and other complicated conditions. As such, it can be a useful tool to help parties realize the purposes of a contract.

Arbitration

6.339 Arbitration is a method to resolve disputes in a contractual, autonomous, and quasi-judicial manner. To adopt arbitration, the parties must have an arbitration agreement, which can come in two forms: An arbitration agreement before the dispute, which is included in the contract; and an arbitration agreement after the dispute, which means that the parties agree after the dispute arises to submit the dispute to the arbitration institution.

6.340 China's domestic arbitration is limited to institutional arbitration. Currently, disputes related to construction project are always submitted to well-organized domestic arbitration institutions, such as the Beijing Arbitration Commission and the China International Economic and Trade Arbitration Commission.

6.341 Arbitration is a final judgment. It costs less time to resolve the dispute and to claim the cost of the project. Thus, arbitration offers the contractor a more efficient and intensive method of dispute resolution.

6.342 In addition, the characteristics of engineering arbitration are that, before engineering disputes become divergent, they often go through a long period of incubation and entanglement. The characteristics of engineering arbitration are as follows.

The Characteristics of Arbitration Cases and Arbitration Request.

6.343 The causes of arbitration can be divided into payment and confirmation. Because the causes are not mandatory in an arbitration institution, the causes of arbitration are flexible in practice.

6.344 Causes of confirmation may include:

- Confirmation of invalidity of the bidding and the contract;
- Confirmation of acceptance of the completed construction;
- Confirmation of qualification of the completion documents;
- Confirmation of a quality defect;
- Confirmation of unsatisfactory quality, or nonconformity of materials, equipment, and products;
- Confirmation of the validity of arbitration agreement or the jurisdiction of arbitration;
- Confirmation of the termination and rescission of the contract;
- Confirmation of the accounting price of the project contract, or the amount of debt during accounting;
- Confirmation of other rights or obligations, such as specific approval for documents and instructions.

6.345 Causes of payment may include:

- Request for rectification of engineering defects within a time limit;
- Request to submit completion materials on schedule;
- Request payment of project progress payment;
- Request payment of project settlement price;
- Request to submit design documents;
- Request payment of interest on arrears, or liquidated damages, etc.;
- Request payment of arbitration fees and attorney fees, etc.

The flexibility of construction project contract arbitration procedures

6.346 In construction arbitration, the arbitration schedule is more flexible than in litigation. Arbitration allows disputes to be resolved more easily and to the greater satisfaction of the parties than is typical in litigation. This increased efficiency and efficacy is due to the following five reasons:

(1) Arbitrator selection. If the arbitration mechanism allows the parties to choose the arbitrator, it can provide the parties with more confidence that the decision will be fair and that it will be based on the merits and the arbitrator's professionalism;

(2) Less restrictive limits on attorney participation. In a litigation, no more than two attorneys are permitted to attend the litigation proceedings according to the "Civil Procedural Law" and other procedural laws. Arbitration institutions are generally more permissive with the number of attorneys that may attend the arbitration proceedings. For example, the Beijing Arbitration Commission and the China Economic and Trade Arbitration Commission do not limit the number of attorneys in the arbitration case, which makes it convenient for the parties and lawyers to appear in arbitration proceedings together;

(3) Acceptance of change arbitration request. The arbitration tribunal considers more about relationship between the change arbitration request and the original arbitration request, rather than mechanically loyal to the procedure. Based on consideration of the rights and obligations of the parties participating in the hearing, the arbitral tribunal considers whether to agree to the change of a request

in the mid or late trial in the view of resolving the disputes, which would satisfy both parties;

(4) Case consolidation. The consolidation mechanism provides procedural efficiency in cases. Criteria vary among different arbitration institutions. The current rules of the Beijing Arbitration Commission stipulate:

> (1) two or more cases will be consolidated when the following conditions are met: 1. arbitration objects are the same type or related; 2. one party initiates and obtains consent from other parties; 3. arbitral tribunals have the same composition; (2) the arbitration tribunal may decide the specific procedures of the trial according to the circumstances.

The arbitration tribunal shall determine whether to consolidate cases by asking for the parties' opinions, verifying the parties in the different cases, and learning the special circumstances of the case. This consolidation mechanism shows the flexibility of arbitration;

(5) Interim decisions. The interim decision is an efficient way to solve disputes between parties. It accelerates the arbitration progress and positively impacts business activities. Interim decisions include determinations on jurisdiction, contract validity, delivery of drawings, and contract termination. Interim decisions play a decisive role in the construction progress, completion, delivery, sale, and other commercial activities. It also can promote the healthy development of the business transaction and help resolve disputes.

The Relationship Between the Settlement and the Administrative Audit of Payment

6.347 Previously, many places such as Jiangxi, Beijing, Shanghai, Hainan, Anhui, Hebei, and Chongqing have promulgated local regulations on auditing, saying that

> for construction projects involving governmental investment or funded mainly by government investment, the construction entity or the agent shall specify in the bidding documents and the contract that an audit shall serve as the basis for final accounting upon completion of the project.

The validity of such local legislation has given rise to numerous disputes. In resolving disputes arising from construction project contracts, whether the conclusion of an administrative audit may serve as the basis for the final accounting or not has become a judicial issue.

6.348 The holdings of the High People's Court of Heilongjiang and the Supreme People's Court clarify that two legal relationships are involved: The administrative legal relationship between the auditing institution and the audited entity; and the contractual relationship between the employer and the contractor. The reasoning of the two courts reflects the fact that the conclusion of an administrative audit may not serve as the grounds for determining the project costs unless the parties agree to it.

6.349 In fact, the judicial opinions are also reflected in the "Telephone Replies of the Supreme People's Court on the Application of Laws on the Inconsistency between the Final Accounting Confirmed by the Parties and the Final Accounting Audited by an Audit Institution in Construction Project Contract Cases" (Min Yi Ta Zi No. 2 of 2001), which states that "after discussion, it is held that an audit is a type of administrative supervision exercised by the state on the project employer, so it does not affect the validity of the contract between the project employer and the contractor". In a construction project contract case, the agreement between the parties is the basis for the court to render judgment. The conclusion of an audit may serve as grounds for judgment only when the contract stipulates it or when the contract is ambiguous or invalid.

6.350 Since then, on 5 June 2017, the Legal Affairs Committee of the Standing Committee of the National People's Congress also responded to the "Response to the Review Recommendations of the Local Regulations Regarding the Audit Results as the Completion and Settlement of Government Investment and Construction Projects". On the basis of full investigation and soliciting opinions, we researched and concluded that the local regulations directly use audit results as the basis for completion settlement and should be stated in the bidding documents or stipulated in the contract that the audit results shall be used as the basis for completion settlement, which restricts civil rights and exceeds the authority of local legislation, and should be corrected.

6.351 In the author's opinion, when handling disputes involving using an audit as the grounds for calculating the project price, the Supreme People's Court's opinion that "the application of an administrative audit shall be subject to agreement between the parties" should be followed. However, the opinion that "audits may be admitted as the grounds for judgment when the contract is ambiguous or void", as stated in the same Supreme People's Court holding, should not be followed because Article 793 of the Civil Code has clearly stipulated that "a construction project construction project contract is invalid, but if the construction project experience is qualified, the contractor can be compensated at a discount according to the contract on the project price". So, even if the contract is invalid, the contract price would still be confirmed. In this sense, as long as the contract does not adopt the administrative audit as grounds for determining the project price, the disputed project price should not be determined by the administrative audit. If the contract does not specify the basis for settlement, the calculation method or calculation standards released by the government should be considered to calculate the payments.

6.352 Furthermore, in the author's opinion, the legal status of audits in construction settlement should strictly follow the Audit Law, the Budget Law and the Construction Law. If there is a need to adjust the status of the audit to affect the legal relationship between parties, it should be specified in laws and regulations; otherwise, the creditor's contractual rights would be in danger.

Engineering Intellectual Property Disputes

6.353 Recent years have seen sustained growth in the number of patent applications in China. China has become one of the largest patent filing countries in the world. According to officials from the Planning and Development Department of the State Intellectual Property Office (SIPO), in 2020, China would have 530 thousand invention patents authorized. As of the end of 2020, the effective number of domestic invention patents in China was 2.213 million. There are 15.8 invention patents per 10,000 people, 2.377 million utility model patents, and 732,000 design patents.

6.354 Intellectual property rights cases related to construction have also increased in number and diversity. As the main implementation body of construction activities, construction enterprises, especially in the design and construction general contracting contract, need to complete process design, special construction methods, patented products, engineering machinery and equipment procurement, etc. Along with the economic reform and technology upgrades in China, all types of construction work may now involve patents, copyrights, and business secrets. Disputes related to this intellectual property can be reduced if construction entities: Take steps to record the original sources of workmanship, construction methods and procurement of equipment; and promptly cease the use of any potentially infringing products, preserve any relevant evidence once they become aware of the potential infringement, and immediately notify the parties concerned.

Conflicts between Limitation of Claims and Remedies for Breach of Contract

6.355 According to international and domestic practice, the contract should stipulate claim and the procedures for bringing a claim, including timing, matters, documents, loss of right. What needs to be pointed out in particular is the statute of the time of claim, which means that if the injured party does not bring a claim in a specified period, then the injured party loses the right to bring the claim. Specifically, Article 19.1 of the 2017 Model Text stipulates: "if the contractor does not bring a claim within 28 days after the contractor knows or should have known about the incident, then the contractor loses the right to bring the claim". The 1999 Model Text had similar text.

6.356 However, after the promulgation of the 2013 and 2017 versions of the Model Text, different interpretations of this provision arose. One opinion argues that the right to claim breach of contract is not waived even if the claim is not brought within the claim period; instead, the claimant loses only the right to claim compensation for that breach.[112] The opposing opinion argues that the claim arising from one incident cannot be separated in this way; thus, the claim for breach would be waived along with the claim for compensation as they really are a single claim.[113] In the author's opinion, this debate can be avoided if the parties agree on this issue in the contract. If the contract says each incident only gives rise to one claim, then the waiving party cannot bring another claim; if the contract says the opposite, then the waiving party can still claim breach.

National Construction Law and International Forms

National Construction Law

6.357 In China, besides the basic law issued by the National People's Congress, there are other rules to regulate the conduct in the Chinese construction industry, including administrative law and regulatory documents of highest organ of state power, administrative regulations, and interpretation and guiding cases of the Supreme Court and so forth.

6.358 The law issued by the National People's Congress to regulate activities of construction mainly includes Construction Law of the PRC (hereinafter referred to as

112 See Jiang Xueping, On the Liability and Claim Management of the Construction Contract, Technology Information, Volume No. 1, 2017.

113 See Yu Aitao, How to Cope with Claims for the Contractor, Technology Information, Volume No. 19, 2013.

"Construction Law"), the Civil Code and Bidding Law of the PRC (hereinafter referred to as "Bidding Law").

6.359 The Construction Law was issued on 1 November 1997 at the 28th Meeting of the Standing Committee of the Eighth National People's Congress and implementation as of 1 March 1998 which is regarded as a basic law in the system of Chinese construction law and regulations. The Construction Law stays a core status in Chinese construction industry law system that instructs other legal regulations of Chinese construction industry. The Construction Law is mainly applied in house building related construction.[114] There are many special laws and regulations for other kinds of construction, for instance some include, Highway Law of PRC,[115] Railway Law of the PRC[116] or Oil and Natural Gas Pipeline Protection Law of PRC.[117]

6.360 The Civil Code was adopted at the Third Session of the Thirteenth National People's Congress on May 28, 2020 and came into force as of January 1, 2021. The Civil Code is implemented later than the issuance of Construction Law of PRC and in Chapter 18 of the Civil Code, it stipulates the rights and obligations of parties in construction contract from a contractual perspective.

6.361 Bidding Law was adopted by the Standing Committee of the Ninth National People's Congress at the 11th Session on 30 August 1999 and came into force as of 1 January 2000. Based on the particularity of offer invitation and acceptance in construction contract, Bidding Law regulates the rights and obligations of bidding parties and covers all the tender and bid activities in China. Furthermore, Bidding Law lists projects for which have to be carried out though bidding and subject to the Bidding Law, the bid can be made by the public notices or special requests.

6.362 Besides, some matters relevant to the construction shall also regulated by the relevant law, such as the Law of the People's Republic of China on Environmental Impact Assessment,[118] the Labour Law of the PRC,[119] and, etc.

6.363 In Chinese construction industry, some regulations or measures issued by the State Council or government department are the crucial rules to regulate conduct during the construction activities. From the view of quality, security and permit, it mainly includes the Regulation on the Quality Management of Construction Projects,[120] the

114 Article 2.2, Construction Law of PRC , reads:

"The term 'construction activities' as mentioned in this Law shall refer to the construction of all kinds of houses and buildings and the ancillary facilities thereof and the installation of their supporting lines, pipes and equipment".

115 Highway Law of the People's Republic of China, Order No. 81 of the President, date of enforcement: 5 November 2017.

116 R January ailway Law of the People's Republic of China, Order No. 25 of the President, date of enforcement: 24 April 2015.

117 Oil and Natural Gas Pipeline Protection Law of the People's Republic of China, Order No. 30 of the President, date of enforcement: 1 October 2010.

118 Law of the People's Republic of China on Environmental Impact Assessment, Order No. 48 of the President, date of enforcement: 1 October 2010.

119 Labour Law of the People's Republic of China, Order No. 24of the President, date of enforcement: 29 December 2019.

120 Regulation on the Quality Management of Construction Projects, Order No.714 of the State Council, date of enforcement: 23 April 2019.

Administrative Regulations on the Work Safety of Construction Projects,[121] the Provisions on the Administration of Credential Evaluation for Construction Enterprises[122] and the Measures for the Administration of Construction Permits for Construction Projects.[123]

6.364 In order to strengthen the administration of construction quality and guarantee the construction quality, in accordance with the Construction Law, the Regulation on the Quality Management of Construction Projects was promulgated by the State Council. It stipulates that all those engaging in activities of the new construction, expansion, change of construction projects as well as supervision and management of the quality of construction projects shall abide by this Regulation and the construction project owners, survey entities, design entities, construction entities and construction project supervision entities shall be responsible for the quality of construction projects.

6.365 In order to strengthen the supervision over and administration of the work safety of construction projects, the Administrative Regulations on the Work Safety of Construction Projects was issued by the State Council. Similar with the Regulation on the Quality Management of Construction Projects, this administrative regulation prescribes that all those who are engaged in the construction of new buildings, the expansion, rebuilding and demolishment of buildings, and the supervision over and administration of the work safety of construction projects shall abide by the present Regulations. The construction entities, survey entities, design entities, construction undertaking entities, construction project supervision entities and other entities related to the work safety of construction projects assume the responsibility for the work safety of construction projects and if they fail to abide this regulation, they shall bear the respective administrative penalty.

6.366 The Provisions on the Administration of Credential Evaluation for Construction Enterprises issued by the Ministry of Housing and Urban Rural Development prescribes the qualifications of construction enterprises. According to this Provision, the qualification of construction enterprises can be divided into general contracting, specialty contracting and labour contracting. Specifically, general contracting includes four grades, special, first, second, and third grades, respectively. The enterprise who has the special grade can undertake all projects. Specialty contracting includes three grades, first, second and third grades respectively and labour contracting includes two grades, first and second grades respectively. The Measures for the Administration of Construction Permits for Construction Projects was promulgated by the Ministry of Housing and Urban Rural Development and subject to it, the construction entity and projects employers shall apply for the Construction Permit before the commencement of construction. If they fail to obtain such permit, the construction will not be allowed to commence.

6.367 The interpretation and guiding cases issued by the Supreme Court also are the evidence for addressing the disputes of construction, especially the Interpretation of the Supreme People's Court on Certain Issues Concerning the Application of Law in the Trial of Cases Involving Project Construction Project Contract Disputes promulgated on

121 Administrative Regulations on the Work Safety of Construction Projects, Order No. 393 of the State Council, date of enforcement: 1 February 2004.

122 Provisions on the Administration of Credential Evaluation for Construction Enterprises, Order No.45 of the Ministry of housing and urban rural construction, date of enforcement: 22 December 2018.

123 Measures for the Administration of Construction Permits for Construction Projects, Order No. 52of the Ministry of housing and urban rural construction, date of enforcement: 30 March 2021.

29 September 2020 . These Interpretations stipulate the practical issues during performing the construction contract, such as the dispute of the actual completion date of a construction project.

6.368 In order to guide the parties entering into a construction contract, the Construction Contract for Construction Project (Model Text) (GF-2013-0201) and Design Contract for Construction Project Model Text (GF-2015-0210) were enacted by Ministry of Housing and Urban Rural Development and former State Administration for Industry and Commerce of PRC (current State Administration for Market Regulation of the PRC). Many construction contracts of local project in China are made based on these model forms.

The Application of International Construction Contract Forms in China

6.369 The huge construction market of China decides the diversity of the entities in construction area. Furthermore, it also makes the diversity of the contract form in Chinese construction area. Except for various model forms, guided by Chinese government,[124] on the basis of different investment subjects, there are many other contract forms applicable in Chinese construction market.

6.370 International construction contract forms are applied mainly in the following projects:

6.371 The funding of construction comes from the project of multilateral bank, such as the World Bank. In such kind of projects, the red book of FIDIC Contract conditions is generally adopted, for example Xiaolangdi Dam water control project in the Yellow River in China, Beijing–Tianjin–Tangshan motorway project, etc.

6.372 The projects initiated by investment entities which come from developed countries such as Britain and the United States. These investment entities prefer their own construction contract forms.

6.373 The overseas construction project which are funded by Chinese government. As Chinese government provides preferential financing for such projects, Chinese government or relevant banks prefers to review such contract. For assuring the quality and efficiency of reviewing, Chinese government always requests a uniform contract context. Recently, the China Import and Export Bank of China is inclined to request the employer or contractor to adopt the FIDIC Contract context for reviewing pertaining to the project financially supported by itself.

The Application of FIDIC Contract Conditions in China

6.374 The application of FIDIC Contract conditions in China includes two parts, indicating FIDIC Contract conditions applied in the construction projects within the territory of China and applied in overseas construction projects.

6.375 The Application of FIDIC Contract Conditions in Chinese domestic construction projects Compared with other international construction contract conditions, the FIDIC

124 For example, the Construction Contract for Construction Project (Model Text) (GF-2013-0201) and Design Contract for Construction Project Model Text (GF-2015-0201) were enacted by Ministry of Housing and Urban Rural Development and State Administration for Industry and Commerce of the PRC. The Standard DB/EPC Tender Document of the PRC was enacted by the National Development and Reform Commission of the PRC and so forth.

Contract conditions are enormously popular in China. In the field of international construction, the person who does not know the FIDIC Contract conditions will be regarded not belonging to the area of construction. In 1996, China Engineering Consulting Association, on behalf of Chinese engineering consulting industry, became the member of FIDIC. Since then, FIDIC Contract conditions have been extensively studied in China.

6.376 Although the Chinese construction industry is keen to learn FIDIC Contract conditions, within the territory of China, the FIDIC Contract conditions are mainly applied in the projects supported by multilateral bank loan or the projects of foreign investment. The reasons include the following aspects:

The Limits by the Chinese Laws and Regulations

6.377 In December 20, 2011, the notice of issuing concise standard DB and EPC tender documents was jointly enacted by several departments of PRC. Subject to the applicable scope and requirement in this notice, the specific projects within the territory shall use the construction contract and design construction contract mentioned in this notice which are not FIDIC Contract conditions. Therefore, FIDIC Contract conditions cannot be applied in such projects.

The Maladjustment of FIDIC Contract Conditions in Chinese Domestic Construction Market

6.378 As former chapter mentioned, the Chinese domestic construction market is regulated strictly and the participants have not enough freedom to choose. However, in the FIDIC Contract conditions, employers, contractors and engineers are granted a wide discretion. Such conditions don't match the Chinese domestic construction market. Thus, although using the FIDIC Contract conditions, it has to make a great modification, which leads to lose the original mechanism of FIDIC Contract conditions.

6.379 As mentioned above, GF-2013-0201 (Model Text) was published by the Ministry of Housing and Urban–Rural Development of the PRC and former State Administration for Industry and Commerce of the PRC (current State Administration for Market Regulation of the PRC), which are usually used in the Chinese construction market. There are several differences between this model form and FIDIC Contract conditions, which can mainly reflect on the following factors.

6.380 First, the engineer in the FIDIC Contract enjoys more power than Chinese Model Text. For example, generally, in FIDIC Contract conditions, unless otherwise specified, the contractor shall obtain the prior consent of engineer before subcontracting. In the Chinese Model Text, the contractor is not entitled to subcontract any part of the construction unless the consent of the employer.

6.381 Second, the body for settling disputes on construction quality is different. In the FIDIC Conditions of Contract for Construction, the engineer has the right to verdict concerning such quality disputes between the employer and contractor. However, in the Chinese Model Text, such disputes shall be settled by the relevant administrative department.[125]

125 Zhicai Zhou, "the research and application of FIDIC Conditions of Contract for Construction in China", [2012] Fujian Jiancai.

6.382 Third, the defects period is quietly different.[126] In the FIDIC Conditions of Contract for EPC/Turnkey Projects, unless otherwise specified, the defect notification period is one year. In Chinese Model Form, the quality warranty period shall be subject to the Regulation on the Quality Management of Construction Projects.[127]

6.383 Fourth, the method of settling disputes is different. FIDIC Contract conditions usually apply the multi-tier mechanism to settle the disputes, for example, setting up Dispute Adjudication Board. In Chinese Model Text, the disputes could be solved by the amicable negotiations or relevant competent department, otherwise, the disputes can be settled through arbitration or litigation.

The Application of FIDIC Contract Conditions in Overseas Construction Projects of Chinese Companies

6.384 The Chinese companies tend to use the FIDIC Contract conditions in their overseas construction projects, which can be divided into two categories: i) The investors of the overseas construction projects are the Chinese companies, which take the FIDIC Contract conditions as the conditions of construction contract; ii) the contractors of the overseas construction projects are the Chinese construction companies, which are willing to accept the FIDIC Contract conditions as the conditions of construction contract. In conclusion, the use of FIDIC Contract conditions in the overseas construction projects of Chinese companies is relatively extensive and easily to be accepted by Chinese companies.

126 Weiguo Min, "The Comparative Study on the Suitability of FIDIC Contract Conditions", Wuhan University, 2013.

127 Regulation on the Quality Management of Construction Projects, Order No. 279 of the State Council, date of enforcement: 30 January 2001.

CHAPTER 7

GCC LAW

Aymen Masadeh and Michael Grose

Contents

DOI: 10.4324/9781315671376-7

History of GCC Countries Law

Sources of Law

7.1 The legal system of the United Arab Emirates and the Arab Gulf states is based predominantly on the civil law model, adapted to reflect the region's Islamic and Arab heritage.[1]

7.2 These states formed a loose political and economic union, known as the Gulf Cooperation Council, in 1981.[2] The GCC comprises Bahrain, Kuwait, Oman, Qatar, Saudi Arabia, and the United Arab Emirates.

7.3 With the exception of Saudi Arabia, the GCC states have each adopted a Civil Code. As these are all modelled on the Egyptian Civil Code (1949), which itself is a derivative of the French Civil Code (1804), the Civil Codes of Bahrain, Kuwait, Qatar, Oman, and the United Arab Emirates[3] are broadly similar. As the Civil Code is the backbone of any civil law jurisdiction it follows that there is a considerable degree of similarity in the principles of law applicable to construction contracts in each of Bahrain, Kuwait, Qatar, Oman, and the United Arab Emirates.

7.4 The KSA Basic Law of Government expresses the role of the Islamic *Shari'ah* in the following terms:

> "The Kingdom of Saudi Arabia is a sovereign Arab Islamic state with Islam as its religion. The Constitution [of the Kingdom of Saudi Arabia] is the Quran and the Sunna of His Prophet, peace be upon him".

7.5 This is more than merely a difference of emphasis, reflecting, instead, a direct application of the Islamic *Shari'ah* to the extent that no relevant temporal laws exist.

Contract Law

The Formation of Contract

7.6 There are three elements for any contract formed under the UAE law; that is, agreement on the essential matters, a legal subject matter and a lawful purpose for the obligations arising out of the contract.[4] The following will discuss the valid agreement and the contract's place and time.

Offer and Acceptance

7.7 Article (125) of the UAE Civil Code states that

1 This civil law system co-exists with a broadly common law system that has been adopted in certain limited geographical areas, such as the Dubai International Financial Centre.

2 Charter of the Gulf Cooperation Council, 25 May 1981.

3 "*Civil Codes of Arab Countries: The Sanhuri Codes*", N Saleh, ALQ, Vol. 8, No.2 (1993), pp. 161–7.

4 Article 129 of the UAE Civil Code states that "The necessary elements for the making of a contract are:

(a) That the two parties to the contract should agree upon the essential elements;
(b) The subject matter of the contract must be something which is possible and defined or capable of being defined and permissible to be dealt in;
(c) There must be a lawful purpose for the obligations arising out of the contract.

> A contract is the coming together of an offer made by one of the contracting parties with the acceptance of the other, together with the agreement of them both in such a manner as to determine the effect thereof on the subject matter of the contract, and from which results an obligation upon each of them with regard to that which each is bound to do for the other.

7.8 Contracts are formed by mutual consent of competent parties who intend to be legally bound by the agreement. Parties' consent is expressed by offer and acceptance. A contract is formed only when the offer is unconditionally accepted.

7.9 The first expression of intent between the parties is called an offer. In order to constitute a legally binding offer, it must contain the essential information of the contract. If an essential element is missing, the agreement between the parties cannot be legally binding under UAE law. Offers do not need to include all elements. Non-essential elements can be provided by supplementary rules that can be found mainly in the Civil Code. They act as gap-filling rules.

7.10 The borderline between essential and non-essential elements can be blurred in some cases. Whether the missing elements are essential or not is a matter of fact that can be determined by the trial judge. Obviously, the significance of information may vary from one case to another.

7.11 The existence of supplementary rules may indicate that the gaps; that is, the missing elements, are non-essential for the validity and enforceability of the contract. In the normal course of circumstances, where the missing elements can be provided by supplementary rules, such missing elements are considered non-essential. Courts can always apply the supplementary rules to fill in the contract's gaps. Thus, missing non-essential elements do not affect the validity and enforceability of the contract. Article 141 of the UAE Civil Code states that

> (a) A contract may only be made upon the agreement of the two parties to the essential elements of the obligation, and the other lawful conditions which the parties regard as essential.
>
> (b) If the parties agree on the essential elements of the obligation and the remainder of the other lawful conditions which both parties regard as essential and they leave matters of detail to be agreed upon afterwards but they do not stipulate that the contract shall not be regarded as made in the event of absence of agreement upon such matters, the contract shall be deemed to have been made, and if a dispute arises as to the matters which have not been agreed upon, the judge shall adjudicate thereon in accordance with the nature of the transaction and the provisions of the law.

7.12 Offers can be made in any form and can be communicated by all means. An offer can be in writing or by word of mouth or even implied.[5] For example, displaying goods with their prices is normally treated as an offer.[6]

5 Article 132 of the UAE Civil Code states that "An expression of intent may be made orally or in writing, and may be expressed in the past or present tense or in the imperative if the present time is intended or by such means as are customary even by a person who is not dumb, or by an interchange of acts demonstrating the mutual consent or by adopting any other course in respect of which the circumstances leave no doubt that they demonstrate mutual consent".

6 Article 134 (1) of the UAE Civil Code states that "An offer of goods or services accompanied by an indication of the consideration shall be regarded as an offer".

7.13 In cases of advertisement or announcement made to the public, offers may be confused with the so-called 'invitation to treat'. The main difference between the two is the intent of the party. Whereas the offer makes a contract once it is properly accepted, the invitation to treat is merely an invitation to make an offer.

7.14 Catalogues, advertisements, announcements and alike are usually considered invitations to the public to make offers. Such expressions are usually used to promote trades with no legal intention to make offers. The UAE Union Supreme Court made it clear that "A publication or advertisement and a current price list at which goods are sold, and any other statement of offer or orders directed at the public or individuals, will not, in the event of doubt, be regarded as an offer, but as an invitation to enter into a contract within the meaning of Article 134 of the Civil Code".[78] However, the wording of the advertisement may indicate otherwise; for example, the advertisement can be considered an offer if it provides a discount for the first certain number of units sold. In this example, the intention to be bound by the advertisement can be seen there as the seller can honour his promise.

7.15 Offers can be terminated by several ways; that is, withdrawal, revocation, rejection, counteroffer, lapse of time, death or incapacity of a party and subsequent illegality.

7.16 The offer can be revoked at any time before the contract is made unless it is irrevocable. An offer will be irrevocable if it states a period of time within which the acceptance must be made.[9] The period may be inferred from the circumstances and nature of the transaction. Such an offer cannot be revoked. In the case no. 255/2007, the Dubai Court of Cassation held that

> Under Article 139 of the Civil Code, if a person makes an offer and specifies a time limit for acceptance, he shall remain bound by his offer until that time expires, and he shall be absolved of his obligation if the response accepting the offer does not reach him within the time specified.[10]

In principle, offers are revocable unless the circumstances show otherwise.[11]

7 Union Supreme Court, 497/Judicial Year 25, WestLaw Middle East publications.

8 Article 134 (2) of the UAE Civil Code states that "A publication or advertisement or a current price list or any other statement connected with offers or orders directed towards the public or individuals shall not in the event of doubt be treated as offers but only as an invitation to enter into a contract".

9 Article 139 of the UAE Civil Code states that

> (1) If a time is fixed for the acceptance to be given, the offeror shall be bound to keep to his offer until such time expires;
> (2) The time may be inferred from the circumstances of the case or from the nature of the transaction.

10 WestLaw Middle East publications.

11 The Abu Dhabi Court of Cassation, in the case 355/Judicial Year 2, held that "Article 139 of the Civil Code shows that the basic rule is that an offer is not binding, and that the offeror may retract it unless it has been accepted. If, however, the offeror has specified a time limit for acceptance, then the offeror will be obliged to keep his offer open throughout the period that he has specified, and no regard will be had to any retraction on the part of the offeror if that occurs before the end of the period, provided that the second party was aware of the offer, because the retraction of the offer before the expiration of the period will not preclude the concluding of a contract if the offer is accepted". WestLaw Middle East Publications.

7.17 Revocable offers can be revoked expressly or impliedly. For example, in sale offers, the offer can be impliedly revoked if the offeror sells the same goods to someone other than the offeree. In cases of several offers, each new offer will cancel the older one.[12]

7.18 Offers, whether revocable or irrevocable, can be withdrawn provided that the withdrawal letter reaches the offeree before the offer. This may occur if the withdrawal letter is transmitted via electronic means and the offer was sent by normal mail. If the withdrawal letter reaches the offeree before the offer itself, the offer will be deemed null even if it was an irrevocable one.

7.19 Offers can be terminated by express or implied rejection. For example, procuring the goods or services from someone other than the offeror will usually mean an implied rejection of the offer. Counteroffers, in effect, terminate the original offers. If the offeree replies by indicating his willingness to accept the offer subject to additions or omissions or any changes, the original offer will no longer exist and the reply will amount to a new offer; that is, a counteroffer. The contract can be formed by accepting the counteroffer. If the offeror turns the counteroffer down, the offeree will not have the privilege of accepting the original offer. If this occurs, the acceptance of the original offer will be considered a new offer, which means that the original offeror will act as an offeree.

7.20 Offers do not last forever. Where parties are in each other's presence, the offer is kept active till they go apart. This is based on the Islamic concept of *Majlis* (a place where people meet for social or business purposes). Article 136 of the UAE Civil Code states that

> the contracting parties shall retain the option (to rescind) from the time the offer has been made until the time the *Majlis* ends, and the offer shall be avoided if the offeror retracts it after making it and prior to its being accepted by the other side or if either of the contracting parties says or does anything to demonstrate that he is resiling from it, and no acceptance made after that shall be of any effect.

7.21 If the offer states a period of time for acceptance, the offer ends automatically once the period lapses. If the offer is silent on this period, the offer will last for a reasonable period of time. Reasonableness is a matter of fact that shall be decided by the trial judge.[13] Any acceptance made after the lapse of such period will be considered as a new offer. It can only form the contract if its accepted by the original offeror.

7.22 Offers are also terminated by death or incapacity or subsequent illegality. If either the offeror or the offeree dies or becomes insane or bankrupt before the contract is formed, the offer is automatically terminated. If the offer becomes illegal due to changes in law, the offer becomes automatically null.

7.23 Acceptance of the offer must be absolute and unconditional. The UAE law adopts the orthodox theory, known as the mirror image theory, which requires the acceptance to mirror all the elements of the offer. Article 140(1) of the UAE Civil Code clearly states that "The acceptance must coincide with the offer".

12 Article 138 of the UAE Civil Code states that "A repetition of the offer prior to acceptance annuls the first offer, and the last made offer shall be regarded as the valid one".

13 Article 139 of the UAE Civil Code states that "(1) If a time is fixed for the acceptance to be given, the offeror shall be bound to keep to his offer until such time expires. (2) The time may be inferred from the circumstances of the case or from the nature of the transaction".

7.24 However, if the acceptance does not mirror the offer exactly and the alterations are in the pure interest of the offeror, the contract can still be formed. For example, where the offer sets a future date for the price and the offeree accepts the offer and adds that the price will be paid in advance, the contract is formed despite the differences between the offer and the acceptance.

7.25 Offers can be accepted by all means unless the offer specifies the method of acceptance. In the latter case, an acceptance through a different method will be considered a counteroffer. Acceptance can be made by words or actions. For example, in works contracts, commencing performance may constitute an acceptance by action.

7.26 Silence or inaction may not constitute an acceptance. However, the offeree's silence may be interpreted as an acceptance where the circumstances or, more specifically, previous dealings, support such an interpretation.[14] For example, if a wholesaler usually delivers the goods within a week after contacting the buyer, the silence of the latter may be interpreted as an acceptance. The frequency, consistency and regularity of the previous dealings shall be taken into account while considering such cases.

7.27 Furthermore, the acceptance must be made by the person to whom the offer is directed. A purported acceptance made by a third party is nothing more than an offer.

7.28 In auctions, unless agreed otherwise, the bidder will make the offer. The bid is cancelled by the higher one. Article 144 of the UAE Civil Code states that

> A contract by way of auction shall only be made by the bid being accepted, and an offer shall lapse upon a higher offer being made even though the higher offer may be void, or upon the auction ending without a bid being accepted.

7.29 Furthermore, effective acceptance determines where and when the contract is formed. Time and place of contract are very significant. They are relied on to determine the governing law, the competency of the parties, the period of the contract, etc. The Contract is formed at the time and place where the acceptance becomes effective.

7.30 Determining the place and time of the contract may vary from one jurisdiction to another if both parties are not in each other's presence. There are four theories around the world for the place and time when the acceptance becomes effective; that is, acceptance expressing, acceptance dispatching, acceptance arrival and offeror's awareness of acceptance. Under UAE law, acceptance becomes effective where and when the offeror becomes aware of the acceptance. Awareness is assumed if it is proved that the acceptance reached the offeror.[15]

---

14 Article 135 of the UAE Civil Code states that

1) A person who remains silent shall not be deemed to have made a statement, but silence in the face of a circumstance in which a statement is called for shall be regarded as an acceptance;
2) In particular, silence shall be deemed to be an acceptance if there has been a prior dealing between the contracting parties and the offer is related to such dealing or if the offer will bring about a benefit to the person to whom it is made.

15 Article 142 of the UAE Civil Code states that

1) A contract made between parties not in each other's presence shall be deemed to have been made at the time and place at which the offeror learns of the acceptance unless there is an agreement or a provision of the law to the contrary;

7.31 In cases of electronic communication, the contract may be made at the time when the acceptance is made if the electronic communications are instantaneous. This may apply to telephone and video calls, live chatting and any similar means.

Intention to Create Legal Relations

7.32 A party's intent to be bound by his promises and expressions is of vital significance for the creation of a binding contractual relationship. In principle, the intention to enter into a legally binding agreement is always assumed in commercial transactions unless the circumstances show otherwise. However, social and family promises are usually not intended to create a legally binding agreement.

7.33 The existence of such an intention is a matter of fact that needs to be decided by the trial judge provided that his decision is based on sound reasoning. The UAE Union Supreme Court held that

> Although it is settled law that findings of fact are an exclusive matter for the trial court, nevertheless the court of cassation may intervene if the grounds on which the judgment relied involve a departure from the law, or a departure from the matters proved in the papers, or if the matters proved are not capable of leading to the result that the court reached, because of a shortcoming in the reasoning or a vitiation of deductions.[16]

7.34 The intention requires a good understanding of the nature of the contract and the obligations of the parties. Where it is proven that the parties did not intend to be involved in a legally binding relationship, the contract will be held void. The UAE Union Supreme Court held that

> The meaning of true consent is that the person making the disposition is of sound mind and intends to make that disposition, which is to say that he understands the nature of the contract and the obligations arising out of it, and that his intention is genuine and is not tainted by any defects in intention, because intention is one of the basic pillars of any legal disposition. A contract based on an intention that does not exist is a void contract, and is not lawful in its essence or in its description, because an element of it or the subject matter or purpose of it, or the form laid down by law for the making of it, is defective in some way, whereby it will produce no result, and may not be rectified by affirmation under Article 210 of the Civil Code.[17]

Capacity

7.35 Article 85 of the UAE Civil Code states that

(c) Every person who has reached the age of majority in possession of his mental powers and who has not been placed under a restriction shall be of full capacity to exercise his rights laid down in this law and the laws deriving from it;

(d) A person shall be of the age of majority upon reaching the age of 21 lunar years.

---

2) The offeror shall be deemed to have learned of the acceptance at the time and place at which such acceptance reaches him unless there is evidence to the contrary.

16 The Union Supreme Court, 226/Judicial Year 24.

17 The Union Supreme Court, 671/Judicial Year 24.

7.36 Under UAE law, the age of majority is twenty-one years. This is the age when the person becomes competent to make all types of contract. Contracts made by minors can be either void or voidable depending on their age and the type of contract.

7.37 A person who is less than seven years old; that is, the age of discretion, cannot make any type of contract. That is to say that all contracts made by such minors are void. If the person is more than 7 years old and less than 21 years old, he may make valid and binding contracts provided that such contracts are in his pure interest, such as accepting a donation. On the contrary, if the contract is purely to his detriment, it shall be void.

7.38 However, most contracts fall between pure benefit and pure detriment, such as sale and rent contracts. Such contracts can be in either the interest or the detriment of the minor depending on whether the minor made a good deal or not. These transactions are subject to the approval of the guardian or the court or the minor once he reaches the competence age.[18] The affirmation of such contracts can be express or implied. Silence may also be interpreted as an affirmation where the circumstances of the case lead to this conclusion. The UAE Union Supreme Court held that "Where affirmation awaits the moment where the person entitled to give it achieves the age of majority, then an acquiescent silence lasting years after the attaining of majority may properly be construed as implied consent".[19]

7.39 The affirmation has a retrospective effect; that is, the contract will take effect backdated to the time it was made. The UAE Union Supreme Court made it clear that:

> The contracting party may in such event require that it be voided, or he may affirm it when he achieves full capacity. In such a case, the contract will have a legal existence until the decision is made to void it. The right to void the contract will cease upon affirmation, and it will then, pursuant to Articles 215 and 217 of the Civil Code, enter into full effect. Any statement expressly or impliedly so indicating may have that effect, and silence may amount to an affirmation if by custom it indicates consent. If the disposition is affirmed, it will take effect backdated to the time it was made, and the subsequent affirmation will be regarded as a prior grant of agency. If the affirmation is refused, the disposition will be void. Affirmation of a contract as a legal disposition implies an extinguishment of the right, and that may be express or implied.
>
> 20

7.40 Having said that, it is important to note that the UAE law adopts the concept of emancipation. Under Article 160 of the Civil Code, the competent court or the guardian may permit the minor who reaches the age of eighteen to receive and administer part or all his property.[21]

---

18 The UAE Union Supreme Court, in the case of 671/ Judicial Year 24, held that "where the disposition ranges between benefit and detriment, then it is voidable, or its effectiveness will be suspended pending affirmation pursuant to article 213 of the Civil Code. The contracting party may in such event require that it be voided, or he may affirm it when he achieves full capacity. In such a case, the contract will have a legal existence until the decision is made to void it".

19 The UAE Union Supreme Court, 671/ Judicial Year 24.

20 The UAE Union Supreme court, 671/Judicial Year 24.

21 Article 160 of the UAE Civil Code states that

1) A guardian may permit a minor who has reached the age of 18 Hijra years to receive all or part of his property to administer it;
2) It shall be permissible for the court upon hearing the evidence of the guardian to permit a minor who has attained the age of 18 Hijra years to receive all or some of his property to administer it;
3) The provisions relating to the above shall be laid down by law.

7.41 In addition to age, capacity is also affected by the mental status of the person. An insane person is treated as a minor with no capacity; that is, a minor who is less than seven years old. That is to say that any contract he makes will be rendered void.[22] If a person has a mental illness, which does not cause absolute insanity but affects the mental ability to make decisions, the legal effects of his actions will be similar to the effects of the minor's acts whose age between 7 and 21.[23]

Formalities

7.42 As a general rule, there is no required formality for making contracts under UAE law. Exceptionally, some contracts require certain formalities for the purpose of their validity. Almost all governmental contracts must be made in writing.

7.43 Dubai laws require real estate contracts, whether off plan sales or ready buildings, to be registered in the Dubai Real Estate Regulatory Agency. If formality is required for making a contract, the absence of such a formality will render the contract void.

7.44 However, formalities may be required for the purpose of proof only. Naturally, evidence is only required in cases of denial. This has nothing to do with the validity of the contract.

7.45 Under Article 35 of the UAE Evidence Law,[24] a civil contract with an undetermined value or with a value of more than five thousand dirhams must be proved in writing. Other civil contracts and commercial contracts can be proved by all means.

Agency

7.46 The principle of ostensible or implied authority is generally recognized, except for a limited class of actions that require actual or specific authority.

---

22 Article 169 of the Civil Code states that "Adult insane persons and imbeciles who are under a restriction shall be of the same status as a minor of no capacity".

23 Article 170 of the CTC states that

1) Dispositions made by an idiot or person suffering from a mental disability occurring after either an application for a restriction has been made or after an order in that behalf has been made or after an application or order for restoration of guardianship has been made shall be subject to the same provisions as govern dispositions made by persons of defective capacity;
2) With regard to dispositions made prior to such restriction, they shall not be void or voidable unless they result from exploitation or conspiracy.

24 Article 35 of the UAE Evidence Law states that

1) In the absence of an agreement or a law provision to the contrary, and excluding commercial matters, evidence as to the existence of an act or as to its extinction may not be established by the testimony of witnesses where the value involved exceeds five thousand Dirham or is of undetermined value;
2) In the assessment of the obligation, its value at the moment of performing the act, without adding the accessories to the principal, shall be taken into account;
3) If the lawsuit includes several claims arising from a number of sources, proof may be established by testimony of witnesses for each claim not exceeding in value five thousand Dirham, although the total value of the claims exceeds this amount, or although they arise from dealings between the parties to the litigation themselves or from transactions of the same nature;
4) For the purpose of establishing partial payment, the value of the principal obligation shall be taken into account.

7.47 A third party is entitled to assume that an agent or representative held out by a company is duly authorized to represent that entity.[25] Accordingly, a company is bound by a contract executed by its employees provided that the position of the employees indicates that they are duly authorized and that the contract is entered into for a purpose that falls within the objects of the company.[26]

7.48 Special care is required, however, in to relation arbitration agreements and settlement agreements, which generally require the signatory to be in possession of an express delegation of authority. In such cases, a valid delegation of authority may take the form of the memorandum and articles of association of a company or a power of attorney, each of which is required expressly to delegate the authority to enter into an arbitration agreement or to settle litigation.

The Content of Contract

7.49 The scope of the contract is not limited to its general and particular conditions. It includes implied terms, mandatory and supplementary rules, customs and all appendices. Article 246(2) of the UAE Civil Code states that

> The contract shall not be restricted to an obligation upon the contracting party to do that which is (expressly) contained in it, but shall also embrace that which is appurtenant to it by virtue of the law, custom, and the nature of the transaction.

Terms of a Contract

7.50 Terms of the contract can be found in the general and particular conditions of the contract. Mandatory rules are part of the contract regardless of whether the contract includes a term to this effect. Any agreement to the contrary of a mandatory rule will be held null and void. In addition, relevant supplementary rules are also enforceable whenever the contract does not address the matters they deal with. In other words, such rules step in to fill the gaps, but they are only applicable if the contract does not provide otherwise.

7.51 Drawing the borderline between mandatory rules and supplementary rules is straightforward in most cases. Whenever the rule governs matters related to public order, the rule is a mandatory one. The Dubai Court of Cassation held that

> It is a settled principle that the rules of law that are regarded as matters of public order and may not be departed from by agreement between the parties are those rules designed to achieve a public political, social or economic interest relating to the higher governance of society, above the interests of individuals.
>
> [27]

7.52 Article 3 of the UAE Civil Code lists examples of public order matters. It states that

> Public order shall be deemed to include matters relating to personal status such as marriage, inheritance, and lineage, and matters relating to sovereignty, freedom of trade, the circulation

25 Article 23 of the UAE Commercial Companies Law 2015.
26 Article 25(1) of the UAE Commercial Companies Law 2015.
27 Dubai Court of Cassation, 280/2008.

of wealth, rules of private ownership and the other rules and foundations upon which society is based, in such a manner as not to conflict with the definitive provisions and fundamental principles of the Islamic *Shari'ah*.

7.53 Nevertheless, determining whether the rule is mandatory or not is still difficult in certain cases. For example, under Article 1099 of the UAE Civil Code, the suretyship shall terminate upon the death of the principal obligor. The wording of this article does not show whether parties can contract out of it; that is, to agree that the suretyship will survive and continue running in case the obligor passes away. This was a controversial point until the Dubai Court of Cassation held that there is nothing in the law preventing such an agreement.[28]

Unfair Contract Terms

7.54 The Freedom of Contract principle is well preserved in UAE and the Gulf region. Under this principle, parties are free to select terms of their choice for their contract as long as such terms are not in conflict with public order and common morals.

7.55 In principle, the court may not amend or reject the enforcement of any contractual term. The same applies even if the terms of the contract seem to be unfair for one party. If a party agrees on the contract with his own free will, the court will have no jurisdiction to amend or deny its enforcement.

7.56 The discretion of court to amend or avoid a contractual term is very limited.

7.57 Having said that, it is important to note that the UAE court can amend the contract or cross out certain contract terms in certain cases related to adhesion contracts, unforeseen circumstances and employment contracts.

7.58 Parties may have recourse to the court in cases of unfair terms of an adhesion contract. In UAE, the court may amend or avoid an unfair term of an adhesion contract in order to protect the adhering party. Article 248 of the Civil Code states that

> If the contract is made by way of adhesion and contains unfair provisions, it shall be permissible for the judge to vary those provisions or to exempt the adhering party therefrom in accordance with the requirements of justice, and any agreement to the contrary shall be void.

7.59 For a contract to be classified as adhesion, its terms must be imposed by one party, there is a kind of monopoly of the goods or service and the adhering party is in a serious need of the service or the goods. Perhaps, the obvious example in UAE is the utilities

28 The Dubai Court of Cassation, in the case of 280/2008, held that "the provisions of articles 1056, 1078 and 1099 of the Civil Code show that a guarantee is a consensual contract of indemnity under which a person guarantees the performance of an obligation by undertaking to the obligee that he will perform that obligation if the obligor himself does not satisfy it. Notwithstanding that the guarantee expires upon the death of the principal obligor, a contract may validly be made that it will continue, in that the guarantor will remain liable to guarantee the debt if the principal debtor dies, on the grounds that that agreement gives rise to a personal obligation of the guarantor. For such a contract to be made, it is sufficient that the parties thereto mutually consent. There is nothing in the law to prevent such an agreement. The obligation of the guarantor will not expire upon his death, but will remain as a liability of his estate and will devolve upon his heirs. If the principal debtor dies before the deferred debt falls due, the debt will be a liability on his estate. The effect of that is that when the date for payment of the debt arrives, the creditor may make a claim against the heirs of the debtor for payment of the debt within the limits that the estate has devolved upon them, or may make a claim against the guarantor if it has been agreed in the deed of guarantee that the obligation of the guarantor will not expire upon the death of the principal debtor, or that he may make a claim against them both together".

contract where there is only one provider of the service. The UAE Union Supreme Court held that:

> Article 248 of the Civil Code provides that if the contract is made by way of adhesion, and it contains arbitrary conditions, the judge may vary such conditions or may exempt the adhering party therefrom as justice may require. However, a contract of lease made between the parties to the dispute is not regarded as a contract of adhesion, because the appellant had the choice whether or not to make the contract or to lease any other property to carry on its business from any other landowner in town.
>
> 29

7.60 Moreover, under the hardship theory, the court may have the authority to amend the contract terms if unforeseen circumstances make the contract hard to perform. UAE law adopts the hardship theory under Article 249 of the Civil Code.[30] Obviously, the hardship has nothing to do with the fairness of the contract terms at the time of making the contract. The theory exists to respond to unforeseen events that affect the balance of the contract and make it very hard for one party or both parties to perform.

7.61 The UAE court has the discretion to amend an employment contract if it does not provide for certain rights required by the law. Employment law provides for the minimum benefits for workers, such as annual leave, gratuity, etc. If the contract provides less benefits, the court has the discretion to amend the contract in order to provide the worker with the minimum protection and benefits stated in the law. This is a matter of public order that cannot be varied by agreement.

Good Faith Obligations

7.62 The requirement to perform the contract in good faith is expressly stated in the UAE Civil Code. Article 246(1) states that "The contract must be performed in accordance with its contents, and in a manner consistent with the requirements of good faith".

7.63 The principle of good faith requires both parties to perform the contract in a way to achieve the best results. One of the main aspects of good faith here is the parties' duty of cooperation. Both parties must execute the contract fairly and responsibly. They need to act fairly in order to reach the best results that they reasonably expected at the time of making the contract. A party to the contract must avoid acts that prevent the other party from carrying out his obligations.

7.64 Contracts may expressly provide for some elements of the good faith principle. This has the advantage that it eliminates the controversies over the interpretation of the principle of good faith and its scope. The cooperation clause in FIDIC books is an example here.

7.65 The principle is designed to prevent one party from misusing the contract terms. For example, if the duty of the contractor is to obtain governmental permits and the

29 Union Supreme Court 472/Judicial Year 27. WestLaw Middle East publications.

30 Article 249 of the UAE Civil Code states that "If exceptional circumstances of a public nature which could not have been foreseen occur as a result of which the performance of the contractual obligation, even if not impossible, becomes oppressive for the obligor so as to threaten him with grave loss, it shall be permissible for the judge, in accordance with the circumstances and after weighing up the interests of each party, to reduce the oppressive obligation to a reasonable level if justice so requires, and any agreement to the contrary shall be void".

employer can help in obtaining such permits, the latter may be expected to do so under the principle of good faith.

7.66 Good faith is about honesty or sincerity of intention. Exercising a right in bad faith occurs in cases where a party's primary goal is to harm the other party, and not to protect his own contractual interests.

7.67 The applications of good faith principle can be found in numerous areas of contract law and property law. For example, it is not permissible to rely on a mistake for the purpose of rescinding a contract if such a reliance is inconsistent with principle of good faith.[31]

7.68 Further, the good faith principle can be used to protect an innocent person who is ignorant of certain realities. For example, payment made by a third party is not refundable if the creditor, acting in good faith, has been deprived of an instrument proving the debt.[32] Good faith principle, in such cases, is related to ignorance of reality. The creditor may not know that payment is made by an unauthorized third person, and thus, his action is made in good faith.

7.69 The principle of good faith may also aim to protect an innocent third party. For example, a sale contract made by a person, suffering from a deadly disease, may be cancelled or amended in certain cases under the UAE law. However, such a contract may not be cancelled if the purchaser has disposed the goods to confer a right on a third party acting in good faith.[33]

7.70 The good faith principle has several applications in property law. They all aim at protecting persons in possession of property in good faith; that is, ignorance of the absence of the right to possess.[34] Article 1312 of the UAE Civil Code is helpful in describing the person who possesses property in good faith. It states that

> A person in possession of a thing shall be deemed to be acting in good faith if he is ignorant that he is infringing the rights of another person, and good faith shall be presumed unless there is evidence to the contrary.

Vitiating Factors under Contract Law

7.71 The contract is a binding agreement between parties who have truly and genuinely given their consent. Defective consent can be caused by mistake or duress or misrepresentation and gross disparity.

31 Article 198 of the UAE Civil Code states that "A person who has made a mistake may not rely on it in a manner inconsistent with good faith".

32 Article 323 of the UAE Civil Code states that "If payment is obtained from a person other than the obligor and the result of that is that the obligee acting in good faith has been deprived of an instrument proving the debt or any security attaching thereto or if he has foreborne to make a claim against the true obligor within the time limit laid down, he does not have to return what he has taken, but the person who has paid may have a recourse against the true obligor for the obligation and render him a guarantor thereof if appropriate".

33 Article 601(1) of the UAE Civil Code states that "It shall not be permissible to cancel the sale of a sick person if the purchaser has disposed of the goods sold in such a way as to confer a right against consideration upon a third party acting in good faith".

34 See Articles 1318, 1325-1327, 1520, 1524 of the UAE Civil Code.

Mistake

7.72 A mistake is an illusion, about a certain matter such as the subject matter of the contract, the parties, the specifications, etc., that leads to the conclusion of the contract. Without such an illusion the party would not enter into the contractual relationship.

7.73 Bilateral mistake can make the contract avoidable. Unilateral mistake is effective only if the party, who is not under illusion, was aware or ought to have been aware that the other party is under an illusion and, due to this illusion, he is entering into the contract. For example, the buyer may return a television; that is, avoiding the sale contract, because he mistakenly thought that the television was a smart one, provided that the seller knew or ought to have known that the buyer was looking for a smart television. Article 193 of the UAE Civil Code states that "No regard shall be had for any mistake save in so far as it is contained in the form of the contract or demonstrated by the surrounding circumstances and conditions, or the nature of things, or custom".

7.74 Only the party who is making the contract under an effective mistake can avoid the contract. Obviously, this choice is not available for the other party who is bound by the contract.[35]

7.75 Effective mistakes may cause the contract to be invalid. Under the UAE law, if there is a mistake as to the type of contract or the subject matter of the contract, the contract maybe held void.[36]

7.76 Having said that, it is important to note that rectifiable mistakes may not be relied on to avoid the contract. This may apply to typos and errors in the contract documents. These mistakes can always be rectified and should not be a reason to avoid the contract. Article 197 of the UAE Civil Code states that "A mere mistake in an account or in a writing shall not affect the contract, and it shall simply be rectified".

7.77 Furthermore, the choice of avoiding the contract must be used in good faith. In the above example of the television sale, if the seller offers to replace the television by the required smart television and under the same contract conditions, the buyer will not have the choice to avoid the contract anymore.[37]

Duress

7.78 Duress is an illegitimate moral or material pressure on someone to do something without free consent. Article 176 of the UAE Civil Code defines duress as a "coercion of a person without the right of so doing to perform an act without his consent. Duress may be forcible or non-forcible, and may be material or moral".

7.79 In order to rely on duress to avoid a contract, it should be clear that:

35 This applies to cases where a party has made mistake in the characteristics of the contract or the other party. Article 195 of the UAE Civil Code states that "A contracting party shall have the right to cancel the contract if he has made a mistake in a desired (non-essential) matter such as a characteristic of the subject matter of the contract or the identity of the other contracting party or as to a characteristic of such person".

36 Article 194 of the UAE Civil Code states that "If there is a mistake as to the identity of the contract or as to one of the conditions upon which it is made or as to the subject matter of the contract, the contract shall be void".

37 Article 198 of the UAE Civil Code states that "A person who has made a mistake may not rely on it in a manner inconsistent with good faith".

(e) the victim would not have consented but for the threat. If it is clear that the victim would have consented to the transaction anyway, the threat cannot be considered as a cause of defective will. Thus, it does not affect the conclusion of the contract. To decide whether the threat was serious enough to force the victim to enter into a contract, one must consider all the circumstances of the case, including "age, weakness, position, rank, influence, the degree to which they are hurt by the duress whether lesser or greater, and by any factor which may affect the seriousness of the duress".[38]

(f) the person, causing the threat, can carry out his threat. If it is clear that the threat is beyond the ability of the person exercising it, it cannot be taken as a cause of defective will. The conclusion of the contract cannot be affected by such a threat.

(g) the victim reasonably believed that that the threat will be carried out immediately. Article 181 of the UAE Civil Code states that

> In order for there to be duress the person exercising it must be capable of carrying out his threat, and the victim must believe that the threat will be carried out immediately if he does not do that which he is coerced into doing.

7.80 Duress can be material such as a threat by using a weapon; or a moral one, such as a threat to disclose a secret. In both cases, the contract will be voidable. The victim may avoid the contract or choose to confirm it expressly or impliedly.

7.81 The confirmation of the contract can be express or implied. If the victim commences performing the contract after the threat disappears, his action will be considered as an implied confirmation of the contract.[39]

7.82 Duress can be made by a third party. A person may not rely on such a threat to avoid the contract unless he can show sufficient evidence that the other contracting party was aware or ought to have been aware of such a threat at the time of making the contract.[40]

Misrepresentation and Gross Disparity

7.83 Misrepresentation occurs "when one of the two contracting parties deceives the other by means of trickery of word or deed which leads the other to consent to what he would not otherwise have consented to".[41]

7.84 Acts of misrepresentation are made in bad faith. However, if the innocent party would have consented even if there was no misrepresentation, the validity and enforceability of the contract will not be affected by misrepresentation.

38 Article 180 of the UAE Civil Code states that "Duress may vary according to different persons, their age, weakness, position, rank, influence, the degree to which they are hurt by the duress whether lesser or greater, and by any factor which may affect the seriousness of the duress".

39 Article 182 of the UAE Civil Code states that "A person who exercises either kind of duress to conclude a contract may not enforce his contract, but the contract will be valid if the victim or his heirs so permit after the threat has ceased, either expressly or by their acts".

40 Article 184 of the UAE Civil Code states that "If the duress is exercised otherwise than by one of the contracting parties, the person coerced into contracting may not claim that the contract is ineffective unless he proves that the other contracting party knew or is presumed to have known of the duress".

41 Article 185 of the UAE Civil Code.

7.85 Means of misrepresentation include actions, documents, word of mouth, etc. A misrepresentation, made by a third party, may not affect the validity of the contract unless the other party was aware of such a misrepresentation at the time of making the contract.[42]

7.86 Silence can also be an act of misrepresentation if it was made on purpose; that is, deliberate silence, and the innocent party would not have consented to the contract if he was aware of the concealed information.[43]

7.87 For misrepresentation to affect the validity of the contract, it must be accompanied by gross disparity/cheating. That is to say that the market/actual value of the subject matter of the contract is substantially different from the contract price. Therefore, misrepresentation, which does not affect the value of the subject matter of the contract, has no impact on the validity and enforceability of the contract.

7.88 Gross disparity/cheating can be defined as the difference between the market price and the contract price. It will be considered gross/substantial cheating if the contract price is beyond the expectations of experts.

7.89 In principle, the combination of misrepresentation and gross cheating will render the contract voidable. The party who is misled by the misrepresentation, can avoid the contract provided that there is also a gross disparity/cheating.[44]

7.90 Gross disparity/cheating may be used alone to avoid the contract if the contract is related to the property of state or minors (persons under restrictions) or the so-called *waqf*.[45]

7.91 Finally, it is worth noting that the reliance on misrepresentation here is used to avoid the contract. If the innocent party wishes to sue for damages, this has to be in a tort action under Article 285 of the UAE Civil Code which states that "If a person deceives another, he shall be liable to make good the harm resulting from that deception".

The Rights and Liabilities of Third Parties

7.92 The privity principle is well-preserved under the UAE law. Only the parties to the contract can seek its enforcement.[46] The contract may not impose a duty on a third party but it may confer a benefit.[47]

---

42 Article 190 of the UAE Civil Code states that "If the misrepresentation is made by a person other than the contracting parties, and the person to whom the misrepresentation was made proves that the other contracting party knew of the misrepresentation, it shall be permissible for him to cancel the contract".

43 Article 186 of the UAE Civil Code states that "Deliberate silence concerning a fact or set of circumstances shall be deemed to be a misrepresentation if it is proved that the person misled thereby would not have made the contract had he been aware of that fact or set of circumstances".

44 Exceptionally, cheating alone, even the slight of cheating, may make the contract voidable if it affected a person under judicial restriction. Article 189 of the UAE Civil Code states that "If the cheating, however, slight, affects the property of a person under judicial restriction on account of a debt or a terminally ill person, and that person's liabilities exceed his assets, the contract shall be dependent upon the cheating being redressed, or the consent of the creditors, otherwise it shall be void".

45 *Waqf* is a property that is devoted for public benefits.

46 Article 250 of the UAE Civil Code states that "The effects of the contract shall extend to the contracting parties and their general successors without prejudice to the rules relating to inheritance, unless it appears from the contract or from the nature of the transaction or from the provisions of the law that the effects were not to extend to a general successor".

47 Article 252 of the UAE Civil Code states that "A contract may not impose an obligation upon a third party but it may create a right in him".

7.93 Parties may agree at the time of making the contract to confer the benefit on a third party. If this becomes the case, the intended third party beneficiary will have the right to sue under the contract and to seek the conferred benefits against the debtor.

7.94 The third party beneficiary has the choice to either accept or reject such a benefit. Unless and until the third party expresses his consent to a conferred right, the creditor may replace the third party beneficiary or may claim the benefit for himself. By doing so, the creditor should not impose any extra burden on the debtor.

7.95 Although the contract needs to clearly state that its subject matter is conferred on a third party, it is not necessary that the latter is mentioned by name. It is enough to state a certain characteristic that will identify the third party, such as the owner, contractor, etc. This may be the case where the contractor agrees with the supplier to extend the quality warranty to the benefit of the employer and subsequent buyers. At the time of procurement, these buyers may not be known. Actually, the third party beneficiary may not be in existence at the time of making the contract, such as a company under establishment.

7.96 Parties may also agree to assign the rights to a third party. Under the UAE law, assignments of obligations and rights are possible. Assignment to a third party requires the consent of the three parties. It is quite common for the employer and the master contractor to agree to assign the rights of the latter against the subcontractor to the employer. Here, the effective assignment requires the consent of the subcontractor as well. The UAE Union Supreme Court held that

> The effect of the provisions of Articles 252, 258 and 265 of the Civil Code is that the effects of a contract do not devolve on a third party who was not party to the contract, whether those effects amount to a right or an obligation, and the third party will not acquire any of the rights arising out of the contract save by the agreement of the parties to the contract, or by the transfer of the right to him in accordance with the law.
>
> *48*

7.97 This is important in cases where the maintenance period under the subcontract is longer than the maintenance period under the master contract. In order for the employer to be able to benefit from the subcontract maintenance period, the contractor needs to assign this right against the subcontractor to the employer.

7.98 A third party beneficiary can also be a successor. If a right is connected to something, the right will be transferred to whoever owns this thing. In sale contracts, all rights connected to the sold object will be transferred to the buyer. The Abu Dhabi Court of Cassation held that:

> the effect of a contract extends to the contracting parties and to a general successor, unless it appears from the contract or from the nature of the transaction or from a provision in the law that such effect will not extend to a general successor. If a contract establishes personal rights connected with a thing that is thereafter transferred to a special successor, such rights will be transferred to the successor at the same time as the thing passes, if it is one of the appurtenances thereof, and if the special successor knows of them at the time of the transfer of the thing to him. So far as concerns obligations created by the contract, they will not pass to a special successor

48 The UAE Union Supreme Court, 135/Judicial Year 21.

unless they are part of the appurtenances of the thing passing to such successor, and are specified in his favour as imposing restrictions or narrowing his scope.

[49]

Performance of Contract

7.99 Parties need to comply with all the terms of contract and carry out all their contractual obligations in good faith.[50] Contractual duties can be either duties of purpose or duties of care.

7.100 In cases of duty of care, the debtor needs only to pay reasonable efforts to reach the hoped outcome. For example, the duty of the physician is to treat the patient according to the required standards. If the patient nevertheless is not cured, the physician will not be legally liable. This may also apply to most duties of the lawyers who are under a duty to pay reasonable care in representing their clients. In such cases, the creditor will need to prove the negligence of the debtor. It is not enough for the creditor to show that the hoped outcome was not accomplished.

7.101 In construction contracts, most contractor's duties are duties of purpose. In other words, if the agreed outcome is not reached, the contractor will be in breach of contract. For such a liability, the employer will only need to show that the performance of contract is defective or not in compliance with the agreed terms.

7.102 Parties need to honour their promises as agreed in the contract. It is well settled under UAE law that the contract cannot be amended unilaterally. It can only be amended by the mutual consent of both parties.

7.103 However, exceptionally, the court may have some discretion to alter some terms of the contract. In the case of unforeseen circumstances, the court can amend the contract in light of the hardship theory. Furthermore, there are also quasi-performance means. Under the UAE law, these include substitute performance, set-off, and merger.

Substitute Performance

7.104 Parties may agree on a substitute subject matter to the contract.[51] In order to so, the original rights must be certain and not be disputed by either party. Such an agreement will terminate the original obligation and replace it with a new one.

49 Abu Dhabi Court of Cassation, 351/Judicial Year 3.

50 Article 246 of the UAE Civil Code states that

1. The contract must be performed in accordance with its contents, and in a manner consistent with the requirements of good faith.
2. The contract shall not be restricted to an obligation upon the contracting party to do that which is (expressly) contained in it, but shall also embrace that which is appurtenant to it by virtue of the law, custom, and the nature of the transaction.

51 Article 365 of the UAE Civil Code states that "An obligee may, in satisfaction of his right, accept another thing or another act performed by the obligor, and the agreement to the substitution shall be subject to the general provisions governing contracts as laid down in this Law".

7.105 In cases of substituted performance, according to Article 367 of the UAE Civil Code,[52] all securities of performance of the original duties will expire and cannot be relied on by the creditor. The UAE Union Supreme Court held that "With such substituted performance, the first obligation with its guarantees will expire, and the right of the obligee will transfer immediately to the substitute".[53]

7.106 Thereupon, parties need to take the securities into accounts when they agree on any substitute performance. For example, parties may need to agree expressly that performance bonds will stay valid and in force even after the agreement on a substitute performance. They may include this point in their agreement for the substitute performance.

Set-Off

7.107 Set-off can be defined as an exchange of rights.[54] This requires both parties' rights to be due and of the same nature and between the same parties.

7.108 If both debts are of the same nature, there will no need for the exchange of payment. The debt will automatically expire to the extent of the lesser debt.[55] However, third parties must not be harmed by such a set-off. The Abu Dhabi Court of cassation held that

> in order for there to be a mandatory set-off by operation of law, or a judicial set-off, it is a pre-condition that that procedure should not prejudice any third party rights, whether the cause of the two debts is the same or different. Further, it is not permissible to conduct a set-off if one of the debts is coupled with a third party right precluding satisfaction of it, and the set-off will not be made in detriment to rights acquired by a third party.
>
> [56]

7.109 If any of the requirements of the set-off is disputed, the court will have the jurisdiction to decide on the availability of the set-off. This is called a judicial set-off. Further, parties may wish to agree on set-off even if not all requirements are met. For example, if one of the debts is not yet due, still both parties can agree on set-off. The same will apply if the nature of the debts differs.[57]

7.110 In brief, set-off may occur by the operation of the law, where all the requirements are met, or by the consent of the parties or by a court order.

7.111 If all requirements are present and, nevertheless, one of the parties choses to pay his debt, he shall not be able to take the benefits of the securities of his rights against the other party, such as personal guarantees. If a party neglects the right to offset his debt, he

52 Article 367 of the UAE Civil Code states that "The original obligation, together with any securities pertaining thereto, shall be extinguished by the substituted performance, and the rights of the obligee shall be transferred to the substitute".

53 UAE Union Supreme Court, 354/Judicial Year 22. Publications of Westlaw Middle East.

54 Article 368 of the UAE Civil Code states that "Set-off is the satisfaction of an obligation of the obligee by an obligation to be performed by the obligor".

55 The Dubai Court of Cassation held that "in order for there to be a set-off both parties must be both the debtor and the creditor of the other, and the debts must be of the same kind and description, and must both be due and of equal strength or weakness, because that is one of the modes of extinction of an obligation, in that instead of each of them making payment of the debt to the other, both debts will become extinguished to the extent of the lesser of them".

56 Abu Dhabi Court of Cassation, 12/Judicial Year 1.

57 Article 369 of the UAE Civil Code states that "Set-off may either be mandatory, occurring by operation of law, or voluntary, occurring by agreement between the parties, or judicial, occurring by order of the court".

will lose all the securities for his corresponding right unless he proves that he did not and had no reason to know of the existence of the corresponding right.

7.112 Finally, it should be noted that, unless the parties agree otherwise, the set-off cannot occur if the corresponding debt is of a deposit nature.[58] In effect, banks may not conduct a set-off among independent accounts of the depositor unless both the depositor and the bank agreed otherwise. The Dubai Court of cassation held that:

> The effect of Article 376 of the Commercial Code is that if one person has more than one current account with a bank, the rule is that each account is independent of the other, unless the customer, the holder of those accounts with the bank, agrees that the accounts should be linked whether by way of allocation of the credit balance by way of collateral for a debit balance on another account, or by way of amalgamation of the accounts, so that they will be treated as one account, irrespective of the type or nature of the accounts. The fact that each account is independent of the other means that there may be no set-off between them. The effect of that is that the bank must pay to its customer the credit balance without being able to rely on a set-off to recover the indebtedness owing to it on an account that is in debit. Likewise, the customer may not withhold payment to the bank of the amount due on a debit account when it is closed, notwithstanding that he may have another credit account, save by way of judicial set-off and by the procedures referred to in Articles 97 and 99 of the Civil Code.
>
> [59]

Merger

7.113 Where the creditor and debtor merge to create a new legal entity, the debt will automatically perish. Merger will in effect cause both the creditor and debtor to disappear in order to make a new form of entity that includes both.

7.114 In cases of takeover where the creditor or the debtor becomes part of the other, the debt will also perish.

7.115 Inheritance may lead to the termination of debt. If the creditor or debtor solely inherits the other, the debt will cease to exist.

7.116 If creditor is not the sole heir, he will be paid back his debt before the distribution of the inheritance among all heirs. On the other hand, if the debtor is not the sole heir, he will have to pay the debt to all heirs after deducting his share of the inheritance.

Termination of Contract

7.117 Contracts can be terminated by either the operation of law or a court order or the mutual consent of the parties.

7.118 In cases of force majeure events, the contract becomes impossible to perform and, thus, it ends. Force majeure circumstances can be natural disasters or law changes that prevent the performance of the contract.

58 Article 373 of the UAE Civil Code states that "If a bailee is under an obligation to his bailor, or if a person who has misappropriated goods is owed an obligation by the person from whom the goods have been misappropriated, and the obligation is of the same nature as the goods deposited or misappropriated, there shall be no set-off save by the agreement of the parties".

59 Dubai Court of Cassation, 141/2008. Westlaw Middle East Publications.

7.119 In this type of termination, the significant issue is whether the contract price remains applicable for the purpose of calculating the contractor's payment for the completed works.[60] The UAE Union Supreme Court held that

> The effect of Article 894 of the Civil Code is that if the contractor is unable to complete the works that he has begun to execute for some force majeure reason in which he played no part, then the contract will be set aside and the positions of the contracting parties will be liquidated. The employer must pay to the contractor the value of the works that he has completed, and what he has expended in executing what has not been completed, to the extent of the benefit devolving on the employer from such works and expenses.
>
> *61*

7.120 According to the above Article, the contractor's payment is capped at the market value of the benefit conferred upon the employer. Contractors may need to pay attention to this risk at the time of calculating the tender price. Parties have the option to contract out of this article as it is not a mandatory rule.

7.121 In cases of defective performance, the contractor may be given a chance to rectify the defect if it is rectifiable. If the defect is substantial and the contractor is either incapable of fixing it within a reasonable period of time and/or announced that he will not fix it or could not fix it within the reasonable period, the employer may claim the termination of contract.[62,63]

7.122 The court may terminate the contract upon the request of either party in cases of substantial breach. However, such a court order may not be obtainable where the breach is negligible or rectifiable within a reasonable period of time.[64] Furthermore, the party who claims the termination in such cases must not be himself in breach of contract.

---

60 Article 894 of the UAE Civil Code states that "If the contractor commences to perform the work and then becomes incapable of completing it for a cause in which he played no part, he shall be entitled to the value of the work which he has completed and the expenses he has incurred in the performance thereof up to the amount of the benefit the employer has derived therefrom".

61 Union Supreme court, 213/Judicial Year 23.

62 Article 877 of the UAE Civil Code states that "The contractor must complete the work in accordance with the conditions of the contract. If it appears that he is carrying out what he has undertaken to do in a defective manner or in a manner in breach of the agreed conditions, the employer may require that the contract be terminated immediately if it is impossible to make good the work, but if it is possible to make good the work it shall be permissible for the employer to require the contractor to abide by the conditions of the contract and to repair the work within a reasonable period. If such period expires without the reparation being performed, the employer may apply to the judge for the cancellation of the contract or for leave to himself to engage another contractor to complete the work at the expense of the first contractor".

63 The Dubai Court of Cassation, in 51/2007, held that "If it appears that he has done what he undertook to do defectively, or otherwise than in accordance with the conditions, then the employer may require that the contract be rescinded immediately if it is not possible to make good the work. If, however, it is possible to make good the work, the employer may require the contractor to abide by the conditions of the contract and to rectify the work within a reasonable period. If that period expires without the rectification being done, it will be open for the employer to apply to the judge for rescission of the contract or that he be given leave to engage another contractor to carry out the work at the expense of the first contractor. Further, the contractor guarantees his work against any defect or loss whether arising through his infringement or default or otherwise, but such obligation will be negated if the incident arises out of something that could not have been guarded against".

64 Article 86 Dubai International Financial Centre Law No. 6 2004 states that:

> "(1) A party may terminate the contract where the failure of the other party to perform an obligation under the contract amounts to a fundamental non-performance.

7.123 Parties may always agree to terminate the contract. Article 268 of the UAE Civil Code states that "The contracting parties may mutually revoke the contract by their mutual consent after it has been concluded". Here, parties may need to agree on the consequences of such a termination. For example, they need to agree on the payment, any compensations, any expenses, etc.

7.124 It is possible to agree expressly by a contractual term that one party or both parties have the right to terminate the contract for no cause; that is, termination for convenience. Although termination for convenience is implemented unilaterally by one party, it is consented mutually by an express contract term. This may fall under the aforementioned Article 268 of the UAE Civil Code.

7.125 Finally, it should be noted that "Anticipatory breach" is not expressly recognized in the UAE Civil Code. However, it seems that the court is willing to terminate the contract if there is sufficient evidence showing that the creditor will not or will not be able to carry out his obligations on time. The Dubai Court of Cassation allowed the termination of sale of off-plan sales on the ground that the employer will not be able to handover the real estate at the agreed time.[65] [66]

Remedies for Breach of Contract

7.126 The primary remedy for breach of contract is specific performance. In other words, the debtor must perform all his obligations and in good faith.

7.127 A court order for specific performance may not be obtainable in certain cases:

(h) The performance of the contract is impossible;
(i) Parties agreed expressly on the type of remedy;
(j) The performance of the contract requires the personal skills of the debtor who refuses to perform.

7.128 In such cases, the court will order damages instead of specific performance. In construction contracts, it is quite common to find a liquidated damages clause. The judge has a full authority to adjust the liquidated damages clause in order to make damages

(2) In determining whether a failure to perform an obligation amounts to a fundamental non-performance regard shall be had, in particular, to whether:

(a) The non-performance substantially deprives the aggrieved party of what it was entitled to expect under the contract;
(b) Strict compliance with the obligation which has not been performed is of essence under the contract;
(c) The non-performance is intentional or reckless;
(d) The non-performance gives the aggrieved party reason to believe that it cannot rely on the other party's future performance".

65 Dubai Court of Cassation, 200/2013.

66 Art. 88 the Dubai International Financial Centre Contract Law No 6 of 2004 provides for right to terminate in anticipation of non-performance. It states that "Where prior to the date for performance by one of the parties it is clear that there will be a fundamental non-performance by that party, the other party may terminate the contract".

equal to the actual loss. Under UAE law, creditors cannot be overcompensated even where there is an agreed damages clause. Article 390 of the UAE Civil Code states that

> (1) The contracting parties may fix the amount of compensation in advance by making a provision therefor in the contract or in a subsequent agreement, subject to the provisions of the law. (2) The judge may in all cases, upon the application of either of the parties, **vary such agreement so as to make the compensation equal to the loss, and any agreement to the contrary shall be void**.
>
> *[Emphasis Added]*

7.129 Article 390 is a mandatory rule and, thus, parties cannot alter or exclude its application by contract. However, this article may not apply to the agreed cap of liability. It is a common practice to disregard Article 390 in governmental contracts. The court may reject the application of this article in governmental contracts due to the difficulties in calculating the actual loss. For example, the actual losses resulting from the contractor's delay in infrastructure projects may not be easy to calculate. The government may not incur a monetary loss but the public may be hurt due to the delay in the project.

7.130 It is quite common in construction contracts to agree on a certain cap for the contractor's liability. This may be considered as a kind of limitation of liability, which is permissible under UAE law in contractual liability that does not result from fraud or gross negligence.[67] Needless to say that any attempt to limit or exempt a tortious liability will be void. Therefore, if a breach of contract amounts to a tortious liability in addition to contractual liability, any exemption or limitation of such a liability will be void.

7.131 Of course, Article 390 has nothing to do with the settlement agreement which parties reach after the occurrence of the breach. The court may not have a discretion to judge on the fairness of such settlements unless the settlement amounts to an adhesion contract or the will of one of the parties or both parties is defective due to mistake or duress or fraud and gross disparity.

7.132 Liquidated damages clauses do not apply after the termination of contract. However, in cases of delay prior to the termination of contract, the liquidated damages clause remains applicable.

7.133 The UAE court recognizes the concept of accrued rights. Accrued contractual rights can still be claimed under the contract even after its termination.

7.134 The quantification of damages is a matter of fact that must be determined by the trial judge. The supreme court will not oversee the quantification of damages as long as it is based on a sound reasoning.

7.135 However, the trial judge needs to expressly state the elements of damages. It is possible to award damages as a total lump sum provided that the elements of loss are expressly stated.

67 Article 383 of the UAE Civil Code states that "(1) If that which is required of an obligor is the preservation of a thing, or the management thereof, or the exercise of care in the performance of his obligation, he shall have discharged that obligation if, in the performance thereof, he exercises all such care as the reasonable man would exercise, notwithstanding that the intended object is not achieved, unless there is an agreement or a provision of law to the contrary. (2) In all cases, the obligor shall remain liable for any fraud or gross negligence on his part".

7.136 Damages for loss of profit resulting from breach of contract are recoverable under UAE law unless the parties agree otherwise.

7.137 Usually parties agree to exclude the contractor's damages for loss of profit in cases of employer's termination of contract for convenience. If the contractor is compensated for all his losses, including loss of profit, resulting from the employer's termination of contract for convenience, there will be no difference between defective termination and termination for convenience. Therefore, parties need to agree on the consequences of the termination for convenience. Standard contracts, such as the FIDIC books, include terms that grant the employer the right to terminate the contract for convenience provided that the contractor is fully compensated for all his losses excluding the loss of profit.

Interpretation of Contract

7.138 Under UAE law, interpretation of contracts is based on the actual will of both parties. If the words of the contract are clear, the court will apply the common meanings of the contract terms. Article 265(1) of the UAE Civil Code states that "If the wording of a contract is clear, it may not be departed from by way of interpretation to ascertain the intention of the parties".

7.139 If there is any term in the contract that can have several meanings, the judge will need to decide on meaning intended by the parties. This is not necessarily the meaning that a layman may intend. Interpretation is conducted under an objective method; that is, what a reasonable person may understand; it is rather the actual will of both parties that govern the interpretation. Article 265(2) of the UAE Civil Code states that

> If there is scope for an interpretative construction of the contract, an enquiry shall be made into the mutual intentions of the parties beyond the literal meaning of the words, and guidance may be sought in so doing from the nature of the transaction, and the trust and confidence which should exist between the parties in accordance with the custom current in (such) dealings.

7.140 Article 265 provides a number of guidelines that may be followed by the trial judge. First of all, the judge needs to reach the intended meaning of the words and not their literal meaning. In doing so, the judge may take into account:

(k) The nature of the transaction;
(l) The trust and confidence between the parties;
(m) The relevant customs.

7.141 All contract documents can be used for the purpose of interpreting any contract term. For example, the judge may refer to an appendix in order to interpret a term in the particular conditions.

7.142 Any ambiguity shall be interpreted in favour of the debtor as no debt is presumed and the person, in principle, is not indebted unless proven otherwise. However, in adhesion contracts, the interpretation shall be in favour of the adhering party even if he is the creditor.[68]

68 Article 266 of the UAE Civil Code states that "(1) A doubt shall be resolved in favour of the obligor. (2) Nevertheless it shall not be permissible to construe ambiguous words in contracts of adhesion in a manner detrimental to the interests of the adhering party".

7.143 Interpretation is a matter of fact that needs to be conducted by the trial judge. The Dubai Court of cassation held that:

> The trial court has complete jurisdiction over the interpretation of the evidence and documents, and over the interpretation of contracts pursuant to the provisions of Articles 257, 265, and 266 of the Civil Code, and in drawing conclusions as it deems closest to the common purpose and intention of the contracting parties, provided that its judgment is founded on sound reasons derived from the matters proved by the papers and that it does not depart from the evident meaning of the expressions used in the contract or the agreement. In so doing, it must take all of the words and expressions of those documents as a whole, and must be guided by the nature of the transaction and the necessary element of confidence and trust between the contracting parties in accordance with the custom prevalent in transactions, and any doubt in the interpretation of the meaning of the words contained in a contract of insurance must not be construed against the assured or the beneficiary, on the grounds that this is a contract of adhesion.
>
> [69]

National Standard Forms of Contract in GCC Countries

Public Procurement and Tender Laws

7.144 Throughout the Gulf a distinction is drawn between public and private sector projects for the purposes of procurement and tendering. Tendering and procurement processes for private sector projects are subject to laws and regulations governing commercial transactions and, accordingly, are lightly regulated. Public projects, in contrast, are subject to a class of laws and regulations that exist specifically and exclusively to regulate the applicable procurement and tendering processes. The status of this class of laws is an area of uncertainty, specifically whether they are limited to serving as internal departmental regulations or operate as laws of specific application.

7.145 In relation to public projects regard should be had to the following laws and regulations:

- (n) Bahrain Decree 36/2002 regulating government tenders and purchases and Bahrain Decree 37/2002 issuing the amending regulations of the law regulating government tenders and purchases;
- (o) Saudi Arabia Royal Decree No. M/58/4 Ramadan 1427H/27 September 2006 government tenders and procurement law;
- (p) Oman Tenders Law No. 36/2008 and Oman Decree No. 29/2010 implementing regulations for the Tenders Law;
- (q) UAE Ministerial Decision No. 20/2000 on rules and procedures for purchase contracts and works contracts;
- (r) Qatar Law No. 26/2005 issuing the tenders and bids regulations law;
- (s) Kuwait Law 37/1967 pertaining to public tenders.

7.146 In general, the above laws mandate that building projects are procured by means of competitive tender through a standardized process which includes imposition of

69 The Dubai Court of Cassation 125/2009.

requirements for bid bonds, disqualification of bidders in certain circumstances and the types of information to be furnished.

Standard Form Construction Contracts

7.147 Traditional forms of procurement are the mainstay of the projects market in the Gulf, with lump sum price and remeasurement remaining common. The suite of contract conditions published by FIDIC satisfies the demand for these conventional forms of pricing.

7.148 Alternative approaches to contracting, such as partnering and public private partnerships have generally failed to overcome the region's attachment to more traditional forms of procurement. Enabling legislation for privately funded infrastructure has been adopted in many Gulf States and has resulted in some progress, notably in the power and water sector but adoption in other sectors has been sluggish. The adoption of public private partnership laws in Dubai[70] and Kuwait[71] reflects cautious progress towards expanding the adoption of this model to other project types.[72]

7.149 A consultant-led procurement model remains deeply entrenched and is reinforced by laws and regulations that enforce a separation of construction and engineering activities. A contractor's commercial licence, for example, cannot combine both general contracting and engineering design throughout most of the Gulf states. Although some workarounds have been found and some limited relaxations have been granted[73] the applicable laws are a further deterrent to a change in procurement methodologies.

7.150 Many of the Gulf states have adopted standard forms of contract for use on public projects. In practice, however, adherence to the mandated forms is patchy. Thus, in Saudi Arabia, government departments and ministries are required by the Government Tenders and Procurement Law to use standard form contracts approved by the Ministry of Finance. Such approved standard form contracts include the construct-only standard form known as the Public Works Contract, which is loosely modelled on the Conditions of Contract for Works of Civil Engineering Construction, published by FIDIC, 3rd edition, 1977. Notwithstanding these mandated forms, many of the kingdom's high-profile mega projects are being procured on forms of contract that have been prepared on a project-by-project basis.

7.151 Regulations applicable in Abu Dhabi, likewise, prescribe the forms of contract for procurement of certain public works. The prescribed forms comprise, in dual English and Arabic, the FIDIC Conditions and the Conditions of Contract for Plant and Design – Build (1999), published by FIDIC, incorporating amendments. These prescribed conditions are not, however, widely used in practice.

70 Dubai Law No. 22/2015.

71 Kuwait Law No. 116/2014.

72 Saudi Arabia published a draft law on private/public sector partnerships in July 2018 and Oman has also indicated an intention to establish a PPP authority.

73 Dubai Municipality allows contractors to design and build steel structures of up to two stories without appointing a consultant.

Construction Law Issues Specific to GCC Countries

Interest and Financing Charges

7.152 The relationship between the laws of Gulf states and the Islamic *Shari'ah* is a defining characteristic of these legal systems. This has potentially significant implications when it comes to the application of contractual interest provisions.

7.153 The Islamic practice of prohibiting the charging of interest in transactions arises from the provision that:

"God deprives usurious gains of all blessing, whereas He blesses charitable deeds with manifold increase".[74]

7.154 The Islamic concept of *riba*, a rough translation of the English "usury", is thus prohibited by the Qur'an. The difficulty arises from the lack of consensus as to what exactly constitutes *riba*. Whilst the charging of excessive interest is widely, but not exclusively, regarded as a defining characteristic of *riba*,[75] it is not universally accepted that the definition is limited to excessive interest or usury.

7.155 In addition to the *Shari'ah* prohibition against *riba*, the UAE, as well as other Gulf States,[76] has enacted both civil[77] and criminal[78] provisions against the practice of *riba* and usury.

7.156 In practice, the impact of these provisions on commercial transactions is largely neutralized in most Gulf States[79] by legislation that is aimed at enabling and encouraging thriving commercial and banking industries. Thus, the UAE Code of Commercial Practice permits the parties to apply interest to loans and other business transactions (including construction contracts).[80] Moreover, in the absence of an agreement, commercial debts attract interest at the prevailing market rate up to a limit of 12% per annum.[81]

7.157 For the purpose of applying interest pursuant to the statutory regime, a distinction is drawn by the UAE courts depending on whether interest is claimed in respect of a debt which is of a fixed amount or on an amount that requires assessment. A court is more likely to award interest if the amount of the debt is fixed on the date it falls due.[82]

7.158 In a construction context, the above rules can be unhelpful to contractors seeking interest on unpaid portions of the contract price. This is because, in terms of its status as a debt, it only becomes crystallized or is fixed upon certification. As contractor claims commonly arise in respect of amounts which have not been certified, interest does not generally accrue on these claims until judgment of the court is issued.

---

74 Qur'an, chapter 2, verse 276.

75 For a discussion and contrary view on the need for excess, at least in relation to interest on loans: "Stipulation of Excess in Understanding and Misunderstanding *Riba*: The Al-Jassas Link", Dr Mohammad Omar Farooq, ALQ 21 (2001).

76 Bahrain Civil Code, Article 228 and Kuwait Civil Code, Article 305.

77 UAE Civil Code, Articles 204 and 714 and "The New Civil Code of the United Arab Emirates", W.M. Ballantyne, ALQ Vol. 1, Iss. 3, p. 263.

78 UAE Penal Code, Article 409. Also, the Bahrain Penal Code, Article 401, makes usury a crime.

79 Saudi Arabia is an exception.

80 UAE Code of Commercial Practice, Article 77. Also, Bahrain Commerce Law, Article 81, and the Kuwait Commerce Law, Article 110.

81 UAE Code of Commercial Practice, Article 76.

82 Dubai Cassation No. 52/1997 dated 6 April 1997.

7.159 The concept of financing charges has, historically, been used by parties seeking to avoid the complications that can arise out of a claim for interest under a contract or at law. Broadly, financing charges relate to the costs of financing incurred by one party which arise out of the failure of the other party to make payment of an amount due, on time. These costs are, most commonly, either borrowing costs or the loss of investment income and, as actual costs, must be properly evidenced as having been incurred.

7.160 The laws of GCC countries do not provide any express prohibition on awarding financing charges. Qatar, in fact, expressly allows such claims.[83] As financing charges are often based on a claim for damages, rather than an express contractual term, a party claiming financing charges is required to prove the actual loss. Provided that such a loss can be proved, financing charges are recoverable, in principle.

Decennial Liability

7.161 The design and construction of safe structures is recognized in the Civil Codes of the GCC states as matter of public policy. In consequence, these Civil Codes allocate the risk of serious structural defects to the consultant and contractor jointly and severally.[84] This marks a notable departure from the corresponding position at common law which does not single out liability for structural failure from liability for defects in general but is consistent with an approach that imposes risk on those that possess a special skill or technical knowledge.

7.162 In the UAE decennial liability runs, as the name suggests, for a period of ten years beginning from the time of handover.[85] Contractors and consultants will be liable jointly and severally to their employers (but not to third parties)[86] for issues relating to the safety or structural integrity of the buildings they design and/or construct. Design consultants who provide designs but do not oversee construction works face liability for structural issues arising from the design, but not workmanship or construction defects.[87]

7.163 Decennial liability will be triggered by the "*partial or total structural collapse*" or "*defects threatening the stability or safety of a structure*".[88] Those terms are not defined in the applicable legislation and have not been clarified significantly by the courts. Whether or not the triggers for decennial liability have occurred will, therefore, likely be determined by the Court of Merits as matters of fact specific to each case.

7.164 It has been confirmed by the Federal Supreme Court in the UAE that decennial liability is strict, and is not dependent upon proof of wrongdoing. The Federal Supreme Court held, in finding against a consultant and a contractor, that "*breach of the obligation is established whenever the result has not been attained without the need to prove*

83 Qatar Civil Code, Article 268.

84 UAE Civil Code, Article 880 and Kuwait Civil Code, Article 692, Oman Civil Code, Article 634, Qatar Civil Code, Article 711 and, to some extent, Saudi Arabia Government Tenders and Procurement Law, Article 76.

85 Federal Supreme Court No. 293/2009 dated 27 May 2009.

86 Dubai Cassation No. 150/2007 dated 7 October 2007.

87 Federal Supreme Court No. 2/21 dated 1 April 2001.

88 UAE Civil Code, Article 880.

any wrongdoing".[89] The required result in terms of decennial liability is the design and construction of a building that is free from defects which threaten its stability or safety.

7.165 Whilst there is no requirement to establish fault, for the purposes of decennial liability, it remains necessary for there to be an element of causation. Therefore, in a case in which it was established that the causes of cracking in a commercial building was the trenching and tunnelling works being carried out at an adjacent property, liability was avoided by the consultant and the contractor.[90] Notably, however, the onus will be on the contractor or consultant to prove that the relevant damage arose due to an external cause.[91]

7.166 A contractor and consultant will be jointly and severally liable to pay compensation, calculated on the same basis as damages for breach of contract, arising out of decennial liability. However, the Federal Supreme Court has confirmed that the courts have discretion to apportion damages between a contractor and a consultant "*pro rata to their respective contribution to the occurrence of damage*".[92] Any apportionment will affect the respective amounts payable by a contractor and consultant, if both parties are solvent, but will not affect an employer's ability to claim full payment from either party, pursuant to the principle of joint and several liability.

7.167 Decennial liability has mandatory status under the UAE Civil Code and, as such "*Any agreement the effect of which is to exempt the contractor or the consultant from liability, or to limit such liability, shall be void*".[93]

7.168 It is, theoretically, possible for contractors or consultants to mitigate the risk of decennial liability through insurance. Although some standard forms of insurance available in the UAE, such as insurance against inherent defects, or professional indemnity insurance, give the appearance of providing coverage for decennial liability, such policies are unlikely to provide an adequate indemnity. Decennial liability cover is a specialized product that is not widely available in the region.

Establishment and Licensing Issues

7.169 Each of the GCC member states has its own distinct corporate licensing regime and as a result the establishment options and licensing requirements vary between the member states. There is not, therefore, a single approach to corporate licensing and establishment in the construction sector which will be universally appropriate or applicable in all GCC member states.

7.170 Typically, a company may only carry on work in the construction sector in a GCC member state (or Emirate, in the case of the UAE) if it has registered a presence in that member state (or Emirate, in the case of the UAE) and obtained a corporate registration which authorizes it to do so. A number of terms are used in the different GCC member states to refer to the document that records a corporate registration, such as an operating licence or commercial registration.

89 Federal Supreme Court No. 336 and 470/21 dated 20 March 2001, previously Federal Supreme Court Nos. 101, 102, and 59/16 dated 28 June 1998.

90 Federal Supreme Court Nos. 722 and 735/22 dated 9 October 2001.

91 Federal Supreme Court Nos. 722 and 735/22 dated 9 October 2001.

92 Federal Supreme Court Nos. 336 and 407/21 dated 20 March 2001.

93 UAE Civil Code, Article 882.

7.171 In most cases, it will not be possible for a company to lawfully employ employees or commence business operations in a GCC member state until it has registered a presence in that GCC member state.

7.172 Corporate registrations in the GCC will ordinarily permit the registration holder to carry on the specific business activities listed on its registration in the GCC member state (or Emirate, in the case of the UAE) in which the registration has been issued.

7.173 Companies can structure their operations in the GCC member states in a number of different ways. The most common structures for companies operating in the construction sector (depending on the work that they carry out in that sector and the GCC member state in which they propose to operate) are typically:

(a) Registering a branch office;
(b) Incorporating a company with limited liability.

7.174 There are restrictions in some of the GCC member states on the type of work that can be performed through each of the above structures, and in some cases, for whom that work can be performed.

7.175 There are also restrictions on foreign ownership which apply, to varying degrees, to companies incorporated with limited liability in each of the GCC member states. Navigating those restrictions is often a challenging priority for investors from outside the GCC who are looking to establish operations in the GCC member states. At the time of writing, foreign ownership regimes are in a period of change in a number of GCC member states.

7.176 The construction sector is regulated in all of the GCC member states, but the extent of that regulation varies depending on a number of factors, including the particular member state and the nature of the work to be performed "on the ground". Ordinarily, a company will not be permitted to obtain or maintain a corporate registration which authorizes the registration holder to carry on work in the construction sector unless approvals from one or more sector specific regulators are obtained. Obtaining those approvals can be challenging. The complexity of the process of obtaining those approvals will vary depending on the GCC member state and the nature of the work to be carried out. Requirements for obtaining construction sector specific regulatory approvals may include any one, or a combination, of capital investment, the employment of individuals with specific qualifications or experience, evidence of prior projects, the employment of certain numbers of employees, the ownership of plant and machinery "in country" and the employment of nationals of the GCC member states (amongst many other things).

7.177 In the GCC member states, there are often restrictions on the combination of work that may be carried out under a single corporate registration. By way of example, it may not be possible for a company to establish a presence in a GCC member state and obtain a corporate registration which authorizes that company to carry on both contracting works and engineering design.

Alternative Dispute Resolution

7.178 There is a commonly held belief that mediation and amicable settlement is an ancient tradition of the Gulf that has been carried forward into the current business practices of the region. Although there is ample evidence that resolving disputes or differences amicably has been part of the local culture for several millennia there are reasons to question whether and to what extent this has survived the transformation of the region's business environment since the discovery and exploitation of the region's natural resources. Indeed, the inevitable formalization of business relationships, the introduction of a substantial body of laws and independent courts in which to resolve disputes are evidence of an economy that has developed well beyond the point at which the traditional notion of mediation continues to have much practical influence over the majority of contentious situations.

7.179 There is, however, a growing recognition that an alternative to litigation and arbitration is needed and which is being reflected in some fledgling schemes to encourage mediation. In a sign that legislators wish to encourage settlement of disputes, conciliation committees were formed in 1999 as part of the UAE Federal Court of First Instance. Any litigation, with limited exceptions such as labour disputes, disputes involving the Government and 'any other matters referred to settlement committees, whatever their description' must be referred to one of the Mediation and Reconciliation Committees prior to filing a case with the Federal courts.

7.180 A broadly similar scheme was introduced in Dubai in 2009, though the mandate of the Centre for Amicable Settlement of Disputes established as part of the scheme is limited to disputes that are voluntarily referred or those with a value of less than AED 50,000. Labour disputes and those involving personal status, such as matrimonial disputes are also excluded from the jurisdiction of the Centre. Prior registration of a case with the Centre for Amicable Settlement of Disputes is a pre-condition fencing formal proceedings in the courts.

7.181 The role of mediation in construction disputes outside the statutory regime outlined above is limited. The courts do not encourage the parties to consider mediation and project participants are, in general, wary of a process that has no protection from disclosure and subsequent use in formal proceedings.

7.182 Unlike in some other jurisdictions, notably the United Kingdom, Australia (New South Wales), Singapore, Malaysia, New Zealand, Germany, and Ireland there is no statutory recognition of adjudication in the United Arab Emirates or other Gulf states.

7.183 In the absence of any statutory framework to support adjudication the process faces a number of problems. In particular, obtaining recognition and ratification of an adjudication award from the domestic courts is likely to prove problematic. An adjudication conducted pursuant to the FIDIC Conditions, which provide for all disputes to be referred to a dispute adjudication board before proceeding to arbitration, is not immune from these difficulties.

Islamic Financing

7.184 Islamic financing is frequently utilized to fund large infrastructure projects in the Middle East. A popular Islamic financing technique used for the purpose construction projects is *Istisna'a* (Commissioned Construction) and (Leasing).

7.185 An *Istisna'a-Ijara* structure incorporates an *Istisna'a* contract that applies to the construction phase of a project, and an *Ijara* contract is put in place for the operations phase. *Istisna'a* is similar to a procurement agreement typically between a special purpose vehicle (SPV) owned by the bank as purchaser and the customer/the project company as seller.

7.186 *Istisna'a* is the most commonly used method in construction project finance to facilitate lending during the construction phase. On project completion, the *Istisna'a* will be superceded by an *ijarah*, which is essentially a lease agreement that kicks in during the operational phase of the project. Under the *Ijarah* agreement, the project company will take a lease of the *Istisna'a* from the SPV in return for lease payments. Under Shariah principles, the SPV (as lessor) is responsible for the major maintenance and insurance of the *Istisna'a* whereas the project company is responsible for the ordinary maintenance. However, the SPV typically enters into a Service Agency Agreement pursuant to which the major maintenance and insurance obligations are outsourced to a service agent.

7.187 This Islamic financing structure is attractive as the combination of the two contracts covers a longer term which is particularly vital for construction projects as it helps to recover the entire financing and profits. In addition, the use of the SPV means that financiers are protected from the risks associated with owning the *Istisna'a* and the seller is protected from direct ownership of the *Istisna'a* by the financiers, which help to mitigate insolvency concerns.

National Construction Law and International Forms

7.188 The FIDIC 4th Edition Red Book was widely adopted in the region in the decades that followed its publication in 1987 and it remains a popular form notwithstanding the publication of the FIDIC 1999 rainbow suite and its updated 2017 edition. Uptake of the 1999 suite was slow but has gathered pace and is now commonly used. Due to the conservative nature of the region's major procurers, the region is likely to be a slow adopter of the FIDIC Conditions, 2017 edition.

7.189 The FIDIC Conditions have various features that make them well-suited to use in the region, notably:

(c) An effort has been made to draft the conditions in a way that is compatible with civil and common law;
(d) The structure, comprising a short form of agreement, tender appendix, general conditions and particular conditions, makes them easy to use;
(e) The suite of forms allows for familiar structure, principles and language to be applied to different procurement and project scenarios;
(f) The central role of the Engineer is consistent with the supervisory role of engineers in region's regulatory regime governing construction.

7.190 These features, whilst cementing the ongoing popularity of the FIDIC Conditions, do not deter parties, especially project owners, from preparing extensive amendments to the standard conditions, a practice that is widely resented (but tolerated) by contractors. The Golden Principles, published by FIDIC in 2018 to accompany the updated rainbow suite, are aimed at discouraging this practice and, in particular, at discouraging any amendments that fundamentally alter the balance of risk established by the standard forms.

CHAPTER 8

North American Construction Law

John B. Tieder Jr., David F. McPherson, and Keith C. Phillips

Contents

DOI: 10.4324/9781315671376-8

History and Sources of North American Construction Law

Federal Systems Generally

8.1 In order to understand properly the sources of North American law, it is first necessary to appreciate that both the United States and Canada are Federal entities. In summary, this means that there are certain laws enacted by the Central Government which affect the entirety of the country and laws enacted by the constituent parts of the country, that is, the individual states of the United States and individual provinces of Canada, which only affect that state or province. Construction law as a subset of contracts law, of course, falls within this division.

US Federal Law

8.2 The basis of US Federal law is the Constitution. The Constitution sets forth in Article I, Section 8 those areas which are subject to Federal law. All other areas are left to the States.[1] Federal law is almost all based on statutes or enacted laws. The interpretation of these laws is carried out by the Federal courts. Federal construction law covers two primary fields: 1) Requirements that affect all or many contracts regardless of who the parties are, and 2) laws that apply to the United States Government in its role as a direct procurer of construction services. Although not limited to the field of construction, Federal law also covers arbitration.

Laws affecting all or most contracts

8.3 The laws of the United States are enacted by the US Congress. Many such laws are very general, and the details are filled in by regulations which are consistent with the basic law. For the most part, the laws affecting all contracts deal with labour and other socio-economic fields instead of the commercial rights and liabilities of the parties to the contract. Some examples are the Davis-Bacon Act of 1931 (which sets forth the policy of the minimum wage rates that can be paid), safety and health legislation, and non-discrimination.[2] Many of these requirements apply to all contracts while others only apply to contracts where the US Government has provided some of the funding.

---

1 US CONST. Amend. X.

2 Davis-Bacon Act, 40 U.S.C. §3141 et seq. (2012); see also Copeland Act, 18 U.S.C. §874 et seq., 40 U.S.C. §3145 et seq. (2012) (making it unlawful to induce, by force, intimidation, threat of procuring dismissal from employment, or otherwise, any person employed in the construction or repair of public buildings or public works, financed in whole or in part by the United States, to give up any part of the compensation to which that person is entitled under a contract of employment); Contract Work Hours and Safety Standards Act, 40 U.S.C. §3701 et seq. (2012) (stating that no labourer or mechanic doing any part of the work contemplated by the contract shall be required or permitted to work more than 40 hours in any workweek unless paid for all additional hours at not less than 1 1/2 times the basic rate of pay); Service Contract Act, 41 U.S.C. §§ 6701-07 (2012) (establishing minimum wage rates and fringe benefits based on those found in the region to be paid to service employees for contracts over $2,500); Walsh Healey Act, 41 U.S.C. §6501 et seq. (2012) (creating "minimum" wages in supply contracts for contracts over $15,000 for the manufacturing or furnishing of materials, supplies, articles, and equipment).

Laws Affecting Direct US Government Construction Contracts

8.4 The US Government is a major procurer of construction services. Its procurement system is governed by a few basic statutes, for example, the Armed Services Procurement Act,[3] the Federal Property and Administrative Services Act,[4] the Competition in Contracting Act,[5] and the Contract Disputes Act,[6] but expanded and supplemented by a system of regulations known as the Federal Acquisition Regulations (FARs). The FARs deal with virtually all aspects of contracting including changes (variations), delay, dispute resolution, etc. These are addressed in more detail in Section C below.

8.5 All disputes between the US Government and its contractors are resolved by either specialized administrative courts known as the Civilian Board of Contract Appeals (CBCA) for contracts with civilian agencies,[7] and the Armed Services Board of Contract Appeals (ASBCA) for contracts with military agencies,[8] or a specialized court known as the US Court of Federal Claims.[9] Appeals from both the two administrative courts and the Court of Federal Claims are appealable only to another specialized court, the Court of Appeals for the Federal Circuit.[10]

8.6 A practical effect of having these specialized courts is the development of a large body of construction jurisprudence. While strictly applicable only to direct Federal government contracts, it has been relied upon by other courts and often by arbitrators, even international arbitrators.[11] It is certainly the largest body of construction law in the US and perhaps the world.

Arbitration

8.7 The US Federal Arbitration Act (FAA), 9 U.S.C.§1 governs all arbitrations which involve more than one state, in effect, virtually all commercial contracts. Of particular importance to the construction community is that the FAA enforces arbitration provisions as agreed to by the parties, including choice-of-law and the site of the arbitration provisions even if a state law purports to limit arbitration to its laws and requires arbitration to be held in that state.[12] In addition, arbitration awards can only be challenged on very limited grounds which would be readily familiar to those who know the UNCITRAL Model Law on Commercial Arbitration and the 1958 New York Convention.[13]

---

3 10 U.S.C. §2302 et seq. (2012).
4 41 U.S.C. §251 et seq. (2012).
5 31 U.S.C. §3551 et seq. (2012).
6 41 U.S.C. §7101 et seq. (2012).
7 41 U.S.C. §7105(b).
8 41 U.S.C. §7105(a).
9 Tucker Act, 28 U.S.C. §1491(a) (2012).
10 28 U.S.C. §1291 et seq. (2012).
11 E.g., *British Caribbean Bank Ltd. v Gov't of Belize* (*Turks & Caicos Is. v Belize*), PCA Case No. 2010–18, ¶ 256 (2014).
12 Convention on Recognition and Enforcement of Foreign Arbitral Awards, 10 June 1958, 330 U.N.T.S. 38 [hereinafter Convention]; see also *Victrix S.S. Co., S.A. v Salen Dry Cargo A.B.*, 825 F.2d 709, 712-13 (2d Cir. 1987) ("We think, however, that the Convention preempts state laws and leaves the entire subject of enforcement of foreign arbitration awards governed by its terms".); *Fotochrome, Inc. v Copal Co.*, 517 F.2d 512, 518 (2d Cir.1975) ("Foreign [arbitral] awards are vulnerable to attack only on the grounds expressed in other articles of the Convention, particularly Article V".)
13 9 U.S.C. §10(a) (2012); see also *Banco de Seguros del Estado v Mut. Marine Office, Inc.*, 344 F.3d 255, 262 (2d Cir. 2003) (citing *Westerbeke Corp. v Daihatsu Motor Co., Ltd.*, 304 F.3d 200, 220 (2d Cir.2002) ("We

State Law

Common Law

8.8 The starting point of state law is that 49 of the 50 states, the exception being Louisiana, and all the Canadian provinces except Quebec are common law jurisdictions. This means that the law has developed through the application of prior decisions on the same subject modified when necessary to fit new, but still analogous circumstances; however, the basic principle is that prior decisions are binding; this is known as "*stare decisis*".

8.9 The law in each state has separately developed. For many the common law of England was the starting point and older English case law like the foreseeability of damages as set forth in *Hadley v Baxendale* 9 Exch. 341, 156 Eng.Rep. 145. (Court of Exchequer, 1854) is still applicable. This, of course, includes construction law.

State Statutes Affecting Construction Law

8.10 For the most part, the parties to a construction contract are free to contract as they choose. In some states, there are statutes which directly affect construction contracts. An example is statutes requiring owners (employers) to pay prime (main) contractors or main contractors to pay their subcontractors within stated periods; these are called "prompt payment" requirements.[14] Some such statutes affect all contracts; others only contracts entered into by the state or other public entities.

Direct state and Local Procurement

8.11 Each state and political sub-division, of each state, for example, cities, highway authorities, etc., has requirements for their direct procurements. This accounts for a vast amount of construction activity; for example, roads, bridges, water treatment and distribution systems, sewage treatment systems, etc. The laws and regulations applicable to these procurements have to be individually ascertained.

Canadian Construction Law

8.12 Canada has a similar Federal system with national laws that affect the entire country and provincial laws which affect only that province. Since Canada is still in the British Commonwealth, its provincial laws are still more directly derivative from English common law then the laws of the states of the United States.

---

have 'consistently accorded the narrowest of readings' to the FAA's authorization to vacate awards pursuant to §10(a)(4)".)

14 E.g., N.Y. State Fin. Law §§ 139-f, 179-f (McKinney 2016) (state agencies); N.Y. Gen. Mun. Law §106-b (McKinney 2016) (municipal agencies); N.Y. Pub. Auth. Law §2880 (McKinney 2016) (public authorities) (for all, owner to prime within 30 days of invoice; prime to sub within 7 days of payment; interest at statutory rate depending on type of public agency); Cal. Pub. Cont. Code §§10261-10265 (West 2016) (state agencies) (owner to prime 30 days after receipt of payment request; interest at 10% per annum; prime to sub within 7 days of payment; interest at 2% per month); Cal. Pub. Cont. Code §20104.50 (West 2016) (local entities) (owner to prime within 30 days; interest at statutory rate); Tex. Gov't Code Ann. §§2251.021-.028 (West 2016) (owner to prime within 30 days of invoice or within 45 days of invoice if contract executed by Political Subdivision which meets once a month or less; prime to sub within 10 days of payment; interest at prime rate on the first weekday of preceding July, plus 1%).

Louisiana and Quebec

8.13 Louisiana and Quebec are civil law jurisdictions with comprehensive civil codes and their legal history is based on the French Civil System. Louisiana has adopted many common law concepts and follows the principle of "*stare decisis*" in the application of its Civil Code. Quebec is more purely a civil code jurisdiction.

Conclusion

8.14 It would seem from the above that construction law in the US and Canada has to be separately ascertained depending on which state law applies and who the particular owner is, especially a public entity. This is true; however, construction law has developed in a similar fashion in the 49 common law states and the concepts set forth in the remainder of this chapter are generally applicable.

Contract law

The Formation of a Contract

Offer and Acceptance

8.15 A contract is at its simplest "a promise or set of promises for the breach of which the law gives a recovery or the performance of which the law in some way recognizes as a duty".[15] The three classic elements for contract formation are an offer, acceptance and consideration. In modern construction contracts, particularly those made by public entities, there are generally two forms of offer and acceptance: Invitation to bid or request for proposals.

8.16 The invitation to bid process typically begins with an owner's issuance of a formal invitation to bid or on a specific project, which includes detailed plans and specifications and the contract terms and conditions under which the owner seeks to procure the project. Contractors then submit sealed bids to the owner. The owner evaluates the bids and selects the lowest priced responsive (strict adherence to the instructions in the invitation to bid) and responsible (a determination of the bidder's ability to perform the work) bid for award of the contract.

8.17 Sealed bidding has long been the generally accepted method by which government (at the Federal, state, and local levels) construction contracts are made and are governed by the Federal Acquisition Regulations and state and local procurement laws and regulations.

8.18 In the past several decades, government entities have increasingly embraced negotiated procurement of construction projects. Under this method, the government issues a request for proposals and allows the contracting officer to select a proposal that offers the "best value" to the government by allowing tradeoffs between price and technical factors related to the procurement. The request for proposals must include a detailed listing of all factors that will be taken account of in making the award. The contracting authority (often known as the contracting officer) evaluates the proposals received, enters into negotiations

15 Restatement Second, Contracts §1.

with one or more contractors to clarify technical and pricing matters, and then awards the contract to the contractor that offers the best value to the government.

8.19 In private construction contracts, an owner is much freer to utilize the method it desires to retain a contractor, and often will solicit proposals or bids from only contractors it is familiar with or knows can perform the work. Regardless, the methods are largely the same as in the government realm but typically without the attendant formality.

Intention to Create Legal Relationships

8.20 In commercial settings, it is presumed that the contracting parties have the intent to create legal relations. Courts apply an objective test and determine whether a reasonable person, after taking into account all the circumstances of the case, believes that the parties intended to be bound.

Capacity

8.21 Capacity to enter into a contractual relationship is required for every party entering a contract. Legal capacity refers to the legal ability to enter into a contract and the competence to perform some act. Capacity to contract is rarely an issue with respect to construction contracts. Note that certain individuals such as minors and those who lack mental capacity cannot enter into binding contracts. Such contracts are voidable, except in circumstances such as contracts for necessities, like food and shelter. Although a contract entered into by a minor may be voidable, if the contract is challenged after the minor reaches legal age, the contract can no longer be voided in most states.

Formalities

8.22 The general rule is that a contract must be in writing and signed by the opposing parties before a court will enforce it. This rule is referred to as the "statute of frauds". The purpose is to prevent the possibility that a non-existent agreement is "proven" by perjury or fraud. All states have a statute of frauds and typically apply for contracts in excess of a certain value, contracts for sale of real property, or contracts that cannot be performed within one year.[16]

Agency

8.23 A contract made by an agent with actual or implied authority is valid and binding. An agent is an individual or firm authorized to act on behalf of another, called the principal. Actual authority arises when a party expressly gives the agent authority to enter into a particular contract. Implied authority arises when the principal places the agent in a position – such as a manager, officer or director – that customarily has the power to enter into contracts. Apparent authority may also suffice. For apparent authority, the principal's acts or words lead another to believe that he has appointed the agent to act on his behalf.

Consideration

8.24 Consideration is the benefit that the parties bargain for in the contract and is one of the basic elements of a valid and binding contract. Consideration must be of value and

---

16 See, e.g., *Yamaha Motor Corp., USA v Calhoun*, 516 US 199 (1996).

is exchanged for the performance or promise of performance by the other party. Also known as "mutuality of obligation" or *quid pro quo*, it is up to the parties to determine the value of the consideration received. The courts largely do not entertain disputes over the adequacy of consideration unless the values are so unequal as to rise to the level of unconscionability.[17] Similarly, promises which are illusory or conditional on events that cannot occur have been found to be unenforceable. Issues of adequacy of consideration rarely arise in construction contracts, although the issue may arise with respect to a particular contract change.

The Contents of a Contract

Terms of a Contract (Express and Implied Terms)

8.25 Simply stated, the express terms of the contract are those contractual duties that are stated in the contract documents. Express terms will be enforced in accordance with their plain meaning. The parol evidence rule prevents a party to a written contract from presenting extrinsic evidence that discloses an ambiguity and clarifies it or adds to the written terms of the contract that appears to be a complete integration of the parties' agreement. Oftentimes, contracts contain an integration clause that states that the written agreement is complete and includes all terms of the parties' agreement and that the parties are not relying on any oral representations or prior negotiations.

8.26 Implied contract terms, on the other hand, are not expressly included in the contract language but are introduced into the contract by courts as necessary to give effect to the intentions of the parties or by statute. The most common implied term is the covenant of good faith and fair dealing that the parties will deal with each other honestly, fairly and in good faith so as not to prevent the other party from enjoying the benefits of the contract. All states have some form of this duty, and it is codified in the Uniform Commercial Code (Section 1-304) and in the Restatement Second of Contracts (Section 205).

Unfair Contract Terms

8.27 The concept of "unfair contract terms" is not a concept typically found in United States construction law. Parties in the United States are largely free to contract as they see fit and the courts are reluctant to not enforce the contract as written, especially when the parties are sophisticated commercial entities. Some state statutes and court decisions do, however, make certain clauses unenforceable as a matter of public policy and deal with issues such as contingent payment clauses (pay-if-paid and pay-when-paid provisions), no damages for delay clauses, and no-lien clauses. These jurisdictions seek to protect contractors and subcontractors from onerous and "unfair" contract provisions.

Pay-If-Paid/Pay-When-Paid Clauses

8.28 Pay-if-paid clauses provide that a general contractor is not required to pay subcontractors unless and until it receives payment from the owner. An example of a pay-if-paid clause:

17 Restatement Second, Contracts §208.

Receipt of payment by the Contractor from the Owner for the Subcontract Work is a condition precedent to payment by the Contractor to the Subcontractor. The Subcontractor hereby acknowledges that it relies on the credit of the Owner, not the Contractor, for payment of Subcontract Work.

8.29 By contrast, a pay-when-paid clause provides that a general contractor will pay the subcontractor within a certain period of time after receiving payment from the owner but does not shift the burden of non-payment to the subcontractor.

8.30 Most states will enforce pay-if-paid clauses if they are explicit – providing language such as "condition precedent", "unless and until", or "if and only if".[18] Certain states, most notably New York and California, either by statute or by judicial decisions, have determined pay-if-paid clauses are not enforceable.[19] These clauses have spawned considerable litigation when subcontractors are not paid and the parties disagree over the interpretation of the clause. Jurisdictions addressing these distinctions tend to interpret any uncertainty as creating a pay-when-paid clause.[20]

No Damages For Delay Clauses

8.31 No damages for delay clauses are enforceable in most states for private contracts where clearly and unambiguously stated.[21] Several general exceptions to the enforceability of these clauses, however, have been recognized by many state courts: "No damage for delay" clauses enforceable, except where the delay is one "(1) not contemplated by the parties under the (no damage for delay) provision, (2) amounting to an abandonment of the contract, (3) caused by bad faith, or (4) amounting to active interference".[22]

8.32 With regard to public construction contracts, a number of states impose restrictions or bans on the use of no damages for delay. For instance, Colorado law states: "Any clause in a public works contract that purports to waive, release, or extinguish the rights of a contractor to recover costs or damages … for delays in performing such contract, if such delay is caused in whole, or in part, by acts or omissions within the control of the contracting public entity or persons acting on behalf thereof, is against public policy and is void and unenforceable".[23] California provides that

> [c]ontract provisions in construction contracts of public agencies and subcontracts thereunder which limit the contractee's liability to an extension of time for delay for which the contractee is responsible and which delay is unreasonable under the circumstances involved, and not within

18 *BMD Contractors, Inc. v Fidelity & Deposit Co. of Maryland*, 679 F.3d 643, 648 (7th Cir. 2012) *as amended* (July 13, 2012).

19 NY General Obligations Law §5-322.1; *West-Fair Elec. Contractors v Aetna Cas. & Sur. Co.*, 661 N.E.2d 967, 971 (1995) (Pay-if-paid clauses are void as against the state's public policy protecting lien rights); Cal. Civ. Code §8126; *William R. Clark Corp. v Safeco Ins. Co.*, 938 P.2d 372 (Cal. 1997).

20 E.g., *Sloan & Co. v Liberty Mut. Ins. Co.*, 653 F.3d 175, 180 (3d Cir. 2011); *DEC Electric, Inc. v Raphael Constr. Corp.*, 558 So. 2d 427, 429 (Fla. 1990).

21 E.g., *K & F Constr. v Los Angeles City Unified School Dist.*, 123 Cal. App. 3d 1063, 1065 (Cal. App. 2d Dist. 1981).

22 *Blake Constr. Co., Inc. v C.J. Coakley Co.*, 431 A.2d 569 D.C. 1980).

23 Colo. Rev. Stat. §24-91-103.5.

the contemplation of the parties, shall not be construed to preclude the recovery of damages by the contractor or subcontractor.

[24]

Note that the Federal Acquisition Regulations do not contain damages for delay clauses.

No-Lien Clauses

8.33 A "no-lien clause" is simply a clause within a construction contract, or a lien waiver document signed before the furnishing of work, whereby a party waives its right to later file a mechanics lien on the project. In other words, the waiving party agrees to perform the work without the security of a potential mechanics lien claim against the improved property if unpaid. These clauses have been looked upon with disfavor and the majority of states have enacted statutes that make pre-work lien waivers unenforceable.[25]

Vitiating Factors under Contract Law

8.34 As noted previously, private parties in the United States are relatively free to contract as they desire. Certain factors, discussed below, are vitiating factors that are common to all contracts and may allow a party to avoid contractual obligations.

Misrepresentation and Mistake

8.35 All states recognize some form of the mistake defense to the enforceability of a contract. The Restatement Second of Contracts provides generally accepted rules by which a party can be relieved of a mutual or unilateral mistake of fact.

- § 152. When Mistake of Both Parties Makes a Contract Voidable
- Where a mistake of both parties at the time a contract was made as to a basic assumption on which the contract was made has a material effect on the agreed exchange of performances, the contract is voidable by the adversely affected party unless he bears the risk of the mistake under the rule stated in §154.[26]
- § 153. When Mistake of One Party Makes a Contract Voidable
- Where a mistake of one party at the time a contract was made as to a basic assumption on which he made the contract has a material effect on the agreed exchange of performances that is adverse to him, the contract is voidable by him if he does not bear the risk of the mistake under the rule stated in §154, and
  - (a) the effect of the mistake is such that enforcement of the contract would be unconscionable;
  - (b) the other party had reason to know of the mistake or his fault caused the mistake.[27]

24 Cal. Public Contract Code §7102; See also *Howard Contracting, Inc. v G.A. MacDonald Constr. Co., Inc.*, 71 Cal. App. 4th 38 (1998) (finding city's no damage for delay clause unenforceable under §7102 because delays were caused by the city and "a basis exists for concluding that the delays were unreasonable and not within the contemplation of the parties").

25 E.g., AZ St. §33-1008(A) (Arizona); Cal. Civ. Code §8124 (California); IL St. Ch. 770 §60/1(d) (Illinois); NV St. 108.2457 (Nevada); NY Lien Law §34 (New York).

26 Restatement Second, Contracts §152; *Leff v Ecker*, 972 So.2d 965, 966 (Fla. 3d DCA 2007).

27 Restatement Second, Contracts §153; *BMW of N. Am. v Krathen*, 471 So.2d 585, 588 (Fla. 4th DCA 1985).

- § 154. When a Party Bears the Risk of a Mistake
- A party bears the risk of a mistake when
  (a) the risk is allocated to him by agreement of the parties;
  (b) he is aware, at the time the contract is made, that he has only limited knowledge with respect to the facts to which the mistake relates but treats his limited knowledge as sufficient, or;
  (c) the risk is allocated to him by the court on the ground that it is reasonable in the circumstances to do so.[28]

8.36 In Federal government contracting, mistakes that are discovered after contract award are very difficult to correct or obtain relief. The Federal Acquisition Regulations provide that if a mistake is discovered after award, a modification to the contract may be made "if correcting the mistake would be favorable to the Government without changing the essential requirements of the specifications".[29] The government may also rescind the contract or reform a contract: "(i) To delete the items involved in the mistake or (ii) to increase the price if the contract price, as corrected, does not exceed that of the next lowest acceptable bid under the original invitation for bids".[30] Contractors seeking relief from bid or proposal mistakes after award bear the burden of "clear and convincing evidence" that a mistake has been made.[31]

8.37 Similar to mistakes, misrepresentations can be a cause to deny the enforceability of a contract. A fraudulent mistake, in which the maker of the representation intends to induce the other party to enter into the contract with an assertion he knows is false or has no basis for making, is in all circumstances, grounds for voiding the contract.[32] Fraudulent representation is an independent cause of action.

8.38 A misrepresentation is deemed to be material if it would be likely to induce a reasonable person to enter into the contract, or if the maker knows that it would be likely to induce the recipient to do so.[33] There is no knowledge or *mens rea* requirement for a misrepresentation to be material. A contract induced by a material misrepresentation is voidable.[34]

Illegality

8.39 If the purpose of a contract is to achieve an illegal end, courts will not enforce the contract, and performance is excused. Illegality is not often seen as an excuse for non-performance in construction contracts, but some instances concerning illegal public contracts due to failure to follow procurement laws do arise.[35] The contractor is generally still able to recover the costs for the work it performed under an illegally awarded contract

28 Restatement Second, Contracts §154.

29 FAR 14.407-4(a).

30 FAR 14.407-4(b). Note that in the event it was a negotiated procurement, the government follows the same procedure for correction/rescission. FAR 15.508.

31 FAR 14.407-4(c).

32 Restatement Second, Contracts §162(1).

33 Restatement Second, Contracts §162(2).

34 Restatement Second, Contracts §164.

35 *Reams v Cooley* (1915) 171 Cal. 150 (1915) (failure to follow competitive bidding requirements).

based on a good faith belief that the contract was valid and if the failure to competitively bid was due to the public agency's actions.[36]

8.40 Moreover, some states have consumer protection laws that protect homeowners by requiring certain formalities in contracts for construction. If the contract does not contain the required provisions, it may be voided for illegality. For example, Connecticut law provides:

> No home improvement contract shall be valid or enforceable against an owner unless it: (i) Is in writing, (ii) is signed by the owner and the contractor, (iii) contains the entire agreement between the owner and the contractor, (iv) contains the date of the transaction, (v) contains the name and address of the contractor and the contractor's registration number, (vi) contains a notice of the owner's cancellation rights in accordance with the provisions of chapter 740, (vii) contains a starting date and completion date, (viii) is entered into by a registered salesman or registered contractor, and (ix) includes a provision disclosing each corporation, limited liability company, partnership, sole proprietorship or other legal entity, which is or has been a home improvement contractor pursuant to the provisions of this chapter or a new home construction contractor pursuant to the provisions of chapter 399a, in which the owner or owners of the home improvement contractor are or have been a shareholder, member, partner, or owner during the previous five years.[37]

Duress and Undue Influence

8.41 Economic duress will make a contract voidable if one party threatens to commit a wrongful act that would put the other party's property or financial well-being in jeopardy and there is nothing the other party can do to avoid the threat other than enter into the contract. Undue influence, on the other hand, is taking advantage of another person through a position of trust in the formation of a contract. Duress is most often invoked as a defense to waiver language in change orders. For example, in *Pellerin Const., Inc. v Witco Corp.*,[38] the contractor signed various change orders that waived any delay or disruption claims that had arisen as of the date of the modification. Pellerin filed a lawsuit and claimed that it signed the change orders under economic duress because the project delays had caused it to incur almost $1 million in additional costs, it was running a $1 million operating deficit on the project, and defendants had not properly paid Pellerin at the time. The Court, while recognizing that Pellerin may have been in financial straits, rejected its claim of economic duress, finding that there were no allegations that defendants improperly threatened Pellerin. The Court stated that "in the absence of evidence that defendants caused delays to put Pellerin in extremis, so that they could thereafter make unjustified demands on Pellerin, there is no duress".

8.42 Improper threats to default terminate a contract unless the contractor signs a no-cost change order have been found to constitute duress.[39] Similarly, the government's

36 Cal. Pub. Cont. Code §5110; Paul *G. Marshall Jr. v Pasadena Unified Sch. Dist.*, 119 Cal.App.4th 1241(2004).

37 CT Gen. Stat. §20-429.

38 169 F. Supp. 2d 568 (E.D. La. 2001).

39 *Universal Sportswear, Inc. v United States*, 145 Ct. Cl. 209, 180 F. Supp. 391 (1959).

insistence that a contractor agree to a change order before a progress payment would be made was improper duress and vitiated the waiver language in the modification.[40]

The Rights and Liabilities of Third Parties

8.43 Third-party beneficiaries are parties other than those entering into the contract but may nonetheless derive a benefit from the performance of the contract. Third party beneficiaries can be intended or incidental beneficiaries. When determining whether the parties to a contract intended to make a third person a third-party beneficiary, courts use an objective standard. Third-party beneficiary status requires an express promise to act for the benefit of the third party and where no such promise existed, that third party cannot maintain an action for breach of the contract. A person who incidentally benefits from the performance of some duty required under a contract has no rights under the contract.[41]

8.44 Construction projects typically involve different parties performing under several different contracts and sub-contracts. A general contractor who has entered into a contract and provided a bond to the owner may contracts with a number of subcontractors and suppliers. In this scenario, one party's performance often depends on timely and complete performance by another party. However, subcontractors, their employees and material suppliers are generally held not to be third-party beneficiaries of the contract between the general contractor and the owner.

8.45 A more complicated situation arises when there are multiple prime contracts. Courts have usually ruled in these situations that absent a clear intent in each of the contracts, the prime contractors cannot sue each other but may sue the owner for failure to coordinate or manage the project.[42] In response to these rulings, owners now often protect themselves by inserting identical provisions in each of the prime contracts stating that if one of the prime contractors causes damage to any of the others, the damaged contractors may only seek recompense from the contractor causing the damage.

Performance of a Contract

Performance

8.46 The performance obligations of each party are set forth in the express and implied terms of the contract. Each party is expected to perform its obligations in a timely fashion and to avoid interfering with the other's performance. Performance discharges the contractual duty, while non-performance constitutes a breach.[43] The performance of a construction contract, no matter the size of the project, is rarely without performance issues. This section discusses frustration and breach and the consequences and remedies available to the parties when performance does not proceed smoothly.

Frustration

8.47 Frustration of purpose is defined as

---

40 *Rumsfeld v Freedom N.Y., Inc.*, 329 F.2d 1320 (Fed. Cir. 2003).

41 *Dynamic Const. Co. v Barton Malow Co.*, 214 Mich. App. 425, 543 N.W.2d 31 (1995).

42 *J.F., Inc. v S.M. Wilson & Co.*, 504 N.E.2d 1266 (Ill. App. 1987).

43 Restatement Second, Contacts §235.

Where, after a contract is made, a party's principal purpose is substantially frustrated without his fault by the occurrence of an event the non-occurrence of which was a basic assumption on which the contract was made, his remaining duties to render performance are discharged, unless the language or circumstances indicate the contrary.

[44]

A breaching party may be excused from a contract based on the frustration of purpose doctrine if it can demonstrate four requirements: (i) The frustrated purpose "must have been a principal purpose of that party" and must have been so within the understanding of both parties; (ii) the frustration "must be so severe that it is not to be regarded as within the risks assumed under the contract"; (iii) "the non-occurrence of the frustrating event must have been a basic assumption [on which the contract was made]"; and (iv) "relief will not be granted if it may be inferred from either the language of the contract or the circumstances that the risk of the frustrating occurrence, or the loss caused thereby, should properly be placed on the party seeking relief".[45]

Breach

8.48 While any failure to perform an obligation under a contract is a breach,[46] and damages, if any, can be recovered therefor, in order to determine whether a contracting party is entitled to terminate the contract and is excused from its performance and may sue for damages, one must determine whether a breach is material. The Restatement Second of Contracts provides in this regard:

In determining whether a failure to render or to offer performance is material, the following circumstances are significant:

(a) The extent to which the injured party will be deprived of the benefit which he reasonably expected;
(b) The extent to which the injured party can be adequately compensated for the part of that benefit of which he will be deprived;
(c) The extent to which the party failing to perform or to offer to perform will suffer forfeiture;
(d) The likelihood that the party failing to perform or to offer to perform will cure his failure, taking account of all the circumstances including any reasonable assurances;
(e) The extent to which the behavior of the party failing to perform or to offer to perform comports with standards of good faith and fair dealing.[47]

8.49 A material breach can give rise to a party's right to terminate the contract, as discussed below, and/or sue for monetary damages. A material breach is often difficult to

44 Restatement Second, Contracts §265; *St. Paul Mercury Ins. Co. v Capitol Sprinkler Inspection, Inc.*, 573 F. Supp. 2d 152, 172 (D.D.C. 2008) ("Under the frustration [of purpose] defense, the promisor's performance is excused because changed conditions have rendered the performance bargained from the promisee worthless").

45 *Next Gen Capital LLC v Consumer Lending Associates LLC*, 316 P.3d 598 (Ariz. 2013) (citations omitted).

46 Restatement Second, Contacts §235.

47 Restatement Second, Contracts §241.

ascertain from minor breaches[48] and is generally understood to be a significant breach that endangers future performance and "defeat[s] the very object of the contract".[49]

Termination

8.50 Termination of a contract will cease all or a portion of the work on the contract. Almost all construction contacts contain clauses that permit the owner to terminate a contract, in whole or in part, for either its convenience or because of a default by the contractor.

Termination for Convenience

8.51 Termination for convenience clauses permit an upstream party to terminate the contract, in whole or in part, for a reason unrelated to the downstream party's breach. The following discussion relates specifically to the Federal government's termination provisions, although similar termination for convenience clauses are found in a number of standard form contracts. In government contracting, it is typical that the owner may terminate for convenience for almost any reason, absent a severe abuse of discretion. In Federal government contracting, the termination for convenience clause reads as follows:

> The Government may terminate performance of work under this contract in whole or, from time to time, in part if the Contracting Officer determines that a termination is in the Government's interest. The Contracting Officer shall terminate by delivering to the Contractor a Notice of Termination specifying the extent of termination and the effective date.[50]

After receipt of a Notice of Termination, the contractor is under a number of obligations:

(1) Stop work as specified in the notice;
(2) Place no further subcontracts or orders (referred to as subcontracts in this clause) for materials, services, or facilities, except as necessary to complete the continued portion of the contract;
(3) Terminate all subcontracts to the extent they relate to the work terminated;
(4) Assign to the Government, as directed by the Contracting Officer, all right, title, and interest of the Contractor under the subcontracts terminated, in which case the Government shall have the right to settle or to pay any termination settlement proposal arising out of those terminations;
(5) With approval or ratification to the extent required by the Contracting Officer, settle all outstanding liabilities and termination settlement proposals arising from the termination of subcontracts; the approval or ratification will be final for purposes of this clause;
(6) As directed by the Contracting Officer, transfer title and deliver to the Government –
    (i) The fabricated or unfabricated parts, work in process, completed work, supplies, and other material produced or acquired for the work terminated; and

48 *Bat Masonry Co., Inc. v Pike-Paschen Joint Venture III*, 842 F. Supp. 174, 182 (D. Md. 1993).
49 *Wells Benz, Inc. v United States ex. Rel. Mercury Elec. Co.*, 333 F.2d 489, 492 (9th Cir. 1964).
50 FAR 52-249-2(a).

(ii) The completed or partially completed plans, drawings, information, and other property that, if the contract had been completed, would be required to be furnished to the Government.

(7) Complete performance of the work not terminated;

(8) Take any action that may be necessary, or that the Contracting Officer may direct, for the protection and preservation of the property related to this contract that is in the possession of the Contractor and in which the Government has or may acquire an interest;

(9) Use its best efforts to sell, as directed or authorized by the Contracting Officer, any property of the types referred to in paragraph (b)(6) of this clause; provided, however, that the Contractor (i) is not required to extend credit to any purchaser and (ii) may acquire the property under the conditions prescribed by, and at prices approved by, the Contracting Officer. The proceeds of any transfer or disposition will be applied to reduce any payments to be made by the Government under this contract, credited to the price or cost of the work, or paid in any other manner directed by the Contracting Officer.[51]

8.52 With respect to compensation for the work performed up to the date of termination, costs continuing for a time after termination, and the costs of settling with subcontractors, the Federal Acquisition Regulations provide that the contractor and Contracting Officer should endeavor to agree on the amount to be paid because of the termination, including a reasonable amount of profit on the work performed, not to exceed the total contract price less the amounts of previous payments and the price of the work not terminated.[52] If the parties are unable to agree, the regulations provide:

If the Contractor and Contracting Officer fail to agree on the whole amount to be paid the Contractor because of the termination of work, the Contracting Officer shall pay the Contractor the amounts determined as follows, but without duplication of any amounts agreed upon under paragraph (f) of this clause:

(1) For contract work performed before the effective date of termination, the total (without duplication of any items) of –

(i) The cost of this work;

(ii) The cost of settling and paying termination settlement proposals under terminated subcontracts that are properly chargeable to the terminated portion of the contract if not included in subdivision (g)(1)(i) of this clause;

(iii) A sum, as profit on subdivision (g)(1)(i) of this clause, determined by the Contracting Officer under 49.202 of the Federal Acquisition Regulation, in effect on the date of this contract, to be fair and reasonable; however, if it appears that the Contractor would have sustained a loss on the entire contract had it been completed, the Contracting Officer shall allow no profit under this subdivision (g)(1)(iii) and shall reduce the settlement to reflect the indicated rate of loss.

(2) The reasonable costs of settlement of the work terminated, including –

51 FAR 52.249-2.

52 FAR 52-249-2(f).

(i) Accounting, legal, clerical, and other expenses reasonably necessary for the preparation of termination settlement proposals and supporting data;
(ii) The termination and settlement of subcontracts (excluding the amounts of such settlements); and
(iii) Storage, transportation, and other costs incurred, reasonably necessary for the preservation, protection, or disposition of the termination inventory.

8.53 Note that under this provision, no anticipated profit is allowed on uncompleted work and in fact a loss factor will be applied in the event the contractor would have suffered a loss on the entire project.

8.54 While other construction contracts in the United States often follow the general outlines of the Federal termination for convenience clause, contractors must be aware of differences and carefully consider how a termination for convenience is handled by the particular contract. Additionally, the contractor must be aware of its liability to third parties, such as its subcontractors and suppliers. A contractor should make certain that it has similar language (or a flow-down provision) in its subcontracts and supply agreements to avoid claims for lost profits or damages the subcontractor suffered because its contract was terminated.

Termination for Default

8.55 Termination for default is a drastic sanction that occurs when the contractor breaches the contract.[53] The contractor forfeits any right to proceed with the work and is liable for excess costs the government may incur in completion of the contract. Default termination clauses in non-government contracts generally contain similar termination for default provisions. The Federal government termination for default clause states:

(a) If the Contractor refuses or fails to prosecute the work or any separable part, with the diligence that will insure its completion within the time specified in this contract including any extension, or fails to complete the work within this time, the Government may, by written notice to the Contractor, terminate the right to proceed with the work (or the separable part of the work) that has been delayed. In this event, the Government may take over the work and complete it by contract or otherwise, and may take possession of and use any materials, appliances, and plant on the work site necessary for completing the work. The Contractor and its sureties shall be liable for any damage to the Government resulting from the Contractor's refusal or failure to complete the work within the specified time, whether or not the Contractor's right to proceed with the work is terminated. This liability includes any increased costs incurred by the Government in completing the work;
(b) The Contractor's right to proceed shall not be terminated nor the Contractor charged with damages under this clause, if–

53 *Mega Constr. Co. v United States*, 29 Fed. Cl. 396 (1993).

(1) The delay in completing the work arises from unforeseeable causes beyond the control and without the fault or negligence of the Contractor. Examples of such causes include –
  (i) Acts of God or of the public enemy;
  (ii) Acts of the Government in either its sovereign or contractual capacity;
  (iii) Acts of another Contractor in the performance of a contract with the Government;
  (iv) Fires;
  (v) Floods;
  (vi) Epidemics;
  (vii) Quarantine restrictions;
  (viii) Strikes;
  (ix) Freight embargoes;
  (x) Unusually severe weather;
  (xi) Delays of subcontractors or suppliers at any tier arising from unforeseeable causes beyond the control and without the fault or negligence of both the Contractor and the subcontractors or suppliers;

(2) The Contractor, within 10 days from the beginning of any delay (unless extended by the Contracting Officer), notifies the Contracting Officer in writing of the causes of delay. The Contracting Officer shall ascertain the facts and the extent of delay. If, in the judgment of the Contracting Officer, the findings of fact warrant such action, the time for completing the work shall be extended. The findings of the Contracting Officer shall be final and conclusive on the parties, but subject to appeal under the Disputes clause;

(c) If, after termination of the Contractor's right to proceed, it is determined that the Contractor was not in default, or that the delay was excusable, the rights and obligations of the parties will be the same as if the termination had been issued for the convenience of the Government.[54]

8.56 Notably, under subparagraph (c) of the default clause, in the event the termination is later found to be improper because the contractor was not in default, the contractor is entitled to compensation in accordance with the termination for convenience provisions. Often times, however, this determination is not made until years later by a court or board of contract appeals, and the contractor may have suffered severe financial consequences in the interim.

Remedies

8.57 In the event a party to a contract does not perform as promised, thereby materially breaching the contract, there are several remedies available to the non-breaching party or parties. Contract remedies are designed to protect the parties' expectation, reliance and restitution interests arising out of the mutual exchange of promises made in the contract.[55]

54 FAR 52.249-10.

55 Restatement Second, Contracts §344.

An expectation interest relates directly to the "benefit of the bargain" each party negotiated in the agreement. When a court awards damages based on a party's expectations, the court is attempting to put the non-breaching party back into the same position the party was in prior to the breach as if the breach never occurred and both parties had performed.[56] On the other hand, a court may award damages based on a party's reliance interest, which includes reimbursement for the non-breaching party's loss caused by reliance on the contract. Reliance damages are intended to put the non-breaching party back into as good position as he would have been in had the contract not been made. Finally, restitution damages are based on restoring any benefits the non-breaching party conferred on the other party.[57]

8.58 Most courts rely upon common law remedies, but parties may agree to what remedies are available in the event of a breach within the contract itself. By far the most common remedy is in the form of monetary damages. Other possible remedies include specific performance, rescission and restitution.

Common Law Remedies

Compensatory Damages

8.59 Compensatory damages, or actual damages, are monetary damages intended to reimburse the non-breaching party for losses incurred as a result of a breach based on the party's expectation, reliance, or restitution interests. There are generally two categories of compensatory damages that the non-breaching party may recover: General damages and special damages. General damages include all costs directly and necessarily incurred by the non-breaching party as a direct result of the breach. These tend to be the most common types of damages awarded and are typically supported by evidence and testimony related to invoices showing costs for materials and labour, as an example. On the other hand, special damages, otherwise known as "consequential damages", are intended to compensate the non-breaching party for losses that were indirectly caused by the breath such as lost rent or lost income as a result of an unfinished building. Notably, particular attention may be paid to the foreseeability of special damages.

Specific Performance

8.60 Specific performance is considered one possible equitable remedy for a non-breaching party to an agreement. Specific performance is considered an alternative to monetary damages and involves a court or arbitrator ordering the breaching party to perform in accordance with the contract. However, orders of specific performance are generally disfavored in the context of construction. A level of distrust by the non-breaching party develops as a result of the breach that undermines the full benefits intended by the bargain for which the parties contracted. From a more practical standpoint, specific performance is disfavored by courts because it requires monitoring and active participation by the court in order to ensure the performance.

56 Restatement Second, Contracts §347, comment a ("An injured party's 'expectation interest' is calculated as: 1. A loss in the value to him of the other party's performance caused by its failure or deficiency, plus, 2. Any other loss, including incidental or consequential loss, caused by the breach, less, 3. Any cost or other loss that he has avoided by not having to perform".)

57 Restatement Second, Contracts §370.

Punitive Damages

8.61 Punitive damages are generally designed to punish and deter egregious conduct. Such damages are typically barred in contract cases, however, unless the conduct constituting the breach is also a tort for which punitive damages are recoverable.[58]

Equitable Remedies

Quantum Meruit

8.62 *Quantum meruit* is an equitable remedy that provides restitution for performance under a contract implied-in-fact. Under the theory of *quantum meruit*, a non-breaching party may be awarded damages in an amount considered reasonable to compensate for the value conferred on the breaching party. Most courts will not consider an award of *quantum meruit* damages when a written, express contract exists between the parties.[59]

8.63 A claim for *quantum meruit* requires a plaintiff to show that it expected compensation for its actions.[60] The measure of *quantum meruit* damages is the "reasonable value of the benefit conferred, either by part performance or reliance".[61]

Unjust Enrichment

8.64 Although commonly confused with *quantum meruit*, unjust enrichment is measured by the value of what was unequitably retained under a constructive contract implied in law.[62] Unjust enrichment is a quasi-contract theory of recovery, and "is an obligation imposed by equity to prevent injustice, in the absence of an actual contract between the parties concerned".[63] Typically, when claiming unjust enrichment, the plaintiff must show that the other party was enriched at the plaintiff's expense, and that "it is against equity and good conscience to permit [the other party] to retain what is sought to be recovered.[64] Unlike a claim in *quantum meruit*, the plaintiff does not have to show that the benefited party had an active role in obtaining the benefit, however.[65] Even an innocent party may be unjustly enriched.[66]

---

58 *Rocanova v Equitable Life Assur. Soc. Of US*, 83 N.Y.2d 603, 612 N.Y.S.2d 339 (1994)(holding that punitive damages are not recoverable for ordinary breach of contract as their purpose is not to remedy private wrongs but to vindicate public rights; however, where breach of contract involves fraud evincing high degree of moral turpitude and demonstrating such wanton dishonesty as to imply criminal indifference to civil obligations, punitive damages are recoverable if conduct was aimed at public generally.); see also, Restatement Second, Contracts §355 ("Punitive damages are not recoverable for a breach of a contract unless the conduct constituting the breach is also a tort for which punitive damages are recoverable".)

59 *A & V 425 LLC Contracting Co. v RFD 55th Street LLC*, 15 Misc. 3d 196, 830 N.Y.S.2d 637 (Sup 2007).

60 *Gidatex, S.r.L. v Camaniello Imports, Ltd.*, 49 F.Supp. 2d 298 (S.D.N.Y. 1999).

61 *Jay Cashman v Portland Pipe Line Corp.*, 559 F. Supp. 2d 85 (D.Me.2008).

62 *See* 6 Bruner & O'Connor Construction Law §19:36 (2016); *Barry v Pacific West Const., Inc.*, 140 Idaho 827, 103 P.3d 440, 447 (2004); *Paffhausen v Balano*, 1998 ME 47, 708 A.2d 269 (Me. 1998).

63 *IDT Corp. v Morgan Stanley Dean Witter & Co.*, 12 N.Y.3d 132, 142, 879 N.Y.S.2d 355, 907 N.E.2d 1104 (2009).

64 *Mandarin Trading Ltd. v Wildenstein*, 16 N.Y.3d 173, 182, 919 N.Y.S.2d 465, 944 N.E.2d 1104 (2011) [internal quotation marks and citations omitted].

65 *Aetna Cas. and Sur. Co. v LFO Const. Corp.*, 207 A.D.2d 274, 615 N.Y.S.2d 389 (1st Dep't 1994).

66 *Cruz v McAneney*, 31 A.D.3d 54, 816 N.Y.S.2d 486 (2d Dep't 2006).

Remedies under Contract

8.65 Most jurisdictions within North American routinely uphold contracting parties' "freedom to contract", meaning, absent promises based in illegal acts or provisions that violate statutes, courts generally enforce contract provisions to the extent they are unambiguous and not inconsistent with other contract provisions. Accordingly, parties may agree ahead of time to a non-breaching party's remedies that shall be imposed in the event of a breach. One very common example of a predetermined contractual remedy is liquidated damages. Liquidated damages are typically tied to the duration of contract performance and represent a pre-determined dollar amount as monetary damages that will be charged to the breaching party per day for the duration of the contract breach. Liquidated damages are intended to replace actual damages associated with construction delays.

Limitation on Remedies

Contractual Limitations

8.66 It is not uncommon for contracts to include provisions that specifically limit damages that may be recovered by the non-breaching party. Waivers of consequential damages are ubiquitous in construction contracts. Similarly, provisions that limit the liability for design professionals are quite common. Courts tend to uphold these types of provisions as considerations of the parties related to risks and benefits negotiated at the time the parties entered the contract.

Foreseeability

8.67 Damages are generally not recoverable for losses that the breaching party did not have reason to foresee at the time the contract was made as a probable result of a breach.[67] A court may consider a loss to be foreseeable as a probable result of a breach as long as it follows from the breach in the ordinary course of business or as a result of special circumstances, beyond the ordinary course of events, that the breaching party had reason to know.[68]

Reasonableness

8.68 The party requesting damages has the burden to prove that the requested amounts are reasonable. An important limitation in this analysis is whether the non-breaching party met its obligation to mitigate the amount of damages to the extent reasonable. Damages cannot be recovered for losses that reasonably could have been avoided or minimized after the breach occurred. If the non-breaching party fails to use reasonable diligence in mitigating its damages, the court may reduce the requested damages in an amount equal to that which could have been avoided. On the other hand, if there are costs related to the mitigation of damages, those costs may be included in the non-breaching party's total damage request.

---

67 Restatement Second of Contracts §351.

68 *Hadley v Baxendale*, 9 Exch. 341, 156 Eng.Rep. 145. (Court of Exchequer, 1854)

Doctrine of Economic Waste

8.69 The Doctrine of Economic Waste applies to cases in which a contractor's performance does not strictly conform to the contractual requirements. This doctrine acts to limit the non-breaching party's damages to the lesser amount of the "cost to repair or to strictly conform to the contract requirements" as compared to the diminution in value attributable to the non-conforming work.[69]

Interpretation of Contracts

8.70 The interpretation of a contract and determination of the meaning of contract language is typically an issue of law for a court to decide.[70] When considering the meaning of contract terms or provisions, a court must follow certain rules of interpretation. The main concern of a court is always to ascertain and give effect to the intention of the parties.[71] The parties' intentions are first to be determined by the plain language used in the contract.[72] The plain, common, or normal meaning of language will be assigned to the words of a contract unless there are circumstances that require a special meaning.[73]

8.71 The contract must also be read as a whole so that every part is interpreted in conjunction with all other parts in order to give effect to the contract's overall general purpose as revealed within its four corners or in its entirety.[74] An interpretation that gives effect to all provisions of the contract should be sought so as to not render any portion superfluous, useless, or inexplicable.[75] If it is impossible to interpret a contract in such a way that does not leave part of the contract ineffective or superfluous, the court will seek an interpretation that will at least effectuate the principal or main purpose of the parties.[76] Similarly, an interpretation of the contract that renders it valid or its performance possible is preferred to one that renders the contract invalid or its performance impossible.[77]

8.72 The *Ejusdem Generis* Doctrine can be particularly useful in the interpretation of construction contracts. Under this doctrine, when general and specific contract clauses conflict, the specific clause governs the meaning of the contract.[78]

8.73 In the event an ambiguity exists within the contract, a court must employ accepted methods of interpretation in order to discern the parties' intent. An ambiguity exists if there is the possibility for a word or phrase to be reasonably or plausibly subjected to more than one meaning. Because the party that drafted the contract was in the best position to control the meaning of the provisions, it is a generally accepted principle that the

69 *Lyon v Belosky Const. Inc.*, 247 A.D.2d 730, 669 N.Y.S.2d 400 (3d Dep't 1998).

70 *Manchester Technologies, Inc. v Didata (NY) Inc.*, 303 A.D.2d 726, 757 N.Y.S. 2d 439 (2d Dep't 2003).

71 *Postlewaite v McGraw-Hill, Inc.*, 411 F.3d 63 (2d Cir. 2005).

72 *County of San Diego v Ace Property & Casualty Ins. Co.*, 37 Cal.4th 406, 118 P.3d 607 (2005); *Beardslee v Inflection Energy*, LLC, 25 N.Y.3d 150, 8 N.Y.S.3d 618, 31 N.E.3d 80 (2015).

73 *City of Fulton v Great American Indem. Co.*, 11 Misc. 2d 536, 174 N.Y.S.2d 690 (Sup 1958), aff'd 7 A.D.2d 832, 181 N.Y.S.2d 780 (4th Dep't 1958).

74 *Riverside South Planning Corp. v CRP/Extell Riverside, L.P.*, 13 N.Y.3d 398, 892 N.Y.S.2d 303, 920 N.E.2d 359 (2009).

75 *LaSalle Bank Nat. Ass'n v Nomura Asset Capital Corp.*, 424 F.3d 195 (2d Cir. 2005).

76 *Farrell Lines, Inc. v City of New York*, 30 N.Y.2d 76, 330 N.Y.D.2d 358, 281 N.E.2d 162 (1972).

77 *Consul Ltd. v Solide Enterprises, Inc.*, 802 F.2d 1143 (9th Cir. 1986).

78 Restatement Second, Contracts §203 (c); *Kayfield Construction Corp. v United States*, 278 F.2d 217 (2d Cir. 1960).

ambiguity shall be construed against the drafter.[79] This rule is frequently referenced by the Latin term *contra proferentum.*

8.74 The court may also look to the parties' actions during the course of performance under the contract in order to reconcile an ambiguity within the contract. The parties' actions may reveal their practical interpretation of the contract during the course of performance and provide give meaning to the parties' intent related to the ambiguous terms.[80] Conduct demonstrating the parties' intent to be bound by the agreement may also be used to enforce a contract that otherwise may have been considered too vague to be enforceable.[81]

8.75 Most jurisdictions have adopted the parol evidence rule to bar the introduction of evidence related to extraneous agreements not formally incorporated into a written contract in the absence of an ambiguity where that intent can be gathered from the instrument itself. More specifically, the parol evidence rule is a substantive rule of law that prohibits the admission of evidence of prior or contemporaneous oral agreements, or prior written agreements, whose effect is to add to, vary, modify, or contradict the terms of a writing that the parties intended to be a final, complete, and exclusive statement of their agreement.[82] Where an ambiguity exists in a contract, however, many courts will allow the introduction of parol evidence including additional promises to complete the entire agreement, custom or practice of the parties, or specific trade usage of certain terms, in order to determine the parties' intent.[83]

---

79 Restatement of Contracts Second §206.

80 *In re Field's Will*, 11 A.D.2d 774, 204 N.Y.S.2d 947 (2d Dep't 1960)(stating, "The interpretation given by the parties themselves, as shown by their acts, will be adopted by the Court, and to this end, not only the acts but the declarations of the parties may be considered ... The courts in determining the obligations of a contract should, when possible, apply the same measure as the parties have applied").

81 *Bohman v Berg*, 54 Cal. 2d 787, 8 Cal. Rptr. 441, 356 P.2d 185 (1960) (citing Corbin, Contracts (1950) s 101, p. 319; 1 Williston, Contracts (Jaeger 1957) s 49, p. 158; the court said: "It is well-settled law that, although an agreement may be indefinite or uncertain in its inception, subsequent performance by the parties under the agreement will cure this defect and render it enforceable. When one party performs under the contract and the other party accepts his performance without objection it is assumed that this was the performance contemplated by the agreement".

"This rule is in accord with the cardinal rule of construction that when a contract is ambiguous or uncertain the practical construction placed upon it by the parties before any controversy arises as to its meaning affords one of the most reliable means of determining the intent of the parties. [In] all cases where the terms of their contract, or the language they employ, raises a question of doubtful construction, and it appears that the parties themselves have practically interpreted their contract, the courts will follow that practical construction. It is to be assumed that parties to a contract best know what was meant by its terms, and are the least liable to be mistaken as to its intention; that each party is alert to his own interests, and to insistence on his rights, and that whatever is done by the parties contemporaneously with the execution of the contract is done under its terms as they understood and intended it should be. Parties are far less liable to have been mistaken as to the intention of their contract during the period while harmonious and practical construction reflects that intention, than they are when subsequent differences have impelled them to resort to law ... The law, however, recognizes the practical construction of a contract as the best evidence of what was intended by its provisions".

"When the parties perform without objection under a contract the terms of which appear to be indefinite, they have indicated that its terms were sufficiently certain so that they, at least, could perform it".

82 *Niagara Mohawk Power Corporation v Graver Tank & Manufacturing Co.*, 470 F. Supp. 1308 (N.D.N.Y.1979); *but see Sterling v Taylor*, 40 Cal. 4th 757, 55 Cal. Rptr. 3d 116, 152 P.3d 420 (2007) (disapproving language in several prior cases and holding that parol evidence may be introduced to explain or clarify the terms set forth in a writing if the writing otherwise contains the essential terms of the alleged contract).

83 *Mejia v Trustees of Net Realty Holding Trust*, 304 A.D.2d 627, 759 N.Y.S.2d 91 (2d Dep't 2003); see also, U.C.C. §2-202, which permits trade usage to "explain" or "supplement" even a fully integrated agreement for the sale of goods; Restatement of Contracts, Second §222.

Standard Forms of US Contracts

US Government Direct Contracts

8.76 As set forth in Section A.2.b above, direct US Government Contracting accounts for a significant amount of construction work. There is no standard form of contract; instead, the FARs specify those clauses which must be included in a contract. There are a variety of different types; for example, Firm Fixed Price, cost reimbursable, and for each type there are required clauses. Many of these clauses are the socio-economic requirements addressed in Section A.2.a above. However, there are also required clauses for the commercial relationship between the US Government and the contractor. Using the Firm Fixed Price format as an example, some of the significant clauses are as follows:

FAR §52.243-4	Changes (Variations)
FAR §52.236-2	Differing Site (Physical) Conditions
FAR §52.242-4	Suspension of Work
FAR §52.249-2	Termination for Convenience
FAR §52.249-10	Termination for Default
FAR §52.211-12	Liquidated Damages
FAR §52.233-1	Disputes

8.77 The inclusion of these and all other Clauses is mandatory. If a particular clause is not set forth or directly referenced in the Contract but required by the FAR's, that clause will be read into the Contract as a matter of law.[84] In addition to being required for direct Government Contracts, many of these clauses are required for contracts where the Government has provided funding.[85]

American Institute of Architects (AIA) Family of Contracts

8.78 The American Institute of Architects (AIA) is a private organization which has developed an entire family of documents covering virtually all construction relationships. They are primarily designed for buildings, as compared to civil works.

8.79 The entire family of documents can be viewed and purchased from the AIA's website, www.aia.org. The documents include those appropriate to conventional Firm Fixed Price contracts, Design Build contracts and several other categories. One of the more widely used forms is AIA201 for Firm Fixed Price contracts. The commercial clauses will be familiar in intent and content, but not necessarily in terminology, to users of the FIDIC documents. For example, a partial list of AIA 201 clauses for Firm Fixed Price contracts and the FIDIC Red Book (1st Ed. 1999)[86] shows the following:

---

84 *G.L. Christian & Associates v United States*, 312 F.2d 418 (Ct. Cl. 1963).

85 E.g., Office of Mgmt. & Budget, Revised Circular No. A-102, Grants and Cooperative Agreements with State and Local Governments (revised 7 October 1994, as further amended 29 August 1997) (requiring agencies to include in their contracts to grantees a clause providing for termination for cause and for convenience and a clause dealing with breach of contract and resulting sanctions).

86 Conditions of Contract for Construction for Building and Engineering Works Designed by the Employer (1st Ed. 1999).

Clause	AIA 201	Red book (1st Ed. 1999)
Changes/variations	Article 7	Articles 13.1 and 13.3
Time extensions	Article 8.3	Article 8.4
Termination of contractor	Article 14.2	Article 15
Termination of employer	Article 14.1	Article 16

There are many others.

8.80 Although the AIA forms are drafted to reflect an integrated approach, in practice they are often modified. As with any integrated contract form, a change in one section often has unanticipated consequences for other sections. Thus, like many other standard forms of contract, it is recommended that no changes be made to the mandatory language.

Engineers' Joint Contract Documents Committee

8.81 The Engineers Joint Contract Documents Committee (EJCDC)[87] has developed a series of documents targeted towards infrastructure, as compared to building projects. There are numerous documents for both Firm Fixed Price contracts and more recently, a series of documents for Design-Build contracts, especially for public–private partnership projects. The documents are available through the EJCDC website, www.ejcdc.org.

8.82 The basic document for Firm Fixed Price contracts is C-700, Standard General Conditions. Like AIA 201, the basic commercial terms will be familiar to those who work regularly with the FIDIC Red Book (1st Ed. 1999) and cover such matters on differing site (physical) conditions, delay, and changes/variations.

Consensus Docs

8.83 A relatively recent entry into the US Construction standard forms of contract for the construction market are the consensus documents. The consensus documents have been prepared by a committee of construction owners, main contractors, subcontractors and suppliers. Some of the members are the Associated General Contractors of America (AGC), Construction Users Roundtable (CURT), National Electrical Contractors Association (NECA) and the Disputes Review Board Foundation (DRBF).

8.84 There is an entire family of documents which can be obtained through the consensus documents website, www.consensusdocs.org. The document for a Firm Fixed Price contract is No. 200 and again many of its concepts will be familiar to anyone who has worked with the FIDIC Red Book (1st Ed. 1999).

8.85 There is also a set of documents for Design Build projects, the 400 series. There has yet to be a wide acceptance of the Consensus forms compared to the AIA or EJCDC documents.

87 The EJCDC is a committee of the leading engineering societies in the US, The American Council of Engineering Companies (ACEC), the American Society of Civil Engineers (ASCE), and the National Society of Professional Engineers (NSPE).

Design Build Institute of America (DBIA) Documents

8.86 The Design Build Institute of America is a relatively new professional organization and as its name suggests, it has developed a series of documents for Design-Build projects. The documents are available through its website, www.dbia.org. Its basic documents are the Standard Form of Agreement between Owner and Design-Build-Lump Sum Contractor (No. 525) and Standard Form of Agreement between Owner and Design-Builder-Cost Plus Fee with an Option for a Guaranteed Maximum Price Contractor (No. 530). The documents are not yet in wide use, but as the Design-Build format of contracting expands in the US, the DBIA documents are also likely to become more widely used.

Industrial Construction

8.87 There are no widely used standard forms for industrial projects. Most industrial owners have their own forms, sometimes closely tied to their proprietary processes. Contracts for electrical generating projects are often performed on an EPC basis and tailored to the major equipment being used; for example, turbines, generators, and boilers.

Canadian Construction Forms

8.88 The Canadian Construction Documents Committee (CCDC)/Comité Canadien des Documents de Construction has a complete set of Contract forms. These include the following:

CCDC – 2 (2008), Stipulated Price Contract
CCDC – 2MA (2016) Master Agreement between Owner and Contractor
CCDC – 3 (2016) Cost Plus Contract
CCDC – 18 (2001) Civil Works Contract

The full set of documents is accessible from www.ccdc.org/document-outlets.

Construction Law Principles

Procurement and Tendering

8.89 Construction contracts are generally awarded to contractors through a competitive bidding or negotiation process. The preferred (often statutorily mandated) method of awarding *public* construction projects is through the competitive sealed bidding process, whereas *private* projects are often awarded through negotiation between the employer and a select group of qualified contractors.

Public Procurement and Tendering

8.90 As discussed, Federal procurement in the US is governed by the Federal Acquisition Regulation (FARs). Although state and local procurement can vary depending on the state and/or locality, state and local projects often follow or incorporate Federal principles of procurement as well. The main characteristics of public procurement through competitive bidding are that the projects are generally open to all companies and projects are awarded to the lowest responsible bidder.

The typical competitive bidding process is outlined below:

- Employer determines the project and availability of funding;
- Employer determines whether competitive sealed bidding is "feasible" and "practicable" for the project at issue. Factors for consideration include the extent of competition, completeness of bid documents, and whether there is sufficient time for bidders to prepare and submit their bids and for proper evaluation of bids;
- Employer prepares invitation to bid package, including detailed and complete plans, specifications, and contract terms and conditions;
- Employer announces/issues solicitation for bids;
- Contractor prepares and submits bid;
- Employer publicly opens bids and evaluates bids for responsiveness to the requirements of the solicitation, responsibility of lowest bids to complete the project, and overall bid pricing considerations;
- Employer awards contract to the lowest responsive bid submitted by a responsible bidder.

Private Procurement and Tendering

8.91 In contrast to public procurement, private companies have the latitude to customize their procurement processes and are not obligated to award projects to the lowest responsible bidder. Private entities need not provide equal procurement opportunities to all companies nor do they need to publish or announce contract awards publicly. Private procurement can involve issuing of solicitations to preferred contractors or suppliers, prequalification of bidders, and awarding of projects based on a scoring system that takes into account more than simply bid price but other factors as well, such as interviews, previous/existing relationships, and value engineering. Furthermore, evaluation criteria need not be made public.

Different Types of Contract (Unit Price, Lump Sum, etc.)

8.92 There are a number of different possible pricing arrangements for construction contracts, whether they are for general contracts, prime contracts, or subcontracts. The following are the main types of pricing arrangements used throughout the United States:

- Fixed price (lump sum), in which the work under the contract is charged one fixed price;
- Unit price, in which work under the contract is charged based on set prices for various units of production;
- Cost reimbursement plus a fee;
- Guaranteed Maximum Price;
- Time and material;
- Force account.

Note that the various types of pricing arrangements (including those not listed above) can be combined in nearly any combination and exist in a single contract.

Nature of Construction Contract

8.93 A construction contract is typically commenced by the employer. The employer will start the process by choosing the project delivery method, type of contract, extent of risk-allocation between the parties, and the solicitation process. It is important to note that in many (if not most) cases, employers wield more bargaining power or leverage over contractors and, as a result, bargaining power for contractors can be relatively limited with respect to the construction contract with the employer. As such, contractors often exert their bargaining power down the line with their subcontractors and suppliers.

8.94 As construction projects rarely proceed as originally anticipated, construction contracts by their very nature should account for and address unexpected events and conditions that occur during any given construction project. Such unexpected events and conditions are typically defined as "changes". Some of these changes include minor design changes; errors and/or omissions in the plans and specifications; changes in laws and regulations; and other events that cause delay or increase costs on a project.

8.95 The changes clause is one of the most important provisions contained in a construction contract. A changes clause can cover numerous areas of disagreement between the parties. In the United States, the changes clause will often permit the employer to make unilateral changes to the work without having to compensate the contractor for time and/or money provided that the change falls within the originally anticipated scope of work. For the contractor, the changes clause provides the right to equitable adjustment of time and/or costs in certain situations, such as employer-directed changes materially affecting design or construction performance or completion; circumstances beyond the control of the parties, such as unforeseen site or weather conditions; that is, force majeure; differences between estimated and actual material quantities; directions necessary to resolve design defects, unavailability of specific materials; or unexpected construction hindrances or interferences.

Design Obligations

8.96 Design obligations on construction projects in the United States typically vary depending on the type of project delivery method and contract. Under the traditional design-bid-build model, the designer or architect contracts directly with the employer to provide the design. Once the contract is awarded to the contractor and construction commences, the designer/architect typically acts as the employer's representative during construction, and the contractor bears no design responsibility.

8.97 On the other hand, under a project delivery method such as design-build where the employer contracts with a single entity to carry out both the design and construction of a project. The contractor and the designer/architect work as part of the same team; thus, the contractor owes obligations for the design to the employer under the main contract. Although it may seem unfavorable for the contractor to shoulder design responsibility, the substantial advantages of the design-build project delivery system with respect to lower project costs and faster delivery time will often outweigh concerns with assuming design obligations.

8.98 With respect to the common law approach to design obligations for a traditional design-bid-build project, the seminal case is *United States v Spearin*, 248 US 132 (1918). In projects where the employer furnishes the design, the employer is obligated under the

Spearin Doctrine to compensate the contractor for additional costs and time arising out of any defects in the design. Simply stated, the *Spearin Doctrine* creates an implied warranty that the plans and specifications provided by the employer are adequate, accurate, and complete such that satisfactory performance of the contract will result if the contractor follows the furnished design documents. If the contractor is bound to build according to plans and specifications prepared by the employer, the contractor has no design obligations and will generally not be responsible for the consequences of defects in the plans and specifications.

Duty to Warn/Check/Review

8.99 The duty to warn/check/review in the United States is best exemplified in Article 3.2 REVIEW OF CONTRACT DOCUMENTS AND FIELD CONDITIONS BY CONTRACTOR of the AIA Document A201 – 2007. Specifically, Article 3.2.1-.2 provides in relevant part:

> **§ 3.2.1** Execution of the Contract by the Contractor is a representation that the Contractor has visited the site, become generally familiar with local conditions under which the Work is to be performed and correlated personal observations with requirements of the Contract Documents.
>
> **§ 3.2.2** Because the Contract Documents are complementary, the Contractor shall, before starting each portion of the Work, carefully study and compare the various Contract Documents relative to that portion of the Work, as well as the information furnished by the Owner pursuant to Section 2.2.3, shall take field measurements of any existing conditions related to that portion of the Work, and shall observe any conditions at the site affecting it. These obligations are for the purpose of facilitating coordination and construction by the Contractor and are not for the purpose of discovering errors, omissions, or inconsistencies in the Contract Documents; however, the Contractor shall promptly report to the Architect any errors, inconsistencies or omissions discovered by or made known to the Contractor as a request for information in such form as the Architect may require. It is recognized that the Contractor's review is made in the Contractor's capacity as a contractor and not as a licensed design professional, unless otherwise specifically provided in the Contract Documents.
>
> **§ 3.2.3** The Contractor is not required to ascertain that the Contract Documents are in accordance with applicable laws, statutes, ordinances, codes, rules and regulations, or lawful orders of public authorities, but the Contractor shall promptly report to the Architect any nonconformity discovered by or made known to the Contractor as a request for information in such form as the Architect may require.

8.100 In short, the contractor is required to carefully study and compare the contract documents, to take field measurements of existing conditions, and to observe conditions at the site affecting that portion of work. This duty arises only after the contractor has been awarded the work. Although such review is not intended for checking the designer's design, any errors, inconsistencies, or omissions recognized by the contractor must be promptly reported to the designer/architect.

8.101 Essentially, the standard AIA language reflects a compromise for all parties: Contractors are not responsible for the errors and omissions of designers/architects, but the employer is also entitled to costs and damages that would have been avoided if the contractor had properly performed its obligations to review, check, and warn. The standard for proper review by the contractor is indicated by the language in Article 3.2.2. stating that review obligations are for the purpose of facilitating coordination and construction by the Contractor. In the event of a dispute as to the adequacy of the review, industry standards would generally apply to determine the sufficiency of the contractor's review.

Employer and Contractor

The Employer

8.102 The employer owns the project and thus is generally the origin of the construction project and its team. The employer may be a public entity (such as a city or county) or a private entity. Two variables are important to the employers: Project (and schedule) predictability and the cost of the project. From a contractual perspective, the employer has significant responsibilities to see that a project is successfully completed.

Some of the principal roles of a project employer include:

- **Provide Information to the Contractor.** The contractor is entitled to several items of information only the employer can provide including affidavits of financial commitments to the project, surveys, utilities, legal descriptions, and geotechnical site investigation reports.
- **Payment of Work Project Fees and Charges.** The employer has a responsibility to pay for approvals, easements, assessments, and other charges and items for which the contractor is responsible.
- **Payments to the Contractor.** These payments are outlined in the employer-contractor agreement.
- **Right to Stop Work.** Under almost all contracts in the United States, work can be stopped by the employer for good cause. Typically, the contract will identify the circumstances under which this right can be invoked.
- **Right to Carry Out the Work.** If the contractor defaults or neglects to perform the work according to the terms of the contract documents, or if the contractor fails to commence the work within a noted period of time, the employer will almost always have the right to take over a portion of the work or terminate the contract and complete the contract by other means.
- **Right to Perform Construction.** The employer may initiate construction according to its own services, but in these instances, the employer is responsible for the coordination of its services with the contractor's work and schedule.
- **Right to Award Separate Contracts.** The employer has the right to divide the project into diverse components and award a separate contract for each component. In such cases, the employer will often require each contractor to agree to cooperate with one another and coordinate their work efforts.
- **Termination Without Cause.** The employer may terminate the contract with the contractor without cause. The conditions of the contract specify the termination procedures and generally prohibit the contractor from recovering profit on the unfinished portion of the work.

The Contractor

8.103 The contractor is responsible for the day-to-day operations and oversight of the construction project, and in many cases direct performance of work on the project. The contractor is also responsible for acting as the intermediary for the various parties to the project (design/architects, subcontractors, supplier, the employer, etc.).

8.104 Some principal responsibilities that a contractor undertakes when entering into a contract in the United States include:

- Site visit and assessments;
- Providing submittals to architects and/or engineers;
- Acquiring necessary permits;
- Producing project schedules;
- Performing or overseeing the performance of all construction work on the project;
- Selecting and overseeing subcontractors to carry out portions of the work on the project;
- Selecting suppliers and procuring all materials and equipment that are necessary for the project.

Consultant's Role and Liability

8.105 The employer of a construction project will typically hire various consultants to oversee and/or provide recommendations for the project, such as design consultants, architecture consultants, and engineering consultants. Liability of such consultants is typically controlled through a contract with the employer in a traditional design-bid-build project or general contractor if contracting directly with the contractor rather than the employer (such as in a design-build project).

8.106 Another type of "consultant" on many constructions projects is a "construction manager at risk" ("CMAR") or a "construction manager not at risk" ("CMNAR"). A CMAR typically enters into a lump sum or guaranteed maximum price contract under which the CMAR provides preconstruction services transitioning the design phase into the construction phase. Then, during construction phase, the CMAR essentially fills the role of a general contractor for the project, most notably by directly entering into various subcontracts and supply contracts in its own name. As such, the CMAR is ultimately liable to the employer for all of the contracted work on the project, including the work carried out by the subcontractors and is also responsible for paying the subcontractors.

8.107 Conversely, a CMNAR (also known as agency construction management) acts as the employer's agent in providing services and consultation to the employer. A CMNAR does not have responsibility for design work or for construction work, and the employer directly contracts with the general contractor for the construction work (rather than through the construction manager). Accordingly, the general contractor is directly responsible for its work to the employer, and the employer is directly responsible for paying the general contractors and subcontractors. A CMNAR bears no risk for the price of the project, but will have direct contact with, and generally control over, the General Contractor as the employer's designated agent.

Subcontracting

8.108 Most construction work on larger-scale construction projects is all or in large part performed by subcontractors. Thus, proper selection of subcontractors by the contractor is essential, as subcontractors can have substantial effects on coordination, project schedule, and project completion – which, if not done properly, can have dire consequences for all parties involved on a project. Accordingly, general contractors must have the ability and experience to evaluate and select qualified subcontractors, as well as to properly manage subcontractors and their work for the duration of the project.

8.109 Typically, contractors are given great flexibility in selecting their subcontractors. In addition, while the contract with the employer may require some clauses set forth in the subcontracts, for the most part the form of the subcontract is left to the control of the contractor.

Unforeseeable Physical Conditions

8.110 A differing site condition is defined as an unanticipated physical condition on the site that existed at the time the contract was awarded but was unknown at the time of bid and could not have been discovered by a reasonable inspection of the site. Examples of unforeseeable physical conditions include soil with deficient bearing capacity, soil that cannot be reused as structural fill, unforeseeable groundwater, quicksand, rock formations or excessive quantities of rock, and artificial subsurface structures or obstacles. The problem of differing site conditions is often addressed by the construction contract through a differing site conditions or changed conditions clause aimed at alleviating some of the risk associated with differing site conditions for both the employer and the contractor.

8.111 There exist two types of differing site conditions in the United States. A Type I differing site condition is a condition that differs materially from the conditions depicted in the contract. A Type II differing site condition is a "catch all" of sorts and is defined as an unknown physical condition at the site, of an *unusual* nature, which differs materially from those ordinarily encountered and generally recognized as inhering in work of the character provided for in the contract.

8.112 Recovery for a Type I changed condition requires a showing of (1) conditions that are depicted by the contract documents; (2) reliance on the physical conditions as depicted in the contract documents; (3) actual conditions; (4) material difference between the conditions as depicted in the contract documents and as actually encountered; (5) notice, as required by the contract, provided or excused; and (6) sufficient documentation or records of additional costs or time incurred.

8.113 Under a Type II situation, it is possible to recover even when the contract is silent about the nature of the condition. To establish a Type II differing site condition, the conditions encountered must be unusual and differ materially from those reasonably anticipated, given the nature of the work and geographical area. Unknown and unusual conditions can include both entirely unanticipated materials, as well as anticipated materials appearing in significantly different proportions or amounts.

8.114 As noted, a differing site conditions clause in the contract grants the contractor the right to an equitable adjustment whenever materially differing site conditions are encountered on the project and those conditions result in an increase in the contractor's cost and/or time. Such a differing site conditions clause is consistent with established US case law that recognizes the need to compensate contractors when differing site conditions are encountered. As touched upon above, when an employer provides information to bidders regarding anticipated conditions on a project, bidders are allowed to reasonably rely upon that information in preparing their bids. Contractors are generally not required to undertake an independent investigation to verify the accuracy of the information provided by the employer.[88] The mandatory nature of the differing site conditions clause is not an accident or mistake. The primary purpose of the differing site conditions clause is to encourage lower bids, by discouraging bid padding or contingency amounts, through an understanding with the contractor that an adjustment to the contract price will be made when differing site conditions are encountered.[89] Essentially, by using a differing site conditions clause, an employer gets a lower price from contractors in exchange for agreeing to pay for the extra costs and time if, and when, differing site conditions impact a project.

Materials and Workmanship

8.115 The typical standard of quality governing a contractor's work, including materials and workmanship, is best represented by Article 3.5 WARRANTY of the AIA Document A201 – 2007. Specifically, Article 3.5 provides:

> **§ 3.5 WARRANTY**
> The Contractor warrants to the Owner and Architect that materials and equipment furnished under the Contract will be of good quality and new unless the Contract Documents require or permit otherwise. The Contractor further warrants that the Work will conform to the requirements of the Contract Documents and will be free from defects, except for those inherent in the quality of the Work the Contract Documents require or permit. Work, materials, or equipment not conforming to these requirements may be considered defective. The Contractor's warranty excludes remedy for damage or defect caused by abuse, alterations to the Work not executed by the Contractor, improper or insufficient maintenance, improper operation, or normal wear and tear and normal usage. If required by the Architect, the Contractor shall furnish satisfactory evidence as to the kind and quality of materials and equipment.

8.116 While many variations of this clause exist, the intended results are almost always the same: The contractor warrants that (1) materials and equipment will be of good quality and new, (2) the work will conform to the requirements of the contract documents, and (3) the work will be free from defects. Thus, a contractor who fails to repair defective work after receiving requisite and proper notice from the employer may be liable for both breach of warranty to perform work free from defects and breach of contract to repair defective work. It is also important to note that even if a contractor performs all work with good workmanship, should the contractor fail to follow the contract specifications it will still be exposed to a claim for breach of contract.

Labour Law Considerations

8.117 Labour laws in the United States tend to be state-specific and must be examined on a state-by-state basis. Certain labour law issues, however, are found throughout the

88 *Foster Const. C. A. & Williams Bros. Co. v U. S.*, 435 F.2d 873, 887 (Ct. Cl. 1970); *see Sierra-Blanca*, Inc., ASBCA Nos. 30943 et al., 91-2 BCA ¶ 23,990 (1991).

89 *James Julian, Inc. v President and Commissioners of the Town of Elkton*, 341 F.2d 205, 209 (1965); *Foster*, 435 F.2d at 887.

US One such issue is the strength and prevalence of labour unions in the construction industry and beyond.

8.118 Generally, labour unions exert significant power in the US construction industry and union workers typically earn more than non-union workers. Unions have a long and storied history in the United States and have exercised over the years an ability to influence the construction industry's hiring requirements. The US Department of Labor's Bureau of Labor Statistics reported in its Economic News Release in 2015 www.bls.gov /news.release/union2.nr0.htm) that the construction industry had one of the top 5 rates of unionization at 13.2%. This percentage varies considerably throughout the US For 2015, all states in the Middle Atlantic and Pacific divisions reported union membership rates above the national average, and all states in the East South Central and West South Central divisions had rates below it. New York has the highest union membership rate in the US and South Carolina has the lowest; the higher the unionization rate of the region, the higher the likelihood that a contractor will have to bargain with a union to find an adequate and qualified labour force.

8.119 The power exerted by unions has significant ramifications for construction projects in the US For instance, employers might restrict procurement to those contractors that employ union workers so as to avoid labour challenges and backlash from the unions. To ensure that contractors will employ only union workers, employers will typically enter into project labour agreements acceptable to the unions and require bidders to comply with these agreements as a condition of award of the contract. An important effect of such union-friendly procurement for a project is that the contractor will pay union wages and benefits in return for agreement by the unions to not strike.

Performance and Take-Over

8.120 Issues relating to a contractor's performance of its work and the right of the employer to take over the work are standard clauses in almost all construction contracts. Some of the most common revisions are found in the AIA Document A201 – 2007. Specifically, in Article 2.3 OWNER'S RIGHT TO STOP THE WORK and Article 2.4 OWNER'S RIGHT TO CARRY OUT THE WORK. Articles 2.3 and 2.4 provide:

> **§ 2.3 OWNER'S RIGHT TO STOP THE WORK**
>
> If the Contractor fails to correct Work that is not in accordance with the requirements of the Contract Documents as required by Section 12.2 or repeatedly fails to carry out Work in accordance with the Contract Documents, the Owner may issue a written order to the Contractor to stop the Work, or any portion thereof, until the cause for such order has been eliminated; however, the right of the Owner to stop the Work shall not give rise to a duty on the part of the Owner to exercise this right for the benefit of the Contractor or any other person or entity, except to the extent required by Section 6.1.3.
>
> **§ 2.4 OWNER'S RIGHT TO CARRY OUT THE WORK**
>
> If the Contractor defaults or neglects to carry out the Work in accordance with the Contract Documents and fails within a ten-day period after receipt of written notice from the Owner to commence and continue correction of such default or neglect with diligence and promptness, the Owner may, without prejudice to other remedies the Owner may have, correct such deficiencies. In such case an appropriate Change Order shall be issued deducting from payments then or thereafter due the Contractor the reasonable cost of correcting such deficiencies,

including Owner's expenses and compensation for the Architect's additional services made necessary by such default, neglect or failure. Such action by the Owner and amounts charged to the Contractor are both subject to prior approval of the Architect. If payments then or thereafter due the Contractor are not sufficient to cover such amounts, the Contractor shall pay the difference to the Owner.

8.121 Article 2.3 is essentially a quality assurance clause and authorizes the employer to issue a written order directing the contractor to stop work where the contractor continually fails to carry out the work as required by the contract documents or fails to correct nonconforming work. Similarly, Article 2.4 authorizes the employer to directly (or through another contractor) correct defective work where the contractor fails to do so after proper notice from the employer to correct the non-conforming work. The employer is then entitled to correct the defective work itself and seek compensation from the contractor for costs incurred by the employer to correct the work.

Contract Price and Payment

8.122 Section D(2) titled "Different Types of Contract", *supra,* outlines some of the various types of pricing arrangements used in construction contracts in the United States.

8.123 With respect to the actual payment processes, provisions in construction contracts typically structure payment as progress payments made on a regular periodic basis (typically monthly). Progress payments may differ, however, depending on the type of contract. For example, progress payments for fixed price contracts are typically based on percentage of project completion involving the use of a schedule of values. Under this process, the contractor indicates the percentage of each line item that has been completed and upon agreement by the Owner or its consultant, is paid the corresponding percentage of the value assigned to each line item. In contrast, for a unit price contract, progress payments are typically based on a calculation of the number of units of quantity of material supplied and/or installed each month.

8.124 In addition to defining how the payment will be calculated, it is typical for the payment provision to set forth the date by which the payment must be made, interest that will apply to late payments, the rights of the employer to withhold portions of a payment and to set forth a list of documents that must be provided with each payment request. The required documents which must be provided as a condition precedent to payment often include lien releases, monthly progress reports and updated schedules.

Defects Liability

8.125 The Federal and individual state laws uniformly require contractors to perform their work in accordance with the project plans and specifications and in a professional and workmanlike manner. In the event that defective construction is discovered, the contractor will be responsible. There are several legal theories employers may utilize to recover against a contractor for defective construction.

8.126 The most common and effective legal theory utilized by employers and contractors to recover the costs of correcting defective construction is negligence. Proof of negligence in the construction defect context requires that plaintiff demonstrate that the defendant fell below established professional standards or failed to meet building code requirements. Under a negligence theory the standard of care, in most cases, be established by expert testimony.[90] In a successful claim under negligence, the insurance carriers for contractors and subcontractors are often responsible for most, if not all of the costs to correct the defects. For many years, the established law in the United States required the "privity doctrine" in order to sue for negligence. Under the prior law, a cause of action for negligence would not lie without a contractual relationship. That "privity doctrine" has not been substantially eroded. The law of negligence has now been expanded to allow various persons to sue third parties with whom they have no contractual privity. For example, the Supreme Court of California, a leader in the expansion of negligence in the United States, determined that a duty of due care will exist in the absence of privity of contract by balancing the following

- The extent to which the transaction was intended to affect the plaintiff;
- The foreseeability of harm to the plaintiff;
- The degree of certainty that plaintiff suffered injury;
- The closeness of the connection between the defendant's conduct and the injuries suffered;
- The moral blame attached to the defendant's conduct;
- The policy of preventing future harm.

8.127 Under the strict liability doctrine, construction defect plaintiffs may recover damages without having to prove breach of duty. Rather, they need only show that a "mass-produced consumer item" is defective and that the "defect" proximately caused injuries.

8.128 Construction contracts typically include provisions requiring competent and defect-free construction practices and warranty obligations. As a result, actions for breach of contract and warranty are often used to pursue defect claims and can enlarge the types of recoverable damages. For instance, many construction contracts contain liquidated damages in the event of late performance. As for warranty obligations, most contracts incorporate express warranties or performance standards which may form the basis of liability in addition to characteristic extended warranties on items such as HVAC, roofing, waterproofing, windows, and mechanical equipment.

Limitation of Liability

8.129 Unambiguous limitations of liability provisions are generally enforceable as long as the terms are not unconscionable or otherwise prohibited by a particular state statute. Limitation of liability clauses are routinely found in design and engineering proposals and negotiated in private design contracts. Some states allow a limitation of liability up to $50,000, the cost of the contract, or whichever amount is greater. Additionally, in order for a limitation of liability clause to be enforceable, some states usually require that both parties clearly state that they both intend to enter into the current contract containing the limitation of liability clause.

---

90 *Miller v Los Angeles County Flood Control Dis.* (1973) 8 Cal.3d 689, 703.

8.130 Where the limitation of liability term is disputed, courts will focus their attention to determine whether or not the limitation of liability clause was located in a conspicuous place in the contract and evaluate whether or not both parties had equal bargaining power. The courts are more likely to enforce the clause if (1) the provision in unambiguous and not unconscionable; (2) the parties' intentions were clearly expressed; (3) the parties had equal bargaining powers or a high level of sophistication; and (4) there is no public policy or statute prohibiting the enforcement of the provision.

8.131 Many owners' contracts include a "no damages for delay" clause in an attempt to shift the financial risks of delay to the contractor. Such a clause usually provides that the contractor is not entitled to any delay damages or alternatively limits the remedy to a non-compensable time extension. A typical clause reads as follows:

> Should the contractor be delayed in the commencement, prosecution, or completion of the work by any act, or failure to act on the part of the Owner, or by any extraordinary conditions arising out of war or government regulations, or by any other cause beyond the contractor's control, none of which are due to any fault, neglect, act or omission on its part, then the contractor shall be entitled to an extension of time only, such extension to be for a period equivalent to the time lost by reason of any and all of the aforesaid causes, as determined by the Owner. Such extension or extensions of time, as determined by the Owner, shall be the contractor's sole remedy. In no event will the contractor be entitled to any costs or damages as a result of such delay.

8.132 Courts generally uphold no damages for delay clauses on the presumption that the parties had equal bargaining power when negotiating the contract. The United States Supreme Court has also approved such a clause in *Wells Bros. Co. of New York v United States* 254 US 83 (1920).

> Men who take $1,000,000 contracts for government buildings are neither unsophisticated nor careless. Inexperience and inattention are more likely to be found in other parties to such contracts than the contractors, and the presumption is obvious and strong that the men signing such a contract as we have here protected themselves against such delays as are complained of by the higher price exacted for the work.

Note, however, that no damages for delay clauses are strictly construed and apply them only when the language is clear and unambiguous. Thus, such clauses will not be enforced if:

1. There is evidence of fraud, bad faith, or malice by the owner;
2. The delay is so long that it justifies the contractor's abandoning the job;
3. The owner actively interferes with the contractor's normal progress.

8.133 In one instance, the California Court of Appeal overturned a no damages for delay cause in a public works contract issued by the City of Los Angeles. The Court reasoned that, while one contract provision only allows a time extension for delays caused by unforeseen events, a related provision created an exception by specifically authorizing payment for unreasonable and unanticipated delays caused by the public entity. The Court of Appeal rejected the City's contention that the contractor had waived its right to delay damages by signing the contract. The court relied, in part, on Public Contract Code Section 7102, which provides:

> Contract provisions in construction contracts of public agencies and subcontractors thereunder which limit the contractee's liability to an extension of time for delay for which the contractee is

> responsible and which delay is unreasonable under the circumstances involved, and not within the contemplation of the parties, shall not be construed to preclude the recovery of damages by the contractor or subcontractor.
>
> No public agency may require the waiver, alteration, or limitation of the applicability of this section. Any such waiver, alteration, or limitation is void. This section shall not be construed to void any provision in a construction contract which requires notice of delays, provides for arbitration or other procedure for settlement, or provides for liquidated damages.

8.134 While the courts will enforce a no damages for delay clause, many contractors have successfully argued that it entered into the contract and accepted the risk of the contract based upon the owner's representation that the plans were complete and accurate. The success of such arguments depends upon the specific facts of each case.

Variations (Changes)

8.135 Every construction project, whether public or private, large or small, will encounter events that require variations or changes to the original construction plans that impact the cost of construction and/or the time to complete the work. Such events include owner-requested changes, correction of design errors, contractor-suggested changes, differing site conditions, and acts of God. Indeed, building designs are never perfect at the outset, and owners want the ability to adjust the design plans throughout the course of the project and to take advantage of better ideas or technological advances. These changes usually impact the cost and/or time of construction.

8.136 The purpose of the change order clause is to vest the owner with the *right* to make changes to the contracted work without invalidating the contract, and to *obligate* the contractor to perform the changed or extra work. The clause should provide a method for calculating the appropriate adjustments to the contract price and/or time caused by the change. The clause should also specify the persons authorized to issue change orders on the owner's behalf, and establish a procedure for requesting, processing, and disputing change orders.

8.137 Absent a change order clause, modifications to a construction contract are governed by general contract modification rules. But these rules only address the *manner* in which modifications can be made to the contract (e.g., a written contract can be modified only by a written modification, but an oral modification to a written contract will be enforceable if it has been fully executed by one party); they do not establish any right to require or obligation to perform the changed work.

8.138 The most important rule in handling potential changes is to strictly follow the contractual change order procedures. Indeed, the majority of litigation involving change order disputes includes circumstances where the parties failed, in some way, to follow the contractual change order procedures. For example, in *Greg Opinski Construction, Inc. v City of Oakdale* 199 Cal.App.4th 1107 (2011), the court held that a contractor could not defend an owner's claim for liquidated damages because the contractor had failed to follow the contractual procedure for requesting an extension of time.

8.139 Following the contractual change order procedures is especially important in the public contract context. In *Amelco Electric v City of Thousand Oaks*, 27 Cal.4th 228, 38 P.3d 1120, 115 Cal. Rptr. 2d 900 (2002), the Supreme Court emphasized that "public works contracts are the subject of intensive statutory regulation and lack the freedom of modification present in private party contracts". For example, Public Contract Code Section 7105(d)(2) mandates that public agency contracts can *only be modified* pursuant to the terms of the contract. That section provides, in pertinent part:

> I. Contracts of public agencies, excluding the state, required to be let or awarded on the basis of competitive bids pursuant to any statute may be terminated, amended, or modified only if the termination, amendment, or modification is so provided in the contract or is authorized under provision of law other than this subdivision. The compensation payable, if any, for amendments and modifications shall be determined as provided in the contract.

8.140 In *Katsura v City of San Buenaventura* 155 Cal.App.4th 104 (2007), the court denied a contractor's claim for payment based on an alleged oral modification of a public contract because oral modifications were not authorized under the change order clause.

8.141 Changes are typically referred to as either (1) Actual or Owner Acknowledged Changes, (2) Constructive Changes, or (3) Cardinal Changes.

Actual or Owner Acknowledged Changes

8.142 Actual or owner acknowledged changes are changes that are either initiated or requested by the owner or its authorized agent (e.g., architect, engineer, or project manager), or suggested by the contractor and approved by the owner. While the owner and contractor may disagree on the amount of the contract price and/or time adjustment, these are changes where the owner does not dispute the contractor's entitlement to the change order. Typically, these are changes made by the owner for its own convenience or preference, or recognition that the construction plans are incomplete or inadequate.

Constructive Changes

8.143 Constructive changes are changes caused by the owner but not acknowledged by the owner as a change. Constructive changes include any action or inaction by the owner or its agents that changes or interferes with a contractor's permitted method of performing the contract but that is not formally implemented or acknowledged by way of a change order. Common constructive changes arise from (1) different interpretations of the plan or specifications, (2) correction of construction errors or omissions in the plans or specifications though the issuance of clarifications or bulletins, (3) owner's improper rejection of conforming work, (4) owner's improper inspections, (5) owner's failure to disclose superior knowledge of site conditions, and (6) accelerations.

Cardinal Changes

8.144 Cardinal changes are material changes that alter the work so drastically that the contractor's performance is significantly different from that contemplated in the original contract. Cardinal changes constitute a material breach of the contract for which the contractor can recover breach of contract damages. Also, a cardinal change will permit the contractor to stop work, despite a change order clause in the contract obligating the contractor to perform changed or extra work. Where excessive changes cause the project to be so fundamentally different from the project on which the contractor submitted its original bid, the contractor may be entitled to relief under the cardinal change doctrine. In *Amelco*, the Supreme Court of California stated that the abandonment and cardinal change theories of liability are "fundamentally different". In contrast to the abandonment doctrine, where the contract is held inapplicable and is set aside, "[u]nder the cardinal change doctrine, the cardinal change 'constitutes a material breach of the contract'. The contractor may recover breach of contract damages for that additional work".[91] The Court acknowledged that the "United States Federal Court of Claims has historically recognized government breach of contract liability under the doctrine of cardinal change".[92]

Delay and Disruption

8.145 See Section 23, *infra.*

Liquidated Damages and Other Damages

8.146 When a contractor inexcusably delays the completion of a project, the owner is entitled to recover damages for that delay. Often, the parties stipulate at the time of contracting an amount of liquidated damages that the parties estimate will reflect the degree of harm the owner will incur in the event of a contractor delay. Liquidated damages clauses set, in advance, an amount to be paid to the owner in the event of a contractor breach. These clauses are particularly advantageous when the amount of damages is uncertain or unable to be measured with any degree of certainty. In construction contracts, the parties frequently include a liquidated damages provision, stipulating a certain amount to be paid by the contractor for each day of delay after the scheduled completion date.

8.147 The law creates a presumption in favor of enforcing liquidated damages clauses. Generally, courts will enforce such provisions and award liquidated damages unless the party seeking to invalidate the clause is able to prove "that the provision was unreasonable under the circumstances existing at the time the contract was made". However, courts may decline to enforce liquidated damages clauses when their enforcement is viewed as a penalty, an unreasonable forecast of just compensation for the harm caused or where the actual harm is difficult or impossible to estimate at the time of contracting.

Insurance

8.148 The parties to the construction contract will strive to secure insurance for most potential risks inherent in construction. A contractor will typically be required to obtain and maintain one or more insurance policies in connection with a particular project. Each policy requires the contractor to pay a premium, usually annually. In the event the project is delayed, a contractor may be required to renew its policies for a period exceeding what it originally anticipated, requiring it to pay additional policy premiums. Where the contractor performs additional or "extra" work, it may be required to obtain additional coverage, potentially resulting in additional costs. Provided the owner caused the delay or the "extra" work, a contractor may recover the entire amount of additional or increased insurance premiums.

91 *Amelco*, 27 Cal.4th at 238.
92 Ibid.

8.149 The contractor's commercial general liability (CGL) insurance covers basic risks including bodily injury and property damage. Most CGL policies also cover a group of tortious conduct and construction risks. Under the terms of most CGL insurance policies, the insurer has the responsibility to defend the insured in litigation and to pay any judgment are award rendered against the insured. However, it is highly important to analyze any lawsuit or claim to determine whether the claims or allegations falls within the basic coverages. Many CGL policies contain coverage exclusions that eliminate insurance coverage for specified items.

8.150 Many owners and lenders will not fund a project without a builder's risk insurance policy. The purpose of builders' risk insurance is to protect against damage to the project during construction. This type of insurance is intended to cover loss or damages resulting from accidents or acts of God, such as floods, rain damage, or fire. Generally, this type of insurance will expire upon the completion of the project.

Suspension

8.151 Most construction contracts allow the owner to suspend construction operations for a limited period of time, either for the convenience of the owner or because of a failure by the contractor in performing the work. The contracts will usually allow the owner to issue an order directing the contractor to cease work. If the contractor is suspended under these terms the contractor may be entitled to an equitable adjustment of the contract price. However, in order to recover for a suspension of work, the contractor must demonstrate that its work was delayed for an unreasonable period of time.

8.152 On occasion, a contractor will receive an oral field directive to suspend work. This would be considered a constructive suspension of work. Constructive suspension of work could also result from acts or omissions of the owner or its agents prohibit the contractor from making progress. One example is where the contractor's work is delayed by the failure of the owner or architect to timely respond to requests for critical information. Where there has been a constructive suspension of the work, the contractor may be entitled to an extension of time and an increase in the contract sum. However, the contractor must be mindful to follow the contract notice requirements and timely notify the owner of the delays that it has caused.

Termination

8.153 There are two general types of contract termination: Termination for convenience and default termination.

Termination for Convenience Clause

8.154 A termination for convenience clause permits the owner to terminate the contract without cause, at its convenience. The clause defines and limits the compensation to which the contractor is entitled when the Owner terminates for convenience. The contractor's compensation due upon termination usually includes the costs of demobilizing and closing out the subcontract agreements, along with some degree of overhead and profit on the work performed. In order to avoid paying the loss of anticipated profit on the portion of the work that has been terminated, the parties must expressly waive the right to recover lost profits.

Default Termination Clause

8.155 Default termination is an extreme remedy available to owners for the actual or anticipated failure of the contractor to perform. A default termination clause usually provides that, if the contractor refuses or fails to pursue the contract work with such diligence as will insure its completion within the time specified, or if the contractor fails to complete the work within such time, the owner may take over and complete the work. Regardless of whether the contractor's right to proceed is terminated, the contractor and its sureties will be liable for any damage the Government may incur from the contractor's failure to complete the work within the specified contract time.

8.156 In Government construction contracts, an owner has three grounds for terminating a contractor for default: (1) Unreasonable delay in completing the project; (2) failure and/or refusal to make progress or "endangering" the timely completion of the project; and (3) breach of other contract provisions. Many of these bases are also available to an owner in a private construction contract. A contractor will not be defaulted if the delay was unavoidable and caused by such factors as strikes, fires, floods, embargoes, unusually severe weather, etc. These are known as excusable delays.

8.157 Because default termination is such an extreme remedy, under both Government and private construction contracts, courts scrutinize the appropriateness of default terminations carefully, with all doubts resolved in favor of the defaulted contractor. Accordingly, an owner should not exercise this remedy rashly, since the consequences will be either the legal conversion of the default to a termination for convenience for the benefit of the defaulted contractor or the owner will be deemed to have breached the contract.

8.158 Additionally, the default termination clause should include language that would convert a wrongful termination for default into a termination for convenience. If the contract includes such language and the court or arbitrator deems the termination for default improper, the claimant's recovery will usually be limited to the damages that it could recover under the termination for convenience clause. This makes the limitations in the termination for convenience provision that much more important. If there is no conversation language, the claimant could seek all actual damages.

Forms of Security – Bonds and Guarantees

8.159 The bond surety plays a key role in the inception, progression, and completion of certain construction projects. Surety bond providers, also known as "sureties" or "surety companies", provide a financial service by guaranteeing to pay and/or complete a contract if the person or business that entered into the contract is unable to do so. This is achieved through the surety's issuance of bonds, which indicates to the owner that the surety has pre-qualified, or guaranteed, the bond principal's (entity on whose behalf the guarantee is made) ability to successfully complete the contract at issue. In other words, through the posting of the bond, the surety reassures the owner that it has thoroughly investigated, through its underwriting practices, the bond principal's financial ability to carry a bonded contract to successful completion.

8.160 A surety is traditionally defined as someone who contracts to answer for the debt or default of another. Section 2(b) of the Restatement of Suretyship describes a tri-partite suretyship contract among the following parties: (1) The primary obligor, or the principal; (2) the secondary obligor, or the surety; and (3) the obligee, or the person to whom the principal and the surety owe a duty. Suretyship is a financial guarantee under which the surety suffers a loss only if the principal fails to perform its obligation and is financially unable to reimburse the surety. In other words, the surety's liability is coextensive with that of the debtor (or bond principal) and arises only when the debtor fails to discharge his or her duties to respond in damages for that failure. In this respect, the surety possesses the same defenses available to the bond principal, and the surety's liability cannot be greater than that of its bond principal.

8.161 Even though they are regulated by the insurance commissioner, sureties differ from traditional insurance carriers. If it is able to determine beforehand that a default will likely occur, a surety can protect itself by either not writing the bond under the circumstances, or obtaining sufficient collateral from the principal during the underwriting process. An insurer, on the other hand, expects that a certain percentage of its insureds will suffer a loss during the policy period and calculates its premiums accordingly. If a covered loss is suffered, the insurer, in effect, has the primary obligation to pay and has no recourse against the insured for reimbursement.

8.162 In general, there are several different types of surety bonds serving a wide variety of purposes. For the construction industry, however, the types of bonds commonly issued are more limited.

Performance Bonds

8.163 A performance bond is a bond issued by a surety to guarantee satisfactory performance by the contractor, or bond principal. In this respect, the purpose of the performance bond is straightforward: It provides available funds to complete the principal's contract should the latter be in default of the performance it owes the obligee. Almost all states require a writing signed by the party to be charged as a condition precedent to enforcement of a promise of suretyship. Like any other surety bond, performance bonds create a tripartite relationship consisting of the bond obligee, bond principal, and the surety.

Labour and Materials Payment Bonds

8.164 A labour and materials payment bond, or "payment bond", guarantees that a contractor will pay suppliers, labourers, and subcontractors (subject to contract terms) for labour and materials. Often, payment and performance bonds are issued together as one bond and termed a "Performance and Payment Bond".

8.165 Since a payment bond guarantees the owner that subcontractors and suppliers will be paid the monies that they are due from the principal, an owner benefits indirectly from a payment bond. With a payment bond in place, subcontractors and suppliers: (1) Are assured of payment; (2) will continue performance; and (3) will refrain from recording liens on the property on a private project, or filing stop payment notices on a public project. If the principal fails to pay the subcontractors or suppliers, they may collect from the principal or surety under the payment bond, up to the penal sum of the bond. The penal sum in a payment bond may be less than the total amount of the prime contract, and is intended to cover anticipated subcontractor and supplier costs.

Indemnity Bonds

8.166 Unlike other performance bonds, a surety's performance obligation under indemnity bonds is limited to reimbursing the obligee up to the penal sum for any cost of completion in excess of the unpaid contract balance at contract termination. Under this scenario, the surety has no control over completion by the obligee and the costs incurred therein. Although completion costs must be reasonable, the surety's burden of proving the unreasonableness may not be easily satisfied. Indemnity bonds have been interpreted by courts to cover consequential damages as well, including, but not limited to, delay and lost profits.

8.167 Typically, the surety's obligation is parallel with that of the principal under the bonded contract, up to the stated penal sum. However, as with all contracts of surety, the scope of a surety's liability under a performance bond is determined by examining: (1) The bond language used; and (2) the circumstances surrounding the issuance of the bond.

Liquidated Damages

8.168 Applying the aforementioned principles, a surety may be liable for *all* of the bond principal's contractual obligations, including, among other things, liquidated damages. The determinative factor is whether the terms of the underlying, bonded contract (which contains a liquidated damages provision) are incorporated into the performance bond itself. If so, the general rule is that the performance bond surety will be liable for liquidated damages in the event the principal, without excuse, delays the completion of the contract. However, because it is generally not liable for anything that is not within the letter of its bonds, a surety may argue that it did not consent to be bound by any damages not set forth in the bond itself.

Attorneys' Fees

8.169 A surety may be liable for attorneys' fees if there is an enforceable attorneys' fees provision in the underlying, bonded contract. Under the same principle, however, the surety may be able to recover its attorneys' fees if it is ultimately determined to be the prevailing party.

Statute of Limitations

8.170 The statute of limitations for initiating an action against a performance bond surety is not clearly defined. Therefore, several sources must be examined before a determination can be made.

8.171 First, the bond may contain language that provides the express time limit during which a claim may be brought against the surety. A contractual stipulation to limit a statute of limitations must be clear and explicit, and is to be strictly construed against the party invoking the provision. However, this rule is simply a general rule of law, which should not be used to destroy the effect of a more specific rule of law that applies to the case.

8.172 Second, the applicable statute of limitations may be provided in the bonded agreement. For instance, subdivision improvement agreements often contain language that states that the public agency must accept the bonded improvements before they are deemed "completed". In such a case, some California courts have held that the surety remains liable until all subdivision improvements are completed and accepted. In this regard, the developer and its surety may also be obligated to maintain and repair any completed improvements until all subdivision improvements guaranteed by security are complete and accepted.

8.173 Third, if the performance bond is required by statute, the applicable statute of limitations may be decided by that particular code section. For example, in California, Under Code of Civil Procedure Section 338(a), the statute of limitations for "an action upon a liability created by statute, other than a penalty or forfeiture" is three years.

8.174 Finally, any bond claimant must comply with all contractual and statutory notice requirements. Otherwise, the bond claim could be deemed invalid.

Claims

8.175 While there are numerous types of claims that owners can pursue, most claims consist of: (1) Delay-related claims related to the contractor's failure to timely perform its work; (2) performance based claims caused by the contractor's failure to complete or properly perform its work; (3) warranty claims based upon the contractor's breach of express or implied warranties; (4) termination claims based upon the owner's decision to terminate the contractor; and (5) claims related to the contractor's submission of false claims.

8.176 Like owner claims, there are also various types of claims that contractors can pursue against an owner. The most common types of claims that are asserted by contractors are: (1) Claims for delay-related damages for which the owner is responsible; (2) claims for damages resulting from acceleration of the contractor's work; (3) claims for disruption and productivity impacts to the contractor's work; (4) claims related to the contractor encountering differing site conditions or extra work; (5) claims related to the owner's failure to timely and properly pay the contractor for its work; (6) claims related to stoppage or a suspension of the contractor's work; and (7) claims related to termination of the contract. All of these claims generally relate to a contractor's entitlement to time or costs in connection with its work on the project. In order to protect the contractor's rights and support any claim for recovery against a project owner, contractors should make a deliberate effort to review, understand and comply with all requirements set forth in the contract documents, including any notice or claim provisions. Contractors should also attempt to identify and document claims or potential claims as soon as possible.

8.177 While the majority of these issues are addressed in other portions of this chapter, special attention should be given to delay claims. Construction delays fall into the following three basic categories: (1) Excusable or inexcusable; (2) compensable or non-compensable; and (3) concurrent.

Excusable vs. Inexcusable Delay

8.178 Excusable delays are delays caused by factors beyond the control of either the owner or the contractor, such as severe weather conditions, strikes, unavailability of materials due to unforeseen and unavoidable conditions, war, government regulations and acts of God (i.e., fire, flood, lightning, landslides, earthquakes, hurricanes, etc.) Due to the fact that neither the owner nor the contractor can control this type of delay, excusable delays will typically result in an extension of the time for performance under the contract and, depending upon the provisions of the contract, may provide for additional compensation.

8.179 In contrast, inexcusable delays are within the control of the responsible party and are delays for which that party has assumed the risk. For example, an owner's claim against a contractor for inexcusable delay will typically be caused by the contractor's failure to properly man the job, failure to properly schedule the work, failure to timely provide equipment or material to the project, failure to meet schedule deadlines for submittals or shop drawings, and other types of delay for which the contractor is responsible. If the owner can prove that a delay was inexcusable, the contractor may not be entitled to time extensions or compensation and the contractor could be liable for damages the owner may sustain as a result of the delay, including liquidated damages, lost rents, lost profits caused by loss of use and potentially extended financing costs.

Compensable vs. Non-Compensable Delay

8.180 Inexcusable delays will either be compensable or non-compensable. Compensable delays will entitle the aggrieved party to additional compensation for the delays, while non-compensable delays will not. In order for a delay to be compensable, it must be caused by the other party or the other party's agent. Regardless of the existence of any contractual provision entitling an aggrieved party to additional compensation due to an inexcusable delay, an aggrieved party may nonetheless be entitled to additional compensation due to duties that are implied by law, such as the implied duty of cooperation or the implied duty of good faith and fair dealing.

Concurrent Delay

8.181 Concurrent delays are delays for which more than one cause results in the delay. It is common, especially in large or complex construction projects, for delays to be caused by numerous events or occurrences that may take place simultaneously or overlap. Often where the simultaneous or overlapping causes of delay are caused by both the owner and the contractor, it is very difficult to determine who should be responsible for the resulting delays and damages. As such, the parties will need to conduct a schedule analysis to attribute fault between the parties. If the parties are unable to apportion fault for the delay, it is likely that neither party will be entitled to compensation for the delay, including any liquidated damages. The current trend is to apportion liability for the delay based upon the relative fault of the parties. As such, it is critical that a thorough schedule analysis be performed in order to determine allocation of responsibility and support a claim of entitlement for additional compensation.

8.182 Regardless of the parties' ability to reach an agreement regarding entitlement and the amount of any additional time or compensation, most contracts normally contain provisions that require the contractor to perform the extra and/or changed work regardless of an agreement between the parties, with the understanding that the contractor may have to pursue a claim at a later date for the additional time or cost associated with the extra or changed work. If the contractor refuses to perform the work, the contractor risks being in material breach of the contract and could face termination and liability for the owner's resulting damages. However, if an owner is unreasonable or the scope of changed or extra work is substantial, the contractor may not be able to finance the extra costs for performing the work by simply waiting to have the matter adjudicated at the end of the project, which could be several years down the road if the dispute goes through to litigation. The contractor will need to conduct a thorough review of the contract documents to ensure that the contractor is aware of the duties of the parties for changed or extra work and will need to make sure to properly document the contractor's position and performance in order to either attempt a resolution with the owner or support a contractor's decision to either wait until the end of the project to pursue a claim or refuse to perform the work and potentially face termination.

8.183 All claims are governed by the specific provisions of the contract. Therefore, it is incumbent upon the parties to be completely familiar with not only the terms of the contract itself but also with all of the contract documents that are typically incorporated therein by reference. Special attention should be given to all notice requirements and the submission of claims documents (i.e., claim narrative, time impact analysis, cost backup). The failure to comply with these provisions could result in a waiver of all or a portion of a claim.

Time-Bar Provisions

8.184 Statutes of limitations are a fundamental aspect of United States contract law. In every state, different causes of action have different statutes of limitations. Statutes of limitations are extremely important – if a person does not bring a lawsuit within the set period, they may lose their right to do so forever. Each state has its own unique statutory scheme relating to the time in which contract claims must be brought. In general, the range is between three and ten years. Most states have longer statutes of limitations for written contracts, and shorter statutes of limitations for oral contracts. In a few states, the time limit is the same for both types of contract. Generally, the statute of limitations for contract actions begins to "run" (the clock starts ticking), once the facts that give rise to an action on the contract, such as breach or grounds for rescission, come into being. It usually does not matter when they are discovered.

8.185 The rules and procedure in this area are complex. The time period might be different for an action against the government. You might have to file a particular kind of claim before initiating a lawsuit. For example, in order to sue a governmental agency in California, one must first file a claim against the agency under California Government Contract Code 910 et. seq. This process takes at least 45 days and must be factored into any statute of limitation. In sum, the statutes of limitation for your particular jurisdiction will control and should be thoroughly analyzed at the outset of any claim.

Disputes – Adjudication and Arbitration

8.186 The claimant has a variety of choices to resolve its disputes. If there is diversity jurisdiction, Federal court is an option. Federal courts are often more expedient and have highly competent judges. However, many Federal court judges lack significant construction expertise. State court is a second option. Each state has its own codes and rules relating to the scope of discovery. Both Federal and state courts have the right to appeal any judgment rendered. However, with the increased caseload clogging the Federal and state courts, a party pursuing a construction claim in court often must wait years for resolution of disputes. Many states have instituted regulations to speed up the process. While these regulations have shortened the duration of cases, in some instances this has equated to incurring the costs of litigation at a faster rate.

8.187 In response, parties continue to turn to arbitration as a means to effectively litigate claims. Arbitration of construction disputes and claims has become ever more popular as a means to handle disputes in a less expensive manner. Arbitration offers a number of advantages in resolving construction disputes including: (1) Less expense; (2) informal pleadings and legal memoranda; (3) potentially less discovery; (4) speedier resolution; and (5) a trier of fact who has construction expertise.

8.188 There are, however, some distinct disadvantages in using arbitration. If a party has a good claim but needs to develop facts through discovery, litigation in court may be a better forum. It is often more advantageous for a party to present a technical defense (i.e., lack of timely notice or waiver) in a courtroom rather than to an arbitrator. Also, a party may decide that it has an advantage with a local jury. In a contract dispute, courts may be less apt to give credence to equitable issues than an arbitration panel.

8.189 All parties should be aware that arbitration has many benefits, but may not be an ideal solution to resolve all disputes. As such, each project must be examined prior to selecting the dispute forum.

Construction Law Issues Specific to North American Common Law

Construction Law in Canada

8.190 The Canadian legal system is highly intricate: Among other things, it is composed of both common law and civil law, maintains separate systems for criminal and civil law, operates in two different languages, and is structured – in a similar manner to the United States – with Federal, provincial, and municipal legal systems. The majority of Canada follows a common law system based on the English legal system, although Quebec adheres to a civil law system.

8.191 Through Canada's Constitution, the judicial system is divided between the Federal government and the ten provincial governments. The Federal branch has the power to appoint judges of provincial superior courts (including the courts of appeal and trial courts of general jurisdiction), authority over remuneration of judges, and even the authority to remove them (although such removal has yet to occur in Canada), as well has power to appoint judges to the Supreme Court of Canada, the tax court, and the Federal court. The provincial governments, however, have authority over administration of its courts, including over both civil and criminal courts and civil procedure.

8.192 A relatively recent development in the Canadian legal system has been the movement towards the adjudication system for construction disputes (among other things) based on English adjudication. In the United Kingdom, adjudication for construction disputes emerged in the 1990s during which legislation, as part of the Housing, Grants, Construction and Regeneration Act of 1996, was passed and implemented. This legislation provided for construction disputes to be determined by an adjudicator for initial decisions that were binding until project completion. In recent years, the U.K.'s adjudication system has influenced Canada's legal system as well.

8.193 An example of Canada's move towards the adjudication system is reflected in the planning and creation of Ontario's revamped Construction Lien Act. On 26 September 2016, the Ministry of the Attorney General issued recommendations relating to the act, including on adjudication processes. Some of the highlights of the proposed adjudication process include the following:

- Parties to a construction contract would be entitled to refer disputes to adjudication that flow from the contract, including monetary claims, set-offs, deductions, and delay claims;
- Adjudication would be intended as an interim binding dispute resolution method;
- Adjudication would be available as a right for both public and private construction projects, but parties may contract out of the adjudication process provided that opt-out provision is consistent with the act;
- Upon delivery of a notice of adjudication the parties have two business days to agree on an adjudicator. Failure to do so would permit either party to request that an adjudicator be appointed within five business days;
- Within thirty calendar days of appointing an adjudicator, the adjudicator would be required to set and execute his/her process for the adjudication;
- The adjudicator's decision would be binding on an interim basis. It may be enforced through an application to the Ontario Superior Court of Justice, if necessary;
- A party's right to preserve and perfect a lien shall not be affected.

8.194 Similar to the English system, Canada's proposed adjudication rules will generally allow adjudicators wide discretion as permitted by law in order to ensure a fair and expeditious resolution of construction disputes. As discussed above, such rules are already being discussed at length in the context of the current lien dispute resolution framework in Canada.

Use and Adaptation of the FIDIC Forms of Contract

8.195 The FIDIC forms of contract are not used internally in the United States. There is not a single reported Federal or state case which addresses the FIDIC forms with the exception of a few international arbitration enforcement actions which simply reference the term.

8.196 Foreign contractors with projects in the United States usually compete for those projects with domestic firms and have no choice but to use the domestic US forms.

8.197 The reasons the FIDIC forms are not used seem to be twofold. First, the role of the Engineer on FIDIC[93] contracts has not developed in the US Second, the risk profile; for example, cost adjustment (FIDIC Art. 13.8) war and revolution (FIDIC Art. 19.1(d)(i) and (ii) changes in currencies of payment (FIDIC 14.15) has little application in the relatively stable US economy and political structure.

93 All FIDIC references are to the Conditions of Contract for Construction for Building and Engineering Works Designed by the Employer (1st Ed. 1999) (Red Book).

CHAPTER 9

South America

Alexandre Aroeira Salles, Federico Allendes, Francisco Ferreira, and Mariana Miraglia

Contents

 DOI: 10.4324/9781315671376-9

History of South American Legal Systems

Introduction

9.1 South America is made up of a diverse range of countries with distinct historical and cultural backgrounds. The manner in which the legal systems across South America developed is heavily influenced by colonization from the Portuguese and Spanish. Brazil is the largest country in South America in terms of size and economy and is the only major South American country to have been colonized by the Portuguese.[1] The other major South American countries were largely colonized by the Spanish and of these countries Chile is recognized as having a particularly sophisticated legal system which has heavily influenced a number of other key legal systems across South America. The Chilean Civil Code, which has its roots in the private law of Castile, Spain, was either fully adopted or heavily influenced the development of the civil codes in a number of South American countries including Argentina, Colombia and Uruguay.

9.2 Given the above context, a specific structure has been adopted in this chapter in order that the content can reflect the position under a broad range of South American countries. Each section and subsection in this chapter begins by setting out the position under Brazilian law followed by commentary on the position under Chilean law highlighting the differences and similarities with Brazilian law. Given the influence that the Chilean Code had on other codes across South America the analysis of the position under Chilean law will serve to give a direction as to the position under many other major legal systems in South America.

Development and International Influences on The Brazilian and Chilean Legal Systems

Brazilian Legal System

9.3 In the 16th century, due to Portuguese colonization, Portuguese Law was applied in Brazil which has its base in Roman Law and the tradition of written regulations.[2] It is interesting to note that Brazil subsequently had some parts of its territory momentarily occupied by the French and Dutch, although the Portuguese always managed to retake the territory and guarantee unity.[3]

9.4 In the early nineteenth century (1807–1808), the Portuguese Court was transferred to Brazil resulting in profound transformations in the colonial legislation with Brazil starting to create its own laws.[4] Various treaties and agreements were also entered into (in particular with England).[5]

1 For historical material on the colonial origins of South American legal systems, see Borchard, *Guide to the Law and Legal Literature of Argentina, Brazil and Chile* (U.S. Library of Congress, 1917).

2 Chaves, "Formação Histórica do Direito Civil Brasileiro" [2000] 95 *Revista da Faculdade de Direito da Universidade de São Paulo* 57 (downloadable at www.revistas.usp.br/rfdusp/article/view/67456).

3 Chaves (n 2) 70.

4 Chaves (n 2) 72.

5 Cunha "A fundação de um império liberal" in Holanda (ed), *História Geral da Civilização Brasileira* (DIFEL, 7th Edition, 1985) 135–78.

9.5 The Portuguese managed successfully to keep the whole of Brazil as its colony until Brazil's independence was declared in 1822.[6] The first Brazilian Constitution came into force soon after in 1824 and determined the creation of a Civil and Criminal Code. Through this process, the same effort towards codification that was underway in continental Europe could be seen in Brazil.[7]

9.6 Many discussions and studies took place in Brazil about the ideal draft for the Civil Code without a consensus being reached.[8] It was only after the constitutional monarchy was overthrown in 1889 that an agreement was reached regarding the Civil Code in 1916.[9] This Code, highly sophisticated and very modern for the time, gave protection to individual rights (family, ownership, and contract) and was influenced by the legal systems of continental Europe, taking into consideration the most advanced academic studies undertaken in France and Germany.[10] The same process of codification can be seen across South America.[11]

9.7 The freedom to contract has consistently been ensured, only limited through public order provisions. During the 20th century, a number of specific uncodified laws were created and several of these laws created public order provisions protecting certain categories of individuals (workers, consumers, tenants, etc.).[12]

- Throughout the post-independence political history of Brazil, the promulgation of other written constitutions did not impact the validity, enforceability, or application of the Civil Code.

9.8 In 1988, a new Brazilian Constitution came into force. The new Constitution broke with the military regime that had governed the country between 1964 and 1985. The Constitution is highly democratic and assures Brazilian citizens political and social rights as well as public services.[13] Under the Constitution, following the tradition of a state-driven economy, the development of key parts of the infrastructure of the country is considered the responsibility of the State.[14]

Over its long existence, in a period of significant civilizational advancements and cultural transformations, the Civil Code had been constantly interpreted and reinterpreted by Brazilian Courts, which also incorporated new general principles inspired by the doctrinal evolution of jurisprudence and comparative law. Nonetheless, it has managed to largely preserve its integrity.

---

6 Chaves (n 2) 78.

7 Alves, "*Panorama do Direito Civil Brasileiro: das origens aos dias atuais*" [1999] 88 *Revista da Faculdade de Direito da Universidade de São Paulo* 185 (downloadable at www.revistas.usp.br/rfdusp/article/view/67220/69830).

8 Alves (n 7) 191–208.

9 Alves (n 7) 208–10.

10 Alves (n 7) 211–14 and 218–21.

11 Morato, "Codificação e Descodificação: uma análise acerca do tema" [2003] 98 *Revista da Faculdade de Direito da Universidade de São Paulo* 95 (downloadable at www.revistas.usp.br/rfdusp/article/view/67581).

12 Tepedino, *Temas de Direito Civil* (Renovar, 4th Edition, 2008).

13 Carvalho, *Direito Constitucional: Teoria do Estado e da Constituição.* (Del Rey, 14th Edition, 2008) ch 13.

14 Soares, "A CF/88 e a Infraestrutura Econômica Brasileira" in Cardoso Jr (ed), *A Constituição brasileira de 1988 revisitada: recuperação histórica e desafios atuais das políticas públicas nas áreas econômica e social* (Ipea, 2009) 37–53.

9.9 In 2002, a new Brazilian Civil Code came into force. The new Code was not a complete break from the previous Code but rather a revised version incorporating interpretations developed through case law and also ideas and principles derived from more recent European Codes. [15]

9.10 This process of development of Brazilian law has resulted in a contractual system whereby, under private law, the provisions relating to contracts are generally suppletive meaning that the parties have the right to derogate from such provisions and determine their own contractual rules. However, there are also certain public order provisions that cannot be derogated from by the parties, as they reflect collective interests. Contracting parties are, therefore, generally free to contract as long as: (1) The general rules contained in the Civil Code are observed; (2) public order provisions are not violated; and (3) the parties act in good faith and the contract fulfils its social purpose.[16]

Chilean Legal System

9.11 The Chilean Civil Code is the result of a long process of maturation and development that culminated with its approval on 14 December 1855. The first expressions of the need to codify the law were made by the Supreme Director of Chile,[17] Bernardo O'Higgins R., who stated "May the five famous codes, so worthy of the wisdom of these latter times, be adopted, and which evidence the barbarity of the former ones!".[18] This proposal was neither accepted nor re-discussed, as the need to systematize the law was already considered as a priority, which could incorporate the necessary innovations and be adapted to the juridical Chilean culture.

9.12 There were many attempts to amend the law at the time, but those efforts were not fruitful for reasons such as the resistance by conservative sectors based on the fact that the codification process could eliminate the positive effects of the laws of the colonial regime currently in force, as well as on the fact that no bill that could seriously be considered had been proposed.[19] It was only in 1833/1834 when Minister Diego Portales[20] privately[21] entrusted Mr Andrés Bello to begin the drafting of a new Civil Code. Subsequently, on 10 September 1840,[22] a committee of deputies and senators was formed among which was Bello. However, since Portales had already requested Bello to draft a code almost seven years earlier, by 1840 he had already drafted the chapter on successions, obligations and contracts wherein these texts were used as references by the commission. Between

15 Baptista, "Dez anos de Código Civil" [2012] 2 *Série Aperfeiçoamento de Magistrados 13* 44 (downloadable at www.emerj.tjrj.jus.br/serieaperfeicoamentodemagistrados/paginas/series/13/volumeII/10anoscodigocivil_volII_44.pdf).

16 Lyra Jr "Os Princípios do Direito Contratual" [2002] 12 *Revista de Direito Privado* 135.

17 The position of Supreme Director consisted of the entitlement of the Administration and existed as such until the year 1826.

18 See O'Higgins's speech of 23 July 1822 in Jaksic, *Andrés Bello: La pasión por el orden* (Editorial Universitaria, 1st Edition, 2001) 189; Alejandro Guzmán B, *La Codificación Civil enIberoamérica. Siglos XIX y XX* (Editorial Jurídica de Chile, 1st Edition, 2000) 351.

19 See Jaksic (n 18) 191–2.

20 Powerful former Minister of the Interior who was one of the fundamental figures in the consolidation of the State of Chile. He was assassinated on 6 June 1837.

21 See Jaksic (n 18) 195–6.

22 Between the date of the assignment of Diego Portales and the creation of the bicameral commission several years later and after an external war between Chile and the Peruvian-Bolivian Confederation had passed.

May 1841 and December 1845, the draft of the chapter on successions and an important part of the chapter on obligations and contracts (as approved by the commission) were published in the newspaper "El Araucano". Following on from this, Bello continued working alone on the drafting project between 1848 and 1852 and finally produced the Civil Code Project, otherwise known as the "1853 Project".

9.13 The final draft civil code prepared by Bello went through a rigorous process of consultation with all State bodies, Courts of Justice and jurists in Chile. This long and arduous process took over 35 years, which evidence that serious efforts were made to thoroughly debate to approve a Civil Code that included the existing national law in force at the time with the necessary reforms, and a systematization and order that allowed a harmonious development of the knowledge and practical application of the law, thus, fulfilling the codifying ideal that began in the 17th century.[23]

9.14 The Civil Code text is eminently a tribute to Roman law but receiving its tradition from the private law of Castile (Spain) with particular emphasis on the Seven-Part Code ("*Siete Partidas*") produced by Alfonso X the Wise. In fact, the prevailing law prior to the country's independence was constituted by a) Pragmatics,[24] notices, decrees and resolutions of the King made known in the Americas by means of the Council of the Indies; b) the Indies Restatement; and c) The Newest Compilation of the Laws of Spain.[25] In a deep sense, Bello was a Romanist. He saw in the institutions of Roman private patrimonial law, the main instruments for the liberal-bourgeois ideology of the nineteenth century, one of the wanted and desired effects of contracts namely, *pacta sunt servanda*, which was incorporated through including the principles of free will and contractual freedom.[26]

9.15 There is no doubt that the Chilean Civil Code was influenced by French Civil Code[27] where French jurists are mentioned in several parts by Bello, "*Delvincourt, Rogron and above all Pothier in his several Traites; also, used Merlin, Favard de l'Anglade, Portalis, Maleville; in the phase of revision of the 1853 Project, Bello consulted works of Troplong, Delangle and Duranton. But, likewise, made use of Savigny in controlled measure*".[28]

9.16 Apart from using parts of the French Civil Code when drafting the Civil Code, Bello relied also on other codified laws of his time:

23 See Ramón Martínez Tapia, "*Leibniz y la Ciencia Jurídica*", Anales de Derecho. Universidad de Murcia, No.14, 1996.

24 Pragmatics were a type of orders promulgated by Spanish Kings.

25 See Luis Claro Solar, "*Explicaciones de Derecho Civil Chileno y Comparado, Volumen I, De las Personas, Editorial Jurídica de Chile/Editorial Temis*" (1992) pp. 9–17; Also, Alejandro Guzmán B., op. cit. pp. 179–96.

26 The character of the Civil Code as eminently receiving Roman and Spanish law is recognized in a letter of thanks from M. Laferriere, member of the Institute of France and Inspector General of Law Faculties, who said, "*It is easy to recognize the origin and character of the peoples to whom the work is destined, by the mixture of Roman law and of Hispanic law that constitute its main provisions*". This letter from Mr. M. Laferriere was forwarded to thank Bello for sending him a copy of the Civil Code. This letter is quoted in Hugo Hanisch Espíndola's "Andrés Bello y su obra en Derecho Romano" [1983] 94 *Boletin de la Academia Chilena de la Historia* 370.

27 "The Code Civil certainly occupied an important place in the Chilean codification; not in terms of the system, which he did not adopt, but as an inspiration to many provisions, especially obligations and contracts ... Rarely, however, Bello copied some provisions of the French code ... it was his constant concern that the norm formally inspired by foreign law had its corresponding material in the national law, by general rule in the *Siete Partidas*" Guzman (n 18) 371.

28 Guzman (n 18) 371.

"*...which he could know, like almost all the codifiers of the second half of the nineteenth century, through the Concordance of Saint Joseph (1840, or its Castilian translation by Verlanga and Muñiz, 1843); that is, the French, Bavarian, Prussian, Austrian, Sardinian, Louisiana, Dutch, Canton of Vaud codes; although several of these texts could have been examined directly by Bello. Later, for the 1853 Project, he scarcely succeeded in employing Garcia Goyena's Civil Code Project and the Civil Code of Peru of 1852.*[29]"

9.17 As it can be noted, Bello reviewed several codes and projects of codes with the object to analyze the innovations contained on these. This arduous work aimed to draft a legal text which considered the Chilean context and could be useful for the country.

9.18 The Chilean Civil Code's influence in the South Americas has been substantial with countries either: 1) Simply adopting completely the Chilean Civil Code and making it their own civil code in all its parts; or 2) drafting their own civil codes under the guidance or heavy influence of the Chilean Civil Code. The primary reason so many Latin America countries using or relying upon the Chilean Civil Code may have been because the code was deeply rooted in Castilian law, and consequently Roman law, which reflected their existing codes at the time.

9.19 Examples of countries fully adopting the Chilean Civil Code as their civil code include Ecuador, Colombia, El Salvador, Venezuela (1862), Nicaragua (1867), Honduras I (1860) and Honduras III (1906), and Panama, although Nicaragua, Panama and Venezuela no longer have the same code. Countries which heavily relied upon or were influenced by the Chilean Civil Code include Uruguay,[30] Costa Rica,[31] Argentina,[32] and Paraguay (although the latter adopted the Argentine Civil Code).[33]

Sources of Law

Brazil

9.20 The Constitution of 1988 is the supreme law in Brazil and determines the organizational structure of the country as a federal republic made up of the federal government, states, federal district, and municipalities.[34]

29 Guzman (n 18) 370.

30 "*The Eastern Civil Code, extracted from the different bodies of law that we inherited from Spain, and from all the codes in force or in the project of the learned peoples, maintains unity and logic in its system and quite clear in its method. The codes of Europe, those of America, and specially the justly praised of Chile*". Report of the Code Commission of Uruguay, quoted in Guzman (n 18) 464.

31 "the Civil Code of Chile, perhaps not directly but through the codes of different countries neighbouring Costa Rica or relatively such, that had adopted it. El Salvador, Honduras, Nicaragua and Colombia" Guzman (n 18) 469.

32 The same draftsman of the Argentine Civil Code, Dalmacio Vélez Sarsfield, said: "*I have been mainly served by the Civil Code Project for Spain by Mr. Goyena, of the Civil Code of Chile, which is so far ahead of European codes, and especially the Civil Code Project that Mr Freitas has been drafting for Brazil*", quoted in Guzmán (n 18) 450. Recently, the Republic of Argentina promulgated a new Civil and Commercial Code. No study has been made as to the extent of the influence that Chilean Civil Code has had in the current Argentine text.

33 See Guzmán (n 18) 455–7.

34 *Constitution of Brazil* [Brazil], 5 October 1988, available from – www.planalto.gov.br/ccivil_03/constituicao/constituicao.htm (last accessed 9 April 2020) Article 18.

9.21 The federal government is composed of three independent branches: Legislative, executive, and judicial.[35] The Brazilian Congress is the legislative branch of the federal government comprising the House of Representatives and the Federal Senate (Article 44 of the Constitution of Brazil). The executive power is vested in the President assisted by their ministers (Article 76). The judicial branch is made up of those courts and bodies set out in Article 92 of the Constitution including the Federal Supreme Court which is the highest court in Brazil for constitutional issues.

9.22 The states, federal district and municipalities all have autonomy to create their own laws subject to their being compatible with the principles of the Constitution and within each of their competencies (Articles 25, 29, 30, and 32). Laws created by municipalities must also be compatible with the principles of the constitution of the state in which they are situated (Article 29).

9.23 The Constitution provides that the legislative process comprises the preparation of constitutional amendments, complementary laws, ordinary laws, provisionary measures, delegated laws, legislative decrees, and resolutions (Article 59). Each of these is considered in more detail below as well as the constitutional rules relating to the passing of laws.

Constitutional Amendments (Emendas *À* Constitui*ção*)

9.24 The Constitution can be amended through a proposal of at least one third of the members of the House of Representatives or of the Federal Senate, the President or more than half of the legislative assemblies of the Brazilian states (Article 60). Once the proposal has been made, it will be discussed and voted in each house of the Brazilian Congress in two rounds, and will be considered approved if it obtains, in both houses, three-fifths of the votes of their respective members (Article 60(2)). The consideration of certain amendment proposals is prohibited such as those that aim to abolish the separation of powers or individual rights (Article 60(4)).

Complementary Laws (Leis Complementares) and Ordinary Laws (Leis Ordin*á*rias)

9.25 The Constitution sets out that certain matters must be regulated by complementary laws. These matters tend to be of great general importance such as rules for cooperation between the federal government, the states, the federal district and the municipalities (Article 23, Sole paragraph). Ordinary laws regulate other matters that have not been specified in the Constitution as being necessarily regulated by complementary laws.

9.26 Another significant difference between complementary and ordinary laws is the type of majority that is required to pass the law. Complementary laws require an absolute majority (more than 50% of the total membership of the house) whereas ordinary laws only require a simple majority (more than 50% of the members present and voting) subject to there being an absolute majority of the members of the house present and voting (Articles 47 and 69).

9.27 The Constitution provides that both ordinary and complementary laws can be proposed by

35 *Constitution of Brazil*, 1988 (BR) Article 2.

any member or commission of the House of Representatives, the Federal Senate or the National Congress, the President of the Republic, the Supreme Federal Court, the Superior Courts, Prosecutor General of the Republic and the citizens, in the form and in the cases considered in this Constitution.

(Article 61).

Where the law relates to certain specific matters, such as the creation of public posts or the organization of the judiciary, it can only be proposed by the President (Article 61(1)).

Provisionary Measures (Medidas Provisórias)

9.28 Where there is a matter of high importance and urgency, the President can issue a provisionary measure to regulate such matter which will have force of law (Article 62). There are a number of restrictions on what provisionary measures can cover such as matters relating to nationality, citizenship and criminal law (Article 62(1)). Once a provisionary measure has been issued, it must be submitted immediately for analysis by Congress (Article 62). Provisionary measures will generally lose force of law if they were not converted into law within a period of 60 days from publication (Article 60(3) and (4)). This period can be extended once for a further period of 60 days where both houses of Congress have not concluded voting on the provisionary measure within the original period of sixty days (Article 60(7)). The provisionary measure will retain force of law during this additional period. Provisionary measures are commonly issued in Brazil with the requirement of importance and urgency not interpreted too restrictively. They are a way in which the Executive can frequently participate in the legislative process.

Delegated Laws (Leis Delegadas)

9.29 In certain cases, the President can ask Congress for the right to create certain laws called delegated laws (Article 68). There are a number of restrictions on such a delegation, for example, where the Constitution specifies that a certain matter should be regulated by a complementary law or where the matter relates to individual rights or the organization of the judiciary (Article 68(1)). Where such a delegation is made, it must be in the form of a resolution of the Congress specifying the content and the terms under which the President may exercise the delegated power (Article 68(2)). Where the resolution of Congress determines that it must approve the bill created by the President, the bill will be voted on by Congress in a single vote without any right to amend its provisions (Article 68(3)).

Legislative Decrees (Decretos Legislativos)

9.30 Legislative decrees detail and make binding certain acts under the exclusive competency of the Brazilian Congress. Article 49 of the Constitution sets out a number of such acts, for example, authorising the President to declare war or making definitive resolutions in relation to treaties, agreements or international acts that involve serious obligations or responsibilities in relation to the national patrimony. Article 62(3) also provides that Congress must, through a legislative decree, determine the legal relations resulting from provisionary measures that are not converted into law. Legislative decrees must be discussed and voted on in both houses of Congress. The President does not participate in this process and does not have the right to veto.

Resolutions (*Resoluções*)

9.31 Resolutions are generally made in order to regulate administrative matters within Congress, the Federal Senate or the House of Representatives. Resolutions, therefore, generally only have internal effect within the Legislative branch and do not require the sanction of the President.

Passing Of Laws

9.32 Articles 65 and 66 of the Constitution set out a number of procedural rules in relation to passing laws in Brazil. Where a bill has been approved by one house of Congress it must be reviewed by the other house in one round of discussion and voting. Where the other house approves the bill, it will be sent on to the President, but where it rejects the bill it will be archived (Articles 65 and 66). Where the bill is amended by the other house, it will be sent back to the house where it was introduced (Article 65, Sole paragraph).

9.33 Where the President agrees to a bill that has been approved by Congress, the President will sanction it (Article 66). If the President considers the bill, in whole or in part, unconstitutional or against the public interest, the President may, within a period of 15 working days from receipt of the bill, veto the bill either in whole or in part (Article 66(1)). Where the President exercises the right to veto, it must inform the Senate President of the reasons for the veto (Article 66(1)). The veto will then be considered in a joint session and can only be rejected through an absolute majority of the members of both houses (Article 66(4)).

Interpretation and application of the law by the Courts

- Judges are, as a rule, free to apply the law according to their convictions, thereby being empowered to recognize, in specific cases, the unconstitutionality of a statute or the contractual provision that contradicts a norm of public order. In this sense, the courts are also empowered to review contracts. Nevertheless, in recent years, there has been a significant development in civil process aimed at ensuring greater uniformity in legal application through the establishment of binding precedents by higher courts. It shall also be noted that arbitration is a growing method of resolving contractual disputes, including in contracts involving the State and public agencies.

Chile

9.34 The system of sources of law of the Chilean legal system is structured on a pyramidal basis, at the top of which is the Political Constitution.[36] Below that, there are rules with legal status, such as laws and statutory decrees.[37] Then, depending on the legal rules, there

36 The current Political Constitution of Chile was approved in 1980 by the Military Board and in a referendum that lacked the most elementary democratic standards, as it was carried out in a state of emergency, without press or expression freedom, without electoral records and through a system that allowed duplication of the vote. It entered into force on 11 March 1981, and since 1989 has had a series of reforms that once returned to democracy in 1990 has been subject of numerous amendments.

37 Statutory Decrees ("*Decretos con Fuerza de Ley*") are regulation issued by the Administration, thus their name of "decree", dealing with law matters, having the Parliament previously passed an empowering law.

are regulations that develop the matters contained in the law, such as enforcement regulations, or that deal with matters that are not matters of law, such as autonomous regulatory power. Finally, there are acts of the administrative authority which can have general or particular effects, that is, in terms of State regulation creation.

9.35 Private law is governed by the principle of autonomy of the will.[38] This means that individuals may do whatever is not expressly forbidden or does not go against public order regulations. This principle arises from several liberties that are guaranteed by the Constitution, such as (i) personal freedom,[39] (ii) freedom of conscience,[40] (iii) freedom of expression,[41] (iv) press freedom,[42] (v) freedom of education, (vi) freedom of reunion,[43] (vii) work freedom,[44] and freedom to unionize,[45] (viii) freedom of association,[46] (ix) freedom and right to require from the public authority,[47] (x) freedom to private initiative in economic matters,[48] (xi) freedom to acquire property of any type of goods,[49] and (xii) property right.[50] It is also manifested in the structure of the juridical act in the Civil Code, as it is ordered based on the expression of the agent's free will and culminates in its legal concretization with the establishment of the principle of *pacta sunt servanda*.

9.36 On the other hand, public law is ordered on a different principle, the so-called principle of legality;[51] that is, the public authority may only perform what it is expressly allowed to do. This principle is established in the Political Constitution and is one of the bases of the institutionality of the Republic.

9.37 Notwithstanding the clear differentiation for performance by State organs and private agents, it is important to note that this does not mean that the rules of private law are never applied to the organs of the State administration. The reason of this is because when the State enters into contracts, of whatever nature, private law rules may be applied, when, in their supplementary role, they turn out to be applicable according to general law or private law in a subsidiary or residual manner.

9.38 It is important to note that the referral to general law will be more or less intense depending on the nature of the contract. Thus, with an eminently public contract such as the concession contract, the contract for the construction of public works, etc., firstly, it will be necessary to resort to the rules and principles of public law and, in what does not conflict with these regulations, general or private law may be drawn upon.

---

38 Articles 1437, 1438, 1444, 1445(1), and (2), 1448, 1453, 1545, and 1560, all from the Civil Code of Chile, are receivers of this idea supporting the manifestation of the will as an entity able to generate, modify or extinguish rights.

39 *Political Constitution of the Republic of Chile* 1980 (CL) (*CPE* 1980), Article 19(7).

40 *CPE* 1980 (CL), Article 19(6).

41 *CPE* 1980 (CL), Article 19(12).

42 *CPE* 1980 (CL), Article 19(12).

43 *CPE* 1980 (CL), Article 19(13).

44 *CPE* 1980 (CL), Article 19(16).

45 *CPE* 1980 (CL), Article 19(19).

46 *CPE* 1980 (CL), Article 19(15).

47 *CPE* 1980 (CL), Article 19(14).

48 *CPE* 1980 (CL), Article 19(21).

49 *CPE* 1980 (CL), Article 19(23).

50 *CPE* 1980 (CL), Article 19(24).

51 *CPE* 1980 (CL) Article 6 and 7.

Contract Law

The Formation of a Contract

9.39 As set out in the previous section, in 1988 representatives democratically elected by the Brazilian people promulgated the current Federal Constitution, establishing a democratic state founded, among other things, in free enterprise (Article 1), while guaranteeing the right to ownership (Article 5) and ensuring the free exercise of any economic activity (Article 170, single paragraph). At the same time, the 1988 Constitution values principles such as the dignity of the human person and those principles aimed at achieving social justice and diminishing social inequalities.

9.40 Furthermore, Article 5 (II) of the Brazilian Constitution expressly states that "no one shall be obliged to do or refrain from doing something except by virtue of the law".[52] This is a fundamental principle of Brazilian law, meaning that the conduct and choices of Brazilians are free, not to be curtailed by the State or other people, except where there are express legal provisions prohibiting someone from acting in a certain way. In practice, however, the Courts may adopt a non-literal interpretation of the law or address a case on a basis of general principles, which may enable fair solutions in concrete cases but also undermine legal certainty.

9.41 Brazilian legislation must be interpreted in accordance with these constitutional provisions; in particular, for the purpose of this section, the Brazilian Civil Code of 2002 and its chapters on the formation of a "legal transaction" which is a broad term including contracts. In this important Code the same principles are maintained as indicated above, of particular note that of free enterprise, which when converted to contractual logic means that the parties in Brazil are free to create between themselves rights and obligations consistent with the national public order. The principle of *pacta sunt servanda*, originating in Roman law, prevails as a general rule.

9.42 In Brazil, there is also an important constitutional regime of Public Law set out in Article 37 of the Constitution and related provisions, which regulates the State's conduct in relation to citizens and legal entities. The Brazilian government can only do what the law expressly determines, that is, the State has no freedom and has no free enterprise. The contracts entered into by the Government are all subjected to rigorous and detailed legislation, with many laws setting out the mandatory procedures and content.

9.43 In Chile, the same constitutional principles of free enterprise (Article 19 (21)), right to ownership (Article 19 (24)) and free exercise of any economic activity (Article 19 (21)) are enshrined in the Chilean Constitution enacted in 1980. However, this text has no provision which aims to obtain a special social outcome when exercising these rights like in Brazil, and the State's role in the economic activities is limited to the regulation of these activities. If the State desires to perform an economic activity, this must be authorized by a special law that needs to be approved by an absolute majority of the members of the parliament with a right to vote. For this reason, the Chilean legal regime may be considered economically more liberal.

52 Law in Brazil means specific introductory instruments of legal norms created by the legislative of the Brazilian State: Constitutional Norm, Complementary Law, Ordinary Law, Provisional Measure, Legislative Decree, and Resolution of the Federal Senate.

9.44 The Chilean private law contained in the Civil and Commercial Codes and their complementary laws are also developed promoting the principles of freedom of contract and *pacta sunt servanda.* However, this situation has been limited by laws like the Consumer Protection Law that creates special protection for consumers[53] in order to prevent abuses. These limitations on the fundamental principles of freedom of contract and *pacta sunt servanda*, mean that contractual terms must be fair and equitable.

Capacity

9.45 In Brazil, individuals aged 18 and over are able to practice the acts of civil life,[54] including entering into contracts. In some situations, set out in law it is possible for people under 18 to get full civil capacity (for example, by capacity being conceded by parents to their children over 16; marriage; or graduating from a higher education course).[55]

9.46 Legal entities such as companies also have rights and obligations, with capacity to enter into contracts. In Brazil there are principally two kinds of legal entities: Those regulated by private law and those regulated by public law. The formal existence of a legal entity under private law begins with the registration of its articles of association on the public record.[56] Legal entities under public law (for example, the federal union, states, municipalities and authorities) are created by law. Legal entities under private law are free to contract and can do anything that is not prohibited by law. The actions of legal entities under public law are fully governed by the law.[57]

9.47 The Chilean Civil Code establishes that capacity has two variants, the first being "capacity to have" and the second one "capacity to exercise". The first is inextricably linked to the possibility of a person to acquire rights, which is an attribute of one's personality that is inalienable; and the second one, "capacity to exercise", consists in the legal ability that the individual has to act in legal affairs. For individuals, the capacity to exercise is acquired at the age of 18 at which time a person reaches maturity under the law.

9.48 With respect to legal entities, they acquire both types of capacities at the time of being constituted, and a distinction can be made between those that are created through the enactment of a law and those that are created as a consequence of the mutual agreement of legal or natural persons.

Intention to Create Legal Relations, Offer, and Acceptance

9.49 In order for any legal transaction to be valid in Brazil, it is necessary, firstly, that the parties have legal capacity. If they do, they will be able to establish mutual obligations, forming a binding legal relationship.

9.50 In addition to the parties having legal capacity, the subject of the transaction, has to be lawful, possible, determined or determinable.[58] If the subject is lawful and the parties

53 Law 20.149 provides that the companies whose turnover is less than US$ 1.000.000. (approximately) can be considered as consumers and, therefore, can exercise the rights conferred by the consumers' law.

54 Federative Republic of Brazil. *Brazilian Civil Code.* Law no 10.406. Chapter I. (2002) Brasília: The Presidency of the Republic of Brazil. Available from – www.planalto.gov.br/ccivil_03/ leis/2002/L10406.htm (last accessed 9 April 2020) Article 5.

55 Further grounds are set out in Brazilian Civil Code, 2002 (BR) Article 5.

56 *Brazilian Civil Code*, 2002 (BR) Article 967.

57 *Constitution of Brazil*, 1988 (BR) Article 37.

58 *Brazilian Civil Code*, 2002 (BR) Article 104.

have legal capacity, the intentions expressed orally or in writing create a contractual legal relationship, establishing binding obligations between the parties, even if a party had "made a mental note of not wanting what he expressed".[59] In the same sense, when a declaration of express will is not required, the silence of a party may denote its consent.[60]

9.51 It is important to note that the validity of the declaration of will of any of the parties does not depend on any determined form, except in cases specifically required under law[61] (such as the obligation to use a "public deed" for the transfer of property rights in relation to real estate).[62] This is because there are two very strong principles in Brazilian law that mean that the will prevails over the form: (i) "regarding declarations of will, the intention contained within them shall prevail over the literal meaning of the language";[63] and (ii) "legal transactions shall be interpreted according to good faith and the customs of the place in which it is entered into".[64]

9.52 It is important to note that the right of freedom to contract must always be exercised reasonably and within the boundaries of the contract's social function.[65,66] In addition, throughout the formation and execution of the contract the parties must comply with the principles of good faith and probity.[67] As mentioned above, general principles, such as these, may be applied by the Courts when interpreting the contract and the behaviour of the parties as well as in enforcing contractual obligations.

9.53 It should also be noted that, under Brazilian Law, an offer is a binding declaration of will, unless stated otherwise or it can be clearly implied by the circumstances that this was not the intention (Civil Code, Article 427). A contract is formed whenever the offer is accepted, or the parties agree to the contract. The acceptance is also a declaration of will. The general rule is that the contract is formed whenever the acceptance is issued, but the acceptance may be withdrawn if the withdrawal is received by the offeror before the acceptance. When the offer is made with no expiration date between people that are in direct and immediate contact, it should be accepted promptly (Civil Code, Article 428). The mutual agreement is, therefore, the basis for the formation of a contract and there is no requirement for consideration.

9.54 The doctrine of *culpa in contrahendo* is also well developed in Brazil. It requires that the parties negotiate in good faith (Civil Code, Article 422) and they may be liable if they induce certain behaviours in the other parties and unreasonably break expectations of good faith negotiations.

9.55 Considering the points raised above, it can be seen that just as the law gives individuals the right to contract, it also enforces upon them responsibilities for what they contract, from the pre-contractual phase through the proposal and other acts until its

---

59 *Brazilian Civil Code*, 2002 (BR) Article 110.

60 *Brazilian Civil Code*, 2002 (BR) Article 111.

61 *Brazilian Civil Code*, 2002 (BR) Article 107.

62 *Brazilian Civil Code*, 2002 (BR) Article 108.

63 *Brazilian Civil Code*, 2002 (BR) Article 112.

64 *Brazilian Civil Code*, 2002 (BR) Article 113.

65 *Brazilian Civil Code*, 2002 (BR) Article 421.

66 According to Statement 21 promulgated by the Center for Legal Studies of the Council of Federal Justice (CEJ) the social function of the contract provided for in Article 421 of the Civil Code does not eliminate the principle of contractual autonomy, but mitigates or reduces the scope of this principle when there are meta-individual interests or individual interest regarding the dignity of the human person.

67 *Brazilian Civil Code*, 2002 (BR) Article 422.

conclusion. A contract proposal, for example, imposes obligations on the party creating it,[68] which are only extinguished on the expiry of its validity period, where it is not accepted or where there was a retraction of the proposal before the other party became aware of it.[69] In a similar manner, the acceptance of a proposal also imposes obligations on the party accepting it.

9.56 Brazilian law also contains provisions relating to preliminary contracts, where the parties agree to create a contract and already establish its core content. If the preliminary contract is entered into and its terms fulfilled, there will be an obligation on the parties to enter into the definitive contract.[70]

9.57 The autonomy of will mentioned above should be construed as a rule of Brazilian law; however, there are important exceptions. These exceptions are expressly set out in laws that limit the autonomy of will of citizens, such as labour laws that give special protection to employees, laws protecting disadvantaged consumers, monetary laws, laws that prohibit the practice of compound interest, laws relating to the right of ownership of assets of public interest, laws regarding succession and marital status, environment laws, among others. In such cases, the parties cannot derogate from the public order rules that apply.

9.58 According to the Chilean Civil Code, for a person to be bound to another it is necessary that they are legally capable, that they manifest their will giving their consent to such act, free of any vice (whether personally or represented),[71] and the act must have a licit object and cause.[72] The object of the contract consists of the obligation assumed thereunder with the purpose of giving, doing, or not doing something,[73] and the cause, the motive which induces to the act or contract.[74]

9.59 Consequently, having fulfilled these requirements, and other established by the law for certain cases, we will be in presence of a binding act or contract for the parties, where the principle of obligatory force of the contracts or so known as *pacta sunt servanda*[75] will be in full force. It is important to note that for the will to create obligations, it must be externalized, so, in general, silence does not have any value. Nevertheless, there are certain situations in which the parties or the law can attribute legal effects to silence.[76]

9.60 As for the way in which the will manifestation must be made, in principle, there is no specific manner, except on cases where the law requires certain solemnities, such as the sale of real property, which must be executed by public deed.[77] Despite the requirement of certain solemnities in specific cases, it is important to bear in mind that in order

68 *Brazilian Civil Code*, 2002 (BR) Article 427; The Superior Court of Justice of Brazil considers that a breach of the duties of loyalty and mutual confidence (objective good faith) is a unlawful act that generates an obligation to repair the damages suffered by the party who has made provisions for the contract and incurred expenses in a fair expectation of the conclusion of the contract created by the other party: See, e.g., *REsp 1051065*, STJ, 21 February 2013.

69 *Brazilian Civil Code*, 2002 (BR) Article 428.

70 *Brazilian Civil Code*, 2002 (BR) Articles 462 and 463; The Superior Court of Justice of Brazil has already decided that a Memorandum of Understanding creates a fair expectation that guarantees the parties the right to obtain via preliminary injunction what was agreed in its terms (*RMS 6183*, STJ, 14 November 1995).

71 Article 1448, Chilean Civil Code.

72 Article 1445, Chilean Civil Code.

73 Article 1460, Chilean Civil Code.

74 Article 1467 paragraph 2, Chilean Civil Code.

75 Article 1545, Chilean Civil Code.

76 Article 2125 paragraph 1, Chilean Civil Code.

77 Article 1801 paragraph 2, Chilean Civil Code

to construe the will of the parties we must consider their intention more than the literal of the words they used;[78] having to, moreover, always execute contracts in good faith, so the contracts will not only bind them to what is expressed in them, but to everything arising from the nature of the obligation, or that by the law or custom belong thereto.[79]

9.61 Where the aforementioned requirements have been fulfilled the act or contract shall be binding on the parties.

9.62 As for the formation of consent, this matter is expressly regulated in Chile, beginning from the moment in which the offeror makes a proposal, whether verbally or in writing,[80] and establishing for the offeree the term he will dispose of to give his answer to the offeror. In the case of verbal offers, the offeree must accept on the spot upon knowing the offer in order to bind the offeror,[81] while in the case of offers made in writing, different terms are established depending on whether or not the offeree resides in the same place as the offeror.[82] Notwithstanding the foregoing, the offeror will be entitled to retract before the offeree's acceptance (except in certain cases), in which case it will have to indemnify the expenses incurred and the damages suffered by the offeree.[83]

9.63 The Chilean Civil Code also regulates the promise to enter into a contract, from which an obligation to do will arise for the parties, consisting in entering into the promised contract.[84] Notwithstanding the foregoing, certain requirements are established for the promise contract to be binding, which are that i) such contract must be in writing, ii) that it is not a contract declared by the law as invalid, iii) the obligation must contain a term or a condition and iv) that it specifies in detail the promised contract.

9.64 Such as it happens in Brazil, despite the autonomy of the will is a widely recognized principle in the Chilean legislation, there are limitations about the content of the acts and contracts entered into by the parties. Thus, the acts and contracts entered into may not be contrary to the law, good conduct or public order,[85] given that in such cases these acts and contracts will be invalid. Moreover, under Chilean law there are several public order rules, which content cannot be modified by the parties. There are examples of this in labour law,[86] consumer's rights law,[87] environmental law, rules on succession upon the death of a person, among others.

Formalities

9.65 As seen above, in Brazil the formation of a legal transaction does not need to follow any specific formality, unless there is an express requirement provided by the law. Contracts can usually be written or oral, and any legal fact can be proved by testimony, documents, witnesses, presumption or by experts.[88] Where there is a requirement for

---

78 Article 1560, Chilean Civil Code.
79 Article 1546, Chilean Civil Code.
80 Articles 97 et seq., Chilean Commerce Code.
81 Article 97, Chilean Commerce Code.
82 Article 98, Chilean Commerce Code.
83 Articles 99 and 100, Chilean Commerce Code.
84 Article 1554, Chilean Civil Code.
85 Article 1467 paragraph 2, Chilean Civil Code.
86 Article 5 paragraph 2, Chilean Labour Code.
87 Article 4, Law No. 19.496 On the Protection of the Rights of Consumers.
88 *Brazilian Civil Code*, 2002 (BR) Article 212.

certain formalities in the creation of a contract, it is essential for the validity of the contract that they are complied with rather than being a mere evidentiary requirement.

9.66 Under the Chilean Civil Code, contracts can be consensual, solemn or real. A consensual contract is one that can be agreed verbally without any formality or solemnity. Solemn contracts are those that must be in writing and in some cases must be recorded in a public deed. Finally, real contracts are those that have full force and effect upon delivery of the good.

Contracts dealing with real estate may only be definitively formed under a notarial service and upon registration, although preliminary contracts may be set by the parties before the formal conclusion of the transfer of real estate rights upon a notarial deed and its registration.

9.67 Under the Electronic Signature Law, electronic medium has the same legal validity as physical documents, and, therefore, it is understood that the contracts that must be in writing comply with this requirement if they are on an electronic medium, such as recordings, videos, etc. They can also be recorded through electronic media that certify the existence of simple or advanced electronic signatures. However, when the law requires the solemnity of a public deed, that requirement cannot be replaced with any other.

The Contents of a Contract

Terms of a Contract (Express and Implied Terms)

9.68 In Brazil, there are a number of provisions of the Civil Code that apply to contractual terms, although in view of the freedom to contract, many of these provisions are suppletive, meaning that the parties can decide how to regulate their relationship. As well as the provisions that apply generally to contracts, the Civil Code also defines certain types of contract with specific provisions regulating each contract type. Examples of such contracts include those for sale and purchase, donations, transport, brokerage, insurance, guarantee, lease, loan, service provision and contract of works. In these cases, if the parties do not establish their own specific rules, the provisions in the Code will apply. It is important to note that under Article 425 of the Civil Code, the parties may also create what is defined as an "atypical" contract and determine between themselves the specific terms of the contract. In this case, the parties must observe the general norms set out in the Civil Code and public order provisions.

9.69 For some types of contract, Brazilian law stipulates in specific statutes that certain mandatory terms should be included, as is the case with consumer, employment, and sale and purchase contracts.

9.70 As an integral element of contracts, the Chilean Civil Code enshrines the principle of objective good faith, and in virtue of this principle it also forms part of a contract the elements that form part of the nature of the contract itself or implicit terms, as well as the elements that are part of the contract due to custom. Good faith, therefore, operates as an integral element of the contract, which will always contain explicit and implicit clauses.

Limitation on Contractual Terms

9.71 It is an explicit norm of the Brazilian Civil Code that the right of freedom to contract must be exercised reasonably and within the limits of the social function of the contract.[89] This means that it is prohibited to create an obligation that goes against the legitimate and protected interests of the collective.[90] This norm should be interpreted in conjunction with Article 422 and also Article 187 which provides that an illicit act will be committed by "the holder of a right that, by exercising it, clearly exceeds the limits imposed by its economic or social purpose, good faith or good practices".

9.72 It is essential to emphasize that these provisions do not undermine the private autonomy of will, when that is consistent with the law in force. Two people can contract anything that does not violate the law that governs them. Contracts must observe, for example, the legal provisions that protect society against the abuse of economic power,[91] or that prohibit contractual terms for the payment of interest above the legal limit.[92]

9.73 For each of the types of contract set out in the Brazilian Civil Code (sale and purchase, donation, transportation, brokerage, insurance, guarantee, leasing, loan, provision of services), there are certain specific limitations on the parties regarding the rights and obligations that can be contracted which are explained in in the relevant articles of the Civil Code, although a detailed analysis of each of these limitations is beyond the scope of this chapter.

9.74 The Chilean legal system, as it has been mentioned, enshrines the principle of autonomy of will, and as such will only recognize limitations in respect of actions prohibited by law, must not be the result of vitiating factors and must have a lawful subject. It also recognizes as a limitation the rules of public order. There are certain types of contract on which the law establishes limitations to the will of the parties. For example, in a loan agreement, an interest rate higher than the conventional maximum cannot be agreed, and the penalty clauses cannot exceed two times the main obligation. The Law on the Protection of Consumer Rights perhaps imposes the greatest number of such limitations, as it has a protective characteristic in favour of the consumer, just like labour law.

Principles of Good Faith

9.75 Brazilian law incorporates the Germanic-Roman legal tradition regarding the interpretation of the law and the application of its principles, such as good faith.

9.76 When considering the hierarchy of legal provisions in this area, one must first look to the constitutional norm that "*no one shall be obliged to do or refrain from doing something except by virtue of law*", together with other constitutional norms that guarantee the principle of free enterprise and ownership.[93]

9.77 Where a party seeks to enter into a contract, it is necessary to confirm whether there is some express provision in the law prohibiting the contract. If there is no such provision, the party should evaluate whether what they intend to contract violates the right of others or goes against the economic or social purpose or the good practices of society.

---

89 *Brazilian Civil Code*, 2002 (BR) Article 421.

90 As established in Statement 23 of the I Civil Law Conference (CJF, 2002): "The social function of the contract, present in Article 421 of the new Civil Code, does not eliminate the principle of contractual autonomy, but it mitigates or reduces the extent of this principle when there are meta-individual interests or individual interest related to the dignity of the human person".

91 *Constitution of Brazil*, 1988 (BR) Article 173(4).

92 *Decree 22,626*, 1933 (BR) Articles 1 and 4.

93 *Constitution of Brazil*, 1988 (BR) Articles 1° (IV) and 170 (II).

Finally, the party must ensure that the principle of good faith is maintained throughout the course of the contract.

9.78 The principle of good faith was recently confirmed in Brazilian contract law through the 2002 Civil Code and has since been widely applied in cases.

9.79 A correct application of the principle of good faith occurs when it is used to overcome contractual loopholes in relation to the conduct of one of the parties in its relationship with the other. Under the principle of good faith, it is not enough that one of the parties is transparent about its own interest, it essentially serves to ensure that the parties consider the interests of each other,[94] to prevent the lack of knowledge of just one of the parties as to facts relevant to the contractual relationship being an unjustified source of benefit to the other. There is a duty to negotiate in good faith, which justifies, for instance, the doctrine of *culpa in contrahendo* mentioned earlier in this chapter.

9.80 The best Brazilian doctrine and jurisprudence recognise the principle of good faith as a principle that is a part of the interpretation of facts and evidence presented in concrete cases, in which the parties are expected to have acted honestly from the formation of the contract.[95]

9.81 Following also the tradition of Western law, and especially that derived from Roman law, the Chilean legal system recognizes the principle of good faith, which is present throughout its legal framework. The principle of good faith has been understood as that which obliges the parties to behave in an honest manner, acting with respect and fidelity in business, and means that trust, loyalty, honesty, and rectitude are fundamental duties that the parties have to each other. The principle of good faith, where it is complied with, necessarily leads to a collaborative relationship and seeks to fulfil one of the fundamental roles of law which is to achieve social peace based on the above-mentioned values.

9.82 Everyday Chilean jurisprudence has given greater importance to this principle, determining that the relevant matter is the behaviour of the parties, which can be measured against an objective standard of conduct, instead of their motivations. This definition has led doctrine and jurisprudence to speak of "objective good faith". In order to modulate this objective criterion, it is necessary to resort, in matters of contractual liability, to the degree of negligence for which the debtor is responsible, which varies depending on the type of contract. Chilean law differentiates three types of intensity in the negligence attributed to the debtor. If a contract does not report any benefit to the debtor, its responsibility will be of less intensity – gross negligence – than the one enforceable in those contracts where the benefit is for both parties, since in the latter they must behave as a good *pater familias*. Finally, the standard will be more severe for that party that is the only one to receive benefits from the legal relationship, who should act with extreme diligence, being this the diligence of a wise person "managing its important affairs".[96]

94 III Civil Law Conference (CJF, 2004) Statement 169: "The principle of good faith must conduce the creditor to avoid the deepening of its own losses".

95 III Civil Law Conference (CJF, 2004) Statement 170: "Objective good faith must be observed by the parties during the preliminary negation phase and after the contract's execution, when such obligation results from the nature of the contract"; V Civil Law Conference (CJF, 2011) Statement 409: "Legal transactions must be interpreted not only according to the good faith and the local customs, but also according to the behaviors usually adopted by the parties".

96 Article 44, Chilean Civil Code.

9.83 It is important to emphasize that the principle of good faith is considered in Chile as an integral element of contractual relationships, but in no case can be interpreted as a norm that can repeal or modify what the parties have expressly agreed. This impossibility to derogate or amend cannot be confused with the fact that the parties in practice, tacitly, many times modify or derogate contractual rules, but this phenomenon is very different to considering that the principle of good faith is a sufficient tool to repeal or modify express contractual agreements agreed by the parties.

Vitiating Factors under Contract Law

9.84 Chapter V Article 166 of the Brazilian Civil Code sets out situations in which a legal transaction will be considered null. These situations include the absolute incapacity of a party; the unlawfulness of the object of the legal transaction; an impossible or indeterminate subject; or where a requirement of the law as to form or formality has not been complied with.

9.85 Any part of a legal transaction which is held to be a "simulation" will also be null (Article 167). This includes a situation where the legal transaction contains a declaration or clause that is not truthful (Article 167, para. 1(I)). In the case of a "simulated" legal transaction, the rights of third parties that have acted in good faith in relation to the contracting parties will be protected (Article 167 (2)).

9.86 Under Brazilian law there prevails the principle that no one can benefit from their own moral turpitude.[97] Therefore, the declaration of nullity of a contract may not favour the person responsible for the grounds of the nullity. Under this premise, the Courts may evaluate the behaviour of the parties in order to resolve a contractual dispute.

9.87 It is important to note that nullities may be raised by any interested party or the public prosecutor (Article 168). Furthermore, as stated in Article 169, where a legal transaction is null it is not possible for it to subsequently become valid whether through the agreement of the parties or the passage of time.

9.88 Under the system of the Chilean Civil Code, legal acts must comply with a series of requirements to be valid, namely: a) The declaration of will should be made by a capable person; b) the declaration of will should not be affected by any vitiating factors, such as error, force or fraud; c) must have a subject which is determined or determinable and also lawful; d) the act must have a cause, and that cause must be lawful; and e) for some cases, the solemnities established by law must be complied with.

9.89 The grounds for nullity are divided into absolute and relative. The former in no case can be made good or ratified by the parties, whereas the latter can be made good or ratified by the party in whose benefit the nullity action is granted. The grounds for absolute nullity are: A) Absolute incapacity; B) lack of will or consent; C) lack of subject; D) illicit subject; E) lack of cause; F) illicit cause; and G) non-compliance with solemnities in the cases required by law. The grounds for relative nullity are: a) Relative incapacity; and b) that the declaration of will is vitiated by error, force, or fraud.

9.90 The nullity must always be declared judicially, as legal acts have a presumption of validity. Any person who has an economic interest in the declaration of nullity can request the declaration of absolute nullity, and also the judge can declare it *ex officio*, but only

97 This principle can be seen, for example, in Articles 150 and 883 of the *Brazilian Civil Code*, 2002 (BR).

when the absolute nullity is evident from the simple reading of the act or contract. The action of absolute nullity is denied to anyone who undertook the act or signed the contract with effective knowledge of the vitiating factor or when, due to its special position, should have been aware of the vitiating factor that invalidated the act or contract. The relative nullity can only be requested by those who are affected by the vitiating factor, that is to say, by those in whose benefit the action of relative nullity has been established.

9.91 The absolute nullity action is extinguished by prescription after ten years from the date of the juridical act or contract. The relative nullity action has a limitation period of four years counted from the date of the act or contract.

9.92 In Chile, there are no express provisions relating to an action for "simulation", and its development has been carried forward by reference to the norms on Theory of Evidence and on Theory of Nullities. According to the Chilean doctrine and jurisprudence, there is simulation when the consent manifested in an act or contract does not correspond to the real will of the party. This means that, in practice, there are two types of simulation: Absolute simulation, when a legal act is undertaken but there is nothing real behind it and it is absolutely fictitious; and relative simulation, when the parties intended to perform an act which is different to the one stated, whether totally, as in the case of a donation disguised as a sale, or only partially, for example, where in a contract one of the clauses has a different content to that agreed, or includes a different benefit than the real benefit agreed by the parties. In the first case, the simulation will result in the absolute nullity of the act or contract for lack of consent, and in the second case; that is, where there is relative simulation, a distinction must be made to determine if the hidden act is a null act or a valid one. In principle, the action of relative simulation aims to make the hidden act prevail over the visible one, but if the said hidden act also has the defect of nullity in its genesis, it must also be declared if requested by the plaintiff.

Misrepresentation and Mistake

9.93 Brazilian law makes a distinction between legal relations that are null and annullable. As seen, where a legal transaction is null it is not possible for it to subsequently become valid. Where a legal transaction is annullable, the parties may confirm it as long as they do not violate the right of third parties in good faith (Article 172).

9.94 Some of the principal grounds under which a legal transaction can be held to be annullable are the relative incapacity of a party; error; deceit; coercion; state of danger; injury and fraud against creditors (Article 171).

9.95 Those that are under sixteen are absolutely incapable (Article 3). The Brazilian Civil Code considers relatively incapable those aged between 16 and 18, as well as those that are held "prodigal", those incapable of expressing their will, habitual drunks, and drug addicts (Article 4). Persons between 16 and 18 years old cannot use their age as a basis for evading their obligations if they have claimed to be over 18 when they entered into the obligation or have concealed their age intentionally when asked by the other party (Article 180).

9.96 There will be an error in the legal transaction when the declaration of will is produced from a substantial error in the subject of the main business, its quality or as to the identity of another person (Article 139).

9.97 A deceit will also be considered a ground for the annulment of a legal transaction and, for example, will occur where one of the parties, or a third party, deliberately remains silent about a fact or a quality which, if revealed, would not have led to the business being undertaken (Article 147). However, if both parties act deceitfully, neither can use deceit as a basis to nullify the business or claim compensation (Article 150).

9.98 Under Brazilian law, in order to vitiate the declaration of will, any coercion must instil in the relevant party fear of imminent and serious injury to themselves, their family or their assets (Article 151). If it relates to another person who is not a family member, the judge will decide based on the circumstances whether there was in fact coercion (Article 151, single paragraph).

9.99 The grounds "state of danger" and "injury" are similar in certain aspects to coercion. They are a means of nullifying a legal transaction where a party takes on an obligation that is excessively onerous or manifestly disproportionate to the value of what they are receiving out of a need to save themselves or someone in their family or out of inexperience (Articles 156 and 157).

9.100 Finally, it is worth mentioning the ground "fraud against creditors", which is where an insolvent party transfers to third parties' assets that should be transferred to creditors at the time of insolvency (Article 158).

9.101 In the case of each one of the grounds above there are important legal consequences and jurisprudential discussions regarding the best way in which they should be applied to specific cases.

9.102 The limitation period for claims to nullify a legal transaction is four years (Article 178). The start date for this period depends on the grounds for the claim. In the case of coercion, the period starts on the day the alleged coercion ceases and where there has been an act of someone incapable, the day on which their incapacity ceases. In other cases, such as error, deceit, and fraud against creditors, the period starts on the day the legal transaction took place.

9.103 Where a legal transaction is nullified, the parties should be restored to the state in which they were before the legal transaction was undertaken or, where this is not possible, they will be compensated with the equivalent amount (Article 182).

9.104 The Chilean Civil Code establishes adult minors as relatively incapacitated, females older than 12 and younger than 18 years old, and males older than 14 and younger than 18. The regulation of the capacity also have specific rules, which are the following: a) Adult minors have the management, use and enjoyment of the goods of their professional earnings,[98] with the exception of selling or affecting real state; b) Administration of certain goods acquired by donation, inheritance or legacy; c) Disposal of their goods in a testament; d) Acquisition of the possession of personal property and e) Extra contractual liability.[99]

98 Professional earnings are the group of assets and liabilities that the minor adult has or acquires as a consequence of the remunerated activities that are carried out.

99 Extra contractual liability commences at the age of 16, and the liability of a minor between 7 and 16 years old requires a judicial declaration concluding that the minor acted with discernment, this means that he was capable of distinguishing between right and wrong.

9.105 An error, in order to annul the contract, has to be related to a fact, as an error of law does not vitiate the consent given;[100] this error has to be fundamental,[101] substantial,[102] or has to be related to a person or a matter that was considered as the main motivation that one of the parties had to conclude the contract (Articles 1453, 1454, and 1455 of the Chilean Civil Code).

9.106 Force may also be grounds to annul an agreement where it is capable of inflicting a material fear in a person, considering their age, sex, lineage, and status; and it is understood that this force exists when inflicted to a person that can have a reasonable fear of being exposed (or have his relatives exposed) to an irreparable and serious damage. It is irrelevant who inflicted the force, as the important matter is that it was exerted (Articles 1456 and 1457, Chilean Civil Code).

9.107 Fraud annuls the contract when it is decisive and committed by one of the parties of the contract. On cases where the fraud is not decisive or is committed by a third party, there will only be an indemnity action against the one who planned and committed the fraud, as well as against the person that benefited from the fraud committed by others (Article 1458, Chilean Civil Code).

9.108 Regarding the term to present the annulment action and from when is this term counted, both Chilean and Brazilian law have the same rules.[103] The term to exercise the relative nullity action is of four years but the moment from which the term is counted will depend on the cause. In case of fraud and error the term is counted from the date of the act or contract; in case of coercion, the term is counted from the date on which the violence ends, and finally, in case of incapacity, the term of four years is counted from the moment the incapacity ends (Article 1691). In this matter, both Chilean and Brazilian law have the same rules.

9.109 The Chilean Civil Code recognizes the existence of an action in relation to the contracts that are entered into in fraud of creditors; this is when the debtor decides to transfer its assets being aware of the bad situation of its business. However, in Chile this is not a cause of nullity, but the contract does not produce an effect in respect of the creditors, which means that it is unenforceable against third parties. For onerous acts, it is necessary that all parties were aware of the bad situation of the businesses, while for gratuitous transferences it is only necessary to prove that the debtor was aware of the bad situation of the businesses, but there must always be a detriment to the creditors.

9.110 Unlike Brazilian legislation, the Chilean Civil Code does not admit annulment as a consequence of a necessity or a danger state.

The Rights and Liabilities of Third Parties

9.111 A contract is meant to produce its legal effects among the contracting parties. Brazilian law, as well as other Romano-Germanic systems, has its contractual legal regime based on the *pacta sunt servanda* principle ("agreements must be kept"), which

100 Article 1452, Chilean Civil Code.

101 An error is fundamental when one of the following circumstances occur: a) The parties in their belief thought that they were celebrating different types of contracts; or b) if the parties committed an error in relation to the identity of the item which was the subject matter of the contract.

102 This case refers to the composition of the items that are the subject matter of the contract.

103 See Article 1691 Chilean Civil Code.

means that a contract, which has been validly entered into by capable parties, is binding between them and, as a general rule, shall not benefit or harm third parties.[104] *Pacta sunt servanda* is not an absolute principle,[105] as agreements may be subject to judicial review, as will be explained below.

9.112 Under certain circumstances, the contract may affect third parties, directly or indirectly. By way of example, Brazilian law expressly allows contracting parties to stipulate a benefit in favour of a third party, who, even not being a party to the contract, may demand it.[106] The consent of the third party is irrelevant for the formation of the contract, but, at the appropriate time, this will be given. The party that has stipulated the benefit may replace the beneficiary when such change is allowed in the contract.[107]

9.113 An agreement in favour of third parties may be extremely complex, for example, in the case of a concession contract[108] under which the government engages a private company to provide public services in favour of the users, generating a series of obligations involving these parties.

9.114 The Brazilian Civil Code also foresees the possibility of a contracting party taking on an obligation to be performed by a third party. In that case, the promisor is liable for the third party's performance, until the third party agrees and binds himself to comply. From that moment on, the promisor is not liable in case of non-performance by the third party.[109]

9.115 In Brazil, there is a legal requirement that a construction company, whenever entering into a construction contract, appoints one or more professionals as technically responsible for the works.[110] These professionals, even though they are third parties still have relevant obligations and responsibilities related to the contract.

9.116 The Civil Code also establishes a liability period of five years, during which the contractor is liable for the solidity and safety of the works.[111] Case law has extended the ambit of this warranty clause to benefit third parties who may be the final recipients of the construction project.[112]

9.117 It is also worth mentioning that the Civil Code specifies parameters of construction to preserve the interests of neighbours.[113] These rules deal with cables and pipes that may be located in neighbouring land, water drainage, distance between windows and balconies between the buildings, among other matters.[114] Neighbours may be considered another category of third parties who have rights that may be enforced against the contracting parties.

104 Gomes, *Contratos* (Forense, 18th Edition, 1999) 167.
105 AgInt no AREsp 1506600, STJ, 9 December 2019 (BR).
106 *Brazilian Civil Code*, 2002 (BR) Article 436.
107 *Brazilian Civil Code*, 2002 (BR) Article 438.
108 Pereira, *Instituições de Direito Civil* (Vol. III, Forense, 10th Edition, 1999) 66.
109 *Brazilian Civil Code*, 2002 (BR) Articles 439 and 440.
110 *Federal Law 5194*, 1966 (BR); *Federal Law 6496* 1977 (BR).
111 *Brazilian Civil Code*, 2002 (BR) Article 618.
112 *REsp 215832*, STJ, 07 April 2003 (BR).
113 Meirelles, *Direito de Construir* (Malheiros, 10th Edition, 2011) 47ff.
114 *Brazilian Civil Code*, 2002 (BR) Chapter V – Neighborhood Rights.

These regulations are distinct from urban planning rules regarding land use, as well as environmental requirements, which tend to be stringent in Brazil and can vary depending on the specific municipality and state involved.

9.118 Finally, the contract may also indirectly impact a third party in several cases. When a party disposes of its assets through a contract, for example, it may affect their solvency in relation to a third party. Brazilian law entitles this third party, in certain situations, to render such contract ineffective.[115]

9.119 The Chilean Civil Code incorporates the Brocard "*res inter allios acta*", according to which contracts only produce rights and obligations for the parties that, personally or represented, concluded the contract. This principle has not been expressly established in the Civil Code, but is a consequence of the correct application of the principle of autonomy of will,[116] which is expressed in the binding force of the contracts, being a contract a law for the contracting parties[117] that does not oblige or confer rights to third parties.

9.120 This principle admits some exceptions, such as the stipulations in favour of third parties,[118] but the third party has to accept expressly or tacitly the right that was conferred and the parties have the right to revoke that right as long as it has not been accepted by the third party.[119]

9.121 Another institution is the promise of an act from a third party, which strictly speaking cannot be considered as an exception to this principle, since the act from the third party has to be ratified by the third party, and if this does not happen, the creditor will only have the right to demand compensation from the party that made the promise.[120]

9.122 Additionally, various provisions of the Chilean Legal System produce *in toto* effects in relation to certain acts or contracts such as the sale of assets of a company, as the purchaser assumes all the labour rights and obligations that arise out of the individual and collective agreements so the workers shall render the services in favour of a company with which they have not made a contract. There is also an exception to the principle on arrangements with creditors as if the majorities required by the insolvency law are obtained, its provisions are also mandatory for those who did not concur and even for those who voted against.[121]

9.123 In relation to the construction of works, and despite the fact that architects, engineers and technical inspectors are not part of the construction contract, the General Law on Urbanism and Construction (GLUC)[122] establishes that these consultants are liable in

115 *Brazilian Civil Code*, 2002 (BR) Article 158; Civil Procedure Code 2015 (BR) (*CPC* 2015), Article 789ff.

116 Jorge López Santa María, Los Contratos, Parte General, Vol. II, Fourth Edition, Editorial Jurídica de Chile, 2005, p. 342.

117 Article 1545, Chilean Civil Code.

118 Article 1449, Chilean Civil Code.

119 Examples of this institution are the life insurance under which a third party will receive certain sum of money in the event the insured passes away, or in contracts for the transport of goods, on which the carrier shall deliver the goods to the consignee, being the beneficiary of the insurance policy and the consignee of the transport contract third parties that were only named on the relevant contracts, but not part of those contracts (Jorge López Santa María, Los Contratos, Parte General, Vol. II, Fourth Edition, Editorial Jurídica de Chile, 2005, pp. 353 and 354).

120 Article 1450 Chilean Civil Code.

121 Jorge López Santa María, *Los Contratos, Parte General, Vol. II, Fourth Edition*, Editorial Jurídica de Chile, 2005, p. 350.

122 Article 18 of Decree No. 458 of 1976 of the Ministry of Housing and Urban Development.

their respective fields for their obligations, and must sign the plans and reports that they have approved, being, therefore, liable for their own acts, omissions or negligence. The liability of the professionals involved is concurrent[123] with the liability of the constructor and the party that requested the works. Moreover, and at least under this act, our courts have held that this is a case of strict liability.[124] The legal actions related to the liabilities mentioned before prescribe depending on the type of damages caused: a) Ten years for structural damages; b) five years for defects on construction elements or in the installations; c) three years for defects that affect the finishing and termination of the works; and d) five years for defects different to the ones listed above.[125] It is important to mention that this is only applicable to constructions that need the approval of the City Hall Works Department, but that the Chilean Civil Code also extends the liability of the construction company to the consultants.[126]

9.124 In conclusion, although Chilean Law incorporates the *res inter allios acta* principle, there are some exceptions to this rule.

Performance of a Contract

Performance

9.125 Once an agreement is reached and a contract is formed, the parties shall perform their obligations with duty and good faith. The fulfilment of all obligations prescribed in the contract is the natural way to render the contract extinguished and the parties automatically discharged.

9.126 Under Chilean Law, Article 1546 of the Chilean Civil Code establishes the obligation of the parties to execute contracts in good faith. In consequence, this implies that not only what is expressly agreed in the contract is binding for the parties, as the obligations of the contract also include that which forms part of the nature of the obligation, or that by law or customs forms part of it. The fulfilment of the obligation extinguishes the obligation, being the natural way to do so.

Force Majeure and Other Justifications for Non-Performance

9.127 According to the Brazilian Civil Code, as a general rule, no one shall be liable for losses resulting from a *Force Majeure* event. The definition of *Force Majeure* in Brazilian Law is a general concept, covering a fact whose effects could not be avoided or prevented,[127] being, therefore, irresistible.[128]

---

123 This means that the innocent party will be entitled to demand the total amount of the indemnity to any of the professionals involved with the damage.

124 Supreme Court, Rol 47.579-2016.

125 These terms start running once the work is approved by the City Hall Works Department, except for letter c) which begins once the property is registered to the name of the buyer in the public registry.

126 Article 2004 of the Chilean Civil Code makes reference specifically to architects but in our opinion, this is also applicable to other consultants. In this respect, Arturo Alessandri Rodríguez, De la Responsabilidad Extra Contractual en el Derecho Civil Chileno, Vol. II, Second Edition, Editorial Jurídica Ediar Conosur Limitada. p. 435; and Enrique Barros Bourie, Tratado de Responsabilidad Extracontractual, First Edition, Editorial Jurídica de Chile. p. 777.

127 *Brazilian Civil Code*, 2002 (BR) Article 393.

128 Silva, *Vocabulário Jurídico* (Forense, 15th Edition, 1999) 366.

9.128 However, if the contractor is delayed in fulfilling its obligation and such fulfilment happens to become impossible due to a *Force Majeure* event, the non-performance will not be excused, unless the contractor is able to demonstrate that the performance would have become impossible even if there were no delay.[129] This is a general rule applicable to any contract as a suppletive provision, meaning that in a construction contract the parties are free to regulate this situation otherwise, if they do so explicitly.

9.129 As per the specific chapter of the Civil Code regulating "contracts of works", which includes certain types of construction contracts, the contractor is allowed to suspend the works in four situations, one of them being a *Force Majeure* event.[130] Such provision is also suppletive and may be derogated by the parties if they prefer to regulate the matter in a different way.

9.130 It is important to keep in mind that, whenever entering into a contract, the parties are free to allocate the *Force Majeure* risk and establish its consequences as they see fit.[131] However, if no provisions are agreed on this matter and the contract is not fulfilled by reasons considered as *Force Majeure* events, all suppletive provisions in the Civil Code will apply and, as a general rule, there will be no penalties or compensation for losses.

9.131 The Chilean Civil Code incorporates the "*res perit domino*" principle, under which the property is lost to the owner. In addition to this, the breach of one party caused by *Force Majeure* or by a fortuitous event does not entitle the other party to claim for compensation.[132] However, this rule can be modified by the parties in the respective contract if the parties agree to make the party or parties liable in the event of *Force Majeure*.

9.132 *Force Majeure* or a fortuitous event is defined in the Chilean Civil Code as an unexpected event that is not possible to resist, such as the sinking of a ship or an earthquake, among others.[133] Therefore, Chilean law establishes two elements of the *Force Majeure* and fortuitous event, which are the impossibility to foresee and to resist such event, elements that shall be proved by the party claiming the *Force Majeure* event on its own benefit and analyzed on a case-by-case basis[134] by the judge.

9.133 There are some exceptions in the Chilean Civil Code[135] to the general rule explained above about *Force Majeure*. For instance, if one of the parties does not fulfil their obligations in time and manner, and the item to be delivered results damaged due to a fortuitous event which would not have occurred if the item had been delivered to the other party on time and manner, the breaching party shall be liable for the damages caused. The same will happen in the event the fortuitous event occurred as a consequence of the negligence of the obliged party.

129 *Brazilian Civil Code*, 2002 (BR) Article 393; V Civil Law Conference (CJF, 2011) Statement 443: "Case fortuit and *Force Majeure* will only exclude legal liability when the fact that generates the damages is not connected to the activity developed".

130 *Brazilian Civil Code*, 2002 (BR) Article 625(I).

131 I Civil Law Conference (CJF, 2002) Statement 34: "With the exception of the guarantee contained in Article 618 of the Civil Code, other articles referring in particular to the contract of works (Articles 610 to 626) will apply only supplementarily to the contractual terms agreed by the parties to complex contracts of engineering and construction, such as EPC, EPC-M and Alliance".

132 Article 1558, Chilean Civil Code.

133 Article 45, Chilean Civil Code.

134 René Abeliuk Manasevich, *Las Obligaciones*, Fourth Edition, Vol. II, Editorial Jurídica de Chile, 2003, p. 746.

135 Article 1547, Chilean Civil Code.

9.134 It is important to mention that, although Chilean authors make a distinction between *Force Majeure* and fortuitous event (e.g., being the first an act of the competent authority and the second an act of nature like an earthquake), this distinction is not incorporated in the Civil Code which assimilates both concepts and assigns them the same effects.

9.135 Our Supreme Court addressed some of these matters on a recent ruling.[136] The Court stated that an event is unforeseeable when it is not possible to detect the damages before these occur; and that to consider an event as irresistible, the measures to be taken to avoid or mitigate the damages should be useful, appropriate, and effective.

Breach

9.136 Under Brazilian law, when one party fails to comply with any of his duties under a contract or performs it in breach of the contract terms, he is liable for losses caused to the innocent party. If the contract establishes specific timeframes and deadlines for the fulfilment of obligations, the contractor will be in breach whenever he fails to comply with such requirements, despite any formality or notification, unless otherwise prescribed by the contract. If no deadline is agreed in the contract, the party will be in breach only after being notified by the innocent party.[137] The party will not, however, be liable for non-performance if he was not at fault, as in the case of *Force Majeure* or where the owner, by his own breach, prevents the contractor from complying with its obligations in a timely manner.[138]

9.137 As a rule, compensation should cover all losses, including not only the direct damages but also the profits that the party may have reasonably lost by virtue of the infraction.[139] It is also important to note that decisions of the Brazilian Superior Court of Justice reinforce that the parties should cooperate with one another and mitigate their own losses in case of breach.[140] Where one party is in breach, the other party may also be entitled to claim specific performance or termination, as will be explained in the sections below.

9.138 Under Chilean Law, when a party breaches the obligations of a contract, the other party has the right to be indemnified for the damages suffered, with the objective that the aggrieved party is compensated in full by the breaching party. The types of damages that may be indemnified are the actual loss suffered, the loss of profits[141] (also known as

136 Chilean Supreme Court of Justice, Rol No. 68818-2016, 27 July 2017.

137 *Brazilian Civil Code*, 2002 (BR) Article 397.

138 *Brazilian Civil Code*, 2002 (BR) Article 396.

139 *Brazilian Civil Code*, 2002 (BR) Article 402. Article 403 provides that losses and damages only include the actual losses and the loss of profits as its direct and immediate effect. This rule results from the adoption by the Brazilian legal system of the theory of direct and immediate damage, which establishes that, among the all of the causal antecedents, only that one that is a necessary cause of damage will create the duty to indemnify. See, e.g., *RE 130764*, STF, 12 May 1992 (BR) and *REsp 1154737*, 21 October 2010 (BR).

140 *REsp 758.518*, STJ, 28 June 2010 (BR).

141 Article 1556, Chilean Civil Code.

lucrum cessans), chance,[142] and the moral damages,[143] but all of these have to be proven by the innocent party in order to be compensated.

9.139 In addition to this, and as a general rule, a party shall only be liable in the event that party breached the contract and the breach can be attributed to that party. Therefore, if a party breached the contract and caused damages to the other party, the breaching party should indemnify the direct damages that were foreseen or that could have been foreseen by the time the contract was signed.[144] The exception to this are the cases were the breaching party acted with wilful misconduct, as on these cases that party will be liable for all the damages that were a direct consequence of the breach or of the delay in the fulfilment of the obligation (i.e., foreseen and unforeseen by the time the contract was signed). It is also important to stress that these rules can be amended by the parties in the relevant contract if they wish to do so.

9.140 To determine when a party is in breach, Chilean Law makes a distinction between the types of obligations in a contract. If the obligation is negative (i.e., to refrain from certain behaviour), a party will breach the obligation by the time the party does what agreed not to do. If the obligation is positive (to do or deliver something), the party will be in breach: i) If this is not done before the agreed deadline, ii) if the thing or act can only be delivered/executed within certain timeframe and this was not done, and iii) in other cases, since legal proceedings were commenced against the breaching party.[145]

9.141 The duty to mitigate damages is not expressly incorporated in the Chilean Civil Code, but this is an expression of the general obligation to execute contracts in good faith.[146]

Termination

9.142 According to Brazilian Law, when one party is in breach, the innocent party has the right to terminate the contract. This is an implied clause to any contract established under the Brazilian Civil Code.[147] Therefore, where there has been a breach and the contract has no provisions regulating termination, the innocent party may submit to the Court a request for termination of the contract. This is just one option for the innocent party, alternatively it may demand that the contract be complied with. In either case, any claimable losses and damages shall also be compensated.

142 Chilean Supreme Court of Justice, Rol No. 9481-2016, and Mauricio Tapia R. Loss of a chance. Its compensation in Chilean Jurisprudence *Revista de Derecho. Escuela de Postgrado* (2012) (2), pp. 251–64.

143 In relation to companies, this is limited to the damages caused to the reputation of the company or the loss of value of the brands of the company. As the acts that affect the reputation of a Company have a patrimonial or monetary effect, Barros wonders if instead of forcing the application of the moral damages to companies it would be better to appraise the damages according to the patrimonial or monetary rules (actual damages and loss of profits) as a company losses clients and business opportunities but does not have a self-esteem. Enrique Barros Bourie, *Tratado de Responsabilidad Extracontractual*, First Edition, Editorial Jurídica de Chile, year 2007, p. 300.

144 Article 1558, Chilean Civil Code.

145 Article 1551, Chilean Civil Code.

146 Boetsch, quoting Saavedra, states that the good faith in the execution of the contract requires the parties to refrain from causing damages to the other party (Cristián Boetsch Gillet, La Buena Fe Contractual, 2015, Ediciones Universidad Católica de Chile. p. 123).

147 *Brazilian Civil Code*, 2002 (BR) Articles 474 and 475.

9.143 As a general rule, the Civil Code also prescribes that, whenever the obligations of one party become excessively onerous in virtue of extraordinary and unpredictable factors, with unreasonable advantage to the other party, the party suffering excessive burden may terminate the contract if the other does not agree to review the contractual terms accordingly. Therefore, termination may be avoided if the parties can agree to review the contract. The Brazilian Civil Code calls it "excessive onerousness".[148]

9.144 Public contracts, however, due to the public interest in their performance, are subject to specific rules, whereby the contractor may only suspend or terminate the contract in certain situations prescribed in the law. Examples include delay in payments, or suspension of the works for a certain time. If it is a concession or public–private partnership contract, the circumstances in which the contract may be terminated due to breach of the public entity are even more limited.

9.145 Finally, it is important to note that termination for convenience is only applicable if expressly stipulated in the contract, in view of the *pacta sunt servanda* principle.[149]

9.146 It should be noted in relation to public contracts that, due to the public interest involved, the Public Entity, as per various regulations, is entitled to unilaterally terminate the contract at any time. As with any public decision, according to the Brazilian Constitution, it must be properly founded and may be challenged by the contractor, for example, if he is able to demonstrate that the reasons for the decision are incoherent and actually not compatible with the public interest. If the Public Entity decides to unjustifiedly terminate the contract, full compensation is due to the contractor.

9.147 In Chile there is a similar provision to the one applicable in Brazil,[150] as if one of the parties breaches a bilateral contract, the other party can demand, at its option, the termination, or the performance of the contract, plus in both cases compensation for the damages suffered. In addition to this, the parties can agree other causes and/or procedures in relation to the termination of the contract (this is a special type of condition subsequent).

9.148 One big difference with the Brazilian Legal System is that under Chilean Law it is not possible to terminate a contract in case the conditions change (as the parties have a constitutional property right over the intangible rights of the contracts),[151] even if the contract becomes excessively onerous in virtue of extraordinary and unpredictable factors. According to the Chilean Civil Code, the contract is a law for the parties (*pacta sunt servanda*), which can only be invalidated by mutual agreement of the parties or by legal causes, and the excessive onerousness is not one of them.

9.149 However, the Chilean Civil Code[152] in works contracts gives the right to the party that requested the works (even in case the agreed price was a lump sum) to terminate the contract by reimbursing the contractor of all costs, paying the value of the work done and the amount that would have been earned by the contractor.

---

148 *Brazilian Civil Code*, 2002 (BR) Articles 478–80; III Civil Law Conference (CJF, 2004) Statement 176: "In attention to the principle of the preservation of legal transactions, Article 478 of the Civil Code should conduce, whenever possible, to the judicial review of contracts and not the contractual resolution".

149 The Superior Court of Justice of Brazil has already recognized the impossibility of the review of the agreement due to the existence of a specific and agreed provision that may cause an excessive burden to one of the parties. *REsp 831.808/SP*, STJ, 18 May 2006 (BR).

150 Article 1489, Chilean Civil Code.

151 Article 19 No. 24, Chilean Constitution.

152 Article 1999, second paragraph.

9.150 It is also important to mention that on some regulations there are certain provisions that allow one of the parties to an early termination of the contract (same as in Brazil, public contracts in Chile are subject to specific rules).

9.151 For instance, the Regulation for Contracts of Public Works,[153] on Article 151 allows the Direction of the Ministry of Public Works to terminate administratively and unilaterally one or more contracts on certain cases (e.g., if the contractor, its shareholders, or directors are sentenced to three years and one day or more of prison; if the contractor is declared in bankruptcy, etc.). Additionally, Article 148 of this regulation entitles the Direction to an early termination of the contract or to suspend the works in the event there are no sufficient funds or when it is recommendable due to its needs (this shall be informed in written to the contractor).

9.152 Similarly, the Regulation which contains the General Conditions for the Works Contracts for the Housing and Development Services (SERVIU)[154] establishes on Article 91 that the SERVIU shall have the right to suspend the works whenever there are no sufficient funds or when it is recommendable due to the necessities of the SERVIU; and if the contract is suspended for more than two months, the contractor shall have the right to demand the termination of the contract.

9.153 Another example of termination can be found on the Law of Concessions of Public Works,[155] as according to Article 28, the President of the Republic of Chile can terminate a concession provided this is convenient for the public interest and other requirements are met. Other case can be found on Article 36, third paragraph, of Law No. 18.695 of City Halls, which allows the city halls to terminate concessions at any time for reasons of public interest.[156]

Remedies

Remedies under Contract

9.154 As set out above, in the case of breach of a private contract, the innocent party is generally entitled to terminate the contract or to demand specific performance. In both cases, the losses to be compensated by the party in breach will include reasonable loss of profits that are directly caused by the breach, unless specified otherwise.[157] If it is a financial obligation, interest and monetary adjustment will be due. However, the parties may agree on specific compensation in case of complete breach, so that the innocent party may choose between demanding the full performance of the obligation or the payment of such specific compensation. In this case, the innocent party does not need to demonstrate any losses to claim the specific compensation, but it shall be understood as full compensation. Supplementary compensation will only be demandable if expressly entitled in

153 Decree No. 75 of the Ministry of Public Works of 2004.

154 Decree No. 236 of the Ministry of Housing and Urbanism of 2003.

155 Decree with force of Law No. 900 of the Ministry of Public Works of 1996.

156 Another case can be found on Article 13 of Law 19.886 (Bases of Administrative Contracts of Supply and Rendering of Services) which establishes that the contracts can be terminated early under certain circumstances. However, according to Article 3 of this law, the contracts related to the execution and concession of public works are specifically excluded from its application.

157 *Brazilian Civil Code*, 2002 (BR) Article 430.

the contract, subject to clear demonstration that the losses were greater than the specific compensation.[158]

9.155 Unless it is specified in the contract,[159] the specific compensation shall not be understood as an option for the party to not perform, meaning that it cannot choose between performing or paying the specific compensation. Indeed, the innocent party may decide to demand performance, including specific execution, or termination and specific compensation.[160] If the specific compensation is agreed in case of delay, specific performance may be demanded together with the specific compensation for delay.[161]

9.156 Similar to Brazilian Law, under Chilean Law the parties may agree in the contract the effects that a breach of contract may have. Examples of this are the early termination of the contract, the obligation to perform an additional action, the application of liquidated damages (which can be demanded by the aggrieved party without the need to prove the damages suffered),[162] among others.

9.157 Once a party is in breach of a relevant part of its contractual obligations, if liquidated damages have been agreed the other party is entitled to require the other party, at its option, to fulfil the original obligation or to pay the liquidated damages. However, the aggrieved party may require both the fulfilment of the original obligation and the payment of the liquidated damages if after reviewing the contract it appears that the liquidated damages were agreed for the event of delay in the fulfilment of the obligations, or if this was expressly agreed by the parties.[163] This is because liquidated damages have three objectives: i) An in advance appraisal of the damages, ii) a guarantee of the obligation, and iii) a civil penalty (being the latter discussed by the authors in Chile).[164]

9.158 It is important to mention that there is a limit for the liquidated damages or penalties that can be agreed by the parties as these cannot exceed the double of the original obligation,[165] and that in the event the actual damages are higher than the amount of the liquidated damages that were agreed, the aggrieved party can claim the actual damages instead of the liquidated damages (however, in this case the actual damages shall have to be proven by that party).

Remedies under Law

9.159 According to the Brazilian Civil Code, as a general rule[166] applicable to private contracts, parties may not, before fulfilling their own obligations, require performance by the other. It means that a party delayed or in breach may not demand performance of the other party.

9.160 If a construction contract is considered a typical contract of works and the suppletive provisions of the Civil Code are not excluded by the parties, then the contractor is

158 *Brazilian Civil Code*, 2002 (BR) Article 416.

159 Nery and Nery Jr, *Código Civil Comentado* (Revista dos Tribunais, 7th Edition, 2009) 518.

160 *Brazilian Civil Code*, 2002 (BR) Article 410.

161 *Brazilian Civil Code*, 2002 (BR) Articles 410 and 411.

162 Article 1542, Chilean Civil Code.

163 Article 1537, Chilean Civil Code.

164 René Abeliuk Manasevich, *Las Obligaciones*, Fourth Edition, Vol. II, Editorial Jurídica de Chile, 2003, p. 801

165 Article 1544, Chilean Civil Code.

166 *Brazilian Civil Code*, 2002 (BR) Article 476.

entitled to suspend the works in certain cases. These would include reasons attributable to the owner and also unforeseen geological or hydrological conditions that render the performance more onerous to the contractor, if the owner does not agree to review the price. The contractor may also suspend the works if the owner requests technical modifications and does not agree to review the contract price accordingly.[167]

9.161 In case of breach, the innocent party is always allowed to demand specific performance in a lawsuit, plus losses, unless performance becomes useless to him and he prefers to demand the payment of damages.[168]

9.162 As per the Brazilian Procedural Code,[169] the Court is allowed to order a series of remedies at the request of the innocent party, where there has been a breach or non-performance. Subject to the evidence presented to the Court, preliminary injunctions may be awarded, including coercive remedies that can lead to the equivalent practical result of specific performance.

9.163 To incentivize performance, the Court may fix a specific fine to be imposed to the party in breach where it does not comply with the measures determined by the Court.

9.164 The demand for performance will not succeed if it is impossible to achieve such a result or if the plaintiff prefers to terminate the contract and demand full compensation for its losses and damages.

9.165 Similar to Brazilian Law, on bilateral contracts under Chilean Law a party that has not fulfilled its obligations is not obliged under the contract if the other party has not fulfilled its obligations as well or if the other party has not performed any acts with the object to fulfil its obligations in time and manner.[170]

9.166 Therefore, if one of the parties in a bilateral contract is in breach and the other party fulfilled its obligations or has performed acts with the purpose to fulfil its obligations, then the innocent party is entitled to demand the termination or the performance of the contract, plus compensation in both cases.

9.167 As mentioned before, the possibility to review the contract in case of excessive onerousness does not exist as a general principle under Chilean Law, although there are some exceptions that will be described in the following title.

9.168 An important case is Article 2003 of the Chilean Civil Code, which refers to construction contracts on which the price agreed is a lump sum. Although the first rule of Article 2003 does not allow the contractor to demand an increase in the price in case the wages of the workers or the materials to be used turn out to be more expensive, the second rule allows the contractor to request the owner to cover expenses that were not foreseeable, provided these were caused by unknown circumstances, such as a hidden vice of the terrain. In the event the owner refuses to approve such costs, the contractor has the right to take this matter to the courts to decide the conflict.

Judicial Review

9.169 Contracts in Brazil are subject to judicial review in various circumstances, particularly if they are considered null or, for any legal reason, defective or ineffective. These

167 *Brazilian Civil Code*, 2002 (BR) Article 625.
168 *Brazilian Civil Code*, 2002 (BR) Article 395.
169 *Brazilian Civil Procedure Code*, 2015 (BR) Articles 300, 301, 497, 499, and 501.
170 Article 1552, Chilean Civil Code.

cases may lead to rescission of the contract, in which case the Court will try to restore the parties to the positions they were in before entering into the contract.[171] The judicial review may address a certain clause of the contract which is considered illegal in which case it may be possible for the agreement to be kept intact.[172]

9.170 The Civil Code also establishes situations where a perfectly valid contract may be adjusted by the Court to meet unforeseen conditions. As explained above, in a situation of excessive onerousness, termination may be avoided if the contract is rebalanced by the parties. According to case law, the Courts may review the contractual conditions when unforeseeable and unpredictable events make them very onerous to perform for one party, to the advantage of the other, and the parties are unable to reach an agreement as to an adjustment to the conditions to take into account these events.[173] Case law shows that, when assessing excessive onerousness, the Courts are much more rigorous in analyzing the unpredictability of the event and the actual impact on the economic balance of the contract than in verifying the advantage to the other party, which tends to be an incidental factor.[174]

9.171 It is important to note that the excessive onerousness provision is mostly understood as a suppletive provision.[175] As explained, in construction contracts, the parties may set their own allocation of risks and this allocation shall be observed by the Court, in such a way that the judicial review would not occur in relation to a circumstance that was agreed to be part of the risk taken on by a party.[176] Furthermore, extraordinary and unpredictable events will not justify a judicial review if that event is covered by risks which are inherent to that specific contract.[177]

9.172 In the chapter regulating "contracts of works", the Civil Code establishes other suppletive provisions under which the contractor is entitled to demand a price review, such as when technical modifications are made at the request of or with the tacit agreement of the owner.[178] On the other hand, if the costs of material or workmanship are reduced by more than one-tenth of the agreed global price, then the owner may demand a price review.[179]

9.173 The Court is allowed under the Civil Code to equitably reduce specific compensation contractually agreed if it was agreed in respect of non-performance of a certain duty and the duty was partially performed. It should also be noted that a contract which is considered a consumer contract will be subject to specific regulations, according to which judicial review will be admitted more broadly, in protection of consumers.

9.174 Finally, it is also important to note that public contracts, according to specific regulations rather than the Civil Code, may also be subject to judicial review in various

171 *Brazilian Civil Code*, 2002 (BR) Article 182.

172 *Brazilian Civil Code*, 2002 (BR) Article 184.

173 *REsp 1321614*, STJ, 3 March 2015 (BR).

174 See Statement 365 in IV Civil Law Conference (CJF, 2007).

175 Cf Martins, "A Onerosidade Excessiva no Código Civil: Instrumento de Manutenção da Justa Repartição dos Riscos Negociais" [2007] 8 *Revista de Direito Privado* 253.

176 See Statements 439 and 440 in V Civil Law Conference (CJF, 2007).

177 Nery and Nery Jr (n 86) 579–81.

178 *Brazilian Civil Code*, 2002 (BR) Articles 619 and 620.

179 *Brazilian Civil Code*, 2002 (BR) Article 620.

circumstances, whenever an extraordinary and unpredictable circumstance affects their economical balance.

9.175 In Chile there is no general rule which allows the judicial review of the contracts. Although a few authors argue that this could be admissible due to the general duty to execute contracts in good faith, this has not been broadly accepted neither by the Chilean courts[180] nor by the major part of the authors.[181] In Chile a contract is a law for the parties which can only be invalidated by mutual agreement or for legal grounds,[182] as the law establishes specific cases on which contracts can be reviewed by the courts.

9.176 For instance, if a contract has a vice that can be considered as a cause of nullity, the parties can start a proceeding to request the judge to declare the nullity of the contract, in full or in part. As mentioned before, Chilean Civil Code distinguishes between absolute nullity and relative nullity; these two types of nullity have different causes and features but once declared have the exact same effect. It is important to mention that on some cases absolute nullity can be declared *ex officio*,[183] whilst relative nullity can only be declared if requested by the parties.[184]

9.177 As to the effects, before a contract is declared null it will be valid and binding for the parties, but if the contract is declared null by the judge, and similar to Brazilian Law, the parties have the right to be restored to the position they would have been had the contract not been made.[185]

9.178 In the Law of Concessions of Public Works there is a provision which allows the concessionaire to demand compensation in the event there is an act of the competent authority that substantially affects the economical regime of the contract and other requisites are complied with.[186] In addition to this, in the relevant works contract other exceptional cases can be agreed by the parties as long as these were part of the terms of the tender, so the possibilities to revise the contract in public contracts are broader than in private contracts.[187]

9.179 Another case would be if the parties agree in the contract that any disputes shall be settled by an *ex aequo et bono* arbitrator, as on these cases the arbitrator will decide the conflict considering his own prudence and equity and not the applicable law.[188] Therefore, this opens the possibility to review the contract in a judicial proceeding, so a party that may be a victim of excessive onerousness could have a way out on these cases.

9.180 Finally, only under Article 2003 No. 2 of the Chilean Civil Code it can be said that the possibility of judicial review exists, since this provision allows the judge to make a decision in the event the owner and the constructor do not reach an agreement. However,

180 Jorge López Santa María, *Los Contratos, Parte General, Vol. II, Fourth Edition*, Editorial Jurídica de Chile, 2005, p. 304.

181 René Abeliuk Manasevich, *Las Obligaciones*, Fourth Edition, Editorial Jurídica de Chile, 2003, Vol. I, pp. 119 and 120, and Vol. II pp. 761 to 763.

182 Article 1545, Chilean Civil Code.

183 Article 1683, Chilean Civil Code.

184 Article 1684, Chilean Civil Code

185 Article 1687, Chilean Civil Code.

186 Article 19 of the Decree with Force of Law No. 900 of the Ministry of Public Works of 1996.

187 Article 19, 2nd paragraph, of the Decree with Force of Law No. 900 of the Ministry of Public Works of 1996.

188 Article 223 paragraph 3, Organic Code of the Courts.

a requirement for the application of this article is that the costs must be a consequence of unforeseeable circumstances.

Limitation on Remedies

9.181 Under the general rule of freedom to contract in Brazil, parties can agree on specific remedies that are suitable to them and limit or extend their liability by incorporating in contracts specific provisions which prevail over the suppletive rules of the Civil Code.

9.182 There is a discussion as to whether parties are able to render inapplicable the legal provisions related to excessive onerousness, as these provisions might be considered as a public order matter. However, as explained above, parties are free to agree on a specific allocation of risks that suit their interests. In this case, if the parties regulate the matter in their own interest, making clear that the excessive onerousness provisions will not apply in the exact terms prescribed in the Civil Code, such agreement is likely to prevail.

9.183 The Superior Court of Justice has also accepted, in some cases, that the substantial fulfilment of an obligation may release the party from claims for remedies, although this situation is not expressly covered in the Brazilian Civil Code. It applies to a situation where a party has not complied with its obligation fully but has done so substantially and, by a proportionality analysis, the contract may keep its full effectiveness in relation to both parties. The Superior Court of Justice understands that the substantial performance theory may be inferred from the principle of good faith,[189] the principal of proportionality and the prohibition of abuse of rights[190] but must be applied with care and sparingly.[191]

9.184 Under Chilean law it is also possible to agree on specific remedies or to limit or extend the liability of the parties in the relevant contract, which is an expression of the principle of party autonomy.

9.185 Since such a concept is not regulated, the abovementioned subsequent excessive burden, does not apply in Chile. Notwithstanding the foregoing, the parties may agree on modifying the contract in case certain events rendered some or all obligations under the contract excessively onerous.

9.186 With respect to contract compliance, and as it occurs in Brazil, substantial compliance of the obligations of one of the parties may release that party from the contractual remedies to which the other party is entitled. An example of that is the *exceptio non rite adimpleti contractus* which is the exception that the defendant bases on the fact that the plaintiff did not fully comply with all of his obligations; however, if the unpaid part is insignificant, this exception should be repudiated as it contravenes objective good faith.[192] In consequence, a party could not be excused from complying with the contract if the other party has substantially complied with its obligations, even though it has not complied fully, to the extent that the unfulfilled part is irrelevant or is not an important

189 IV Civil Law Conference (CJF, 2009) Statement 294: "Substantial performance results from the general contractual principles, in a way to preponderate the social function of the contract and the principle of objective good faith, balancing the application of Article 475".

190 *Brazilian Civil Code*, 2002 (BR) Article 187, which prescribes that anyone who, exercising his right clearly exceeds the limits imposed by its economic or social purpose or by good faith also commits an unlawful act.

191 *REsp 1581505*, STJ, 28 September 2016 (BR).

192 Jorge López Santa María, *Los Contratos, Parte General*, Vol. II, Fourth Edition, Editorial Jurídica de Chile, 2005, p. 557.

obligation, as it has been declared by the Supreme Court.[193] This should be analyzed on a case-by-case basis by the judge, who shall determine whether the unfulfilled part of the obligation is or not essential.

9.187 As has been pointed out, it is possible to extend or limit the liability of the parties,[194] provided that this does not alter public order rules.[195]

Interpretation of Contracts

9.188 The Brazilian Civil Code prescribes that contracts shall be interpreted in good-faith and considering the local common practices.[196] It is also prescribed that the intention of the parties shall prevail over the literal meaning of the language.[197]

9.189 However, it should be noted that the goal of contractual interpretation is not just to understand the innermost thoughts and wishes of the parties, but rather to ascertain the aim of the agreement, starting from the meaning of the words and phrases used in the contract, and, whenever necessary, considering the economic and social context, the participants' qualifications,[198] and the other circumstances under which each agreement was made.

9.190 Some specific statements should be interpreted restrictively, such as renouncements and waivers.[199] In this sense, if a statement discharges a party from a specific obligation, declaring that it has been fulfilled, it shall be interpreted strictly so that it does not cover other obligations.

9.191 It is important to mention that there is nothing in Brazil similar to the parole evidence rule meaning that the parties can rely on letters, meeting minutes and witness evidence relating to the pre-contractual and contractual phases to support a certain contractual interpretation. A judge may also give preference to an interpretation that produces an effect rather than the one that does not produce one, and may also conduct a systematic analysis of the contractual provisions so that there is a correlation between the different clauses. Finally, where there is doubt the general rule is that an interpretation that benefits the party that did not draft the clause will be made.[200]

---

193 Chilean Supreme Court role No. 4693-2006 (grounds 5° and 7°), and role No. 951-2013 (ground 11°).

194 Article 1547 final paragraph, Chilean Civil Code.

195 Regarding liability limitations, they are also admitted, but with certain exceptions, such as Article 1465, according to which remission of future wilful misconduct is not valid, a prohibition that would extend to gross negligence, since in civil matters gross negligence is equivalent to wilful misconduct (Article 44). Nor is it possible to establish clauses limiting damages caused to persons, such as injury or death, since they are not in the trade and, therefore, are not disposable (Hernán Corral Talciani, *Cláusulas De Exención, Limitación y Agravación De Responsabilidad Civil EnPerjuicio Del Consumidor, First Edition,* in Estudios de Derecho Civil VI, JornadasNacionales de Derecho Civil, Olmué 2010, Editorial Abeledo Perrot 2011, p. 664).

196 *Brazilian Civil Code*, 2002 (BR) Article 113.

197 *Brazilian Civil Code*, 2002 (BR) Article 112.

198 Venosa, Direito Civil (Atlas, 3rd Edition, 2003) 451.

199 *Brazilian Civil Code*, 2002 (BR) Article 114.

200 The need to ensure a more favorable interpretation of the contract to the party who's agreed to the contractual terms drafted by the other derives from the objective good faith (Article 422 of the *CC* 2002 (BR)); as established in Statement 26 of the I Civil Law Conference promulgated by the Center for Legal Studies of the Council of Federal Justice of Brazil (CJF) in 2002: "The general clause contained in Article. 422 of the new Civil Code requires the court to interpret and, when necessary, supplement and correct the contract according to objective good faith, understood as the requirement of the parties' fair behavior".

9.192 The Chilean Civil Code has similar provisions to the Brazilian Civil Code, as once the intention of the parties is clearly known it shall prevail over the wording of the contract.[201]

9.193 Additionally, and as an integrating element, there is the application of the principle of good faith to interpret contracts, given that contracts must be executed in good faith, and, therefore, do not only oblige to what expressed therein but to all things that by the nature of the obligation arise therefrom, or that by the law or custom belong thereto.[202]

9.194 Other rules provide that the interpretation that can produce an effect shall be preferred over the interpretation that causes no effect whatsoever;[203] and that the clauses in a contract shall be interpreted considering the contract as a whole, even allowing the parties to consider other contracts between the same parties as long as these refer to the same subject matter.

9.195 The clauses of the contract can also be interpreted considering the practical application that the parties have given to these, or by one of the parties with the approval of the other party, which is an expression of the doctrine of own acts (estoppel).

9.196 In the event it is not possible to apply the rules mentioned above of the Civil Code, there is a subsidiary article which provides that the ambiguous clauses shall be interpreted in favour of the debtor, and that the ambiguous clauses drafted by one of the parties shall be interpreted against that party as long as the ambiguity was due to the lack of explanation from that party[204] (*contra proferentem* rule).

9.197 With respect to the interpretation of contracts, this is a matter of fact which is not subject to the cassation control of the Supreme Court. Notwithstanding the foregoing, if due to the interpretative labour the contract is denatured, it is possible that the Supreme Court annuls that kind of decisions.

Construction Law Principles

Procurement and Tendering

9.198 Brazilian construction law is essentially divided into two different systems – public and private. The public system is generally more relevant due to the strong participation of the State in the national development.

9.199 The key principle that should be understood when talking about public contracts in Brazil is that the regime grants the Public Administration the power to modify several aspects of the contract in benefit of the public interest,[205] for example, to terminate the contract or to modify its scope. The Federal Constitution does, however, protect the

---

201 Article 1560, Chilean Civil Code.

202 Article 1546, Chilean Civil Code.

203 Article 1562, Chilean Civil Code.

204 Article 1566, Chilean Civil Code.

205 "It should be clear that the Public Administration cannot change the contract on its own convenience, to satisfy the State's exclusive interests (e.g., merely financial interests not linked to actual collective interest). In order to be legitimate, the modification must be motivated by obtaining benefits to society or improvements to the construction, service or supply. The contract's modification is always related to the correct performance of the contracted object. It is bound to the public objective of the contract, and not to the Public Administration's interests". Klein, Reisdorfer and Olbertz, "Government Contracts in Brazilian Law" in Marçal and Pereira (ed), *Infrastructure Law of Brazil* (Fórum, 2nd Edition, 2010) 151.

original economic-financial balance of the contract, which must be maintained, even if the Public Administration exercises one of its prerogatives of modification.[206] This regime, therefore, establishes the need for an equivalence of the mutual consideration provided by the parties at the outset of the agreement and throughout contract performance. In practice, in construction contracts, this means that the parties are under the constant obligation to maintain this equilibrium.

9.200 As for public procurement and tendering of construction works and engineering services, the federal, state and municipal public authorities are subject to the same law[207] which provides general rules for procurement, tendering, formation, modification, termination, suspension, including in relation specifically to construction contracts.

9.201 Under Brazilian private law, the provisions relating to contracts are in general suppletive meaning that the parties have the right to derogate from such provisions and determine the rules for their particular relationship. However, there are certain provisions (called "public order provisions") that cannot be derogated from by the parties as they reflect precepts relating to collective interests that transcend those of the parties directly involved.[208] This means that, although the parties are free to choose contractual forms and their contents, there are universal contractual rules set out by statutory law that must be followed. Moreover, the parties must act in good faith,[209] and the contract must fulfil its social purpose.[210]

9.202 In Chile, like in Brazil, there is also a private and a public construction regime, being the latter's regulation much more detailed than the private regimes.

9.203 For public construction contracts there are rules that regulate the power of the State to modify the contract or to terminate it in certain cases and upon compliance with certain requirements, but *ius variandi* is not considered as a generic right for the State that may be exercised in any situation (it is worth noting that such right does not exist under the private regime of the Civil Code).

9.204 In Chile, there are certain principles applicable to the procurement process and tendering, among which we find the principles of strict subjection to the bidding rules, equality between bidders, free competition to tender, legality or lawfulness, efficiency, and transparency.[211]

9.205 Finally, although in Chile contracts must be executed in good faith, it is not a requirement that the contract complies with a social role, since it can be perfectly entered into by the mere particular interest of the parties. However, public contracts must be based on a public need.

---

206 *Constitution of Brazil*, Article 37 (XXI).

207 *Law 14133 2021* (which replaced *Law 8666* 1993) (BR).

208 "Although the most important rule is that of party autonomy, there are restrictions imposed by social interest laws, preventing arrangements that go against morality, public order and good practice, which are not subject to the will of the parties" Rizzardo, *Contratos* (Forense, 12th Edition, 2011) 21.

209 *Brazilian Civil Code*, 2002 (BR) Article 422.

210 *Brazilian Civil Code*, 2002 (BR) Article 421.

211 These principles are found in the following legal instruments: Law 19,886 on the Bases on Administrative Contracts for Supply and Provision of Services; the Law on Concessions of Public Works (Statutory Decree No. 164 of 1991) and its regulations (Supreme Decree No. 956 of 1999); the Supreme Decree No. 75 of the Ministry of Public Works of 2004 that approves the Regulation for Public Works Contracts; the Supreme Decree No. 236 of 2003 approving the General Rules Regulations for the Contracting of Works for Housing and Urbanization Services (SERVIU); and Law No. 19,865 on Shared Urban Financing.

Different Types of Contract (Unit Price, Lump Sum, etc.)

9.206 The public procurement law in Brazil sets out broad definitions of the contract types for unit price, lump sum and "*empreitada integral*" which can be loosely translated as turn-key. There is also a relatively new model for public EPC contracts called "*contratação integrada*"[212] which has been introduced in Brazil in specific cases, usually for major and priority government projects. This new model of public contracting is still subject to the constitutional protection of the original economic-financial balance of the contract.

9.207 Regarding private contracts there are very few limitations on the contract types that can be entered into under the principle of party autonomy.[213]

9.208 Under the Chilean Civil Code, there is freedom of contract for the parties to enter into the contracts they deem relevant, save for some exceptions, and to include the terms they freely agree upon. Notwithstanding the foregoing, the Civil Code contains certain provisions regarding works construction contracts, that refer to specific contracts or under specific terms such as the lump sum contract,[214] regulating some particular rules for them.

9.209 On the other hand, Supreme Decree No. 75 establishes certain contractual categories, setting out different payment methods for the contracts entered into, such as delegated administration, lump sum proposal, proposal of series of unitary prices and the compensated budget.[215] Likewise, the Supreme Decree No. 236[216] also incorporates some of these definitions[217] and indicates that the hiring systems that may be used are the lump sum, series of unitary prices and delegated administration.[218]

9.210 In a different way than Supreme Decrees No. 75 and 236, the Law of Concessions of Public Works establishes that the concessionaire will receive as only compensation for the services rendered the mutually agreed price, fee or subsidy, as well as other additional benefits expressly agreed upon,[219] not including, therefore, the contractual categories aforementioned. Definitely, regarding the object of the concession contract, the Law of Concessions of Public Works is similar to a turnkey contract, given that the concessionaire must comply with the level of service and technical standards determined by the concession contract, being at his cost and risk the necessary works to comply with such requirements.

Nature of Construction Contracts

9.211 In Brazil, public construction contracts will generally be construed as administrative contracts, subject to a specific regime and regulations.

9.212 Private construction contracts, on the other hand, are subject to civil regulation. Among the contract types provided for in the Civil Code, the one applicable to

212 *Federal Law 12462* 2011 (BR) Article 9.

213 Among the many precedents in this sense: *REsp 1388972*, STJ, 13 March 2017 (BR).

214 Articles 1999 and 2003, Chilean Civil Code.

215 Article 4, Supreme Decree No. 75.

216 Article 6 of Supreme Decree No. 236 also considers another manner, which is the Bidding Offers, which consists in the attendance of business teams to tenders for Housing and Urbanization Services, which will be tendered exclusively by the system of lump sum price.

217 Article 2, Supreme Decree No. 236.

218 Article 5, Supreme Decree No. 236.

219 Article 11, Law of Concessions of Public Works.

construction projects is the "*empreitada*",[220] which can be loosely translated as a contract of works. It should be noted, however, that the rules defining contracts of works do not encompass the complexity of large construction projects. One of the implications of this lack of legislation is that there are no specific legal provisions for prevailing international contract models such as FIDIC. While there are differing and conflicting views on how construction contracts are dealt with in the Civil Code, as typical or atypical contracts,[221] this distinction should be given a great deal of attention when negotiating private construction contracts in Brazil as it may have a significant impact on risk management.

9.213 As in Brazil, in Chile the public construction contract is considered an Administrative Contract,[222] which is governed by the regulatory bodies previously detailed (laws and regulations). Notwithstanding this, in the Chilean Civil Code there are rules regarding contracts for the building of material works, which are applicable to any type of construction contract, except for certain articles referred to specific cases.[223]

9.214 Private contracts are regulated by the rules of the Civil Code and provisions that for those purposes the parties agree upon, which reflects the principle of autonomy of the will. Given that in Chile, the regulation of the private construction contracts is relatively scarce, this gives a more important role to what the parties agree upon in the respective contracts, and, therefore, more room for international construction contract models, to the extent these do not modify Chilean public order rules.

Design Obligations

9.215 In Brazil, in order to create equal conditions for bidders for public projects, the State is obliged to provide the bidders with a project design. Therefore, public construction contracts are generally restricted to procurement and construction, and do not feature the engineering activities, as in a typical EPC contract. The exception is the new EPC model mentioned above, in which the Contractor is responsible for the concept and designs (basic and executive), however, the possibility of amendment to these public contracts is restricted to cases of *Force Majeure* and technical adaptation of the project requested by the government.

9.216 Regarding private contracts, based on the principle of party autonomy, Brazilian legislation does not restrict whether the contractor may or may not also be in charge of the concept, engineering and design processes.

9.217 In Chile, Supreme Decree No. 75[224] establishes procurement and construction from the contractor's perspective, who must carry out the work in accordance with the

220 *Brazilian Civil Code*, 2002 (BR) Articles 610-626.

221 "Engineering is considered an atypical contract of the mixed contract type, in the sense that it results from the juxtaposition of features representative of different typical contracts. Some authors qualify it, however, as a special kind of contract of works ("*empreitada*"), and others believe that it merges with the so-called mixed contract of works ("*empreitada mista*"), forming an unique entity" Gomes, *Contratos* (Forense, 26th Edition, 2009) 579.

222 Mauricio Viñuela Hojas, *El Contrato de Concesión de Obra Pública. Una Ratificación Legislativa de las Categorías Conceptuales del Contrato Administrativo*, Revista de Derecho Administrativo, No. 1, 2007, p. 39 and following (Thomson Reuters online quotation code: CL/DOC/168/2011).

223 As Articles 2003, 2004 (which refer to the lump sum construction contract), and 2005.

224 In other sense of DS 75 we have the Supreme Decree 108 of 2009 dictated by the Ministry of Public Works that approves the General Administrative Bases for Contracts for the Execution of Works by Payment System Against Reception, which establishes that in those contracts governed by this Supreme Decree, all

administrative bases, technical specifications, general and detailed plans, profiles and specifications of the project.[225] However, this decree allows tenderers to submit modifications to specific parts of the project to the extent that they mean savings for the Treasury and that is authorized by the administrative bases,[226] which can also be done during the performance of the contract.[227]

9.218 Supreme Decree No. 236 contemplates different manners and allows, according to the respective tender, to define if the design will be presented by the contractor or delivered by the public institution.

9.219 On the other hand, in the Law of Concessions of Public Works the contract is a true turnkey contract, so the regular practise is that the Ministry delivers a referential a project.

9.220 In relation to private contracts, and as in Brazil, in Chile what the parties agree on the design and engineering of the Project will be applicable, which is an expression of the principle of autonomy of the will.

Duty to Warn/Check/Review

9.221 The contractor and engineers in a construction contract under Brazilian law have an obligation as to the result of the project,[228] meaning that they are obliged to deliver the works in accordance with the agreed time, quality, safety and other specifications, which implies that the constructor also has a general duty to warn, check and review. Moreover, the principle of good faith and the liability for the solidity and safety of the works applicable to both public and private contracts[229] reinforce this general duty. In the case of private contracts for works everything that is paid is presumed verified,[230] which implies that the owner has a duty to check.[231]

9.222 Under Chilean law the duties are the same ones. The Law of Urbanism and Construction[232] establishes a strict liability regime[233] in case of flaws or defects of construction that have caused damages,[234] so that in order not to fall into default, the obligation must be fulfilled comprehensively. This law also extends this liability to the professionals who have intervened in the works, establishing a concurrent liability[235] with respect to the

responsibility for the design, even based on erroneous antecedents provided by the Ministry will be the responsibility of the contractor.

225 Article 142 Supreme Decree No. 75.

226 Article 79, Supreme Decree No. 75.

227 Article 107, Supreme Decree No. 75.

228 "Since the contract of works creates an obligation of result, the contractor has the duty to deliver the work free from any defects, incurring in contractual fault if the agreement is breached" – *AREsp 348764*, STJ, 4 September 2013 (BR).

229 *Brazilian Civil Code*, 2002 (BR) Article 618.

230 *Brazilian Civil Code*, 2002 (BR) Article 614(1).

231 "If the owner receives the works and pays for what has been delivered, the works are presumed to be verified and in order" – *REsp 1446315*, STJ, 11 September 2015 (BR).

232 Statutory Decree No. 458 de 1976, Ministry of Housing and Urbanism,

233 Hernán Corral Talciani. *Responsabilidad civil en la construcción de viviendas. Reflexiones sobre los regímenes legales aplicables a los daños provocados por el terremoto del 27 de febrero de 2010*. p. 2. Available at: www.scielo.cl/pdf/rchilder/v37n3/art03.pdf.

234 Article 18, Statutory Decree No. 458.

235 This liability arises from different causes and allows the aggrieved party to claim the full amount of the damages from any of the parties to which it applies.

architect, civil engineer or civil constructor, who must be individualized in the respective construction permit. The law does not make the involved parties as jointly and severally liable, but the provision has a similar effect as the innocent party will be able to claim the total amount of the damages from any of the parties to which it applies.[236]

9.223 On the other hand, the Chilean Civil Code establishes in its Article 2003 No. 3 the objective liability of the constructor in case the building perishes or threatens ruin,[237] in all or in part, due to a flaw in the construction, a defect in the soil that the builder should have known or in the materials, unless they are supplied by the owner (in which case a special rule applies). Therefore, the builder has the duty to properly carry out the construction, to duly review the soil and the materials to be used, and to act diligently in the fulfilment of his obligations. In addition, the Civil Code establishes in matters of torts liability that the assessment of the damage is subject to reduction if the person who suffered it was exposed to it recklessly,[238] a principle that could be considered as related to the general duty to prevent and mitigate damages.

9.224 DS No. 75 establishes the obligation of the contractor to timely warn the Ministry of Public Works about mistakes in the designs of the Ministry. If this is done, the repair of the flaws will not be borne by the contractor; otherwise, the degree of liability of the contractor should be determined for not having detected and reported said design mistakes, which may be up to 50% of the works repair costs.[239]

Consultant's Role and Liability

9.225 In the case of both public and private construction contracts, the architectural and engineering services, including consultancy, are subject to the technical terms of responsibility before the Regional Board of Engineering, Architecture, and Agronomy.[240] The contractor and engineers responsible for the execution of the works will always have certain responsibilities to the private owner[241,242] or the public authority in case of defects and be responsible for the safety and solidity of the works. However, the consultant may be also liable to the extent that the defects arise from the failure of the consultancy provided.

9.226 In Chile, as mentioned above, the General Law on Urbanism and Construction establishes the liability of professionals, who will have a concurrent liability for damages and injuries suffered by the works, in the terms indicated in Article 16 et seq. of the law (it is worth noting that this legislation is applicable to works that require municipal authorization). Furthermore, this law regulates the liability of the independent auditor, who will be subsidiarily liable for the architect who carries out the project, in relation to

236 Hernán Corral Talciani. *Obligaciones por el total no solidarias u obligaciones concurrentes*. En Estudios de Derecho Civil X, Legal Publishing Chile, 2015, p. 466.

237 The threat of ruin also refers to the functional ruin of the work, that is, when it has lost a significant part of its capacity to provide the service that it must fulfil. In this sense, Enrique Barros points out that "*the flaws of a construction can be understood ... as that quality that prevents it from its natural destination*" (Enrique Barros Bouric, op. cit. p. 773).

238 Article 2330, Chilean Civil Code.

239 Article 150, final paragraph, DS No. 75.

240 *L6496* 1977 (BR).

241 *Brazilian Civil Code*, 2002 (BR) Article 618.

242 *AgRg no AREsp 176664*, STJ, 28 February 2014 (BR).

the construction project and that its works comply with the applicable legal, regulatory and technical standards.[243]

9.227 On the other hand, the Civil Code establishes that the rule of Article 2003 No. 3, to which we have already referred, is also applicable to professionals who participate in the design or construction of the works as consultants.[244]

Sub-Contracting

9.228 In Brazil, in relation to public contracts, the contractor is generally entitled to subcontract parts of the construction, under the conditions provided by the law, and that every request for subcontracting must be submitted for approval to the relevant public body. This provides a significant restriction for subcontracting in the case of public construction contracts which may become a burden for large projects. It should also be noted that subcontracting does not exempt the contractor from legal liability of the subcontracted parts. As a result, the contractor shall be held accountable for any damages resulting from parts of the project that have been subcontracted.

9.229 Regarding private construction contracts, there is no general limitation for subcontracting works and the parties will be able to agree on whether subcontracting is possible and the extent to which this may be done. It should be noted that the contractor in a private contract is generally liable for damages incurred by the owner and third parties, even if some parts of the works are subcontracted.[245] Moreover, the subcontractor will be jointly liable for the works performed.

9.230 It is important to note that there may be labour law limitations regarding outsourcing of activities understood to be the core business of the construction company, which may be relevant when defining what parts of the works may be subcontracted or outsourced.

9.231 Chilean law allows, as a general rule, to subcontract, which may be done in whole or in part. However, there are certain limitations and restrictions regarding public contracts, especially in the field of construction.

9.232 The Law of Concessions of Public Works allows the concessionaire to subcontract all or part of the design, construction, and/or exploitation of the works. In case of subcontracting the construction, this shall be done only with contractors registered in the registry of the Ministry of Public Works.[246]

9.233 According to DS 75,[247] the contractor may only subcontract part of the works to the extent that he is authorized to do so, being understood that he shall remain liable for all obligations contracted with the Ministry. Likewise, subcontractors must be registered in the relevant registry, and may subcontract up to 30% of the total value of the contract.

---

243 Article 116 bis, New General Law of Urbanism and Construction.

244 Article 2004 of the Chilean Civil Code, which also makes rules No. 4 and 5 of Article 2003 applicable to architects.

245 "In a contract of works in which parts of the construction have been subcontracted, the legal relationship is formed between the general contractor and the subcontractor. There is no legal bond between the subcontractor and the owner, unless the owner has effectively participated in the subcontracting of the construction" – *APL 0010783-64.2007.8.08.0048*, TJES, 27 March 2013 (BR).

246 Article 22 second paragraph, Law of Concessions of Public Works.

247 Article 101, Supreme Decree No. 75.

It is worth noting that the use of subcontractors without having obtained the respective authorization is a cause of early termination of the contract.

9.234 Under DS 236, and more broadly than DS 75, the contractor may subcontract part or all of the works, according to the tender rules and prior authorization of the SERVIU, but the contractor shall be liable for all obligations entered into with that entity.[248] It is worth noting that although it is possible to subcontract all of the works, in some cases it will be necessary for the subcontractor to be registered in the National Registry of Contractors, and also that in case there are unreported subcontractors, the SERVIU may terminate the contract administratively, without the contractor being entitled to compensation of any kind.[249]

9.235 Similarly, in private contracts there is no general limitation to subcontract, but the parties may limit such possibility contractually. The exception to this is *intuito personae* contracts, in which a person is contracted due to the special conditions that that person has, not being possible, thus, to subcontract the services of another person.

Unforeseeable Physical Conditions

9.236 In relation to public construction contracts in Brazil, the law provides for the possibility of contractual amendment in cases where the economic financial balance of the contract has changed due to "unpredictable events" such as unforeseeable physical conditions. This may vary depending of the allocation of risks and the contract model, within the models prescribed by the law, adopted in each case. It is important to note that, in order for this rule to apply, the conditions must genuinely have been unforeseeable and not attributable to any of the parties.

9.237 Regarding private contracts, the parties will be generally free to allocate risks relating to physical conditions and modify the suppletive rules set out in statute. If the parties do not specifically allocate any of the risks, the general rules from the Civil Code and other applicable laws will regulate the agreement. There is a standard provision in the Civil Code (Article 626) applicable to "contracts of works" whereby the contractor is allowed to suspend the works when geological conditions create unforeseeable difficulties, rendering performance excessively onerous, and the owner does not agree to review the price accordingly. However, as explained above, the parties may agree on different terms, particularly in complex construction contracts that are considered atypical.

9.238 One important general rule is the five-year liability of the constructor for soundness and safety of the works relating to materials and soil, which tends to be applicable to all construction contracts due to its nature as a public order rule.[250] [251]

9.239 In Chile there is no general regime on unforeseen conditions of the soil, and, therefore, it is necessary to review each legal and regulatory text.

248 Article 55, Supreme Decree No. 236.

249 Article 55, Supreme Decree No. 236.

250 *Brazilian Civil Code*, 2002 (BR) Article 618.

251 "The constructor's liability for the quality of the works is laid out on Article 618 of the Civil Code, which provides for a guarantee period of five years from the delivery of the works, and, during the interregnum, the constructor is obligated to ensure the soundness and safety of the construction, being liable for any defects that may appear. The 5-year liability is a legal guarantee of public order, and may not be derogated by the parties" – *AC 151633-54.2015.8.09.0051*, TJGO, 19 July 2016 (BR).

9.240 Under the Chilean Civil Code, Article 2003 No. 2 of the Civil Code establishes that if unknown circumstances, such as a hidden flaw of the soil, causes costs that could not be foreseen, the constructor must be authorized to incur them, being entitled to appear before the judge so that he settles the dispute in case of the owner's refusal.

9.241 There is no specific reference to this matter in the Law of Concessions of Public Works. Such law is built upon a system in which the concessionaire must meet the service levels and technical standards established in the tender rules, and the concessionaire cannot require for additional economic compensation than the one agreed upon, except for exceptional cases provided in the tender conditions.[252] It is worth noting that during the construction phase, the works will be carried out at the full risk of the concessionaire, who must make the disbursements arising from fortuitous or *Force Majeure* events. However, the concessionaire may be entitled to payment from the Treasury for the damages caused by fortuitous or *Force Majeure* events, if this is established in the tender rules.[253] Therefore, the concessionaire would not have the possibility to allege unforeseeable physical conditions (or that would be at least questionable), unless for example the Ministry of Public Works had delivered incorrect information that was difficult or impossible to notice for the concessionaire, in which case it could eventually be exempted from liability.

9.242 DS 75 obliges the bidder only to carry out a careful visual inspection, and also requires him to comply with the general conditions of the project.[254] This is treated differently in DS 236, since this decree obliges the bidder to submit a statement declaring having visited the site and knowing its relief, topography, quality and all other surface, geological, climatic characteristics or others that may have a direct impact on the execution of the works.[255] Consequently, if there were soil characteristics that could not be detected through a careful visual inspection, the constructor could be exempted from liability according to the DS 75, but not under DS 236.

Material and Workmanship

9.243 In private contracts of works, the contractor may provide workmanship only or workmanship and materials.[256] There are several general rules in the civil code applicable to material supply in respect of contracts of works and they will be applicable if the parties do not derogate from them. As a rule, the obligation of providing materials in such contracts derives from the law or the parties' will.[257]

9.244 There is a generally applicable rule that the contractor supplying materials bears the risks of such materials until delivery and is liable for five years regarding the soundness and safety of the works due to the materials.[258]

9.245 In Chile, DS 75 and DS 236 establish that the provision for the materials will be borne by the contractor, not being the public institutions obliged to provide them, unless they are expressly obliged to do so, or this is stipulated in the respective conditions.[259] The

252 Article 1 paragraph 2 and Article 19 paragraph 2 of the Law of Concessions of Public Works.
253 Article 22 No. 2 of the Law of Concessions of Public Works.
254 Article 76, No. 1 letter b) No. 2), Supreme Decree No. 75.
255 Article 31 No. 1.2 letter b), Supreme Decree No. 236.
256 *Brazilian Civil Code*, 2002 (BR) Article 610.
257 *Brazilian Civil Code*, 2002 (BR) Article 610 (1).
258 *Brazilian Civil Code*, 2002 (BR) Article 618.
259 Article 141, DS No. 75 and Articles 88 and 99, DS No. 236.

materials used must be of good quality and come from the quarries or factories indicated in the contract, and in the absence of stipulation in this respect they must be of the best quality and provenance in their type.[260] Additionally, these decrees establish the obligation of the contractor to rebuild the works or replace the materials that have not been accepted by the relevant inspector.[261]

9.246 On the other hand, the Civil Code distinguishes whether the materials have been supplied by the constructor or by who commissioned the work: In the first case the constructor is the one who must respond if the work perishes or threatens ruin, while in the second case the constructor will not be liable unless he should have known the flaw or if knowing about it has not given timely notice.[262]

Labour Law Considerations

9.247 In Brazil, labour rights are established in the Constitution and regulated by federal law. The Brazilian labour laws are applicable to all employees and there are extensive social security laws and labour regulations on work shifts, wages and salaries, benefits and contributions, health and safety, and termination of a labour contract. Trade unions are very active and participative in respect of labour relations and also play an important part in the construction industry and regulation.

9.248 Issues deriving from labour regulations such as minimum wages, transportation costs, unemployment insurance programs, outsourcing restrictions and strikes must be considered when assessing costs and risks in construction contracts in Brazil.

9.249 In Chile, principles of freedom of association and freedom of work are guaranteed by the Constitution,[263] regulating the labour and collective relations in the respective Labour Code and in the International Treaties in force in Chile. The Labour Code is applicable to all workers in the private sector, since the public sector is governed by a special statute. Nevertheless, it is worth noting that although workers for a specific project or service are entitled to bargain collectively, they cannot exercise the right to strike,[264] having to, in case of conflict, recur to compulsory arbitration established by the law.[265]

9.250 With regard to labour obligations of a monetary nature, including social security contributions, under Chilean legislation, the employee is entitled to an action against his employer, being able to sue the principal or owner of the works jointly or subsidiarily. The principal will be jointly and severally liable when he has not exercised the right to be informed or nor has withheld the monies owed to the workers.

9.251 In issues regarding occupational accidents, there is a concurrent liability of the owner of the works, as well as of its contractors and subcontractors.

Performance and Taking-Over

9.252 In Brazil, public construction contracts must be performed according to the designs, bidding documents and contract. As a general rule, taking-over by the public

260 Article 144, DS No. 75 and Article 84, DS No. 236.
261 Article 113, DS No. 75 and Article 84 paragraph 2, DS No. 236.
262 Articles 1671, 2000 and 2003 of the Civil Code.
263 Article 19 No. 16 of the Constitution of the Republic of Chile.
264 Article 365, Chilean Labour Code.
265 Article 386, Chilean Labour Code.

administration occurs provisionally and (ii) definitively by a government official or a commission designated to analyze that the works have been delivered in accordance with the terms of the contract.

9.253 The owner of a private contract for works is obliged to receive the works once they have been completed according to the contract, or in accordance with the customs of the place in which the works are executed.[266] The owner may reject the works if the contractor fails to meet the instructions received and the plans given or fails to comply with the technical rules governing such works. Instead of rejecting the works, the owner may accept them at a reduced price.[267]

9.254 In private contracts in Chile, the work must be built according to the terms agreed upon in the respective contract and must be received by the person who commissioned it once it has been completed. This is without prejudice to the liabilities that may arise according to Article 2003 of the Civil Code and to the General Law of Urbanism and Construction. It is worth noting that according to the Civil Code, the receipt granted by the owner after completion of the work, only means that the owner approves the works as externally compliant to the plan and the rules of such art. Consequently, in construction contracts, the constructor is not discharged from liability imposed by Article 2003 No. 3, to which we have already referred.[268]

9.255 According to DS 75, the contractor must execute the works in accordance with the contract.[269] Once the work is completed, the reception of the work will be required by the inspection authority, who will verify the completion, being the provisional acceptance made by a commission, which must evacuate its report within a period not exceeding 20 days counted from their designation.[270] As for the final acceptance, this will be done in the same way as the provisional one after the warranty period has expired, which will be one year or six months computed from the date of completion of the works, depending on whether the works are major or minor.[271]

9.256 Under DS 236 the system is similar, since the contractor must execute the works in accordance with the contract.[272] Once the works have been completed, the contractor must request the acceptance of the works to the SERVIU, through the Technical Inspection of the Work, being such acceptance made by a commission designated for such purposes. The works will be accepted by the designated commission within a period not exceeding of two working days from the date of the report of the Technical Inspection of the Works.[273]

9.257 On the other hand, the Law of Concessions of Public Works establishes that in the concessions granted, the concessionaire must comply, throughout the concession, with the levels of service and/or technical standards established in the respective tender terms.[274] The said law and its regulations refer to the commissioning of the work, which

266 *Brazilian Civil Code*, 2002 (BR) Article 615.
267 *Brazilian Civil Code*, 2002 (BR) Article 615.
268 Article 2003 No. 4, Chilean Civil Code.
269 Article 142, DS No. 75.
270 Article 166, DS No. 75
271 Articles 170 and 176, DS No. 75.
272 Article 74, DS No. 236.
273 Article 123 paragraph 2, DS No. 236.
274 Article 1 paragraph 2, Law of Concessions of Public Works.

must be authorized by the Ministry of Public Works.[275] Provisional commissioning, in whole or in part,[276] may only be requested if this is established by tender rules, provided the operating guarantee is delivered[277] and prior approval of the service regulations for the works.[278] Regarding the final acceptance of the service, the concessionaire must request it within the term established in the tender conditions, which shall not be longer than one year, counted from the provisional authorization for the implementation of the service for the whole works.[279]

Contract Price and Payment

9.258 In Brazil, in a public construction contract the contract price is determined during the bidding process and is one of the aspects considered in the economic financial balance which must be observed throughout the contract. The bidding documents and the contract will also establish the terms of payment. The bidding documents will also determine the disbursement schedule per period, in accordance with the public budget, the criterion for financial updating of amounts to be paid and financial compensation for delays, discounts, and advanced payments.

9.259 In relation to private contracts, under the principle of party autonomy, the parties are free to agree on price and payment conditions, observing general rules and principles such as good faith, legality and equality. If the contract is one where works are being continually undertaken, if the performance by one of the parties becomes excessively onerous, imposing an extreme advantage to the other, due to extraordinary and unforeseeable events, the disadvantaged party may request the termination of the contract, or the parties may agree to modify the conditions of the contract equitably.[280] Where the contract is considered a contract of works, if there is a decrease in the price of the material or labour exceeding one-tenth of the agreed global price, the contract price may be revised, at the request of the owner.[281]

9.260 Under Chilean law, the prices will be fixed in the respective tender and the payment balances shall be payable according to the contract and the respective tender terms. DS 75 states that the payments will be made through a fortnight or monthly payment basis, according to the minimum established in the contract and the limits established by said regulation. In the event of failure to pay the respective payment balance within 30 days of the date therefrom, an interest will accrue for said delay until the payment date[282] (this being the only applicable interest), and the contractor will not be entitled to terminate the contract.

9.261 DS 236 also establishes the payment by means of payment balances, which will be based on the items approved by the Technical Inspection of the Work which, with certain

275 Article 17, Law of Concessions of Public Works.

276 The implementation of the service may be carried out partially, to the extent that they constitute in themselves units capable of independent exploitation, and conform to the conditions established by the tender terms (Article 17, Law of Concessions of Public Works).

277 Article 35 No. 2, Regulations of the Law of Concessions of Public Works.

278 Articles 55 No. 1 and 57 No. 4, Regulations of the Law of Concessions of Public Works.

279 Article 56 No. 1, Regulations of the Law of Concessions of Public Works.

280 *Brazilian Civil Code*, 2002 (BR) Article 478 and 479.

281 *Brazilian Civil Code*, 2002 (BR) Article 620.

282 Article 156, DS No. 75.

exceptions, cannot be presented with a frequency of less than 14 days nor more than 28 days.[283] Failure to pay the payment balances within 30 days from the date thereof, for reasons not attributable to the contractor, shall be paid adjusted to the value of the UF,[284] this being the only compensation to which the contractor is entitled for this concept.[285]

9.262 In private contracts, the price will be freely agreed upon by the parties, this being consequence of the principle of autonomy of will. In case of failure to comply with obligations that consist in paying a sum of money, the legal or the conventional interest (if agreed) must be paid, not being necessary for the creditor to justify damages when it only collects interest.[286] The Civil Code establishes limitations to the amount of conventional interest that can be fixed by the parties in the loan agreement, which cannot exceed the maximum agreeable interest rate,[287] being indicated by the doctrine that this rule is extendable to all type of interests.[288]

9.263 As previously stated, there is no possibility in Chile of modifying or terminating the contract in the event of excessive onerousness. Nevertheless, for the construction contract under the Civil Code, there is a possibility of recovering from the person who commissioned the work, the costs that could not be foreseen, in case there were hidden flaws in the soil.[289]

Defects Liability

9.264 In Brazil, as a rule, the Civil Code establishes a five-year liability period of the contractor for soundness and safety of the works due to materials and soil, which tends to be applicable to all construction contracts due to its nature as a public order rule. To benefit from this provision, the owner must, however, file a suit against the contractor within 180 days following the appearance of any defect.[290]

9.265 In Chile, the Civil Code establishes a term of guarantee of five years subsequent to the delivery of the works, within which the ruin or threat of ruin of the work must occur. On the other hand, the GLUC establishes different limitation periods depending on the type of flaw or defect in place, to which we have previously referred.

9.266 DS 75 establishes the liability of the contractor for damages caused by defects in the construction of the work or in the materials used, for a period of five years counted from the provisional reception. The exception to this rule would be the case where the damage arises from the poor quality of the materials that have been supplied by the State, on cases where the contractor is obliged to use these materials.[291]

9.267 It is worth mentioning that this regulation establishes the obligation of the contractor to maintain for a certain period the guarantees that secured the contract, which

283 Article 114, DS No. 236.

284 *Unidad de Fomento* is a monetary measure used in Chile and equals approximately USD 34.

285 Article 121, DS No. 236.

286 Article 1559, Chilean Civil Code.

287 Law 18.010, Article 6, final paragraph.

288 René Abeliuk Manasevich, *Las Obligaciones*, Fourth Edition, updated and expanded, year 2003, Vol. I, p. 356.

289 Article 2003 Rule 2, Chilean Civil Code.

290 *Brazilian Civil Code*, 2002 (BR) Article 618 (*sole para*).

291 Article 150 paragraph 3, DS No. 75.

must be understood without prejudice to the period of legal guarantee of five years established in Article 2003 No. 3 of the Chilean Civil Code.

9.268 On the other hand, DS 236 states that in case the damage arises from a defect in the construction of the work or in the materials used in it, the contractor will be liable according to Article 2003 No. 3 of the Civil Code, with the exception of cases where the damages arise from the poor quality of the materials supplied by the SERVIU and where the contractor is obliged to use these materials.[292] Likewise, these regulations require a guarantee bond to be kept validly for a certain period to respond for the good performance of the works, but this is without prejudice to the period of legal guarantee of five years that regulates Article 2003 No. 3.[293]

Limitation of Liability

9.269 In Brazil, as a general rule, the parties to a construction contract may claim losses and damages, including lost profit.[294,295] Even where there is wilful misconduct, the losses and damages are limited to the actual losses and the lost profits due to the direct and immediate effect of the misconduct.[296] The parties may also agree on other limitations of liability in the Contract.

9.270 In Chile, the general rule in contractual matters is that the debtor must be liable for the damages that are a direct consequence of their non-compliance and that were anticipated or could have been foreseen at the time of the contract. Notwithstanding the foregoing, in case of wilful misconduct on the debtor's part, the debtor will be liable for all damages that are an immediate or direct consequence of not having fulfilled the obligation or delayed its compliance,[297] including, therefore, the foreseen and unforeseen damages. It should be clarified that this does not include any indirect damage that may have occurred, since in Chile one is only liable for damages that are an immediate or direct consequence of the non-compliance. Consequently, indemnifiable damages are those that have a reasonable causal proximity to the harmful event.

9.271 Finally, it must also be borne in mind that the parties may contractually limit their liability, subject to certain restrictions, such as those relating to unavailable property such as life and physical integrity and limitations that may be contrary to the public order.

Variations

9.272 In Brazil, administrative contracts may be subject to change orders by the public party when there is a modification of the project or the specifications for better technical adaptation to its objectives (qualitative variation) or when it is necessary to modify the contract value due to the increase or decrease in the quantity of what is being delivered (quantitative variation). These variations are subject to limitations under the law and the economic financial balance of the contract must always be maintained. This type of contract may also be subject to bilateral variation in the cases set out in the law, for example,

292 Article 100 paragraph 2, DS No. 236.
293 Article 126 paragraph 3, DS No. 236.
294 *Brazilian Civil Code*, 2002 (BR) Article 402.
295 Among the many precedents in this sense: *AREsp 1083279*, STJ, 7 June 2017 (BR).
296 *Brazilian Civil Code*, 2002 (BR) Article 403.
297 Article 1558, Chilean Civil Code.

in order to maintain the initial economic and financial balance of the contract, in the event of unforeseeable or unpredictable events delaying or impeding the performance of the contract, or, in case of *Force Majeure* or government acts.

9.273 As for private contracts of works, the contractor will be entitled to a variation of the contract if modifications are made to the design as a result of written instructions from the owner or if there are increases or additions to the project which, even if they were not explicitly ordered, were accompanied by the owner, who could not ignore what was happening and never protested.[298] The parties may, however, decide not to incorporate these terms, particularly in complex contracts that do not fall within the "contract of works" category.

9.274 Under Chilean law there are certain rules that make the modification of the contract possible, being such rules of exceptional character, since the Chilean legal system does not regulate the *ius variandi* in general terms; additionally, the authority cannot alter unilaterally the contract without granting something in exchange, being this a limitation to the *ius variandi* on administrative contracts.[299]

9.275 The Law of Concessions of Public Works establishes the authority[300] of the Ministry of Public Works to modify the characteristics of the contracted works and services, in order to increase the service levels and technical standards established in the tender rules. This can also be made if there are other reasons of public interest that are duly founded. However, the concessionaire shall have the right to be duly compensated for the additional costs when applicable.[301] These variations cannot exceed the amount established in the tender rules, which in any case may exceed 15%[302] of the official budget for the work, nor may they be required on a date subsequent to the fulfilment of three-quarters of the term of the concession, unless otherwise agreed in writing with the concessionaire.

9.276 In the event of need for a redesign or complementation where the additional investments exceed 25% of the official budget for the work, and for reasons of public interest, the Law of Concessions of Public Works regulates the possibility of contracting such works with the concessionaire, subject to the fulfilment of certain requirements established by law.[303]

9.277 The Regulations of the Law of Concessions of Public Works establishes the power of the Ministry of Public Works to replace or carry out additional works on the proposal of the General Director of Public Works or of the concessionaire, insofar as they do not imply a variation in the economic conditions of the contract.[304]

298 *Brazilian Civil Code*, 2002 (BR) Article 619 (main section and sole para).

299 Contraloría General de la República, Ruling No. 34.523 of 04-VI-2013.

300 Article 20 of such law also considers the possibility that the concessionaire and the Ministry agree to modify the characteristics of the works or services contracted with certain limits, in order to increase the levels of service and technical standards established in the tender rules, which will be materialized through a complementary agreement of the concession contract.

301 Article 19 paragraph 3, Law of Concessions of Public Works.

302 In the event that additional investments during the exploitation stage exceed 5% of the official budget of the work or such are above US$ 4,000,000, such works must be tendered by the concessionaire under the supervision of the Ministry of Public Works, except in exceptional cases (Article 19, paragraph 5, Law of Concessions of Public Works).

303 Article 20 bis, Law of Concessions of Public Works.

304 Article 68 No. 1, Supreme Decree No. 956 de 1999.

9.278 DS 75 and DS 236 allow the administrative authority to increase or decrease the works, but always with the obligation to compensate the contractor.[305] Both regulations establish limits to this power, which are expressed in a percentage of the official budget.

9.279 The Civil Code establishes the possibility of requesting price increases of lump sum contracts in the case of additions or modifications to the original plan, to the extent that a particular price has been adjusted due to such additions or modifications.[306]

Delay and Disruption

9.280 In Brazil, the duration of public construction contracts must be compliant with so-called budgetary credits. This means that the public entity is restricted to establishing contractual deadlines in accordance with the public funding it receives.[307] The law does, however, cover the possibility of contractual time extension. The law very clearly establishes that the contractual deadline may be extended without prejudice to other aspects of the contract in situations of *Force Majeure*, where the public entity alters the project or if there is any impediment to the execution of the works not attributable to the contractor. In these cases, the economic financial balance of the contract will have to be maintained. If a delay is caused by the contractor, the law establishes the penalties the contractor will be subjected to where it fails to conclude the works on time.

9.281 Disruption is not expressly dealt with in the law applicable to public construction contracts, but it will be covered by the contractor's general right for adjustment of the economic financial balance of the contract if caused by the public entity or if it is otherwise not attributable to the contractor.[308]

9.282 Under Brazilian private law, there is no specific provision addressing delay and disruption in relation to contracts of works and the parties are free to agree on terms to cover these matters.[309] [310]

9.283 In Chile, the Law of Concessions of Public Works establishes that in case of delays attributable to the Treasury during the construction phase, the concessionaire will enjoy a term increase of a time equal to the period of obstruction or paralysation, without prejudice to any compensations that may be applicable.[311]

9.284 On the other hand, the regulation of said law refers to compliance with the term, stating that the concessionaire is obliged to complete the works and put them into service at the dates and time limits determined in the tender rules or in their offer as may be applicable, and that the tender rules will indicate the sanctions and/or fines in case

305 Articles 102, 104, 105 and 106 of DS No. 75; and Articles 103 paragraphs 1 and 3 and Article 104 del DS No. 236.

306 Article 2003 No. 1, Chilean Civil Code.

307 "The validity of the contracts is subject to the respective budgetary credits" – *Acórdão 1683*, TCU, 27 October 2004 (BR).

308 "Although the interruption is legitimate, the losses incurred as a result of the halt must be compensated in order to safeguard the maintenance of the economic financial balance of the contract" – *REsp 734696*, STJ, 7 July 2009 (BR).

309 "In the event that the completion of the works has been delayed by the contractor, there is no legal obligation to readjust the contract without specific contractual provision" – *REsp 104522*, STJ, 09 December 1996 (BR).

310 *RC 71004368320*, TJRS, 26 November 2013 (BR).

311 Article 22 No. 3, Law of Concessions of Public Works.

of non-compliance.[312] The regulation also establishes that in case of delays caused by a fortuitous event or *Force Majeure*, the concessionaire must present his justification in writing within 30 days, and the Director General of Works will decide whether to accept or reject the extension of the term.[313]

9.285 It is worth mentioning that the delay could constitute cause of extinction of the concession in case that is so agreed in the tender terms, or in case that could be considered like a serious breach of the obligations of the concessionaire.[314]

9.286 Additionally, in case the concessionaire left the work or unjustifiably interrupts the services, the Ministry of Public Works must file a requirement with the Arbitration Commission to so declare it and so that it is authorized to designate an intervener, in which case it will be deemed a serious failure to comply with the concession contract.[315]

9.287 Under DS 75 and DS 236, in the event of a delay of more than 15 days in the commencement of the work, or interruption of the same number of days that was not caused by *Force Majeure* or unforeseeable circumstances, or justified to the inspector, the Administration shall be entitled to terminate the contract.[316] In addition, in case of delays in the work program, the authority will be entitled to take the necessary measures to regularise the pace of work,[317] being able even to an early termination of the contract and to impose fines in the event there is an unjustified delay which exceeds 30% with respect to the progress of the work program.[318]

9.288 Notwithstanding the foregoing, if the land is not put at the disposal of the contractor for events not attributable to him, certain damages will be compensated, and the term of the contract will be increased.[319] Likewise, in case the contractor should use materials provided by the authority and their delivery causes delays in the work programme, the authority will authorize the increase of the term.[320]

9.289 Finally, it is worth mentioning that under DS 75 and DS 236, the authority is entitled to stop the works when funds are not available to carry them forward or when this is advisable considering the needs of the authority.[321]

9.290 In private contracts, what the parties agree will prevail, so they must comply with the established deadlines, milestones, progresses and other agreed conditions, together with the respective legal effects that they have agreed (indemnities, fines, among others).

Liquidated Damages and Other Damages

9.291 In relation to public contracts in Brazil, penalties for when the contractor fails to conclude the works on time for reasons not attributable to the public body may range from a warning or monetary fine to the suspension of the right to contract with the public administration and will be regulated in the bidding documents.

312 Article 52 No. 1, Supreme Decree No. 956 de 1999.
313 Article 52 No. 2, Supreme Decree No. 956 de 1999.
314 Article 27 No. 3 and 4, Law of Concessions of Public Works.
315 Article 37, Law of Concessions of Public Works.
316 Article 139 final paragraph, DS No. 75, and Article 81 paragraph 2, DS No. 236.
317 Article 143 paragraph 2, DS No. 75, and Article 83, DS No. 236.
318 Article 161 paragraph 2, DS No. 75, and Article 82 paragraph 1, DS No. 236.
319 Article 138, DS No. 75, and Article 92, DS No. 236.
320 Article 145, DS No. 75, and Article 88, DS No. 236.
321 Article 148 DS No. 75 and Article 91 DS No. 236.

9.292 In relation to private contracts, a contractor delayed in completing a construction contract due to its own actions or omission, will generally be liable for the corresponding and effective damages and lost profits. It should be noted that the parties are subject to a general duty to mitigate losses which derives from the principle of good faith.[322] Parties to private contracts are free to decide on specific terms relating to damages including provisions relating to the exclusion of a party's responsibility, liquidating damages or a cap on liability. Moreover, the parties may agree on a specific compensation clause, limited to the agreed value of the main obligation under the contract,[323] although it is important to note that the specific compensation may be reduced by a judge if the main obligations under the contract are fulfilled or if the specific compensation is considered excessive in view of the nature and purpose of the contract.[324] The parties may also stipulate in the contract that damages arising out of or in connection with the contract may be claimed in a court of law. In this case, the amount of any liquidated damages provided for in the contract will have to be regarded by the judge as the minimum compensation, unless the clause is purely punitive whereby the amounts could be claimed together with the main obligation (specific performance).[325]

9.293 In Chile, under the Public Works Concessions Law, liquidated damages are not regulated. Nevertheless, the State is empowered to collect the fines provided for it in the tender rules and the regulations,[326] which will be imposed by the Direction of the Ministry of Public Works (with the approval of the Conciliation Commission in certain cases).

9.294 A system is established under DS 75, by which fines will be applied to the contractor in case the latter fails to comply with the orders of the inspector. The amount will vary depending on whether they are contracts of the Minor, Major or Special Works Registries,[327] establishing also that the fines of said regulation may be modified by the tender rules but with certain limits.[328] Moreover, daily fines are set for the case where the contractor does not deliver the work fully completed within the contractual term, establishing in the regulations the formula for calculating the damages, and also a limitation to the amount of the total fine, which may not exceed 15% of the value of the contract.

9.295 DS 236 also establishes daily fines to the contractor that does not deliver the work on the date set or does not comply with the partial deadlines when applicable, which amount may be modified in the special administrative rules.[329]

9.296 In private contracts, and similarly to the case of Brazil, in case of delays attributable to the contractor, the contractor shall be liable for the damages caused, including any loss of profits. Although Chilean law does not explicitly provide for the duty to mitigate damages, it could be deemed incorporated as a consequence of the obligation to execute

322 "Precept derived from the principle of objective good faith. Duty to mitigate the loss. The contractors must take the necessary and possible measures so that the damage is not aggravated. The party that benefits from these losses cannot remain deliberately inert in before the damages" – *REsp 758518*, STJ, 28 June 2010 Article (BR).

323 *Brazilian Civil Code*, 2002 (BR) Article 412.

324 *Brazilian Civil Code*, 2002 (BR) Article 413.

325 *Brazilian Civil Code*, 2002 (BR) Articles 411 and 416 (sole para).

326 Article 18 and 29 paragraph 3, Law of Concessions of Public Works.

327 Article 111, paragraph 2, DS No. 75.

328 Article 135, DS No. 75.

329 Article 86, DS No. 236.

the contracts in good faith. In addition to the above, the parties may set liquidated damages, which may not exceed twice the amount of the main obligation.[330]

Insurance

9.297 In Brazil, the Decree-Law No. 73/66 (regulated by Decree No. 61,867/67) establishes, among other things, the mandatory insurances applicable for construction contracts which include those relating to: (i) Civil liability for real estate contractors of urban zone constructions with respect to bodily injury and physical damage injuries and property damage; and (ii) guarantee of compliance with the obligations of the real estate developer and constructor.

9.298 In the case of public construction contracts, the contractor may be required to comply with additional insurance obligations set out in the bidding documents. These requirements have become more rigid in the recently enacted Law 14133, which regulates public tenders and contracts. In large-scale engineering works a performance bond equivalent to up to 30% (thirty percent) of the initial contract value may be required.[352]

9.299 In relation to private contracts, the parties are free to determine the specific insurance obligations.

9.300 In Chile, under the Law of Concessions of Public Works, the concessionaire is liable for the fortuitous event or *Force Majeure* during the construction phase (unless the tender rules establish otherwise);[331] thus the contracting of insurance by the concessionaire is fundamental. According to the regulations of said law, the concessionaire must hire insurance policies that cover civil liability[332] for damages caused to third parties and catastrophic risks that may occur during the period of the concession. The tender rules will specify the terms, conditions and other clauses that such policies must contain, and these rules may also require other types of insurance policies.[333]

9.301 On the other hand, DS 75 establishes that the administrative rules may require the contractor to have civil liability insurance, which is extremely relevant for the contractor, since, in principle, any damage caused to third parties is under his responsibility. Similarly, and considering that the contractor must respond for any damage caused to the works, including a fortuitous event or *Force Majeure*, the said regulation entitles him to contract the insurance policies he deems pertinent.[334]

9.302 In private contracts there is no obligation to contract specific insurance, so it will not be mandatory unless the parties expressly stipulate it in the respective contract. Notwithstanding this, it is advisable for the contractor to contract certain insurance policies based on a program that covers the different risks, paying particular attention to the particular conditions relating to franchises, deductibles, guarantees, limits and sub-limits.

Suspension

9.303 In relation to public contracts in Brazil, the public authority may suspend a contract for up to one hundred and twenty days without the contractor obtaining the right to

330 Article 1544, Código Civil.
331 Article 22 No.2, Law of Concessions of Public Works.
332 This type of insurance is regulated in Article 570 et seq. of the Code of Commerce.
333 Article 36, Supreme Decree No. 956 of 1999.
334 Article 134, DS No. 75.

terminate, although it will have the obligation to indemnify the contractor for additional costs resulting from the suspension.[335] The contractor to a public contract may only suspend the works in case of: (i) A delay of more than two months of payments due from the public authority;[336] (ii) default from the public authority in complying with its obligation of releasing areas, objects, supply or sources of natural materials specified in the design and that are necessary for the execution of the works;[337] or (iii) suspensions of the works or part thereof by the public authority for more than ninety business days, altogether.

9.304 In relation to private contracts, aside from *Force Majeure*, the Civil Code establishes general rules regarding when the contractor may suspend the works in the situations where: (i) The owner opposes a price adjustment due to unforeseen geological or hydrological conditions that render the contract excessively onerous to the contractor; or (ii) the owner requests disproportionate modifications to the approved design, even if willing to increase the contract price.[338] These hypotheses apply to typical "contracts of works" and the parties can, therefore, derogate from them, particularly in more complex construction contracts that do not fall under this category.

9.305 In Chile, under DS 75 and DS 236, the possibility of suspending the contract by the State is quite broadly regulated, since it establishes the right of the Ministry of Public Works and the SERVIU respectively to stop works when the funds are not available to carry them forward or when their needs so dictate, in which case the contractor must be compensated.[339] Furthermore, these two regulations establish the possibility of suspending, in qualified cases, the liquidation of the contract, when the same contractor has other contracts pending liquidation.[340]

9.306 In the Law of Concessions of Public Works, the concession may be suspended in case of war, internal commotion or *Force Majeure* that prevent the provision of the service; partial destruction that makes its use temporarily unfeasible and for other causes that are established by the rules.[341]

9.307 The Chilean Civil Code incorporates the rule *exceptio non adimpleti contractus* for bilateral contracts, by virtue of which none of the contractors is in arrears failing to comply with the agreement, while the other does not comply with its part or is not willing to comply in a fully and timely fashion.[342] Consequently, outside the cases that may be expressly agreed in the contract, if neither party complies with or is willing to fulfil its obligations, the performance of the contract will be suspended. It is worth mentioning that in case of an event of *Force Majeure*, the contractor could suspend the work, to the extent that it is not responsible for the *Force Majeure* or unforeseen event, and that in Chile, unlike Brazil, it is not allowed to modify the contract in case of excessive onerousness.

---

335 *L8666* 1993 (BR) Article 78 (XIV).
336 *L8666* 1993 (BR) Article 78 (XV).
337 *L8666* 1993 (BR) Article 78 (XVI).
338 *Brazilian Civil Code*, 2002 (BR) Article 625.
339 Article 148 DS 75 and 91 DS 236.
340 Article 188, DS No. 75 and Article 132, DS No. 236.
341 Article 26, Law of Concessions of Public Works.
342 Article 1552, Chilean Civil Code.

Termination

9.308 In Brazil, the law sets out where default and public interest may be grounds for termination of public contracts. It is provided that a public authority may terminate a public contract through agreement with the contractor or unilaterally. The contractor, however, must request termination before a court of law. The law also regulates the consequences of the termination of a public contract including payments, devolution or execution of guarantees, take-over, retention of credits, fines and penalties.

9.309 In the case of private contracts, the parties may stipulate the grounds for termination or be subjected to the general rules set out in the Civil Code. According to the Civil Code a private contract may be terminated by agreement between the parties,[343] in case of default or if the performance of one of the parties becomes excessively onerous, with great advantage to the other, due to extraordinary and unforeseeable events.[344]

9.310 In Chile, under DS 75, the power of the Direction of the Ministry of Public Works to early terminate the contract is broadly regulated. This can be done when there are no funds available to carry it forward or when it is advisable considering its needs, in which case the contractor must be compensated.[345] Additionally, the Ministry is entitled to an early termination of the contract based on a material breach of the contract.[346]

9.311 With regard to DS 236, the SERVIU may early terminate under certain circumstances related to the contractor, such as bankruptcy, if he does not concur to receive the land, among others.[347]

9.312 On the other hand, the Law of Concessions of Public Works establishes the power of the President of the Republic to early terminate the concession, insofar as the public interest so requires and complies with the other requirements established by the law (that the work became unnecessary or required a substantial redesign or complementation, among others). This power can only be exercised during the construction stage and will entitle the concessionaire to be compensated.[348]

9.313 Under the Chilean Civil Code, it is not possible to terminate contracts in case of failure to comply by one of the parties, since this will also require an enforceable judicial sentence.[349] The latter will not be necessary when the parties have agreed in the contract the possibility for the innocent party to terminate without the need for judicial authorization. In relation to the possibility to terminate a contract for subsequent excessive onerousness, and unlike Brazil, this institution is not recognized by the Civil Code in Chile, so this circumstance must be borne by the party that is affected by it, unless the same could be qualified as a fortuitous event or *Force Majeure*.

343 *Brazilian Civil Code*, 2002 (BR) Article 472.
344 *Brazilian Civil Code*, 2002 (BR) Article 478–80.
345 Article 148, DS No. 75.
346 Article 151, DS No. 75.
347 Article 134, DS No. 236.
348 Article 28 ter, Law of Concessions of Public Works.
349 Article 1489, Chilean Civil Code.

Forms of Security – Bonds and Guarantees

9.314 In the case of public contracts in Brazil, the bidding documents will generally establish the requirements for guarantees of performance, which may vary from cash deposits to bank guarantees or insurance bonds.

9.315 In the case of private contracts, a performance bond is not mandatory but is fairly common in construction contracts and may be a bank guarantee or an insurance bond.

9.316 In Chile, under the Public Works Concessions Law and its respective regulations, the concessionaire's obligation to provide a guarantee of seriousness of the offer is regulated, which will be replaced once the construction guarantee is delivered; and this, in turn, will be replaced by the operating guarantee. Said guarantees must be granted in the terms, form and amount established by the tender rules.[350]

9.317 DS 75 establishes that in the tender rules a performance bond may be required to guarantee the seriousness of the offers, the amount of which is specified in the regulations but may be modified by the respective administrative rules.[351] In addition, it is established that the contractor must present a guarantee of faithful compliance with the contract consisting of a bank performance bond or an insurance policy,[352] detailing in the regulations the amount and term that must have (which will depend on the type of work in question), and further indicating that such amounts and terms may be increased in administrative rules.[353]

9.318 Under DS 236 it is established that prior to the signing of the contract, a bank performance bond must be delivered to respond for the timely and complete compliance with the agreement. The amount of said guarantee will be fixed in the special rules, with a minimum of 3% and maximum 5% of the contract amount[354]. Once the works have been received, the contractor must deliver a bank performance bond to guarantee the good performance of the works and their proper execution, at which time the guarantee previously delivered to guarantee the timely and full compliance with the contract will be returned[355].

9.319 Under the Civil Code no guarantees are required, but the parties are free to expressly agree them on the contract, which is common in large private contracts where performance bonds are usually required from the constructor party to ensure the faithful performance of the contract.

Claims

9.320 In Brazil, the grounds for claims relating to public contracts are generally that the economic financial balance of the contract has been disrupted due to supervening unpredictable facts, which may have delayed or hindered the execution of the contract as initially agreed, including *Force Majeure* and government acts[356].

350 Articles 20 and 33, Supreme Decree No. 956 of 1999.

351 Article 76, DS No. 75.

352 In case of opting for this policy, only the specific wording mentioned in the Regulations can be used.

353 Article 96 first paragraph, DS No. 75.

354 Article 50, DS No. 236.

355 Article 126, DS No. 236.

356 "If the public services company does not demonstrate the occurrence of an economic-financial imbalance in the contract, the public entity is under no obligation to reimburse any losses that the company may have incurred in complying with the contract" – *APC 20130110039812*, TJDF, 03 November 2015 (BR).

9.321 Private contract claims will often provide that the conditions agreed for the execution of the works have not been met for reasons attributable to the other party. As a general rule, claims for losses and damages may include effective losses and lost profits [357]which are subject to monetary updating in line with official indexes, including interest, costs and lawyer's fees, without prejudice to any agreed penalty[358].

9.322 In general terms, Chilean law does not confer the parties the right to file a claim based on supervening conditions.[359] Only in concessions of public works it was argued in the past, and with relative success, the necessity that the contract had an economic - financial balance, since the courts decided cases *ex aequo et bono*. However, with the entry into force of Law 20.410, the grounds for claims related to events that caused changes in the circumstances and allowed the revision of the contract were drastically restricted. In Chile the principle of intangibility of contracts (i.e. that the contract is an actual law for the parties) is a fundamental principle in the law of contracts.

9.323 Therefore, the analysis to be carried out in respect of claims must first be made by reviewing the contractual provisions to determine which of the parties has assumed the risk on which the claim is based, but to be successful the claim shall also comply with the general requisites applicable. In any case, claims will normally be made on the basis of two concepts that may concur or not, which are: (a) An extension of the term; and/or (b) a monetary compensation.

9.324 In order for a claim to be successful, it will be necessary that: (a) The claimant had acted in such a way that the occurrence of the claimed event is not of his responsibility; (b) the risk of the event that caused the damages was assumed by the party receiving the claim, whether that assumption is either a consequence of a legal or contractual provision; (c) the cause is not attributable to the fault or wilful misconduct of the person making the claim; (d) the claimed event caused damages, which can be compensated with time and/or monetarily compensated; and (e) that there is a causal relation between the fact and the loss in time and/or the monetarily loss.

Time-Bar Provisions

9.325 In Brazil, there are different time limitations for making claims in relation to construction contracts provided for in the law. The applicable limitation period will generally depend on the contracting parties, the nature of the contract, the nature of the claim and the moment the damage or loss is identified and will generally vary from one to ten years.[360] There are differing and conflicting interpretations of these limitations and their deadlines in doctrine and jurisprudence, which demand careful analysis of the specific context of a given contract. It is important to note, however, that the contractor will be liable for the solidity of the works for five years, as provided by law.[361]

---

357 *Brazilian Civil Code*, 2002 (BR) Article 402.

358 *Brazilian Civil Code*, 2002 (BR) Article 404.

359 Chilean Courts have rejected the possibility to review contracts accepting expressly the principle of intangibility of the contracts (Patricia López Díaz, *El Principio de Equilibrio Contractual en el Código Civil Chileno, y Su Particular Importancia Como Fundamento De Algunas Instituciones Del Moderno Derecho De Las Obligaciones En La Dogmática Nacional*. Revista Chilena de Derecho Privado, No. 25, Fundación Fernando Fueyo, p. 143).

360 *Brazilian Civil Code*, 2002 (BR) Article 205 and 206.

361 *Brazilian Civil Code*, 2002 (BR) Article 618.

9.326 In Chile, the Law of Concessions of Public Works establishes a period of two years for the parties to submit their claims to the Arbitration Commission. The law distinguishes the facts or acts that take place during the stage of construction from those that occur during the stage of exploitation, noting that claims relating to the first must be filed within two years counted from the final commissioning of the work, while those of the latter, within two years counted from the occurrence of the fact or since it had notice of the fact as duly proven.[362]

9.327 In the event of termination of a contract for serious breach by the concessionaire, a period of expiration of ten days is granted to the concessionaire to appeal to the Arbitration Commission in case of disagreeing with the amount set by the Technical Panel.[363] If the concessionaire does not resort to such commission within the indicated period, it shall be deemed that the concessionaire accepts the highest amount offered by the Ministry of Public Works.[364] A similar provision applies in case the State rescues the concession for reasons of public interest, in which case the concessionaire will also have 10 days to appeal to the Arbitration Commission if it does not agree with the recommendation of the Technical Panel.[365]

9.328 In addition, this law establishes as a general rule that the term to file a claim against resolutions of the Ministry of Public Works is of 1 year, except for resolutions imposing fines, since in that case it will be of 120 days.[366]

9.329 DS 75 states that in case of damages that are caused by flaws in the construction of the work or the materials used, the contractor will always be liable for the term of five years counted from the date of provisional acceptance (unless caused by materials supplied by the Treasury that the contractor is obliged to use).[367]

9.330 The DS 75 and the DS 236 establish that the works have a guarantee of five years counted from the date in which the works are delivered.[368]

9.331 In private contracts, it is necessary to distinguish between the limitation period of the obligations of the contract, and the warranty period that Article 2003 No. 3 of the Civil Code regulates for construction contracts. Regarding the first, the general rule in contractual matters is that the obligations prescribe within five years from the time they become due.[369] On the other hand, the five-year period of Article 2003 No. 3 has been understood as a guarantee period (although the doctrine is not unanimous); so if, during the five years following its delivery, the work collapses or is in danger of collapsing, it is only then that the five-year limitation period applicable to the contractual regime starts to run.

---

362 Article 36 bis paragraph 9, Law of Concessions of Public Works.

363 The Technical Panel is an institution which purpose is to know the technical or economic discrepancies between the parties, produced during the execution of the contract.

364 Article 28 paragraph 5, Law of Concessions of Public Works.

365 Article 28 ter paragraph 7, Law of Concessions of Public Works.

366 Article 36 bis paragraph 10, Law of Concessions of Public Works.

367 Article 150 paragraph 3, DS No. 75.

368 Article 170, DS No. 75 and Article 126, DS No. 236.

369 Articles 2514 and 2515 of the Civil Code.

Disputes – Adjudication and Arbitration

9.332 In Brazil, arbitration is regulated by Federal Law[370] and is allowed in the case of both public and private construction contracts. Although arbitration involving the government is generally admissible, there are limitations on the use of arbitration in respect of disputes relating to public unalienable rights and interests.[371] Arbitral awards issued in Brazil are immediately enforceable and are not subject to judicial review or ratification, while foreign arbitral awards must be approved by the Brazilian Superior Court of Justice.[372] Such approval does not evaluate the merits, but rather the formal validity of the award.

9.333 The Brazilian judiciary has consistently honoured arbitral awards. In general, the only situation where the judiciary may annul an arbitral award is where there has been a relevant violation of due process issues related to bias and the impartiality of the Tribunal. These hypotheses are presented in an exhaustive list.[373]

9.334 Although adjudication is possible as a means of dispute resolution for private construction contracts in Brazil, it is still more common for the parties to choose arbitration. It is important to note that alternative dispute resolution is growing in Brazil, including dispute boards and mediation. There is no provision regarding adjudication for public construction contracts.

9.335 Under Chilean law, the Treasury is not allowed to go to arbitration, unless there is a special law that allows it, as it is the case of the Law of Concessions of Public Works. This law establishes that disputes or claims arising from the interpretation, application or execution of the concession contract may be settled by an Arbitration Commission or by the Court of Appeals of Santiago.[374] It is worth mentioning that in this law there is also a Technical Panel, which is qualified to hear the technical or economic discrepancies between the parties during the execution of the concession contract.[375] Although the Panel does not exercise jurisdiction and its recommendations are not binding to the parties, such parties may only bring to the Arbitration Commission or the Court of Appeals the knowledge of technical or economic aspects of a dispute, insofar as these matters have previously been submitted to the Technical Panel.[376]

9.336 As for private contracts, there are in Chile matters that are of forced arbitration, of prohibited arbitration and matters in which arbitration can be freely agreed upon.[377] In the case of private construction contracts, the parties may freely agree to arbitration if it is deemed appropriate and may even appoint an arbitrator or arbitrators in the same contract.

370 *Federal Law 9307* 1996 (BR).
371 *Federal Law 9307* 1996 (BR) Article 1 (1).
372 *Federal Law 9307* 1996 (BR) Article 34.
373 Federal Law 9307 (BR) Article 32.
374 Article 36 bis, Law of Concessions of Public Works.
375 Article 36, Law of Concessions of Public Works.
376 Article 36 bis first paragraph, Law of Concessions of Public Works.
377 Article 227 et seq., Organic Code of the Courts.

National Construction Law and International Forms (Emphasis FIDIC) – How do FIDIC and Other International Forms Operate?

9.337 The use of international forms of construction contract in Brazil has been greatly affected by national infrastructure investment policy and how such contracts are regulated under the national law. International forms have been used relatively infrequently in Brazil as investment in complex infrastructure projects has been made to a great extent by the state and public contracts fall under specific rules contained in the legislation. Traditionally high levels of investment have been made in complex and high value infrastructure projects contracted by the state using public funds or funds from public banks.[378]

9.338 As a general rule, international standard form contracts may be used in Brazil as Brazilian private law, which provides for the freedom to contract, allows the parties to create their own contractual forms and obligations. However, some consideration is required as to how the national law may impact on the interpretation and application of the contract. The parties should consider: (1) The general principles in the Civil Code that may be applicable; (2) whether their intention of derogating from any suppletive laws and creating an atypical contract is clear and effective; (3) any misunderstandings that may be caused from using translations of foreign standard form contracts and the implications of using imported international legal concepts that may not be considered in Brazilian law; and (4) any public order provisions that may be applicable.

9.339 By way of example of an area in which care should be taken when using international forms in Brazil, the Brazilian Civil Code contains a provision which states that if there is reduction in the price of material or labour of more than one-tenth of the agreed global price, then the owner may make a claim for a price revision (Article 620). It is easy to see that it may not be clear if this provision is applicable to a complex contract which does not have a specific clause covering this situation. Greater legal certainty can be achieved by ensuring that, where the parties decide not to adopt or to alter certain suppletive rules, this is made clear in the contract.

9.340 When considering the use specifically of FIDIC standard contracts in Brazil, as an initial point, it is important to note that the versions of FIDIC in Portuguese are translations of the versions in English. Careful consideration should, therefore, be given to the language used in the FIDIC contract and how it could be interpreted within the relevant Brazilian legal provisions.

9.341 Further points for consideration in relation to the use of FIDIC contracts include the defects liability period. Brazilian law considers a period of five years for guarantees relating to the safety and solidity of works.[379] Some other liability periods may also be applicable, for example, in relation to hidden defects.

9.342 In Chile it has not been very common to use international forms of construction contracts. These have been used mainly on projects developed by European companies, on which many times important amendments have been made to the forms. This idea of

378 PwC, "Infraestrutura no Brasil" (2013) (downloadable at www.pwc.com.br); Ministério da Fazenda, "Infraestrutura no Brasil: Projetos, financiamento e oportunidades" (March 2013). (downloadable at www .fazenda.gov.br).

379 *Brazilian Civil Code*, 2002 (BR) Article 618.

customizing or adapting the contract is not always convenient as it could affect the principles on which the international forms are based in.

9.343 Under Chilean Law, the international construction contract forms are perfectly applicable in private contracting, since in such contracts party autonomy prevails, and there are no substantial restrictions that prevent the application of these international forms, with the exception of public order rules. Therefore, any of the different international contract models can be used in private contracting, as Article 1545 of the Civil Code establishes the principle of intangibility of the contracts, which means that contracts are a law for the parties, and also Article 1546 of the Civil Code that establishes the principle that contracts must be executed in good faith.

9.344 In terms of public contracts, some provisions of the international forms could be included in the Bidding Rules, but the major part of these will have to be carefully adapted to the provisions of public regulations, as the latter cannot be waived by the contracting entities. These limitations can be found especially in the works contracted by the Ministry of Public Works and the SERVIU under DS 75 and DS 236 respectively.

9.345 However, it is always necessary to bear in mind that international forms must be respected in their essence, as if the modifications made to the terms and conditions of these forms affect their principles, the expected outcome will not be achieved and even worse, it may cause greater distortions. Adaptation is a difficult task that requires a fine balance between the applicable legal provisions and the international models, especially considering its philosophy, principles and purposes.

9.346 Additionally, in the regime of the Law of Concessions of Public Works it would be very difficult to adapt an international form as the law incorporates a specific system of risk allocation, variations, claims, dispute resolution mechanisms, time bar, etc.

9.347 It is important to mention that FIDIC contracts establish actions that the contractor must take in the event archaeological remains are found. However, it is important to mention that in the event archaeological remains are found on the construction site, Chilean Law provides that it will be necessary to suspend the works and to notify immediately the administrative authority[380].

9.348 Another very relevant matter to be considered is related to translations, as there may be words or concepts that when translated to Spanish or other languages may cause conflicts. Therefore, in the event a dispute arises due to an ambiguous translation, the original English text should prevail, being recommendable to include this form to solve the conflict on the particular conditions of the contract.

9.349 FIDIC forms are balanced contracts and, in consequence, Chilean Law applicable to private contracts recognize these contracts as an expression of party autonomy. In effect, the regime of rights and obligations that the parties have on the different forms, even in the Silver Book, is consistent with the Chilean provisions applicable to this matter. In this sense, the Chilean Civil Code allows the parties to allocate the risks involved including fortuitous events and *Force Majeure*.[381]

380 Article 26, Law 17.288.

381 Article 1547 final paragraph, Chilean Civil Code.

CHAPTER 10

Nordic Law

Sylvie Cécile Cavaleri and Herman Bruserud

Contents

DOI: 10.4324/9781315671376-10

History of Nordic Law – Sources of Law

10.1 The Nordic countries include Denmark (including the partially autonomous territories of Greenland and the Faroe Islands), Finland, Iceland, Norway, and Sweden, whereas the cultural and linguistic region usually called Scandinavia is limited to Denmark, Norway, and Sweden.

10.2 Denmark, Norway, and Sweden were united under the Kalmar Union, a state that brought them together under the Danish monarch, from 1397 to 1523, after which Sweden became independent following a liberation war; the union then came to an end. In 1814, the King of Denmark had to cede Norway to Sweden, and Norway gained independence in 1905. Finland was part of Sweden from the 13th century until 1809 where a major part of the territory was ceded to the Russian Empire; Finland declared its independence in 1917. Norway included the Faroe Islands, Greenland, and Iceland until 1814. In 1814 Iceland became part of Denmark. It gradually gained more and more independence, until it in 1944 became an independent republic. This closely intertwined history as well as their geographical isolation explain the pronounced ties uniting the Nordic countries on many levels, which results in the same type of societal organization characterized by strong welfare states financed by a relatively high level of taxes.

10.3 Similarities between the Nordic countries can be observed from a legal point of view as well. In the 13th and 14th centuries, Nordic laws were codified on a provincial basis. In 1683, a general code of law, the Danish Code 1683 (*Danske Lov*), which consolidated most of the regional legal regimes from the Middle Ages in force at that time,[1] was adopted by the Danish monarch. Since Norway was a part of Denmark at that time, the Danish Code was also put into force in Norway as the Norwegian Code (*Norske Lov*).[2] Although it is called a code, *Danske Lov* differs from a proper code in the ordinary civil law sense on several aspects. First of all, it does not systematically regulate the main areas of law, but is a compilation of rules on scattered subjects such as civil and criminal procedure, religion and clergy and maritime matters.[3] Second, its rules are of casuistic nature, giving examples of application of rules rather than exposing them in a general and abstract manner. In Sweden, a code compiling the medieval rules was enacted in 1734. Like the Danish and Norwegian codes, it contains rules of both private and public law nature; it extended to Finland and is still valid in both countries as the latest global restatement of the law. A few rules of the original Nordic Codes are still in force but most of them have been overridden by more recent and more specialised legislation or became obsolete. Since the Nordic codes regulated specific areas of law in a fragmented way, there was at their time no codification of the general law of obligations.

10.4 A Nordic legislative cooperation was driven by the Convention of Nordic Lawyers regularly held every third year since 1872 and created in the context of a political movement

1 Ole Lando, *A Short Survey of the Laws of the Nordic Countries – The Laws in General and Contract Law in Particular* in O. Lando, M.-L. Holle, T. Håstad, B.-E. Konow, P. Møgelvang-Hansen, S. Nysten-Haarala, Á.Ólafsdottir, and L. Zackariasson (Editors), *Restatement of Nordic Contract Law*, Copenhagen, 2016, p. 14.

2 Mads Bryde Andersen & Eric Runesson, *An Overview of Nordic Contract Law* in Torgny Håstad (ed.), *The Nordic Contract Act – Essays in Celebration of its One Hundredth Anniversary*, Copenhagen, 2015, p. 15.

3 Bryde Andersen and Runesson, op. cit., p. 16.

called Scandinavism[4] which was based on the idea of a Nordic federation.[5] Within the framework of the Convention, Nordic lawyers and academics, inspired by the movement leading to the adoption of the German BGB, attempted to codify various part of private law. The most significant achievement of its collaboration was the adoption of Sales of Good Acts and Contracts Acts which had almost identical content in all the Nordic countries. The unity remains when it comes to the Contracts Act, while the unity was partly disrupted in sales law during the 1980s.

10.5 The Contracts Act and the Sales of Goods Acts are the most important legislative sources of Nordic private law, which is generally divided into two distinct disciplines.

10.6 The first, called *contract law*, covers the formation, invalidity, and interpretation of contracts as well as agency; it is governed by the different Contract Acts adopted in the Nordic countries between 1915 and 1929.

10.7 The second is the *law of obligations*, and covers matters of performance, breach of contract and corresponding remedies, including termination. This part is not on a general level codified in legislation, but based on general principles, either judge-made and/or founded in legal doctrine. Due to this absence of specific legislation corresponding to the Codes of Obligations of many countries of continental Europe, some of the provisions of the Sales Acts are applied by analogy to contracts other than sales contracts.[6]

10.8 Construction law in the Nordic countries is not regulated by statute as for instance sales law is. Although some statutes are relevant to construction matters (for instance legislation concerning environmental protection or health and safety), they do not directly regulate construction contracts.[7] The absence of legislative provisions regulating commercial[8] construction contracts has led to the adoption of standard contracts in this area. Each Nordic country has its own set(s) of national standard construction contracts which have the character of agreed documents and are the results of negotiations between organizations representing the interests of all parties involved in the construction industry.[9] This means that they are generally considered as providing balanced solutions which do not favour one party over the other.[10] In order to be applicable, standards have to be formally incorporated into individual contracts; however, some of the rules contained in the standards are considered as a codification of court made general principles of construction law and consequently apply even if the parties did not incorporate the standard into their contract.[11] Since their provisions are not negotiated individually by the parties and consequently do not reflect their particular intentions, standard contracts are in the Nordic countries interpreted based on objective criteria; subjective interpretation criteria such

4 Bryde Andersen and Runesson, op. cit., p. 17.

5 Ruth Nielsen, *Contract Law in Denmark*, Aalphen aan den Rijn, 2011, p. 23.

6 Ruth Nielsen, op. cit., p. 25.

7 Torsten Iversen, *Entrepriseretten*, 1st ed., Copenhagen, 2016, p. 53.

8 Several Nordic countries have legislative provisions concerning construction services provided to *consumers*. For instance, Norway has legislation about consumer construction contracts in form of a statute governing the construction of residential dwellings and a statute on services provided by craftsmen to consumers, and Denmark has a specific standard contract for construction services provided to consumers. The focus of the present chapter is on commercial construction contracts and these statutes will, therefore, not be dealt with here.

9 Erik Hørlyck, *Entreprise*, Copenhagen, 2014, p. 19.

10 Robert Deli, *Kommersiell byggjuridik i praktiken*, Stockholm, 2012, p. 21.

11 Iversen, op. cit., p. 55.

as the *contra proferentem* rule do not apply to such standards.[12] One may, however, quite often see that the parties make deviations from the standards, and in these situations subjective interpretation criteria may come into play.

10.9 Together with case law and academic doctrine; the standard contracts represent the main sources of Nordic construction law. The nature and availability of construction case law depends of the country in question. In Denmark, a large majority of construction disputes are settled through a system which is a hybrid between arbitration and State proceedings, since the standard contracts contain clauses stating that disputes related to contracts based on the standards shall be finally settled by the Building and Construction Arbitration Court in Copenhagen, a dispute resolution institution which only deals with construction disputes. This system shares only a few, but important common features with what is traditionally understood as arbitration, as its jurisdiction depends on the existence of an arbitration agreement between the parties and as awards rendered under the auspices of this institution are final. However, the system also differs from arbitration in that the parties do not choose their arbitrators, who are appointed by the institution from a permanent panel composed of civil judges and members of technical professions. Furthermore, the procedure and, until recently, the type of evidence allowed under this system completely mirrors state court procedure.The most important decisions rendered under its system are published in one of two specialized law journals,[13] which means that a significant body of case law is available in comparison with countries where most disputes are settled by ADR not leading to published decisions. In the other Nordic countries, various dispute resolution models exist and the availability of published decisions depends on various factors such as the model chosen by the parties – keeping in mind that mediation is growing in importance in the Nordics as much as in the rest of the world – and whether the standard adopted by the parties proposes court proceedings as standard dispute resolution.

Contract Law

The Formation of a Contract

Offer and Acceptance

10.10 The starting point in all the Nordic countries when it comes to formation of contracts is the regulation in the common Contracts Act enacted in different countries in the period 1915 to 1929.[14] The national laws were the result of cooperation between the countries and – apart from on some issues – still are almost identical.

12 Denmark: Hørlyck, op. cit., p. 19. Norway: Henning Nordtvedt, Dag Arne Ruud, Olav Bergsaker, Arve Martin Bjørnvik and Johnny Johansen, *NS 8407 Kommentarutgave*, Oslo, 2013, p. 24. Sweden: Per Samuelsson, *Entreprenadavtal – särskilt om ändrade förhållanden*, Stockholm, 2011, p. 37.

13 Kendelser for fast ejendom (KfE) = decisions on real estate law and Tidsskrift for Bolig- og Byggeret (T:BB) = Journal of Tenancy and Construction Law.

14 The Swedish Contracts Act (*Lag (1915:218) om avtal och andre rättshandlingar på förmögenhetsrättens område*, in abbreviated form *avtalslagen*)was enacted on June 11, 1915 and its current text can be found at www.riksdagen.se/sv/dokument-lagar/dokument/svensk-forfattningssamling/lag-1915218-om-avtal-och-andra-rattshandlingar_sfs-1915-218. The Danish Contracts Act (*Lov 1917-05-08 nr. 242 om Aftaler og andre Retshandler paa Formuerettens Omraade*, abbreviated *Avtaleloven*, was enacted on May 8, 1917 and its current text can be found on the following link: www.retsinformation.dk/forms/r0710.aspx?id=177079. The Norwegian Contracts Act (*Lov om avslutning av aftaler, om fuldmagt og om ugyldige viljeserklæringer,*

10.11 Thus formation of contracts in all the Nordic countries is based on the exchange of an offer and a mirroring acceptance between an offeror and an offeree.[15] An offer will be binding on the offeror according to its own terms, but if no specific terms are expressed the offer will be binding for a period allowing for the exchange of the offer and possible acceptance and proper time for the offeree to evaluate the offer made.[16] An offer may, therefore, not be revoked by the offeror within this timeframe, unless the revocation reaches the offeree at least at the same time as the offeree gains knowledge of the offer.[17] If an offer is made orally, an acceptance must, however, be made immediately if there is no indications to the contrary from the offer or the circumstances.

10.12 A late or deviating acceptance constitutes a new offer from the offeree.[18] The original offeror – receiving the late or deviating acceptance – must, however, warn the original offeree if the offeror, from the circumstances, ought to realize that the offeree assumes that the acceptance was timely or in accordance with the original offer.[19]

10.13 The offer and acceptance model of formation of contract – if, however, widely accepted as the starting point also outside the Nordic countries – may not offer the best model of understanding the diversity of situations where contractual obligations may arise. Especially where a contract gradually grows from continuous negotiations between the parties, a binding effect may arise even though it is hard to explain this by applying the traditional offer and acceptance model. Different tests as to whether the binding effect has arisen have been suggested in legal doctrine, for instance whether the parties have reached agreement on the substantial terms of the contract.[20] This test will, however, most often only apply to contractual relationships of a rather simple nature, while it usually will not be sufficient to establish a contract in more complex relationships. Basically the underlying question is whether the parties have reached a point where it is reasonable to expect that the parties have concluded a contract. In complex contractual relationships, this will be a hard test to pass.

Capacity

10.14 The capacity of the contracting parties is one of the conditions of substantive validity of a contract under Nordic law. The incapacity of a contracting party can derive from two main causes. First, a party's incapacity can be due to his or her age (the legal majority is set to 18 years old in all the Nordic countries) or to health or behavioural reasons making the person unfit to look after his or her own affairs; in these cases, the person can only be bound by a legal act if the act is executed by the person's guardian.

10.15 Second, and most importantly in the context of this chapter, a party's incapacity can result from the fact that the person who signed the contract on behalf of one party does not have the authority to bind this party.[21]

---

abbreviated *avtaleloven*, was enacted on May 31, 1918 and its current version can be found here: https://lovdata.no/pro/#document/NL/lov/1918-05-31-4.

15 See the Contracts Act, Chapter 1.

16 Cf. the Contracts Act sec. 3.

17 Cf. the Contracts Act sec. 7.

18 Cf. the Contracts Act sec. 4 and 6.

19 Cf. the Contracts Act sec. 4 and 6.

20 See, for instance, Geir Woxholth, *Avtalerett*, 2015, p. 268.

21 Nielsen, op. cit., p. 131.

10.16 A contract entered into by a person without authority is invalid and the parties must return what they have received under the contract, or compensate the other party for the value of his or her performance if the latter cannot be returned.[22] For these reasons, and due to the high values often at stake in construction contracts, it is recommended that each party requires and obtains documentation as to the capacity of the person(s) executing the contract on behalf of the other party.

Formalities

10.17 Generally, there are very few examples of formal requirements for a contract to come into existence in Nordic contract law.[23] An oral agreement is thus, as a starting point, just as binding as a written contract. This also applies to other acts of contractual importance, such as a for instance a notice of non-conformity. The fact that no written contract has been issued may – depending on the issue at hand – indicate that the parties had no intention to enter into a binding contract, but there are no formal limitations on which evidence may be presented to the effect that a contract has come into existence.

10.18 There are some statutory exemptions from this starting point. Most of these exemptions are generally aimed at protecting a weaker party or making sure that the parties realize the seriousness of the relationship they are about to enter into. In Sweden, Finland, and Iceland there is, for instance, a general exemption applying to contracts for the sale of real property. These contracts must always be made in writing.

10.19 The general approach also applies to unilateral promises – an oral promise of a gift is thus binding under Nordic contract law. Under Swedish and Finnish law a promise of a gift is, however, not binding until it has been fulfilled, unless it has been given in a deed or announced publicly.[24]

Agency

10.20 The starting point for agency under Nordic contract law is the common regulations in the Contracts Act chapter 2 generally addressing the issue of direct representation (where the agent acts in the name of the principal), even though each country also has more specific regulations of the issue in more specialized legislation for instance relating to company law issues. Further Sweden, Denmark and Norway have – at least to a large extent – common regulations on indirect representation (where the agent acts in his or her own name). Iceland and Finland have no such regulation, but seem to apply principles of the same kind.[25] Only direct representation will be dealt with below. Additionally, authority may be based on general principles beyond these regulations, where the acts or omissions of the principal – after an *in casu* broad evaluation of the facts – gives a third party good reason to believe that such an authority exists.

10.21 If a principal has authorized an agent, the principal will be bound towards a third party by the acts made by the agent on the former's behalf within the authority given. The authority of the agent is either communicated only to the agent or (also) to a third party,

22 Nielsen, op. cit. p. 131.

23 Cf. O. Lando, op. cit., p 75 ff. and Art. 1 of the Danish Code of 1683 and the Norwegian Code of 1687.

24 Cf. O. Lando, op. cit., p 76.

25 See Lando, op. cit., p. 128.

and a communication to a third party may also lie in an appointment of a person where the position, by custom or law, entails an authorization to act on the employer's behalf.

10.22 If the agent goes beyond his mandate, but still acts within his authority, for instance where the principal has made limiting instructions to the agent, the principal will be bound by the agent's acts if the authority has been communicated to the third party and the latter does not know – and should not have known – of the restrictions in the mandate. For instance, if the employer gave the project manager the authority to approve the contractor's variation proposals but only until a certain value but this limit has not been communicated to the contractor, the employer will be bound by the approval of the variation given by the project manager even though the value of the variation is higher than the limit.

10.23 The agent is generally not personally liable towards a third party. Nevertheless, an agent will be liable towards a third party for loss the latter suffers as a consequence of an exceedance of the agent's authority. The agent, thus, may be held to guarantee that he or she has the necessary authority to act on behalf of the principal covering the acts actually made. An agent may also become liable towards his principal if he or she has exceeded the mandate given by the principal.

The Contents of a Contract

Terms of a Contract (Express and Implied Terms)

10.24 The terms of the contract are principally determined by an interpretation of the contract at hand. The Nordic contract drafting tradition is, however, based on a notion that the parties' rights and obligations will be a result of a close interplay between the individual contract and the default rules offered by the law. Contracts drafted under Nordic contract law will, therefore, very often appear as short and rudimentary compared to for instance contracts drafted under an Anglo-American legal system. Absent any evidence to a different intent of the parties, the default rules in Nordic contract law would be implied, they hence play an important role in the interpretation of contracts.

10.25 In some instances, statutory default rules are of a mandatory nature, and thus will override any individual deviating regulation. As a general rule, mandatory rules are enacted to the benefit of consumers. Examples of statutes of this nature can be found for, for instance, sales contracts,[26] service contracts,[27] real estate sales,[28] and construction contracts.[29] Outside consumer contracts mandatory regulations are scarce.

26 See, for instance, the Norwegian law on consumer sales contracts of 21 June 21 2002 no. 34 and the Danish law on sales contracts of 17 February 2014.

27 See, for instance, the Norwegian law on consumer service contracts of 16 June 1989 no. 63 and the Swedish law on consumer service contracts (1985: 716).

28 See, for instance, the Norwegian law on the sale of real estate of 3 July 1992 no. 93.

29 See, for instance, the Norwegian law on consumer construction contracts of 13 June 1997 no. 43.

Vitiating Factors under Contract Law

Misrepresentation and Mistake

10.26 Art. 30 of the common Nordic Contracts Act deals with fraudulent misrepresentation and its consequences. The first part of the provision states that a declaration of intention is not binding on the promisor if the promisor was induced to make the declaration by fraud on the part of the promisee or if the promisee realized or ought to have realized that the declaration was induced by fraud on the part of a third party. The second part of the provision contains a rebuttable presumption. In fact, it states that if the promisee fraudulently misrepresented circumstances that may be deemed to affect the declaration or fraudulently failed to disclose such circumstances, the promisor shall be regarded as having been induced to make the declaration by the fraudulent conduct, unless it is demonstrated that the fraudulent conduct was unlikely to have affected the declaration.

10.27 As mentioned in the provision, fraud can consist in either express or implied misrepresentation or in fraudulent non-disclosure of relevant circumstances.[30] In commercial matters, a duty of disclosure exists when reasonable commercial standards of fair dealing dictate that particular circumstances be disclosed;[31] such standards can vary between different branches of trade.[32]

10.28 The consequence of fraudulent misrepresentations or fraudulent non-disclosure of relevant circumstances is the invalidity of the contract if it is the fraudulent misrepresentation or non-disclosure that caused the promisor to enter into the contract;[33] that is, if the promisor would not have contracted in absence of the fraudulent circumstances.

10.29 Besides misrepresentation, several types of *mistakes* can affect the validity of a contract. Art. 32 of the common Contracts Act deals with the *error in expression*; that is, the situation where a person (the promisor) made a declaration of intention which terms do not express his intentions as a result of a clerical error or other mistake on his part. In this case, the provision states that this person, the promisor, is not bound by the terms of his declaration if the person to whom the declaration was made realized or ought to have realized that an error or mistake had been made (i.e., if the promisee is acting in bad faith).[34] The provision is not meant to apply in situations of *errors as to the motives*; that is, where the promisor misunderstood the factual or legal circumstances which led to his declaration of intention.

10.30 The consequence of a person not being bound by the terms of a declaration affected by an error in expression is not that the person is not bound at all and the declaration rendered invalid. The declaration of intention must instead be assigned the meaning that the promisor meant it to have, or which the promisee must have understood that the promisor intended.[35] If the promisee acts in good faith and has no reason to detect the mistake, the promisor is bound by the terms of the erroneous declaration. The question of whether the promisee is justified in not being able to detect the mistake is assessed by

30 Nielsen, op. cit., p. 134.
31 Nielsen, op. cit., p. 134.
32 Mads Bryde Andersen, *Grundlæggende aftaleret*, 4th ed., Copenhagen, 2013, p. 382.
33 Bryde Andersen, op. cit., p. 375.
34 Bryde Andersen, op. cit., p. 387.
35 Bryde Andersen, op. cit., p. 389.

comparing his behaviour to that of a *bonus pater*; that is, a reasonable person placed in the same circumstances.[36]

Illegality

10.31 Surprisingly, the list of invalidity grounds contained in the Nordic Contracts Act does not mention illegality. However, it is generally accepted that Art. 5-1-2 of the old Nordic code of the 1680s which states that contracts which are not contrary to law and morality must be enforced according to their terms, still applies. This provision is interpreted as meaning that contracts contrary to law and morality are invalid.[37] As an example of a recent application of this provision, a judgment rendered by the Danish Western District Court (one of the two Danish courts of appeal) on 4 July 2013 can be mentioned. In this case, a plumber had carried out some works in connection with the building of a couple's villa. The plumber and its clients had agreed that part of the contract sum would be paid in cash and without invoice in order to keep it out of the knowledge of public authorities. A dispute arose between the parties as to which works were comprised in the original contract and the plumber sued the clients, claiming the payment of a part of the contract price as well as for additional works. The plumber won on first instance and the clients appealed. In its judgement, the Western District Court stated the following:

> The District Court assumes, based on [the respondent's] explanations and exhibit [...] that a significant part of the price for the plumber works were according to the parties' agreement to be paid in cash and in such a manner that this part of the price would not come to the knowledge of public authorities [...] Since the agreement on the cash payments violates law and morality pursuant to Art. 5-1-2 of Danske Lov, the plumber's claims, which are based on this agreement, cannot be enforced by the courts.
>
> [38]

The decision rendered on 25 September 2007 by the Danish Supreme Court and according to which an agreement between an energy company and its client concerning the delivery of oil at a particulary advantageous price, which could not be approved by the Energy Agency, could not be enforced in court because the lacking approval of the agency made the contract illegal,[39] is another example of application of this provision.

10.32 Not every agreement breaching legal rules can be considered invalid on the ground of illegality. Contracts aiming at criminal actions (for instance a contract for the sale of stolen goods) are clearly invalid, and so are the contract breaching rules expressly stating that their breach results in invalidity, such as for instance public procurement rules stating that no contract can be entered into during a standstill period. As far as other rules are concerned, the consequence of their breach on the validity of the contract has to be assessed by balancing the general motives underlying the rules (consideration of public

36 Bryde Andersen, op. cit., p. 390.

37 Lynge Andersen and Bo Madsen, op. cit., p. 239.

38 U (Ugeskrift for Retsvæsen).2013.2978, p. 2985, free translation.

39 U.2007.3102.

interest) and the parties' interest in being able to rely on their contracts (consideration of individual will and expectations).[40]

Duress and Undue Influence

10.33 Duress is present under Nordic law when a person enters into a commitment under an influence to his will or body which deprives him from his freedom of action or influences him in such a way that he does not have any actual choice. The law does not sanction any kind of influence, but only the types of influences that can be qualified as improper or unacceptable from a moral or societal point of view. Certain cases of duress can fall within the scope of application of the general clause of the Contract Act regarding unconscionability (Art. 36 of the Contracts Act) discussed below.[41]

10.34 The Nordic Contract Act distinguishes between violent duress (Art. 28) and simple duress (Art. 29). Violent duress is present when a declaration of will has been wrongfully obtained by actual or threatened imminent violence; it is a so-called strong invalidity ground in that the declaration of will is not binding on the coerced person (Art. 28 s. 1 of the Contracts Act). If the duress is exercised by a third party and if the person to whom the declaration was made acted in good faith, the person coerced must, if he intends to rely on the duress, inform the receiver of the declaration without undue delay after the duress has ceased to operate. If the coerced person fails to do so, he is bound by his declaration (Art. 28 s. 2 of the Contracts Act).

10.35 Simple duress is present when a person is induced by acts not falling within the scope of application of Art. 28 (i.e., violent duress) to make a declaration of will by the person to whom the declaration of will was made or if the latter realized or ought to have realized that the declaration was wrongfully obtained as a result of coercion by a third party (Art. 29 of the Contracts Act). This type of duress is a weak invalidity ground in that it can only be invoked if the promisee was aware or should have been aware of the circumstances constituting duress.[42]

10.36 Whereas cases of violent duress are relatively easy to identify, the scope of application of simple duress is less clear. A detailed discussion of this subject would go beyond the goal of this chapter. However, it is useful to mention that a threat to do something that one is legally allowed or entitled to do (for instance to notify the police of criminal handlings or to sue a contract party and claim remedies) does not constitute duress as far as the circumstances justifying the action actually exist.[43]

10.37 Following the same line of reasoning, undue influence (called "exploitation" in the Nordic languages) is present when a person unreasonably takes advantage of another person's significant economic or personal difficulties, lack of knowledge, thoughtlessness or of an existing relation of dependence in order to obtain or contract for a benefit which is substantially disproportionate to the given consideration or for which no consideration is given. Provided that the promisee is aware of the exploitation, exploitation makes the

40 Bryde Andersen, op. cit., p. 406–7.
41 Bryde Andersen, op. cit., p. 376.
42 Lynge Andersen and Bo Madsen, op. cit., p. 163.
43 Bryde Andersen, op. cit., p. 377–9.

promise invalid (Art. 31 of the Contracts Act). In practice, courts sometimes increase the agreed remuneration (consideration) instead of declaring the whole contract invalid.[44]

10.38 Exploitation is the private law equivalent of the criminal law provisions on usury.[45]

Unconscionability

10.39 The Nordic Contracts Act has since the mid-1980s had what is generally referred to as a "general clause" in its Section 36 on unconscionability. There are some minor differences in the wording of the sections in the different countries' statutes, but the concept of the regulation is the same in all countries: If a term or contract has unconscionable effects, it may be set aside or be amended to cure the unconscionability. The regulation thus seemingly gives the courts a broad competence to intervene in contractual relationships. An examination of the background of the regulation and court decisions dealing with the regulation reveals, however, that the threshold to be met for a court to intervene – especially in contractual relationships between professional parties – is very high. Most of the cases where a court has intervened has been to the benefit of a consumer towards a professional party. This was the intention when enacting the regulations, to protect the weaker party if, however, not formally restricted to these situations.

10.40 Court practice shows a wide variety of situations where the regulation may be applicable. Especially in Sweden it has been applied to arbitration clauses in contracts with consumers or people in similar positions. In Danish courts one finds a few examples of application on liquidated damages clauses, where the applicable damages have been reduced. In Norwegian courts it was from an early stage applied to increase the remuneration in long term land lease contracts where the remuneration was not originally subject to indexation and, therefore, had lost a significant part of its value. When evaluating whether a term or a contract is unconscionable, a court will typically put weight to the position of the parties involved, and thus its core field of application is to the benefit of consumers, even though it is applicable in other instances as well. The extent of deviation of the contract in question from what would have otherwise applied (i.e., if the default rules applied) is usually of significant importance in the application of this section. Other important factors will often include whether the contractual relationship is of a strict commercial nature, the acts and omissions of the parties during the negotiations and under the contract and whether the contract is in accordance with established practice in the relevant branch of business, as such, the application of the unconscionability principle depends on a broad evaluation of the circumstances of each case

The Rights and Liabilities of Third Parties

10.41 The doctrine of privity of contract, according to which a contract only produces effects between its parties, applies as the main rule in Nordic law of contract. However, there are exceptions to this rule; for instance, the parties may have agreed on clauses

44 Bryde Andersen, op. cit., p. 385.
45 Lynge Andersen and Bo Madsen, op. cit., p. 163.

granting rights to third parties or allowing for the transfer of contractual rights to third parties.[46]

10.42 As opposed to other jurisdictions such as English law, Nordic law does not require consideration as a condition for the validity of a contract. For this reason, there is no fundamental objection in Nordic law to the validity of stipulations in favour of third parties even though the latter do not provide a consideration for the benefits/rights they receive[47] under the contract.

10.43 There are three main types of legal acts involving rights and liabilities of third parties in a contractual context: 1) A contract or clause granting rights to a third party; 2) the performance of the contract by a third party, and 3) the transfer of contractual rights under a contract.

10.44 First, a stipulation in favour of a third party grants this third party a right if his right has been expressly agreed upon between the promisor and the promisee, or when such third party right must be inferred from the purpose of the contract or the circumstances of the case. Typical examples of such case are a life insurance policy under which the beneficiary acquires an irrevocable right upon the death of the promisee, or the fact that under Danish sales law, the seller's warranty to the buyer extends to members of the buyer's household. In some situations, the promisor and the promisee may agree that the promisor's promise to perform an obligation to the benefit of a third party grants the latter an independent right to enforce such promise.[48]

10.45 Second, is the situation where the contract is performed by a third party, which is for instance the case when a main contractor hires a subcontractor to perform part of the main contractor's obligations. As a rule, the promisee cannot refuse performance by a third party, unless the contract provides otherwise or if personal performance by the promisor is implied by the nature or purpose of the contract, such as for instance a contract for the performance of a concert by a famous musician.

10.46 Third, some contracts can provide for the transfer of contractual rights and duties to third parties. An example of this is Art. 5, s. 1 of the Danish standard construction contract AB 92, which provides that the parties may assign their rights under the contract, and according to s. 3 of the same provision, neither party may transfer its obligations to a third party without prior consent from the other party.

Performance of a Contract

Performance

10.47 Most contractual rights are discharged through performance. A contractual right ceases to exist when: 1) It has been performed in accordance with the contract, 2) at the right time and in the right place, and 3) performance has been effected to the obligee or the person who is legitimately entitled to receive the performance[49] (for instance, a person stated in the contract as a third party beneficiary).

46 Lynge Andersen and Bo Madsen, op. cit., p. 334–5.

47 Nielsen, op. cit., p. 155.

48 Nielsen, op. cit., p. 156.

49 Bernhard Gomard, *Obligationsret 2. del*, 4th ed.by Torsten Iversen, Copenhagen, 2011, p. 21.

10.48 Whether a contract has been performed properly depends, first; on the provisions of the contract and on the legal rules applying to all types of contracts, such as the law provisions on contracts' formation and validity in the common Nordic Contracts Act, or those of the statute of limitation. Such rules can be mandatory, meaning that they apply regardless of what the parties agreed on, or dispositive meaning that they only apply if the parties did not agree otherwise.

10.49 Non-performance or improper performance constitutes breach of contract, which is sanctioned by the remedies described below.

Breach

10.50 Under Nordic contract law, for a breach of contract to occur giving the injured party a right to damages generally two criteria must be met, these are:

10.51 First; there must be a deviation from the contractual requirements to performance, and second, the deviation may not be attributable to something which the other party bears the risk of. The first criterion is based on a comparison between the contractual requirements and the performance presented, and any deviation could – in principle – constitute breach of contract.

10.52 The latter criterion – that the deviation may not be within the other party's share of risk covers a number of different situations, and is quite dependable on the type of the contractual relationship in question. One category of situations is when one party is in breach of its obligations giving rise to remedies for the other party, for instance the right to withhold its own performance. This might be the case when payment is delayed. Another category would be when the end result is dependent on input or deliveries from both parties, as is the case in a construction contract. If a party's defective performance is the result of failing to provide the required input or deliveries from the other party, the defective performance will not constitute a breach.

10.53 Generally speaking, the non-performance of a contract can consist both in the obligor's culpable or excusable failure to perform or in the obligee's failure to accept performance. The obligor' failure to perform can consist both in a delay in performance or in premature delivery, or in performance not complying with the parties' agreement, for instance defects, seller's lack of title or deviation from the agreed quantity (a seller who delivers too little or too much raw materials).[50]

10.54 In case of breach of contract, the obligee can safeguard its interests by requesting/claiming different types of remedies. The victim of the breach can either request one of the so-called *performance remedies*; that is, remedies aiming at proper performance of the contract, such as requesting a new delivery in a sales contract, or requesting that the contractor remedies defects in a construction contract. Depending on the provisions of the parties agreement and on the applicable legal rules, which can vary significantly between different types of contracts, the obligee can also request to postpone the performance of his own obligations or to be partly or fully released from performing such obligations; withhold his own performance; reduce his remuneration paid to the party in breach or

50 Gomard, op. cit., p. 28.

terminate the contract.[51] Furthermore, the party which failed to perform and acted wrongfully may be liable in damages for the other party's economic loss. This liability is however sometimes dependent on the nonperforming party's negligence or wilful misconduct. These remedies are described briefly below.

Termination

10.55 An obligee cannot always protect himself against losses and inconveniences resulting from the obligor's breach of contract by exercising remedies aiming at full performance of the contract by the obligor. The obligee can in some situations safeguard his interests in a quicker and more effective manner by requesting to be released from a mutually binding contract which has been fundamentally breached. Examples of such situations are cases where a request for full performance is without prospect of success; where late performance has no value for the obligee (e.g., a birthday cake delivered too late), or when the obligee reasonably does not want to waste resources to try and enforce a claim against a company with which he has no intention to conduct further business. The obligee can in these cases, provided that the conditions for termination are fulfilled, give notice of termination to the obligor and bring both parties' main obligations to an end.[52]

10.56 The conditions and effects of termination can vary between different types of contracts. In the general Nordic law of obligations; it is accepted that a party's right of termination is conditional upon the other party's fundamental breach of the contract. In some areas of law, as the law of sales, the notion of fundamental breach is further defined by statute (see: Art. 21, s. 2 of the Danish Sales Act). Furthermore, the obligee requesting termination must give both a notice of breach and a notice of termination indicating the grounds justifying termination.[53]

10.57 The effect of termination is to put an end to the parties' main obligations, while some ancillary obligations (such as an obligation not to compete with a former employer or the obligation to refer any dispute to arbitration) survive the termination.[54]

10.58 For sales contracts, termination has retroactive effect, meaning that both parties must restitute what they received under the contract. For other types of contracts, the main rule is that termination affects only obligations yet to be carried out.[55]

Remedies

Remedies under Contract

10.59 The remedies described in the following section (Remedies at Law) are general rules which apply unless the parties agreed otherwise.[56] Parties can make agreements concerning remedies in their contract in several ways. First, they can add remedies not

51 Mads Bryde Andersen and Joseph Lookofsky, *Lærebog i obligationsret I – Ydelsen, Beføjelser*, 4th ed., Copenhagen, 2015, p. 179.

52 Bryde Andersen and Lookofsky, op. cit., p. 212.

53 Gomard, op. cit., p. 115 19.

54 Gomard, op. cit., p. 116.

55 Bryde Andersen and Lookofsky, op. cit., p. 213.

56 Bryde Andersen and Lookofsky, op. cit., p. 404.

provided for by the law (e.g., liquidated delay damages in construction contracts). Second, they can exclude the application of certain remedies or create a hierarchy between legal remedies so that certain remedies cannot be resorted to before others have been already exhausted. Third, they can modify the legal conditions that must be fulfilled in order to request a remedy, for instance, by stating that any delay, fundamental or not, gives the other party the right to terminate the contract immediately.[57] Finally, some clauses purport to exclude any remedy, such as clauses according to which an object is sold "as is". Whether such clauses actually protect the seller against any claim depends on the very circumstances of the case, but it is generally accepted that they do not protect a seller acting in bad faith; who should know that the object was defective but does not draw the buyer's attention to the defect in violation of the seller's loyal duty of information or in cases of fundamental hidden defects.[58]

10.60 Such agreement(s) on remedies can be found both in contracts based on standard forms and in bespoke ones. For instance, the Danish standard construction contract AB 92 provides that in case of defective works, the contractor has both a right and a duty to try and remedy the defects before the employer can request other remedies such as a price reduction and/or terminate the contract.[59] Another example is contract clauses providing for the allocation of liability on a knock-for-knock basis, meaning that in case of losses caused to one of the contract parties, the aggrieved party shall bear his own losses regardless of who caused them, effectively barring the aggrieved party from claiming any kind of damages, under tort or contract, from the other party.[60]

10.61 The validity of agreements concerning remedies, especially those limiting the access to certain remedies, are to be assessed in light of the general provisions concerning contract validity, especially Section 36 of the Contracts Act regarding unconscionability.

Remedies at Law

10.62 In the Nordic law of obligations, remedies available to a party against another party in breach of his obligations can derive either from applicable statutes (for instance, the Sales Act or the Tenancy Act) or be based on principles established by case law and legal doctrine. These remedies at law can be classified in three categories.

10.63 First, the so-called *performance remedies* aim at having the party in breach perform the contract properly (specific performance); remedying of defects in construction law, or requesting new delivery in a contract of sales are examples of such remedies.

10.64 Second, the so-called *reciprocity remedies*, based on the fact that the contract imposes obligations on both parties. Examples of such remedies are a party's right to suspend his own performance until the other party has offered to perform, provided that the contract provides for simultaneous performance; termination or a proportionate reduction of the price.

57 Gomard, op. cit., p. 300.
58 Gomard, op. cit., p. 308.
59 AB 92 §31, s. 1 and 4.
60 Gideon Parchomovsky and Endre Stavang, Contracting Around Tort Defaults: The Knock-for-Knock Principle and Accident Costs, CREE Working Paper 14/2013, p. 3, available at www.cree.uio.no/publications/CREE_working_papers/pdf_2013/knock_for_knock_stavang_cree_wp_14_2013.pdf.

10.65 Third, and often provided that the breach constitutes wrongful behaviour of the party in default, the aggrieved party may claim damages.[61]

10.66 The availability and conditions of requesting *performance remedies* vary greatly depending on the type of contract at hand; the nature of the obligation breached, and the type of breach. If the breach consists a failure to pay; a claim for payment will be filed through a request for a summary judgment ordering the defaulting party to pay the due sum, interest as well as debt collection expenses, will, if necessary, be enforced through seizure and forced sale of the debtor's assets. If the breach is a an obligation to deliver goods not effected at the agreed time for performance (delayed performance), the creditor will simply request performance; that is, delivery of the agreed goods. If the breach is defective performance (i.e., that the performance does not comply with the parties' agreement with respect to quantity and/or quality, etc.), the obligee can either request a new performance (as provided for in Art. 43 of the Danish Sales Act) or the remedying of defects (as provided for in consumer sales in Art. 78 of the Danish Sales Act). An obligee has, in principle, the right to specific performance, but this main rule has many exceptions, namely in cases where it is practically or economically impossible for the obligor to perform.[62]

10.67 The right to retain one's performance until the other party has performed his obligations is an important remedy if the parties agreed they should perform simultaneously or if such simultaneity of performance is not excluded by agreement or by the circumstances of the case. If not excluded by agreement or the circumstances, the right to retain performance presupposes correlation between the parties' obligations; that is, that the parties' mutual obligations derive from the same legal relation (for instance, a contract).[63] In addition to the condition of correlation, the existence and conditions of application of a retention right depends on the type of contract at hand. In construction law, the contractor's right to suspend performance of his own obligations materializes in his right to suspend the works if the employer does not pay the agreed instalments (see, for instance, in Danish law §22 and 23 of the standard contract AB 92).

10.68 If there is defective performance (e.g., if the sold goods do not comply with the contractual specifications) and the obligee cannot or does not want to terminate the contract, he may have the possibility to request a reduction in the price. Such remedy is provided for by law or standard contracts in some areas (see: Art. 42, 43, 78 and 79 of the Danish Sales Act, Art. 11 of the Danish Tenancy Act and §31, s. 4 and 32, s. 4 of the Danish standard construction contract AB 92). Such remedy is only relevant if the defect(s) actually reduce the value of the deliverables. When such is the case, the goal of the remedy is to re-establish the balance that the parties agreed on; if the object of the contract is worth less than what it was sold or rented for, the remuneration can be adapted accordingly. The amount of the reduction corresponds to the difference between the agreed contract price (i.e., the value of the proper performance according to the parties' agreement) and the actual value of the performance. In many cases, the amount of the reduction can correspond to the cost of remedying the defects, provided that such costs were justified.[64]

61 Gomard, op. cit., p. 33 to 37.
62 Bryde Andersen and Lookofsky, op. cit., p. 203.
63 Gomard, op. cit., p. 33.
64 Bryde Andersen and Lookofsky, op. cit., pp. 239–43.

10.69 Finally, if the breach gives rise to the liability of the obligor, the obligee can request compensatory damages to cover the losses that the breach of contract caused him. The obligor is liable for both his own and his employee's wrongful acts. The burden of proof is often reversed so that the obligor's behaviour is presumed to be wrongful unless he proves otherwise (presumed liability). The law also contains rules according to which certain obligors are strictly liable, such as a seller who sells goods over which he has no title (Art. 59 of the Danish Sales Act). The aggrieved party will generally calculate his claim to damages as amounting to his positive performance interest; that is, request to be economically placed in the same situation as if the contract had been properly performed. In some situations, he may have an interest in claiming his negative contract interest; that is, to be placed in the same situation as if the contract had never been entered into.[65] The basis of the liability of the obligor for damages is subject of debate; his liability is a consequence of the breach of his contractual obligations and can, therefore, be said to be of contractual nature, but some types of wrongful behaviour can also be a matter of tort. The distinction is relevant in relation to contractually agreed limitations of liability, which as a main rule only can exclude or limit contractual liability, but not tort liability.[66]

Limitation on Remedies

10.70 As they often provide a limitation or exclusion of liability for the party benefitting from them, limitation on remedies are, in Nordic law, subject to a validity control which is effected in three steps.

10.71 First, a judge or adjudicating authority will investigate whether the limitation has been validly adopted by the parties. This question is very often raised in relation to limitations of liability contained in standard contract terms, especially if those are meant to be incorporated into the contract by way of simple reference. The answer to this question depends on the circumstances of the case, but it is generally accepted that limitation of liability must be highlighted for the other party, or his attention must be otherwise brought to the limitation clause for the latter to be valid.[67]

10.72 Second, clauses purporting to limit a party's liability must be *restrictively interpreted*; if a clause is unusual or places an unusual burden on a party, the clause must be very clear and highlighted for this party for it to be valid. An example of restrictive interpretation is that a clause restricting a party's liability for negligence is not deemed to cover gross negligence.[68]

10.73 Finally, the substantive validity of the clause has to be assessed. In this regard, it is important to note that under Nordic law, certain types of liability such as liability under the Product Liability Directive cannot be excluded. The same will probably apply for liability attributable to certain types of behaviour such as wilful misconduct.[69] The question of validity will often be discussed in light of Art. 36 of the common Nordic Contracts Act sanctioning unconscionable contracts or clauses.

65 Gomard, op. cit., pp. 35–6.
66 Gomard, op. cit., p. 36.
67 Bryde Andersen and Lookofsky, op. cit., p. 411.
68 Gomard, op. cit., pp. 313–14.
69 Gomard, op. cit., pp. 314–16.

Contract Interpretation

10.74 The practical main rule and the starting point of the interpretation of any contract is the plain and natural meaning of the wording of the contract. If no clear plain and natural meaning is identifiable, the decisive point which a decision maker has to look in order to ascertain the meaning of a contract is the parties' coinciding understanding when entering into the contract. This rule is, however, very rarely applied, as it is often very difficult to bring the evidence which is necessary to reach a conclusion in this respect.

10.75 When establishing the natural meaning of a contract term, not only the words of the term in question are of importance. The term must be read in light of the other terms of the contract, the purpose of the term and the contract as such. One must also properly consider the reasonability of the possible different interpretations.

10.76 The practical starting point of the plain meaning of the wording will be deviated from where a party to the contract realized-or at least should have realized-that the other party had a diverging opinion of the content of the parties' rights and obligations than what otherwise can be inferred from the contract. This is often referred to as part of a party's continuous obligation of loyalty, which applies from the pre contractual phase and throughout the contractual phase, and even continues after the contractual relationship has been brought to an end. This rule, as described, allows for/permits deviation from the literal interpretation of the wording of the contract. The party's deviating opinion can, then, be understood as "realizable" from a broader context other than just of the default rules of law, namely; what happened during negotiations.

10.77 If neither the rule on the parties coinciding understanding or the rule on a realizable interpretation gives a basis for an interpretation, and a clear interpretation of the contract's wording cannot be established, the interpretation is most often decided on an application of risk-based considerations. An application of these considerations will typically end up with a distribution of the risk of unclear terms according to which party should have avoided-or at least addressed-the situation. There are different versions of this kind of considerations, but typically what will be important will be who drafted or introduced the term in question.

Standard Forms of National Contracts

10.78 As mentioned above, each Nordic country has its own set(s) of national construction contracts. This paragraph is thus dedicated to a brief overview of these national standards.

Denmark: The AB Standard Contracts

10.79 The Danish standard contracts mainly giving rise to disputes and case law are the following at the time of this writing[70]: AB 92 – *Almindelige betingelser for arbejder og leverancer i bygge- og anlægsvirksomhed*, which can be translated as General Conditions for the Provision of Work and Supplies within Building and Engineering, which covers the

70 The content of this chapter was last updated on 16 August 2019.

traditional "build-only" model where the employer provides the design and the contractor executes the works. The ABT 93 standard – *Almindelige betingelser for totalentreprise*, regulates turnkey contracts where the contractor designs and executes the works. Finally, technical advice by architects and engineers is regulated by the standard ABR 89 – *Almindelige betingelser for teknisk rådgivning og bistand*, General Conditions on technical advice and assistance.[71] The number contained in the standard contracts' abbreviations indicates the year of adoption of each standard.

10.80 The above-mentioned standard contracts were recently replaced by new revised versions made public on 21 June 2018 and which their drafting committee recommends parties to apply from 1 January 2019. These standard contracts are AB 18 ("build only"), ABT 18 (turnkey) and ABR 18 (consulting services).[72] Simplified versions of AB 18 (titled "*AB Forenklet*", AB simplified),[73] and ABR 18 (*ABR Forenklet*)[74] also exist. The simplified AB 18 is meant to be used when the works are small and/or of simple nature whereas the simplified ABR can be applied for consulting services where the consultant does not assume design responsibilities or only to a limited extent

10.81 In addition to these standard contracts, the AB system has been extended with four standard contract appendixes intended to be used in specific situations. The APP Design Development[75] (*APP Projektudvikling*)[76] contains additional conditions to AB 18 or ABT 18 which can be applied when the contractor is required to participate at an early stage to the development of the design being produced by the consultant. The APP Design Optimization[77] (*APP Projektoptimering*)[78] contains additional conditions to

71 Iversen, op. cit., pp. 56–9. Digital versions of the Danish standard construction contracts are freely available at the following links. AB 92: www.danskbyggeri.dk/publikationer-og-blanketter/byggejura/ab-92-og-abt-93/ab-92-a4-format/ (Danish version) and www.danskbyggeri.dk/publikationer-og-blanketter/byggejura/ab-92-og-abt-93/ab-92-engelsk-udgave/ (English version). ABT 93: www.danskbyggeri.dk/publikationer-og-blanketter/byggejura/ab-92-og-abt-93/abt-93-almindelige-betingelser-for-totalentreprise/. ABR 89: www.danskeark.dk/content/abr-89 (Danish version) and www.frinet.dk/kontrakt-og-udbud/vaerktoejer/regler-og-love/aftale-kap-9-general-conditions-for-consulting-services-(abr-89) (English version).

72 The new standard contracts are freely available on different websites, for instance the following: AB 18 in Danish at www.retsinformation.dk/Forms/R0710.aspx?id=202695 and in English at www.trafikstyrelsen.dk/~/media/Dokumenter/09%20Byggeri/Byggeriets%20aftalevilkaar%20AB%20system/AB%2018%20English/2019_03_08_AB_18_EN.pdf; ABT 18 in Danish at www.retsinformation.dk/Forms/R0710.aspx?id=206410 and in English at www.trafikstyrelsen.dk/~/media/Dokumenter/09%20Byggeri/Byggeriets%20aftalevilkaar%20AB%20system/AB%2018%20English/2019_02_07_ABT_18_EN.pdf; ABR 18 at www.retsinformation.dk/Forms/R0710.aspx?id=206408 and in English at www.trafikstyrelsen.dk/~/media/Dokumenter/09%20Byggeri/Byggeriets%20aftalevilkaar%20AB%20system/AB%2018%20English/2019_02_07_ABT_18_EN.pdf.

73 The simplified AB 18 in Danish can be accessed at www.retsinformation.dk/Forms/R0710.aspx?id=206415. An English translation of this standard contract, titled AB Abridged, can be accessed at www.trafikstyrelsen.dk/~/media/Dokumenter/09%20Byggeri/Byggeriets%20aftalevilkaar%20AB%20system/AB%2018%20English/2019_02_07_AB_Abridged_EN.pdf.

74 The simplified ABR 18 can be accessed at www.retsinformation.dk/Forms/R0710.aspx?id=206416 and its English translation, titled "ABR Abridged", can be accessed at www.trafikstyrelsen.dk/~/media/Dokumenter/09%20Byggeri/Byggeriets%20aftalevilkaar%20AB%20system/AB%2018%20English/2019_02_07_ABR_Abridged_EN.pdf.

75 English version: www.trafikstyrelsen.dk/~/media/Dokumenter/09%20Byggeri/Byggeriets%20aftalevilkaar%20AB%20system/AB%2018%20English/2019_02_07_AB_APP_Design_Development_EN.pdf.

76 Danish version: www.retsinformation.dk/Forms/R0710.aspx?id=206288.

77 English version: www.trafikstyrelsen.dk/~/media/Dokumenter/09%20Byggeri/Byggeriets%20aftalevilkaar%20AB%20system/AB%2018%20English/2019_02_07_AB_APP_Design_Optimisation_EN.pdf.

78 Danish version: www.retsinformation.dk/Forms/R0710.aspx?id=206413.

AB 18 or ABR 18 which can be applied when the contractor is required to review the design and make optimization proposals in relation to time, price and/or quality. The APP Operational Requirements[79] (*APP Driftskrav*)[80] contains additional conditions to AB 18 or ABT 18 and can be applied when operational requirements apply to the works but can only be tested after a period of operation subsequent to taking-over. Finally, APP Incentives[81] (APP Incitamenter)[82] is a catalogue of optional provisions which can be added to AB 18, ABT 18 or ABR 18 when the parties wish to agree on bonuses under specific conditions.

10.82 There is understandably little available case law on these new standard contracts and appendixes yet, but the below comments will endeavour to point out when and how they are expected to modify the current practice. In this respect, our observations will to a large extent be based on the explanatory report published by the standard contracts' drafting committee together with the contracts and appendixes (hereafter the "Report").[83]

10.83 The successive versions of the Danish standard contracts were issued either by the Ministry for Housing (AB 92, ABT 93, ABR 89) based on drafts submitted by a committe composed of representatives of the various organizations promoting the interests of the different professions in the construction industry, or directly by such drafting committee, appointed by the Climate, Energy and Housing Minister, as he then was.[84] They, therefore, belong to the category of standard contracts called agreed documents[85] and aim at achieving a reasonable balance between the interests of the parties to construction contracts.

10.84 As a matter of principle, the Danish standard construction contracts only apply if the parties choose to incorporate them to their contracts; however, a significant part of the rules contained in these standard contracts are deemed to constitute a codification of general rules of the Danish law of obligations and, therefore, apply regardless of whether the parties incorporated the standard into their contract or not. Until January 2019, the use of the national Danish standard contracts was imposed by a government circular on all public or publicly financed projects; according to guidelines issued in May 2019 by the Danish Building and Property Agency and addressed to all public employers, the latter are advised to apply a "follow or explain" principle, meaning that any total or partial derogation from the AB standard contracts must be argued for in tender documents.[86] In the private sector, the parties are free to choose their standards contracts but the national

79 English version: www.trafikstyrelsen.dk/~/media/Dokumenter/09%20Byggeri/Byggeriets%20aftalevilkaar%20AB%20system/AB%2018%20English/2018_12_17_AB_APP_Operational_Requirements_EN.pdf.

80 Danish version: www.retsinformation.dk/Forms/R0710.aspx?id=202700.

81 English version: www.trafikstyrelsen.dk/~/media/Dokumenter/09%20Byggeri/Byggeriets%20aftalevilkaar%20AB%20system/AB%2018%20English/2018_12_17_AB_APP_Incentives_EN.pdf.

82 Danish version: www.retsinformation.dk/Forms/R0710.aspx?id=206432.

83 The document is titled *Betænkning nr. 1570 2018 – Almindelige betingelser i bygge- og anlægsvirksomhed* (Report nr. 1570 2018 – general conditions in the building and engineering sector) and can be accessed in original Danish language at www.trafikstyrelsen.dk/DA/Byggeri/Byggeriets-aftalevilkar/~/media/25F62FD1A7CF4BE1ACE6A0C979E174D2.ashx At the time of this writing (August 2019), no English translation of this document exists.

84 Hørlyck, op. cit., p. 18. Erik Hørlyck, *Entreprise – AB 18*, Copenhagen, 2019 (hereafter "Hørlyck-2019"), p. 47.

85 Hørlyck, op. cit., p. 19. Hørlyck-2019, p. 47.

86 Bygninsstyrelsens Bygherrevejledning 2019 (Employer Guidelines 2019 by the Danish Building and Property Agency, p. 3, www.bygst.dk/media/735036/Bygherrevejledning-2019.pdf.

standards are quite popular as well and are incorporated into a large majority of contracts (and virtually all the large ones).

Norway: Distinct Standards for Onshore and Offshore Construction

10.85 Since an important part of Norway's GDP is derived from oil from the North Sea, a lot of offshore construction is taking place along Norway's coasts and in Norwegian territorial waters. Specific standards contracts; the NF and NTK contracts, apply in the offshore sector, whereas another set of standards, the NS family of contracts, apply to land construction. Recent evolution shows that offshore standards are increasingly applied to land projects as well, most likely because they are seen as more professional and providing the parties with a higher level of certainty, especially with respect to contract management in a broad sense and dispute resolution. Still, however, the NS contracts dominate the land projects.

Land Construction: The NS Family of Contracts

10.86 Like it is the case in the other Nordic countries, Norway has a long-standing tradition of using standard contracts in the construction sector, it is the "NS" family of contracts. The acronym "NS" in the standard contracts names stands for *Norske Standarder*; the Norwegian Standards. They are drafted and revised by committees appointed by the organization Standard Norge, previously known as the Norwegian Council of Building Standardization (*Norsk Byggestandardiseringsråd*). Like in other Nordic countries, the NS standards are the result of trade collaboration.

10.87 The first standard contract, NS 401, directed at build-only projects where the design is provided by the employer, dates back from 1938 and came out in subsequent versions in 1961 (NS 401 A), 1969 (NS 3401) and 1991, revised in 1994 (NS 3430).[87] The first standard contract for turnkey projects, NS 3431, came out in 1992 with a second edition in 1994. NS 34030 was extensively revised as the result of a procedure which started in 1996 and concluded with the publication of the new standard contract NS 8405 in 2004, with a new edition in 2008. A committee composed of members representing architects, contractors, private and public employers and other actors with interests in the construction industry was constituted in 2008 in order to revise the turnkey standard contract; the committee's work led to the current NS 8407, in force since 1 July 2011.

10.88 Specific standard contracts for subcontracts exist for both the build-only model (with subcontract standard NS 8415) and the turnkey model (subcontract NS 8417), and simplified versions exist for both the build-only model (NS 8406) and the build-only subcontract (NS 8416). In addition to the named build-only and turnkey contracts and subcontracts, the NS family contains standard contracts on consultancy contracts: NS 8401 (design assignment), NS 8402 (consultancy assignment with remuneration on an hourly basis), NS 8403 (project manager assignment) and NS 8404 (independent controller assignment).

87 Nordtvedt et al., op. cit., p. 21.

10.89 As opposed to Denmark where some aspects of tender procedures; for instance, the requirements set to the content of tender documentation are (summarily) regulated in the turnkey and build-only standard contracts,[88] Norway has specific rules which can be used by employers conducting tender procedures in the private sector: NS 8400 (Conditions for acquisitions for building services and engineering in the context of tender procedures) and NS 8410 (Conditions for acquisitions for building services and engineering in the context of tender procedures with negotiations). The latter can apply to cases where the commissioning party is allowed to negotiate with the tenderers about the contents of their bids but not of tendering documents.[89] NS 8400 and NS 8410 are not standard contracts, but sets of rules which private employer can, but are not obligated to, follow when they conduct competitive tender procedures. However, their use is recommended to guide these employers, which can otherwise risk being exposed to significant damages claims from tenderers believing that they have been evicted in violation of general principles governing tender procedures (for example the principle of equal treatment of the tenderers, which applies as a general principle of law, whether or not the procedure is subject to a specific set of rules).

10.90 Finally, the NS family counts three standard contracts which regulate specific matters and procedures: General conditions for the purchase of building materials (NS 8409), general conditions for the regulation of the contract price based on indexes (NS 3405, which provides for the procedures to be followed when the parties agreed that the contract price should be adapted to follow indexes) and NS 8430, which describes procedures to be followed when building and engineering works are taken over by the employer.

Offshore Construction: The NF Family of Contracts

10.91 The NF standards are standard contracts regulating the production and supply of large components for the petroleum industry on the Norwegian continental shelf.[90] The family is composed of two main types of contracts. First, the NF 2015 (*Norsk Fabrikasjonkontrakt*) is designed to regulate contracts concerning only the manufacture of large components produced for the Norwegian petroleum industry.[91] As it is understandable from its name, the latest version dates from 2015. Second, the NTK (*Norsk Totalkontrakt*) applies to more extensive deliveries which comprise design, procurement, construction and possibly installation (i.e., it is an EPC(I) standard). The latest version of NTK (NTK 2015) is flanked by three specific contract versions. The NTK 2015 MOD (Norsk Totalkontrakt Modifikasjon) is meant to regulate contracts concerning large modifications of offshore installations if the "contractor" (called "supplier" in these standards) is in charge of the design, procurement, construction and installation of the modified parts. If the modification also comprises a new module, a third contract, the NTK 2015 Module and Modification, which exists in two versions (one with single delivery of the entire con-

88 See §2 to 4 in AB 92 and §2 to 4 in ABT 93.

89 Viggo Hagstrøm and Herman Bruserud, *Entrepriserett*, Oslo, 214, p. 118 (description of the types of tender procedures in the public sector) and p. 133-134 (standard conditions on tender procedures in the private sector).

90 Knut Kaasen, *Petroleumskontrakter – med kommentarer til NF 05 og NTK 05*, Oslo, 2006, p. 19.

91 Kaasen, op. cit., p. 21.

tract object, and one with separate deliveries of module, prefabricated items and offshore permanent works) should be applied.

10.92 The Norwegian offshore standard contracts are inspired by and share common features with Anglo-American contracts: They contain long and detailed provisions, many definitions and cross-references and place a strong emphasis on contract management. However, they also possess typical Norwegian features such as a terminology and structure influenced by Norwegian contract law and a heavier reliance to the background law[92] than normally is the case with standards deriving from common law.

Sweden: The AB Standards

10.93 Similarly as in Denmark, commercial construction contracts are dominated in Sweden by three standard contracts: The AB 04 (*Almänna Bestämmelser för bygg-, anlägning och installationsentreprenader* – build-only model), the ABT 06 (*Almänna Bestämmelser för totalentreprenader avseende bygg-, anläggnings og installationsarbeten* – turnkey model) and the ABK 09 (*Almänna Bestämmelser för konsultuppdrag inom arkitekt- og ingenjörsverksamhet* – consultants). The number in the standards' titles indicates the year of the latest version.

10.94 The contracts are drafted by the Contract Committee of the Construction Association (*Föreningen Byggandets Kontraktskomitté*, BKK). The association's members are representatives of employers and contractors as well as several public authorities.[93] The Swedish standards belong, therefore, also to the category of agreed documents and are interpreted consequently.

10.95 As it is the case in Denmark, the Swedish standard contracts are broadly applied. A large majority of commercial construction contracts and almost all public ones are based on these standard contracts.[94]

10.96 Another standard contract; the ABA 99 – *Almänna Bestämmelser för leverans av industriella anläggningar*, general conditions for the supply of industrial plants, is relatively broadly used for the supply of such projects in or for Sweden, especially for energy production plants. The standard is produced by *Teknikforetägen*, an employer trade union; its standard contract is, therefore, not an agreed document and is known to be relatively supplier-friendly.[95]

Finland

10.97 Two main standard contracts are in use in Finland: The YSE 1998 – General Conditions for building contracts, which is meant for the build-only model but can be modified to regulate turnkey contracts as well, and KSE 2013 – general conditions for consulting for consultancy contracts. Both are agreed documents negotiated between the relevant actors across the construction industry.

92 Kaasen, op. cit., p. 21.
93 Deli, op. cit., p. 21.
94 Samuelsson, op. cit., p. 21.
95 Deli, op. cit., p. 24.

Construction Law Principles

Procurement and Tendering

Public Procurement

10.98 With the exception of Norway and Iceland,[96] the Nordic countries are members of the EU. Norway and Iceland are members of the EEC. The rules governing public procurement are thus to a large extent directly dictated by EU directives, mainly the classical public sector directive,[97] the utilities directive[98] and the concessions directive[99] (all last revised in 2014) as implemented in national law. These directives are also applicable in the non-EU states under the EEC agreement.

10.99 The implementation of directives can take place in several forms. In Denmark, for instance, the previous versions of the public sector directive were implemented by simple ordinance stating that the directive was valid law in Denmark, whereas the 2014 version is implemented through a distinct statute, the Danish Public Procurement Act ("*Udbudsloven*") as is the case in Norway as well.[100]

10.100 The prescriptions deriving from the directives and the implementing national legislation are only applicable if certain criteria are met, among others if the value of the contract exceeds a certain threshold.[101] The conditions of award of public contracts with values lower than the specified thresholds are regulated by national statutes.[102]

10.101 A detailed discussion of the rules governing public procurement goes beyond the scope of the present work. Generally, one can say that the rules are meant to ensure an efficient use of public resources, transparency of processes and equal and fair treatment of the bidders.[103] This is ensured by subjecting public procurement procedures to requirements which must secure a competition based on objective and transparent criteria[104] for example price and quality. The most recent version of the directives also aims at ensuring greater inclusion of common societal goals such as environmental protection, social responsibility, innovation, combating climate change, employment, public health, and other social and environmental considerations in the procurement process.[105]

10.102 The correct enforcement of the public procurement directives is dictated by two additional directives commonly called the control directives. Concretely, this goal is ensured by the creation of complaint boards which are competent to investigate claims of

96 However, Hagström and Bruserud state that the Norwegian rules on public procurement are to a large extent also an implementation of EU rules: Hagström and Bruserud, op. cit., p. 115 ff.

97 Directive 2014/24/EU on public procurement.

98 Directive 2014/25/EU on procurement by entities operating in the water, energy, transport, and postal services sectors.

99 Directive 2014/23/EU on the award of concessions contracts.

100 Lov 17. juni 2016 nr. 73 om offentlige anskaffelser.

101 Peter Stig Jakobsen, Sune Troels Poulsen, Simon Evers Kalsmose-Hjelmborg, *EU Udbudsretten*, Copenhagen, 2016, p. 48.

102 See, for instance, the Danish Act on Invitations to Tender in the Building and Engineering Sector (*Lov om indhentning af tilbud i bygge- og anlægssektoren*, commonly called "*Tilbudsloven*").

103 See, for instance, §1, s. 1 of the Norwegian Public Procurement Act (*Lov om offentlige anskaffelser*), which states the goal of public procurement rules as being to contribute to increasing the creation of value in society by ensuring the most effective use of resources in public acquisitions as possible based on professionalism and equal treatment (our translation).

104 Hagstrøm and Bruserud, op. cit., p. 114.

105 http://ec.europa.eu/environment/gpp/eu_public_directives_en.htm.

violations of the directives and/or the national implementation legislation.[106] In Denmark, for instance, this function is exercised by the Public Procurement Complaint Board,[107] which has its Norwegian equivalent – The Norwegian Complaints Board for Public Procurement.[108]

Private Procurement

10.103 The procurement of private construction projects is not subject to the above-mentioned rules of public law. However, and especially for larger projects, private employers often make use of processes similar to public procurement procedures in order to reach the same advantages, mainly obtaining the best possible value for their investments through a formalised competition between bidders. In this respect, the applicable rules and principles depend on the country at stake.

10.104 The Danish standard construction contracts contain rules dictating, among other things, the content of the employer's invitation to tender; the conditions of validity, and the required content of the contractor's tender.[109] To quote a few of these rules; the employer's invitation to tender must be clear and unambiguous and contain a project time schedule as well as information as to the respective weighting that will be given to each of the unit prices if the tender has to be structured with unit prices. The provision on the contractor's tender mentions that the contractor's reservations or derogations to the tender materials must be indicated clearly in his tender, and specifies the period of time during which tenderers are bound by their tenders. These rules are applicable regardless of whether the invitation to tender has been sent out based on EU or national rules governing public procurement[110] or whether the employer decides on his own free will to apply a tender procedure to the project in question.

10.105 As opposed to Denmark where these matters are regulated in the turnkey and build-only standard contracts, and as already mentioned, Norway has specific standards governing tender procedures in the private sector: NS 8400 and NS 8410, where the latter applies to cases where the commissioning party is allowed to negotiate with the tenderers about the contents of their bids but not aboutthe tendering documents.[111]

Different Types of Contracts

10.106 As opposed to, for instance, the UK, where the choice of the right standard form within a family often depends among other criteria on how the price and payment structure of the works is to be regulated,[112] the Nordic standard contracts are rather classified

106 Jakobsen, Poulsen, and Kalsmose-Hjelmborg, op. cit., p. 48–9.

107 *Klagenævnet for Udbud.*

108 Klagenemda for *offentlige anskaffelser.*

109 See §4 and 5 in both standard contracts AB 18 and ABT 18.

110 Hørlyck, op. cit., p. 44.

111 Hagstrøm and Bruserud, op. cit., p. 118 (description of the types of tender procedures in the public sector) and p. 133–4 (standard condition on tender procedures in the private sector).

112 See, for instance, the standard contracts published by the Joint Contracts Tribunal (JCT), where the issue of pricing and valuation often stands explicitly in the form's title: Measured Term Contract, Prime Cost Building Contract and Standard Building Contract with or without Quantities/with Approximate Quantities.

according to the allocation of responsibilities, especially those related to design, between the parties.

10.107 As detailed above, in Sweden and Denmark three standard contracts forms are used, two for construction works (build-only on one hand and turnkey on the other) and one for consultancy services. In Denmark and since the latest revision of the standard contracts in 2018, simplified versions of the build only and of the consultancy contracts also exist.

10.108 As far as land construction is concerned, Norway has a broader range of standard forms including, in addition to the minimal build-only, turnkey and design, consultancy, simplified forms and subcontracting forms, as well as specific forms for project manager and independent controller assignments. The range, also, includes standard contract forms or sets of rules describing procedures (contract price regulation, taking-over, private procurement). In Norwegian offshore construction, as mentioned above, the traditional Nordic divide between build-only and turnkey is retained, and a specific standard contract concerning projects of modifications of offshore platforms has three different variants.

Nature of Construction Contracts

10.109 The absence of codes of obligations in the Nordic legislations means that construction contracts are not defined and regulated by law as is the case in many jurisdictions of continental Europe, where the different types of contracts are listed and regulated in the code. In such codes, construction contracts are generally qualified as contracts by which one party undertakes to bring about a specific work result in exchange of an economic compensation which the other party undertakes to pay,[113] which has its roots in the Roman law notion of *locatio conductio operis*.[114]

10.110 In spite of this absence of legislative regulation, the systematic categorization of construction contracts is conceptually not much different in the Nordic countries than in continental Europe. In fact and until the development of construction law as a distinct discipline of contract law, contracts concerning building and engineering works were dealt with in Nordic literature and case law as contracts the correct performance of which depends on the bringing about of a specific *result* – an *obligation de résultat*, as opposed to the contracts stipulating an obligation to exercise best efforts in order to try and obtain a result, but where such result is not part of the obligation – *obligation de moyen*. These contracts containing an obligation to produce a result were designated under the common name of labour contracts ("*værksleje*").[115] The obligation to produce a result, as well as the fact that the contractor performs its work as an independent tradesman and not an employee,[116] allow the distinction between construction contracts and employment contracts.

113 See, for instance, the definition of the *Werkvertrag* – contract for works – in Art. 363 of the Swiss Code of Obligations.

114 Samuelsson, op. cit., p. 13.

115 Iversen, op. cit., p. 28 to 32.

116 Hagström and Bruserud, op. cit., p. 20.

10.111 The second important distinction is between construction contracts and commissioned sales; that is, contracts for the supply of movable goods to be manufactured or produced by the seller. The major differences between these and construction contracts are: First, that commissioned sales contracts are to be performed on real estate belonging to the party who ordered the works, and second, different rules apply to the two types of works; in fact, the Nordic Sales of Goods Act, which apply to the manufacturing of movable goods by the seller, mentions that its provisions do not apply to contracts for the construction of buildings or other facilities on *immovable property*.[117] The fact that the real property on which the works are to be carried out belongs to the employer allows the distinction between construction contracts and real estate sales, which is the qualification to be given to a contract where a contractor sells a property including a building which he carried out on a real estate ground that he previously acquired.[118]

10.112 The last defining feature of construction contracts, which depends on the way the "result" to be produced is described, is that such contracts concern the *bringing about* of concrete works, as opposed to their design and/or to the scheduling of the carrying out activities, even though design and scheduling are in fact part of the commissioned work in case of a turnkey construction contract.

10.113 A construction contract can thus be defined in Nordic law as a contract where one party, the contractor, undertakes as an independent tradesman, to carry out building works, possibly together with engineering works,[119] in exchange of economic compensation to be paid by the other party, the employer.

Design Obligations

10.114 The function of providing the design ("all necessary design in order to be able to deliver the object of the contract in conformity with the contract", as expressed in the Norwegian turnkey standard NS 8407) is not always precisely defined, but is generally meant to include the provision of necessary drawings, descriptions and calculations.[120] The distinction between build-only and turnkey contracts is: Which party assumes the design obligation. A turnkey setup, where the contractor is responsible for both design and construction, does not exclude the use of external design consultants, as the turnkey contractor does not necessarily have the competence or resources to assume the whole of the design obligation on his own.

10.115 The exact content of the design obligation varies depending on the contract in question. It is generally accepted that for the party responsible for the design to fulfil his obligations, such design must comply with legislation and other prescriptions of public law; be in accordance with the contract; be conducted in conformity with good design practice and follow the state of the art knowledge in place at the time when the design is being produced. The design must be clear, exhaustive, unambiguous and understandable.[121]

117 See, for instance, Art. 2, s. 1 of the Danish Sales of Goods Act.
118 Hagström and Bruserud, op. cit., p. 19–20.
119 Hagstrøm and Bruserud, op. cit., p. 19.
120 Nordtvedt et al., op. cit., p. 234.
121 Vagner, op. cit., p. 245.

Duty to Warn/Check/Review

10.116 It is a generally accepted rule in Nordic contract law that a contract party owes the other party general duties of loyalty and collaboration, meaning that it must have reasonable regard to its counterpart's interests.[122] This general obligation translates in construction law into several secondary duties[123] among which the duty to inform and counsel the other party and, as the case may be, request its instructions when some situations occur.

10.117 Such duties can concern either circumstances present from the start of the project (such as errors and inconsistencies in the design information) or circumstances appearing during the course of the project which make its execution impossible or significantly more difficult than planned (such as the impossibility to procure the prescribed materials), or where there is a risk that the employer may suffer a loss or incur liability towards a third party (such as, for instance, in case of risk of water leakage or a risk of damage to adjacent buildings).[124]

10.118 All Nordic standard construction contracts contain rules imposing an obligation on the contractor to inform the employer without delay about inconsistencies or errors in the contract and design documentation (for instance, incorrect information about soil conditions) received from the employer, or if the said contract or the design documents are insufficient to serve as a guideline for the carrying out of the works.[125]

10.119 The question is when does this obligation arises, especially in case of design errors. In Danish practice, it is generally accepted that the contractor must inform the employer about errors and inconsistencies that are so obvious that they should be immediately noticed by a competent contractor.[126] Such obligation concerns mostly errors and inconsistencies noticed during the construction phase; literature and case law generally agree on the fact that the contractor does not have sufficient time to notice and mention such errors during the tendering phase.[127]

10.120 Unless the contract states otherwise, the obligation to inform the counterpart about errors and inconsistencies does not imply an obligation to *investigate* whether the assumptions contained in the project documents are correct.[128] In Swedish law, this conclusion can be derived from the text of the provision imposing the obligation to warn, which states that the contractor has a duty to warn about the circumstances that he "detected".[129] However, the duty to inform about errors and inconsistencies can in some cases be interpreted as comprising a duty to advise *against* some solutions chosen or proposed by the employer, but such duty can already be inferred from the positive duty to propose an adequate solution.[130] The party's duty to conduct and participate in a review of the project documentation, introduced in the latest version of the Danish build only stand-

122 Hørlyck, op. cit., p. 220.

123 Hagstrøm and Bruserud, op. cit., p. 375.

124 Hørlyck, op. cit., p. 225.

125 Denmark: AB 18, §26 sect. 1 and 2;; Norway: NS 8405 Art. 21.1, 2nd section; Sweden: AB 04 Chap. 2, §9.

126 Iversen, op. cit., p. 408 to 411.

127 Iversen, op. cit., p. 413–14.

128 Hørlyck, op. cit., p. 222.

129 Deli, op. cit., p. 81, free translation.

130 Hagstrøm and Bruserud, op. cit., p. 377.

ard contract aims at an early detection of errors and inconsistencies and at a clarification of their consequence. In fact, it impose an obligation to rectify to the party responsible for the design, and an obligation for the contractor to give written notice of claims for modifications of the contract in relation to price, time or security if such modifications are made necessary by the correction measures adopted by the design team and approved by the employer.[131]

10.121 In the turnkey model, some standards such as the Norwegian NS 8407, explicitly provide that the turnkey contractor has a duty to advise and guide the employer to a reasonable extent, to evaluate and point out alternative solutions and give an assessment of the solutions proposed by the employer. According to literature, these duties also exist in build-only construction contracts, but the question is not uncontroversial. The contract model will of course, in any event, have a heavy influence on defining the content of such an obligation.

10.122 The first consequence of not complying with the duty to warn about design errors is that the contractor must carry out the construction in accordance with the rectified project without extra economic compensation or with a reduced additional compensation. The omission to name potentially problematic issues, such as insufficient foundations or inappropriate choice of materials, may also lead to the contractor's liability for defects[132] and thus the obligation to carry out remedial works without additional economic compensation, a liability which in Denmark at least is generally borne jointly and severally with the technical consultant (e.g. architect) who is responsible for the defective design.[133]

10.123 In Sweden, the build-only standard contract expressly states that a party must without delay inform the other party if it discovers inconsistencies, inaccuracies or errors in the contractual documentation, if instructions or information given during the execution of the project are inconsistent with the contract, or generally if circumstances decisive for the project occur or change. This provision states that a party who does not comply with these obligations is liable to cover the damages caused by this omission.[134]

10.124 This provision is tightly linked to §§6 to 8 in the first chapter of the standard AB 04 which allocate the responsibility for the correctness of the information given in the precontractual phase, especially with respect to the soil conditions and other circumstances related to the construction site. A liability provision is contained in §9, last section of Chapter 2 of AB 04, which states that a party who does not comply with his duty to warn must compensate the damage arising out of its omission, which means that a contractor can obtain additional economic compensation for a variation made necessary by errors in the design material but that he is liable for the extra costs arising out of the fact that he did not point out the errors in due time. According to an author, it cannot be excluded that the consequence of this liability rule may be that a contractor can be liable towards the employer for part or the totality of the costs of the extra works if the latter could have been avoided if the contractor had informed the employer of the errors in due time.[135] This interpretation does not seem to be supported by court practice (yet); in this respect,

131 AB 18, §19.
132 Hagstrøm and Bruserud, op. cit., p. 375.
133 Hørlyck, op. cit., p. 223.
134 AB 04, chap. 2, §9.
135 Deli, op. cit., p. 81.

it is, however, useful to note that most of construction disputes are in Sweden settled by arbitration and that practice, therefore, remains to a large extent unpublished.[136]

10.125 The relation between the contractor's omission to warn the employer and defect liability is made explicit in the Norwegian turnkey standard, which states that if the contractor does not warn the employer within the specified deadline, the employer may claim compensation for the damage that could have been avoided had the warning been given in time.[137]

10.126 In case of circumstances that hinder/obstruct the works or make it significantly more difficult, or in case of risk of damages of any kind, the contractor must inform the employer to allow the latter to take the necessary steps to safeguard its own interests. In urgent situations where the instructions of the employer cannot be obtained on time and according to the Danish standard contract, the contractor must take initiative and act as the employer's spontaneous voluntary agent (in compliance with the Roman law institution of the *negotiorum gestio*). In such case, and in cases where the employer order specific measures to be taken, the contractor may claim an extension of time and additional economic compensation if the measures undertaken render this necessary.[138]

Employer and Contractor

10.127 In the Nordic countries, as in other parts of the world, the parties to a construction contract are the employer (also sometimes called the client, such as, for instance, in the Finnish standards), for whose benefit the works are carried out, and the contractor who carries out the works[139] and, in a turnkey contracts, also designs them. The parties are sometimes explicitly defined in a preliminary definition chapter in the standard contracts, as, for instance, in the Norwegian turnkey standard (NS 8407), or the definition of the parties can be implicit like in the Danish standards, where the standards are structured around subjects (contents of the contract, securities and insurance, performance of the works, etc.).

10.128 As opposed to Anglo-American standard contracts, the Nordic standard contracts do not contain sections dedicated to the general obligations of the parties. These obligations are included in the provisions concerning the parties' specific obligations. For instance, the contractor's obligations to execute the works in accordance with the contract and to remedy all defects, as for example stated in Sub-C. 4.1 of the FIDIC Red Book, are stated in AB 18 in the rules defining defective work as work which is not carried out in accordance with the contract, good professional practice or the client's instructions,[140] and in the contractor's duty and right to remedy defects.[141]

10.129 As far as the manner in which the parties are to perform their obligations is concerned, their mutual duty of loyalty, which derives from the general law of obligations

136 Hedberg, op. cit.,

137 NS 8407, Art. 25.1.2.

138 Iversen, op. cit., p. 166–7.

139 Comparatively in common law: Stephen Furst and Vivian Ramsey (eds.), *Keating on Construction Contracts*, 9th ed., Sweet & Maxwell, 2012, p. 2.

140 See AB 18 §47, s. 1 and §12, s. 1.

141 See AB 18 §48, s. 1.

which serves as background law of the contract, is generally translated into specific contractual obligations, such as the above-mentioned contractor's obligation to inform the employer of the design errors which the contractor notices during the course of his work. Some standard construction contracts state the mutual duty of loyalty expressly; for instance, Section 3 of the Norwegian NS 8407 states that the parties are obligated to collaborate and to show loyalty during the carrying out of the contract.

Consultant's Role and Liability

10.130 In addition to the parties to the construction contract, technical consultants such as architects and engineers are very often involved in construction projects. These consultants are generally engaged by the employer, but they can also be the contractor's counterpart; for instance, when a turnkey contractor hires an architect or an engineer to fulfil his design obligations.

10.131 All Nordic countries have specific standard forms for contracts with technical consultants.[142] The Danish, Swedish, and Finnish consultancy standard contracts cover all types of technical consultants,[143] whereas Norway has distinct standards for independent controllers, construction and project managers, the latter being split in two standard forms according to the chosen mode of remuneration of the project manager.[144]

10.132 The main obligations assumed by technical consultants, quite often towards the employer, are design and supervision obligations.[145] The most important technical consultants are architects, who are in charge of designing the main lines of the project as well as drawing building plans, and engineers, who make the necessary calculations to ensure the feasibility of the project.[146] The technical consultant's role and liability depend on and are defined by the contract at hand. When he assumes the function of project supervisor, he acts as the employer's representative. His functions are typically to send and receive messages and notices on behalf of the employer; approve or discard materials or works; give instructions as to the coordination of the different contractors' work, convene the periodical site meetings and draft the minutes of the meetings; answer the contractor's queries concerning project materials and takes position on the contractor's requests for extensions of time and additional economic compensation.[147]

10.133 Unless the contract states otherwise, the liability of the technical consultant is in principle a fault-based liability, meaning that the consultant is liable for errors and omissions in the exercise of his functions. This liability is assessed in comparison with the usual benchmark of qualifications and care in the profession in question. The technical consultant is liable if he did not carry out his tasks with the care and professional competence which the client could reasonably demand from a professional consultant.[148] The content and extent of the consultant's obligations is defined in the contract, often through

142 See above in the section titled "Standard forms of national contracts".

143 Deli, op. cit., p. 216 states that the Swedish standard expressly mentions that it applies to all kinds of consulting tasks from preliminary drawings to detail design at the end of the construction phase.

144 Hagstrøm and Bruserud, op. cit., pp. 85–6.

145 Vagner, op. cit., p. 236.

146 Iversen, op. cit., p. 195.

147 Vagner, op. cit., p. 237.

148 Iversen, op. cit., p. 794 to 796.

reference to standard services descriptions drafted by branch organizations,[149] such as the Danish Association of Architectural Firms or the Danish Association of Consulting Engineers. The area generating most case law with respect to technical consultants' liability is that of design defects which covers a broad range of specific issues, such as choice and use of materials; budget overrun as well as building ground or soil adequateness. Yet there is also significant case law on the issue of defective project supervision.[150]

10.134 In Denmark and Norway, if one of the standard forms ABR 18 or NS 8401/8402 is part of the contract, the consultant's liability is limited to five years from the date at which the consulting task ended. If the consulting task was related to the carrying out of building or engineering works, the limitation period, according to ABR 18, would run from the date of taking-over of the works. These limitation periods do not apply if the consultant is guilty of fraud or gross negligence.[151]

Sub-Contracting

10.135 Subcontracting, by which a contractor delegates part of the works he undertook to carry out, to one or several subcontractors, is frequent in all Nordic countries both in build-only and in turnkey models. The contractor's right to subcontract part of its scope of work is expressly mentioned in several Nordic standards,[152] and Norway uses specific standard forms for subcontracts drafted to provide coherence with the main contract. Subcontracting does not alter the content of the contractor's obligation towards the employer; in other words, the main contractor is liable towards the employer for the acts and omissions of the subcontractor as if they were his own.[153]

10.136 As a matter of principle, it is the main contractor's prerogative to choose the subcontractor(s),[154] but this freedom can be limited in different ways. In Norway, the standard conditions provide that the contractor must inform the employer of his intention to use subcontractors and name the relevant parts of the works as well as the intended subcontractors' names before the contract is entered into. The employer can refuse to approve the subcontractors named by the contractor within a certain deadline, but unless the employer can demonstrate that his refusal is based on objective grounds, the contractor can claim that the change of subcontractor be treated as a variation[155] and, therefore, potentially give rise to an extension of time and/or an additional economic compensation. The Finnish standards, also, state that the employer must approve the most important subcontractors and suppliers chosen by the main contractor but that the employer's refusal to approve a subcontractor must be based on valid grounds.[156]

149 Vagner, op. cit., p. 241.

150 For a detailed discussion of these issues under Danish law, see Iversen, op. cit., p. 808 to 818.

151 Vagner, op. cit., p. 255.

152 See, for instance, Art. 15.1, first sentence of the Norwegian build-only standard NS 8405, and §8, Section 1 of the Danish build-only standard AB 18, stating that the contractor can sublet the performance of the works to others to the extent that it is customary or natural for such work to be performed under a subcontract.

153 Hagström and Bruserud, op. cit., p. 78–9. Hørlyck-2019, p. 136.

154 Iversen, op. cit., p. 72.

155 See, for instance, NS 8405, Art. 15.1, second section and Art. 15.2.

156 YSE 1998 §7, s. 3.

10.137 It is, also, common for the employer to insert provisions in the contract allowing him to choose the subcontractors (nominated subcontractors). Such choice can have the consequence of limiting the main contractor's liability for the actions and omissions of the nominated subcontractor.[157] In Denmark, for instance, there is case law establishing that the main contractor is not liable for defects in works carried out by the subcontractor; in cases where the materials and work methods had been agreed on between the employer and the nominated subcontractor.[158]

10.138 The Danish standard contracts provide the employer with the right to make *direct claims* regarding defects against a subcontractor or a supplier if it is demonstrated that the claim cannot or only with great difficulty can be pursued against the main contractor;[159] for instance, in case if the latter has become insolvent. Furthermore, the newest version of the Danish standard contracts introduced a right for the employer to demand, upon written notice, that a subcontractor or supplier be deprived of his right to carry out work or deliver materials, if the subcontractor or supplier has failed materially to comply with applicable rules or agreed terms and conditions on social responsibility, including rules on health and safety at work. Under the same conditions, the employer is entitled to summarily dismiss individuals and order them to leave the construction site.[160]

Unforeseeable Physical Ground Conditions

10.139 Unforeseeable ground conditions appear in Scandinavia as frequently as in the rest of the world. In Denmark, issues are often related to the ground being too soft and making deeper pile driving necessary, whereas rock formations often disturb works in Norway;[161] the pollution risk also increases with time everywhere. As a matter of principle, the risk of unforeseen physical ground conditions is in Nordic law assumed by the employer, but the issue is delicate and calls for the following qualifications.

10.140 The Scandinavian standard construction contracts express the main rule in different manners.

10.141 In Denmark, the standard contracts state that the tender documentation must contain adequate information about investigations conducted in relation to physical ground conditions, pollution, cables and other obstacles, and that if it is not the case, the measures to be taken to overcome such obstacles must be paid as additional work.[162] However, unforeseen obstacles which appear although the adequate investigations have been made and giving rise to public bans or orders making the continuation of the works

157 Hagstrøm and Bruserud, op. cit., p. 80, mention that the extent of such consequence is unclear. In Denmark, scholarly literature states that in some cases where the employer has demanded that a specific subcontractor be used, such obligation can have the consequence that the "sub"contractors must be considered as a side contractor, whom the "main" contractor is not responsible for: Hørlyck 2019, p. 138 and Iversen, p. 721 to 726.

158 Hans Henrik Vagner, *Entrepriseret*, 4th ed. by Torsten Iversen, Copenhagen, 2005, p.223–8.

159 AB 92 §5, Section 5. Iversen, op. cit., p. 72. AB 18, s. 8, st. 4 and 5. Hørlyck-2019, p. 139–144.

160 AB 18 §59, s. 2.

161 Iversen, op. cit., p. 362.

162 See, for instance, AB 18 §26, s. 3.

difficult or unreasonably burdensome for the employer give the latter the right to cancel the contract under certain conditions.[163]

10.142 The delicate issue consists in defining the exact content of some of the terms used in this provision, namely what is unforeseen and what should be considered as adequate information. In relation to the unforeseeability, two elements must be taken into account. First, a scholar, commenting on available case law, argues that a distinction must be made between contractors carrying out excavation, road, sewer, decontamination or coast protection works on one hand, and building contractors on the other, as the former must be able to adapt to more severe difficulties in relation to ground conditions.[164] Although the standard contract text refers to unforeseen rather than unforeseeable ground conditions, there seems to be a normative aspect in the evaluation of what a given contractor should expect. Second, a turnkey contractor has a stricter investigation duty in relation to the ground as he is also providing the design.[165] Information provided by the employer will be considered adequate if it allows the bidders to calculate their price accurately, without having to make reservations or add a mark-up to their price to cater for unforeseen ground conditions.

10.143 The Norwegian standard contracts state that the employer assumes the risk for ground conditions to the extent that they deviate from what the (turnkey) contractor had grounds to rely on when he prepared his tender.[166] Here as well, what the contractor had grounds to rely on is assessed based on a general evaluation mostly depending on two elements. These are first the employer's duty to inform in the tender documentation on the ground conditions he knew or should have known about,[167] and second, the contractor's duty to investigate the site and its surroundings and obtain information from state authorities concerning the ground to the extent that this information is not already provided by the employer.[168] When the employer bears the risk, the contractor is entitled to an additional payment and/or to an extension of time if the risk materializes.

10.144 In the Swedish standard contracts, provisions concerning the ground conditions are contained in the first chapter of the standard contracts, more precisely in the provisions stating the assumptions on which the contract is based. These assumptions have a double function as they both allocate risks between the parties and define the extent of the works comprised under the contract.[169] Like in Norway, the risk allocation depends on the fulfilment by the parties of their duties; that is, the employer's duty to inform in the tender documentation about the state of the ground on which the works will be carried out,[170] and the contractor's duty to obtain before the submission of his tender the knowledge of the ground which is necessary to assess what is required to carry on the works.[171] The

163 AB 18 §26, s. 4.

164 Hørlyck-2019, p. 288–9.

165 Hørlyck-2019, p. 295.

166 Turnkey: NS 8407, 23.1, 1st para Build-only: NS 8405 19.3, 2nd para, with a slightly different formulation (the employer bears the risk that the ground conditions are such as the contractor had grounds to rely on. on considering the contract, the nature of the assignment and the general circumstances.

167 NS 8407,23.1, 3rd para, Nordtvedt et al., op. cit., p. 336 to 338.

168 NS 8407,23.1, 2nd para, Nordtvedt et al., op. cit., p. 332 to 336.

169 Deli, op. cit., p. 62.

170 AB 04 Chap. 1 §6.

171 AB 04 Chap. 1 §7.

contractor's duty of investigation is limited to the information that can be collected from a site visit. Like in Norway, the Swedish standards state that works which are carried out because the information delivered by the employer was not correct or which result from the construction site and other important elements not being as assumed by the contractor have to be remunerated as extra works[172] and the contractor may also be entitled to an extension of time.[173]

10.145 Employer frequently attempt to transfer the ground conditions risk to contractors by contract, often by imposing on the contractor a duty to investigate the ground conditions and to give notice of certain circumstances within a certain deadline.[174] The treatment of such clauses varies from one country to the other. In Denmark, adjudicating authorities generally do not give effect to such clauses.[175] In Norway, the turnkey standard contract expressly addresses this situation by stating that even if the parties agreed that the contractor bears the ground conditions risk, the contractor can in any case invoke that such conditions diverge fundamentally from what the contractor had grounds to rely on.[176] Furthermore, such agreed risk allocation does not free the employer from the risk of the consequences of the inaccuracy of the information he delivered.[177] Since the parties are free to deviate from the standard contracts, this does not mean that they cannot agree on a more radical transfer of risk to the contractor, but such transfer should be made very clear in the contract, possibly by stating the transfer of risk as an independent item in the price list, and could under specific circumstances be considered unreasonable by an adjudicating authority and modified through the application of Art. 36 of the Contracts Act.[178]

Material and Workmanship

10.146 Like in many other countries, the contents of each contract sets the requirements with regards to material and workmanship. What is required in each case is, therefore, primarily a question of contract interpretation.[179]

10.147 Several Nordic standard contracts state that unless specific quality requirements are set in the contract, the applicable requirements are those which are *usual* for the type of works in question.[180] For instance, the Danish build-only standard contract states that the works must be carried out with the correct workmanship and that the materials must be of customary good quality, which is interpreted in literature as meaning normal solidity and fitness for the usual or contractually agreed purpose for the type of works concerned.[181]

10.148 Such general criteria, leading to an objective assessment of possible defects based on industry practice and customs, have limited practical relevance especially in build-only projects where the subject matter of the contract is generally defined in great

172 AB 04 Chap. 2 §4.
173 AB 04 Chap. 4 §3.
174 Hørlyck-2019, p. 295.
175 Hørlyck-2019, p. 295.
176 NS 8407,23.2, 1st para.
177 NS 8407,23.2, 2nd para.
178 Nordtvedt et al., pp. 339–41.
179 Hagstrøm and Bruserud, op. cit., p. 367.
180 Denmark: AB 18 §12, s. 1. ; Norway: NS 8405 11.1; Sweden: AB 04 Chap. 2, §1, etc.
181 Hørlyck, op. cit., p. 134. Deli, op. cit., p. 111.

detail, thereby considerably reducing the contractor's freedom of choice.[182] If the material to be used and methods to be followed are defined in the contract; the contractor cannot choose otherwise and works not complying with the contractual specifications will, to start with, be qualified as defective and raise the contractor's liability,[183] unless the contractor can demonstrate exceptional circumstances, for instance, that it was objectively impossible to procure the prescribed materials. In such cases, the contractor is allowed to use other materials with similar properties and quality.

10.149 Due to the occurrence of disputes related to the use of new materials which proved to be inadequate, at least under the Danish climate, and to uncertainties as to which party should bear such development risk, the newest version of the Danish standard contracts contain a provision stating that the contractor must notify the employer in writing about any use of methods and materials that are not thoroughly tested, including any associated risks, unless such use is prescribed by the employer.[184]

10.150 Objective criteria related to material and workmanship are more important for turnkey projects where the subject-matter of the contract is often defined by its function, and where designing the project and choosing the right material and work methods are part of the contractor's contractual duties.[185]

10.151 It is generally the contractor's obligation to provide the material.[186] The Danish standard contracts prohibits the contractor from supplying material with a *property reservation*; they state that the material become the employer's property upon delivery to the site. It is, however, doubtful that such provision can bind suppliers who, as third parties, do not generally make the standard construction contracts part of their supply contracts.[187] Denmark, also, has specific rules stating that material must be supplied with a five-year guarantee counting from taking-over of the works (corresponding to the contractor's defect liability period), but at the supplier's liability ceases at the latest six years after delivery of the goods at a warehouse or to a third party and that the supplier must accept that defects can be invoked against him directly by the employer.[188] The contractor can be exempted from securing that the supplier complies with these requirements in special circumstances, namely if they would cause significant additional costs or delay or if abiding by these requirements would be difficult to control; for example, in cases of minor deliveries.[189] This special Danish solution is the result of the transcription into the standard contracts of rules previously applying to acquisitions in the public sector; it does not have an equivalent in other Nordic countries.

Labour Law Considerations

10.152 In his role as employer in the labour law sense, it is each contractor's responsibility to ensure that the work conditions on the construction site are fully adequate from

182 Hagstrøm and Bruserud, op. cit., p. 367.
183 Hørlyck, op. cit., p. 136.
184 AB 18 §12, s. 3.
185 Hagstrøm and Bruserud, op. cit., p. 373.
186 See, for instance, in Denmark: AB 18 §12, s. 2.
187 Hørlyck, op. cit., p. 153.
188 AB 18 §12, s. 5 Hørlyck, op. cit., p. 156–7.
189 AB 92 §10, s. 5.

the point of view of health and safety; the contractor can incur criminal liability if he does not comply with the relevant rules.[190] In Denmark, rules governing work conditions are contained in the Working Environment Consolidated Act as well as in several ministerial orders; among others the ministerial order concerning construction and engineering works and the ministerial order concerning the employer's duties.[191]

10.153 The contractor's responsibility is partly shared in this respect with both the employer and the party responsible for the design. First, the employer must coordinate the measures taken to ensure the workers' health and safety, he is in this respect responsible for appointing a safety coordinator and ensuring that safety meetings are held on the site.[192] Second, the party in charge of the design also bears part of the responsibility for the working environment, as he is responsible for the approval of the project by the authorities in all aspects, including health and safety. He must also make sure when choosing the specifications for the project that the relevant health and safety rules can be respected in relation to the carrying out of the project as well as the maintenance of the works.[193]

10.154 The starting point is that the contractor must bear the costs linked to complying with an injunction from the Danish Working Environment Authority. However, if an order is extraordinary and unforeseeable, the employer may be ordered to cover part or all of such costs.[194] In a case from 1983 where the Authority had ruled that workers may not work more than 3 hours a day in a crawlway, the employer was ordered to cover the major part of the costs, while a minor part was attributed to the contractor who was deemed not to have organized the work adequately.[195]

10.155 Norwegian law has the same features when it comes to labour law considerations described under Danish law. Further, there are rules on the general application of collective agreements on construction works in Norway. There are no statute rules on minimum wages, but rules to that effect will apply as an effect of decisions made by the Tariff Board.[196]

Performance and Taking Over

10.156 As mentioned above, the standard of performance of a construction contract depends on the content of the contract. In fact, all standard contracts state that works must be performed according to the contract as well as customary standards in the concerned industry. Under the general heading of performance, contracts mostly contain various provisions concerning the organization of the works and the administration of the construction site, including parties' representatives and communication between them during the course of the project and periodical meetings, as well as procedures for tests to be carried out. Such provisions are in most cases self-explanatory and do not require detailed review.

190 Hørlyck, op. cit., p. 247.

191 Arbejdsmiljøloven and bekendgørelse no. 1516 of December 16, 2010 as amended by bekendtgørelse nr. 115 of February 5, 2013.

192 Hørlyck, op. cit., p. 249.

193 Hørlyck, op. cit., p. 247.

194 Hørlyck, op. cit., p. 247.

195 KfE 1983.69.

196 See the General Application Act of 4 June 1993 no. 58.

10.157 A more important question, often discussed in relation with the performance of the works, is the issue of possible damages to or destruction of the works during the construction period. The general rule is that damages affecting the works before taking-over (or in certain cases, before the employer starts to use them, which often the equivalent of taking-over in the context of the passing of risk), the contractor has the duty to make good these damages (i.e., reinstate the works) at no additional costs for the employer. In other words, the contractor bears the risk of any damage to the material and the works until they are taken over or taken in use[197] by the employer, unless the damages are caused by the employer[198] or by circumstances or persons for which the employer is contractually responsible.[199] In the case of *Force Majeure* events,[200] the risk of damages or destruction of the works during the construction period is in the majority of cases covered by insurance which is made mandatory by the standard form provisions.[201]

10.158 All Nordic contracts provides for a formal *taking-over procedure*, which according to the newest version of the Danish standard contracts must start with a preliminary review of the works[202] conducted between the notice of completion and the handing-over meeting The contractor must give notice of completion[203] and one of the parties (which varies depending on the standard/country in question) calls the handing-over meeting[204] where the parties meet at the construction site and inspect the works in search for possible defects.

10.159 In the meeting, the parties establish and sign a *handing-over report* which content can vary according to the jurisdiction in question, but always contains at least a list of the defects observed at handing-over and an indication as to whether taking-over is considered to have taken place or not. In fact, all standard contract forms state that taking-over is deemed to have taken place at the handing-over meeting, unless fundamental defects are recorded then.[205] Instead of using the elusive term of fundamental defect, the Norwegian standards further define the defects allowing the employer to refuse to take-over the works; that is, defects which or the remedying of which prevent the intended use of the works.[206]

10.160 When the employer refuses to take over the works, the contractor must remedy the defects observed at the handing-over meeting within a reasonable deadline set by the employer[207] and a new handing-over meeting must be called. In addition to the passing of risk to the employer as mentioned above, the main effects of taking-over is that potential liquidated damages stop running; the contractor's obligation to insure the works come to an end; the securities given by the contractor must be progressively released and the defect notification period start running.

---

197 Denmark: AB 18 §27, s. 1. Sweden: AB 04 5, §1, s. 1.
198 Denmark: AB 18 §27, s. 2. Sweden: AB 04 5, §1, s. 2.
199 Denmark: AB AB 18 §27, s. 2. Norway: NS 8405 Art. 17, s. 2.
200 Denmark: AB 18 §27, s. 2. Norway: NS 8405 Art. 17, s. 3. Sweden: AB 04 5, §1, s. 3.
201 See section on insurance below.
202 AB 18 §44.
203 Denmark: AB 18 §45, s. 1. Norway: NS 8405, Art. 32.2, s. 1. Sweden: AB 04 Chap. 7, §2.
204 Denmark: AB 18 §45, s. 1. Norway: NS 8405, Art. 32.2, s. 1. Sweden: AB 04 Chap. 7, §2.
205 Denmark: AB 18 §45, s. 2. Sweden: AB 04 Chap. 7, §12, s. 1.
206 NS 8405, Art. 32.5, s. 1.
207 Denmark: Hørlyck-2019, p. 464. Norway: NS 8407 42.3.3, 1st para Sweden:

Contract Price and Payment

10.161 The price to be paid for construction or engineering works is calculated in the Nordic countries according to models that also apply in the rest of the world. There are two fundamentally opposed price calculation principles which can be combined in large and complex projects.

10.162 The two fundamental principles are *lump sum contracts* on the one hand, and *measurement or value contracts* on the other. In a lump sum contract, where the contractor undertakes to carry out (and design, as the case may be) the works for a fixed sum (save variations and extra works), the contractor bears the measurement risk; that is, of not being able to carry out the works for the agreed price because the evaluation of the quantities made in his tender proved to not be accurate. In this model, the contractor covers its risk by adding a margin to its expected costs, which explains why this model is not necessarily the most economically advantageous for the employer.[208]

10.163 In a measurement contract, which can take different forms, the contractor is remunerated for its actual costs (building materials, employees' wages, equipment, etc.) plus a fee which can be fixed or a percentage of the actual costs, meant to cover the contractor's indirect costs, risk and profit.[209] Measurement contracts are more risky for the employer since the latter has to pay for the costs invoiced by the contractor unless the employer can prove that they are unnecessary, which is difficult to demonstrate. This mode of calculation is the main rule in Norway, at least for build-only projects, turnkey projects being more often carried out on the basis of lump sum contracts.

10.164 An intermediary form is *unit price contracts*, where the works are divided into measurable elements (for instance, a fully assembled window or a square meter of fitted parquet flooring) with a fixed price for each element; the final contract price is then reached by adding up the units actually applied.[210]

10.165 Both the Norwegian and Swedish standard contracts contain rules concerning different pricing methods. The Danish standard contracts do not take position on how the price of the works is to be calculated and the parties must, therefore, agree on particular conditions on this subject. However, it is clear from provisions in the standard contracts concerning other topics, such as the provision on variations and their pricing, that they are meant to be applied to lump sum contracts.

10.166 All national standard contracts also provide for the possibility of the *indexation of prices* which is especially relevant for long-term contracts subject to price variations on key elements such as materials and workers' wages. Such indexation applies as a starting point to contracts based on the Norwegian NS standards, unless the parties agree otherwise,[211] whereas parties to Swedish and Danish contracts must expressly stipulate such indexation.

10.167 It is also usual, especially in larger contracts, for the parties to provide economic incentives for the contractor. A possible form is the Norwegian "target sum", where

208 Hørlyck, op. cit., p. 258.

209 Hagstrøm and Bruserud, op. cit., p. 311.

210 Hagstrøm and Bruserud, op. cit., pp. 316–17. About the different pricing methods in Danish law, see Iversen, op. cit., pp. 149–55.

211 Hagstrøm and Bruserud, op. cit., p. 321–2.

parties agree on a goal price and the contractor, who is involved in the design phase, gets a share of the savings if the project ends up being carried out for a lesser amount thanks to contractor's initiatives.[212]

10.168 Unless the contract states otherwise, the standard solution in Nordic contract law is that payment is to be effected upon the creditor's demand, which the creditor can only present once he has performed his own obligations[213]. According to this main rule, the contractor is not able to claim payment before he hands over the works. However, and since construction projects are generally long-term undertakings where big sums are involved, the contractor needs to be able to finance its costs and thus in some situations obtain payment before performance. Consequently, the vast majority of construction contracts entered into in the Nordic countries provide for mechanisms according to which the contractor can claim payments on a continuing basis while the works are being carried out.

10.169 All the Nordic standard contracts[214] provide for such periodic payments combined with a final invoice comprising all the amounts which the contractor considers owed after taking-over.

10.170 By way of example, the Danish standards contain two options: The contractor can either make bimonthly payment requests requesting payment for the works carried out during the preceding fortnight[215] (i.e., practically, since the last invoice was sent), or payments are to be effected according to a payment plan which follows the project's time schedule or provides for payment when certain concrete milestones are reached[216] (foundations rate, roof rate, etc.). In both options, payment is dependent upon the progress actually achieved on the construction site. The works completed can be evaluated based on the provisions concerning the payment deadlines: In the bimonthly payment system, the employer has to pay within 15 days of reception of the invoice[217] "*for works and materials in conformity with the contract*";[218] the provision concerning the payment plan uses a similar wording.[219] If the employer is of the opinion that part of the payment requested is not due, he must inform the contractor thereof, but in any case, pay the amount which is not disputed. In case of disagreement relating to payments, each of the parties has the right to start an accelerated dispute resolution process called expert determination which leads to a decision within a short period of time.[220]

10.171 The system with bimonthly payments is the most frequently used and is the solution by default if the parties include the standard contract in their contract without making special provisions concerning payment; payment plans are less frequent and are more often applied to private and minor projects.[221]

212 Hagstrøm and Bruserud, op. cit., p. 320–1.
213 Gomard, op. cit., p. 40.
214 Norway: NS 8405 Chapter V and NS 8407 Chapter VI. Denmark: AB 918, §36; ABT 18 §34.
215 AB 18 §36, s. 1.
216 AB 18 §36, s. 3.
217 AB 18 §37, s. 1.
218 AB 18 §36, s. 1.
219 AB 18 §36, s. 3 in fine: "provided that the work concerned by the payment request is performed", free translation.
220 For more details on the expert determination, see below in the "Dispute resolution" section.
221 Vagner, op. cit., p. 76.

10.172 In Norway, the rules concerning payments following the progress of the works only apply to works comprised in the original contract price, while variations and extra works are paid in a different manner.[222] Both Norway and Sweden apply a system according to which the contractor must deduce "outstanding amount", as a starting point 10% in Norway, from each of its invoice, until the said outstanding amount reaches 5% of the original contract amount; the outstanding amount can only be claimed with the contractor's final invoice, and functions as an extra security for the employer, in addition to the usual performance guarantee given by the contractor.[223]

10.173 Special rules apply in Denmark to the payment for material. The contractor is allowed to request the payment for the material that he bought but not yet delivered to the construction site. If the employer effects such an early payment, he is allowed to request a security corresponding to the amount of its payment.[224]

Defects Liability

10.174 In all Nordic countries, the definition of a defect depends primarily on the contract, as all standard contracts state that a defect is present if the works or parts of them are not in conformity with the contract or, as far as Swedish standards are concerned, not carried out at all.[225] The observations made above in the section on material and workmanship, which define the required quality standards of these elements, can be referred to for a detailed understanding of the meaning of contract conformity.

10.175 Norwegian law adds a second step to the analysis of whether a defect is present by adding that the non-conformity with the contract must be due to circumstances for which the contractor bears the risk. Identifying such circumstances depends on the allocation of responsibilities between the parties in the contract. In fact, liability follows responsibility: If the employer is, for instance, in charge of providing the design, he is in principle liable if the design is defective or not provided at the right time.

10.176 The circumstances that the contractor bears the risk for with respect to defects are the same that the contractor bears the risk for in other instances, for example concerning delay.[226] Consequently, non-conformity with the contract is considered a defect in Norwegian law if it is caused by circumstances for which the contractor would not be entitled to an extension of time, had a delay occurred instead of a defect. The circumstances typically entitling the contractor to an extension of time may be the following: Variations, delay, or default in case of employer supplies or other employer duty (provide the design, the site, in some situations the materials, public permits to build and coordination of the different actors working on the project), and other acts preventing the contractor from carrying out the works and for which the employer bears the risk.

10.177 Although this is not expressed in the standard contract's provisions, the contractor can under Danish law and similarly to Norwegian law avoid to be held liable for defects if he proves that the defect is caused by circumstances that the employer is responsible for

222 Hagstrøm and Bruserud, op. cit., p. 324.
223 Hagstrøm and Bruserud, op. cit., p. 324–5.
224 AB 18 §36, s. 1.
225 AB 18, §47, s. 1 to 3. NS 8405 Art. 36.1. Sweden: AB 04, definition chapter.
226 Hagstrøm and Bruserud, op. cit., p. 379.

(e.g., defective design) or that the works were carried out correctly in accordance with the state of the art at the time at they were carried out.[227] Danish law has specific and more detailed provisions with respect to defects linked to the *material* used. In fact, the material is deemed to be defective if they are not as agreed or not of the customary good quality, unless the contractor proves that materials conforming with the contract do not exist or could not be procured because of *Force Majeure*-type of circumstances such as war or import bans[228], or unless the materials prescribed by the employer cannot be provided due to circumstances that the contractor ought not to have foreseen at the time of the conclusion of the contract[229]. Furthermore and in cases where a material proves not to be fit for the purpose that it was used for, the contractor can escape liability if he demonstrates that the material was considered as adequate according to the state of the art, or if the employer prescribed that a specific material or an equivalent be used and the contractor indeed used such material.

10.178 In Swedish law as well, the contractor is liable for defects unless he can prove that the defect is caused by circumstances which the employer is responsible for.[230]

10.179 The standard defect liability period according to the Nordic standard construction contract is five years from taking-over,[231] with the following modifications.

10.180 In Denmark, and if the contractor has remedied defects invoked by the employer, a new five year time limit for the submission of claims related to the remedied defects, starting at the completion of the defect rectification, applies; however, and in any case, the contractor's liability expires after a maximum of three years after the expiry of the initial five-year time limit.[232] If the employer's claim against the contractor on grounds of defects concerns movable objects or fixtures which are not specially adapted or permanently fixed, the liability period is reduced to two years.[233] Furthermore, the employer's five-year deadline to invoke defects does not apply if the contractor has contractually agreed to a longer liability period; if it is established at taking-over that agreed quality assurance measures have failed materially or if the contractor is guilty of gross negligence.[234]

10.181 According to the Swedish standard contracts, the contractor is fully liable for five years if the defect is due to the contractor's workmanship but only two years (or a longer liability period granted by the supplier to the contractor) for materials and goods.[235] When these periods have expired, the contractor's liability can only be invoked in case of material defects and if the defect is caused by the contractor's negligence.[236] The Finnish standard contracts provide for a similar gradation of the contractor's defect liability with a full liability during a two-year guarantee period and a liability limited to defects caused by the contractor's gross negligence for up to ten years from taking-over.[237]

227 Hørlyck, op. cit., p. 376.
228 AB 18 §47, s. 2, lit (a).
229 AB 18 §47, s. 2, lit (b).
230 AB 04 Chapter 5, §5
231 Denmark: AB 18 §55, s. 1. Norway.
232 AB 18 §55, s. 2.
233 AB 18 §55, s. 3.
234 AB 18 §55, s. 4.
235 AB 04 Chap. 4, §. 7.
236 AB 04 Chap. 5, §6.
237 YSE 1998 §29 and 30.

10.182 *Defect notification rules* apply in all Nordic jurisdictions. In Denmark, the employer must give written notice of a defect which was not noticed at taking-over within reasonable time after the defect was or ought to have been discovered, but these rules do not apply if the defect is due to the contractor's gross negligence.[238] In Norway, the employer must give notice of defect without undue delay and in any case within five years from taking-over, but these notice provisions – which, as discussed below in the section "time-bar provisions", are actual time-bar rules – do not apply if the defect was caused by the contractor's gross negligence or wilful misconduct.[239]

10.183 In all Nordic countries, the primary remedy for defects is *specific performance*: The contractor has both a right and a duty to carry out remedial works before other remedies are considered. There are though exceptions to this principle. First of all, if the costs of remedial works would be disproportionately high in relation to the expected benefit;[240] the remedy seems unreasonable due to other circumstances[241] or, in Finnish standard contracts, if the defect does not hinder the use of the works;[242] the contractor is not obligated to carry out remedial work, but the employer is entitled to a price reduction instead.[243] Second, and according to the newest version of the Danish standard contracts, if at the defect rectification review meeting or after the expiry of a deadline for rectification, the employer finds that the defects have not been rectified, he must give the contractor a written notice stating the outstanding defects; the employer is then entitled to have the defects in question rectified at the contractor's expense or be granted a reduction of the contract price. However, if the contractor has sought to remedy all the defects and the outstanding defects only represent a small proportion of them, the contractor is nevertheless entitled to rectify such defects, provided that this rectification is initiated immediately after the employer's notice.[244]

10.184 Finally, the contractor can in some situations be liable to *pay damages* in case of defects. If a defect causes consequential damages or injury (to the works themselves or to the employer's or a third party's), the solution varies according to the country in question. In Sweden, the contractor is bound to compensate consequential damages caused by a defect which the contractor is liable for.[245] In Norway, the contractor is liable to pay for the costs of remedy of damages which are caused to parts of the works not comprised in the contract[246] by a defect caused by the contractor's negligence. Furthermore, if the defect caused a loss to the employer which is not covered by the provision just mentioned, the employer can claim that the contractor should compensate such loss but only if the defect

238 AB 18 §49, s. 2.

239 NS 8405 Art. 36.7.

240 AB 18 §51. Norway: NS 8405, §36.2, s. 1.

241 Sweden: AB 04, Chap. 5, §18, states that the contractor is not obligated to remedy defects which do not essentially influence the state, the appearance or the possibility to use the works for the intended purpose to the extent that such remedial work would be unreasonable having regard to their costs or other circumstances.

242 YSE 1998 §29, s. 3.

243 Denmark: AB 18 §51 and 52, s. 1. Sweden: AB 04, Chap. 5, §18, 2nd section. Norway: NS 8405 Art. 36.4.

244 AB 18 §50, s. 1 and 2.

245 AB 04 Chapter 5 §8.

246 As seen above, the risk of damages to the works themselves remains with the contractor until taking-over and is covered by insurance during the construction period.

is due to the contractor's wilful misconduct or gross negligence.[247] The level of fault the contractor is guilty of thus determines the extent of his liability for damages in case of defects. In Denmark, the contractor is liable to cover consequential damages caused by defects which are the result of the contractor's errors or omissions or if the defects relate to properties that must be considered as warranted under the contract[248] (for instance, if a roof collapses because it does not have the guaranteed load bearing capacity).[249] As opposed to what the wording of the clause suggests, this provision does not only concern consequential damages caused by defects in the works, but also by the contractor's activity in relation to the contract in general; literature quotes the example from case law of a contractor obstructing a sewage pipe while pouring foundations piles.[250] However, the contractor is not liable for operational losses; losses of profits or other indirect losses.[251]

Limitations of Liability

10.185 All Nordic standard contracts provide for limitation of liability, and parties often agree to additional limitations. Such limitations are either of quantitative or qualitative nature.

10.186 As far as quantitative limitations are concerned, several contracts state that liability is limited to a certain percentage of the contract sum.[252] Qualitative limitations generally concern excluding liability to certain types of damages. For instance, the Danish standard contracts exclude the contractor's liability for certain types of consequential damages by stating that the contractor cannot be held liable for operational losses; loss of profit or other indirect losses.[253] Furthermore, the provisions, present in most Nordic standard contracts, according to which agreed liquidated damages shall be the only damages that the employer may claim in respect of delay,[254] also represent a limitation of liability where the employer's losses are higher than the liquidated damages.

10.187 A common and important feature of limitation of liability in the Nordic countries is that their validity can be challenged to the extent that they purport to exclude liability for wilful misconduct and in some situations, also, gross negligence. In fact, there are authorities in literature and examples in case law where such exclusion of liability were deemed invalid.[255] This important limitation applies if it is explicitly stated in the contract, like it is the case where a provision of the Swedish standard construction contract stating that the various limitations of liability contained therein do not apply when the liable party is guilty of gross negligence.[256] The validity limitation can also apply indirectly by virtue of the "general clause" contained in Art. 36 of the Nordic Contract Act, stating that

247 NS 8405, Art. 36.5.

248 AB 18 §53, s. 1.

249 Hørlyck, op. cit., p. 432.

250 Hørlyck, op. cit., p. 432.

251 AB 18 §53, s. 2.

252 Sweden: AB 04 Chap. 5, §11, limiting the contractor's liability to 15% of the contract sum; the provision only applies to a limited type of damages. Norway: NS 8405 §34.3, s. 3, limiting the contractor's global liability for liquidated damages to 10% of the contract sum.

253 AB 18 §53, s. 2.

254 See, for instance, NS 8405 §34.1, s. 3 and AB 18 §40, s. 2.

255 Bryde Andersen and Lookofsky, op. cit., pp. 412–13.

256 AB 04 Chapter 5, §11, s. 2.

a contract may be modified or set aside, in whole or in part, if it would be unreasonable or contrary to the principle of good faith to enforce it and which adjudicators can use to strike out liability limitations which are deemed too far-reaching.

Variations

10.188 Since construction projects are very often long-term the needs or budget of the employer may vary over time; all construction contracts provide the employer with the right to require variations. There are different kinds of variations; the main categories are change orders (for instance, a change of material for parts of the works) and additional works or the contrary; that is, omissions, where part of the original scope of work is removed from the scope of work.[257] Variations concern the works' *nature or extent* and variation orders cannot normally be used to change contract conditions such as the project's time schedule or payment structure,[258] but the Norwegian standard contracts state that if the contractor is entitled to an extension of time, the employer may in certain circumstances use the variation procedure to request acceleration measures.[259]

10.189 Since variations can result in significant shifts in the balance of the contract, variations are only authorized within certain *limits*; for instance, certain contracts provide that variations cannot amount to more of a certain percentage of the original contract price,[260] and most contracts state that the employer cannot take part of the works out of the original scope in order to have that part performed by another contractor. This is an illustration of the basic principles concerning variations: The employer has the right to request variations and the contractor has both the right and the duty to carry out the varied works,[261] unless the employer demonstrates special circumstances justifying to let another contractor carry out the works;[262] for instance, if the first contractor is already in delay.[263] Furthermore, the general rule is that in order to qualify as a variation, extra works required by the employer must be in a natural connection[264] with the original works.

10.190 Most contracts provide a detailed variation procedure. Such procedure generally starts with a request in writing[265] and some standard contracts allow such request to be implicit; for instance, the requirement of written request is deemed to be respected in Sweden if the employer hands over drawings containing a variation to the contractor.[266]

257 See, for instance, in Norway NS 8405 Art. 22.1, 2nd section.

258 Hørlyck, op. cit., p. 190.

259 NS 8405 Art. 22.2.

260 See, for instance, in Norway NS 8405 Art. 22.1, 3rd section, providing that unless agreed otherwise, the employer cannot impose on the contractor a variation amounting to a raise of more than 15% of the original contract price.

261 Explicit in the Danish standard: AB 18 §23, s. 1 and 2.

262 AB 18 §23, s. 2 in fine.

263 Hørlyck, op. cit., p. 191.

264 See, for instance, in Denmark AB 18 §23, s. 1, first sentence: " The client may order variations to the works when such variations are naturally linked to the services agreed upon". And in Sweden AB 04 Chap. 2 §3.

265 Sweden: AB 04 Chap. 2 §6. The Danish standard contracts also provide for variation orders to be presented at a construction meeting: AB 18 §23, s. 3.

266 Deli, op. cit., p. 68.

10.191 Variations often (but not always) have impact on the project's time schedule and/or on the contract price. Contracts must, therefore, provide for mechanisms allowing or imposing an exchange of views between the parties on these issues, including the question of whether an order or instruction given by the employer is a simple clarification within the context of the original works or constitutes a variation. Standard contracts have several methods to deal with such issues. The most recent version of the Danish standard contracts provides that any claim by a party concerning amendments to the contract in terms of price, time and security resulting from a variation must be submitted as soon as possible, and that this requirement also applies to a party's claim for amendments to the contract resulting from an approved proposal from the contractor or an instruction issued by the employer which the contractor considers to be a variation to the works, even if the proposal or instruction does not state that a variation is involved.[267] The contract also states that the parties must as soon as possible enter into an addendum to the contract concerning the variation and its consequences in terms of price, time and security, but that negotiations about this addendum must not delay the works.[268] However, the contractor is not obliged to commence the work on the variation before the employer has responded as to whether he considers an order or approval as a variations entailing amendments to the contracts in terms of price, time or security.[269] Read together, these provisions mean that the contractor has the right to refuse to start working on the varied works until the employer has acknowledged in writing that the required works constitute a variation, but that the contractor cannot wait to have a full agreement concerning all the consequences of the variation.[270]

10.192 Norwegian standard contracts and the Swedish turnkey standards also both contain provisions according to which the contractor has the duty to give notice without delay to the employer if the contractor considers that an order given constitutes a variation or entitles the contractor to an additional payment.[271] In Sweden, unless special circumstances are present, the contractor loses his right to extra payment or other consequences linked to a variation if its notice is not given.[272] This is the general rule only if certain circumstances are present justifying the contractor not following the general rule; for instance, if the works have to be carried out in emergency and the contractor cannot wait for an agreement with the employer on the nature of the works.[273] Upon reception of the notice, the employer must reply without delay, by stating whether he wishes the works to be carried out as a variation or not, and in Norway the employer's reply would be either issuing a variation order in writing or rejecting the contractor's claim. In case of disagreement between the parties, the Norwegian standard contracts state that the contractor must carry out the ordered works but that he can request a security from the employer corresponding to the value of the disputed claim.[274]

267 AB 18 §25, s. 1.
268 AB 18 §25, stk. 4
269 AB 18 §25, stk. 2 and 4.
270 Hørlyck, op. cit., p. 193.
271 NS 8405, Art. 23.2 and ABT 06 Chapter 2 §7.
272 NS 8405, Art. 23.2 and ABT 06 Chapter 2 §8.
273 ABT 06 Chapter 2 §8. Deli, op. cit., p. 68.
274 NS 8405, Art. 26.1.

10.193 The question of whether an instruction given by the employer constitutes a simple clarification and/or an elaboration of the works within the contractor's scope of work or a variation and the directly related question of whether a variation entitles the contractor to additional payment and/or an extension of time are of the issues generating most of the case law in Nordic construction matters.

10.194 Generally speaking, the contractor has to demonstrate that a variation has an actual impact on the time schedule or the contract price in order to obtain an extension of time or an additional payment; this is expressed in standard contracts in the provisions on extension of time or additional payment, stating that these can be requested in case of delay or increase in costs *caused* by variations.[275]

Delay and Disruption

10.195 Time is one of the most essential factors in a construction project. Delay in the carrying out of the works can have extensive economic consequences for both parties. The employer risks losing the income he is expecting to earn (e.g., by renting the completed building and facing claims for delay damages from tenants or buyers supposed to take over the works at a certain point in time) and the contractor will in all likelihood owe delay damages to the employer, face costs linked to his prolonged presence on the site and possibly lose income if he cannot dedicate his resources to a planned subsequent project.[276]

10.196 Parties to a construction contract almost always agree that the works have to be completed within a certain period of time. If delay arises, two situations must be distinguished. If the delay was caused by circumstances contractually defined as excusable, the contractor (and in some situations also the employer) can be entitled to an *extension of time*, and in some cases also to an economic compensation. If there is no ground for an extension of time, the party in delay will, in the majority of cases, owe *delay damages* to the other party. Due to the difficulty in proving the actual loss suffered in case of delay, parties most often provide for standardized (liquidated) amounts of damages to be paid by the contractor for definite periods of delay, usually one day and often expressed as a percentage of the contract sum (for instance, 1‰ of the contract sum per day of delay).

10.197 Rules concerning the circumstances giving rise to extensions of time for the contractor can be found in all Nordic standard contracts, and can be classified into two main categories: Circumstances related to the employer (such as variation orders or late delivery of design documents in the build-only model or delay caused by another contractor hired by the employer)[277] on the one hand, and on the other hand events generally termed neutral events because they are not related to or caused by any of the parties to the construction contract and beyond the latter's control. This second category namely encompasses *Force Majeure* type of circumstances such as war, natural catastrophes; fire or exceptionally adverse weather conditions, as well as several types of labour disputes

275 See, for instance, in Norway NS 8405, Art. 24.1 "*som følge av*" ("as a consequence of") and Art. 25.1 "*som endringer medfører*" ("which the changes cause").

276 See, for instance, Deli, op. cit., p. 92.

277 Denmark:AB 18, §39, lit (a) and (b). Norway: NS 8405 Art. 24.1. Sweden: AB 04 Chapter 4, §3 s. 1.

such as strikes or lockouts or authorities interventions such as public bans and orders[278] as long as they are not caused by the contractor's behaviour. Danish contracts explicitly mention that the contractor is liable for delay caused by circumstances which do not entitle it to an extension of time,[279] but this conclusion is implicit in most contracts.

10.198 Delay, defined as the overrun of a contractually agreed deadline, must be distinguished from *disruption*, which is the disturbance or interruption of a contractor's work progress resulting in lower efficiency or productivity than originally expected.[280] Disruption does not necessarily lead to delay; for instance, if the contractor works extra shifts in order to counter the effect of disruptive events. Rules on the circumstances causing delay on the one hand and disruption on the other are often discussed in the same context, although they have different consequences: Circumstances leading to delay may give rise to an extension of time and only sometimes also an economic compensation, whereas disruption understood as a loss of productivity can in some circumstances give rise to economic compensation because it causes additional work and expenses.[281] This difference can be observed in the structure of the Swedish and Norwegian standard contracts: The rules concerning acts of prevention leading to delay are found in the chapter concerning time whereas the rules addressing disruption are located in the chapter regulating the project's economic aspects.[282] Disruption claims are often linked with difficulties, in particular in respect to evidence; in case of loss of productivity, the contractor will often have trouble proving which part of the loss is caused by circumstances that the employer bears the risk of, such as variations, unforeseen ground conditions or employer's breach of his obligations, and which part is due to circumstances related to the contractor, which the latter has to bear. Methods to prove such claims are discussed in practice, and Norwegian courts have often criticized the method consisting in comparing the contractor's expected productivity with the productivity actually attained, or the productivity that would have been attained without the circumstances attributable to the employer, as it supposes that the contractor's expectations as to productivity be reasonable and realistic. In a case decided in January 2009, the Agder Court of Appeal admitted that the contractor was entitled to compensation of additional costs caused by unfavourable mountain ground conditions, but did not follow the contractor in relation to the quantum of the claim. In fact, the court noted that the contractor's plan to dig the tunnel in 50 weeks was not realistic and had not been substantiated by the contractor, so that some of the acceleration costs had to be considered as caused by the contractor.[283]

278 Denmark AB 18, §39, lit (c), (d) and €. Norway: NS 8405 Art. 24.3. Sweden: AB 04 Chapter 4, §3 s. 2 and 3.

279 AB 18 §40, S. 1.

280 Keith Pickavance, *Delay and Disruption in Construction Contracts*, Informa Professional, London, 2005, p. 838.

281 See, for instance, the Norwegian standard NS 8405, Art. 25.3, s. 2 (b), enumerating the situations in which the contractor must give a specific notice, namely if its claim for additional payment is based on, among others, the ground of disruption.

282 Deli, op. cit., p. 105. Norway: NS 8407 Art. 34.1.3, 2nd para.

283 Agder Court of Appeal, judgement of 22 January 2009, published at LA-2008-52830, commented by Nordtvedt et al., p. 516–17.

Delay Damages

Liquidated Damages

10.199 All Scandinavian standard contracts provide for *liquidated damages* as standard solution in case of contractor's delay. The possibility of claiming non-standardized delay damages is only mentioned in the Danish contracts which state that if no liquidated damages or other specific sanctions are agreed on, delay damages are calculated according to general principles of Danish law.[284] In Sweden, liquidated damages are presented as the usual remedy in case of contractor's delay, but the parties must agree on a rate or calculation method in order for the standard liquidated damages clause to apply.[285] The Norwegian and Finnish standard contracts function differently since they provide for a per default rate of liquidated damages per day of delay, which means that the parties do not need to make express provisions in order to apply liquidated damages, but in the contrary explicitly opt out if they intend delay damages to be calculated according to general rules concerning assessment of damages.[286] If the parties do not agree on liquidated damages in case of contractor's delay, the employer can claim the damages he actually suffered as a consequence of a delay, calculated according to general rules on damage assessment.[287]

10.200 Liquidated damages on one hand and general damages on the other are generally considered as alternatives: When liquidated damages are agreed on, the main rule is that the employer is barred from claiming additional damages on the account of the contractor's delay.[288] The Norwegian standard states that the employer can claim damages instead of liquidated damages if the delay is caused by the contractor's gross negligence or wilful misconduct.[289] No corresponding rule exists in Denmark, and in Danish case law there is one case only where an employer was unsuccessful in trying to obtain higher damages than the liquidated damages based on the argument that the contractor intentionally caused the delay;[290] a renowned scholar suggested that a rule similar to the Norwegian rule be inserted in the Danish standard,[291] but his suggestion was not followed in the most recent version of the standard released in 2018. The Swedish standard contract does not contain an exception to the main rule for the situations where the delay represents gross negligence or wilful misconduct from the contractor's side, but it is suggested in literature that in certain situations; for instance, if the contractor deliberately dedicates resources to another project, it could be reasonable to let the employer claim general damages instead of liquidated damages.[292] Such a solution could be inferred from the "general clause" contained in Section 36 of the Nordic Contract Act allowing for the setting aside of unfair and/or unreasonable contract clauses and in some situations interpreted as containing a prohibition of exclusions of liability for wilful misconduct and gross negligence. This

284 AB 18 §40, s. 6.

285 AB 04 Chap. 5, §3.

286 Norway: NS 8405 Art. 34.3. Finland: YSE 1998 §18.

287 See, for instance, the Danish AB 18 §40, s. 6.

288 See, for instance, the Danish AB 18 §40, s. 2.

289 See NS 8405 Art. 34.1, third part.

290 Decision published at T:BB 2000.518 (2) VBA.

291 Torsten Iversen, *Nogle bemærkninger om dagbod* in *Festskrift til Det Danske Selskab for Byggeret*, Copenhagen, 2009, p. 124.

292 Deli, op. cit., p. 102.

provision and its consequences for limitations of liability, in general, are discussed below in the section concerning limitations of liability.

10.201 The Norwegian standard contracts expressly limit the contractor's liability for delay to 10% of the contract sum.[293] This limitation does not exist in other Scandinavian standards but corresponds nonetheless to a market standard and is, therefore, frequently inserted by parties in their contracts.

10.202 In situations of excusable delay, the contractor may be entitled to an extra *economic compensation* in addition to an extension of time. The Danish standards provide for two different types of additional economic compensation depending on the circumstances causing the delay. In fact, the contractor can either claim full compensation for its delay-related costs (prolongation costs) plus its loss of profits ("*erstatning for det lidte tab*", meaning compensation of the loss suffered)[294] or only an indemnity covering his delay-related costs but not its loss of profits ("*godtgørelse*", literally meaning "making good again").[295] In short, the main criterion distinguishing the two types of grounds is fault; if the employer or a contractor the actions or omissions of which the employer is contractually responsible delays another contractor by a faulty conduct (for instance, by not securing sufficient workforce on the site), the delayed contractor is entitled to a full indemnity including his loss of profits, but he can only claim a simple indemnity if neither the employer nor one of the co-contractors is at fault. Finally, if the delay is caused by a neutral event, the contractor is entitled to an extension of time, but no additional economic compensation,[296] meaning that the parties share the overall risks of such events.

10.203 In Norwegian law, the standard contracts list a series of grounds based on which the contractor may claim an adjustment of his remuneration, among others delay or other default by the employer.[297] The contracts contain detailed provisions on how the adjustment may be calculated,[298] and the leading principle is that the contractor must be fully compensated for the consequences of the delay.[299]

10.204 In Swedish law, the contractor is as, a matter of principle, entitled to an economic compensation to cover the costs caused by employer-related circumstances, among other employer-related delay.[300] However, if the employer can prove that he could not reasonably have expected, prevented and overcome the hindrance, the related costs must be shared equally between the parties.[301]

Insurance

10.205 Since construction works present risks of damage to the works themselves, the employer's property as well as third parties, all Nordic standard contracts contain

293 NS 8405 Art. 34.3, s. 1.

294 AB 18 §43, s. 1.

295 AB 18 §43, s. 2.

296 AB 18 §43, s. 3. Sylvie Cavaleri, *Concurrent Delay in Construction Disputes*, Denmark, 2015, pp. 142–7.

297 NS 8405 Art. 25.2.

298 NS 8405 Art. 25.7 to 25.9.

299 Hagstrøm and Bruserud, op. cit., p. 269.

300 AB 04 Chapter 5, §4, referring to Chapter 4 §3 s. 1 related to employer-related circumstances.

301 AB 04 Chapter 5, §4, second sentence.

provisions obligating the parties to take out insurance. Two different types of insurance are generally relevant in relation to a construction project. First, *all-risk insurances*, which are property insurance of the object of the construction contract, cover all damages to the latter except those risks expressly excluded from the insurance. Generally, the insurance policy runs from the commencement date until that of taking-over or until the remedial works are completed. All-risk insurances are generally taken out by the contractor but the employer must be co-insured under several standard forms.

10.206 Second, contractors are generally required to take on *liability insurance* covering the damage they and/or their subcontractors may cause to the employer or third parties' property or persons in relation with the performance of their duties under the construction contract.

10.207 The regulation of these matters, namely the question of which party is responsible for the insurance, differs between the Scandinavian countries. In Sweden, the contractor is responsible for taking out both the all-risk insurance[302] and professional liability insurance.[303] As far as the all-risk insurance is concerned, the default provision, which apply unless the parties agrees otherwise, stipulates that the employer must be named as co-insured; that the insured amount must correspond to the costs of reinstatement of the works in case of damages, and provide for a maximum amount for the deductible. The provisions also state a minimum insured amount and a maximum amount for the deductible for the contractor's liability insurance.

10.208 The Norwegian solution resembles the Swedish in that the contractor is also responsible for taking out both the all-risk[304] and the professional liability insurance.[305] The Norwegian regulation of insurance is quite detailed and contains rules as to the exact object covered by the all-risk insurance (the works and the materials that the employer has either made an advance payment for or put at the disposal of the contractor); the kind of risks that the insurance policy must cover (fire, water damage, vandalism and theft caused by forced entry on the site, etc.) as well as the fact that the insurer must waive the right to invoke certain objections stated in Norwegian insurance legislation in order to reduce payouts under the insurance policy as well as the right to negotiate with or make payouts to the insured without the employer's consent. As for the professional liability, similar provisions exist concerning the minimum insured amount and the relation to Norwegian insurance legislation concerning the aggrieved party's rights vis-à-vis the insurer.

10.209 The Norwegian and Danish standard contracts contains specific provisions concerning alteration works and obligating the employer to take out insurance covering the parts of the building not included in the construction contract.[306]

10.210 In Denmark, the insurance provisions in the standard contracts differ from the other Scandinavian countries in that they impose an obligation on the *employer* to take out insurance covering fire and storm damages from the beginning of the construction operations until remedial works are completed.[307] In case of alteration works, this insurance

302 AB 04 Chapter 5, §22, s. 2.
303 AB 04 Chapter 5, §22, s. 3.
304 NS 8405 Art. 10.1.
305 NS 8405 Art. 10.2.
306 Norway: NS 8405 Art. 10.4.Denmark: AB 18 §11, s. 1.
307 AB 18 §11, s. 1.

must cover the works as well as the building or the installation which is being altered.[308] This obligation to take out insurance only applies to private employers.[309] In fact, public employers can demand to be placed in the situation of self-insured, meaning that they must place the contractor or his sub-contractors in the same position as they would have been had the employer taken the usual fire and storm insurance – or in other words, cover damages caused by such events if they occur.[310] As mentioned above, this employer insurance obligation constitutes a mitigation of the extensive risks taken on by the contractor since he retains the risk for the state of the works until taking-over, unless damage is caused by circumstances outside of its control.

10.211 In addition to this specific insurance, *employers* (as opposed to contractors) often take out all-risk insurances covering all types of damages to the works not specifically excluded in the policy. Such all-risk insurances do not usually cover fire and storm risks in Denmark, which means that an all-risk does not per se fulfil the employer's obligation to take out fire and storm insurance,[311] hence the employer must take an additional insurance covering these two risks, or have them added to the all-risk policy.

10.212 Finally, contractors and subcontractors are obliged, under the Danish standard, to take out the usual professional and product liability insurance.[312] This insurance does not cover the contractor's liability pursuant to the construction contract, but liability under Danish general professional liability and product liability legislation. Since insurance policies covering professional liability and product liability in Denmark generally exclude coverage for damages caused to objects that the insured has undertaken to install, repair, assemble or in any way process or treat in the course of the insured's work, and in general also exclude coverage for a significant number of construction activities such as excavation, ground water lowering, etc., such insurances are of limited practical relevance for contractors.[313] However, the product liability insurance may become more important as contractors are more and more often held liable pursuant to product liability rules, and since the newest version of the Danish standard contract provide that the contractor's product liability is limited to the amount covered by his product liability insurance.[314] This new clause is a reaction to an evolution observed in practice where employers would frequently frame their claims against contractors as product liability claims because the exclusion of the contractor's liability for indirect losses, contained in the former version of the standard contracts, was not always deemed to apply to product liability, which is not purely contractual in nature.[315]

Types of Damages

10.213 There are four types of damages: Damages to the works themselves; damages to the contractor's property (equipment, materials, etc.), damages to the employer's property in the broad sense (including damages to adjacent buildings and to materials and/or

308 AB 18 §11, s. 1.
309 AB 18 §11, s. 2.Hørlyck, op. cit., p. 122.
310 Iversen, op. cit., p. 276.
311 Hørlyck, op. cit., p. 126.
312 AB 18 §11, s. 3.
313 Hørlyck, op. cit., s. 128.
314 Se AB 18 §54, s. 1 and 5.
315 Hørlyck-2019, p. 551.

equipment provided by the employer) and damages to third parties' property. Since most construction contracts provide for various types of insurance obligations for the parties, the damages just mentioned are quite often covered by insurance.

DAMAGES TO THE WORKS

10.214 As noted above, the contractor bears the risk for the material and the works until they are taken over or taken in use;[316] he is naturally liable for damage to the works that he causes before taking-over. This rule applies unless the damage are caused by the employer[317] or persons for which the employer is contractually responsible[318] or by certain *Force Majeure*-type of circumstances.[319] The newest version of the Danish standard contracts introduced an important exception to the contractor's liability, since if the works are being carried out in a building or plant which is in use during construction, the contractor is only liable for damages caused by another contractor and which is not a consequence of circumstances pertaining to the employer. The employer is liable for other damages, especially damages caused by the users of the building or plant.[320]

10.215 In case of damage caused to the works by the employer or persons for whom the latter is contractually responsible, Nordic standard contracts provide for different solutions.

10.216 In Sweden, a general provision states that the contractor is not liable for damages to the works caused by the employer.[321] It is complemented by a mutual provision concerning general liability for damages, which states that each party must compensate for the damages this party caused to the other party's work by performing his duties negligently,[322] this is interpreted as making the employer liable for damages he causes to the works when the employer's behaviour amounts to negligence.

10.217 The Norwegian solution to this issue is closely linked to insurance provisions. As an exception to the rule according to which the contractor bears the risk for the works until taking-over; the contractor does not bear the risk for damages to the works caused by the employer or his employees or delegates in the exercise of their functions. If such damages are covered by the contractor's mandatory insurance and the contractor's insurance deductible is not covered by the person causing the damages or his insurance, the deductible must be, up to a certain amount defined (and updated annually) by Norwegian legislation, covered by the employer.[323]

10.218 In Denmark until recently the only damages to the works which the contractor was not liable for were those caused by the employer and/or his employees or delegates, which had to be be covered by the employer.[324] Damages to the works caused by *Force Majeure* type of circumstances were also part of the contractor's risk. Although it was mitigated by the employer's obligation to insure the works against fire and storm damages,

316 Denmark: AB 18 §27, s. 1. Sweden: AB 04 5, §1, s. 1.
317 Denmark: AB 18 §27, s. 2. Sweden: AB 04 5, §1, s. 2.
318 Denmark: AB 18 §27, s. 2. Norway: NS 8405 Art. 17, s. 2.
319 Norway: NS 8405 Art. 17, s. 3. Sweden: AB 04 5, §1, s. 3. Denmark: AB 18 §27, s. 2.
320 AB 18 §27, s. 6.
321 AB 04 Chapter 5, §1, s. 2.
322 AB 04 Chapter 5 §9, s. 1.
323 NS 8405 Art. 17, s. 2.
324 AB 92 §12, s. 1: "unless the damages can be imputed to the employer".

this solution was unusual and literature suggested that it should be modified in order to align with other Nordic countries.[325] In fact, the employer bears the (most often insurance-covered) risk of damages to the works caused by *Force Majeure* circumstances in both Sweden[326] and Norway.[327] The drafting committee of the newest versions of the Danish standard contracts followed these scholarly suggestions and these contracts now provide that the contractor does not bear the risk of damage or loss due to consequences of exceptional external events beyond his control (*Force Majeure*), including war, riot, acts of terrorism, and acts of God.[328] Both the report and an author though stress that the definition of *Force Majeure* is narrower and covers less situations in relation to the passing of risk than it does in relation to extensions of time.[329] This is the situation under the Norwegian standard contracts as well.

Damages to the Employer's Property

10.219 The employer's property most likely to suffer damages during the course of construction works are materials, and in some situations also equipment, delivered by the employer to the construction site. As far as materials are concerned, the risk of damage follows the general rule; the contractor bears the risk for the whole of the works until taking-over. In Norway[330] and Denmark,[331] this contractor's liability is strict, whereas the Swedish contracts state that the liability depends upon the contractor's negligent omission or lack of care for property put at his disposal by the employer.[332]

Damages to the Contractor's Property

10.220 The Swedish contracts are the only Scandinavian contracts directly addressing this matter by stating that the employer must insure against damages that he or his employees cause to both the contractor's work and/or property (equipment, materials, etc.). This employer's liability supposes that the employer acted negligently causing damage to the contractor's works,[333] and a failure to exercise the required level of care on the employer's part in case of damage to materials, equipment or goods belonging to or provided by the contractor.[334] In this second situation, literature suggests it is unclear whether a simple omission or lack of care is sufficient to trigger liability, or whether the employer's behaviour must be reprehensible.

10.221 In the other Nordic countries, construction contracts do not contain specific provisions concerning damages caused by the employer to the contractor's property. It must consequently be solved according to the usual rules and principles of liability in tort and/or contract.

325 Hørlyck, op. cit., p. 168.
326 AB 04 Chapter 5, §1, s. 3.
327 NS 8405 Art. 17, s. 3.
328 AB 18 §27, s. 2.
329 Report, p. 130-131. Hørlyck-2019, p. 305.
330 NS 8405 Art. 17, s. 1.
331 AB 18 §27, s. 1.
332 AB 04 Chap. 5, §9, s. 2 and §10 discussed by Deli, op. cit., p. 126.
333 AB 04 Chap. 5, §9, s. 1.
334 AB 04 Chap. 5, §9, s. 2.

Damages to Third Parties Properties

10.222 The relevant issues do not properly belong in a construction contract which regulates the relationship between the employer and the contractor, and consequently cannot impose obligations or restrictions on third parties. This basic principle is expressed in provisions such as §27, s. 3 in the Danish AB 18; stating that damage caused by a contractor to the works, materials, or equipment of other contracts is of no concern to the employer.

10.223 However, some standard contracts, such as the Swedish AB, contain provisions concerning the parties' situation in relation to third parties claim based on national law. Chapter 32 of the Swedish environmental regulations gives an aggrieved third party (for instance, one of the employer's tenants suffering noise or vibration nuisances caused by works on a construction site adjacent to their habitation) the choice to sue either the employer or the contractor, thereby creating the need to regulate the parties' related rights and obligations in the construction contract. The relevant general provision states that the contractor is liable towards the employer for claims made by third parties as a consequence of the construction activities, unless the contractor can prove that he could not have reasonably prevented or limited the damage.[335] As far as damages pursuant to the environmental legislation, the employer must as a starting point hold the contractor harmless of claims made by third parties for such damages if the contractor can prove that he could not have prevented or limited the damage.[336]

Suspension

10.224 Since the most usual payment arrangements in construction contracts in the Nordic countries is that the employer is to effect a monthly payment, and since the contractor's invoices often provide for a payment deadline of 30 days, the contractor often gives considerable credit to the employer, in that he carries out works for which he will first obtain payment up to two months after performance. To counterbalance this risk; all Nordic construction contracts provide the contractor with the right to interrupt his performance of the works in order to exercise pressure on the employer in case the employer breaches his payment obligations. Such suspension always represents a significant standpoint risk: If the suspension is justified, the contractor will obtain an extension of time and delay damages, but if it is not, the contractor is in breach of his contract and thereby exposes itself to various sanctions, from liquidated damages, other damages and possibly termination by the employer. This contractor's right of suspension is regulated slightly differently from one Nordic country to another.

10.225 In Denmark, the contractor can exercise his right of suspension in two main situations. First, the contractor can do so with three working days' notice[337] in case the employer has not fulfilled his payment obligation within the relevant deadline.[338] Second, the contractor can stop working immediately if the employer is declared bankrupt or subject to reconstruction proceedings, or if the employer's financial situation in general proves to

335 AB 04 Chapter 5, §13, s. 1 and 2.

336 AB 04 Chapter 5, §13, s. 3.

337 The deadline is of five working days for public employers and social housing organizations: AB 18 §38, s. 1 in fine.

338 AB 18 §38, s. 1.

be of such nature that he must be assumed to be unable to fulfil his obligations under the contract, unless the employer has provided adequate security for the performance of the remaining part of the contract. If the employer provides such security immediately, the contractor must resume work.[339] The newest version of the Danish standard contains a provision stating that if the contractor is entitled to stop work because of the employer's economic situation, the contractor may demand that the employer immediately provide adequate security for the performance of the remaining part of the contract.[340] The Report mentions that this provision is only applicable if it does not violate mandatory provision of the Danish Bankruptcy Act concerning the right to step in a contract or carry a contract forward, if the bankruptcy estate decides so or if the debtor chooses so with the consent of the reconstruction administrator.[341] The author of the commentary of the standard contract argues that claiming such a security against a debtor in reconstruction who chose with the reconstruction administrator's approval to carry a contract forward or against the bankruptcy estate having chosen to step in the contracts will always infringe on mandatory provisions of the Danish Bankruptcy Act, and that the new provision of the Danish standard construction contract must, therefore, be applied with caution.[342]

10.226 In Norway, the contractor's right of suspension is to be exercised with 24 hours' notice in writing if the employer *substantially* breaches his payment obligations or if it is obvious that such breach is *imminent*[343] – in case of such anticipatory breach, literature sets a high threshold of proof to be provided by the contractor, stating that the anticipated breach must be of such "degree of likelihood very close to certainty".[344]

10.227 In Sweden, the contractor's right of suspension exists not only with respect to the employer's breach of payment obligations, as in other Scandinavian countries, but also in case the employer substantially breaches his other obligations deriving from the construction contract; for instance, his duty to provide the contractor with adequate security, or if the employer transfers his rights under the contract or the contract itself to a third party and this has significant consequences for the contractor. Contrary to other Scandinavian standard contracts, the Swedish standard contract states that suspension may not exceed one month, during which the contractor must inform the employer of his intention to either resume work or terminate the contract.[345]

10.228 As opposed to some Anglo-Saxon contracts such as FIDIC, the starting point of Scandinavian contracts is that a contractual time schedule is binding for both parties, with the consequence that unless specifically agreed, the employer is not allowed to unilaterally order a temporary suspension of the works, even if the contractor is granted an extension of time and prolongation costs on that account. In Denmark, the question of whether the employer could request modifications of the time schedule through a variation has been raised but the general opinion is that he cannot, the variation procedure addressing changes in kind or in extent/quantities and not to other contract conditions

339 AB 18 §38, s. 2.
340 AB 18 §38, s. 3.
341 Report, p. 148.
342 Hørlyck-2019, p. 381–2.
343 NS 8405 Art. 30.2.
344 Nortvedt et al., op. cit., p. 415.
345 AB 04 Chapter 8, §3.

such as time schedule or payment terms.[346] If the employer meets adverse circumstances, he can in some situations obtain an extension of time, which will in some cases entitle the contractor to an additional economic compensation, but that does not equal the employer's unilateral right of suspension stipulated in FIDIC, which does not require a specific cause.

Termination

10.229 In addition to performance in the wide sense, which is the most usual way to bring contracts to an end, Nordic construction contracts consider two ways of ending construction contracts. First, the employer can for various reasons lose interest in the contract and seek to *cancel* it; such cancellation without valid ground would potentially constitute a breach of contract and entitles the contractor to payment for the works carried out until the cancellation as well as an additional economic compensation, the extent of which is often difficult to define and it can vary from one country to another. Second, both parties can *terminate* the contract if some critical circumstances arise, for instance, in case of substantial breach(es) of contract by the other party or based on the latter encountering financial difficulties; for example, insolvency or bankruptcy.

10.230 The employer's right to terminate the contract for convenience is explicitly provided for in the Norwegian standard contracts. In the Danish ones, termination for convenience is explicitly provided for in one specific situation; that is, when unexpected circumstances related to ground conditions give rise to public bans or orders which hinder the continuation of the works or make it unreasonably burdensome for the employer.[347] Although a more general cancellation right is recognized in case law and literature, there are uncertainties as to the elements to be included in the compensation which the contractor is entitled to in case of cancellation by the employer.[348] Swedish construction contracts do not provide for such a right; if the employer terminates the contract without a valid cause, it will be treated as an unauthorised termination and will entitle the contractor to damages.[349]

10.231 In Norwegian law, the employer's right to cancel the contract is restricted in that the employer cannot terminate the contract to award the works to another contractor who would carry them out at a lower price. The nature of the economic compensation due to the contractor depends on how the purported cancellation is qualified. In fact, cancellation in Norwegian law is tightly linked to the notion of variations, which are only allowed within certain limits. If those limits are exceeded, the purported variation will be considered as a cancellation of (part of) the contract and entitle the contractor to additional compensation. As mentioned above, Norwegian standard contracts limits the extent of variations, unless otherwise agreed, to no more than 15% net of the contract price.[350] Consequently, the provision on termination stipulates that if the deduction from the contractor's aggregated remuneration calculated after adding the cost of the additional works and subtracting the value of the omissions related to variations amounts to less than 15% of the contract sum,

346 Hørlyck, op. cit., p. 191.
347 AB 18 §26, s. 4.
348 Hørlyck-2019, p. 295 to 301.
349 Deli, op. cit., p. 187-188. Samuelsson, op. cit., p. 311.
350 NS 8405, Art. 22, s. 3.

such reduction must be dealt with as a variation, whereas reductions exceeding 15% are to be treated as a cancellation of (a part of) the contract.[351] In case of actual cancellation, the contractor is, in addition to payment for the parts of the works already carried out,[352] entitled to the compensation of the economic loss he suffers as a consequence of the cancellation.[353] This compensation is calculated as the positive contract interest; meaning that the contractor must be placed in the same situation as if the contract had been duly performed, but he generally has a duty to mitigate his loss, namely by seeking to use the resources left free due to the cancellation of works.[354]

10.232 In the specific situation of a long-term suspension of the works due to circumstances qualifying as *Force Majeure*, both parties are entitled to terminate the contract, but at conditions different than those applying in case of ordinary termination for convenience just described, in that the contractor is allowed to a payment for the works already carried out, but not for his loss of profits due to the termination.[355]

10.233 As far as termination for cause is concerned, some causes are common to most Nordic standard contracts. They can be classified into three main groups: First, fundamental breach of contract obligations, including fundamental delay or default in providing the contractually agreed securities, by the party against which termination is invoked,[356] second, financial difficulties experienced by that party, such as bankruptcy or insolvency[357] and finally, in certain situations also *Force Majeure* type of circumstances;[358] for example, when parts of the works not yet taken over by the employer suffer extensive damages because of *Force Majeure*; that constitutes a fundamental change of circumstances disturbing the essential premises of the contract.[359]

10.234 Since termination is a radical measure with far-reaching consequences for both parties; contracts generally pose conditions as to when and how termination can be effected. For example, the Norwegian standard contracts provide that before termination can occur, the terminating party must give the other party a reasonable deadline to remedy the situation warranting termination, and that termination cannot take place if the party in breach gives the other party adequate security or proves that the contract will be performed adequately.[360]

10.235 In case of termination, most standard contracts provide for a status meeting to be held on site, namely to determine the stage of advancement of the works already carried out and the amount of the payment due to the contractor for these works.[361] Apart from pay-

351 NS 8405, Art. 38.1, s. 3.

352 Hagstrøm and Bruserud, op. cit., p. 301.

353 NS 8405, Art. 38.1, s. 4.

354 Hagstrøm and Bruserud, op. cit., p. 301–2.

355 NS 8405, Art. 38.2.

356 Denmark: AB 18 §59 (breach by the contractor) and §60 (breach by the employer).Norway: NS 8405, Art. 39.1, also if such fundamental breach has not occurred yet but is imminent. Sweden: AB 04 Chapter 8, §1, s. 1–3, 5–8 (breach by contractor) and §2, (breach by the employer)

357 Denmark: AB 18 §61. Norway: NS 8405, Art. 39.1. Sweden: Chapter 8, §1, s. 4 and §2, s. 2.

358 Sweden: AB 04, Chapter 8, §1, and §2, s. 7–9. In Norway, such circumstances causing a long-term suspension of the carrying out of the works do not warrant termination for cause, but a mutual right of cancellation of the contract: NS 8405 Art. 38.2.

359 Sweden: AB 04 Chapter 8, §1, s. 9 and §2, s. 7.

360 NS 8405 Art. 39.1, s. 2 and 3.

361 Norway: NS 8405, Art. 39.7. Denmark: AB 18 §63, s. 2 to 4.

ment for the works already carried out until termination, which is a logical consequence of the fact that the parts of the works already performed cannot be returned to the contractor, the consequences of termination vary much depending on the cause of termination and the circumstances of the case at hand. When termination is triggered by a fundamental breach by one party, the other party can most often claim damages to compensate for the losses caused by termination (higher financing costs for the employer, loss of profits for the contractor, etc.).[362]

Forms of Security – Bonds and Guarantees

10.236 All Nordic standard contracts contain provisions according to which parties to a construction contract provide one another with financial securities as guarantees for the performance of their respective obligations.

10.237 In Danish law, the contractor must, unless agreed otherwise, provide the employer, within eight working days from contract execution, with a guarantee for the performance of his obligations. If the contract sum is less than DKK 1 million, the contractor must only provide a performance bond if the employer required so in the tender documents.[363] The guarantee can take the form of a bank guarantee, a third party surety or any other adequate instrument, and must amount to 15% of the contract sum until taking-over. After taking-over, the percentage is reduced to 10% until one year has passed since taking-over.[364] When the deadline of one year expires, the guarantee is reduced to 2%, unless the employer has made a claim for the remedy of defects; if he did, the reduction operates once the defects are remedied.[365] The guarantee expires five years after taking-over, unless the employer has made a claim for the remedy of defects; if he did, the guarantee expires once the defects are remedied.[366] The deadline matches the duration of the contractor's defect liability period.[367] The newest versions of the Danish standard contracts introduced specific provisions concerning the regulation of the security amount in case of variations, which now only takes place at handing-over and only if the employer expressly requests it.[368] New provisions also applies to the release at delivery of the security provided by the contractor for specific works for which no defects can occur after handing-over,[369] for instance, demolition work or scaffolding contracts, or for works postponed for later handover[370] or handed over in stages.[371] Finally, a new provision states that in case of termination of the contract by the contractor, the security provided by the contractor expires three months after the date of the termination, unless the termination is contested in dispute resolution proceedings.[372]

362 See, for instance, in Denmark AB 18 §63, s. 6.
363 AB 18 §9 s. 1.
364 AB 18 §9 s. 2 and 3.
365 AB 18 §9 s. 5.
366 See AB 18 §9, s. 6.
367 See the section on defect liability above.
368 AB 18 §9, s. 3.
369 AB 18 §9, s. 7.
370 AB 18 §9, s. 9
371 AB 18 §9, s. 10.
372 AB 18 §9, s. 8.

10.238 The Swedish standard contracts contain the possibility for parties to provide guarantees if such guarantees are agreed on in the contract; as opposed to Danish standard contracts the provision of a guarantee by the contractor is not a rule applying per default and the parties must actively agree on securities. The system is otherwise very similar to the Danish contractor guarantee, with the exception of the percentage of the contract sum suggested by the standard, which is 10% instead of 15%.[373]

10.239 The employer willing to obtain payment under the guarantee must make a written claim addressed to both the contractor and the guarantor and indicating in detail the nature and extent of the breach justifying the call of guarantee as well as the amount claimed. Payment must be effected within ten days from the reception of the claim by the guarantor, unless the contractor has within this deadline requested an expert determination on the question of whether the employer's claim is justified.[374]

10.240 According to several Nordic standard contracts, the employer must also provide the contractor with a guarantee for the performance of the employer's obligations. In the recent past the Danish contracts stated that the contractor had to expressly request such security, but it has been made automatic in the newest versions of the standard contracts.[375] The possibility to request a guarantee only exist against private employers, public law employers being presumed to always being solvent enough to fulfil their payment obligations.[376]

10.241 Since tender documents are drafted by employers, they very often strike out the standard provision concerning the guarantee to be provided to the contractor and this is generally accepted by bidders, which means that having a guarantee provided by the employer is largely a theoretical possibility without much practical significance.[377]

10.242 If the employer provides the contractor with a security under the Danish standard contracts, this must take place within eight days from contract execution. The amount of this bond corresponds to the average payment for a three-month period calculated by dividing the contract sum evenly by the number of months stipulated in the contract for the performance of the works, though a minimum of 10% of the contract sum must be covered.[378] The contractor may request an increase of the bond in case the contract is modified to include extra works but only if the remuneration for all unpaid extra works exceeds the average payment of the contract sum for half a month; conversely, the employer may demand that the performance bond be reduced if the bond exceeds the unpaid part of the contract sum and the extra works.[379] The procedure to be followed by the contractor to claim payment under the guarantee is identical to when payment is claimed under the contractor's guarantee: The contractor presents a written and substantiated claim to both the employer and the guarantor, and the latter must pay within ten workdays of receipt of the notification unless the employer requests an expert determination on the question of

373 See AB 04 Chapter 6, §21.

374 The expert determination is provided by §67 of AB 18 and is described in more detail below under the section "Dispute Resolution".

375 AB 18 §10, s. 1.

376 AB 18 §10, s. 1 and Hørlyck, op. cit., p. 117.

377 Hørlyck, op. cit. p. 117.

378 AB 18 §10, s. 3.

379 AB 18 §10, s. 3.

whether the contractor' call on the guarantee is justified.[380] The performance bond ceases when the contractor has submitted the final account and has no unsatisfied claims.[381]

10.243 The system established in the Norwegian standard contracts is very similar to that in the Danish standard contracts. The security for the contractor is 10% during the construction period, and 3% after take-over with a duration of three years. In EPC contracts the rate for the employer's guarantee is 17.5% and in contracts where the contractor has not taken on engineering works, the rate is 15%.

10.244 The Norwegian statutes on consumer construction contracts also contain rules on security of a mandatory nature. Unless the scope of work is small, the contractor must provide security in form of a bank guarantee. During the construction period, the security must amount to 10% of the contract sum, and after take-over the security must amount to 5% and be valid for five years.[382] There are no mandatory rules on security by the employer, but it may be set as a condition in individual contracts.

Claims

10.245 As opposed to common law inspired standard construction contracts, the Nordic standards, with the exception of Norwegian standard contracts, do not contain general sections concerning the formal requirements and procedures applying when a party has a claim against the other. Such requirements and procedures are thus described in the sections concerning each particular type of claim (additional payment, extension of time, etc.). Such claim clauses are often quite simple in that they only state that a party which considers himself entitled to an extension of time or an additional payment must inform the other party thereof in writing without undue delay, and in some cases an indication of the consequence of non-compliance with such notice requirements.[383]

10.246 This absence of systematized claim procedures is mainly due to the fact that the institution of the engineer, and especially his function to agree or determine claims presented by the parties, are unknown to the Nordic countries. Parties present their claims to one another, and in case of disagreement, they have no other choice than commencing dispute resolution proceedings.

10.247 However, Norwegian contracts contain a systematic and coordinated claim procedure which is closer to FIDIC than other Scandinavian contracts. Schematically, a contractor which considers himself entitled to an extension of time or an additional remuneration must first present a neutral claim[384] only mentioning the subject-matter of the claim, and only as a second step a particularized claim containing a detailed explanation

380 AB 18 §10, s. 5.

381 AB 18 §10, s. 4.

382 See the Norwegian act on consumer construction contracts of 13 June 1997 no. 43 Section 12.

383 See, for instance, the Swedish AB 04, Chapter 2, §7 and 8 on the contractor's duty to request the employer's opinion as to whether the circumstances invoked by the contractor justify the application of the provisions concerning variation and the contractor's loss of right to additional payment in case of non-compliance with such requirement.

384 Hagstrøm and Bruserud, op. cit., p. 265 and NS 8405 Art. 24.4 (extension of time) and 25.3 (additional compensation).

of the claim and the grounds thereof,[385] which corresponds to the obligation to present claim particulars under FIDIC contracts.

Time-Bar Provisions

10.248 The issue of time-bar provisions illustrates the huge differences in construction contracts' practice and culture between the Nordic countries. In fact, if all Nordic standard contracts contain requirements for notices to be given in writing within a certain deadline in some situations, for instance, when the employer orders a variation or the contractor claims an extension of time. The way such requirements are interpreted and enforced varies, however, from one country to another.

10.249 In Denmark, it is a well-known fact that even though some clauses are formulated in the standard contract as time-bar provisions, they are not enforced as such; scholarly literature refers to the Danish practice related to formal requirements as "pronounced pragmatism".[386] The report drafted by the committee in charge of the revision of the Danish standard contracts in 1992, to which reference is often made in matters involving the interpretation of these contracts, also mentions that the requirement that the employer's requests for variations be made in writing should only be given evidential value.[387] Case law follows this line in a large majority of cases, regardless of whether formal requirements are contained in a standard contract or whether parties have drafted bespoke provisions with the intention of giving them preclusive effect.[388] The report accompanying the newest editions of the Danish standard contracts states that the contracts' drafting committee considered whether the absence of compliance with formal notice requirements should in the future result in the loss of rights by the defaulting party, but answered the question in the negative, stressing that the consequences of such lack of compliance should be assessed on a case by case basis and based on a global evaluation of the relevant circumstances.[389] It is thus to be expected that the pragmatic stance observed in practice until now will continue prevailing.

10.250 Norwegian standard contracts have evolved to become quite the opposite. Notice requirements were in older times considered an expression of the parties' mutual duty of loyalty, and their violation was merely sanctioned by damages, but since the 1990s, and more particularly since the latest version of the standard contracts, a complete change of system occurred, leading to notice requirement provisions included in the contracts and generally enforced as condition precedent.[390] An example of this is the provision concerning the contractor's obligation to warn the employer that he considers an employer's

385 Hagstrøm and Bruserud, op. cit., p. 265 and NS 8405 Art. 24.6 (extension of time) and 25.4 (additional compensation).

386 Ole Hansen, *Formkrav og frister i entreprisekontrakter – en analyse af præklusion som retligt redskab til styring af ændringer i byggeaftaler* i Ole Hansen (red.) *Ændringsregler i længerevarende kontrakter*, Copenhagen, 2014, p. 56–8.

387 *Betænkning nr. 1246 afgivet af Udvalget vedrørende revision af almindelige betingelser for arbejder og leverancer*, p. 60.

388 Hansen, op. cit., p. 56–7.

389 Report, p. 18–19.

390 Hagstrøm and Bruserud, op. cit., pp. 267–9.

instruction as a variation order, which states that if the contractor does not comply with its requirement, he loses the right to claim the said order is a variation order.[391]

10.251 The Swedish system can be placed somewhere between these two extremes. The provision concerning the contractor's duty to inform the employer that he considers an instruction as a variation or that he believes that data provided by the employer is inaccurate and that extra works are needed as a consequence, states that variation works carried out without an order or an approval from the employer do not entitle the contractor to additional economic compensation, unless such consequence would be unreasonable. Scholarly work states that there is uncertainty as to the severity with which non-compliance with such requirements should be sanctioned.[392]

Dispute Resolution – Adjudication and Arbitration

10.252 As far as dispute resolution in construction matters is concerned, there are again both significant differences and similarities between Nordic countries. All of them feature various dispute resolution mechanisms that can be classified into four categories. In the first category, one can find systems aiming at obtaining an expert opinion on factual matters, in particular the issue of whether works are affected with defects – such systems are not properly speaking ADR, but rather means of proof, but they can contribute in solving the parties' dispute by bringing clarity about their respective legal position. Second, systems aiming at assisting the parties in finding a consensual solution to their dispute, such as different forms of mediation, exist. The dispute resolution "ladder" introduced in the latest version of the Danish standard contracts, which prohibits the initiation of any kind of dispute resolution method before mandatory negotiation attempts have been conducted between the parties,[393] also belongs to this category. Third, ADR aiming at an actual decision, (temporarily) binding or not, by a neutral third party after an expedited procedure, similar to adjudication processes known in common law countries, can be found. Finally, all Nordic standards propose traditional dispute resolution models aiming at final and enforceable decisions, such as court proceedings and arbitration.

10.253 Both Denmark and Sweden practice *inspections and survey by experts*, which are defined in the contracts as means of dispute resolution but are in fact means of evidence; they are different in their functioning. In Denmark, the inspection and survey by an expert, renamed "expert appraisal" in the latest versions of the standard contracts[394] implies an inspection of the works by an expert and the drafting of a report containing the expert's conclusions based on questions drafted by the parties. This institution, which is mostly used to assess the existence of defects, can be used either as a stand-alone procedure, allowing the parties to evaluate their legal position(s);secure a piece of evidence, or serve as a means of evidence within the framework of arbitral proceedings.[395]

10.254 In Sweden an institution called "over-inspection" is used. It is a process in which one expert or a panel of experts are appointed to scrutinize and render a second opinion

391 NS 8405 Art. 23.2, s. 1.

392 See Hansen, op. cit., p. 63.

393 See, for instance, AB 18 §64, discussed in more details below.

394 AB 18 §66. §45.

395 Sylvie Cavaleri, *International Construction Disputes in Denmark*, [2016] ICLR 39 at 42–3.

on an inspection report produced by a neutral third party appointed by the employer or the parties in common within the context of one of the inspection models provided for in the standard contract; for instance, the final inspection.[396] The only possible objective of such over-inspection is to determine whether the works are affected with defects.[397]

10.255 Second, all Scandinavian countries offer the possibility of *mediating* construction disputes. There again, the modalities of using this type of ADR differs from one country to another. In Denmark, the Arbitration Board for Building and Engineering, a special institution administrating construction disputes in this country, offers two different forms of mediation; that is, mediation on the one hand and conciliation (*mægling*) on the other. A mediator only facilitates settlement discussions between the parties (facilitative model), whereas a conciliator actively advises the parties and can upon request provide a settlement proposal (evaluative model).[398] Since these ADR as well as two others[399] were until the latest version of the standard contracts not mentioned in the latter, but only in the institution's catalogue, parties have insufficient knowledge of their existence, which may explain why they are used quite rarely, nonetheless mediation seems to be on the rise. The newest edition of the Danish standard contracts contain express provisions on mediation.[400] Several of these rules or their exact meaning and consequences, appear controversial,[401] such as the right of an arbitral tribunal seized of a dispute to refer the dispute to mediation without the parties' consent, or the obligation of parties to participate in the mediation and the corresponding prohibition to initiate or continue arbitration until the mediation process is completed, and it remains to be seen how these provisions will be applied. The same can be said of the new provision imposing a dispute resolution ladder, according to which a party willing to initiate dispute resolution proceedings must request negotiation as a first step between the parties' project managers,[402] and as a second step between the parties' management representatives,[403] and can only start proper dispute resolution proceedings after such negotiations are completed. In fact, the standard contracts do not mention the consequence of a complete passivity or non-cooperative attitude from the defendant's side, and it is, therefore, to be feared that these mandatory negotiation steps be used by bad faith defendants to stall proceedings.

10.256 Mediation is not mentioned in standard construction contracts in Sweden either, but its possibility exists under the name of "special mediation" in the Swedish Administration of Justice Act.[404] Finally, the Norwegian turnkey contract provides for

396 As provided for in AB 04 Chapter 7, §2.

397 Deli, op. cit., p. 196.

398 See the definition of these two ADR on the Arbitration Board's website: http://voldgift.dk/maegling-og-mediation/?lang=en.

399 These were the anticipatory dispute resolution (*foregreben tvistløsning*), renamed as informal evaluation (*uformel bedømmelse*) in October 2015, where an expert gives an oral non-binding opinion as to how a dispute should be solved and the expedited arbitration (*forenklet voldgift*): Cavaleri in ICLR, op. cit., p. 43.

400 See, for instance, AB 18 §65.

401 Sylvie Cécile Cavaleri, *Parterne ved bedst – nogle kommentarer om tvistløstningsbestemmelserne i udkastet til AB 18*, in Torsten Iversen (ed.), *Udkast til AB 18 og ABR 18 af 2. februar 2018*, Tidsskrift for Bolig- og Byggeret, special issue, April 2018, p. 412–13.

402 AB 18 §64, s. 1. After handover has taken place, this step is unapplicable, though, and parties must revert directly to negotiations between management representatives pursuant to the second section of this provision.

403 AB 18 §64, s. 2.

404 Deli, op. cit., p. 196.

the possibility of *project-integrated mediation*, according to which a panel of experts is nominated as soon as possible after the conclusion of the contract to assists the parties in finding amicable solutions to disputes as they arise during the course of the project.[405] Probably because of the significant costs linked to this model, project-integrated mediation is not provided for in the Norwegian build-only model, which provides for amicable settlement, stating that until a dispute is referred to either court proceedings or arbitration, a party may request the holding of a dispute settlement meeting between representatives of the management of both the employer and the contractor.[406]

10.257 Parties to Scandinavian construction disputes may, also, request an actual expert decision/determination or at least opinion on their disagreements. All Nordic countries accommodate this need but in different ways. In Denmark, several possibilities exist, one of them introduced in 2018 by the newest version of the standard construction contracts. First, parties can ask for a decision on a security provided,[407] where an expert is at the request of either party appointed by the Danish Building and Construction Arbitration Board and renders a decision on the payment under, reduction or cessation of a security provided after a (in principle at least) brief and mainly written procedure (the expert may carry out on-site inspections but no expert appraisal as described above may take place). The decision of the expert is binding on the parties "in the same way as an arbitral award[408]" according to the newest version of the Danish standard contractsunless one of the parties brings the decision before an arbitral tribunal no later than eight weeks before it was made. However, the actual enforceability of the decision is dubious; in fact and according to the relevant provision of the Danish Administration of Justice Act, Danish courts can enforce decisions rendered by courts or authorities which decisions can be enforced according to the legislation;[409] since the standard construction contracts are not legislation, the enforceability of the decision on security will depend on it being qualified as an arbitral award under the Danish Arbitration Act, which is not necessarily a given. In comparison, decisions taken after similarly short and summary proceedings in construction disputes, such as statutory adjudication decisions in the UK[410] or dispute board decisions in FIDIC,[411] are neither considered arbitral awards nor judgments and, as far as FIDIC dispute board decisions are concerned, must be validated in an arbitral award prior to being enforceable in court. It will, therefore, be interesting to see whether Danish

405 NS 8407 Art. 50.2.

406 NS 8405 Art. 43.1.

407 AB 18 §67.

408 AB 18 §10 and Report, p. 193, which states that the decision on security provided is a binding decision on a dispute between the parties and must, therefore, be considered as an arbitral award under the Danish Arbitration Act.

409 See Art. 478, s. 1 of the Danish Administration of Justice Act.

410 VHE Construction plc v RBSTB Trust Co. Ltd. [2000] EWHC Technology 181 at §54: "Enforcement proceedings are proceedings to enforce a contractual obligation, namely the obligation to comply with the adjudicator's decision. The adjudicator's decision does not have the status of a judgment and there was no provision in the 1996 Act to correspond to Section 66 of the Arbitration Act 1996, under which, by leave of the court, judgment may be entered in terms in terms of an arbitral award or the award may be enforced in the same manner as a judgment".

411 See FIDIC Red Book, 2nd ed. 2017, Sub-Cl. 21.4.3: "The DAAB proceedings shall not be deemed to be an arbitration and the DAAB shall not act as arbitrators".

courts accept to enforce decisions on securities as described, or whether they will demand that they be first validated in a judgment or an arbitral award.[412]

10.258 Second, Danish parties may also request a speedy resolution of their dispute.[413] The speedy resolution is a newly introduced ADR method strongly inspired from common law adjudication; that is, a quick and relatively cheap method of dispute resolution leading to a decision which is binding unless and until reversed by a subsequent judgment or arbitral award. However, the Danish speedy resolution differs from adjudication in several ways. First, and unless both parties agree to adjudication or the amount in dispute is low, it is only possible if the subject matter of the dispute is one of those enumerated in the relevant provision of the standard contract.[414] Second, the procedure is as a principle only written; site inspections are allowed but not expert appraisals.[415] Third, the Danish standard contract allows one of the main parties to bring other parties into the proceedings through third party notices; this seems to be in contradiction with the prohibition placed on the respondent to bring any other dispute in the proceedings.[416] Last and most importantly, the decision on a speedy resolution case is deemed to be binding on the parties in the same way as an arbitral award;[417] the comments made above about the decision on security provided are also applicable here.

10.259 Norway knows a similar institution of the "*oppmann*" (umpire), which is also a neutral third party rendering a rapid decision on any dispute which the parties may submit before him. In the build-only model, the decisions of the umpire are not binding upon the parties unless, in distinct situations,[418] the decision(s) are temporarily binding and are to become finally binding if they are not contested in court proceedings or arbitration within six months. In the same manner, Sweden knows the institution of *simplified dispute resolution*, which also provides for the issuance of a decision by a neutral third party after short summary proceedings, yet with the significant difference that the decision of the umpire is binding unless contested in court or arbitration proceedings within one month from the communication of the decision to the parties.[419]

10.260 As for final means of dispute resolution, both the Swedish and the Norwegian standard contracts provide that unless agreed otherwise, the amount in dispute determines whether the dispute shall be settled by ordinary court proceedings or arbitration.[420] Both sets of standards provide for a specific amount, specified in national legislation and is annualy updated. The Danish system is different and quite peculiar; unless otherwise agreed between the parties or unless one of the ADR methods mentioned below finally settle the dispute, construction disputes must be finally settled under the auspices of an institution named the Arbitration Board for Building and Construction through an ADR

412 AB 92 §46. Cavaleri in ICLR, op. cit., p. 43.

413 AB 18 §68.

414 AB 18 §68, s. 1.

415 AB 18 §68, s.6.

416 AB 18 §68, s. 4

417 AB 18 §68, s. 9.

418 When the parties are in disagreement as to whether an order constitutes a variation or whether the employer is guilty of delay or default in the performance of its obligations under the contract and, if both parties agreed to it, the pecuniary consequences of a decision on these subjects: NS 8405 §26.2. Same grounds in the turnkey model 8407 Art. 50.3.2 with an addition, a decision as to which part must cover the oppmann's fees.

419 AB 04 Chapter 10, §1.

420 Norway: NS 8405 Art. 43.3 and 43.4. Sweden: AB 04 Chapter 9, §1.

mechanism named "arbitration" but is actually a hybrid between arbitration and court proceedings.[421] In this setup, the parties do not choose their arbitrators which are civil judges and technical experts appointed by the institution and the parties have limited possibilities to choose their own expert witnesses, the standard solution in relation to expert evidence being an expert appraisal by a single joint expert appointed by the institution.[422]

Construction Law Issues Specific to Nordic Law

10.261 Issues encountered in Nordic construction law are generally the same as in other parts of the world. However, two points must be emphasized in order to promote a correct understanding of Nordic law in general and Nordic construction law in particular.

10.262 First, it is commonly accepted by jurists from outside of the Nordic countries that Nordic law belongs to the civil law family. Some solid arguments support this opinion. Among other the facts; that Nordic law does not apply the *judicial precedents* rule and does not function with a pre-determined hierarchy of the sources of law known in common law countries. Furthermore, Nordic law uses legal concepts which are greatly inspired by continental Europe, in particular the German BGB. However, it is important to point out that large parts of Nordic law, and in particular the law of obligations, the general law applying to construction contracts, are not systematically codified like it generally is in civil law countries. When looking for the answer to a legal question, Nordic jurists often employ analogies and case law or literature-based rules and reasoning; an approach very similar to common law methodology. The Nordic law family is, therefore, very often understood as forming a category of its own at the crossroads between civil and common law.

10.263 Second, and as far as construction law is concerned, it is a misconception to consider Nordic law as a homogenous entity. In fact, the discussion of selected subjects conducted above showed significant disparities between the standard contracts of the different Nordic countries. For instance, Norwegian law appears to have/share, to a certain extent, similarities with international contracts such as FIDIC, with clear and detailed procedures aimed at handling the parties' respective claims due to changing circumstances occurring during the course of a project. On the contrary, Danish construction law presents in a significant number of issues, (for instance, the guarantee related to materials as well as dispute resolution) some purely national solutions which do not have an equivalent in other Nordic countries. Added to the fact that the Danish standards are not comprehensive as such, with a significant number of rules established by case law and related literature, coupled with a very pragmatic application of the law by Danish construction arbitrators, it can be quite difficult for parties to Danish construction disputes to predict the outcome of their cases. Parties intending to contract for Nordic construction works should, thus, adjust their expectations and gain understanding of the conditions of the exact country in which their project is to be carried out.

421 AB 18 §69.

422 A more detailed description of the system under the former set of standard contracts can be found in Cavaleri in ICLR, op. cit., p. 39–66.

National vs. International Construction Law in Scandinavia

10.264 Although this is difficult to establish with certainty due to the confidentiality generally surrounding international construction projects and the related dispute resolution, it is the general view among construction scholars and practitioners that Nordic practice revolves around the national forms of contract and that international forms such as FIDIC are very rarely used, if at all.

10.265 The explanation for this situation is that FIDIC is considered foreign to Nordic contract culture for a number of reasons. First, FIDIC standards forms aim at regulating the whole contractual relationship between employer and contractor and to detach it from the background law to the largest extent possible. On the contrary, Nordic standards contracts rely, often quite heavily, on the national law under which they were created to operate.

10.266 Second, the FIDIC institution of the Engineer, which carries the double function of being on one hand the employer's representative and on the other hand a (in theory at least) independent and impartial primary adjudicator when making determinations on the parties' claim, is unknown to Nordic construction law. All Nordic standard contracts operate with parties' representatives, but none of them is granted the competence to make first instance decisions on disagreements; if a dispute arises, it has to be settled or mediated by a neutral third party.

10.267 Third, the drafting language of FIDIC forms is technical and complex, with long and detailed provisions and many definitions and cross-references; this is in stark contrast with Nordic forms the language of which is generally more plain and simple, save for the exception of Norwegian standard contracts which have evolved to become closer to Anglo-American standards in general.

10.268 Finally, and though this argument is mostly applicable to Danish law and much less to Norwegian law, FIDIC forms show a high level of formalism and presupposes heavy contract administration which is contrary to the Scandinavian legal pragmatism, where judges and arbitrators are focused on *practical reasonableness* rather than formal requirements and consequently refuse to enforce the latter as condition precedent. It has been repeatedly pointed out in scholarly works that the Danish reluctance towards employing formal requirement(s) is an example of the underdevelopment of Danish construction law[423] and that the pragmatic application of the law operated by Danish construction arbitrators is an obstacle to the internationalization of the Danish construction industry.[424]

423 Hansen, op. cit., p. 70.
424 Cavaleri in ICLR, op. cit., p. 55.

CHAPTER 11

Russian (and Central Asian) Law

Nikolay Scherbakov

Contents

 DOI: 10.4324/9781315671376-11

History of Russian (and Central Asia) Law

Sources of Law

11.1 The formation of Russian civil law in modern history can be divided into several stages.

11.2 Stage 1. First half of the 19th century. The beginning of the establishment of modern Russian civil law is credited to the Russian Emperor Alexander I and a member of the Russian Academy of Sciences M.M. Speranskiy, whom Alexander I, in 1804, charged with the creation of the Legal Code of the Russian Empire. This was actually little more than the systematization of the existing statutes on civil law. In this work M.I. Speranskiy actively used the European, and in particular French, experience for obvious reasons. Here is what leading commentator of modern Russian civil law, A.L. Makovskiy, writes in this respect:

11.3

> Up until his death M.M. Speranskiy occupied high public office and supervised the work on systematization of the Russian legislation. The result was Complete Collection of Laws in 45 volumes (1830) and then Code of Laws of the Russian Empire in 15 volumes (1832–1839). In Part I of Volume X of the Code of Laws various Russian civil statutes, published at different times and for lots of different reasons (specific, as a rule), were systematized. As such, obvious gaps were filled in by new rules of law, and for some rules of law which were too narrow in content, M.M. Speranskiy tried to assign more general tenor. In either event the French Civil Code was widely used, as well as French literature in civil law. [1]

11.4 Stage 2. Second half of the 19th century – 1917. During this period, Russian civil law started to be greatly affected by Roman law, and later also by the German Civil Code. Russia was actively preparing its own Civil Code, which was successfully completed, but was not adopted as a result of the revolution of 1917. Here is how A.L. Makovskiy characterizes this stage:

11.5

> Every Article in the draft Civil Code is supplied with the most detailed commentaries and the table of those articles from 10–12 foreign Codes, Civil or Trade, which resolved the similar issues. Quite often the drafted rule of law if it was not taken from the Russian legislation, represented an indivisible "marriage" of provisions taken from codes of different countries. Of course, the newest for that time Western European Codes – BGB and *Code Civil* of Switzerland were used the most. What contributed to the high quality of the project was the fact that all the time it was the focus of attention of the Russian civil law and was subject of earnest discussions. [2]

11.6 Stage 3. Soviet time – 1917–1991. During the time of the Soviet Union, several significant revisions of the civil law took place. These were Civil Codes (CC) of 1922 and

---

1 A.L. Makovskiy. On Civil Law Codification. Moscow. Statute, 2010. It is necessary to note that in such context Russian civil law in the process of its formation was historically greatly affected by FCC. Suffice it to say that even now in Russia there functions an alternative system of demesne as of fee: *Tradicio* as a general rule and consensus as contractual exception (Art. 223 of the RCC).

2 Ibid.

1964. If it cannot be said that, at this time, the connection between Russian civil legislation and the European tradition did not end, it certainly grew weaker due to the ideological differences of the time. On the one hand, it resulted in the development of Russia's civil laws lagging behind its European counterparts. On the other hand, Soviet civil lawyers did not seek to turn their backs on their European experience – a number of authors applied comparative law research methods (beginning with M.M. Agarkov, V.A. Oygenzikht, and some others). At the same time a number of valuable and original papers on civil law were written (these are papers by S.N. Bratus on responsibility, V.P. Gribanov on the limits of civil rights' performance). But in general, one must acknowledge the fact that private law was affected considerably by the ideology and principles of public law.

11.7 Stage 4. Modern era. 1991–today. During this period the existing CC was created (comprising four parts (1994–2006)). This represented the rebirth of civil law in Russia; during the preparation of the Code, the Russian experience, both pre-revolutionary and the Soviet one was influential, as well as foreign systems of justice, particularly those of Germany and the Netherlands. Since 2013 a trend has evolved during a process of further development of the Russian Civil Code (RCC) – the implementation of Anglo-Saxon law. Therefore, modern Russian law tries to accommodate classical construction of the German and French law with peculiarities of the Soviet era law and the common law. The merit of the RCC is its continuity, and its ability to embrace the spectrum of ideological and legal development throughout its history, as well as incorporating a foreign influence.

11.8 Among the sources of civil law (including construction law), the statute comes first. At the same time, according to the RCC[3] civil legislation and regulations contained in other statutes or presidential decrees, beside the Civil Code, must comply with it. Consequently, in Russia there is an established priority of the RCC regulations, which permits setting forth a clearly defined system of legislation. The RCC contains the majority of regulations, relating to construction law, both in the Property Law and Law of Obligations Sections. Additionally, other statutes, relating both to private and public law contain legal rules, regulating construction law (for example, the Law "On Investment Activity in the Russian Federation", the Urban Development Code of the Russian Federation). Here, the Soviet tradition of state influence (for example, the Urban Development Code) over private legal relationships is the issue. In particular, Art. 1 of the Urban Development Code requires the customer to exercise professional supervision over the construction. In practice, this obligation deforms the structure of contractual links under construction contract. At the same time literature and judicial practice actively discuss wisdom of public laws' interference with private affairs in certain cases.

11.9 Judicial practice is the second of importance source of civil and construction law. Since Soviet times explanatory statements (*razyasneniya*) of the supreme judicial authority (currently the RF Supreme Court)[4] regarding issues of judicial practice (resolutions

3 Art. 3, cl.3, RCC.

4 Before 2014 there existed two supreme judicial authorities – Supreme Arbitration Court of the Russian Federation (RF SAC) and RF Supreme Court (RF SC). By extension, the first was the supreme authority for disputes between entrepreneurs, the second one – between citizens. In 2014 RF SAC was abolished, its powers were delegated to RF SC. At the same time RF SAC explanatory statements (*razyasneniya*) have remained valid.

of the Plenum of the RF SC and RF SAC,[5] information letters[6] and digests of case law of Presidiums of the RF SC and RF SAC[7] are among such explanatory statements) have been most influential. As a rule, these explanatory statements are judicial opinions relating to the interpretation of the rules of law and are binding on lower courts. These judicial opinions are general in nature and are not drafted with regard to the facts of a particular case.

11.10 Over the last 5–7 years, judicial opinions, set forth by courts during particular case handlings have been of growing in importance. The significance of such judicial opinions depends on the authority that handled the particular dispute. In this respect decisions of the RF Supreme Court, which also form the uniform application of statutes, enjoy the greatest prestige and are the most influential. Such influence of the court decisions has evolved in practice; legislation does not establish the indicated significance of court decisions. Aside from historical reasons, the important role of judicial practice is related to the necessity of providing uniformity in the application of the law. In country as vast as Russia, with its various, and sometimes remote regions, uniformity is of paramount importance. Such uniformity ensures the economic unity. Additionally, judicial interpretation permits the development of law and overcoming possible shortcomings of abstract or ambiguous provisions of the law.

11.11 After the downfall of the Soviet Union, the old Soviet civil law faced the necessity of considerable modernization, which was carried out partly through the creation of the RCC and its subsequent revisions. Through the implementation of the judges' experience and the efforts of the academic community, it was possible to employ both Russian and foreign legal doctrines in the creation of modern civil law in Russia. This was the reason of the doctrine's great significance in consideration of civil law disputes. The doctrine helps parties in court trial, and the court – in statute interpretation.

11.12 There is no construction law as such in the Russian Federation. In recent years, there has been a movement to establish a body of construction law in Russia that includes not only contractual law issues (for example, the construction contract), but also property (for example, construction object status, its connection to the land plot etc.) and other areas of law.

Impact Of Russian Law on Other Countries/Jurisdictions

11.13 After the demise of the USSR, the Russian Federation, along with 14 other independent states, were formed, each of which had been former Soviet republics. Each of those republics has adopted the civil code. For a number of historical reasons the Russian Federation has preserved its influence over the formation of civil legislation only approximately half of the new states.[8] This influence is primarily based in the political relationships between the RF and the various states at the time they created new civil codes. Additionally, there remained close contacts in academic circles.

11.14 The model code of the CIS countries, drafted mainly by Russian specialists on the basis of the current RCC, formed the basis for the civil codes of those

5 Hereinafter PPl. RF SC, PPl.

6 Hereinafter IL. RF SC, IL. RF SAC.

7 Hereinafter D. RF SC, D. RF SAC.

8 Such influence has been preserved over civil legislation of the following states: Belarus, Ukraine, Armenia, Uzbekistan, Kazakhstan, Kyrgyzstan, Tadzhikistan, Turkmenistan.

states. The Model Civil Code of the CIS countries is composed of seven parts. It was drafted by the Scientific Advisory Council of the CIS countries and adopted by the CIS Interparliamentary Assembly piece by piece over a 12-year period, between October 1994 and December 2006.[9]

Contract Law

The Formation of a Contract

Significant Conditions of Contract

11.15 General provisions of the RCC on contain provisions for concluding contracts. First of all, the Statute establishes the essential elements; that is, conditions, of a contract. Among these essential elements of any contract are the subject matter, any conditions the law deems essential for such a contract, and the terms by which a party or the parties set forth for the conclusion of the contract.[10] Should a contract be found not to have been concluded then it follows that no contractual relationship exists between the parties. Furthermore, if either party performs, under the general rule rules of law on unjust enrichment shall be applied, as it is considered that performance was provided without legal foundation.

11.16 The procedure of conclusion a contract is traditional and consists of the following stages: 1) Precontractual contacts of the parties (negotiations); 2) offer; 3) consideration of the offer; and 4) acceptance of the offer.

11.17 By an offer[11] a proposal to conclude a contract is meant; the proposal should also meet the following mandatory criteria: Firstly, it should be addressed to a specific person (persons); secondly, it should be sufficiently comprehensive; thirdly, it should express intention of the person who made it to conclude a contract with the addressee, who will accept the proposal; fourthly, contains indication on essential conditions on which it is offered to conclude a contract. Acceptance; that is, response of the person to whom the offer is sent, of its terms and conditions should be full and unconditional, under the general rule, acceptance in the form of silence is prohibited.[12] Contract may be concluded both as a single document and through the exchange of documents via different modes of communication.

11.18 One of the main innovations contained in the RCC is the introduction of general rules of law on precontractual responsibility, something which had never been done before in Russia. For example, in accordance with Article 431.1. of the RCC:

11.19

> When entering into negotiations on conclusion of a contract, during conducting and upon completion of negotiations the parties shall act in good faith, in particular, avoid entering negotiations on conclusion of a contract or their prolongation if there is known absence of the intention

9 Legal Code (LC). 1994. No. 32. Art. 3301, 3302: LC. 1996. No. 5. Art. 410, 411; LC. 2001. No. 49. Art. 4552, 4553; LC. 2006 No. 52 (Part I). Art. 5496.

10 Art. 432, RCC.

11 Art. 435, RCC.

12 Art. 438, RCC.

to reach agreement with the other party. The following actions can be considered to be unfair ones during negotiations:

- Providing a party with incomplete or incorrect information, including non-disclosure of circumstances, which due to the contract nature must be brought to the notice of the other party;
- Sudden and unjustified termination of negotiations on conclusion of a contract under such circumstances, under which the other party could not reasonably expect it.
- The party conducting or terminating negotiations on conclusion of a contract in bad faith shall be obliged to reimburse the incurred losses to the other party.

Expenses incurred by the other party during conducting negotiations on conclusion of a contract as well as due to the loss of the possibility to conclude a contract with a third party shall be recognized losses to be reimbursed by the unfair party.

11.20 It is noteworthy that the nature of precontractual liability, in particular its delict nature is determined at the level of judicial practice:

11.21 "Rules of law indicated in Chapter 59 of the RCC with the exceptions established by Article 431.1. of the RCC shall be applied to the relations associated with the harm-doing by behavior in bad faith during negotiations".[13]

11.22 In accordance with the RCC,[14] the subject matter and dates of the performance of the works form the essential conditions of a construction contract. The subject matter of a construction contract includes of the available technical documentation approved by the parties. Among the essential conditions one can require of both commencement and completion dates be mutually approved by the parties. In accordance with Cl. 1, Art. 743, the contractor undertakes to carry out the works in accordance with the detailed price (*smeta*), determining the cost of the works. In the context of general rules concerning essential conditions,[15] these conditions should also be considered as essential, as they are necessary for such type of contracts. At the same time, judicial practice does not accept price as an essential condition of a contract.[16]

11.23 There is no statutory requirement for the form of construction contracts. Therefore, the general rule applied to construction contracts is that the contract shall be concluded in a simple written form.[17]

WORKS (TECHNICAL DOCUMENTATION)

11.24 In accordance with Art. 743 of the RCC, the parties themselves must determine the composition of all technical documentation and the time limits for its approval. This

---

13 Clause 19, Resolution of Plenum of the RF Supreme Court dated 2416 No. 7 (Chapter 59 of the RCC is dedicated to delict obligations).

14 Art. 702, 708, 743, RCC.

15 Art. 432, RCC.

16 Clause 11 of Information Letter of the RF SAC Presidium dated 20 January 2000 No. 51. Here the RF SAC Presidium agreed with the court stand that qualified the contract where the customer was obliged not to pay for the works completed by the contractor but to transfer certain things, as a construction contract, not as a mixed contract. This stand evoked the approach in accordance with which the subject matter of the customer's obligation had no legal bearing for qualifying the contract as a construction contract. In our opinion, such approach is highly questionable and does not conform to the statute (Art. 743, RCC).

17 Art. 160, 161, RCC.

means that during negotiation of the contract the parties are not bound by any statutory requirements imposed on technical documentation through urban development legislation. In practice, this regularly results there being two sets of technical documentation. The first set is the, so called, operational documentation, approved by the parties. The actual construction is carried out in accordance therewith. The second set of documentation is the proper technical documentation, which undergoes relevant expert review (often on a stage-by-stage basis) for the purpose of obtaining a building permit. The problem of unauthorized construction is one common result of such lack of coordination. The second part of the regulation formalizes the established practice, whereby the parties to the contract establish a deadline for the submission of the technical documentation. This means that until the expiry of the approved period the contract is deemed concluded, which permits the contractor to engage in pre-construction activities.

11.25 The statute specifies the instances when technical documentation may be altered during contract performance. The first instance is a change in technical documentation initiated by the contractor.[18] While performing the contract, the contractor may identify the need to perform off-design works (if they are not performed, the result will not be achieved). Under the said Article, the additional works shall only be paid for if they are performed with the customer's consent. In practice, this means that the contractor, who identified the need for additional works, must immediately suspend the work and inform the customer about such need. In such case, the customer may either agree with the contractor, or repudiate the contract.[19] The exception is accident prevention works, the urgency of which makes their performance necessary even without the customer's consent. The second instance is a change in technical documentation initiated by the customer.[20] As the commercial beneficiary of the construction, the customer is granted the right to change, and particularly increase, the scope of works, and, therefore – to change technical documentation. If such change does not exceed 10% of the overall construction cost, the contractor shall not be entitled to reject the unilateral change in the subject matter. If the 10% threshold for the relevant works is exceeded, the contractor's consent is required. This regulation is aimed at balancing the customer's and the contractor's interests.

Time Limits

11.26 The initial, final and interim time limits are calculated in accordance with general rules for setting time limits. They are stated in minutes, hours, months, years, etc. The parties mostly have no problems in agreeing upon the time limits. However, setting a time limit with a reference to a certain event, the occurrence of which is uncertain, constituted a significant problem. For example, the parties agree that the initial time limit for the performance of works shall be 10 days after the customer has effected the advance payment, or has made the site available to the contractor. This rule does not comply with the rules for setting time limits, under which the parties may only agree upon the time limit provisions by referring to an event, which will inevitably occur[21]. It was a common reason for the court to declare the contract not concluded. Therefore, as part of the current reform,

18 Art. 743, RCC.
19 Art. 716, RCC.
20 Art. 744, RCC.
21 Art. 190, RCC.

the RCC was amended to include a regulation, under which the time limit for the obligation may be calculated from the time when the other party has fulfilled its obligation, or any other circumstances provided by the statute or the agreement have occurred[22]. On the one hand, the amendments contributed to stabilization of the contract; however, they simultaneously added uncertainty in terms of the interrelation between the condition and the time limit, which use different civil law regimes. In view of the foregoing, the parties often lay down the time limit provisions using the structure of cross-obligations arising out of the contract they entered into.[23]

Price

11.27 The construction contract price determines the cross-performance by the customer and constitutes a part of the synallagma while performing a function similar to the "consideration" concept in common law. The construction contract price includes the compensation for expenses of and remuneration payable to the contractor. The parties generally agree upon the price by drawing up a *smeta*. The price (estimate) may be approximate or fixed if a fixed price is presumed. The main difference is that the contractor is not entitled to demand any increase in the fixed price, and the customer may not demand its reduction, even if providing for the complete scope of works to be performed or expenses required for that at the time of concluding the contract was impossible. The only opportunity to increase the price in such case is to refer to material changes in circumstances caused by a substantial increase in the cost of materials and equipment supplied by the contractor and services provided to the latter by third parties.[24] However, such increase must comply with all criteria of a material change in circumstances.[25] As for the approximate price, the contractor may demand its change having warned about such change in a timely manner. In such case, the customer is entitled to repudiate the contract having paid to the contractor part of the price for the works performed.[26] The statute provides for the consequences of contractor's savings. Unless such savings affect the quality of works, the contractor preserves the right to be paid for the works at the initial price. This rule is discretionary, which is explicitly specified by its text containing the expression "except as otherwise provided by the agreement of the parties".

Formalities

11.28 The general rule is that the contract is concluded in plain written form.[27] The written form condition is also deemed to have been complied with if the contract is concluded by means of exchange with relevant information, rather than in the form of a single document. Judicial practice has long been taking a formal approach to the assessment of contract existence. The text of the contract was supposed to contain all essential conditions. Their absence resulted in the contract declared to be not concluded; that is, in its non-existence as such. In recent years, a pronounced tendency towards abandoning such

22 Art. 314, Cl.1, RCC.
23 Art. 328, RCC.
24 Art. 709, Cl. 6, RCC.
25 Art. 451, RCC.
26 Art. 709, Cl.5, RCC.
27 Art. 158, RCC.

formalism is being observed. In assessing whether a particular condition has been agreed upon by the parties, courts focus on revealing the genuine common will of the parties, with such will being also identified as at the time of the trial. In other words, if the parties fail to agree upon any essential condition in the contract, in the future, they can make up for this deficiency of will by their actual deeds. For example, the parties have not agreed upon technical documentation at all, having just indicated the subject matter in general. Formally, the contract is not concluded, but the customary practice is such that, if the parties sign the acceptance certificate after the works have been completed, the contract may no longer be declared not concluded, because the result is of consumption value for the customer. For example, in one of its explanatory statements (*razyasneniya*), RF SAC stated:

11.29 "The absence of technical documentation approved in accordance with the established procedure shall not serve as absolute grounds for declaring a contract not concluded".[28]

11.30 The court found that since

11.31

> The Parties had no disagreements on the subject matter, and they thought fit to proceed to its performance. The Customer accepted the work results against the certificate. The totality of the circumstances specified does not give grounds to declare the contract not concluded due to the absence of technical documentation.
>
> [29]

11.32 On the one hand, such approach is flexible and enables reaching a fair decision. On the other hand, while countering the uncertainty as to the existence of the contract, the approach produces yet another uncertainty as to understanding which actions following the conclusion of the contract are relevant for the assessment of the genuine will, and which are not. For example, legislative rules may be nullified by judicial discretion. As mentioned above, any additional works initiated by the contractor shall only be paid for with the customer's consent. In practice, the contractor often performs additional works without asking for the customer's consent. Thereafter, such works are included into the acceptance certificate, alongside with those originally determined, and the customer signs it as is. The question of whether such action represents the customer's consent to the performance of and payment for additional works is widely debated in literature; and judicial practice predominantly supports the positive answer to this question assuming that any act in the performance process is of legal nature and represents the expression of will.[30] This approach is highly questionable and dangerous for construction contracts, because in Russia, the acceptance certificate under a contract of work, as different from that under a sale contract, does not generally represent the expression of will and technically certi-

---

28 Clause 11 of Information Letter of the RF SAC Presidium dated 20 January 2000 No. 51.

29 Ibid.

30 For example, resolution of the Presidium of the RF SAC dated 20 September 2011, 1302/11, definition of the RF SC dated 21 January 2015 No. 308-ES14-2538. In theoretical terms, the resolution of this issue depends on whether Russia accepts the theory of *Verfügungsgeschäft*, typical of Germany, as well as on the applicability of the said theory to continuing obligations, including contractor's obligations to perform work. For more details, please refer to, e.g., E.A. Sukhanov. On Types of Deals in German and Russian Civil Law.// Bulletin of Civil Law. 2006, No. 2. Prof. E.A.Sukhanov is one of the leading commentators of Russian civil law.

fies the acceptance in terms of quality and scope. In such case, by signing the acceptance certificate as is, the customer only confirms that an additional scope of works exists, without providing customer's subsequent consent for its performance. Such consent must be explicitly expressed or follow from the assessment of the cumulative evidence.[31] Thus, the breakaway from the formal approach to the assessment of non-existence of a contract in the Russian judicial practice and doctrine so far has failed to reach its aim – to ensure stable relations between the parties.

The Contents of a Contract

Terms of a Contract (Express and Implied Terms)

11.33 The majority of conditions in a construction contract in Russia are express. These are conditions about technical documentation, time limits, work schedule, quality requirements for the works being performed, materials and equipment being used, consequences of a breach of contract by the parties, and many other. According to the Russian doctrine, implied conditions cover several groups of conditions. The first group, a peculiarity of the civil law regulation, is discretionary rules present in the law of obligation, particularly in its provisions regulating construction contracts. Discretionary rules are rules of conduct comprising a non-mandatory stipulation similar to "except as otherwise provided by the contract". If no "otherwise" is specified in the contract, the discretionary rule of the statute shall be in effect, which was implied by the parties, who did not state otherwise. The number of such cases in contractual practice is rather large – parties often rely on numerous discretionary rules.

11.34 The aforesaid approach is typical of the Russian doctrine:

11.35

> In literature, the conditions being included into the contract at the discretion of the parties are often called **accidental** as opposed to **ordinary** conditions, which are not subject to any agreement by the parties (and may be absent from the text of the contract), but form part of their contractual obligations. The latter traditionally include conditions envisaged by discretionary rules for the majority of contracts (for example, the condition about the place of performance). It is easy to see that accidental contract conditions being suggested for agreement by one of the parties are, therefore, always material (para 2, Art. 432, Cl. 1, RCC), while ordinary conditions either become material (if the parties directly choose the relevant option provided by a discretionary rule), or are not subject to any agreement by the parties. For this reason, legislation does not make use of the concepts of ordinary and accidental conditions.
>
> *32*

11.36 Lately, in literature one may see a suggestion of reproach to the legislator that, in terms of that peculiarity, the Civil Code bears a resemblance to a textbook for the parties. However, taking into account the country-wise specifics, such a detailed regulation currently appears justified (not everybody is ready to work with an intricate text of the

31 Interestingly, a similar position is expressed in the RF SAC documents, in particular, in Clause 10 of Information Letter of the RF SAC Presidium dated 20 January 2000 No. 51. Such lack of uniformity is primarily related to the absence of construction law in Russia.

32 Civil Law. Text book. Volume 2. Law of Obligations. Edited by Professor E. A. Sukhanov, M, Statute, 2011/.

statute). The second group of implied conditions comprises conditions that stem from the order established as between the parties, if they have had long-term single-type relations under different contracts. This group of conditions makes wider use of the concept of implied conditions; that is, conditions that arise in the course of contract performance. Practical actions of the parties either change the conditions contained in the contract, or introduce new conditions, which originally were not part of the contract. Still, no special agreements on changing contractual terms are to be signed.[33] The number of such instances is great, and there are various practices in assessing which practical actions of the parties lead to the change in (creation of) a condition deemed implied, and which do not.[34]

Unfair Contract Terms

11.37 The concept of unfair contractual terms became part of the Russian law only in 2015.[35] Apparently, judicial practice has not yet been able to articulate a list of construction contract's terms and conditions ranging among "unfair". However, the fact that the unfair terms and conditions doctrine emerged quite late does not mean that previously courts performed no checks of terms and conditions for their fairness. Regulations of Art. 10, RCC concerning the abuse of law institute served as legal framework for such checks. Since the mid-2000s, in assessing whether abuse of law did or did not take place when laying down a specific condition, courts have started to rely on the good faith principle, which was not part of the statute at that time as a general principle. Specific unfair terms were recognized invalid, because any acts of abuse of law are prohibited.[36] In addition, such practice was dissimilar and uncommon at the level of supreme judicial authorities, where, in the opinion of legal community, the list of unfair terms and conditions should be articulated.[37] Still, in general, one can provide an example of an unfair term. Among those often recognized unfair are the terms and conditions of a subcontractor's agreement that make the payment for the works performed by the subcontractor dependent on the receipt of funds by the general contractor from the customer.[38]

---

33 In the Russian doctrine, such conditions are called "*obyknovenie*" (usage). Here is what the most credible textbook on civil law in Russia states in this regard. "Traditionally, customs are distinct from usage. **Usage** is an established rule, which the parties to a specific contract agreed to rely on, and this is the only reason why it acquires legal effect for them ... Technically, usage represents an **implied contractual condition** (partners' agreement). If the contract does not contain references to such condition, or the parties' intention to rely on it has not been proved, usage is not taken into consideration as an obligatory rule even if no special legislative or contractual guidelines are available". Civil Law. Textbook. Volume 1. General Provisions. Edited by Prof. E. A. Sukhanov. M., Statute, 2011.

34 For example, see above about the controversial judicial practice on payment for additional works initiated by the contractor.

35 Art. 428, RCC. In accordance with this rule of law, unfair contractual conditions are conditions of a contract, which "have been determined by one of the parties, while the other party, due to its clearly lower negotiating power, was put into a position that substantially prevents it from insisting on a different content of certain contractual conditions".

36 Art. 10, cl.1, RCC.

37 The situation has changed with the adoption of Information Letter dated 25 November 2008 No. 127 by the RF SAC Presidium. This explanatory statement (*razyasneniye*) describes the application of the rules of law on abuse of the right (good faith) and has become a catalyst for the application of the corresponding rules of law by courts. Since 01 March 2013, certain amendments to the RCC have come into force and ratified the good faith principle as one of the core principles of civil law.

38 E.g., Clause 9 of Information Letter of the RF SAC Presidium dated 20 January 2000 No. 51.

Vitiating Factors under Contract Law

Non-Concluded Contract

11.38 The judicial practice review shows that, since the mid-1990s of the 20th century, there has been quite a large number of cases, in which a construction contract was declared not concluded. Under Russian law, if a contract is deemed not concluded, it does not exist as a juridical fact, and, therefore, no obligations exist either. The consequences of a contract being declared not concluded are only considered in the context of the rules of law concerning unjust enrichment. In practice, it particularly resulted in a partially fulfilled contract, which was subsequently declared as not concluded, being subject to neither the contractual terms and conditions (e.g., as to liability), nor the rules of law (e.g., as to the warranty period). However, the non-existence of a contract often stemmed from, as demonstrated above, a formal application of the statute, notably initiated by the party in bad faith. Here is a classic example: The parties failed to properly agree upon the conditions about the time limit for work completion. Meanwhile, the works have been completed, but the customer, having accepted the works, does not pay for them. In response to the contractor's claim for the collection of debt and penalty for the delay in payment, the court satisfies the cross (counter) claim brought by the customer seeking to declare the contract not concluded and dismisses the contractor's claim.[39] Such decisions were unfair. As demonstrated above, moving away from a formal application of the statute has contributed to easing the situation.[40] The new RCC rule of law has become the second way to improve the situation; it essentially provides that the party, which accepted the performance under the contract, or otherwise confirmed the contract's validity, shall not be entitled to raise any claim seeking to declare such contract not concluded, if such claim contradicts the good faith principle.[41]

39 E.g., decision of the Federal Arbitration Court of Moscow district dated 10 September 2009, No. KG-A40/7627-09-P expresses the legal stance stating that "having determined the contract dated 10 January 2006 No. 08/06 as a contract of work only, in the absence of a condition setting the time limit for work completion in this contract as provided by Article 708 of the Civil Code of the Russian Federation, the court of appeal was not entitled to consider the contract to be concluded and rely on any of its conditions, including those about the cost of work". At the same time, it appears from the case files that the parties determined the commencement date for the works – the time of prepayment transfer to the contractor, which formally contradicted Article 190 of the RCC. Accordingly, even if the works have been performed, the contractor would have no right to recover the cost of work relying on the contractual provisions. Consequently, given that the contract has not been concluded, the rules on unjust enrichment should have been applied, which presupposes a more complex process of proving.

40 For example, in its Resolution dated 18 May 2010 No. 1404/10, the RF SAC Presidium indicated that "civil legislation requirements on determining the time limit for work completion under contracts of work as an essential condition of such contracts were set in order to prevent the uncertainty in legal relations between the parties. If the start of the period is determined by reference to an action of a party or any other person, particularly to the time of advance payment transfer, and such actions were performed within a reasonable time, the uncertainty as to the duration of works shall be eliminated. Consequently, in such case, the condition on the time limit for work completion shall be considered to be agreed upon, and the contract shall be deemed concluded. As found by courts and confirmed by case files, the partnership effected the advance payment in accordance with the contractual conditions. In such circumstances, the courts of appeal and cassation wrongfully declared the contract of work to be not concluded".

41 Art. 432, cl.1, RCC; Federal Law dated 08 March 2015 No. 42-FZ. However, so far, judicial practice has not elaborated the criteria of misconduct.

Illegality

11.39 All general provisions about transactions, including those concerning invalidity of transactions, apply to construction contracts, just like to any other transactions. In other words, a construction contract may be declared invalid on any grounds of invalidity, the list of which generally corresponds to the canonical list of European Codes.

11.40 Meanwhile, the judicial practice review gives grounds to claim that over the past 20 years, the courts declared construction contracts invalid on very rare occasions. An exception is invalidity of contracts concluded in violation of tendering procedures (these are typically construction contracts awarded by the government). Such violation is recognized as affecting third party rights and interests and leading to anticompetitive outcomes and ineffective spending of budgetary funds.

The Rights and Liabilities of Third Parties

11.41 In a construction contract, "third parties" may refer to the following persons. First, if a construction contract is classified as a contract concluded in favour of a third party, this refers to such third party. In such case, the regime of a contract in favour of a third party shall apply, under which such third party has rights, but no obligations, with respect to the parties to the construction contract. In particular, such third party is entitled to make a claim in respect of the discharge of an obligation in his favour.[42] However, one can hardly find contracts of work in favour of a third party. Second, a subcontractor engaged by the general contractor is a third party in relation to the customer. Subcontractor's legal status is governed by special regulations on subcontractors (see the relevant section hereof) and the general concept of performance of obligations by a third party.[43] Third, persons that are not legally related to the conclusion and performance of the construction contract may act as third parties. Here are two examples. A third party – a contractor's ill-wisher – impedes the contract performance by the contractor, which results in the latter's failure to meet the time limits for work completion. Under Russian law, the contractor shall be responsible for such failure to meet the time limits, save where, in response to third party's actions, the contractor suspends works and informs the customer to that effect, expecting for the latter to take the corresponding measures.[44] It begs the question whether the customer (under this exception) or the contractor (if the contractor fails to perform the obligation specified in RCC Art. 716) may claim damages from the third party under tort regulations. The overwhelming part of the doctrine answers in the negative proceeding from the relativity of obligations principle. Meanwhile, in resolving this issue, judicial practice often disagrees with the doctrine. In other words, the problem is far from being solved. The same is true when a construction object put into operation inflicts damage on third parties due to poor quality of work performed or mistakes in its design. This poses the question: Are third parties entitled to demand compensation for damage inflicted from the contractor or the designer as a delinquent, or are they only entitled to address their counterparty under the contract (e.g., if damage was inflicted during a dramatic performance)? The assumption is that only a contractual suit; that is, a suit

42 Art. 430, RCC.
43 Art. 313, RCC.
44 Art. 716, RCC.

against the theatre, may be brought. However, this issue is widely discussed, which may soon affect the resolution of specific disputes.[45]

Performance of a Contract

11.42 RCC dedicates a fair amount of rules of law to general provisions on the performance of obligations.[46] Structurally, legislative materials are arranged in a manner traditional for a pandect system. From the doctrinal point of view, the nature of performance of obligations is the most controversial issue – whether the performance is a deal, legal action, or a physical act. The issue of correlation between cross-performance of obligations and conditional performance is also relevant in this context of a conditional transaction structure. So far, neither the doctrine, nor judicial practice has reached common ground on these issues.[47]

Obligation to Achieve the Result

11.43 In Russia, both in judicial practice and in the doctrine, obligations are often divided into obligations to achieve the result and obligations to use every reasonable effort.[48] Obligations to achieve the result essentially rely on the premise that the lack of the result leads to the failure to perform obligations and, as a consequence, to debtor's liability. Speaking of an obligation to use every reasonable effort, the lack of the result does not entail liability of a debtor acting in good faith. Obligations under a contract of work, including that arising from a construction contract, are the classic example of obligations to achieve the result.[49] The contractor's liability for the failure to achieve the result is very strict. First, as a professional participant of property circulations, a civil engineering contractor being an entrepreneur is held liable regardless of the guilt.[50] Second, it is the contractor who bears the risks of accidental destruction of, or damage to, materials and work results (see below). Third, the contractor is liable to the customer for actions of third parties involved by the former (e.g., suppliers, subcontractors, etc.), as if they were

45 For example, the modern doctrine proceeds from the inadmissibility of competition between contractual and tort claims: "The scopes of application of contractual and tort obligations, and, therefore, contractual and tort liability shall be **delimited** as follows: if damage (loss) arises from the failure to perform or properly perform a contractual obligation, tort liability rules shall not apply, and damage shall be compensated for in accordance with the rules on liability for the failure to perform a contractual obligation, or in accordance with the terms and conditions of the contract between the parties". Civil Law. Textbook, Volume 2. Law of Obligations, Edited by Prof. E.A. Sukhanov, M., Statute, 2011. Yet, even M.M. Agarkov, an outstanding Soviet civil lawyer, based on the European sources, acknowledged exceptions from the relativity of obligations principle. M.M. Agarkov. Obligation under Soviet Civil Law. Moscow, 1940.

46 Art. 309-328, RCC

47 For example, S.V. Sarbash. General Teaching on the Performance of Contractual Obligations. M., Statute, 2005.

48 See, e.g., Resolution of the RF SAC Presidium dated 21 January 2012 No. 11563/11. This Resolution particularly specifies that obligations to use every reasonable effort and to achieve the result provide for "different degrees of diligence in the performance of obligations". Interestingly, the Resolution of the RF SC Plenum, binding on courts, also reads that "to the extent provided by the statute or following from the nature of the obligation, a party may be held responsible for the occurrence or non-occurrence of certain circumstances, including those beyond its control. Technically, under the result achievement model, the parties may build any obligation whatsoever. In this sense, obligations under a work contract are non-monopolistic.

49 Art. 702, RCC reads that the contractor's obligation is the obligation "to deliver the work result to the customer", rather than, for example, to simply perform the work.

50 Art. 401, RCC

his own actions. Finally, the contractor is generally held liable for the failure to achieve the result due to reasons beyond contractor's control. In this context, the contractor incurs professional risks, but, as contrary to the customer, the contractor is a specialist in construction and a stronger party to the contract in this respect.

Allocation of Risks, Rights of Ownership in a Contract

11.44 In construction contracts in Russia, one traditionally identifies three types of risks.[51] First, it is the risk of accidental destruction, of or damage to, materials supplied for the construction. Conventionally, works are performed by contractor's work and labour, from contractor's materials, by efforts and at the expense of the contractor. However, the contract may envisage that materials shall be partially provided by the customer. In accordance with RCC, Art. 705, the risk of accidental destruction of, or damage to, materials shall be borne by the party that provided the materials, since such party is the owner of the materials, regardless of which party eventually paid for the material and which party possesses it. For example, the facts that the possession of the material purchased by the customer was transferred to the contractor, or that the contractor purchased the materials out of the advance payment received are not relevant for the resolution of the ownership issue. In the first instance, the customer remains the owner, and in the second one – the contractor becomes the owner.

11.45 Since bearing the risk of accidental destruction of, or damage to materials is related to the ownership, the following question takes on special importance: Until what time does the party that provided the material remain its owner and bear the risk of its accidental destruction or damage? In practical terms, the issue becomes relevant if the party that provided the material becomes bankrupt, or its debts are recovered as part of enforcement proceedings. Judicial practice has elaborated the following rule in this regard. The party that provided the material is the owner of the material and bears the risk of its accidental destruction or damage until the time of its actual use in work. From that time, the material is legally lost as a subject of civil law rights and becomes part of the construction object. Consequently, from that time, there is no object, with respect to which rights may be established, or risks may be allocated. The rights and risks apply to the construction object in general.[52]

11.46 Second, this refers to the risk of accidental destruction of, or damage to the result of works (construction object). This risk is borne by the contractor until the works have been delivered to the customer.[53] In this context, for the risk of accidental destruction to be transferred, the delivery of works should mean signing an act equivalent to the acceptance certificate (see (d)).

11.47 One peculiarity of Russian law is that, from the time when an interim work result becomes qualified as immovable property, the construction object becomes subject to

51 On this issue, see: M.I. Braginskiy. Contract of Work and Similar Contracts. M., Statute, 1999. It should be noted that the contributions of M.I. Braginskiy are all but only authoritative works in the field of construction law. Prof. M.I. Braginskiy (1925–2009) is the first Soviet and post-Soviet Russian specialist on construction contracts.

52 Resolution of the RF SAC Presidium dated 26 October 1999 No. 3655/99.

53 Art. 741, RCC.

civil rights (an immovable thing).[54] It is called an incomplete construction (*obekt nezavershennogo stroitelstva*). However, the criterion for qualifying facilities as immovable property is of physical nature. Facilities that cannot be moved without causing disproportionate damage to their purpose are recognized as immovable property.[55] The status of the object of uncompleted construction as immovable property is not related to the state registration of title.[56] State registration of title to an incomplete construction does not create an immovable thing or any right thereto, but it enables the right holder to make disposal arrangements with respect to such thing. By virtue of RCC Art. 747, the customer has a binding obligation to transfer the possession of a land plot to the contractor, which implies that the customer has the right to such land plot being developed. The contractor, in turn, only possesses the land plot de facto. It follows that, by virtue of the *superficio solo cedit* principle, it is the customer and not the contractor who owns the object being constructed under the construction contract.[57] This approach is currently considered established, but its emergence was subject to multiple debates concerning the incomplete construction concept and the role of state registration of rights to immovable property.

11.48 Third, the statute allocates the risks of contractor's failure to achieve the result due to circumstances beyond contractor's control.[58] The said article states that if the contractor discovers any circumstances that are beyond contractor's control and endanger the achievement of the work results, the contractor shall immediately suspend the works and notify the customer to that effect. Such circumstances may be associated with defects in the customer's order (errors in technical documentation), unsound materials provided by the customer, and third party actions that impede the work performance. This list of circumstances is not exhaustive. There have been long debates in judicial practice about who bears the risk of failure to discover the said circumstances. Currently, it is generally accepted that such risk rests with the contractor as the professional. In this context, the contractor bears the professional risk of consequences of contractor's activities. For the contractor, bearing the risk of failure to discover such circumstances means that the contractor is liable for any unfavorable consequences of their occurrence. At the same time, if the customer fails to undertake relevant measures within a reasonable period, the contractor shall be entitled to repudiate the contract and claim damages.[59]

Contract of Construction Work and Supply Contract

11.49 As demonstrated above, one does not raise the question of correlation between a pure construction contract and a sales contract or a supply contract, as the customer, while

54 Art. 130, RCC.

55 Art. 130, Cl.1, RCC.

56 Cl. 38 of Resolution of the RF SC Plenum dated 23 July 2015 No. 25 specifies that "by implication of Article 131 of the RCC, for the purposes of stability of civil turnover, the statute establishes the necessity of state registration of title and other important property rights to immovable things, as well as restriction, origin, transfer and termination of such rights. However, conventionally, state registration of the jus in rem is not a mandatory condition for recognizing it as immovable property (Art. 130, Cl. 1, RCC). That is why ... a rightfully erected building or construction is an immovable property object, including before the title thereto is registered in the name of the person that lawfully possesses it".

57 Cl. 21 of Information Letter of the RF SAC Presidium dated 20 January 2000 No. 51 ("the title to uncompleted construction as to immovable property shall accrue to the customer").

58 Art. 716, RCC.

59 These rules are of paramount importance for understanding the essence of contracts of work in Russia.

having the right to the land plot, acquires the title to the construction object on the original grounds. However, as part of the task set by the customer (e.g., plant construction), it is necessary to create (purchase) new things (e.g., industrial equipment, doors, windows, etc.) and subsequently assemble them. By their legal nature, such things are movable property. The existence or absence of the customer's rights for the land plot does not affect the ownership of these things. In practice, the parties conclude either a mixed contract (for delivery and assembly of equipment, windows, etc.), or a contract of work for creation and assembly of equipment. In the latter case, the contract of work has two subject matters and two tasks: First, the creation of equipment and second – its assembly. That is when the question of correlation between a supply contract and a contract of work raises – as part of resolution of disputes arising from such types of contracts. The key issue faced here is the difference between the contract for supply of future things and the contract of work for creation of the same things.

11.50 The practice and doctrine use two approaches to this matter. Under the first one, the contractor is the owner of things created under the contract of work, and, together with the result, the contractor also transfers to the customer the title to the thing. Legal grounds for such approach are provisions in Cl. 2, RCC Art. 703, under which the contractor transfers to the customer the rights to the thing created under the contract of work for creation of such thing.[60] Under the second approach, when creating a new thing at the instruction of the customer, the contractor destroys the material from the time when such material is used, thus losing the right to it. That being the case, the customer becomes the owner from the time of appearance of the object being created on the original grounds. The basic rule of law about the acquisition of title (under which a person that created a new thing acquires the title to it, if it was created for such person) forms grounds for such approach.[61] In this context, the ownership of the material used for the creation of the thing is of no legal effect. The contractor creates a thing at the request of the customer, rather than for the contractor's personal use, and the contractor has no independent interest in the thing being created.[62]

11.51 The first approach has a drawback – it conciliates a contract of work for creation of things with a supply contract, the subject matter of which may particularly be a future thing; that is, the thing, which will be created by the supplier in future.[63] As a result, the person, who invested in the creation of a new thing, loses the guarantees that are common to a contract of work and are absent from a supply contract. Besides, the problem aggravates if the supplier becomes bankrupt, especially where an advance payment has been made.

11.52 Recently, one often finds differences between the two contract types in the will of the contracting parties. If the will expressed by the parties is to have the title to the thing

60 One supporter of this approach was M.I. Braginskiy, who stated: "It follows from the very nature of a contract of work that it is the customer who should be generally acknowledged as the owner of the newly created thing prior to its transfer. Hence, it particularly follows that a thing created by the contractor under the agreement with the customer may be subject to collection under contractor's debts". M.I. Braginskiy. Contract of Work and Similar Contracts. M., Statute, 1999.

61 Art. 218, Cl. 1, RCC.

62 For more details, see: N.B. Shcherbakov. Comments to §3 of Chapter 37 of the RCC "Construction Contract".// Comments to RCC. Part 2. Edited by P.V. Krasheninnikov. M., Statute, 2011.

63 Art. 455, Cl. 2, RCC.

being created initially accrued to the paying party, it is a contract of work, and if they agree on the derivative emergence of title, it is a supply contract.[64]

Delivery and Acceptance of the Work

11.53 The general rule is that the acceptance of work is effected through signing an acceptance certificate. Such certificate has a standardized form, which is used for accounting and taxation reasons. For the purpose of civil law, the certificate may be executed in any form suitable for the parties.

11.54 Signing the acceptance certificate pursues several goals. First of all, the acceptance certificate acts as an acceptance certificate for the work performed.[65] The certificate signed by the parties plays the role of an acceptance confirmation to the extent as follows: If it is the final acceptance certificate for the work performed; if it is a preliminary acceptance certificate for a specific stage of work; and if it is any other certificate, which the parties regard as an acceptance certificate (e.g., the acceptance certificate for specific concealed or critical work items). Having signed the acceptance certificate, the customer loses its right to refer to defects in the work performed and accepted, which could have been discovered during the acceptance procedure using the method specified by the parties in their contract and if no such method is specified, using the method common to the relevant work. Therefore, the contractor that has delivered the work shall not be liable for explicit defects in its work that were not discovered by the customer during the acceptance procedure, but shall be liable for latent defects. Still, judicial practice demonstrates that the acceptance certificate may not serve as the only proof of work performance, as well as of its quality and scope. The court assesses the acceptance certificate in conjunction with other evidence.[66]

11.55 The certificate also plays another role: Its execution signifies the accrual of obligations to pay for the works performed.[67] It is important to note that such settlements-related role is common not only to acceptance certificates in their proper sense, but also to certificates signed monthly or every ten days for the purpose of making settlements. A certificate may be difficult to refer to this category because, in the majority of cases, the form of such settlements certificate coincides with the form of an acceptance certificate in its proper sense.

11.56 The acceptance certificate also has the third role to play: Signing such certificate constitutes grounds for the transfer of the risk of accidental destruction of, or damage to, the work results from the contractor to the customer. It is important to note that signing a certificate that is not an acceptance certificate in its proper sense does not result in the transfer of the accidental destruction risk.[68]

11.57 Following the acceptance, the customer may perform one of the following actions: First, sign an acceptance certificate without reservations; second, sign a certificate with reservations challenging the quality or scope of works presented for acceptance by the contractor. In such case, the customer has no obligation to pay for the disputed works, and

---

64 See: Cl. 6 Resolutions of the RF SAC Plenum dated 11 July 2011 No. 54.
65 Art. 720, 753, RCC.
66 Cl. 12, 13, 18 of Information Letter of the RF SAC Presidium dated 20 January 2000 No. 51.
67 Cl. 8 of Information Letter of the RF SAC Presidium dated 20 January 2000 No. 51.
68 Art. 753, Cl. 3, RCC.

the rule on liability for improper performance of works shall apply. Third, the customer may refuse to sign the acceptance certificate for cause. Such causes must justify the materiality of defects in the work result. In addition, Art. 753 of the RCC contains a special rule of law related to the consequences of customer's unreasoned refusal to accept the work and sign the certificate. In such case, the contractor notes in the certificate that, despite the fact that the customer had been properly informed about the necessity of acceptance, the customer failed to accept the work and to provide causes for refusal of such acceptance. Such unilateral certificate plays an important role: If the contractor files a debt recovery claim with the court with respect to the completed works, which were not accepted, the works specified in the certificate are believed to have been performed in full compliance with the contractual conditions. The customer (defendant in the case) is provided with an opportunity to prove that the customer refused of the acceptance due to material violations on the part of the contractor. It is the general rule that, for example, if the customer signs a certificate with reservations, the burden of proof as to the customer's opinion discrepancy with the reality lies on the contractor (in a potential dispute on debt recovery). Thus, an unreasoned refusal to sign the certificate transfers the burden of proof as to the lack of the required scope or quality of works to the customer.[69]

11.58 One more role of the acceptance certificate, which is widely discussed today, is related to the possibility of its classification as a transaction, for example, as an agreement for changing the terms of obligations. Judicial practice on this issue is controversial; this issue stems from the ongoing debates on the presence or absence of *Verfügungsgeschäft* and its concept in Russian law.

Breach

11.59 Russian law traditionally regards a breach of contract as a violation of law. The main consequence of committing a violation of law is the imposition of civil liability. Such liability includes damages, charge of penalty, and payment of legitimate interest for the failure to perform monetary obligations. However, alongside this, a breach of contract may provide the person, whose rights have been violated, with other possibilities, including, in particular, the right to unilaterally repudiate the contract, the right of retention (lien), and a number of other rights.[70]

Termination

11.60 The RCC contains a great number of rules, which provide both the contractor and the customer with the right to unilaterally repudiate the contract of work.

11.61 Typical instances of such repudiation on the part of the customer are as follows. First of all, by virtue of Art. 717 of the RCC, the customer is entitled to unilaterally repudiate the contract without cause at any time. If this is the case, the customer pays to the

69 Cl. 14 of Information latter of the RF SAC Presidium dated 20 January 2000 No. 51 ("The court may invalidate a unilateral acceptance certificate for work results only if it upholds the reasons for refusal to sign the acceptance certificate. This rule of law means that the certificate issued in accordance with this procedure is a proof of contractor's performance of obligations under the contract, and if the customer refuses to pay, the court is obliged to review the customer's arguments justifying the latter's refusal to sign the acceptance certificate for the work results".)

70 For more details, please see below.

contractor a part of the price proportional to the work actually performed by the time of such unilateral termination, and compensates the contractor for damages to the extent of the difference between such part of the price and the overall contract price. However, this rule only specifies the upper threshold of potential damages, which are to be proved in accordance with general rules.[71] This right of the customer characterizes the latter as the initiator of works and beneficiary of their result. For example, in a new construction, the customer will generally be the owner of the newly created immovable property object. In so far as no ownership may be imposed on a person, the right to the customer's unreasoned repudiation of the contract cannot be excluded by mutual agreement of the parties. The second most popular instance of unilateral repudiation is the repudiation on grounds provided by Art. 715 of the RCC. Pursuant to this article, if the contractor has not started the work, or has been working so slowly that the work would obviously not be completed on time, the customer shall be entitled to repudiate the contract and claim damages. Judicial practice has revealed a problem: The contractor may challenge these grounds for unilateral repudiation by proving that the work was not performed that slowly to make it obvious that it would not be completed on time. For example, the contractor was far behind the work schedule at a certain stage, but had all the possibilities to close the gap during the subsequent stages, without breaching the deadline for completion. If the contractor succeeds in proving the customer's mistake in the reason, the court does not reject the very will of the customer for unilateral repudiation, but reclassifies it from reasoned[72] to unreasoned,[73] which turns the customer from a creditor into a debtor in terms of the obligation to compensate for damages.[74]

11.62 The RCC also specifies a number of grounds for unilateral repudiation of the contract for the contractor. However, such repudiation must always be reasoned. Unreasoned repudiation of the contract by the contractor is prohibited.

11.63 In particular, the contractor is granted the right to repudiate the contract, if the customer informed by the contractor about the discovery of circumstances beyond the contractor's control that impede the achievement of the result, fails to take relevant measures to eliminate the same. Unilateral repudiation is accompanied by the contractor's right to claim damages.[75] The contractor is entitled to repudiate the contract and claim damages to the extent where the customer fails to perform its cross-obligations, which impedes the performance of the contract.[76] A classic reason for such unilateral repudiation is a lengthy delay in transferring technical documentation or its next scheduled part by the customer to the contractor. However, in practice, contractors exercise the right to unilateral repudiation of the contract on rare occasions due to certain business reasons.

71 Cl. 19 of Information letter of the RF SAC Presidium dated 20 January 2000 No. 51.

72 Art. 715 of the RCC.

73 Art. 717 of the RCC.

74 RF SAC Presidium, Regulation dated 23 September 2008 No. 5103/08: "Taking into account the established circumstances, courts of first instance and cassation concluded that the enterprise had no reasons to repudiate the contract of work under Article 715 of the Code and wrongfully validated the contract. However, the unilateral repudiation of the contract by the enterprise took place and resulted in the contract termination under the rules and involving the implications determined by Article 717 of the Code".

75 Art. 716, RCC.

76 Art. 719, RCC.

Remedies

Remedies under a Contract

11.64 A penalty is the principal and universal contractual liability for the failure to perform obligations. A penalty is an amount of money specified by the contract to be paid in the event of non-performance or improper performance of obligations.[77] In Russia, no commodity penalty is recognized. The performance of any contractor's or customer's obligation may be secured by a penalty. A penalty has two forms: Late fee (calculated for each day of delay) and fine (an originally specified amount of money payable for the delay on a one-off basis). Late fees and fines are extensively used in drafting contracts in favour of both the customer and the contractor. The advantage of a penalty compared to damages is that one does not need to prove the amount of damages inflicted on the creditor. The mere fact of delay is sufficient. In other words, a penalty may sometimes be charged even if the creditor incurred no damages.[78]

11.65 In determining the penalty amount, the parties rely on the freedom-of-contract doctrine.[79] In practice, it often results in setting extremely high amounts of penalties comparable to the overall contract price. Russian judicial practice traditionally pays closer attention (in detriment of the freedom-of-contract doctrine) to the amount of penalty claimed. For this purpose, courts proceed from the provisions of Art. 333 of the RCC, under which the court is entitled to reduce the penalty, the amount of which is excessive and evidently does not correspond to the consequences of the violation of obligations for the creditor. For a long time, courts were having powers to reduce penalty amounts at their own discretion. Consequently, given the difficulty in proving damages a penalty stopped playing the role of an adequate compensation mechanism. Therefore, as part of the latest reform, Art. 333 of the RCC was essentially amended as follows. A penalty amount may only be reduced at the defendant's initiative, and the latter is obliged to prove explicit inconsistency between the penalty amount and the consequences of violation of obligations for the creditor; however, as the statute goes, such reduction is only possible in exceptional circumstances.

11.66 In this respect, the RF SC Plenum indicates:

11.67

> When assessing the adequacy of a penalty to the consequences of the violation of obligations, it is necessary to take into account that no person shall be entitled to benefit from such person's unlawful behavior, and that an illegal use of other people's funds shall not be more advantageous for a debtor than the conditions of their legal use.
>
> [80]

11.68 As demonstrated below, the charge of interest as specified in Art. 395 of the RCC represents universal liability for the failure to perform monetary obligations. However, the statute enables the parties to set the interest rate by themselves. The parties generally

---

77 Art. 330, RCC.

78 "In resisting the claim to decrease the penalty amount, the creditor shall not be obliged to prove that it incurred losses (Art. 330, Cl.1, RCC)". (Cl. 74 of the Resolution of the RF SC Plenum dated 24 March 2016 No. 7).

79 Art. 421, RCC.

80 Cl. 75 of PPl. RF SC dated 24 March 2016 No. 7.

set a higher rate of such interest than that established by the statute. In such case, the payment of interest for the failure to perform monetary obligations acquires the meaning of a contractual penalty, which may also be reduced in accordance with Art. 333 of the RCC.

Remedies under Law

11.69 As discussed above, Art. 395 of the RCC specifies the rate of interest payable for the failure to perform monetary obligations. Such interest rate is determined based on average bank interest rates for retail deposits at the creditor's location. The Bank of Russia monthly publishes these average rates, which are extremely low. By its legal nature, interest under Art. 395 of the RCC is a lawful penalty for the failure to perform monetary obligations. It is considered that a contractual penalty may not be reduced under Art. 333 of the RCC to the amount below the interest rate specified in Art. 395 of the RCC.

11.70 A penalty under law; that is, an amount of money to be paid by the debtor for the breach of debtor's obligations represents liability established by the statute.[81] However, the RCC does not specify lawful penalties for contracts of work (except for those involving consumers).

11.71 Damages are a universal type of liability for the violation of obligations. Parties had long faced serious difficulties in claiming damages in court. It was due to an extremely complicated procedure for proving the amount of damages. As part of the RCC reform, amendments were introduced, which made proving damages easier. Now the court may not refuse of awarding damages if no proof of their exact amount has been provided. In such case, the court independently determines the amount of damages to be recovered based on the principles of justice, reasonableness and balance of interests of the parties.[82]

11.72 Besides, new rules were introduced to the RCC[83] concerning damages in the event of contract termination. For the first time, the statute introduces a general rule about an abstract and specific method for calculation of damages.

11.73 In the Russian theory and practice, the admissibility of the customer's remedy of specific performance (in relation to work performance) is controversial. Courts had long dismissed such claims, because in accordance with the Russian legislation, judicial acts forcing the contractor to perform certain works are unenforceable. That is why a court decision to force the performance of works may not be implemented. In accordance with the Russian doctrine, courts must not pass unenforceable judgments. However, as part of the RCC reform, a heated discussion thrived about practicability of legalizing such remedy. Eventually, it was decided to allow the customer to use this remedy having employed the French institution of *l'astriente*. Now, in accordance with Art. 308.1 of the RCC, the creditor is generally entitled to demand specific performance of any obligation, and the court, at creditor's request, is entitled to award in the creditor's favour an amount of money to be paid if the judicial act has not been implemented, determined by the court based on the principles of justice, proportionality, and inadmissibility of making profit out of unlawful or unfair conduct. For example, Resolution of the RF SAC Plenum dated 24 March 2016 No. 7 reads:

---

81 Art. 330, RCC.
82 Art. 393, RCC.
83 Art. 393.1.

11.74

> Payment of an *astreinte* shall not entail termination of the principal obligation, release the debtor from its specific performance and from imposition of sanctions for the failure to perform or properly perform the same. Awarding an *astreinte* must make the implementation of a court decision obviously more advantageous for the defendant than the failure to implement it.[84]

11.75 At the same time, such monetary amount is regarded as a penalty. So far, it is not clear how this institution will function in practice.

11.76 The statute establishes a number of special remedies for the parties to a construction contract. For example, Art. 723 of the RCC particularly states that if the contractor has performed the work with deviations from the construction contract, which worsened the work result, or with any other defects, which make it unsuitable for the intended use, the customer shall be entitled, unless otherwise stipulated by law or by the contract, at customer's discretion, to demand that the contractor eliminate such defects free of charge within a reasonable time period, provide the proportionate reduction in the contract price, or compensation for customer's expenses for eliminating such defects, if the contract provides for such right of the customer. In accordance with Art. 719 of the RCC, the contractor is granted a widely used remedy – the right to suspend works. For example, if the customer fails to perform or properly perform its obligations, which renders the performance of works impossible, or impedes the performance of works by the contractor, the contractor shall be entitled not to start works and to suspend the work in process without the risk of delay.[85]

11.77 In quite a large number of instances, when the other party violates its obligations, both the contractor and the customer are granted the right to repudiate the contract and claim damages.[86]

Remedies Agreed by the Parties

11.78 Two institutions representing remedies of parties to a contract stand somewhat apart. The first one has long been provided by the RCC. For example, in accordance with Art. 757, a construction contract may specify the contractor's obligation to eliminate, at customer's request and at customer's expense, defects, for which the contractor is not liable. The contractor is entitled to refrain from the performance of this obligation, or rather, reject the relevant offer of the customer, if the elimination of such defects is either not directly related to the subject matter of the contract, or may not be performed by the contractor for reasons beyond contractor's control. Therefore, the construction contract enables imposing the risks of adverse consequences resulting from works, which arise due to the circumstances beyond contractor's control, on the contractor. In other words, this refers to the contractor's increased risk of occurrence of adverse circumstances, rather than to contractor's liability. However, the contractor apparently eliminates such defects for a fee.

84 Cl. 28, 32.
85 Art. 719, RCC.
86 E.g., Art. 705, 716, 719, RCC.

11.79 The second institution appeared recently due to the RCC reform. It got the name "compensation for losses incurred due to the circumstances provided by the contract".[87] This institution inherently represents the English institution of *Indemnity* adapted to the Russian legal framework. It essentially states that, in their business activities, the parties to the obligation may stipulate, by mutual agreement, an obligation for one party to compensate for other party's losses incurred due to certain circumstances not related to the violation of obligations by the parties. However, in accordance with the statute, the court may not reduce the amount of losses determined by the parties, save where their amount was intentionally increased by a party to the contract. Essentially, this refers to internal insurance, where bearing the risk of losses will evidently affect the amount of consideration. This novelty may enable, for example, obliging the contractor to eliminate without charge any defects in the work result, for which the contractor is not liable. However, the expert community has certain apprehensions as to how this institution of common law will function against the Russian civil backdrop.[88] In particular, they forecast that parties will use abusive practices in determining the amount of losses, provided that courts will generally have no right to assess such amount.

Limitation on Remedies

11.80 To begin with, a number of remedies provided to contractors and customers by the statute are discretionary by their nature; that is, may be excluded by mutual agreement of the parties. In particular, this refers to the application of remedies with respect to defective work as indicated in Art. 723 of the RCC (see above). Furthermore, the parties may exclude a wide range of instances of unilateral repudiation of the contract by one party if the other party violates its obligations.[89]

11.81 Besides, there is a general rule concerning either limitation or exclusion of liability for the violation of obligations. The general rule is that such agreements are allowed, but shall be invalid if they represent a previously concluded agreement for exclusion or limitation of liability for an intentional breach of obligations.[90] In practice, it turns out to be extremely difficult to prove the debtor's intent to violate debtor's obligation. That is why, in assessing the validity of such agreements, judicial practice tends to judge from the principle of good faith, rather than from the presence or absence of intent.[91] Thus, Russian judicial practice becomes more consistent with the practice of assessment of such agreements common to PECL. However, the RCC provisions on construction contracts contain a special rule, in accordance with which the construction contract conditions on releasing the contractor from liability for certain defects shall not release the contractor from liability, if such defects have been proved to arise as a result of the contractor's guilty activity or failure to act. Thus, as we can see, this rule is stricter than the general rule.Interpretation of Contracts

87 Art. 406.1, RCC.

88 M.A. Pshenichnikov. Comments to Article 406.1 of the RCC. Indemnity Obligations.// Bulletin of Civil Law. 2017. No. 1.

89 E.g., Art. 719, RCC.

90 Art. 401, Cl. 4, RCC.

91 For example, see decision of the Federal Arbitration Court of Moscow district dated 23 March 2011 No. KG-A41/2151-11-P, decision of the 9th Arbitration Court of Appeal dated 24 July 2015 No. 09AP-25496/2015.

11.82 In accordance with Art. 431 of the RCC, when interpreting contractual conditions, the court relies on the literal meaning of the words and expressions contained therein. In case of ambiguity, the literal meaning of contractual conditions is established by comparison with other conditions and the purport of the contract in general. However, if these rules do not allow determining the contract content, it is necessary to reveal the genuine common will of the parties, taking into account the contract objectives. For this purpose, all relevant circumstances, including negotiations and communications preceding the contract, practice established between the parties, customs, and subsequent behavior of the parties are taken into account.

11.83 Thus, the statute establishes a certain hierarchy in the use of interpretation methods, from literal to systematic, teleological, and systematic teleological.

11.84 Following the settled Soviet tradition, courts had long focused on literal interpretation. In recent decades, such approach has been repeatedly criticized as being excessively formal. Therefore, in the past 5–10 years, judicial practice of supreme judicial authorities has been aimed at shifting from formal contract interpretation to interpretation, which takes into account all circumstances of relations between the parties, allowing identification of their genuine will. For example, in the contract signed by the parties, one essential condition is absent. Formally, it entails recognizing the contract as not concluded. However, if one compares the contractual conditions with the subsequent behavior of the parties, it will become evident that, by their subsequent actions, the parties agreed the essential condition in question, which means that the claim seeking to declare the contract as not concluded shall be dismissed. Here is an example from construction practice. A construction contract has been concluded, but design documentation has not been agreed upon. The contractor completed the works and delivered them to the customer. Having failed to receive payment for his works, the contractor files a claim in court, and the customer files a counter-claim seeking to declare the contract as not concluded. In accordance with the Soviet tradition, it is necessary to grant the counter-claim and to dismiss the primary claim, since the parties failed to agree upon such essential condition as the subject matter of the works (technical or design documentation). In accordance with the current practice,[92] the court delivers a decision to the contrary: Though the parties failed to agree upon the condition on the subject matter in the contract, their subsequent actions (acceptance of the work result as is by the customer) clearly show that the parties virtually agreed upon that condition on the subject matter during the contract performance.

11.85 At the same time, in recent years, there has been an emerging trend towards an excessive enhancement in interpretation of a contract contrary to grammatical interpretation of its conditions.[93] Communications, behavior of the parties upon conclusion of the contract may overweigh conditions clearly agreed upon by the parties in the contract. On the one hand, it makes law a more flexible tool of regulation of relations, and on the other hand, such flexibility results in increased legal uncertainty. Presently, the doctrine and judicial practice are in search of the balance between the explicit will of the parties expressed in the contract and their genuine will demonstrated during the contract

92 IL. RF SAC No. 51. This IL. RF SAC is devoted to construction contract issues.

93 Resolution of the RF SAC Presidium dated 20 September 2011 No. 1302/11.

performance as identified by the court. In this process, the principle of good faith[94] introduced as a general principle as part of the ongoing RCC reform plays an important role. These rules introduce the obligation to take good faith into consideration both when concluding the contract, during its performance and upon termination of relations between the parties. Essentially, German law (paragraph 242 BGB) has had a great influence on the introduction of the principle of good faith. In Russia, the principle of good faith was regarded as a method of legal regulation and interpretation of a contract by the court, which was actually granted the right, in order to deliver a fair court decision, not to apply the rule subject to application, to change its disposition and to introduce a new rule. Similarly, this right is also applicable to interpretation of contractual conditions based on the principle of good faith and fairness.[95] On the one hand, the active use of the principle of good faith allows achieving specific fairness. However, the reverse side of this feature is legal uncertainty for the parties to the contract.[96] Under such circumstances, other methods of interpretation start to play a more important role. In particular, in Russia, the contractor (unlike the customer) is considered to be a professional participant of construction relations and therefor, due to possessing relevant competences, a stronger party. Consequently, the contractor has to bear the professional risk, which implies, among other things, that if the court has doubts, the contractual conditions must be interpreted not in contractor's favour. On the other hand, contracts of affiliation are often applied in relation to construction contracts. The contract is drafted by the customer, and the contractor has no actual opportunities to influence on its most important conditions. If this is the case, unfair contractual conditions may be imposed on the contractor, which may be classified as conclusion of a contract in bad faith. Besides, the method of interpretation used here provides that if the contractual conditions are uncertain, the contract shall be interpreted not in favour of its originator (in this case – the customer). The two latter methods obviously contradict each other in part, but unfortunately, though realizing the complexity and importance of resolving the interpretation problems, so far, the Russian doctrine and judicial practice are only looking for such resolution.

Standard Form of National Contracts

11.86 In the Russian practice, there are no general standard forms of construction contracts, which could, for example, have the status of usage. This owes to the following circumstances. First of all, the very construction law is at its onset. The Russian doctrine is only taking its first steps along the path of studying foreign and international experience, where there is an abundance of standard forms. Besides, in Russia, there is yet no

94 Art. 1, 10, 307, RCC.

95 For example, A.M. Shirvidt, based on the comparative legal analysis, ponders that "one should consider actual practice of overcoming rigidity of law by courts with a reference to good faith to be a sign of operation of the 'principle of good faith'". A.M. Shirvidt. Principle of Good Faith in the RCC and Comparative Law.// From friends and colleagues to the 50th anniversary of Professor D.V. Dozhdev. M., Statute, 2014.

96 However, so far, judicial practice is limited to general considerations about criteria for good faith. "In assessing actions of the parties as good faith or bad faith, one should proceed from the behaviour expected from any civilian participant, taking into account the rights and lawful interests of the other party assisting it, *inter alia*, in obtaining the necessary information". (Cl. 1 of Resolution of the RF SC Plenum dated 23 June 2015 No. 25).

properly formed community of construction entities capable of generalizing practice to compile standard forms.

11.87 Still, standard forms of contracts do exist in Russia. We are talking about construction contracts concluded for state needs as part of tendering procedures. However, even for such contracts, there is no generally accepted or mandatory form of a standard contract either. In particular, different forms are used at the federal level and at the level of constituent entities of the federation. There is no standard form in horizontal relations as well; that is, different government authorities (governmental customers) may have their own recommended standard forms.

11.88 Developing the national form of a contract as usage is an important task. It may only be implemented based on the thorough understanding of international and foreign experience by both Russian practitioners and scientists, which will require a certain amount of time.

Construction Law Principles

Procurement and Tendering

11.89 Procurement and tendering in Russia are not legal categories and are considered as part of general management in construction and construction procedure management.

Different Types of Contract (Unit Price, Lump Sum, etc.)

11.90 Russian law does not identify different types of contracts of work depending on peculiarities of agreeing on price terms and conditions (unit price, lump sum, etc.). More importantly, the price is not regarded as an essential condition of the contract. If no contractual price is specified, it is determined by the court based on the cost of similar works under comparable circumstances.[97] In such case, the court makes the decision based on judicial expert review results. However, it must be admitted that instances where no price is specified in contract are very rare.

Nature of a Construction Contract

11.91 A construction contract is a consensual, commutative, and synallagmatic contract. Furthermore, it is classified among contracts with intended continuing duration. A construction contract belongs to contracts that create obligations to perform works.

11.92 In addition, by virtue of the very definition of a contract, the contractor undertakes to perform certain works at the customer's order, and deliver the result to the customer who must accept such result and pay for it. Therefore, the contractor's obligation is to achieve the result specified in the customer's order, for example, to build an immovable property object.[98] It follows that the lack of the result represents the failure to perform the obligation. The risk of the failure to achieve the result is borne by the contractor. In particular, it the contractor who bears the risk of an accidental destruction or damage of the work result.[99] Besides, the contractor is liable to the customer for the failure to achieve the

97 Art. 424, RCC.
98 Art. 702, RCC.
99 Art. 705, 741, RCC.

result regardless of contractor's guilt.[100] Finally, the contractor bears the risk of the failure to achieve the result due to circumstances beyond contractor's control. For example, in accordance with Art. 716 of the RCC, if the contractor discovers any circumstances that are beyond contractor's control and endanger the achievement of the result, the contractor shall immediately suspend the work and notify the customer to that effect. The said circumstances include, *inter alia*, defects in the customer's order (design documentation), defects in the materials provided by the customer, and any other circumstances, including third party actions, impeding the achievement of the result. For this purpose, the risk of the failure to discover the circumstances in question rests with the contractor. In fact, it is the contractor's responsibility to discover obstacles to achieving the result (for example, the contractor is obliged to have the construction project submitted by the customer examined). This rule is regarded as mandatory.

Design Obligations

11.93 A construction contract does not create the contractor's obligation to perform project design work. Project design work is performed under a separate contract, which is called a contract for design and survey works.[101] Under such contract, the contractor (designer) undertakes to develop technical documentation at the customer's order, and the customer undertakes to accept and pay for the result.[102] This means that the risk of the failure to achieve the result, just like in the construction contract, is borne by the contractor (designer).[103] The designer shall be liable for defects in technical documentation, including defects revealed in the process of construction and operation of the facility.[104]

11.94 There are several models of involving designers.

11.95 The first model implies that the customer concludes a separate contract with the designer who develops design documentation. Thereafter, the customer involves the contractor under the construction contract providing such design documentation as the order. As discussed above, by virtue of Art. 716 of the RCC, the contractor bears the risk of the failure to discover project defects that impede the achievement of the result in the course of works (implementation of the design developed by the designer). This raises the question of proportion of liability to the customer attributable to the designer who made mistakes in the design and the contractor who failed to discover them. This issue is controversial, but lately there have appeared grounds for classifying such liability as solidary (joint, joint and several).

11.96 The second model implies that project design work is performed by the contractor. In such case, the contract between the customer and the contractor providing that the contractor will perform both design and construction and related works represents a mixed contract. As such, the contractor may either independently perform design works,

100 Art. 401, RCC.

101 Paragraph 4, Chapter 37, RCC.

102 Art. 758, RCC.

103 The doctrine regards such contract as a type of a construction contract. See V.V. Vitryanskiy, M.I. Braginskiy. Contract Law. Book 3, M., Statute, 2012.

104 Art. 761, Cl. 1, RCC.

or engage third parties to perform the same. In the latter case, the contractor acts as the general designer whose status is similar to that of the general contractor.[105]

11.97 In practice, the second model is considered preferable, as only one person is responsible for the result to the customer, and may not shift his/her/its responsibility to any third party, using interpretation of the statute or the contract.

Duty To Warn/Check/Review

11.98 In accordance with Art. 715 of the RCC, the customer is entitled to exercise control and supervision over the construction, while not interfering with the contractor's activity. At the same time, the customer is entitled to determine the scope of its control over the performance and quality of works, taking into account the above restriction. The customer may not be deprived of this right upon mutual agreement of the parties. It is important to note that civil legislation grants the right, and not the obligation to exercise such control. Nevertheless, public legislation (the Urban Development Code) contains regulations obliging the customer to exercise control and supervision over the construction (for more details, see Sections *Employer and Contractor* and *Consultant's Role and Liability*). At the customer's order, this obligation is often performed by a special agent – a technical customer (See Section *Consultant's Role and Liability*).

11.99 Alongside this, control and supervision over the construction are exercised by government agencies and municipalities, which must enforce relevant rules and regulations into the construction process, and ensure that the works performed correspond to the design documentation.

11.100 The Civil Code does not contain any customer's liabilities on warning the contractor about any given circumstances. On the contrary, pursuant to Art. 716 of the RCC, it is the contractor who must immediately notify the customer and suspend work until the contractor receives instructions from the latter, when the contractor discovers unsuitability or bad quality of the materials, equipment, or technical documentation provided by the customer; potential adverse consequences of implementation of the customer's instructions; other circumstances that are beyond contractor's control, which endanger the achievement of the result, or the failure to meet the deadline for achieving the result. The risk of the failure to discover such circumstances rests with the contractor (see Section *Employer and Contractor*); that is, the contractor will be liable, for example, for the failure to discover defects in the customer's order in the course of work performance. The Russian doctrine considers this provision to be one of those critical to a construction contract. Such approach proceeds on the basis that the contractor, as different from the customer, is a construction professional.

Employer and Contractor

11.101 Any person, whether an individual or a legal entity, may act as the customer under a construction contract. Legislation does not set any special requirements to the customer. Thus, Russian civil law proceeds on the basis that the customer does not need to have any special knowledge in terms of construction. However, public legislation, and primarily the Urban Development Code, does de facto set certain special requirements to

105 Art. 706, RCC.

customer.[106] In particular, the customer must exercise construction control and supervision over the work performance, take measures to prevent causing environmental damage during the construction, etc. Apparently, to discharge such functions, the customer must at least be aware of construction peculiarities. This also underlies the fact that the customer, along with the contractor, is liable for damage inflicted on third parties, environment, etc., during the construction works. This fact dissatisfies customers not being professional customers, since they are deprived of the actual opportunity to discharge these functions. For example, how can a bank willing to construct a new building for itself exercise professional supervision over the safety of works at the construction site? This entails the appearance in the structure of contractual relations for the object construction of new agents instructed to discharge the said functions. One example of such agent is the technical customer not provided by the RCC.

11.102 One important feature of the customer status is that, in accordance with the RCC,[107] the customer must possess the right to the land plot to be developed. Consequently, rights in rem to the facilities created on such land plot accrue to the customer on the original grounds.[108] This circumstance distinguishes the construction contract from the sales contract for a future immovable property, under which the payer obtains the title on derivative grounds.

11.103 Unlike the customer, the contractor is a professional player in the construction market that must have special knowledge. Previously, the contractor's activity was licensable. Nowadays, due to the ineffectiveness of licensing, a new system of self-regulation has been introduced in the construction sector: Each contractor must be a member of a self-regulated organization, which must exercise control over the contractor's activity, and form an insurance fund out of contributions of its members to cover potential future damage inflicted on third parties through improper work performance.[109]

Consultant's Role and Liability

11.104 The RCC provides for the concept of a consultant engineer. For example, in accordance with Art. 749 of the RCC, to exercise control and supervision over project construction and to make decisions as part of relations with the contractor on customer's behalf, the customer may independently, without the contractor's consent, conclude a contract for such services to the customer with the relevant engineering organization. However, the very name of a consultant engineer did not take root in practice. Such agent is called a technical customer.[110]

11.105 In practice, there are two main models of involving technical customers.

106 Art. 1, Cl. 16, Art. 60, RCC.

107 Art. 747, RCC.

108 For example, Clause 6 of Resolution of the RF SAC Plenum dated 11 July 2011 No. 54 specifies that "to the extent where under the contractual conditions a party having title or any other rights to a land plot provides it for construction of a building or structure, and the other party undertakes to carry out construction works, the rules of Chapter 37 of the RCC, including rules of paragraph 3 of the mentioned Chapter ('Construction Contract') shall apply to relations between the parties to the contract".

109 Art. 55.1-55.23, UDC.

110 Recently, the technical customer concept appeared in the Urban Development Code (Art. 1, Cl. 22, UDC).

11.106 The first model provides that the customer involves a technical customer under a separate paid services agreement. In such case, the construction contract articulates the rights and powers, which the technical customer has in relation to the contractor. The following had long been the shortcoming of this model. The service supplier was considered to be not responsible for the result, but only be responsible for making every reasonable effort, which restricted the technical customer's liability. However, given the recent judicial practice, paid services agreements may provide for the service supplier's obligation to achieve the result.[111] Furthermore, the failure to achieve the result entails claiming damages. Thus, it has become possible to oblige the technical customer to achieve the result similar to that indicated in the contract of work. There are grounds to believe that in such case, the technical customer and the contractor are jointly liable.

11.107 The second model provides that the technical customer acts as a commission agent instructed by the customer to involve a contractor under the construction contract and to take certain practical steps, for example, in terms of control and supervision over the construction. The drawback of this model is that in accordance with the Russian civil legislation, a commission agent is responsible for making every possible effort, but not for the result. Besides, the commission arrangement is not in full compliance with the rules of the Urban Development Code concerning the status of the technical customer as a customer's delegate.[112]

Sub-Contracting

11.108 The majority of construction contracts are drawn up in accordance with the model of a general construction contract. The customer concludes a contract with the general contractor, which does not undertake to perform the works using its own resources and is entitled to involve third parties (subcontractors) in the performance of work. Subcontractors are involved through independent construction contracts. The doctrine and judicial practice proceed on the basis that the system of general construction contracts lacks components of an agency agreement (e.g., commission contract). General construction contracts and subcontractor construction contracts are independent construction contracts. In this context, the general contractor performs two functions: For the customer, it acts as the general contractor, and for the subcontractor, it acts as the customer. Furthermore, by virtue of express reference by the statute,[113] the general contractor is responsible for the performance of obligations by the subcontractor to the customer and vice versa. The general rule is that the subcontractor has no rights to raise claims against the customer and the customer may not raise claims against the subcontractor. There is an exception to this rule. If so provided for in both the general construction contract and subcontractor construction contract, the customer is entitled to raise claims directly against the subcontractor and vice versa. It begs the question of interrelation between general construction contract and the commission contract. However, such instances are extremely rare, since the customer is considered to be interested in having a single debtor and creditor represented by the general contractor. At the same time, the customer is

111 For example, decision of the RF SC dated 22.01.2015, No. 306-ES13-1977.
112 Art. 1, Cl. 22, UDC.
113 Art. 706, RCC.

mostly not involved in the selection of subcontractors. General contractors select them independently.

11.109 So-called "double", "triple", etc., subcontracts amplify the contractual relations structure. The essence of this model is as follows. The subcontractor is not obliged to perform the works using its own resources and involves subcontractors (second-level subcontractors). Thus, a "double" subcontract is formed. In turn, second-level subcontractors involve third-level subcontractors, thus forming a "triple" subcontract, etc. Such amplification of the structure results in multiplied of the general construction contracts with customers, general contractors, and subcontractors available at different levels. Still, the foundation of the general construction contract system is preserved.

11.110 Two peculiar problems in subcontracts should be noted. The first one is of a general nature and is confined to the following. In considering a dispute involving a subcontractor, should the court only judge from the conditions of the contract concluded with the latter, or should it assess the overall system of contracts concluded in pursuance of the customer's order? In general, judicial practice tends to use the second approach. For example, if there is a dispute between the general contractor and the subcontractor regarding the quality of works performed by the latter, relations between the general contractor and the customer are taken into account as well. For instance, if the customer accepts such work as is, the general contractor will be unable to lodge any subsequent claim against the subcontractor concerning the quality of such work.

11.111 The second problem is as follows: In a great number of subcontracts, payment for the works performed by the subcontractor and accepted by the general contractor is conditional on the works acceptance by the customer or on the receipt of funds from the customer by the general contractor. Courts consistently declare such conditions invalid. At the same time, they rightly judge from the premise that such conditions alter the binding regime of the general construction contract system. The general contractor is to bear the risk of non-payment by the customer, as well as the risk of non-acceptance of the relevant works by the latter.[114]

Unforeseeable Physical Conditions

11.112 Some unforeseeable physical conditions are classified as *Force Majeure*. By virtue of Cl. 3, Art. 401, RCC, *Force Majeure* shall include extraordinary events that could not have been prevented in the circumstances. The contractor is not liable for the occurrence of such events. In judicial practice, instances of *Force Majeure* occurrence are very rare. Russian law distinguishes between *Force Majeure* events and events, though unavoidable in the circumstances, which a party could have and should have foreseen. Essentially, we are talking about a haphazard (casus). The risk of accidental destruction of, or damage to, the relevant construction object is borne by the contractor.[115] Here is an example of a construction object destruction due to the event, for which the contractor is liable. The parties concluded a construction contract for a riverside wharf. During the construction, due to the river overflow, the construction object was destroyed. If river overflows are not common for this area and are classified as extraordinary and unforeseeable events, we

114 Cl. 9 of Information Letter of the RF SAC Presidium dated 20 January 2000 No. 51.

115 Art. 705 and 741, RCC.

deal with *Force Majeure*, which releases the contractor from liability. However, in this case, it was commonly known that the river floods the nearby lands from time to time, of which the contractor was aware or should have been aware. That is why the court held the contractor liable for the construction object destruction.[116] In other words, the contractor should have taken measures to prevent damage to the construction object that could be caused by a possible river overflow. If the project submitted by the customer did not cover the relevant works, the contractor should have suspended the work and warned the customer about the necessity to perform additional works to protect the construction object.[117] In response, the customer had to either agree with the contractor, or to repudiate the contract and compensate the contractor for damages. If such obligation has been performed, the contractor will be released from liability; otherwise, the contractor will be held fully liable for the destruction.

11.113 At the same time, the customer is liable for a number of unforeseeable physical conditions. We are talking about unforeseeable ground conditions. By virtue of Art. 747 of the RCC, the customer holds the right to the land plot to be developed and transfers the actual lawful possession of such land plot to the contractor. Furthermore, the land plot must be transferred to the contractor in the condition suitable for the performance of works being the subject matter of the customer's order.[118] Theoretically, before proceeding to both design and construction works, the customer must involve, based on the contract for survey works,[119] a specialist to perform survey works; that is, exploration of the land plot, its geological and other peculiarities to determine initial data for designing the construction object with due regard to potential geological risks. Only the holder of the right to the land plot allowing its development (for example, ownership or lease) may conclude such a contract. The failure to take measures on the exploration of the land plot peculiarities is the customer's risk. However, this risk is confined to the provisions of the abovementioned Article 716 of the RCC compelling the contractor to suspend the works and inform the customer if any circumstances threatening the result are discovered. One may call such decision controversial. Currently, the doctrine is in search of a more justified arrangement for allocation of risks between the parties.

Materials and Workmanship

11.114 The work is generally performed using the contractor's materials, resources and means. Furthermore, the contractor is liable for improper quality of materials and equipment provided by it, as well as for the provision of materials and equipment encumbered with third party rights.[120]

11.115 The contract may stipulate that the customer is to provide part of materials or equipment. In such case, the customer is responsible for the proper quality of such materials and equipment, but this responsibility is confined to the abovementioned provisions

---

116 Cl. 18 of Information letter of the RF SAC Presidium dated 20 January 2000 No. 51.

117 Art. 716, RCC.

118 Art. 747, Cl. 1, RCC specifies: "The area and condition of the land plot provided shall correspond to the terms and conditions contained in the construction contract; and in the absence of such terms and conditions, it shall ensure the timely commencement, normal performance and timely completion of works".

119 Paragraph 4, Chapter 37, RCC.

120 Art. 704, RCC.

of Art. 716 of the RCC assigning the risk of the failure to discover relevant defects to the contractor.

11.116 In the Russian Federation, construction is carried out based on design documentation, with respect to which a positive expert opinion was received, subject to the construction permit issued by public authorities.[121] The availability of the construction permit means that the government guarantees that if the construction project is properly implemented, the construction object will comply with all quality requirements. That said, under Art. 754 of the RCC, the contractor is liable to the customer for any deviations from the requirements stipulated by the technical documentation and mandatory technical standards and regulations, as well as for the failure to achieve the construction characteristics contained in technical documentation; for example, plant capacity. During reconstruction (alteration, renewal) of an immovable property object, the contractor is liable for the reduction in or loss of strength, stability or reliability of the construction object or any part thereof. However, the contractor is not liable for minor deviations made without the customer's consent, if the contractor proves that they did not affect the quality of the construction object.

11.117 Improper quality of works (e.g., substantial violations of the technical standards and regulations committed by the contractor) entails classifying the construction object as an unauthorized construction and, therefore, subject to demolition.[122] If the quality of works performed, for which the contractor is responsible, is poor, the customer is entitled to demand, at its own discretion, that the contractor proportionally cut the price, eliminate the defects free of charge, or compensate for the customer's expenses for elimination of such defects, if the contract provides for such right of the customer.[123] Furthermore, if the contractor fails to eliminate the defects within a reasonable period at the customer's request, or if such defects are substantial and non-recoverable, the customer is entitled to repudiate the contract and claim damages. The latter right is normally exercised if the construction object is classified as an unauthorized construction.

11.118 The contractor shall be liable for defects revealed within the warranty period, unless the contractor proves that they occurred due to normal wear and tear of the construction object or any part thereof, its improper operation, incorrect instructions elaborated by the customer, or improper quality of construction object repairs performed by the customer.[124]

11.119 The maximum warranty period is five years.[125] However, the warranty period may be extended by mutual agreement of the parties.

Labour Law Considerations

11.120 In Russia, there is a clear distinction between civil law contracts and labour contracts. Civil law contracts are concluded between equal civil turnover participants. The principles of freedom of disposition, autonomy of will and freedom of contract are fully

121 Art. 47-55, UDC establish exactly the same procedure for construction.
122 Art. 222, RCC.
123 Art. 723, RCC.
124 Art. 755, RCC.
125 Art. 755, 756, RCC.

operational here.[126] Labor contracts are concluded between an employee and an employer. The operation of the mentioned principles in labour law is restricted; an intricate system of guarantees of employee's rights is envisaged. In the construction sector, the parties legalize their relations through civil law contracts, the main one being the construction contract. The customer and the contractor are independent legal entities. These legal persons and their employees mostly legalize their relations through labour contracts. It is also necessary to note that concluding a civil law contract is more advantageous judging from the tax legislation provisions. In Russia, labour law is excluded from construction law.

Performance and Taking-Over

11.121 In accordance with Art. 702 of the RCC, the contractor shall deliver to the customer the result of works performed at the customer's order. The work result may be final or interim (referring to the work result for a specific work stage determined by the parties). Acceptance of the works performed is always formalized by an acceptance certificate, which often has a recommended standardized form in Russia. It is recommended to use the corresponding form of certificates (e.g., KS-2, KS-3, KS-11, and KS14) for accounting and taxation reasons. In legal terms, the certificate may be executed in any other form.

11.122 While performing the contract, the parties sign hundreds of acceptance certificates. Does it mean that signing any certificate signifies acceptance? No, it does not. In accordance with judicial practice,[127] only the following certificates signify acceptance: Final acceptance certificate, interim acceptance certificate for a specific work stage determined by the parties, acceptance certificate for other works, which the parties treat as the acceptance certificate (e.g., an acceptance certificate for specific works on critical structure erection). Other certificates, often signed on a monthly basis or every ten days, do not signify acceptance and are methods to settle accounts between the parties. For example, during one month, the contractor completed 5% of the total scope of work and 5% of the total contract price are payable to it. In practice, it is not easy to determine which certificate the court deals with: The acceptance certificate or the settlement certificate.[128] To determine the significance of the certificate, it is necessary to compare the work indicated in such certificate with the technical documentation and contractual conditions. Recognizing a certificate as an acceptance certificate comes down to three consequences. First, the customer, having signed the acceptance certificate as is, has no right to subsequently refer to poor quality or deficiency of work, which the customer could have identified during the acceptance procedure using the method specified in the contract. In other words, after the customer has signed the acceptance certificate as is, the contractor shall only be responsible for latent defects in its work.[129] Second, the signing of the acceptance certificate signifies the transfer of the risk of accidental destruction of accepted works

126 Art. 1, RCC determines these principles of civil law.

127 IL. RF SAC No. 51.

128 The RF SAC Presidium specified: "Certificates, to which the plaintiff is referring, only confirm the completion of intermittent works for the purpose making calculations. They are not certificates of preliminary acceptance of the result of a specific work stage". (Cl. 18 of Information Letter of the RF SAC Presidium dated 20 January 2000 No. 51).

129 General Rule of the RCC states that:

"The Customer shall be entitled, within the time limit and in the procedure provided by the contract of work, to inspect and accept the work performed (its result) with the contractor's participation, and if any

from the contractor to the customer (this rule is discretionary).[130] Third, the signing of the acceptance certificate creates the obligation to pay for the accepted works.[131]

11.123 The customer may sign the acceptance certificate as is. However, it may also put forward comments to the certificate without refusing acceptance in general. For example, the customer has comments about quality of individual works submitted for acceptance. In such case, no obligation to pay for the works being challenged accrue to the customer. It results in one of the two consequences. The contractor may agree with the defects and the customer's demand with respect to poor quality identified (see section *Materials and Workmanship*). However, the contractor may elect not to agree with the customer's opinion and file a legal claim for the recovery of debt for the works performed being challenged by the customer; in such case, the burden of proving the compliance of the works with the quality requirements lies with the contractor.

11.124 The customer is vested with the right[132] to refuse acceptance of works if the contractor commits a substantial violation of technical documentation requirements, which makes the result unsuitable for use. In such case, the customer repudiates the contract and claims damages.

11.125 There are multiple instances when customers refuse to accept works performed by the contractor for no reason. In such case, the statute[133] entitles the contractor to execute the certificate unilaterally, and such certificate becomes effective as if it were a bilateral one, if it is proved that the customer was properly informed about the readiness of works for acceptance, but failed to accept them or to provide reasons for refusal of such acceptance. The statute indicates that such unilateral certificate may be recognized invalid. In accordance with judicial practice, it signifies the transfer of the burden of proof from the contractor to the customer. As discussed above, if the customer has reasons for signing the certificate with reservations, or for refusing to sign the certificate, the contractor is entitled to prove in court the erroneousness of customer's reasons. A unilateral certificate implies that the works submitted for acceptance were performed in accordance with the contractual requirements. The customer (defendant in the lawsuit on debt collection) is

---

deviations from the contract deteriorating the work result or any other defects in work are revealed, to immediately report this to the contractor.

2. Upon revealing defects in the work during its acceptance, the Customer shall have the right to refer to them, if such defects or the possibility of a subsequent request to eliminate them were specified in the certificate or any other documents proving the acceptance.

3. Except as otherwise provided by the contract of work, the customer that accepted the work without inspection, shall lose the right to refer to the defects in the work, which could have been revealed during the regular procedure of its acceptance (apparent defects).

4. If after the acceptance the customer reveals deviations from the contract of work or any other defects, which could not have been identified during the regular procedure of acceptance (latent defects), including those intentionally hidden by the contractor, the customer shall inform the contractor to that effect within a reasonable period of time following the reveal thereof". (Art. 720, RCC).

130 Art. 753, Cl. 3, RCC.

131 That is exactly what the RF SAC (Cl. 18 of Information Letter of the RF SAC Presidium dated 20 January 2000 No. 51) specified. Meanwhile, this stand appears to be inaccurate. The delivery of work does not give rise to the obligation to pay, but makes the obligation to pay enforceable. Such approach fully corresponds to the construction contract's classification as a consensual contract, in which all rights and obligations arise upon entering into the contract.

132 Art. 720, RCC.

133 Art. 753, RCC.

entitled to overcome this presumption.[134] Practice has shown that in most cases, it is the contractors who win such disputes.

11.126 Lately, there have been ample discussions as to attaching to the acceptance certificate the significance of a transaction (declaration of will at law). Under such understanding, the acceptance certificate may be classified as an agreement for amendment of contract conditions. For example, the contract sets a fixed budget of 100 Rubles; the acceptance certificate is signed for 120 Rubles; the fixed budget has not been altered in the procedure prescribed by the statute. The court may consider that by signing the acceptance certificate for the amount exceeding the one specified in the contract, the parties concluded an agreement on price increase. Such approach is attributed to uncritical and inaccurate perception by Russian judicial practice of individual components of the German concept of *Verfügungsgeschäft*. Such judicial practice gives rise to fair criticism. In actual practice, the mere signing of the acceptance certificate does not mean making a transaction and focusing will on relevant consequences (in the example provided – on the price increase). It means that, having signed the acceptance certificate for 120 Rubles, the customer does not express his will to amend contractual conditions, but states that the performance of works costed 120 Rubles to the contractor; however, it does not entail the increase in the fixed price, which can be increased in accordance with the binding procedure provided by the statute. Currently, judicial practice on this issue is in chaos.[135]

Contract Price and Payment

11.127 As discussed above, pursuant to judicial practice, the price is not an essential condition of a construction contract. In the absence of a contract price, it is determined by court based on the cost of similar works under comparable circumstances. To determine the price, the court generally commissions an expert assessment of the works performed. Meanwhile, by virtue of Art. 743 of the RCC, the contractor undertakes to perform the work in accordance with the *smeta*, which determines its cost. It follows that the legislator nevertheless relies on the need to agree upon not only the price, but also the *smeta* as a method of its calculation. In most contracts, the parties agree upon the price, since such an agreement would meet the interests of both the contractor and the customer. In accordance with Art. 709 of the RCC, the work price (*smeta*) may be approximate or fixed. Unless otherwise indicated in the contract of work, the price is fixed. The peculiarity of the fixed price is that the contractor is not entitled to demand its increase, and the customer – its reduction, including, inter alia, if at the time of concluding the contract of work, it was impossible to provide for the complete scope of work to be performed, or expenses required for that. The contractor has the right to demand an increase in the fixed

134 Cl. 14 of Information Letter of the RF SAC Presidium dated 20 January 2000 No. 51.

135 See: Cl. 18 of Information Letter of the RF SAC Presidium dated 20 January 2000 No. 51 (against the transactional nature of performance under the contract of work), Cl. 7 of Information Letter of the RF SAC Presidium dated 25 February 2014 No. 165 (for the transactional nature of performance under the contract of work). In the latter case, the RF SAC Presidium indicated: "The delivery of the work result by the person, which performed the work in the absence of a contract of work and its acceptance by the person, for which such work was performed, shall mean a conclusion of an agreement between the parties. Obligations arising from such agreement shall be equivalent to obligations arising from the contract of work performed by the contractor. In such case, the obligations to pay for the work and to ensure its quality arise between the parties after the work has been performed, just like if the parties have originally had a contract of work concluded between them".

price only in the event of a substantial increase in the cost of materials and equipment provided by the contractor, as well as of services provided to it by third parties, which could not have been foreseen at the time of entering into the contract. Should the customer reject the demand for the fixed price increase, the contractor is entitled to demand contract termination due to an essential change in the circumstances.

11.128 If the parties have agreed upon the approximate *smeta* and the need for any additional works and, hence, for a considerable increase in the price arises, the contractor must timely inform the customer to that effect. The customer has the right not to agree with such increase and repudiate the contract. In such case, the contractor has the right to demand that the customer pay the price for the scope of work performed. However, if the contractor fails to timely inform the customer of the need to exceed the approximate price, the contractor shall be obliged to perform the contract at the originally determined price. The RCC provides for the rules concerning contractor's savings. For example, in particular, by virtue of Art. 710 of the RCC, if contractor's actual costs turn out to be less than those estimated when determining the work price, the contractor reserves the right to be paid for the work at the price originally specified the contract, unless the customer proves that savings obtained by the contractor have affected the quality of the work performed. This is a discretionary rule.

11.129 The general rule on the procedure for payment for work specifies that the payment for work is effected after the final delivery of its results, provided that the work has been performed properly and within the agreed time limit. However, this rule is also discretionary. Construction contracts generally provide for the customer's advance payment to the contractor. It is important to note that one exception to the general rule is that the contractor is entitled to claim advance payment in court, should the contract grant him such right. Still, the general rule[136] is that the party that failed to start the performance of its obligation is not entitled to claim advance payment in court. This is due to a specific understanding by the Russian legislator of the synallagmatic relation in contracts. Besides the advance payment, the majority of construction contracts provide for the consecutive performance of works and payment therefor. For example, the parties agree upon the need to sign acceptance certificates on a monthly basis. Such acceptance certificates are not acceptance certificates in their proper sense, but they signify that the contractor has completed a certain percentage of the overall scope of work over the relevant month and demands payment of the proportionate share of the total price. However, signing such certificates does not exclude the final settlement of accounts between the parties by work stage (if distinguished) and/or after the final delivery of the result by the contractor.

11.130 In legal and technical terms, while approving the fixed or approximate *smeta*, the parties always indicate the total cost of works. Taking into account the long-term nature of the construction contract, against the background of ever-changing economic situation and weather conditions, such initial price-fixing cannot withstand the test of time. That is why in construction contracts, the parties often agree upon the application of various cost increase indices (seasonal, regional, etc.) to the established fixed price. In Russia, drawing up a *smeta* is not a legal job. Dedicated specialists – budget officers – who draw up and agree upon *smetas*.

---

136 Art. 328, RCC.

11.131 Practice examination results show that most disputes concerning the price derive from the scope of work performed. In particular, any additional works performed by the contractor, both initiated by the latter or by the customer, result in a price increase.

11.132 Resulting from the stand of judicial practice that considers the price to be a non-essential condition of the contract, the nature of consideration provided by the customer for the work performed by the contractor had long not been deemed essential for the status of the contract.[137] For example, a contract was recognized to be a construction contract, if by virtue of it the contractor undertakes to perform certain work (for example, apartment house construction), and the customer undertakes to transfer a certain amount of apartments in the new house, rather than a certain amount of money. Such approach was recognized as erroneous by Resolution of the Plenum of the Supreme Arbitration Court of the Russian Federation No. 54, which classified such contract as mixed; that is, containing components of both a construction contract (in terms of the work performed) and a sales contract for a future immovable thing (in terms of the obligation to transfer future apartments).[138] Such approach, in turn, has peremptorily posed a question of correlation between such type of a mixed contract and a simple partnership agreement, which implies a completely different civil law regime and approach to risk allocation among the parties. Currently, judicial practice proceeds on the basis that it is the presence or absence of a shared objective for the parties that distinguishes between these contracts. The presence of a shared objective signifies that the parties have concluded a simple partnership agreement.[139] For this purpose, the court determines if such objective is present or absent based on the presence or absence of cross-obligations of the parties (the absence of cross obligations points to simple partnership agreements) and grounds for acquisition by the 'contractor' of title to future apartments. The initial acquisition is indicative of a simple partnership agreement.

Defects Liability

11.133 The contractor is liable for the quality of works performed. This liability may be characterized as extremely strict (see above). The party that provided the materials shall generally be liable for the quality of the materials provided for the performance of the contract. At the same time, when the materials are supplied by the customer, the contractor bears the risk of the failure to discover defects (see above for the application of Art. 716 of the RCC). Liability for design documentation defects was discussed in the relevant section.

Limitation of Liability

11.134 The RCC contains general rules concerning permissibility of concluding agreements for limitation of liability, as well as special rules on the limitation of liability in relation to construction contracts. In general, to assess the legislation and judicial practice on this issue, it should be noted that they are quite cautious about such types of agreements if concluded in advance. In this context, their validity is considered through the lens of

137 Cl. 11 of Information Letter of the RF SAC Presidium No. 51.

138 Cl. 6 of Resolution of the RF SAC Plenum dated 11 July 2011 No. 54.

139 Cl. 7 of Resolution of the RF SAC Plenum dated 11 July 2011 No. 54.

compliance with the principle of good faith. At the same time, it is possible to conclude an agreement for limitation of liability, which has already occurred due to the debtor's failure to perform or properly perform its obligation. In such case, agreements for limitation of liability no longer receive special attention from the legislator and are considered as forgiving part of the debt. For example, a penalty of 1,000,000 Rubles is charged for the violation of an obligation; upon mutual agreement of the parties, the penalty amount is reduced to 500,000 Rubles. Such agreement is classified as an agreement for forgiving part of the debt.[140] Just like for other types of contracts, the presumption of their compensatory nature is in force for such agreements; but if it is proved that the creditor forgave part of the debt for the purposes of gift giving, such agreement will be invalidated, because in Russia, gift giving between commercial organizations is prohibited.[141]

Variations

11.135 In accordance with the general provisions of the RCC, any contract may be amended by mutual agreement of the parties.

11.136 The rules regulating construction contracts provide for only one opportunity to make a unilateral amendment to such contracts. We are talking about the customer's right to unilaterally change the scope of work to be completed for an amount not exceeding 10% of the estimate of the entire contract.[142] In such case, the contractor is entitled to deny additional works only to the extent that such works alter the nature of the works provided for by the construction contract. Amendment to a contract made by the court at the request of either party due to an essential change in the circumstances stands somewhat apart. For example, the court has the right to amend the terms and conditions of the contract if its termination either contradicts public interests, or inflicts losses on the parties that considerably exceed the expenses required for the performance of the contract on the conditions as amended by the court.[143] However, to do so, it is necessary to establish the presence of essential changes in circumstances, for which it is required to meet four conditions at the same time. First, at the time of entering into the contract, the parties proceeded from the premise that no such change in the circumstances would take place. Second, changes in the circumstances occurred for the reasons, which the interested party was unable to overcome after they had arisen while displaying the degree of care and diligence expected from it according to the nature of the contract and conditions of civil turnover. Third, the performance of the contract without amending its provisions would largely upset the balance of property interests of the parties to the contract and would inflict extensive damage on the interested party, such that the party would have been to a considerable extent deprived of what it could have counted upon when concluding the contract. Fourth, neither from the customs of the business turnover, nor from the substance of the contract does it follow that the risk of a change in the circumstances shall be borne by the interested party.

140 Art. 415, RCC.

141 Art. 575, RCC; Cl. 3 of Information Letter of the RF SAC Presidium dated 21 December 2005 No. 104.

142 Art. 744, RCC.

143 Art. 451, RCC.

Delay and Disruption

11.137 A delay in the performance of an obligation may be committed by both the contractor and the customer. The contractor is strictly liable for the violation of both intermediary and final deadlines for work performance. The contractor is liable for both its own actions and actions of third parties (for example, subcontractors and suppliers) that caused such delay. Moreover, the contractor bears the risk of accidental destruction of, or damage to the work result, as well as the risk of the failure to discover the circumstances, which are beyond its control, but may impede the timely completion of work.[144] Such circumstances include unsuitability of, or the defects in, the customer's order, third party actions, and any other circumstances. The contractor is also liable for the delay caused by accidental destruction of, or damage to the work result.

11.138 However, there is a number of grounds for relieving the contractor from liability for the delay. These are instances when the work is suspended by the customer, or due to the discovery of circumstances threatening the work result or timely achievement thereof (see above). The contractor is also relieved from liability for the delay if the delay results from the customer's failure to perform its counter obligations, which makes it impossible to start or continue the works.[145] Such obligations include obligations to make an advance payment, and to provide technical documentation, materials and equipment.

11.139 Both the contractor and the customer are held liable for the delay (see above).

Liquidated Damages and Other Damages

11.140 The Russian doctrine and judicial practice do not use the concept of "liquidated damages". However, in Russian law, one may find a kind of an analogue of liquidated damages. We are talking about an exclusive penalty; that is, a penalty, which, if charged, excludes damages. The general rule involves the principle of penalty set-off; that is, the penalty initially determined by the contract does not exclude damages in the amount not covered by such penalty. Furthermore, the set-off penalty does not exclude claims for specific performance. To make it an analogue of liquidated damages, the contract must provide for not only the exclusive nature of the penalty, but also the condition that charging the penalty excludes any claim for specific performance. In such case, the exclusive penalty becomes some sort of accord and satisfaction.[146] However, one rarely comes across such a structure in practice.

11.141 For information about other types of damages, please see above.

Insurance

11.142 The RCC enables providing for insurance as part of a construction contract. For example, in accordance with Art. 742 of the RCC, a construction contract may stipulate the obligation of the party either bearing the risk of accidental destruction of, or damage to, the construction object, materials, equipment, or any other property used during the construction, or being liable for damage inflicted on other persons in the construction process, to insure the relevant risks.

144 Art. 716, RCC.

145 Art. 719, RCC.

146 Art. 409, RCC. See also decision of the RF SC dated 13.04.2023, No. 306-ES22-18849.

11.143 Thus, the statute allows concluding various types of insurance agreements with various subject matters, if the insuring party has property interest in such insurance. In Russian law, property interest is traditionally understood as the relevant party's interest in not bearing the risk of adverse pecuniary consequences that result from the occurrence certain circumstances (insurance risk).[147]

11.144 Property insurance should be classified as the first type of insurance in the construction sector. The party to a construction contract that bears the risk of accidental destruction of, or damage to, the construction object, materials or equipment is interested in preserving property. The risk of accidental destruction of, or damage to, the construction object is generally borne by the contractor until the work result has been delivered to the customer. The general rule is that, under the property insurance contract, the beneficiary under Russian law is the insuring party itself. The contractor bearing the risk of accidental destruction of the construction object has interest in insurance because, if such risk occurs, the contractor incurs adverse property consequences in the form of rebuilding the destroyed construction object at its own expense, or in the form of paying compensation for damages to the customer. Russian law does not enable the contractor to insure the risk of construction object destruction in customer's favour, because the statute[148] does not allow insurance against liability under the construction contract. Furthermore, the payment of insurance benefit to the customer apparently deprives the latter of the right to file a claim against the contractor, which essentially allows regarding it as insurance against liability under the contract. Such approach may be attributable the fact that the extensive application of contractual liability insurance may result in the lack of insuring party's diligence in obligation performance as a debtor under an obligation. Lately, such position has been criticized in literature. Thus, the contractor may insure its risk of accidental destruction of, or damage to, the construction object in its favour.

11.145 As demonstrated above, the customer as the owner of the construction has interest in insurance, as if the risk occurs, the customer will lose the subject of its right. In the Russian doctrine, the indisputable conclusion is that the owner always has interest in insuring owner's thing, even if the risk of its accidental destruction is assigned to the contractual counterparty. Thus, both the contractor (bearing the risk of accidental destruction of, or damage to, the construction object) and the customer (regardless of bearing the said risks), having the property interest in preserving the construction object, are entitled

147 One may probably find interesting the statutory dedicated to the concept of a property insurance contract:

"1. Under the property insurance contract, if an event stipulated by the contract (ensured event) occurs, one party (the insurer), for the fee stipulated in the contract (insurance premium), shall compensate the other party, in favour of which the contract is concluded (the beneficiary), for damages caused to the ensured property due to such event. or damages related to any other property interests of the insuring party (to pay the insurance benefit) up to the amount stipulated in the contract (amount of coverage).

2. Under the property insurance contract, the following property interests may be insured, in particular:

1) Risk of loss (destruction), shortage of, or damage to certain property (Article 930);

2) Risk of liability under obligations arising due to harm inflicted on other people's life, health, or property, and to the extent provided by the statute, risk of liability under contracts – private liability risk (Articles 931 and 932).

3) risk of losses from entrepreneurship activities due to breach of obligations by entrepreneur's counterparties, or changes in the environment of such activities for reasons beyond entrepreneur's control, including the risk of loss of profit – entrepreneurial risk (Article 933)". (Art. 929, RCC).

148 Art. 932, RCC.

to insure it in their favour. However, in accordance with one of the principles of Russian insurance law, it is impossible to insure an object in excess of its insurable value regardless of the number of insuring parties, each of which has its own interest in the object preservation.[149] It results in the following situation: If the contractor has insured the object for its full value, the customer becomes unable to insure it in its favour. Lately, such approach of Russian insurance law has also been the central point of fierce discussions.[150]

11.146 Insurance of property by both the contractor and the customer against different risks is an isolated instance of insurance. For example, in accordance with the construction contract, the risk of accidental destruction of, or damage to, the construction object is borne by the contractor; however, this risk is transferred to the customer upon signing the acceptance certificate for the specific work stage determined by the parties.[151] In such case, the contractor bearing the risk of accidental destruction with respect to the works performed, but not accepted yet, insures them in its favour for the full value. In the meantime, the customer is entitled to insure the same works, but after they have been accepted. For this purpose, separate insurance agreements may be concluded, but it is also possible to conclude a single contract, which sometimes is documented by a bearer insurance certificate. The person that has insurance interest at the time of occurrence of the insured event shall be the beneficiary under the contract.

11.147 Equipment, materials and other property are insured under similar rules.

11.148 The second type of insurance is insurance against the risk of harm inflicted on third parties by the construction. Such insurance essentially covers the risk of tort liability. By virtue of previously mentioned specific nature of the Russian legislation, not only the contractor, but also the customer may be held liable for harm inflicted on third parties. Consequently, both of them are entitled to have insurance against the risk of harm inflicted on third parties. On this point, one of the most authoritative Russian civil lawyers V.V. Vitryanskiy mentions the following:

11.149

> Upon agreement of the parties, the construction contract may also provide for the contractor's obligation to maintain insurance against the third party liability risk for inflicting damage inflicted during the construction (Art. 742, Cl. 1, RCC). Such insurance is primarily maintained in favour and to the benefit of the persons that may be subject to such damage. The contractor being held liable to the injured person for inflicting harm on the latter, is interested in such insurance because, if such liability is insured against based on the relevant provision of the construction contract, the insuring party's (contractor's) expenses for payment of insurance premiums to the insurance company may be included in the budget of the construction project.
>
> *152*

149 Art. 951, RCC.

150 Such discussions generally take place as part of various conferences and round tables and unfortunately, they are by no means always manifested in competent publications.

151 Art. 753, Cl. 3, RCC.

152 V.V. Vitryanskiy. Construction Contract and Other Contracts in Construction.// Economy and Law. 2005. Attachment No. 7.

Suspension

11.150 One may identify several instances of work suspension. In the first instance, the work is suspended by the contractor due to the circumstances, for which the latter is responsible. In such case, the customer has the right to repudiate the contract and claim damages. This right is conditioned by the following: The contractor has not started the work on time, or has been working so slowly that the work would obviously not be completed on time. In the second instance, the contractor suspends the work having discovered the circumstances, which threaten the suitability of the work result, regardless of whether they are within or beyond its control,[153] which may include defects in the technical documents, etc.[154] Having suspended the work, the contractor shall immediately notify the customer of such circumstances discovered and suggest options for solving the problem, and shall not resume the work until it receives the corresponding notification from the customer. Such notification may involve either the customer's repudiation of the contract, or its agreement to search for the solution to the difficulty faced. Should the circumstances discovered by the contractor indeed threaten the work result or its timely achievement, all losses related to the work suspension shall be borne by the customer. If the contractor was mistaken in assessing the seriousness of the circumstances discovered, it makes the contractor liable for breaching the time limits for work performance. Third, the work may be suspended due to the customer's failure to perform its obligations, which renders the start or continuation of work impossible. In particular, this refers to the customer's failure to provide the contractor with the materials and equipment, which the customer must supply.[155] This is a remedy to protect contractor's rights and interests, as in such case, all negative consequences of work suspension are within the customer's pecuniary domain. Moreover, if the customer fails to perform its obligations, the contractor is granted the right to repudiate the contract and claim damages.

11.151 Besides, by their mutual agreement, the parties may provide for the contractor's obligation to suspend the work at the customer's initiative. In such case, such suspension would apparently be charged to the customer's account. Work suspension may also be caused by *Force Majeure*. In such case, the suspension will be charged to the customer's account (conventionally, the contractor is not liable for *Force Majeure*).[156]

11.152 It is also necessary to point out that work suspension may entail the need to lay up the construction object. Such laying-up is carried out at the expense of the party that incurs the adverse consequences of work suspension in a given instance, and if the work suspension is caused by *Force Majeure*, the expenses for laying-up are borne by the customer.[157]

Termination

11.153 In accordance with general provisions of the RCC, any contract may be terminated by mutual agreement of the parties. For this purpose, the parties determine the consequences of such termination at their own discretion. However, the statute or the contract

153 Art. 716, RCC.
154 See Art. 716, RCC.
155 Art. 719, RCC.
156 Art. 752, RCC.
157 Art. 752, RCC.

may provide for unilateral contract termination (repudiation of the contract). With regard to construction contracts, the RCC specifies a considerable number of circumstances, which allow unilateral repudiation of the contract both by the contractor and the customer (for more details, see above). Instances of contract termination due to essential changes in the circumstances (for more details, see the Variations section) stand somewhat apart.

Forms of Security – Bonds and Guarantees

11.154 Accessory suretyship and independent guarantees are the primary ways to secure obligations under construction contracts. In Russia, an accessory suretyship is referred to accessory methods of providing security for a party's obligations. The surety's obligations arise from the contract concluded between the creditor and the surety. The surety in surety obligation mostly vouches for the debtor at the latter's request. Such request may be based on fiduciary relationships, the debtor and the surety being members of the same holding structure, but in most instances, it is a fee-based surety contract that underlies the relations between the debtor and the surety. The surety's obligation is of an independent nature, but the debtor and surety are generally held jointly liable. In this respect, Russian accessory suretyship is described as joint in terms of liability, which is always monetary, rather than in terms of debt. The amount of such liability equals to the amount of debtor's liability for the failure to perform or properly perform its obligation. However, the surety also independently liable for the delay in performance of its obligation to be held liable for the debtor. The surety is entitled to object creditor's claims using the same objections as the debtor does. It is important to note that, as a result of the RCC reform, this rule has become mandatory. Russian civil law does not provide for non-accessory suretyship. The performance of its obligation by the surety entails the transfer to the latter of the creditor's claim against the debtor, which was secured by the surety contract (subrogation). Accessory suretyship is regulated by paragraph 5, Chapter 23 of the RCC.[158]

11.155 Still, in the construction sector, independent guarantees are a more common method of providing security for a party's obligations.[159] Under an independent guarantee as specified in Art. 368 of the RCC, the guarantor undertakes, at the request of another person (principal) to pay to the third party (beneficiary) indicated by the principal a certain amount in accordance with the terms of the undertaking given by the guarantor, regardless of the validity of the obligation secured by such guarantee. By its legal nature, an independent guarantee is a unilateral transaction. Independency from the obligation it secures constitutes the key advantage of an independent guarantee. In this area, Russian law has been greatly affected by *lex mercatoria*, in particular, the rules for independent guarantees of the International Chamber of Commerce in Paris (issue No. 458). Independency of such a guarantee manifests in not only the absence of any connection between the validity of the obligation it secures and the obligation of the guarantor himself. The main distinctive feature of an independent guarantee under Russian law is that no circumstances associated with relations between the debtor and the creditor (e.g., guarantor's objections that it is aware of debtor's proper performance of its obligation)

158 The foregoing in terms of accessory suretyship is fully confirmed by judicial practice – see Resolution of the RF SAC Plenum dated 12 July 2012. No. 42.

159 Paragraph 5, Chapter 23, RCC

may serve as grounds for refusal to pay under the independent guarantee. At first glance, it may seem that operation of the guarantee independency principle may result in the creditor receiving double performance. In this respect, judicial practice had long considered it inadmissible to satisfy the beneficiary's claim against the guarantor in defiance of guarantor's objections associated with relations between the beneficiary and the principal. A reference to the beneficiary's unfair practices served as grounds for such refusal. However, in recent years, the RF SAC has developed practice aimed at strict observance of the guarantee independency principle. The doctrine and judicial practice have acknowledged that the guarantee independency principle turns the guarantee into a quick method of providing security for a party's obligations, and the essence of the guarantee is revealed by the phrase "pay, then argue", since afterwards, having paid (unfairly, in the guarantor's opinion) to the creditor the amount due, the guarantor is entitled to file a relevant claim against the creditor or the debtor. During the relevant trial, the payment reasonableness will be considered in the most careful manner. However, the consideration of all peculiarities of relations between the debtor and the creditor, reasonableness of guarantor's objections against creditor's claims will only prolong the trial, thus resulting in the loss of the main independent guarantee's advantage – quick obtaining of security.[160]

11.156 In almost every construction contract, the parties provide for a non-defined way to secure obligations, such as guaranteed retention, which was discussed above.

11.157 Pledges and retention are not common in the construction sector.

Claims

11.158 One peculiarity of Russian law is the so-called pre-court dispute settlement procedure. It provides that the pre-condition for filing claims with the court is sending a complaint to the debtor, which describes the essence of and grounds for the claim, as well as the request to meet the claim on a voluntary basis. The statute prescribes the obligation to observe the pre-court dispute settlement procedure on very rare occasions. There is no relevant statutory reference applicable to construction contracts. However, the parties often include the obligation to observe the pre-court dispute settlement procedure in their

160 For example, in its Resolution dated 02.10.12 No. 6040/12, the RF SAC Presidium defined the below legal stance:

"*From the principle of independency of a bank guarantee enshrined in Clause 'b' of Article 2 of the Uniform Rules and Article 370 of the Code, as well as the provisions of Clause 2 of Article 376 of the Code compelling the guarantor to satisfy the duplicative claim raised by the beneficiary, even if it is aware that the principal obligation, in full or in the relevant part, has been performed, terminated on other grounds, or become invalid, it follows that objections raised by the bank, based on the assessment of the circumstances around the performance of the principal obligation may not be viewed as a good reason for a refusal to pay.*

The rule requiring indication of the fact and nature of violation of the obligation in the claim submitted by the beneficiary, as specified in Article 20 of the Uniform Rules and Article 374 of the Code, does not impose the obligation to verify such fact on the guarantor. This rule allows the guarantor to determine on its face whether the claim for payment was submitted with respect to the very violation committed by the principal, for which the guarantor undertook to be liable to the beneficiary ...

Under the guarantee, the beneficiary's property interest lies in the possibility to obtain the performance as quickly as possible, without fearing debtor's objections, where the creditor assumes that the due time or any other circumstances with respect to the obligation, for which the creditor gained security, have occurred. Only the circumstances related to the failure to observe the conditions of the guarantee itself may serve as grounds for dismissal of beneficiary's claims".

contracts, which is, most likely, a nod to the Soviet practice. As for other claims, which are usually filed with the court, we have described them in detail above.

Time-Bar Provisions

11.159 The Russian law prescribes the general term of limitation of actions to be three years.[161] The term of limitation is generally calculated from the time when a person learned or should have learned about the violation of such person's rights.[162] Stipulating a so-called objective term of limitation, which may not exceed ten years from the day, on which the right protected by such time bar was violated, is an important novelty in the RCC.[163] In this area, Russian law happened to be influenced by informal codifications of European law of contracts and, in particular, PECL. The practicality of introducing such time bar causes doubts among the professional community.

11.160 Alongside the general term of limitation, special terms of limitation are set. A special term of limitation is particularly set for contracts of work. The term of limitation for claims raised due to the improper quality of work performed under a contract of work, is one year from the date of general acceptance of the work result.[164] However, in relation to buildings and structures as the work result, the general term of limitation is preserved. It is important to stress that, in establishing the warranty period prescribed by law for the work result under construction contracts (see above), the term of limitation starts from the date of complaint about defects.

11.161 One must distinguish between the term of limitation and the term for discovering the improper quality of work. The general rule[165] is that the customer is entitled to file claims related to the defects in the work result discovered within the warranty period.

Disputes – Adjudication and Arbitration

11.162 The majority of disputes between contractors and customers are tried in state courts, and those related to business practice – in commercial courts (state arbitration courts), which have jurisdiction over disputes arising from business legal relations.

11.163 At the same time, arbitration clauses, by which the parties provide for referring disputes to arbitration institutions, become increasingly popular. Usually named as advantages of arbitration proceedings are shorter hearing periods as compared to those in state courts, higher professionalism of arbitrators and high degree of privacy in hearing cases. Indeed, excessive load on judges in state courts does not always allow them dedicating enough time to complicated disputes, which, in entrepreneurs' opinion, often has an adverse effect on the quality of court proceedings and well-foundedness of judicial acts. Load on an arbitrator is incommensurable to that on a state judge, and besides, arbitrators are generally well-known specialists in the professional community having positive reputation. The composition of an arbitral tribunal is determined by the parties themselves: They select arbitrators from the arbitrator list of a specific arbitral institution.

161 Art. 196, RCC.
162 Art. 200, RCC.
163 Art. 196, cl. 2, RCC.
164 Art. 725, RCC.
165 Art. 724, RCC.

If the parties do not exercise this right, an arbitrator(s) is (are) appointed from the relevant list by such arbitral institution itself.[166]

11.164 An arbitral award is final, unless otherwise provided by the parties in the arbitration agreement. This rule means that the award delivered by the arbitral tribunal may not be challenged on the merits in state courts. The only control measure exercised by state courts over arbitral awards, which are conclusive, is that they consider cases involving enforcement of such awards. Furthermore, refusals to enforce an arbitral award are limited in scope. In principle, grounds for refusal to enforce an arbitral award are as follows: The arbitral tribunal commits a gross violation of the established procedure (e.g., the case was considered by an improper panel of arbitrators); the arbitral award violates the fundamental principles of Russian law; the award was delivered in violation of arbitral tribunal's competence.[167]

11.165 The International Commercial Arbitration Court at the Chamber of Commerce and Industry of the Russian Federation is the oldest arbitral institution in Russia, which was created back in the Soviet era. This arbitral institution considers cases involving a foreign element in accordance with the special statute. Internal arbitral procedures are carried out by multiple arbitral panels that can be divided into two groups. First, these are arbitral tribunals created by large Russian legal entities (e.g., Gazprom PJSC, Rosatom State Atomic Energy Corporation, and some others). Second, unfortunately, in Russia, a great number of so-called "puppet" arbitral tribunals were created, which often violated the principles of justice. It resulted in the need to set forth the legal stance at the level of RF SAC judicial interpretation that virtually excluded the enforcement of awards of the majority of arbitral tribunals in Russia, including those, the fairness of which raised no doubts, mainly due to the authority and reputation of their arbitrators (e.g., arbitral tribunal of Rosatom, Gazprom, and some other legal entities).[168] Subsequently, the Constitutional Court of the Russian Federation took their stand.[169] In their legal opinion,

> the current legal regulation does not provide grounds to conclude on the impossibility to refer to a permanent arbitral tribunal founded under an independent non-profit organization a dispute under civil law, one of the parties to which is the founder of such independent non-profit organization.
>
> *(Cl. 3.2)*

Furthermore,

> independence of an arbitrator selected (appointed) to the composition of a permanent arbitral tribunal on behalf of the organization that founded such arbitral tribunal is secured by the prohibition to interfere with tribunal's activities on hearing the dispute and decision-making in the case imposed on bodies, officials and employees of such organization, which is only authorized to approve the rules of procedure for the relevant activities and the list of arbitrators.
>
> *(Cl. 3.1. of the said Resolution)*

Due to the problems identified in judicial practice, the legislator has reformed the laws concerning arbitration in order to secure independence of arbitral tribunals. For example, the new

166 Article 11, Federal Law No. 382-FZ "On Arbitration (Arbitration Proceedings) in the Russian Federation".

167 Article 233, Arbitration Procedural Code of the Russian Federation.

168 E.g., Decision of the RF SAC Presidium No. 8443/13.

169 Resolution dated 18 November 2014 No. 30-P.

2015 Law on Arbitration provides for new requirements to arbitral institutions, tougher control over their activities, while attempting not to interfere with arbitral tribunal's activities. Currently, the accreditation of all arbitral institutions with the Ministry of Justice is underway, as part of which they check the compliance of arbitral institutions with the new statute. So far, it is hard to say what the results of this reform will be. The main point is to liquidate shady arbitral tribunals in the course of the reform, while preventing state dictatorial interference with and control over the activities of arbitral institutions.

Construction Law Issues Specific to Russian (and Central Asia) Law

Federal Legislation Concerning Procedure of Government Contracts Formation

11.166 One Russia's peculiarity is the availability of federal legislation that governs entering into contracts (including construction contracts) for state needs. Its purpose is to ensure efficient spending of budgetary funds, to secure competition in terms of admission to public procurement, and to fight against corruption. In 2015, to improve the efficiency of public procurement, the relevant legislation was reformed, which resulted in the adoption of Federal Law No. 44-FZ "On the Contract System in State and Municipal Procurement of Goods, Works and Services".

11.167 The key provisions of the legislation in question centre on the following.

11.168 The contract system in procurement is based on the principles of openness, transparency of information about the contract system in procurement, competition, customer's professionalism, and encouragement of innovations, unity of the contract system in procurement, liability for the performance in state and municipal procurement, and efficient procurement. This implies a peculiar feature of the public procurement system, in particular, customer's professionalism. Unlike regular relations, the customer must be a professional participant in the sector where the procurement is made (in our situation, the construction sector). To attain these goals, special internal subdivisions for procurement are created at the level of relevant state and municipal bodies, including in the construction sector – so called capital construction departments. Special legal persons with relevant competences in construction are often created to exercise the functions of the public sector customer.

11.169 State supervision over the compliance with the legislation begins at the stage of procurement formation and justification, but the key role in the system of ensuring transparency of public spending is assigned to the control over the procurement procedure itself; that is, the selection of contractors (suppliers). Public procurement is performed either through tendering procedures, or by selecting the single supplier. Furthermore, the statute imposes certain requirements on the procurement parties, the list of which is rather ample. Let us quote the most prominent of them. In particular, legal entities, which have conflicts of interests with the customer, senior executives of which were convicted of economic crimes, or which have taxes and levies in arrears, may not be parties to procurement. Particular emphasis needs to be placed on the rule, in accordance with which offshore companies may not participate in public procurement. This novelty in the new statute is part of the general economy deoffshorization program. At the same time, the rule compelling the respective authorities to engage small enterprises as participants in procurement procedures was introduced, which is intended to support the latter and to prevent excessive participation of major companies in the budget funds allocation.

11.170 Article 24 of the said statute acknowledges the following competitive methods of determining suppliers (contractors, executors): Tenders (open tenders, selective tenders, two-stage tenders, closed competitive tenders, closed selective tenders, closed two-stage tenders), auctions (online auctions (hereinafter – e-auctions), closed auctions), requests for quotations, requests for proposals. For this purpose, "tender" means a method of determining suppliers (contractors, executors), where the winner is the procurement party that offered the best conditions for contract performance, and "auction" means a method of determining suppliers (contractors, executors), where the winner is the procurement party that offered the lowest contract price.

11.171 The statute contains the general rule governing procurement through open tenders, while other competitive procurement procedures or procedures for procurement from the single supplier are only articulated in specific cases. The statute clearly identifies open tender stages and procedures: Tender documentation development, tender announcement publication, filing of bids by interested parties, award of, and entering into a public contract with, the winner. A contract with the single supplier is concluded to the extent strictly defined and under special rules. In particular, these are instances when only one bid is submitted, or the winner refuses from entering into the contract (therefore, the contract is concluded with the runner-up).[170]

11.172 A special procurement system also intended to ensure efficient public spending of on a competitive basis was established in 2011 for certain types of legal entities, in particular, government-owned corporations, state-owned companies, unitary enterprises and some other.[171]

11.173 The practice of application of the abovementioned laws in Russia is rather diverse and extensive. The most acute problems identified through practice in terms of construction contracts concluded in accordance with the said laws are as follows.

11.174 First, such contracts are traditionally classified as contracts of affiliation, since in practice, participant of the tender, for example, cannot influence the contract provisions drafted by the public sector customer. Therefore, as revealed by judicial practice, the contractors that concluded contracts on the terms of the offer (tender documentation containing the draft contract), often refer to unfairness of certain provisions offered by public sector customers, which the contractor as a bidder could not alter. Judicial practice for this category of disputes is controversial. On the one hand, indeed, public sector customers are inclined to specify contract provisions that are only favorable for them, which results in the courts supporting contractors. On the other hand, a dispute generally arises during the implementation of the debatable provision, rather than at the stage of concluding such contracts. This demonstrates the inconsistence of contractor's behavior, which concluded a contract with the unfair (in its opinion) provision, but, nevertheless, proceeded to the implementation thereof. Many people understand such behavior as evidence of Estoppel, a common law doctrine, which was accepted by the Russian legislator as part of the latest reform of the RCC.[172]

170 Article 55 of the Law.

171 Federal Law No. 223-FZ "On Procurement of Goods, Works, and Services by Certain Types of Legal Entities".

172 Art. 166, cl. 5, RCC, 2016.

11.175 Second, in literature and judicial practice, the issue of whether legislation on public procurement excludes the application of specific provisions of the RCC concerning construction contracts to contracts for construction of facilities for state needs is controversial. In particular, one central point in assessing bids is the price for works, which is put up for tender. This raises the question of whether it is admissible to apply, for example, the provisions of the RCC (Art. 743) concerning an increase in the cost of work due to additional works performed by the contractor. An affirmative answer to this question will result in an increased price, which will put the winning contractor at an advantage over other participants of the tender. A negative answer may result in the impossibility to complete the works at the initial price if additional works are required (see above). So far, the Russian law is in search for an optimal solution to this problem.

11.176 The Republic of Kazakhstan has effective legislation governing public procurement.[173] In spite of certain differences, conceptually, this law is very similar to the relevant Russian law. For example, this law is essentially based on the same principles as those underlying the Russian one. These principles particularly include: Optimal and efficient spending of funds used for public procurement; equal opportunities in public procurement procedures for potential suppliers; fair competition among potential suppliers; openness and transparency of public procurement; support to domestic manufacturers and domestic suppliers of works and services to the extent that it does not contradict international treaties ratified by the Republic of Kazakhstan; liability of parties to public procurement; inadmissibility of corrupt practices; acquisition of innovation and hi-tech goods, works and services (Art. 4). The rules governing procurement procedures are also similar. In the Republic of Uzbekistan, the legislation on public procurement is less developed – there is no special statute, and relevant relations are regulated by resolutions of the Cabinet of Ministers.[174] Currently, in Uzbekistan, they actively work on drafting a special law based on the analysis of best world practices in arranging public procurement. The Kyrgyz Republic has lately adopted the Law on Public Procurement (Law dated 03.04.2015 No. 72). The Law governs public procurement relations using the same principles and approaches as applied by the relevant legislation in Russia and Kazakhstan. Among the peculiarities of the Kyrgyz legislation compared with, for instance, the relevant Russian and Kazakhstan laws, it is necessary to point out that in Russia and Kazakhstan, public procurement procedures are elaborated in more detail. Besides, in contrast to Russia, in Kyrgyzstan, the legislation concerning public procurement does not cover procurement directly associated with national defense and security, protection of state secrets, and natural disasters.

Peculiar Features of Construction Law in Certain Central Asian Countries

11.177 Civil Codes of the Republics of Kazakhstan,[175] Uzbekistan,[176] and Kyrgyzstan[177] were developed based on the Model Civil Code of CIS countries (adopted by Interparliamentary Assembly of the CIS Member Nations on 29.10.1994 (General Part)

173 Law of the Republic of Kazakhstan No. 434-V dated 2015 "On Public Procurement".
174 In particular, Resolution No. 397 dated 14 August 1997.
175 Hereinafter RK CC.
176 Hereinafter RU CC.
177 Hereinafter RKz CC.

and 13 May 2005 (Special Part)), which, in turn, is based on the RCC, as noted above. This explains their conceptual similarity and the fact that all these codes use the pandects system and structurally duplicate the RCC system. Moreover, most articles in these codes are textually similar to the revenant articles in the RCC. Yet, one can find certain differences in details of legal regulation and sometimes – in conceptual terms. This refers to both the rules dedicated to contracts of work, especially to construction contracts, and the rules of the common part of law of obligations.

11.178 In particular, the rules concerning construction contracts specify that the contractor is the owner of the incomplete construction until it has been deliver and the works have been paid for;[178] a similar rule is contained in the RU CC.[179] At the same time, both Codes proceed on the basis that the land plot used as a construction site belongs to the customer.[180]

11.179 Thus, the legal regulation suggested by Kazakhstan and Uzbekistan is starkly different from the Russian regulation, under which, as was discussed above, the title to buildings and structures being created on such land plot, is originally vested with the customer, rather than the contractor. What is more, it is considered as one of the essential elements inherent to a construction contract as a type of contract and distinguishing a construction contract from a sales contract for a future thing. Both contracts are akin in the fact that they represent different civil law methods of meeting the same demand – to acquire the title to a construction object, which does not exist yet at the time of concluding the contract. The fundamental difference between contracts under Russian law is seen in grounds for acquisition of title – under a construction contract, the contractor acquires such title on the original grounds, while under a sales contract for a future thing — on the derivative grounds. Consequently, the customer does not bear the risk of contractor's bankruptcy while the buyer does bear the risk of seller's bankruptcy. Taking into account the long-term nature of legal relations on the creation of immovable property objects, this practical difference seems to be quite significant. As it appears from the abovementioned rules, in Kazakhstan and Uzbekistan, the title to the construction object is vested with the contractor on the original grounds; consequently, the contractor is obliged to transfer the title to the thing to the customer, which, from the point of view of Russian law, leads to the confusion of construction contracts and sales contracts for future immovable property. However, if the contractor becomes bankrupt, in the said countries, the construction object will apparently be recognized as part of the contractor's bankruptcy assets. Interestingly, in such case, the contractor acquires the title to the construction object in the absence of the right to the land plot, which makes the principle of superficio solo cedit inoperative in these countries.

11.180 This peculiar feature of construction law in Kazakhstan and Uzbekistan enables making another conclusion. From the rules discussed, we can see that the statute associates the transfer of the title to the construction object to the customer not only with its transfer to the latter, but also with the payment for the work result by the customer. In the countries in question, a situation when the work result has been transferred to the customer, while the title thereto has not been transferred, because the customer failed to

178 Art. 651, cl. 4, RK CC.
179 Art. 666, RU CC.
180 Art. 658, RK CC; Art. 674, RU CC.

perform its obligation to pay for the works in full, appears to be quite common. Thus, here one can see a special method of securing customer's obligations to pay for the works performed – clause of reservation of title by the contractor. The RCC does not provide for such method of securing customer's obligations. However, the RCC employs this method under sales contracts (clause of reservation of title by the contractor),[181] which makes one once again wonder about the correlation between construction and sales contracts in Kazakhstan and Uzbekistan. In Kyrgyzstan, there are no rules similar to those discussed above.

11.181 Kazakhstan statutorily prescribes a separate type of construction contracts – turn-key construction contracts. However, the legislator confines itself the definition of such contract, which is understood as a contract, under which "the contractor assumes all obligations on the construction and support thereof and shall deliver to the customer a fully operational object in accordance with the contractual provisions".[182] Furthermore, under such contract, the contractor bears "all potential construction risks".[183] The laws of Russia, Uzbekistan, and Kyrgyzstan do not directly regulate such contracts. At the same time, such contracts are actively used in practice by virtue of the freedom-of-contract doctrine. Usually, they not only vest all construction-related risks with the contractor, but also provide for contractor's obligations to design the construction object (for more details, see above).

11.182 Peculiarities of construction law in Kazakhstan and Uzbekistan also include provisions of the CCs of these countries stating that liability for construction safety is borne by the contractor.[184] This rule implies that the customer is not liable for violations in the construction process, which resulted in damage inflicted on, say, third parties. Such approach probably relies on the premise that the customer does not need to be a construction professional and is not obliged to supervise construction works; the customer is only entitled to exercise control and supervision over the construction, without interfering with the contractor's business activities.[185] In Russia, the application of such approach, which should be recognized as correct, is blocked by the absence of a special rule in the RCC similar to the RK CC and RU CC rules in question, and by the public legislation literally compelling the customer to exercise control and supervision over the construction in public interests.

11.183 Certain differences between Russia and Kazakhstan, Uzbekistan, and Kyrgyzstan can be seen in terms of general provisions on obligations; this primarily refers to the ways to secure obligations and protection measures.

11.184 With respect to the former, in Kazakhstan, one should note a different (compared to Russia) understanding of methods of providing security for a party's obligations, such as accessory suretyship and guarantees. For example, Article 329 of the RK CC, while rejecting independency of a guarantee, provides for its accessory nature. Furthermore, the difference between an independent guarantee and an accessory suretyship comes down to the fact that under an independent guarantee, the guarantor and the debtor are jointly

181 Art. 491, RCC.
182 Art. 651, Cl. 3, RK CC.
183 Art. 652, Cl. 4, RK CC.
184 Art. 653, RK CC; Art. 668, RU CC.
185 Art. 676, RK CC; Art. 660, RU CC.

liable, and under accessory suretyship, the surety is subject to subsidiary liability for debtor's obligations.[186] Besides, surety's liability under an accessory suretyship is limited to the amount stipulated by the contract, while the guarantor's liability under the guarantee is uncapped in the sense that the guarantor is liable for any consequences of debtor's failure to perform its obligations.[187] Kazakhstan's legislator[188] sees the subsidiary nature of surety's liability in the fact that, prior to addressing the surety, the creditor must take reasonable measures to make the debtor meet the corresponding claim, in particular, by offsetting cross-claims and by properly enforcing debtor's assets. Hence, it follows that, since a levy on debtor's assets is only possible after the claim has been granted by the court, addressing the surety under Kazakhstan's statute requires the creditor to not only file the corresponding claim against the debtor with the court, but also to try to enforce the judicial act delivered. Only if enforcement proceedings do not result in the claim satisfied, in whole or in part, the creditor will become entitled to address the surety. In Russia, Uzbekistan, and Kyrgyzstan, there is no such rule – to address the surety without observing any formalities, it would be enough for the creditor to not obtain satisfaction from the debtor within the time limits stipulated by the contract.

11.185 Finally, in the countries in question, the novelties that appeared in Russia in recent years, including the results of the RCC reform, are not in force. This is primarily about wide practical application of the objective good faith principle.[189] This principle is familiar to the Central Asian countries, but they treat it with caution, reasonably believing that its application may result in excessive court activity in interpreting the statute and in unauthorized appropriation by the judiciary system of legislator's powers. On the other hand, the failure to apply this principle affects flexibility of law enforcement. Furthermore, the status of application of the legislative recognition of protection measures and liability in these countries is at the level that existed in Russia before the RCC reform. For example, in Kazakhstan,[190] Uzbekistan,[191] and Kyrgyzstan,[192] courts play rather an active role in reducing penalties set by the parties; and such reduction is not an exceptional measure, as it is in Russia, where its application requires a number of conditions to be met (see above). It should also be noted that there are no rules that allow facilitating the recovery of damages. The lack of evidence of debtor's unlawful conduct, the causal connection between such conduct and consequences, and the exact amount of damages forms good and sufficient reason for dismissal of an action for damages.

National Construction Law and International Forms (Emphasis FIDIC) – How Do FIDIC and Other International Forms Operate?

11.186 It is well known that many major contracts in the construction sector are drafted on the basis of FIDIC standard forms. By their nature, such forms may be classified as

186 Art. 330, RK CC.
187 Art. 332, RK CC.
188 Art. 332, RK CC.
189 Art. 1, 10, RCC.
190 Art. 297, RK CC.
191 Art. 326, RU CC.
192 Art. 323, RKz CC.

usage (*obyknovenie*). They take effect if a reference to the application of the relevant form is made in the contract itself. In this sense, FIDIC standards forms, if the parties have agreed to rely on them, acquire the significance of contractual terms. In spite of being widespread in construction activities, in judicial practice, the application of FIDIC forms has been considered on rare occasions. Suffice to say that in Russian legal data bases, one would hardly find more than several dozens of judicial acts containing references to such forms (for information: Commercial courts (state arbitration courts) alone yearly consider around 2,000,000 cases). This circumstance is attributable to the fact that contracts based on FIDIC forms mostly specify English law as applicable law; they also contain the arbitration clause that provides for referring a possible dispute to international arbitration tribunals or to other jurisdictions.

11.187 Such state of things primarily stems from the concern of international legal companies operating in Russia as to the compliance of FIDIC standard forms with Russian law. For instance, in literature, it is noted that FIDIC standard forms may come into collision with a number of peculiarities of Russian law.[193] We will only provide the key examples.

11.188 Lately, the opinion has been often expressed that state arbitration courts extensively apply reductions in contractual penalties (liquidated damages in FIDIC terminology),[194] which contradicts the spirit of FIDIC forms.[195] Meanwhile, such practice has started to change since 2011, after the adoption of Information Letter of the RF SAC No. 81, which has considerably restricted courts in delivering decisions to reduce penalties; besides, in 2015, a new version of Article 333 of the RCC ("Penalty Reduction") was adopted, which treats the penalty reduction by the court as an exceptional measure (see above).

11.189 FIDIC standard forms are quite often said to contain a number of conditions providing for the waivers of various rights by a party to the contract.[196] Indeed, such waiver had long been restricted under Russian law. However, for several years, a new approach, currently enshrined in the RCC, has been in effect, which legalizes the waiver of contractual rights, in particular, upon occurrence of an event initially determined by the parties (Article 450.1 of the RCC).[197,198]

---

193 B. Braig, I.M. Mutay. *Lex publica lex mercatoria* in FIDIC forms and the RCC.// Bulletin of Economic Justice. 2016, No. 1.

194 There is no conceptual difference between a penalty and liquidated damages, since a penalty, in accordance with the Russian doctrine, represents the amount of liquidated damages (evaluation theory of a penalty).

195 B. Braig, I.M. Mutay, *Lex publica lex mercatoria* in FIDIC forms and the RCC.// Bulletin of Economic Justice. 2016, No. 1.

196 In particular, on this occasion, B. Braig and I.M. Mutay state:

"Concerns of foreign investors related to possible incorrect application of Russian law to FIDIC contracts are based, among other things, on the opinion of FIDIC inconsistency with the very provisions of the RCC in the form of impossibility to waive the right.

In accordance with cl. 2 of Art. 9 of the RCC, the waiver of individuals and legal entities of enjoyment of their vested rights does not entail termination of these rights, save to the extent provided by the statute. The very RCC rule is quite questionable, because it (and often the practice based on it) does not provide space for a method of termination of rights and obligations, such as a contract".

B. Braig, and I.M. Mutay, Op. cit.

197 Introduced by Federal Law dated 08.03.2016 No. 42-FZ.

198 Let us quote this rule of law:

"Unless otherwise provided by this Code, other statutes, other legal enactments, or the contract, if a party engaged in entrepreneurial activities, upon occurrence of the circumstances provided by this Code, other statutes, other legal enactments, or the contract and serving as grounds for exercising a certain right under the

11.190 Similar doubts may be caused by other obstacles to wide application of standard forms, including FIDIC forms, in Russian courts under the applicable Russian law (e.g., in terms of limitation of liability, pricing, warranty periods, and some others).[199] In any case, in the absence of relevant judicial practice, all these concerns are hypothetical. Besides, they do not take into account the latest changes in the RCC and actual law enforcement practices. Hence, it is necessary to continue the discussion on correlation between FIDIC standard forms and the Russian legislation at a higher professional level.

contract, waives such right, subsequently, this very right may not be exercised on the same grounds, save where similar circumstances occur again". Cl. 6.

199 B. Braig, I.M. Mutay. Op. cit.

CHAPTER 12

International Construction Arbitration

Philip L. Bruner

Contents

 DOI: 10.4324/9781315671376-12

Introduction to International Construction Arbitration

12.1 Those who engage in the in the field of international engineering and construction recognize that major construction projects can "generate major litigation" and that "the management of either is perilous".[1] Major disputes arising on international construction projects typically are resolved through negotiation, mediation, or binding international arbitration rather than through courtroom litigation.

Origins of International Arbitration

12.2 International arbitration traces its lineage back three millennia to patriarchal tribunals whose judgments for settlement of disputes were accepted by tribes and tribal members as peaceful alternatives to what might otherwise have led to resort to arms or other breaches of the peace.[2] About 2,400 years ago Aristotle advised his fellow Athenians:

> [I]t is equitable … to be willing to appeal to the judgment of reason rather than violence; to prefer arbitration to the law court, for the arbitrator keeps equity in view whereas the [court] looks only to the law, and the reason why arbitrators were appointed was that equity might prevail.[3]

12.3 Through the centuries arbitration has remained the distinctive hallmark by which international and domestic commercial disputes between merchants were resolved. By the early Middle Ages, informal "courts" were employed by merchant guilds throughout Europe to reach prompt settlements of disputes arising at international and domestic trade fairs. Dispute resolution in those merchant "courts" was presided over by trusted persons who were selected by the parties and who dispensed equity with speed and informality in accordance with a practical "law of the shop" rather than the strict "law of the court".[4]

---

1 *Morse/Diesel Inc v Trinity Indus Inc 67 F 3d 435, 437* (2d Cir 1995); See also, *Certified Power Systems, Inc. v Dominium Energy Brayton Point, LLC, 2012 WL 384600 *18* (Mass. Super. Ct. 2012), in which a pipe fitter foreman with over 32 years of construction experience testified about the large project he was working on as follows: "Every job has its problems. I mean, its construction. It never works right. It's very, very rare that it goes the way it's supposed to go. But there are some that just don't go at all. This [project] was certainly one of them".

2 See Earl S. Wolaver, The Historical Background of Commercial Arbitration, 83 U. Pa. L. Rev. 132,134 (1934) (noting that patriarchal tribunals offered the earliest ADR processes); Margit Mantica, Arbitration in Ancient Egypt, 12 Arb. J. 155, 155–9 (1957); Henry T. King Jr. and Marc A. LeForestier, Arbitration in Ancient Greece, 49 Disp. Resol. J. 38 (September 1994). Historians of early Rome also report that "the earliest judges derived their judicial authority, not from the state, but from the voluntary submission of the parties". See J.B. Moyle D.C.L., Imperatoris Justiniani Institutionum 633 (5th ed. 1912); Derek Roebuck, Roman Arbitration (2004).

3 Kaja Harter-Uibopuu, Ancient Greek Approaches Toward Alternative Dispute Resolution, 10 Willamette J. Int'l L. & Dispute Resol. 47, 55 (2002). Also reported is the quotation of an Athenian law of private arbitration enacted in 403/2 B.C., which was quoted by the orator Demosthenes as follows:

"If any parties are in dispute concerning private contracts and wish to choose any arbitrators, it shall be lawful for them to choose whomsoever they wish. But when they have chosen by mutual agreement, they shall abide by his decisions and shall not transfer the same charges from him to another court, but the judgments of the arbitrators shall be final".

See also, Derek Roebuck, Ancient Greek Arbitration (2001).

4 See Harold J. Berman, Law and Revolution: The Formation of the Western Legal Tradition 347 (1983) ("In all types of [merchant] commercial courts the procedure was marked by speed and informality. Time limits were narrow; in the fair courts justice was to be done 'from tide to tide', in guild and town courts 'from day to day'. Often appeals were forbidden. Not only were professional lawyers generally excluded but also technical legal argumentation was frowned upon. The court was to be 'ruled by equity … whereby every man

Illustrative of the world-wide acceptance of arbitration in the Middle Ages is a treatise on England's Law Merchant – the *Lex Mercatoria* – written in 1622 by a London merchant for the benefit of "all judges, lawyers, merchants and all others who negotiate in all parts of the world". The author advised that the method then ordinarily employed to resolve international and domestic commercial disputes between merchants was binding arbitration:

> [The] ordinary course to end the questions and controversies arising between merchants is by way of *Arbitrement*, when both parties do make choice of honest men to end their causes, which is voluntary and in their own power, and therefore is called *Arbitrium* or of free will, whence the name Arbitrator is derived: and these men (by some called Good men) give their judgments by awards, according to Equity and Conscience, observing the Custom of Merchants, and ought to be void of all partiality of affection more nor less to the one than to the other: having only care that right may take place according to the truth, and that the difference may be ended with brevity and expedition; insomuch that he may not be called an arbitrator who (to please his friend) makes delays and propagates their differences, but he is rather a disturber and an enemy to justice and truth.[5]

12.4 Consistent with this general tradition of using arbitration to settle commercial disputes, it is not surprising that the international construction industry is one of the foremost users favoring resolution of disputes by binding arbitration.

What Makes an Arbitration "International"?

12.5 An arbitration generally is understood to be "international" when at least two parties are from "different countries". Whether an arbitration is "international" so as to invoke the New York or other international conventions, or is merely "domestic" so as to be subject solely to the local arbitration laws of the nation in which the arbitration is venued, invariably is determined by considerations such as whether the disputing parties are "resident" in different countries, "organized or headquartered" in different countries, owned and controlled by parties organized to headquartered in different countries, or engaged in "international trade".[6]

---

will be received to tell his facts … and to say the best he can 'in his defense'".) See also, Leon Trakman, Ex Aequo Et Bono: Demystifying an Ancient Concept, 8 Chi. J. Int'l L. 621, 629–30 (Winter 2008) ("The rationale behind this process of [merchant judges] reaching decisions was that itinerant merchants who travelled with their goods from guild to guild, fair to fair, and port to port should receive an expeditious remedy before a merchant court without having to delay their mercantile journey. So significant was this interest in expedited resolutions of disputes that Medieval Law Merchant courts in parts of what are now France were named pie-powder or "dusty feet" courts, presumably obligated to provide remedies before the merchant parties could shake the dust off their feet").

5 Gerard Malynes, Consvetvdo, Vel Lex Mercatoria, or The Ancient Law-Merchant 447 (1622). This tradition continued to be followed by merchants for centuries. See also, Wyndham Beawes, Lex Mercatoria: Or a Complete Code of Commercial Law 498 (1st ed. London 1752) (6th ed. London 1813) (recommending that merchants employ arbitration to "prevent many suits at law").

6 See Hinchey and Harris, International Construction Arbitration Handbook (2016), §1:2 ("The term 'international,' as applied to construction arbitrations, is to distinguish construction arbitrations that transcend national boundaries from those that are primarily national or domestic in character … Unfortunately, there is no universally accepted definition of "international" in the context of international construction arbitration, and each country or state can establish its own definition for determining whether an arbitration award is "domestic" or "foreign".); Lamm, Hellbeck and Tsolakidis, International Arbitration in a Globalized World, 20

Modern Treaties Supporting International Arbitration

12.6 The world-wide acceptance of the common vision of dispute resolution by modern international arbitration was encouraged by the promulgation in 1958 of the United Nations Convention on Recognition and Enforcement of Foreign Arbitrable Awards (the "New York Convention"),[7] to which every major trading nation in the world has subscribed.[8] The New York Convention has been amplified by regional conventions, such as the European Convention on International Commercial Arbitration and the Inter-American Convention on International Commercial Arbitration (the "Panama Convention"). Signatory countries have implemented the New York Convention by adopting local laws, such as the United States Federal Arbitration Act.[9] To promote such implementation globally, the United Nations Commission on International Trade Law has promulgated the UNCITRAL Model Law on International Commercial Arbitration,[10] which has been adopted by many of the signatory countries. There has been sufficient international arbitration activity to have established some modern "norms",[11] and international arbitration awards are enforceable today throughout most of the world, subject only to the *vacatur* provisions of the New York Convention or other governing international arbitration treaties.

Why Today's International Construction Industry Favours Resolution of Disputes by Arbitration Rather than by Court Litigation

12.7 International construction arbitration is showing significant growth.[12] What commends international arbitration to the modern construction industry as more suitable than litigation for the resolution of construction disputes are eight generally accepted perceptions:

Disp. Resolution (No. 2) 4 (Winter 2014); UNIDROIT Principles, Preamble, §1 ("The international character of a contract may be defined in a great variety of ways. The solutions adopted in both national and international legislation range from a reference to the place of business or habitual residence of the parties in different countries to the adoption of more general criteria such as the contract having "significant connections with more than one State", "involving a choice between the laws of different States", or "affecting the interests of international trade". The Principles do not expressly lay down any of these criteria. The assumption, however, is that the concept of "international" contracts should be given the broadest possible interpretation, so as ultimately to exclude only those situations where no international element at all is involved; i.e., where all the relevant elements of the contract in question are connected with one country only").

7 21 U.S.T. 2517, 33 U.N.T.S. 38 (10 June 1958).

8 See the list of the 156 signatory nations as of March 2017 at www.uncitral.org/uncitral/en/uncitral_texts/arbitration/NYConvention_status.html.

9 9 U.S.C.A. &ss;§§201 to 208.

10 The United Nations Commission on International Trade Law (UNCITRAL) has published various Model Laws and rules regarding international arbitration, including its Model Law on International Commercial Arbitration (updated 2006) and Arbitration Rules (updated 2010). See www.uncitral.org.

11 See generally, Hinchey and Harris, International Construction Arbitration Handbook (2016 edition); Mouawad, How "International" is International Arbitration? 10 World Arb. & Med. Rev. 69 (2016). Such "norms" also are promoted by bar associations, such as the International Bar Association, which has promulgated IBA Guidelines on Party Representation in International Arbitration (2013), IBA Guidelines on Conflicts of interest in International Arbitration (revised 2014), IBA Rules on the Taking of Evidence in International Arbitration (2010), IBA Rules of Ethics for International Arbitrators (1987), and IBA Guidelines for Drafting International Arbitration Clauses (2010).

12 See Angus McFadden and Gregory Smith, Issues and Solutions in International Construction Contracting, 36 Constr. Law. 7 (Fall 2016) (reporting on growth of construction arbitrations in various countries).

Arbitration Awards Are Enforceable Throughout Most of the World

12.8 Since the promulgation in 1958 of the New York Convention, international arbitration awards are enforceable throughout most of the world, subject to *vacatur* upon limited grounds.[13] Enforceability of foreign court judgments, however, is another matter.[14] For example, the United States, concerned over the lack of due process in some countries, is not a signatory to the United Nations Convention for the Enforcement of Foreign Judgments. Conversely, when the United States became a signatory to the New York Convention, the United States Arbitration Act was amended to conform federal law to the convention.[15] Foreign arbitrable awards issued by tribunals in nations that have subscribed to the convention are routinely enforced in the United States.

Construction Is Technologically Complex

12.9 Construction comprises a host of applied sciences, such as architecture: The engineering disciplines of civil, soils, structural, electrical, mechanical, and others; the materials sciences that govern the extraction, formulation and manufacture of building materials; and, principles of construction and construction management that address the practical building process. Construction's technological complexity is amplified by its uniqueness – most projects are unique, built to a unique design, on a unique site, by a unique aggregation of companies, operating without economies of scale in an uncontrolled environment, where productivity is affected by weather, geology, local labour skills and availability, local building codes, site accessibility. [16]

---

13 The New York Convention contains seven defences to enforcement. Article V of the New York Convention establishes seven defences with which a party may block enforcement of an arbitral award. The court may raise the last two of these grounds *sua sponte* to decline enforcement. These grounds are:

The absence of a valid agreement to submit the dispute to arbitration;

(2) The lack of proper notice or opportunity to present a case;

(3) The arbitral award exceeds the scope of the issues properly submitted to arbitration;

(4) Improper composition of the arbitral panel;

(5) The award is not yet binding or has been properly set aside;

(6) The subject matter of the award is not arbitrable under the law of the enforcing country;

(7) Recognition and enforcement would be contrary to the public policy of the enforcing country.

These grounds to set aside arbitral awards are also incorporated, with minor modifications, into the Model Law on International Commercial Arbitration adopted in 1985 by the United Nations Commission on International Trade Law ("UNCITRAL"). The biggest *vacatur* problem is presented by the "public policy" exception, since countries have different views of "public policy". See Haridi and Wahab, Public Policy: Can the Unruly Horse Be Tamed? 83 Arbitration 35 (February 2017) (reviewing the different "public policy" views in Egypt, Lebanon, Qatar, Saudi Arabia, and the UAE; Bruner and McCormick, Enforcement of Foreign Arbitral Awards: The US View of International Arbitration's "Final Frontier", 11 Int'l Constr. L. Rev. 128 (1994).

14 See Oestreicher, "We're On the Road to Nowhere" – Reasons for the Continuing Failure to Regulate Recognition and Enforcement of Foreign Judgments, 42 Int. Law. 59 (Spring 2008); Nelson, Down in Flames: Three US Courts Decline Recognition to Judgments From Mexico, Citing Corruption, 44 Int'l Law. 897 (Summer 2010); Moedritzer, Whittaker, and Ye, Judgments; "Made in China;" But Enforceable in the United States?: Obtaining Recognition and Enforcement in the United States of Monetary Judgments Entered in China Against US Companies Doing Business Abroad, 44 Int'l Law. 817 (Summer 2010).

15 9 U.S.C.A. &ss;§§201 to 208.

16 The judiciary itself has embellished this legendary reputation for complexity. See, e.g., Erlich v. Menezes, 981 P. 2d 978, 987 (Cal. 1999) in which the Supreme Court of California observed:

12.10 International construction can add exponential complexities, such as multiple languages and modes of communication, local labour productivity, local customs and practices, material acquisition and delivery through local supply chains, and other issues arising out of the project location and local cultural sensitivities.[17] Internationalization of design and construction in the 21st century is being encouraged by (1) advances in communication which allow instantaneous (or at least overnight) transmission of large volumes of information to any place in the world, (2) trends towards democratization of national governments willing to promote international competition for their public work, (3) increased political stability and military security in large parts of the world, (4) heightened global financial and economic interdependencies in trade and banking, (5) rise of large competitive construction and engineering firms willing and able to seek work internationally, (6) pressure on international private owners to control project costs and time of completion by obtaining lowest prices from the best and most competent sources located anywhere in the world, and (7) increasing size and complexity of international projects, which compel, from financial and other perspectives, the spreading and sharing of risk. "Spreading and sharing of risk" remains the 21st century's global watchword because international design and construction involve substantially greater risks than domestic construction.

The Construction Industry Is Huge in Size, Regulated by Governments, Specialized Along Lines of Labour Crafts and Professional Disciplines, Subject to Its Own Trade Customs and Usages, and Undergoing Rapid Change

12.11 Construction is one of the largest segments of the production sector of the world economy. The global construction industry comprises millions of companies that employ many millions of people with various skills and levels of competence.

12.12 Over the past century the industry has witnessed a veritable explosion in construction knowledge: New techniques, materials technologies, geotechnical exploration methods, soils classifications, and environmental monitoring facilities heretofore unknown. This explosion of knowledge has led to the creation of a host of specialized engineering disciplines and construction trades to design and install modern systems – heating and ventilating, plumbing, electricity, lighting, telephones, fiber optic cables, deep caissons, elevators and escalators, fire retardation, building controls, curtainwall. Such advances in construction knowledge have lead (a) to new types of construction projects (hundred-story office towers, interstate highways with cloverleaf interchanges, massive bridges, dams and power plants, airports, subways and tunnels); (b) to new trade customs, usages and language by which those in the industry effectively communicate with each

[T]he [owners] may have hoped to build their dream home and live happily ever after, but there is a reason that tagline belongs only in fairy tales. Building a house may turn out to be a stress-free project; it is much more likely to be the stuff of urban legends – the cause of bankruptcy, marital dissolution, hypertension, and fleeting fantasies ranging from homicide to suicide. As Justice Yegan noted below, "No reasonable homeowner can embark on a building project with certainty that the project will be completed to perfection. Indeed, errors are so likely to occur that few if any homeowners would be justified in resting their peace of mind on [its] timely or correct completion".

17 See Philip L. Bruner and Patrick J. O'Connor, Bruner & O'Connor on Construction Law, §20:2 (2002, supplemented annually).

other;[18] and, (c) to evolving electronic and other methods used for design, construction, and communications. One consequence of the increased industry size, specialization, and rapid change has been heightened concern for public safety that in turn has lead to governmental regulation of construction industry practices through legislative imposition of minimum qualifications and standards enforced through building code permitting requirements, construction safety regulations, and designer and contractor licensing laws.

"Construction Law" Has Become "A Separate Breed of Animal"

12.13 As a consequence of construction's technological complexity, size and uniqueness, the law governing construction necessarily has become more complex[19] and has evolved into what some in the judiciary describe as a "separate breed of animal".[20] Construction law today is a specialized subject of legal study that comprises centuries-old legal theories fortified by statutory law and seasoned by contextual legal innovations reflecting broad factual "realities" of industry experience, custom and usage, specialized language, implied duties and unique concepts of foreseeable risk allocation perceived as invoking the "law of the shop" more frequently than of the "law of the court".[21] Construction law addresses the complex web of legal relationships between and among the multitude of parties involved in the construction project – owners, architects, engineers, contractors, sub-contractors, material suppliers, sureties, insurers, lenders, code officials. Those specialized relationships in turn invoke a multitude of legal rights and remedies arising out of common disputes.[22]

---

18 See David Ratterman, Codification of Trade Custom and Usage as a Viable Supplement to Construction Contracts, 11 J. ACCL 1 (Winter 2017).

19 See Rt. Hon. Beverley McLachlin, Chief Justice of Canada, Judging the "Vanishing Trial" in the Construction Industry, 2 Faulkner L. Rev. 315 (Spring 2011), 5 Construction L. Int'l 9 (June 2010) and 3 JAMS Global Constr. Solutions 1 (Winter 2010). Chief Justice McLachlin reminds us that:

> "Construction Law" … is a "capstone" subject, a towering legal edifice built out of modern statutes, "contextual" common law principles of and foundational legal concepts sustaining and binding the multitude of parties – architects, engineers, contractors, subcontractors, material suppliers, material manufacturers, sureties, insurers, code officials and tradesmen.

20 *Paul Hardeman, Inc. v Ark. Power & Light Co., 380 F. Supp. 298, 317* (E.D. Ark. 1974) ("Construction contracts are a separate breed of animal; and, even if not completely sui generis, still … [the] law must be stated in principles reflecting underlying economic and industry realities. Therefore, it is not safe to broadly generalize").

21 See Philip L. Bruner and Patrick J. O'Connor Jr., Bruner & O'Connor on Construction Law (2002, supplemented annually).

22 Such rights and remedies can include: (1) Express and implied contractual relationships invoking implied "contextual" rights and duties, (2) tort relationships in the absence of contractual privity, (3) equitable principles governing surety subrogation and indemnification rights and contractor quantum meruit recoveries, (4) statutory rights and obligations created by statues governing mechanics liens, claims against surety bonds, sales of goods under the Uniform Commercial Code, and awards of public contracts, (5) public duties created by building codes, licensing laws and health and safety laws, (6) common law principles unique to construction, such as those addressing design errors, implied obligations and impacts of time involving project delay, suspension, acceleration and disruption, and (7) specialized damage concepts unique to construction, such as the doctrines of substantial performance, economic waste, betterment, total cost, and other approaches to damage measurement that recognize construction's imperfect world.

Proof of Complex Construction Claims and Damages Typically Requires Specialized Expertise

12.14 Because of construction's technological and legal complexity and uniqueness, legal proof of causation and quantification of damages necessarily relies heavily upon opinion testimony of experts.[23] This feature of construction disputes indeed can be frustrating to judges inexpert in construction.[24] All too frequently the detailed factual records of construction dispute proceedings appear "formidable" to trial finders of fact[25] and to reviewing appellate judges.[26] When overseen by selected peers knowledgeable in industry customs and practices, arbitration has been viewed universally as an option superior to submission of disputes to judges and juries inexpert in the construction process. Judges themselves often have recognized the wisdom of submitting complex construction disputes to knowledgeable arbitrators or mediators rather than to the courts. Illustrative is the sage advice offered by one US federal judge to parties before him at a pretrial conference:

> Being trained in this field [of construction], you are in a far better position to adjust your differences than those untrained in [its] related fields. As an illustration, I, who have no training whatsoever in engineering, have to determine whether or not the emergency generator system

23 See James Schenck and Kelli Goss, Liability for Construction Defects That Result from Multiple Causes, 9 ACCL J. 2 (January 2015) ("When a structural failure or other construction defect causes harm, what caused the defect and who should bear responsibility are not always apparent. Investigations ensue, and the usual suspects – inadequate design, incompetent construction, material failure, etc. are examined. Experts opine, blame is case, responsibility is often denied, and so litigation begins").

24 See Philip L. Bruner, The Historical Emergence of Construction Law, 34 William Mitchell L. Rev. 1 (2007).

25 Although some jurisdictions such as England and Singapore have an established specialized construction court to hear construction disputes, judges in other jurisdictions lacking such specialization and expertise have a more difficult time adjudicating construction disputes. See *Blake Constr. Co. v C. J. Coakley Co., 431 A. 2d 569, 575* (D. C. 1981):

[E]xcept in the middle of a battlefield, nowhere must men coordinate the movement of other men and all materials in the midst of such chaos and with such limited certainty of present facts and future occurrences as in a huge construction project such as the building of this 100-million-dollar hospital. Even the most painstaking planning frequently turns out to be mere conjecture and accommodation to changes must necessarily be of the rough, quick and ad hoc sort, analogous to ever-changing commands on the battlefield. Further, it is a difficult task for a court to be able to examine testimony and evidence in the quite of a courtroom several years later concerning such confusion and then extract from them a determination of precisely when the disorder and constant readjustment, which is to be expected by any subcontractor on the job sit, became so extreme, so debilitating and so unreasonable as to constitute a breach of contract between a contractor and a subcontractor. This was the formidable undertaking faced by the trial judge in the instant case.

See also, *Kiewit-Atkinson-Kenny v Massachusetts Water Resources Authority, 2002 WL 31187691 *12* (Mass. Super., 3 September 2002) in which the court expressed its frustration at the parties' requests for the court's interpretation of technical contract language:

The contract language … is sprawled over hundreds of pages and contained in several documents, not all speaking consistently with one another; and the "record" is massive, covering literally thousands of pages. The burden placed on this court is immense, and, it fears, after all of its attempts to give fair attention and correct rulings to the various issues, whichever side does not prevail will first seek reconsideration and thereafter will ultimately appeal, and may well argue that material facts remain in dispute. In short, this memorandum and the orders it produces may turn out to be an exercise in futility driven by a hugely over-litigated case.

26 *See Decker & Co. v West, 76 F. 3d 1573, 1577* (Fed. Cir. 1996):

This is one of those messy government [construction] dispute cases in which, during the performance of the contract, neither of the parties acquitted themselves with pure grace. Working through the detailed record of such a case causes one to understand better the ancient curse of "a plague o' both their houses". See William Shakespeare, Romeo and Juliet, act 3, sc. 1. Nevertheless, since the parties could not resolve their dispute, we must.

> proposed to be furnished ... met the specifications, when experts couldn't agree. This is a strange bit of logic ... The object of litigation is to do substantial justice between the parties' litigant, but the parties' litigant should realize that, in most situations, they are by their particular training better able to accomplish this among themselves.[27]

Local Fact-Finders Can Hold Views Reflecting Local Prejudices and Biases

12.15 Arbitration allows parties to place disputes into the hands of independent impartial neutrals beyond the reach of local biases and prejudices.

Court Systems Can be Frustrating, Slow, and Expensive

12.16 Major complaints about courtroom litigation as a dispute resolution method are time, expense and procedure. In 1985, Warren E. Burger, Chief Justice of the United States Supreme Court, offered this compelling advice to the American legal profession:

> The obligation of the legal profession is, or has long been thought to be, to serve as healers of human conflicts. To fulfil that traditional obligation means that there should be mechanisms that can produce an acceptable result in the shortest possible time, with the least possible expense and with a minimum of stress on the participants. That is what justice is all about.
>
> My overview of the work of the courts from a dozen years on the Court of Appeals and now sixteen in my present position, added to twenty years of private practice, has given me some new perspectives on the problems of arbitration. *One thing an appellate judge learns very quickly is that a large part of all litigation in the courts is an exercise in futility and frustration. A large proportion of civil disputes in the courts could be disposed of more satisfactorily in some other way.*
>
> *My own experience persuades me that in terms of cost, time, and human wear and tear, arbitration is vastly better than conventional litigation for many kinds of cases.* In mentioning these factors, I intend no disparagement of the skills and broad experience of judges. I emphasize this because to find precisely the judge whose talents and experience fit a particular case of great complexity is a fortuitous circumstance. This can be made more likely if two intelligent litigants agree to pick their own private triers of the issues. This is not at all to bypass the lawyers; they are key factors in this process. The acceptance of this concept has been far too slow in the United States.[28]

12.17 This advice rings as true today as it did forty years ago.[29] It is not uncommon among the world's judicial systems for litigated cases to take four or more years to reach

27 *E.C. Ernst, Inc. v Manhattan Construction Co., 387 F. Supp. 1001, 1006* (S.D. Ala. 1974).

28 Warren E. Burger, Chief Justice of the US Supreme Court, Remarks before the American Arbitration Association and the Minnesota State Bar Association: Using Arbitration to Achieve Justice (21 August 1985), in 40 Arb. J. 3, 6 (1985). (Emphasis added.). See also, Warren E. Burger, Isn't There a Better Way? 68 A.B.A.J 274, 275 (1982) (quoting Abraham Lincoln: "Discourage litigation. Persuade your neighbors to compromise whenever you can. Point out to them that the nominal winner is often the real loser – in fees, expenses and waste of time").

29 See Roy Weinstein, Cullen Edes, Joe Hale and Nels Pearsall, Efficiency and Economic Benefits of Dispute Resolution through Arbitration Compared with US District Court Proceedings (March 2017) (a multi-year study of average time to complete cases in federal court and arbitration, and concluding with this result: "[O]n average, US district court cases took more than 12 months longer to get to trial than cases adjudicated by

a final judgment following trial and appeal. In comparison, most complex construction arbitrations can be heard and decided within a year or two.

Arbitration is a Process Amenable to Maintaining Business and Personal Relationships

12.18 Arbitration is regarded as "well-suited to the task of blurring the distinction between victor and vanquished, so that the parties could continue their relations within the community".[30] Parties have their disputes heard and decided with promptness in confidential proceedings by knowledgeable experts.

12.19 It is no wonder, then, that the construction industry, as well as many in the judicial process, have perceived construction disputes well suited for settlement by arbitrators who are (1) experienced in the construction process, (2) expert in industry practices invoking the "law of the shop", (3) skilled in management of construction dispute resolution practices, and (4) beyond the influence of local prejudices and biases.

Recent Industry Concerns About Arbitration

12.20 In the past two decades international arbitration, as an ADR alternative to litigation, has been questioned as to whether it remains the best method to satisfy the construction industry's demands for efficient and cost-effective ADR.[31] At the heart of industry's recent dissatisfaction with arbitration has been the perceived "judicialization" of arbitration, difficulties with consolidation of cases and joinder of non-signatory parties, limited scope of appellate review, and poorly drafted arbitration clauses.

12.21 In addition, some parties complained of poor experience with arbitrators selected by institutional providers from lists, where the arbitrators on occasion demonstrated (1) inadequate skills for management of complex cases with competing tensions between efficiency and "due process", (2) inadequate requisite expertise in substantive construction law, industry practice and arbitration hearing management, (3) inadequate time to hear a case through to conclusion without interruption, and (4) unwillingness or inability to follow and enforce the contract. Arbitrations, not properly controlled by the tribunal, all too frequently assumed the trappings of unwanted judicial proceedings, characterized by over-lawyering, unlimited discovery, extensive motion practice, liberal hearing "due process", repeated pre-hearing and hearing delays, extensive post-award disputes over confirmation of binding awards, heavy expense, and long delay in resolution.[32] This "judi-

arbitration (24.2 months v 11.6 months); when the comparison involved time through appeal, US district and circuit court cases required at least 21 months longer than arbitration to resolve (33.6 months v 11.6 months)".

30 Bruce H. Mann, The Formalization of Informal Law Arbitration Before the American Revolution, 59 N.Y.U. L. Rev. 443, 455 (June 1984) (observing that continuing relationships were enhanced by arbitration being "expeditious and inexpensive", "less public and less adversarial than litigation", "permeated with notions of compromise and reconciliation" inherent in the initial decision to submit to a voluntary, mutual process, and emphasizing "ties to the community").

31 See Thomas J. Stipanowich, Arbitration and Choice: Tanking Charge of the "New Litigation", 7 DePaul Bus. & Com. L. J. 383 (Spring 2009) ("Dispute meaningful efforts to promote better practices and ensure quality among arbitrators and advocates, criticism of American arbitration is at a crescendo").

32 Ibid., at 401.

cialization" of arbitration, combined with deficiencies in arbitrator selection processes, produced a new round of construction industry demands both for more cost-effective, expedited, and innovative arbitration,[33] and for efficient early "rapid resolution" ADR methods employing peer expertise.

12.22 "Fixes" to address the construction industry's dissatisfaction with binding arbitration already are being proposed.[34] Parties who continue to use arbitration are those who know how to assure its efficiency and cost-effectiveness.[35] Critical elements in assuring satisfactory use of arbitration are (1) pre-contract planning for conflict management with competent counsel,[36] (2) drafting a well thought out arbitration agreement that confirms applicable law[37] and rules,[38] and defines the powers of the arbitrators[39] and other conditions, (3) selecting arbitrators with requisite skill and expertise in construction industry practices, construction law and case management, (4) filing (or otherwise making early disclosure of) detailed statements of claims and defenses, (5) requiring information exchanges and limiting document and deposition discovery to the issues,[40] (6) encouraging pre-hearing dispositive motions, (7) promoting joinder of parties, (8) creating set

33 See The College of Commercial Arbitrators Protocols for Expeditious, Cost-Effective Commercial Arbitration (2010), of which Professor Thomas J. Stipanowich is Editor-in-Chief. JAMS also has issued expedited arbitration rules and recommended arbitration discovery protocols. See also, JAMS Recommended Arbitration Discovery Protocols for Domestic, Commercial Arbitration (2010) at www.jamsadr.com.

34 See The College of Commercial Arbitrators Protocols for Expeditions, Cost-Effective Commercial Arbitration (2010); Thomas J. Stipanowich, Revelation and Reaction: The Struggle to Shape American Arbitration in CONTEMPORARY ISSUES IN INTERNATIONAL ARBITRATION AND MEDIATION: THE FORDHAM PAPERS (2010); Richard Chernick and Zela Claiborne, What Providers can to do Promote Efficiency, The National Law Journal (22 November 2010)("As criticism of costly arbitration has grown stronger, some providers are also responding by offering more than one kind of arbitration procedure and revising their rules with the goal of helping parties design a process to fit the case").

35 See Zela Claiborne, Designing a Cost-Effective Construction Arbitration, 3 JAMS Global Construction Solutions 10 (Spring 2010); Thomas J. Stipanowich, Arbitration: The Choice is Yours, 3 JAMS Global Construction Solutions 7 (Winter 2010); Michael Timpane and Linda DeBene, Reshaping ADR Strategies for Today's Global Engineering and Construction Market, 2 JAMS Global Construction Solutions 1 (Summer 2009).

36 See Celeste M. Hammond, The (Pre) (as) summed "consent" of commercial Binding Arbitration contracts: An Empirical Study of Attitudes and Explanations of Transactional Lawyers, 36 J. Marshall L. Rev. 589 (Spring 2003) ("The thesis of this article is not that transactional attorneys perpetrate legal malpractice when they advise business clients about pre-dispute arbitration provisions. Instead, the thesis is that where the lawyer, as advisor/counselor, is egregiously incorrect in her own understanding and expectations, the client has not 'knowingly' assented to arbitration and the agreement to arbitrate is not legally enforceable".)

37 See James F. Nagle, ADR in Federal Contract Disputes: What Law Applies? 4 JAMS Global construction Solutions 13 (Winter 2010) (addressing prime and subcontract issues over law applicable in Federal procurements).

38 See, e.g., JAMS Construction Arbitration Rules, JAMS Construction Rules for Expedited Arbitration, and JAMS Rules for International Arbitration and International Mediation at www.jamsadr.com; AAA Construction Industry Arbitration Rules (regular track, fast track, and large complex case procedures), AAA Construction Industry Mediation Rules, ICDR International Arbitration and Mediation Rules at www.adr.org.

39 See *David Co. v Jim W. Miller Constr. Inc., 444 N.W.2d 837* (Minn. 1989) (upholding an arbitration award, rendered under an arbitration clause covering "all claims, disputes and other matters in questions … arising out of or relating to the contract documents or the breach thereof", that required the contractor to buy at the developer's full resale price the project it defectively built).

40 See JAMS Recommended Arbitration Discovery Protocols (2009). See also, 2010 Revised IBA Rules of Evidence for International Arbitration; Nathan O'Malley, An Annotated Commentary on the 2010 Revised IBA Rules of Evidence for International Arbitration, 27 Int'l Constr. L. Rev. 461 (October 2010). See also, Richard Chernick, Discovering New Ways to Make Arbitration More Attractive, The Recorder (April 12, 2010) (discussing new rules for streamlining the discovery process proposed by international ADR groups).

points for exploration of settlement before the arbitration hearing,[41] (9) permitting effective arbitrator control of the hearing, (10) allowing use of written witness statements and affidavits, subject to live cross-examination, (11) using a "chess clock" procedure to control hearing time, (12) requiring written expert reports and rebuttals,[42] subject to live cross-examination, (13) requiring a reasoned award addressing all issues presented for determination, and (14) providing for appeal to an appellate arbitrator where there is concern over the limited statutory scope of judicial review.[43]

12.23 Selection of arbitrators, who are expert in the *substantive law of construction* (to reach a correct decision) **and** *procedural management of cases* (to control and move the hearing along to expeditious conclusion), **and** who *possess the trust and respect of the parties*, is critical to the parties' ultimate willingness to accept any award.[44] Definition of arbitrator powers and parameters of the arbitration process also is vital. Careful delineation of issues to be submitted to and decided by the arbitrators is essential. Agreement on arbitration rules – which can vary considerably[45] – is imperative. Today, counsel for parties intending to arbitrate large and expensive matters typically follow the "party appointment" process, under which each party selects one arbitrator, and the selected arbitrators appoint a third as chair (all three arbitrators being deemed and treated as "neutrals" throughout the proceedings).[46] That process offers the parties the greatest confidence that the right arbitrators have been selected to hear their particular disputes.

Crafting an Effective International Construction Arbitration Clause: The Key Essentials

12.24 Arbitration is founded upon the mutual consent of the contracting parties to have their disputes resolved by a private process under which the arbitrators are selected by the parties themselves and pursuant to an arbitration process agreed by the parties and governed by accepted rules and procedures. The cardinal precondition to international arbitration is a written agreement of the parties to submit disputes to arbitration.[47]

41 See Harvey J. Kirsh, Arbitration & Settlement, 4 JAMS Global Construction Solutions 10 (Winter 2010).

42 See Jesse B. Grove III, An Arbitrator's Tips on Experts to Avoid, 2 JAMS Global Construction Solutions 1 (Spring 2009); Barry Brower, Paul Ficca and Neil Gaudion, Why is an Expert's Evolving Role Important in the Construction Arbitration Process? 2 JAMS Global Construction Solutions 1 (Spring 2009).

43 See JAMS Optional Arbitration Appeal Procedure (2003) at www.jamsadr.com.

44 See John W. Hinchey, Selecting Qualified Arbitrators is the Key to Success in International Construction Cases, 1 JAMS Global Construction Solutions 1 (Fall 2008); Michael J. Altschuler, Arbitrating Before a Non-Attorney Construction Industry Neutral, 63 Disp. Resol. J. 60 (January 2009).

45 See, e.g., JAMS Expedited Construction Arbitration Rules; and the "Fast Track" Procedures of AAA Construction Industry Arbitration Rules and Mediation Procedures. See also, Jesse B. Grove III, New Rules for Expedited Construction Arbitration in the United States, 24 Int'l Constr. L. Rev. 136 (Spring 2007).

46 See John W. Hinchey, Selecting Qualified Arbitrators is the Key to Success in International Construction Cases, 1 JAMS Global Construction Solutions 1 (Fall 2008); Christopher R. Seppala, Obtaining the Right International Arbitral Tribunal: A Practitioner's View, 25 Int'l Constr. L. Rev. 198 (Spring 2008).

47 See United Nations Convention on Recognition and Enforcement of Foreign Arbitral Awards, Art. II (1) (10 June 1958):

> Each Contracting State shall recognize an agreement in writing under which the parties undertake to submit to arbitration all or any differences which have arisen or which may arise between them in respect to a defined legal relationship, whether contractual or not, concerning a subject matter capable of settlement by arbitration.

12.25 The arbitration clause, subject to prevailing law, is the instrument that creates the arbitral tribunal's jurisdiction and empowers the arbitral tribunal to act. The arbitration clause necessarily should address these critical issues: (1) Scope and types of issues to be decided by arbitration; (2) choice of substantive and procedural law; (3) choice of language; (4) choice of international arbitration center to administer proceedings; (5) choice of arbitral rules; (6) choice of venue (the "seat" of the arbitration); (7) type of binding or non-binding arbitral process, such as a dispute review board or adjudicator to hear disputes as these arise during construction, or traditional arbitration; (8) pre-conditions to arbitration such as mediation or other non-binding ADR proceeding; (9) remedies such as specific performance, restitution, and exemplary damages; (10) number, nationality, and qualifications of arbitrators; (11) consolidation with related arbitrations; (12) joinder of non-signatory parties; and, (13) supplementation of the arbitral rules selected to govern the proceedings.[48]

12.26 For traditional international arbitration, the arbitration clause should address the following:

Scope and Types of Arbitrable Issues

12.27 Unless otherwise required, the scope of the arbitration clause should broadly include all claims and disputes of every type that arise out of or are related to the contract and its performance. Such broad clauses have been interpreted to include within the Tribunal's jurisdiction not only claims for breach of contract, but claims articulated as negligence, violation of statutory duties, breaches of implied contractual duties, bad faith, fraud and other legal causes of action. Failure to articulate a broad scope of arbitral issues can lead to an expensive process of "piecemeal resolution" in different forums.[49] Joinder of claims is promoted by arbitration clauses that broadly define "claims" and require arbitration of all claims[50] "arising out of or related to" the contract or "the breach, termination or invalidity thereof", under arbitration rules authorizing broad arbitrator jurisdiction,[51] and judicial rulings that view joinder of claims as a procedural issue to be decided by the arbitrators.[52]

48 See generally, IBA Guidelines for Drafting International Arbitration Clauses (2010). See also, Peter Sheridan and Alex Linhardt, Managing the Battlefield: Using Uniform Multi-Party Construction Arbitration Agreement, 11 ACCL J. 39 (January 2017).

49 See Philip L. Bruner, Dual Track Proceedings in Arbitration and Litigation: Reducing the Peril of "Double Jeopardy" by Consolidation, Joinder and Appellate Arbitration, 31 Int'l Constr. L. Rev. 537 (October 2014).

50 See American Institute of Architects, AIA A201-2007, General Conditions of Contract for Construction, Section 15.1.1 ("A Claim is a demand or assertion by one of the parties seeking, as a matter of right, payment of money, or other relief with respect to the terms of the Contract. The term 'Claim' also includes other disputes and matters in question between the Owner and Contractor arising out of or relating to the Contract".)

51 See JAMS Engineering and Construction Arbitration Rules and Procedures, Rule 1(c) (giving the arbitrator jurisdiction over arbitrability issues) at www.jamsadr.com under "Rules".

52 See *BG Group PLC v Republic of Argentina, 134 Sup. Ct. 1198, 188 L. Ed. 2d 220* (2014) (confirming that arbitrators should decide issues of procedural arbitrability, while courts should decide substantive arbitrability, and holding that the issue of joinder of claims was one of procedural arbitrability to be decided by the arbitrators).

Substantive Law of the Contract

12.28 The arbitration clause, if not otherwise addressed elsewhere in the contract, should designate the jurisdiction whose substantive law will govern the contract. Absent such designation, the contract's governing law likely will be that of the jurisdiction in which the contract will be or is performed. With respect to how the contract may be interpreted, keep in mind that there traditionally have been marked differences in approach to contract interpretation between civil law ("subjective") and common law ("objective") jurisdictions[53] and, where possible, designate a standard of contract interpretation in the arbitration clause that may be in harmony with the governing law. With regard to modern trends for interpretation of international construction contracts, it is important consider the following:

Traditional Interpretative Differences Between Common Law and Civil Law Jurisdictions

12.29 The traditionally perceived differences between contract interpretation in Common Law and Civil Law jurisdictions have been described as follows:

> [I]nternational commercial contracts are often written on the basis of Common Law contract models. Not only are they written in the English language, they frequently also adopt the Common Law legal terminology and legal structure.
>
> The Common Law of Contracts is based on the principles of certainty and predictability. The parties are presumed to be able to assess the risks connected with the transaction and to provide for appropriate regulation of the relationship and allocation of risk. The contract, therefore, is deemed to be sufficient to regulate the transaction between the parties
>
> The law of contracts in Civilian systems, on the contrary, is concerned with ensuring that justice is rendered in the specific case. The contract is interpreted in the light of implied principles of reasonableness, good faith or fair dealing (in different degrees in the respective national systems), thus permitting to avoid unjust solutions that might be based on a literal interpretation of the contract ... [A] party from a Civilian system might have a certain expectation of interference by the governing law [and judge], either to integrate or to correct the contractual regulation.[54]

Trends Toward Harmonization of Contract Interpretation Under the Common Law and Civil Law

12.30 For over 100 years, the development of contract law in common law and civil law countries has crept along a path leading from "text" towards "context", and from "sanctity" towards "fairness". In common law jurisdictions, the traditional Doctrine of Sanctity

53 See Moss, Swiss Law vs. English Law on Contract Interpretation: Is Swiss Law Better Suited to the Realities of International Construction Contracts? 32 Int'l Construction L. Rev. 470 (October 2015); Mulcahy, What Does It Mean? Contractual Interpretation in International Commercial Arbitration, 9 Disp. Resol. Int'l 15 (May 2015); Henriques, Pathological Arbitration Clauses, Good Faith and the Protection of Legitimate Expectations, 31 Arb. Int'l 349 (2015).

54 Moss, International Contract between Common Law and Civil Law: Is Non-State Law to Be Preferred? The Difficulty of Interpreting Legal Standards Such as Good Faith, 7 Global Jurist 1 (2007).

of Contract[55] has given way to recognition of many "implied obligations and conditions", that have narrowed the interpretive differences between the Common Law and Civil Law. Construction contracts in many Common Law jurisdictions today are construed to include a host of implied obligations, such as: (1) The employer's implied warranty of the adequacy of its detailed design; (2) the employer's implied duty of full disclosure; (3) the contractor's implied obligation to seek clarification, before contracting, of patent ambiguities in the employer's detailed design; (4) the parties' mutual implied obligation of cooperation and non-hindrance; (5) the parties' mutual implied obligation of good faith and fair dealing.[56] The Common Law's acceptance of the concept of implied obligations and conditions has narrowed considerably differences in interpretive approaches between the Common Law and the Civil Law.

12.31 Further promoting the harmonization of the Common Law and Civil Law[57] approaches to interpretation of commercial contracts are two important initiatives resulting in draft uniform "restatements" and model "codifications" of international commercial contracts: (1) The UNIDROIT Principles,[58] and (2) The Principles of European Contract Law.[59] These initiatives have received wide recognition by law faculties, and both sets of Principles are gaining significant legal influence. Whereas legislation or treaties require broad consensus prior to their adoption, the Principles are expected to insinuate themselves into the contract law of all nations by the force of fairness and reason alone. This process of insinuation was well described in 1998 by Professor Lookofsky of the University of Copenhagen Law Faculty regarding the UNIDROIT Principles (before the Principles of European Contract Law had been published):

> [S]ince my colleagues and I on the University of Copenhagen Law Faculty consider the [UNIDROIT] Principles to be a most significant and persuasive international Restatement, we now make sure that all our students are introduced to the UNIDROIT Principles, inter alia, as

55 Illustrative of the Common Law's Sanctity of Contract Doctrine in the 19th century is *Dermott v Jones*, 69 US (2 Wall.) 1 (1864), in which the United States Supreme Court said:

> It is a well settled rule of law that if a party by his contract charge himself with an obligation possible to be performed, he must make it good, unless its performance is rendered impossible by the act of God, the law, or the other party. Unforeseen difficulties, however great, will not excuse him … [This rule] rests upon the solid foundation of reason and justice. It regards the sanctity of contracts. It requires parties to do what they have agreed to do. If unexpected impediments lie in the way and a loss must ensue, it leaves the loss where the contract places it. If the parties have made no provision for a dispensation, the rule gives none. It does not allow a contract fairly made to be annulled, and it does not permit to be interpolated what the parties themselves have not stipulated.

56 See Philip L. Bruner and Patrick J. O'Connor, Jr., Bruner and O'Connor on Construction Law (2002, supplemented annually), §§3:1 et. seq.

57 See Wilets, Unified Theory of International Law, the State and the Individual: Transnational Legal Harmonization in the Context of Economic and Legal Globalization, 31 U. Pa. J. Int'l L. 753 (Spring 2010) (adopting as "the central thesis that economic globalization is not happening in a vacuum, and is engendering legal globalization, much in the way that centralized regulation followed trans-state economic globalization within the United States and Europe".)

58 International Institute for the Unification of Private Law (UNIDROIT), Principles of International Commercial Contracts (3dth ed. 2010). See www.unidroit.org/instruments/commercial-contracts/unidroit-principles-2010. See also, Michaels, The UNIDROIT Principles as Global Background Law, 19 Unif. L. Rev. 643 (2014); Philip L. Bruner and Patrick J. O'Connor, Jr., Bruner and O'Connor on Construction law, §§20:4 – 20:7.

59 Commission on European Contract Law, The Principles of European Contract Law. See www.trans-lex.org/400200_/pecl/#head_8.

part [of] their required courses in Contracts and Sales. In this way, we openly acknowledge that the greatest influence on our domestic law of contract now comes from outside.

[I]t would seem to follow that an important purpose of the Principles should be to serve as just such a Restatement, i.e., as a persuasive source of internationally accepted principles of contract law, Lex Mercatoria and the like.

This source-of-law function (purpose) of the Principles seems particularly important in systems where great reliance is placed on uncodified, essentially judge-made rules of law. In Denmark, for example, where the bulk of our existing contract law is not to be found in statutes, it seems unlikely that our Parliament would make much use of the Principles as a model for future legislation: Our Contracts Act ... is not currently up for revision and – in the absence of any European commandment – Denmark would hardly elect to codify the rest of its Contract law, let alone enact an even broader Civil Code.

What does, however, seem very likely is that some UNIDROIT Principles will rub off on, and thus become part of our own judge-made contract law. We in Denmark predict, for example, that our domestic rules on liability will drift towards the international formulations in UNIDROIT and CISG. And indeed, as we academics write about the Principles (and require students, the future Danish judges, to absorb the message), our prophecy begins to fulfill itself![60]

12.32 Notwithstanding the promulgation of the UNIDROIT and European Contract Law Principles, choice of law clauses remain important for international contracts entered into in the European Union and elsewhere. Under EU Regulation No. 593/2008 promulgated by the European Parliament and Council (known as "Rome I"), which applies to conflicts of laws affecting "contractual obligations in civil and commercial matters", the parties may select the governing law of the contract. If parties fail to contractually designate the governing law, Regulation Article 4, 1 (b) provides that a contract for the provision of services or sale of goods shall be governed by the law where the service provider or seller of goods "has his habitual residence". Regulation Article 12 makes clear that the applicable governing law shall govern the contract's "validity", "interpretation, "performance", "breach", "damages", but notes that with respect to the "manner of performance" and "defective performance", "regard shall be had to the law of the country in which performance takes place". On a multi-party construction project, it thus is critical for the contract to specify the "governing law".

"Seat" of the Arbitration and Procedural Law Governing the Arbitration

12.33 The arbitration clause should designate the jurisdiction and location in which the arbitration will be held. This location is called the "seat" of the arbitration. Designating an appropriate "seat" is important because the "procedural law" of the "seat" of the arbitration (as distinct from the substantive contract "governing law"), typically governs the

60 Lookofsky, The Limits of Commercial Contract Freedom: Under the UNIDROIT "Restatement" and Danish Law, 46 Am. J. Comp. L. 485, 488 (1998). See also, Saidov, Cases on the Sales Convention and the UNIDROIT Principles Decided in the Russian Federation: An Update, 9 VJ 1, 15–16 (2005) (With respect to various cases decided in the Russian Federation, "it was not necessary for the arbitrators to refer to the UNIDROIT Principles to reach this decision as the provisions of the Resolution and the Civil Code were sufficient. It seems, therefore, that the reference to the Principles has been made to demonstrate that the decision made on the basis of domestic law was in line with the internationally accepted standards".)

tribunal's jurisdiction, interpretation of arbitration rules, and the process for *vacatur* or enforcement of any award.

"Ad Hoc" or Institutional Arbitration Administration, and Arbitration Rules

12.34 The arbitration clause should address whether the arbitration will be administered "ad hoc" by the arbitral tribunal or under the aegis of an institutional administrator. If "ad hoc", rules governing the arbitration must be established by the parties, left to the tribunal, or incorporated by reference to the UNCITRAL model laws and rules[61] or CPR rules[62] that address "ad hoc" arbitration.

12.35 Although "Ad Hoc" arbitration has an ancient history, a large majority of participants in international arbitration prefer institutional administration[63] by a well-established arbitral organization, such as The International Chamber of Commerce (ICC),[64] JAMS International,[65] the London Court of International Arbitration (LCIA),[66] the International Dispute Resolution Center of the American Arbitration Association (ICDR),[67] the Arbitration Institute of the Stockholm Chamber of Commerce (SCC),[68] the Hong Kong International Arbitration Centre (HKIAC),[69] the Singapore International Arbitration Centre,[70] the China International Economic and Trade Arbitration Commission (CIETAC),[71] and others. There are fundamental differences between the rules and administration practices of each institution, which merit careful study before selecting and referencing a particular institution and its rules in the arbitration clause.[72]

Language of the Arbitration

12.36 The arbitration clause should designate the language in which the arbitration proceedings will be conduction and the award rendered.

---

61 See UNCITRAL Model Law on International Commercial Arbitration (updated 2006) and Arbitration Rules (updated 2010) at www.uncitral.org

62 See Blacker, Making the Case for the Self-Administered Case: Adopting the CPR International Arbitration Model in Selected Circumstances, 23 Int'l Lit. Q. 16 (Summer 2007) ("Law firms and corporations drafting ADR clauses and international business contracts should consider self-administered international arbitration as an efficient, lower-cost alternative to administered arbitrations ... where all counsel to any future arbitration will be experienced international ADR counsel, and where it is felt that pre-screening of all arbitrator candidates for conflicts and calendar availability before nomination is preferred").

63 See Queen Mary University of London and Price Waterhouse Surveys at www.arbitration.qmul.ac.uk /research/2015/; Rawding and Reed, the Freshfields Guide to Arbitration Clauses in International Contracts (3rd ed. 2011).

64 See www.iccwbo.org.

65 See www.jamsinternational.com and www.jamsadr.com.

66 See www.lcia.org.

67 See www.icdr.org, and www.adr.org.

68 See www.sccinstitute.com.

69 See www.hkaic.org.

70 See www.siac.org. See also, Christopher Boog, Arbitrating in Singapore – The 2016 SIAC Rules, 84 IPBA J. 36 (December 2016).

71 See www.ceitac.org.

72 See Granof and Aliment, An Introduction to Alternative Dispute Resolution in International Business Transactions, ABA Section on Dispute Resolution Committee News (Fall 2016).

Selection of Arbitrators

12.37 Arbitrator selections typically are made either by "party appointment" or from an institutional list of panelists. Most parties engaged in international arbitrations eschew the limitations of the institutional lists, and prefer to select arbitrators by the historic "party-appointment" process under which each party appoints one neutral arbitrator and the two arbitrators appoint a neutral tribunal chair, usually with the prior consent of the parties.[73] This process offers the parties the assurance that the arbitrators who will hear and decide their disputes have the critical expertise in the technical and legal subjects related to the disputes, and is said to offer the greatest likelihood that the parties will have confidence in and will accept the Tribunal's final award. Such assurance cannot be offered by courtroom litigation where judges are not appointed based on subject-matter expertise.

Powers of Arbitral Tribunal

12.38 The arbitration clause should address the powers conferred on the arbitral tribunal with respect to powers to grant injunctive relief or impose sanctions and remedies, such as punitive damages. Unless remedies are circumscribed by the clause, courts will allow the tribunal freedom to craft any reasonable remedy it may deem appropriate under the circumstances.[74]

Consolidation of Multiple Arbitrations, and Joinder of Non-signatory Parties

12.39 In international construction, arbitration is considered the best dispute resolution option and litigation in foreign jurisdictions is not often viewed favorably. When intertwined multi-party construction disputes arise, however, all too often they are resolved on a "piecemeal" basis because not all parties are found amenable to the jurisdiction of the same forum – some parties are found to have agreed to arbitrate with different parties in separate arbitrations, while others have assumed no contractual obligation to arbitrate and look to litigation for recourse.[75]

---

73 See Friedland and Templeman, The 2012 International Arbitration Survey: Current and Preferred Practices in the Arbitral Process, JAMS Global Construction Solutions 4 (Spring 2013) (reporting that 76% of international respondents participating in the survey preferred selection of the "party-appointment" process for neutral arbitrators.)

74 See, e.g., *David Co. v Jim W. Miller Const., Inc., 444 N.W.2d 836* (Minn. 1989) (upholding a domestic arbitration award in favour of a project owner that required the contractor to buy from the owner the defective project it built for the full resale price that the owner would have received if the project had been properly constructed, and construing the broad discretion and extensive powers conferred upon arbitrators under the American Institute of Architects' arbitration clause).

75 See *Moses H. Cone Mem'l Hosp. v Mercury Constr. Corp., 460 US 1, 20; 103 S. Ct. 927; 74 L. Ed. 2d 765* (1983) (opining that the possibility of the plaintiff having to resolve its disputes in two forums – one in state court and one in arbitration – where one of the parties to the underlying dispute was not a party to the arbitration agreement, "occurs because the relevant federal law requires piecemeal resolution when necessary to give effect to an arbitration agreement" (emphasis in original). The court expressed its strong support for arbitration, but recognized that such judicial support enhances the peril of "Double Jeopardy". See also, *State ex rel. Johnson Controls, Inc. v Tucker, LLC, 729 S. E. 2d 808* (W. Va. 2012) (reversing a trial court order that required seven defendants to litigate a complex construction dispute together before the court, and compelling arbitration of the plaintiff's claims against three of the seven defendants – the prime contractor and two subcontractors – in accordance with the arbitration clauses in their respective contracts).

12.40 Such "piecemeal" resolution causes multi-party disputes and claims arising out of the same intertwined facts (1) to be decided by different arbitrators or judges in separate arbitration or litigation trial forums,[76] and (2) to be reviewed and enforced by different appellate courts under different scopes of judicial review,[77] This uncertainty of outcomes is known as the dispute resolution peril of "Double Jeopardy" – the peril of economically inconsistent decisions. Accepting litigation to reduce the risk of "Double Jeopardy" through enhanced rights in court of joinder and consolidation of parties, however, creates a Faustian Bargain: The litigation option cannot assure that the assigned judge has knowledge of construction industry customs and practices and requisite expertise in deciding complex construction disputes. The risk of "Double Jeopardy" arising out of inconsistent outcomes in "piecemeal" arbitrations, litigation and appeals, combined with the added cost and delay inherent in dual track proceedings, is one major objection often voiced by parties who eschew domestic arbitration in favor of litigation.[78]

12.41 The "jeopardy" risk can be minimized by contract drafters, who craft broad arbitration clauses[79] with expansive joinder, consolidation and appellate arbitration provisions that endeavor to bind all project parties to arbitrate their disputes and claims against each other under the same arbitration rules and before the same tribunal. Such broad clauses, along with broad arbitration rules,[80] endeavor to confirm the authority of the arbitral tribunal or the arbitral administrator (1) to decide challenges to the arbitral tribunal's jurisdiction regarding any issues arising out of or relating to the arbitration, (2) to consolidate multiple arbitrations before a single arbitral tribunal, (3) to join necessary non-signatories in the arbitration proceeding (or otherwise bind such signatories by findings and conclusions in the arbitral tribunal's award), (4) to decide all claims, counter-claims and cross-claims arising out of or related directly or indirectly to the same factual and legal issues

76 See *Grover-Diamond Assocs. v American Arbitration Ass'n, 211 N.W. 2d 787, 788* (Minn. 1973) ("The owners are entitled to arbitrate their dispute with the contractor and their dispute with the architect. There is no suggestion that the architect and contractor are obliged to arbitrate their differences in that [consolidated] proceeding [because neither the contractor nor architect has agreed to arbitrate with the other]. The only question is whether the two arbitration matters demanded by the owners should be heard at the same time and place or whether they should be heard separately').

77 See *Hall Street Associates LLC v Mattel, 552 US 576, 128 S. Ct. 1396, 170 L. Ed. 2d 254* (2008) (confirming the limited scope of judicial review of arbitration awards under the Federal Arbitration Act, and refusing to allow parties to enlarge by agreement the statutory scope of judicial review of arbitration awards under the Act.)

78 See Andrew McDougal, The "Business Case" For and Against International Arbitration, Rocky Mountain Mineral Law Foundation Conference, 2013 RMMLF–INST Paper 11, page 10 (Westlaw)("[T]he simplest and most effective way to account for the business risks posed by multiple parties is to account for them in the arbitration agreement. To be effective, multi-party arbitration clause should provide that each party consents to arbitration against every other party, ensures that every party is given notice of the arbitration proceedings, and provide a mechanism for appointing the arbitrators. Providing a mechanism for the appointment of the arbitral tribunal is particularly important because the traditional appointment method whereby each side selects an arbitrator and then those two parties or their two party-names arbitrators select the chair is ill-suited".)

79 See *Slutsky-Peltz Plumbing & Heating Co., Inc. v Vincennes Community School Corporation, 556 N.E. 2d 344* (Ind. App. 1990) (The arbitration clause authorized joinder of "the Owner, the Contractor and any other persons substantially involved in a common question of fact or law, whose presence is required if complete relief is to be accorded in the arbitration".)

80 Compare the international arbitration rules of JAMS International, ICC, ICDR, HKIAC, LCIA and CIETAC for their somewhat different approaches to consolidation and joinder. See also, Tao and Zhong, A Quick Read of the CIETAC Arbitration Rules 2015, 31 Arb. Int'l 455 (2015).

in dispute – whether asserted as claims in contract, tort, equity, or statute – in one binding award, and (5) to permit any party to appeal an award to an appellate arbitration panel before proceeding with judicial confirmation of the award.

Consolidation of Separate Pending Arbitrations

12.42 Consolidation generally is treated today under arbitral statutes and rules as a procedural issue for arbitrators to decide rather than a substantive issue of arbitrability for the courts.[81] Many courts construe standard arbitration clauses, arbitration statutes and arbitration rules broadly to authorize arbitrators or arbitration administrators to order consolidation of arbitrations having common issues of fact or law.[82] Where consolidation is upheld, a major issue is (1) whether two or more arbitrations are consolidated merely for hearing by their separate tribunals sitting together to hear the evidence and then writing their own awards, or (2) whether the arbitrations are consolidated for all purposes and assigned to with one of the tribunal panels selected to hear and decide all disputes, claims, cross-claims, and counterclaims asserted among all parties. Some jurisdictions have restrictive statutes[83] or case law that deny consolidation absent the express consent of all parties or authorization by other contract or statute.[84] Problems are likely to arise (1) when arbitration clauses are written to require consent of all parties to arbitrate in consolidated proceedings, (2) when agreed arbitration rules fail to address consolidation, or (3) when arbitration clauses are infected by drafting ambiguities.

12.43 The arbitration rules of some institutional administrators, such as JAMS and JAMS International, LCIA, ICDR and ICC, do address consolidation. The broadest consolidation rights appear in the *JAMS Engineering and Construction Arbitration Rules and Procedures (2009)*,[85] Rules 6(e) and 11, which empower JAMS as tribunal administrator to consolidate separately commenced arbitrations involving claims of different parties that have the same "common issues of fact or law", and to designate administratively which selected tribunal will hear the consolidated matters. Once consolidated, parties in both arbitrations are treated for all purposes as parties in one arbitration, and may assert claims and cross-claims against any and all consolidated parties. The JAMS Rules also empower

81 See *Nath v Merrill Lynch, Pierce, Fenner & Smith Inc., 2014 WL 2438435, *4* (N.Y. Sup., May 21, 2014) ("[T]he question of whether arbitration proceedings should (or should not) be consolidated is a procedural matter to be decided by the arbitrators, not by the court").

82 See also, Howes and Stowell, The Consolidation Dilemma: Is there Finally a Pragmatic Solution? 10 Disp. Res. J. 3 (April 2016).

83 See English Arbitration Act 1996, Section 35(2) (allowing consolidation with other arbitral proceedings only if the parties agree to confer such powers upon the tribunal).

84 See *Georgia Casualty & Surety Co. v Excalibur Reinsurance Corp., 2014 WL 996388* (N.D. Ga. March 13, 2014)(denying motion to consolidate two arbitrations arising out of the same transaction, because neither of the respective arbitration clauses nor state statute nor the Federal Arbitration Act expressly authorized the court to order consolidation); *Baesler v Continental Grain Co., 900 F. 2d 1193, 1195* (8th Cir. 1990)(supporting the "view that the Federal Arbitration Act precludes federal courts from ordering consolidation of arbitration proceedings").

85 See JAMS Engineering and Construction Arbitration Rules and Procedures (2009) at www.jamsadr.com under "rules", and JAMS International Arbitration Rules (2011) at www.jamsinternational.com. The American Arbitration Association Construction Arbitration Rules, Rule R-7 provides for AAA appointment of a special independent arbitrator to decide parties' objections to consolidation or joinder.

the arbitrators "to resolve all disputes regarding the interpretation and applicability of these Rules".

12.44 Consolidation rights under international arbitration rules are less definitive. *ICC Arbitration Rules*, Article 10, allows consolidation only where the parties agree, or where all claims are asserted under the same agreement, or, if claims are asserted under separate agreements, where the parties and their legal relationships are the same.[86] *UNCITRAL Arbitration Rules*, Articles 23 and 17.5, and LCIA Arbitration Rules, Articles 23 and 22.1(h), empower the arbitral tribunal to decide its own jurisdiction, allow joinder of additional parties, but do not expressly mention consolidation of separate related arbitration proceedings.[87] The *Canadian Arbitration Association Arbitration Rules* make no mention of either consolidation or joinder, but do empower arbitrators under Rule 7 to hear challenges to their jurisdiction.[88]

Joinder in Arbitration of Non-Signatory Parties

12.45 Like the issues of consolidation and joinder of claims, the issue of joinder of non-signatory parties is controlled (1) by statutes, (2) by the arbitration clause,[89] (3) by the arbitration rules accepted by the signatory parties,[90] and (4) by principles of law.[91] At the heart of the issue is the arbitrators' jurisdiction to decide this joinder issue under the applicable arbitration clause and rules.[92]

---

86 See ICC Arbitration Rules (2017) at www.iccwbo.org.

87 See UNCITRAL Arbitration Rules (2010), Articles 23 and 17, paragraph 5 at www.uncitral.org; ; LCIA Arbitration Rules (1998), Article 23, at www.lcia.org.

88 See Canadian Arbitration Association Arbitration Rules, Rule 7 at www.canadianarbitrationassociation.ca. under "regular arbitration rules".

89 See *Cape Romain Contractors, Inc., v Wando, 747 S.E. 2d 461* (S.C. 2013) (Arbitration clause provided: "Any party to an arbitration may include by joinder persons or entities substantially involved in a common question of law or fact whose presence is required if complete relief is to be accorded in arbitration, provided that the party sought to be joined consents in writing to the joinder). See also, Tamara Lindsay, Compelling Arbitration By and Against Nonsignatories, 36 Constr. Law. 16 (Summer 2016).

90 See JAMS Construction Arbitration Rules, Rule 6(f), and JAMS International Arbitration Rules, Rule 7.3. Compare UNCITRAL Arbitration Rules, Article17.5, and LCIA Arbitration Rules, Article 22.1(h) (empowering the arbitral tribunal to decide its own jurisdiction, and to allow joinder of additional parties). See also, A.H. Gaede and Luke D. Martin, Arbitration Third-Party Joinder after GE ENERGY POWER, 14 J. ACCL 71, 103–8 (Summer 2020). (Discussing nine "state law" joinder principles as well as the institutional international joinder rules of JAMS, ICLR, CPR, ICC, LCIA, UNCITRAL, Swiss Rules, Stockholm Rules, Vienna Rules, CIETAC, Hong Kong, and Singapore. Of those international arbitration rules, the authors conclude: "Assuming the law develops as anticipated, the JAMS Rules and the Swiss rules could, and should, serve as models".)

91 See *GE Energy Conversion France SAS. Corp. v Outokumpu Stainless USA, LLC, 140 S. Ct. 1637* (2020) and *Arthur Anderson LLP v Carlisle, 556 US 624,631* (2009). (A non-signatory to a contract may bind a signatory to arbitrate a dispute when "traditional principles of state law allow a contract to be enforced by or against nonparties to the contract through "assumption, piercing the corporate veil, alter ego, incorporation by reference, third-party beneficiary theories, waiver and estoppel".) See also, Pedro Martinez-Fraga, The Dilemma of Extending International Commercial Arbitration Clauses to Third Parties: Is Protecting Federal Policy While Accommodating Economic Globalization a Bridge to Nowhere?, 46 Cornell Int'l L. J. 291, 319 (Spring 2011)(proposing a broad comprehensive balancing test for joinder in international arbitration based on an "inextricability" standard, and observing that "adherence to the 'traditional principles' of contract law for the purported protection of non-signatories creates a doctrinal test that does not promote symmetry (equitable treatment) between signatories and non-signatories seeking extension of an arbitral clause and undermines federal policy favoring arbitration".

92 See *Zurich American Ins. Co. v Heard, 740 S.E. 2d 429* (Ga. App. 2013) (Denying joinder where the arbitration agreement provided: "No arbitration arising out of or relating to the Contract shall include, by

12.46 US and state courts, for example, support joinder under arbitration clauses and rules that broadly define the jurisdiction of arbitrators to decide the procedural issue of joinder of non-signatory parties.[93] Illustrative of such a rule is *JAMS Engineering and Construction Arbitration Rules and Procedures (2009)*, Rule 6(f), which provides:

> Where a third party seeks to participate in an Arbitration already pending under these Rules or where a Party to an Arbitration under these Rules seeks to compel a third party to participate in a pending Arbitration, the Arbitrator will decide on such request, taking into account all circumstances the Arbitrator deems relevant and applicable.[94]

12.47 Where joinder of non-signatory parties is not restricted by statute or arbitration clauses or rules, courts traversing the widening road from "text" to "context" and from "formalism" to "fairness" may apply one or more of eleven legal doctrines to justify a pro-joinder decision by the arbitrators. These doctrines are articulated under United States law as:

Assumption

12.48 Non-signatories, such as performance bond sureties or contract guarantors who have taken over and completed contracts after default of their principles, and such as lenders who foreclose on defaulting owners' construction loans and must complete projects under construction, often end up assuming obligations to arbitrate with signatory parties under the defaulted contracts.[95] Upon assumption of a contract, an assuming party as an equitable subrogee ordinarily "steps into the contractual shoes" of the defaulting party.[96]

"Piercing the Veil"

12.49 Where a corporate contracting party lacks independent control and substance of its own, its corporate form may be "pierced" and the controlling person or entity may be forced to arbitrate the controlled party's claims and obligations.[97]

---

consolidation or joinder or in any other manner, the Architect, the Architect's employees or consultants, except by written consent containing specific reference to the Agreement and signed by the Architect, Owner, Contractor and any other person or entity sought to be joined".)

93 See *Eckert/Wordell Architects, Inc. v FJM Properties of Wilmar, LLC, 2014 WL 2922343* (8th Cir., 30 June 2014) (affirming an arbitrator's jurisdiction under AAA arbitration rules to order joinder of a non-signatory party).

94 See JAMS Engineering and Construction Arbitration Rules and Procedures (2021) at www.jamsadr.com.

95 See *Employers Ins. of Wausau v Bright Metal Specialties, Inc., 251 F. 3d 1316* (11th Cir. 2001) (by executing a takeover agreement upon default of its principal under the bonded contract, the surety had assumed the principal's obligations under the contract, including the obligation to arbitrate its claims and defences); *United States Fidelity and Guaranty Co. v Bangor Area Joint School Authority, 355 F. Supp. 913* (E.D. Pa. 1973) (compelling a surety to arbitrate its claims against the owner, where the contract was binding on successors and assigns and the surety was a "subrogated" successor).

96 See *Employers Ins. of Wausau v Bright Metal Specialties, Inc., 251 F. 3d 1316* (11th Cir. 2001) (by executing a takeover agreement upon default of its principal under the bonded contract, the surety had assumed the principal's obligations under the contract, including the obligation to arbitrate its claims and defences); *Town of Berlin v Nobel Ins. Co., 758 A. 2d 436* (Conn. Ct. App. 2000) (same).

97 See *Clark Rigging & Rental Corp. v Liberty Mutual Ins. Co, 118 N.Y.S. 3d 337* (N.Y. Sup. 2020) (reviewing veil piercing legal requirements under New York law); *Wm. Passalacqua Builders, Inc. v Resnick Developers South, Inc., 933 F. 2d 131* (2d Cir. 1991.)

Alter Ego

12.50 An alter ego is bound in the same respect as a contracting party it controls.[98] In addition to being used to "pierce the corporate veil", the alter ego principle can be used to impose obligations upon non-corporate "alter ego" entities and individuals as well.[99] A nonsignatory alter ego who controls a signatory party can be held to the same arbitral obligations as the signatory party and may be liable for the signatory party's debts. A non-corporate alter ego may be a nonsignatory joint venture, partnership, limited liability partnership, sole proprietorship, or individual person who controls or is jointly liable for the debts of the signatory.[100] The alter ego status depends only on proof of control or joint liability for debts and does not require proof that the contracting entity was a corporation used for illegal purposes.[101]

Third Party Beneficiary

12.51 An "intended" third party beneficiary (as distinguished from an "incidental" beneficiary) may compel or be joined in arbitration with a signatory of a contract containing an arbitration clause.[102] Whether a third party is an "intended" or "incidental" beneficiary is determined by the parties' intentions as of the time contract execution as inferred from the contract's terms and surrounding circumstances.[103] The Third Party Beneficiary theory, for example, has been applied in condominium defect disputes to allow non-signatory subsequent unit purchasers to arbitrate warranty claims asserted against the original contractor under the original owner-contractor contract providing for arbitration of disputes.[104] The theory also is applied in the context of owner–subcontractor disputes (1) to allow a nonsignatory subcontractor to arbitrate claims that are brought by or against a signatory owner, and that arise out of the owner-contractor contract,[105] or (2) to allow a

98 See *Lancaster v Harold K. Jordon and Co., Inc., 2014 WL 2568567* (N.S. Super., 5 June 2014) (holding owners of a privately held company bound by an arbitration award as "alter egos"); *British Marine PLC v Avanti Shipping & Chartering Ltd., 2014 WL 24575485* (E.D.N.Y., 2 June 2014) (staying arbitration of alter ego claims against non-signatory parties, but noting the preclusive effect of an arbitration award).

99 See *Church Joint Venture LP v Blasingame, 947 F. 3d 925, 930* (6th Cir. 2020) ("As an initial matter, claims of 'alter ego' and 'veil piercing' are not exactly the same. A veil piercing claim seeks to hold a second party liable for another's debt, while an alter ego claim asserts that the two parties should be treated as the same party, so the liability is direct, not vicarious").

100 See *Lancaster v Harold K. Jordon and Co., Inc., 2014 WL 2568567* (N.J. Super., 5 June 2014) (holding owners of a privately held company bound by an arbitration award as "alter egos"); *British Marine PLC v Avanti Shipping & Chartering Ltd., 2014 WL 24575485* (E.D.N.Y., 2 June 2014) (staying arbitration of alter ego claims against non-signatory parties but noting the preclusive effect of an arbitration award upon them).

101 See *Gartner v Snyder, 607 F. 2d 582, 586* (2d Cir. 1979) ("Because New York courts disregard corporate form reluctantly, the do so only when … the corporation has been so dominated by an individual or another corporation … and its separate identity so disregarded, that it primarily transacted the dominator's business rather than its own and can be called the other's alter ego".)

102 See *Superior Energy Services LLC v Cabinda Gulf Oil Company, Ltd., 2013 WL 6406324* (N. D. Cal., 6 December 2013) (reviewing the doctrines of third party beneficiary, incorporation by reference and equitable estoppel under California law, but finding them inapplicable to compel a non-signatory to arbitrate under an arbitration agreement).

103 See *Harland Clarke Holdings Corp. v Miller, 997 F. Supp. 2d 581* (W.D. Tex. 1984).

104 See *Home Corp. v Bay at Cypress Creek Homeowners Ass'n, Inc., 118 So. 3d 957* (Fla. App. 2013).

105 See *Reliable Energy Solutions v Amalfi Apartment Corporation, 2017 WL 3412198* (S.D. Tex., 3 July 2017) (requiring a signatory owner to arbitrate with a nonsignatory subcontractor found to be a third party beneficiary of the owner's obligations under the prime contract); *Asselin & Vieceli Partnership, LLC v Washburn,*

nonsignatory owner to arbitrate claims by or against a signatory subcontractor that arise out of the contractor-subcontractor subcontract .[106]

Incorporation by Reference

12.52 Nonsignatories to a contract frequently are successful in compelling arbitration or joining in arbitration of common disputes under an arbitration clause that has been incorporated by reference into their separate contract.[107] Key issues often are the extent of the parties' understanding of trade custom and usage applicable to "flow down" provisions,[108] the extent to which an arbitration clause in an incorporated document is apparent,[109] and the strictness of contractual interpretation of the incorporated contract and the arbitration clause.[110] Strict judicial interpretation of the language of the incorporated contract without consideration of industry customs and practices can push claims into litigation.[111] More liberal interpretations are based on the "heavy presumption" of arbitrability under federal law and the common construction industry practice and equitable relationships lead to proper joinder results.[112] Major construction industry incorporation by reference issues affect sureties and subcontractors whose obligations typically include performance of prime contract responsibilities incorporated by reference into their respective bonds and subcontracts.[113]

2017 WL 3174502 (Conn. Sup., 20 June 2017)(a contractor could compel a nonsignatory entity to arbitrate because it was a third party beneficiary of the construction contract).

106 See *Hautz Construction LLC v H & M Department Store, 2012 WL 5880370* (D.N.J., 20 November 2012) (ruling that a signatory owner was a third party beneficiary of a subcontract and could compel the subcontractor to arbitrate its claims against the owner under the subcontract's arbitration clause.

107 See *Kvaerner ASA v Bank of Tokyo-Mitsubishi, Ltd., 210 F. 3d 262* (4th Cir. 2000) (an arbitration clause in the guaranty agreement was incorporated by reference into the construction contract,); *Advance Tank and Const. Co., Inc. v Gulf Coast Asphalt Co. LLC, 2006 WL 253600* (Ala. 3 February 2006) (an arbitration clause in an attachment to the prime contract was incorporated by reference into a subcontract and allowed the employer to arbitrate with the subcontractor).

108 See David Ratterman, Codification of Trade Custom and Usage as a Viable Supplement to Construction Contracts, 11 J. ACCL 1 (Winter 2017).

109 See *G & C Builders, Inc. v Lawson, 238 W. Va. 280* (W.Va., 2016) (holding that an employer could not be compelled to arbitrate with a contractor, because the contractor prepared the contract and "failed to provide the detail necessary to ensure that [the employer] was aware of ... the arbitration provision").

110 See Simon Allison and Kanaga Dharmananda, Incorporating Arbitration Clauses: The Sacrifice of Consistency at the Alter of Experience, 30 Arb. Int'l 265 (No. 2, 2014) (tracing the development of England's strict interpretation of arbitration clauses incorporated by reference and concluding: "Attitudes towards arbitration have changed significantly over time. A general contra proferentum approach to arbitration clauses, analogous to the treatment of exclusion clauses, can no longer be sustained. Certainty must be balanced with accuracy, fairness, and recognition of the realities of modern business").

111 See *Schneider Electric Buildings Critical Systems, Inc. v Western Surety Co., 149 A. 3d 778* (Md. App. 2016) (surety not compelled to arbitrate, even though bonded contract contained an arbitration clause and was referenced in the bond).

112 See *Developers Surety and Indemnity Co. v Resurrection Baptist Church, 759 F. Supp. 2d 665* (D. Md. 2010) (construing an arbitration clause, which required arbitration of "any claim arising out of or related to the contract" and which was incorporated by reference into the surety's bonds, as permitting a performance bond surety to arbitrate its claims against the owner and its construction lender); *US Surety Co. v Hanover R.S. Ltd. Partnership, 543 F. Supp. 2d 492* (W.D.N.C. 2008) (surety was compelled to arbitrate pursuant to a subcontract arbitration clause, which was incorporated by reference into its subcontract performance bond).

113 For an extraordinary illustration of the impact of strict versus liberal approaches to judicial interpretation regarding whether a performance bond incorporated by reference an arbitration clause in the bonded contract, see the contrasting judicial opinions involving the same parties in *Developers Surety and Indemnity Co. v Carothers Construction, Inc., 2017 WL 3054646* (D. S.C., 18 July 2017) (surety compelled to arbitrate

Agency

12.53 Non-signatory agents, who carry out contractual duties on behalf of their contracting principals and who are charged with malfeasance by signatories to an arbitration clause having arbitrable disputes, may compel and join in an arbitration between the signatories. The critical nexus is the agency relationship.[114] Agents have a right to join in arbitrations to defend themselves against allegations of malfeasance that form the basis of claims against their principals or to join with their principals in asserting affirmative claims against other arbitrating parties.[115]

Equitable Estoppel

12.54 Non-signatory parties without an agency relationship also may compel or be joined in arbitrations where claims allege their misconduct in performance of duties intertwined with claims asserted against signatory parties under agreements authorizing arbitration.[116] The doctrine of equitable estoppel is available to non-signatories who wish to stay litigation pending arbitration, and to compel arbitration of allegations of malfeasance related to the contract authorizing arbitration, and asserted by a signatory to the contract engaged in litigation.[117] The signatory is said to be "equitably estopped" to avoid arbitration. The Doctrine is stated thusly:

---

under liberal interpretation finding an incorporation by reference of an arbitration clause into the performance bond), and *Developers Surety and Indemnity Co. v Carothers Construction, Inc., 2017 WL 3674975* (D. Kan., 24 August 2017) (refusing to compel arbitration based on strict interpretation regarding incorporation by reference of the arbitration clause into the performance bond).

114 See *Provenzano v Ohio Valley General Hospital, 121 A. 3d 1085, 1097* (Pa. Super. 2014) ("Pennsylvania law has held that non-signatories to an arbitration agreement can enforce the agreement when there is an 'obvious and close nexus' between the non-signatories and the contract or the contracting parties ... One 'obvious and close nexus' between non-signatories and the contract or the contracting parties arises from the relationship between a signatory principal and a non-signatory agent".)

115 See *Leighton v Chesapeake Appalachia, LLC., 2013 WL 6191739* (M. D. Pa., 26 November 2013) (ruling that under agency theory, non-signatory subsidiaries of the respondent, which carried out respondent's duties in performing fracking operations, could join in the arbitration and compel the claimants to arbitrate their claims against them pursuant to the arbitration agreement).

116 See *Renewable Energy Products, LLC v Lakeland Development Co., 2011 WL 68394* (Cal. Ct. App., 28 February 2011) (reversing the trial court, and compelling the claimant to arbitrate claims with signatory and non-signatory parties); *Grigson v Creative Artists Agency LLC, 310 F. 3d 524* (5th Cir. 2000) ("The linchpin for equitable estoppel is equity – fairness. For the case at hand, to not apply this intertwined-claims basis to compel arbitration [with a non-signatory] would fly in the face of fairness"); *MS Dealer Services Corp v Franklin, 177 F. 3d 942, 947* (11th Cir. 1999):

> Existing case law demonstrates that equitable estoppel allows a non-signatory to compel arbitration in two difference circumstances. First, equitable estoppel applies when the signatory to a written agreement containing an arbitration clause must rely on the terms of the written agreement in asserting its claims against the nonsignatory. When each of a signatory's claims against a non-signatory makes reference to or presumes the existence of the written agreement, the signatory's claims arise out of and relate directly to the written agreement, and arbitration is appropriate. Second, application of equitable estoppel is warranted when the signatory to the contract containing an arbitration clause raises allegations of substantially interdependent and concerted misconduct by both the nonsignatory and one or more of the signatories to the contract. Otherwise the arbitration proceedings between the two signatories would be rendered meaningless and the federal policy in favour of arbitration effectively thwarted.

117 See *Pritzker v Merrill Lynch, Pierce, Fenner & Smith, Inc., 7 F. 3d 1110, 1112* (3d. Cir. 1993) (holding that claims against non-signatory "corporate sister" of signatory corporation fell within the scope of an arbitration agreement because plaintiff's theory of liability demonstrated that corporate sister's interests were "directly related to, if not predicated upon" the alleged wrongful conduct). Any other result would permit a party to "obviate the effect of the agreement merely by finding a way to join another party"); *Arnold v Arnold*

Where a signatory to a contract containing an arbitration agreement has sued a non-signatory, equitable estoppel allows the non-signatory to compel the signatory to arbitrate in two circumstances: (1) when the signatory has raised allegations of substantially interdependent and concerted misconduct by both the non-signatory and one or more of the signatories to the contract; or (2) when the nature of the signatory's claims against the non-signatory requires reliance on the agreement containing an arbitration provision. In other words, the non-signatory is bound to arbitrate if its claim seeks to enforce the terms containing the arbitration provision. The non-signatory cannot enforce specific terms of the agreement while seeking to avoid the arbitration provision. The application of this doctrine falls with the trial court's discretion.[118]

12.55 Non-signatories, however, may not use equitable estoppel affirmatively to compel arbitration of their own claims without signatories first having commenced litigation against them. To that extent, the right of arbitration remains consensual.

Assignment

12.56 A legal assignment permits the assignee to enforce contractual rights of its assignor against other parties to the assigned contract. This includes arbitration rights contained in the assigned contract.[119] Assignments of contract rights routinely are invoked expressly in settlement of affirmative claims by non-signatory parties, where the settlement is less than full value, to preserve recourse for the unpaid balance against third parties. Typically, the settlement agreement expressly conveys the assignor's contract rights against third party signatories, including the right to arbitrate.[120] Assignment also can occur as a matter of law, where a surety or guarantor completes the guaranteed contract upon the principal's default.[121]

Corp., 920 F. 2d 1269, 1281 (6th Cir. 1990) ("[I]f appellant can avoid the practical consequences of an agreement to arbitrate by naming non-signatory parties as defendants in his complaint, or signatory parties in their individual capacities only, the effect of the rule requiring arbitration would, in effect, be nullified".)

118 See *Cappadonna Electric Management v Cameron County, 180 S.W. 3d 364, 373* (Tex. App. 2005). See also, *Corporate America Credit Union v Herbst, 397 Fed. Appx. 540* (11th Cir. 2010) ("Equitable estoppel precludes a party from claiming the benefits of a contract while simultaneously attempting to avoid the burdens that contract imposes. The purpose of the doctrine is to prevent a plaintiff from, in effect, trying to have his cake and eat it too; that is, from relying on the contract, when it works to his advantage by establishing the claim, and repudiating it when it works to his disadvantage by requiring arbitration"); *Waterhouse Const. Group, Inc. v 5891 SW 64th Street, LLC, 949 So. 2d 1095* (Fla Dist. Ct. App. 2007)(non-signatories could compel arbitration of RICO claims brought in connection with a construction project, where the non-signatories were officers, directors or agents of the construction company and assumed duties under the contract containing an arbitration clause).

119 See *Cone Constructors, Inc. v Drummond Community Bank, 754 So. 2d 779* (Fla. App. 2000) (upholding a bank's right to compel arbitration under an assigned contract).

120 See *Robert Lamb Hart Planners and Architects v Evergreen, Ltd., 787 F. Supp. 753* (S. D. Ohio 1992) (upholding a contractor's right to arbitrate its claims against an architect based on an assignment from the owner of its claims against the architect, even though the Owner-Architect contract precluded joinder and arbitration of claims with anyone not a party to the contract).

121 See *United States Fidelity and Guaranty Co. v Bangor Area Joint School Authority, 355 F. Supp. 913* (E.D. Pa. 1973) (compelling a surety to arbitrate its claims against the owner, where the contract was binding on successors and assigns and the surety was a "subrogated" surety).

Successor in Interest

12.57 A legal successor in interest by operation of law has the same contractual rights against signatory parties as the party to whose interests it bound to its contractual obligations succeeds. That includes any right of arbitration. [122]

"Inextricable Nexus"

12.58 Non-signatory parties, whose claims and defenses have an indisputably "inextricable nexus" to claims in arbitration can join and be joined.[123] This principle has been articulated as follows:

> This "inextricability" component [after confirmation of the operative arbitration agreement] represents a non-contractually based, flexible approach that is fundamentally premised on the connections between the non-signatory and the underlying instrument comprising an arbitration agreement, as well as to the claims asserted. Essential to this analysis is strict scrutiny of the commercial effects of the transaction at issue. This approach invites tribunals to weigh and consider the actual workings of a transaction at a micro level between the signatories and from a more macro perspective touching non-parties to the agreement. Certainly, it would not be altogether implausible for a tribunal to focus on issues pertaining to industry sectors or broader market considerations. A "connectivity" review of the claims to determine whether a specific non-party is materially affected, or affected at all by the operative averments, also challenges the tribunal to undertake (i) joinder, (ii) indispensable party, (iii) standing, and (iv) third-party related analyses.[124]

12.59 Although this "intertwining" principle is often stated as a stand-alone concept, the concept is in reality the second prong of the Doctrine of Equitable Estoppel, and often is recognized by courts as equitable estoppel. This principle is particularly helpful to compel arbitration of related affirmative claims between signatories against non-signatories on a multi-party project, where the arbitration clauses allow joinder of "any other persons substantially involved in a common question of fact or law, whose presence is required for complete relief".[125]

---

122 See *Saxa, Inc. v DFD Architecture, Inc., 312 S. W. 3d 224* (Tex. App. 2010) (allowing successors to the owner's interest to arbitrate claims against an architect, because the owner-architect contract called for arbitration of "any claim, dispute or other matter in question arising out of or related to" the contract).

123 *Great American Insurance Co. v Hinkle Contracting Corp., 497 Fed. Appx. 348, 2012 WL 5936178* (4th Cir., 2012)(requiring a performance bond surety for a subcontractor to arbitrate its "surety defenses" to its bond liability with the general contractor, because the defenses bore a "substantial relationship" to a change order issued under the bonded subcontract that contained an arbitration clause); *Giller v Cafeteria of South Beach LTD., 967 So. 2d 240* (Fla. App. 2007)(allowing a non-signatory architect to demand arbitration with an owner under an architectural services agreement between his employer and the owner, "because there is an indisputable nexus between these claims and the Professional Services Agreement").

124 Pedro Martinez-Fraga, The Dilemma of Extending International Commercial Arbitration Clauses to Third Parties: Is Protecting Federal Policy While Accommodating Economic Globalization a Bridge to Nowhere?, 46 Cornell Int'l L. J. 291, 319 (Spring 2011)(proposing a broad comprehensive balancing test for joinder in international arbitration based on an "inextricability" standard, and observing that "adherence to the "traditional principles" of contract law for the purported protection of non-signatories creates a doctrinal test that does not promote symmetry (equitable treatment) between signatories and non-signatories seeking extension of an arbitral clause and undermines federal policy favoring arbitration. ").

125 See *Slutsky-Peltz Plumbing & Heating Co., Inc. v Vincennes Community School Corporation, 556 N. E. 2d 344* (Ind. App. 1990) (Multi-prime contractors where compelled to join an arbitration between one of the contractors and the owner, where the claims involved responsibility for project delays. The arbitration clause

Waiver

12.60 Like any contract right, the right to arbitrate disputes or the right to avoid arbitration may be waived expressly[126] or by conduct.[127] Thus, a party may waive its right to arbitrate a dispute by joining and participating without objection in litigation adjudicating the dispute or may waive its right not to arbitrate a dispute by joining and participating without objection in the arbitration addressing the dispute.

Subrogation

12.61 Nonsignatory sureties, insurers or guarantors who pay sums for and on behalf of a contractor have rights of subrogation. Sureties who suffer loss under their construction bonds, insurers who pay sums to protect their insureds under their property and liability policies, or guarantors who pay off their contractor loans, are said to "stand in the shoes" of the contractors and thus are subrogated to the rights of the contractors to pursue claims to recover their losses. Subrogation is said to result in an "implied assignment" of a contractor's contract rights and claims against others to the extent of their losses. This "implied assignment" also occurs as a matter of law, where a surety or guarantor completes the guaranteed contract upon the principal's default.[128] Courts have allowed subrogated parties to exercise the contractors' arbitration rights under the contract out of which their losses arose.[129]

"Vouching-In" Rights Against Indemnitors

12.62 "Vouching-in"[130] is an important common law concept in construction arbitration that can bind third party nonsignatory indemnitors to factual determinations of an arbitration award or court judgment – ***whether or not*** *they are joined as parties*. Contractors and subcontractors commonly enter written contracts containing arbitration clauses, as well as express indemnity, insurance, guarantee, warranty and surety obligations benefitting other contract signatories. When disputes arise regarding the work, one or more arbitrating contract signatories may seek to join nonsignatory parties owing indemnity obligations, such as sub-subcontractors, suppliers, insurers, sureties, material warrantors, and sub-tier sureties, to avoid dual proceedings and to minimize the risk of inconsistent find-

authorized joinder of "the Owner, the Contractor and any other persons substantially involved in a common question of fact or law, whose presence is required if complete relief is to be accorded in the arbitration").

126 See *American Express Co. v Italian Colors Restaurant, 133 US 2304 2013* (upholding signatory parties' express waiver of class arbitration).

127 See *Nucor-Yamato Steel Co. v J.D. Fields & Co., Inc., 2016 WL 6156188* (E.D. Ark., 2 February 2016) ("A party may waive the right to arbitration if the party: (1) knew of an existing right to arbitration; (2) acted inconsistently with that right; and (3) prejudiced the other party by these inconsistent acts").

128 See *United States Fidelity and Guaranty Co. v Bangor Area Joint School Authority, 355 F. Supp. 913* (E.D. Pa. 1973) (compelling a surety to arbitrate its claims against the owner, where the contract was binding on successors and assigns, and the surety was a "subrogated" surety).

129 See *Equistar Chemicals LP v Hartford Steam Boiler and Inspection Company of Connecticut, 883 N. W. 2d 740* (Ill. App. 2008) (allowing an insurer to exercise its insured's arbitration right under the contract); Blumenthal-Kahn Elec. Ltd. v American Home Assur. Co., 236 F. Supp. 2d 575 (E.D. Va. 2002) (ruling that a contractor's surety could pursue a subcontractor to recover its losses pursuant to the arbitration clause in the contractor-subcontractor agreement.)

130 See *Philip L. Bruner and Patrick J. O'Connor, Jr., Bruner and O'Connor on Construction Law §§10:95–10:101.* (2002, supplemented and updated annually). See also, *Fidelity and Deposit Co. of Maryland v Parsons & Whittemore Constructors Corp., 397 N.E. 2d 380, 383* (N.Y.1979);

ings. Should such nonsignatory parties have actual or constructive notice of the arbitration and fail to do so, they risk being bound by the award.[131]

12.63 If the joinder effort is unsuccessful, the nonsignatory indemnitor may still be bound to the factual determinations of an adverse arbitration award by invoking at an early stage the procedure of "vouching-in" as follows:

> "Vouching-in" is a common-law procedural device by which a defendant notifies another: (a) of the pendency of a suit [or arbitration} against him; (b) that if liability is found, the defendant will look to the vouchee for indemnity; (c) that the notice constitutes a formal tender of the right to defend the action; and (d) that, if the vouchee refuses to defend, it will be bound in any subsequent litigation between them to the factual determinations necessary to the original judgment [or award].

***

Voucher is usually employed in situations where the vouchee is not subject to personal jurisdiction. The procedure has also been employed where it is not possible to obtain jurisdiction over all the relevant parties in one proceeding because of the existence of arbitration provisions prohibiting joinder.[132]

12.64 A third-party indemnitor will not be bound by factual determinations in an arbitral award, if the nonsignatory indemnitor's refusal to join in the arbitration was based on an express contractual reservation[133] or if the arbitration award contains no factual findings.[134]

Implied Consent

12.65 The Doctrine of Implied Contract infers contractual rights and duties from conduct and the contextual transaction rather than from formal contractual expressions of parties. The doctrine has not often been invoked to compel joinder of non-signatories in arbitration. This doctrine, however, has been invoked repeatedly to find implied modifications of express contract, implied warranties and duties of design and construction,

131 See *United States and Skip Kirchdorfer, Inc. v M. J. Kelley Corp., 995 F. 2d 656* (6th Cir. 1993) (individual sureties who had actual or constructive notice of an arbitration against its bond principal and failed to appear were bound by a default award against the sureties' principal when the principal failed to appear); Duferco Int'l Steel Trading v T. Klaveness Shipping A/S, 333 F. 3d 383 (2d Cir. 2003).

132 Philip L. Bruner and Patrick J. O'Connor, Jr., Bruner and O'Connor on Construction Law §§10:95. (2002, supplemented and updated annually). See also, *Duferco International Steel Trading v T. Klaveness Shipping A/S, 333 Fed. 3d 383, 386* (2d Cir. 2003) ("Vouching-in is a common law procedural device that allows a party to arbitration to join a nonparty alleged indemnitor, referred to as the vouchee, by notifying the nonparty of the pendency of an arbitration that might obligate the vouchee to indemnify the defendant ... Vouching-in is used where the vouchee cannot be impleaded because of defects in personal jurisdiction. The purpose of this legal device is to avoid duplicative litigation and the attendant possibility of inconsistent results").

133 See, e.g., Application of Perkins and Will Partnership, 502 NYS 2d 318 (App. Div. 1986) (denying the preclusive effect of an arbitration award against an architect, where vouching-in was unavailable because the architect's contract with the owner expressly rejected arbitration with any party other than the owner without its written consent).

134 See *Guy. C. Long, Inc. v Insul/Crete Co. Inc. 1993 WL 218901* (E.D Pa., 18 June 1993) (arbitration award contained no factual findings and thus had no preclusive effect).

implied duties to cooperate and not hinder or delay the other party, implied authority to bind an employer, and implied waiver of rights.

12.66 The Implied Contract Doctrine has been invoked to suggest, among other things, that parties who engage in large multi-party projects under individual contracts that include the same standard terms, conditions and arbitration clauses, and that contain expressions of third-parties' roles and duties on the project, and who perform under such contracts, "impliedly agree" to arbitrate with non-signatory third parties performing the other individual contracts. On virtually all large construction projects involving multiple parties, standard contract documents routinely refer to the duties of other parties.[135] This implied contract theory, although not widely articulated by the judiciary, has proponents. Opining that the "implied contract" theory was more appropriate than equitable estoppel or other theories as justification for joining a non-signatory party in an arbitration, one judge wrote:

> An agreement implied in fact is founded upon a meeting of minds, which although not embodied in an express contract, is inferred, as a fact, from conduct of the parties showing, in the light of surrounding circumstances, their tacit understanding ... [Here] the same contract designated a nonsignatory party as construction manager and outlines the duties of the owner, construction contractor, construction manager, and in one case, the architect, with respect to the construction project. The construction managers in both cases [in litigation] had not signed the owner-contractor agreement but had signed separate contracts containing similar arbitration clauses with either the owner or the owner's architect. By performing duties and accepting benefits under the interlocking and integrated system of contraction contracts and relationships the contractors impliedly agreed to be bound to arbitrate disputes with the construction managers concerning the performance of the managers' duties assigned by and performed under the owner-contractor agreement, although the managers had only signed the related but separate contract documents between themselves and the owner or its architect. [136]

"Good Faith"

12.67 Although not commonly invoked to compel or reject joinder of non-signatories, the common law doctrine of good faith and fair dealing warrants observation. Recent commentary espouses "good faith" as an overarching doctrine (more expansive than the principle of equitable estoppel or "alter ego") to govern arbitration issues including compelling or denying joinder of non-signatories.[137] In many common law jurisdictions,

135 See, e.g., the American Institute of Architects, Conditions of Contract for Construction, Document A201-2007, (defining the roles and duties of the owner, contractors and architect, and providing for arbitration of disputes unless opting for litigation).

136 *Grigson v Creative Artists Agency LLC, 210 F. 3d 524, 533–4* (5th Cir. 2000). The court's approach does not go as far as the "Group of Companies" theory accepted in France and India but not the United States or England. For more on this theory, see Charlie Caher, Dharshini Prasad and Shanelle Irani, The Group of Companies Doctrine – Assessing the Indian Approach, 9 Indian J. Arb. Law Issue 233 (2019) and *Peterson Farms, Inc. v C & M Farming Ltd.*, [2004] EWHC (Comm) 121 (Eng.).

137 See Christina Perry, Good Faith in English and US Contract Law: Divergent Theories, Practical Similarities, 17 Bus. L. Int'l 27 (January 2016); Stefan Leupertz, The Principle of Good Faith in German Civil Law, 33 Int'l Constr. L. Rev. 67 (January 2016); Bernardo Cremades, Good Faith in International Arbitration, 27 Am. U. Int'l L. Rev. 761 (2012); Aubrey Thomas, Comment: Nonsignatories in arbitration: a Good-Faith Analysis, 14 Lewis & Clark L. Rev. 953 (Fall 2010) ("This Comment proposes that US Courts should apply the principle of good faith to determine whether arbitration including a nonsignatory is appropriate. Essentially, courts should utilize the equitable principle of good faith to analyze both the contractual language as well as

an implied duty of good faith is read into every contract as a matter of law.[138] In many civil law jurisdictions, the principle of good faith is paramount.[139] Implication of the doctrine to joinder issues suggests that nonsignatory persons or entities intimately involved with or benefitted by contractual negotiation or performance may join or be joined in an arbitration.

12.68 Like the issues of consolidation and joinder of claims, the issue of joinder of non-signatory parties is controlled (1) by statutes, (2) by the arbitration clause,[140] (3) by the arbitration rules accepted by the signatory parties,[141] and (4) by principles of law.[142] At

---

the conduct of the parties during negotiation and performance of the contract to determine whether the nonsignatory may compel or be compelled to arbitrate".)

138 See *MSC Mediterranian Shipping Co., v Cottenex Anstalt, 2015 EW HC 283* (recognizing the existence of an "organizing principle of good faith"). See also, *Bannum v US, 80 Fed. Cl. 239* (2008) ("In every contract there exists an implied covenant of good faith and fair dealing. In a government contract, an implied covenant of good faith and fair dealing requires the government not to use its unique position as sovereign to target the legitimate expectations of its contracting partners … For the plaintiff to successfully assert a claim for breach of the implied covenant of good faith and fair dealing respecting a contract with the government, he or she must allege and prove facts constituting a specific intent to injure the plaintiff on the part of the government official"). See generally Uniform Commercial Code, Section 2-103(1) (good faith means "honesty in fact and the observance of reasonable commercial standards of fair dealing"); Restatement (Second) of Contracts, Section 205, cmt. a ("Good faith performance or enforcement of a contract emphasizes faithfulness to an agreed common purpose and consistency with the justified expectations of the other party; it excludes a variety of types of conduct characterized as involving 'bad faith' because they violate community standards of decency, fairness or reasonableness".)

See also, UNIDROIT Principles (2010), Article 1.7, at www.uncitral.org (general principle of good faith); Uniform Commercial Code, Section 2-103(1) (good faith means "honesty in fact and the observance of reasonable commercial standards of fair dealing"); Restatement (Second) of Contracts, Section 205, cmt. a ("Good faith performance or enforcement of a contract emphasizes faithfulness to an agreed common purpose and consistency with the justified expectations of the other party; it excludes a variety of types of conduct characterized as involving 'bad faith' because they violate community standards of decency, fairness or reasonableness").

139 See *Motorola Credit Corp. v Uzan, 388 F. 3d 39* (2d Cir. 2004) (applying Swiss law, and ruling that a nonsignatory "alter ego" could not compel arbitration with a signatory where the nonsignatory had failed to act in good faith and had violated the equitable principle of "unclean hands"). See also, Stefan Leupertz, The Principle of Good Faith Under German Law, 33 ICLR 67 (January 2016); *MSC Mediterranean Shipping Co., v Cottenex Anstalt, 2015 EW HC 283* (recognizing the existence of an "organizing principle of good faith" under English law).

140 See *Cape Romain Contractors, Inc., v Wando, 747 S.E. 2d 461* (S.C. 2013) (Arbitration clause provided: "Any party to an arbitration may include by joinder persons or entities substantially involved in a common question of law or fact whose presence is required if complete relief is to be accorded in arbitration, provided that the party sought to be joined consents in writing to the joinder".) See also, Tamara Lindsay, Compelling Arbitration By and Against Nonsignatories, 36 Constr. Law. 16 (Summer 2016).

141 See also, UNCITRAL Arbitration Rules, Article 17.5, and LCIA Arbitration Rules, Article 22.1(h) (empowering the arbitral tribunal to decide its own jurisdiction, and to allow joinder of additional parties).

142 See *Arthur Anderson LLP v Carlisle, 556 US 624,631 (*2009) (A non-signatory to a contract may bind a signatory to arbitrate a dispute when "traditional principles of state law allow a contract to be enforced by or against nonparties to the contract through "assumption, piercing the corporate veil, alter ego, incorporation by reference, third-party beneficiary theories, waiver and estoppel".) See also, Pedro Martinez-Fraga, The Dilemma of Extending International Commercial Arbitration Clauses to Third Parties: Is Protecting Federal Policy While Accommodating Economic Globalization a Bridge to Nowhere?, 46 Cornell Int'l L. J. 291, 319 (Spring 2011)(proposing a broad comprehensive balancing test for joinder in international arbitration based on an "inextricability" standard, and observing that "adherence to the 'traditional principles' of contract law for the purported protection of non-signatories creates a doctrinal test that does not promote symmetry (equitable treatment) between signatories and non-signatories seeking extension of an arbitral clause and undermines federal policy favoring arbitration".

the heart of the issue is the arbitrators' jurisdiction to decide this joinder issue under the applicable arbitration clause and rules.[143]

Appellate Arbitration: Overcoming Disparities in Scopes of Judicial Review and "Getting the Arbitration Award Right"

12.69 The arbitration clause should consider appellate arbitration. A major concern often raised by parties opposed to binding arbitration of complex disputes is the limited statutory scope of judicial review available to vacate an adverse arbitral award when arbitrators "get it wrong". A 2011 landmark survey of corporate counsel in Fortune 1000 companies identified "leading concerns about binding arbitration [as] the lack of judicial review on the merits, the qualifications of arbitrators, and the belief that arbitrators tend to compromise and ignore legal norms [rather than enforce the contract according to applicable law]".[144]

12.70 Under the New York Convention, the grounds for vacation of an arbitration award are limited to arbitrator misconduct, exceeding powers, corruption, fraud, evident partiality, and public policy.[145] Such grounds are far more limited than those available for judicial

---

143 See *Zurich American Ins. Co. v Heard, 740 S.E. 2d 429* (Ga. App. 2013) (denying joinder where the arbitration agreement provided: "No arbitration arising out of or relating to the Contract shall include, by consolidation or joinder or in any other manner, the Architect, the Architect's employees or consultants, except by written consent containing specific reference to the Agreement and signed by the Architect, Owner, Contractor and any other person or entity sought to be joined").

144 See Thomas Stipanowich and Ryan Lamare, Living with ADR: Evolving Perceptions and Use of Mediation, Arbitration and Conflict Management in Fortune 1000 Corporations, 19 Harv. Negotiation L. Rev. 1 (Fall 2014). Professors Thomas Stipanowich and Ryan Lamare advise that such concerns can be addressed as follows:

[C]oncerns about arbitrators' conformance to legal norms may be addressed by selecting experienced lawyers or former judges as arbitrators (now the prevailing norm in commercial arbitration), through competent legal advocacy ... and by imposing contractual standards for award-making in accordance with applicable law. Despite statutory limitations on judicial scrutiny of the merits of arbitration awards, some organizations publish appellate arbitration rules offering different models for review of arbitration awards. Concerns about arbitrator compromise may be allayed by better information about award-making, more specific guidance for arbitrators regarding award-making, and relying on single arbitrators in lieu of multi-member panels that might be tempted, for example, to rely on compromise to fix damages.

145 See Bruner and McCormick, Enforcement of Foreign Arbitral Awards: The US View of International Arbitration's "Final Frontier", 11 Int'l Constr. L. Rev. 128 (1994). Article V of the New York Convention establishes only seven defences with which a party may block enforcement of an arbitral award. The court may raise the last two of these grounds *sua sponte* to decline enforcement. These grounds are:

(1) The absence of a valid agreement to submit the dispute to arbitration;
(2) The lack of proper notice or opportunity to present a case;
(3) The arbitral award exceeds the scope of the issues properly submitted to arbitration;
(4) Improper composition of the arbitral panel;
(5) The award is not yet binding or has been properly set aside;
(6) The subject matter of the award is not arbitrable under the law of the enforcing country;
(7) Recognition and enforcement would be contrary to the public policy of the enforcing country.

These grounds to set aside arbitral awards are also incorporated, with minor modifications, into the Model Law on International Commercial Arbitration adopted in 1985 by the United Nations Commission on International Trade Law ("UNCITRAL"). The "public policy" exception to enforcement has been of ambiguity. See IBA Subcommittee on Recognition and Enforcement of Arbitral Awards, Report on the Public Policy Exception in the New York Convention (October 2015).

appellate reversal of judgments on the merits, such as mistakes, errors of law, insufficiency of evidence or correction of other substantive or procedural legal deficiencies.

12.71 Because of the stringent statutory limitations on judicial vacation of arbitral awards, construction parties have endeavored for years to enlarge by agreement the statutory scope judicial review of arbitral awards. Parties' consensual enlargement of the scope of judicial review of arbitral awards, however, has been roundly rejected by the United States Supreme Court.[146] Other countries purporting to grant arbitrating parties broader statutory scopes of judicial review of arbitral awards do so by statutes that still are unclear and somewhat restrictive.[147] Canadian law, for example, empowers Canadian courts to vacate arbitration awards for errors on "questions of law" and "questions of fact" only if the parties so provide in their arbitration agreement.[148] Where the arbitration agreement does not so provide, parties may still appeal an arbitration award on a "question of law", but the standard of judicial review is not *de novo*, and is restricted to a standard of "reasonableness", unless the court determines the question of law to be of "central importance to the legal system … and outside the … specialized area of expertise of the administrative decision maker", in which case the standard for review is "correctness". To confuse matters further, relief for errors of law or errors of fact can only be granted on questions not presented to the arbitral tribunal for decision.[149] As a consequence, it is difficult even for a Canadian arbitration award to be vacated for ordinary legal or substantive errors.[150] The enunciated Canadian scope of judicial review suggests that – absent a clear agreement of the parties in the arbitration clause and a clear reservation of an appealed question of law from the arbitral tribunal – an arbitral award likely will not be vacated unless the award is infected by a critical error or law of central importance to the legal system, or is clearly "unreasonable"; that is, near arbitrary and capricious.

12.72 To avoid entirely this issue of the limited scope of judicial review in North America and elsewhere – and to assure decisions by experts on the merits – parties are beginning

146 See *Hall Street Associates LLC v Mattel, 552 US 576, 128 S. Ct. 1396, 170 L. Ed. 2d 254* (2008) (holding that parties could not enlarge by agreement the scope of judicial review of arbitration awards under the Federal Arbitration Act.) A few state courts construing arbitration statutes not preempted by the Federal Arbitration Act and addressing only intra-state commerce, still allow parties to enlarge by contract the state's statutory grounds for award *vacatur*. See *Cable Connection, Inc. v DIRECTTV, Inc. 44 Cal. Rptr. 4th 1334* (2008) (holding that parties may enlarge by agreement the scope of judicial review of arbitration awards under the California Arbitration Act).

147 See England's Arbitration Act 1996, Sections 69 and 70, which limit appeals of questions of law arising out of an arbitral award to those to which all parties consent or with leave of court upon a judicial determination that the tribunal's decision is "obviously wrong" and substantially affect the rights of one or more parties. See also, Tweeddale, Section 69 of the English Arbitration Act 1996 – When Fact and Law Collide, 80 Arbitration 136 (April 2014).

148 See *Dunsmuir v New Brunswick, 2008 SCC 9* [2008]. A standard of "reasonableness" means that the award "falls within a range of possible, acceptable outcomes which are defensible in respect of the facts and the law".

149 See, e.g., Alberta Arbitration Act, Rev. Stat. Alberta 2000, Chap. A-43, Section 44.

150 See *Homexx v Nelson, 2013 ABQB 513* (11 September 2013), in which both arbitrating parties sought vacation of an arbitration award rendered on a dispute over the construction of a home at a wrong elevation lower than contractually specified, which caused ponding. The arbitrator found the contractor in breach of its contract, but rejected the owner's requested recovery of "cost of repair" in favour of ordering the contractor to change the grade around the house and driveway. Both the homeowner and contractor appealed this award. The Court of Queen's Bench of Alberta denied both appeals and confirmed the award, because no question of law of "central importance to the legal system has been raised" and because any other question of law was mixed with fact and had been presented to the arbitrator for decision.

to recognize the wisdom of using Appellate Arbitration.[151] Appellate Arbitration allows the parties to maintain control over the scope of review, and to select appellate arbitrators with recognized expertise in construction law, customs and practices, and management of arbitration proceedings. Pursuant to the parties' agreement, the arbitral tribunal reviews the appealed arbitral award promptly and efficiently under an agreed scope of review.

12.73 The *JAMS Optional Arbitration Appeal Procedure*[152] promulgated in June 2003 offers one example of a formal appellate arbitration process. Such a standard of review affords *de novo* review of issues of law, rather than more limited statutory grounds for *vacatur* of an arbitral award. Unless the parties agree otherwise, the *Procedure* provides for a scope of arbitral review identical to that of appellate courts in the same jurisdiction at the seat of the arbitration. As a starting point, *Procedure* Rule (D) states:

> The Appeal Panel will apply the same standard of review that the first-level appellate court in the jurisdiction would apply to an appeal from the trial court decision.

12.74 The appellate arbitration process undercuts objections to arbitration by maintaining party control over the scope and procedure for review, and appointing experts of their choice to assure enforcement of the contract in accordance with applicable law. With the added oversight of the expert appellate arbitrators, all parties can have confidence that the award when reviewed and perhaps modified has "gotten it right". Instead of an appeal process dragging on for years, the appellate award is rendered promptly on such record as the parties present. The reviewed award is much more likely to be confirmed and not vacated by a court. This likely is the wave of the future.

The Practical Arbitration Process

12.75 The process of arbitration is described in detail in the arbitration rules of institutional administrators.[153] The fundamental purpose of the process is to provide the parties with "due process" consistent with their agreement to arbitrate.

12.76 The process begins with the service of by the claimant of a notice (sometimes described as a demand) for arbitration upon one or more respondents. The respondents then have a designated time in which to answer the demand and, where appropriate, to serve an objection challenging jurisdiction. Arbitrators are then selected by the parties. The arbitrators then must submit disclosures of potential conflicts. After considering the disclosures,[154] any party may challenge appointment of any arbitrator based upon justifiable doubts as to an arbitrator's impartiality and independence. After deciding any challenge, the institutional administrator or other "appointing authority" confirms the appointment of the arbitrators.

151 See Judge Rudolph Kass, A Private Path to Appellate Arbitration, 50 Fed. Bar. J. 35 (January/February 2006) (Appellate arbitration "dodges the considerable uncertainty of being able to obtain judicial review of an arbitral award, and fashions a mechanism to correct serious errors".)

152 JAMS Optional Arbitration Appeal Procedure (June 2003) at www.jamsadr.com. See also, AAA/ICDR Optional Appellate Arbitration Rules (2013).

153 See UNCITRAL Arbitration Rules (2010), Articles 17–43; JAMS Engineering and Construction Arbitration Rules 16–33; JAMS International Arbitration Rules 21-39; ICC Arbitration Rules, Articles 16–37; LCIA Rules 14–22, and arbitration rules of other institutional administrators.

154 See, e.g., IBA Guidelines on Conflicts of Interest in International Arbitration (2014).

12.77 Following selection and appointment of the arbitral tribunal, and submission of parties' formal statements of claims and defenses, a preliminary conference is held by the tribunal and the parties to establish a list and schedule for preparatory activities leading up to the arbitration hearing, and the date of the hearing. Such scheduled activities typically include the exchange of documents, exchange of fact witness lists, fact witness discovery,[155] amendment of claims and defenses, exchange of expert disclosures, discovery of experts, exchange of expert reports, expert conferencing (if desired), tribunal site visit (if desired), filing of dispositive motions, exchange of final witness and exhibit lists, exchange of hearing briefs, and agreed procedures for the final arbitration hearing (such as days and times of hearing, order and admission of evidence,[156] transcription of proceedings, and the like).

12.78 Upon the tribunal's closure of the hearing, following submission of post-hearing written briefs or oral argument, the tribunal decides and issues its award, which may take the form either of a single final award, or an interim award on the merits of the disputes issues followed a final award addressing costs of the arbitration.

12.79 Upon rendition of the Final Award, a party may Petition of tribunal for correction of the clerical errors in the award. If appellate arbitration is provided for in the arbitration clause or agreed by the parties, an appellate tribunal may be appointed to review the award on its merits within the scope authorized by the parties. If appellate arbitration is not provided, a party may seek confirmation or *vacatur* of the award in a court of competent jurisdiction at the seat of the arbitration upon grounds set forth in the New York Convention or other governing law. Confirmation or *vacatur* of the award by a court at the seat of the arbitration does not always mean that courts in other foreign jurisdictions will accept the local court's judgment and enforce the award.[157]

Professional Conduct of Counsel

12.80 In recent years, attention has focused on counsel conduct and party representation in arbitration proceedings. All too often counsel in international arbitrations have found themselves confronting diverse and potentially conflicting rules and norms of professional conduct. To address this issue and in an endeavor to harmonize such rules and norms, the International Bar Association in 2013 promulgated guidelines addressing party representation in international arbitration aimed at preserving the integrity of the arbitration process.[158] Among other things, the Guidelines direct counsel and other party representatives to avoid *ex parte* communications with arbitrators, to disclose any potential conflicts of interest with any arbitrator for clarification by the arbitrator, to advise the client on its duty to preserve and produce evidence, to discourage witnesses from giving false testimony, to assure that an expert report contains the opinion of the expert, and

155 See Patricia Galloway, Streamlining the Arbitration Process Through Innovative Methods of Handling Fact Witnesses, 11 Constr. Law Int'l 11 (June 2016).

156 See IBA Rules on the Taking of Evidence in International Arbitration (2010).

157 See Tweeddale, Cutting the Gordian Knot: Enforcing Awards Where an Application Has Been Made to Set Aside the Award at the Seat of the Arbitration, 81 Arbitration 137 (May 2015).

158 IBA Guidelines on Party Representation in International Arbitration (2013).

to recognize that the arbitral tribunal has the inherent power to sanction unprofessional conduct.

Conclusion

12.81 Arbitration continues to be the preferred method for resolving disputes among parties on international construction projects. Given arbitration's consensual nature, however, the arbitration clause remains the critical contractual provision upon which turn the rights and duties of arbitrating parties. Thus, expansive arbitration provisions and rules of selected institutional administrators assure that the arbitration process can best satisfy its promise of being able to resolve disputes with efficiency of time and cost and with confidence in the ability of their selected arbitrators to "get it right". As observed by Chief Justice Burger of the United States Supreme Court, arbitration is well suited to "produce an acceptable result in the shortest possible time, with the least possible expense and with a minimum of stress on the participants. That is what justice is all about".[159]

159 Warren E. Burger, Chief Justice of the US Supreme Court, Remarks before the American Arbitration Association and the Minnesota State Bar Association: Using Arbitration to Achieve Justice (21 August 1985), in 40 Arb. J. 3, 6 (1985).

SUBJECT INDEX

Made in the USA
Monee, IL
13 September 2026

62980178R00367